NEWSWEEK CONDENSED BOOKS

A. E. MAXWELL and IVAR RUUD

A. E. HOTCHNER

C. D. B. BRYAN

PETER COLLIER and DAVID HOROWITZ

THE YEAR-LONG DAY

DORIS DAY
HER OWN STORY

FRIENDLY FIRE

THE ROCKEFELLERS
AN AMERICAN DYNASTY

NEWSWEEK BOOKS, New York

The original editions of the books in this volume
are published and copyrighted as follows:

The Year-Long Day
Published by J. B. Lippincott Company
Copyright © 1976 by Evan Maxwell and Ann Maxwell

Doris Day, Her Own Story
Published by William Morrow and Company, Inc.
Copyright © 1975 by Doris Day

Friendly Fire
Published by G. P. Putnam's Sons
Copyright © 1976 by Courtlandt Dixon Barnes Bryan

The Rockefellers, An American Dynasty
Published by Holt, Rinehart and Winston
Copyright © 1976 by Peter Collier and David Horowitz

CONTENTS

THE
YEAR-LONG DAY

A condensation of the book by

A. E. MAXWELL and IVAR RUUD

Eighteen fox pelts, half a year's work for Ivar

AFTERNOON

Far out on the slate-blue water, amid glacier calves floating low and cold and translucent, the governor's ship began to move. The man on shore could not hear the big diesels over the wind and waves rushing against Hornsund Fjord's rocky beach, but he could see the ship come about slowly and head west, toward the mouth of the fjord and the Arctic Ocean beyond. Next summer, when the ice broke up again, Ivar Ruud would search hungrily for the first sign of the returning ship, but today he did not regret the disappearance of human company. He was ready to be alone.

There was no time to savor the feeling of freedom. Not yet. Not until his supplies were safe from the August whims of high Arctic weather. He flexed his back and shoulders, testing his tiredness. He had not slept in twenty-four hours, and the last ten hours had been spent hauling more than two tons of heavy crates and bags from ship to rowboat and from rowboat to beach.

Ivar's legs and feet were cold where water had topped his rubber boots as he unloaded the yellow rowboat. Usually he could unload just below his cabin, but a late summer wind had herded glacier calves and fractured ice floes onto the north shore of Hornsund Fjord.

He had searched the shoreline for a mile on either side of Main Cabin before finding a place where he could land. Ironically, the only ice-free beach was beside one of the glaciers that had been so busy sending calves out to sea.

From far out over the water, a pitch above the sound of the wind, Ivar heard a last salute from the ship as it moved out against the tide. One blast on the air horn: Good luck; see you in a year; good hunting. And then quiet, but for the wind and chunks of ice mumbling together as they rode the waves.

He turned to the waiting pile of supplies. He had carefully packed them into loads of approximately 100 pounds, as much as he could comfortably carry—not expecting to have to carry each load a mile. A year's amenities like books and margarine and Scotch, necessities like guns and medicine and skinning knives. The wooden case of guns and ammunition went into the cabin first. Without that case, the rest was meaningless.

Out of old habit Ivar glanced around him, watching for the swift creamy shadow that could be a polar bear. *Ursus maritimus* usually went north with the pack ice in summer, but Ivar had to be wary of the occasional bear that stayed behind. Such bears became as much scavengers as predators, but were no less formidable for the change.

After a last look around, he settled the awkward gun case into carrying position and walked toward the cabin. As he moved slowly up the mile of shoreline, a large German shepherd came running down the rocky beach to greet him. Naika looked him over with alert dark eyes, shook a shower of icy sea water over his legs and dashed back to rejoin the huskies at the cabin.

The distant huskies ignored Ivar for now . They had attention only for the tantalizing scent trails around the cabin. He had expected nothing different. His summer holiday in Norway had meant the huskies' imprisonment in Longyearbyen, the nearest settlement on Spitsbergen Island. While he drank beer and learned again to talk to other human beings, the huskies grew restless and surly behind kennel fences.

By Ivar's third trip with a load of supplies, the huskies had worked off their first excitement and were slowly quartering the area around the cabin. Svarten marked cabin corners and other salient points with a few drops of urine, warning all comers that this territory was occupied. He disciplined the more aggressive males, but none of the fights drew blood; the huskies had no real doubts as to which dog led them.

When the huskies finally had matters settled to their satisfaction, they noticed their empty bellies and came trotting back to Ivar. They even submitted to the collar and chain in order to be fed. After the supplies were safe inside the cabin, he would free them again, but the last thing he wanted was a pack of hungry huskies rummaging in his provisions. Naika gave him a hurt look when he chained her, for normally she ran free.

Ivar started back for another load. First the guns, then the food, then the books, then the rest of the supplies must be carried to the cabin. The rock salt and coal would be covered with a tarpaulin and left where they were for awhile, but even so he had at least fifteen round trips, or 30 miles, to walk, 15 with nothing to carry but his increasingly tired body, 15 with ever heavier 100-pound loads.

By the sixth trip he was too tired to curse the rocks that rolled perversely under his heavy feet. By the eighth, he had stopped carrying his rifle. By the eleventh, he was an automaton; except for the part of him that watched for white shadows, he was effectively deaf and blind. The only real memory he had of the final mile was weary relief when he dumped the last 100-pound load on the cabin floor.

Sleep dragged at his body, but he could not give in yet. There were a few small things to take care of. Household chores. Though he had been gone only six weeks, Main Cabin had paid for his absence. A storm had stripped a swath of tar paper off the roof over the storeroom, and the exposed planks had leaked generously.

Even at that, the cabin looked better than the first time Ivar had seen it. It had been built in 1957 for scientists who lived in Hornsund for a few months during the International Geophysical Year. At the end of summer, the cabin was abandoned and had stayed empty for a decade, testimony to the wastefulness of wealth—such a cabin for a few summer months. When Fredrik Rubach and Ivar had come to Hornsund three years ago, the long, shedlike cabin was a wreck; polar bears had ripped off doors and smashed in windows, allowing storms free entry. But the basic structure was still sound. After a lot of repairs, the cabin had served them well. Fredrik no longer used Main Cabin, preferring to live instead farther north at Cabin Bay, beyond Hornsund's wide mouth, on the shores of the stormy Arctic sea.

Ivar shivered in the damp and cold inside the cabin walls. He gave the iron stove a long look. As he expected, it was bright with rust despite its heavy coat of oil. But rust or no, the stove would heat, and heat would dry out the living quarters. The roof of the storeroom could wait until he had slept, but if he did not get the living room dried out, he would lose a year's supply of flour.

After weeks without dry heat, ceiling, walls, floor, furniture, everything was coated with cabin sweat. The sweat turned into hoarfrost when the temperature went below freezing, but even the high Arctic thawed in summertime. All exposed metal was a garish orange. For most of the metal, rust was merely an aesthetic problem. The stove was another matter. Because of repeated heatings and coolings, the stove was most vulnerable to real damage.

Ivar had given it a coat of blubber oil before he left. Not high-grade machine oil, to be sure, but just as effective. He had also laid the fire before he left, driftwood kindling topped with a layer of coal. Now all he needed was some blubber on top. As the wood burned, the blubber would melt into the coal and the coal would burn hotly. By the time the blubber was spent, the coal would be able to sustain its own fire.

The only blubber available, short of going out and peeling a seal, was the cache of dog food he had left over from last year. He climbed up on the cabin roof where he kept the cache. Most of the seal carcass was still there. With a determined effort not to smell the rotting flesh, he carved off a slab of blubber. In a few weeks at most, he would have to get fresh seal for the dogs. Not that his huskies disliked high meat; they relished it. But the seal was a small one. Barely enough remained for two weeks, or perhaps three if the dogs went on short rations. He would have to go seal hunting sooner than planned.

Grasping the blubber firmly, he descended the ladder and went back inside. He quickly oiled the stove and put the remainder of the blubber on top of the coal. He lit the fire, unconsciously holding his breath. He was used to the odor of burning blubber, but this slab was really rancid.

He fought the smell for half an hour, then gave up. He stoked the stove to bursting and retreated to the tiny shack he used as a bolt-hole. There were always enough supplies in the shack for an emergency trip to his Bird Mountain cabin, if he should lose Main Cabin to fire or storm or polar bears.

The shack was damp and cold and decrepit, but it was better than the frigid mist outside. And it certainly smelled better than the cabin. He curled up in clammy blankets and slept.

By the time he woke up, both the cabin and his thoughts were sweeter. The sun was up, of course. The sun was always up during the months-long Arctic afternoon. The dogs were also up—and hungry. Ivar fed them, and himself, before he tackled the remaining ton of coal and salt. The tide had taken away much of the shore ice; he could use the rowboat instead of his back for hauling.

A meal, a little more rest, a lot more work, and the supplies were all under a roof. Now . . . the other cabin, while the wind was still on his side. The fjord was nearly clear of ice; he could unload supplies practically at the doorstep of his Bird Mountain cabin—if the wind did not shift.

Maintaining and supplying two cabins made for logistical difficulties. Main Cabin was about 7 miles inside Hornsund's mouth. Bird Mountain Cabin was over 9 miles farther east, close to the fjord's inland terminus. A man traveling on foot or skis or dogsled could take hours to cover a single mile, especially when the weather fell apart. Along Hornsund's rugged length, a map mile became at least 2 walking miles, and sometimes 3. But the extra cabin was well worth the extra trouble. The wider his range, the greater his chances of taking fox and polar bear. He could have camped out during his hunts, but a tent or a snow cave was a poor substitute for cabin walls, and it was far easier to stock Bird Mountain's provision shelves in summer than to carry a backpack full of food through winter storms.

Most important, during the long night of winter, when his mind was both not enough and too much company, when "cabin fever" was not a joke, he simply fled to a different cabin.

Within a short time he had the boat loaded with food and tar paper and a few lengths of cut pine board. He launched the boat and pointed it directly out into the fjord. After a mile or so, he would turn east, toward Bird Mountain and the steep headlands that overlooked the chill fjord.

Above, high overhead, the distant calls of white-cheeked geese poured down on him, and their bodies made clean black lines against the cloudless sky. Ivar watched them for a few moments, envying their flight and warm feathers and air of majestic ease.

The sea hissed gently as it was divided by the yellow prow of the boat. The water hissed less gently as it met the obstruction of barely submerged rocks. Though Hornsund was a wide and lovely fjord, it had more than its share of teeth. Rock reefs and sea stacks paralleled the shoreline out to a distance of a mile. And ice was always a hazard, even in the warmest summer months.

Once through the reefs, he opened up the throttle and headed out to the center of the fjord. For the next 3 miles he scanned the sea, hoping for a glimpse of beluga whales on their way down to the closed end of the fjord. But he saw none of their gliding white shapes this time, not even so much as a sudden gush of silver breath condensed above the dark waves.

But he did spot game. The slick brown head of a ringed seal broke water 30 feet off the bow. Round dark eyes watched Ivar for an instant, then vanished beneath the sea. Immediately, Ivar shut off the motor, raised his rifle, and waited motionlessly for the seal's return. The huskies needed food and his fires needed oil; that sleek brown flash represented 200 pounds of meat and blubber. The rowboat lifted and fell and lifted and fell as Ivar sat noiselessly, his light-blue eyes scanning the sea for a shining dark head.

There—20 yards to the right.

Ivar aimed smoothly, quickly, and just as quickly decided no, not this time. Too easy to miss in the rolling sea, too easy to kill instead of stun, and if he killed, the seal would sink before he could reach it. The seal's death would be wasted.

Ivar set the rifle aside and started the motor. In a few weeks, when the ringed seals' blubber thickened against winter and the glaciers no longer diluted the buoyant seawater, dead seals would float, and hunting would be easier. His huskies could not wait that long, but he would have other chances, better chances, to take a ringed seal.

The boat wallowed slightly, then slid into a course parallel to Hornsund's north shoreline. Ivar still watched for telltale patches of foam, but the danger from rocks and reefs was not so great here as closer to shore. He had time to look back at the ragged slice of land that was home.

Even with light and good weather and a machine doing all the work, Hornsund seemed huge. Most maps showed little dots for the Svalbard Islands, and Hornsund Fjord—if it showed at all—was a nameless slit in Spitsbergen's lower half.

But maps were only one kind of reality. Mapmakers floated by the islands in a ship or flew over in a plane, cameras clicking. Ivar used their maps, understood their limitations, and laughed or swore over the mistakes he found.

Just east of Main Cabin there was a beautiful twin-peaked mountain. In summer the peaks were a deep chocolate color, and along the mountain's west side Hans Glacier grumbled to the fjord. A hard landmark to miss, but one mapmaker succeeded. Ivar called the error Missing Mountain. Other mapmakers had found and named it Fannytoppen, but it would always be Missing Mountain to Ivar.

He did not hesitate to give personal names to Hornsund's landmarks, names such as Fox Valley and Goose Bay and Bear Bay and Omelet Slope and Sonofabitch Pass. Where the mapmakers flew or floated, he skied or walked or crawled. His Hornsund was different from theirs, and he knew the area far more intimately than they did.

Yet he had almost missed knowing Hornsund at all. The Svalbard Islands, of which Spitsbergen was one, were under the administration of the Norwegian government. Before Ivar could hunt or trap, he had to receive permission from the government. When he first came to Longyearbyen, the governor of Svalbard refused to grant that permission. The reason given was that Ivar was ill prepared to meet Arctic exigencies.

Ivar disagreed, loudly and at length, with the governor. It was futile, Ivar was only nineteen and, as he later realized, tactless. Nothing in his life had prepared him to deal successfully with the proud obstructions of a bureaucracy. When he was fourteen he had left home, over no one's objections, and lived on the streets of Oslo with children older but no wiser than he was. As soon as he turned fifteen, he joined the merchant marine. He saw Rome, Paris, London, New York, Rio de Janeiro—and most of the whores and bars between. It was all very exciting for a Norwegian farm boy.

There was a problem, though. Ivar was 5 feet 8 inches tall, weighed 140 pounds and was touchy about his size. In time, he learned that fighting had no future. The last lesson came in a Brazilian bar. Two crews were there, Ivar's and one from another ship. He was not sure how that fight started, but it was fast, ugly and final. The bar was destroyed. Not a chair, not a bottle, not a glass was left intact. Nothing. He crawled out of the wreckage very sober and grateful to be moving at all.

It was the first time Ivar had ever been pleased to be alive.

By the time he signed on for the last Norwegian whaling expedition to Antarctica, he had learned to control his temper. For seven months he saw only the ship and other men. No ports, no women, no time off. The months would have been endless if he had not met Fredrik Rubach. Fredrik had lived on the Svalbard Islands for many years and enjoyed talking about his experiences. Ivar enjoyed listening. By the end of the expedition, they had agreed to be partners for a year of trapping on Hornsund Fjord.

Ivar still wondered why Fredrik had wanted him as a partner. Fredrik had enough money and more than enough experience to trap by himself. Ivar knew the older man preferred trapping alone. The only possible answer was that Fredrik liked Ivar. At the time, Ivar found that hard to believe; no one else liked Ivar back then, including himself.

The plans they made led them to Longyearbyen—and the governor. Ivar had purchased all the supplies Fredrik's years of experience said were necessary. The governor had a different list.

A bedpan was high on his list. What would happen to poor Ivar if Fredrik were at one cabin and Ivar were at another, injured or too sick to get up and use the honey bucket? Ivar pointed out that if all that happened, a smelly bed would be the least of his problems. The governor said Ivar must, repeat must, have a bedpan. There was not even one bedpan for sale in Longyearbyen, and no time to ship one in from Norway.

The bedpan was only one of many obstructions. When Ivar should have been repairing cabins and fixing traps and hunting food for himself and the dogs, he was shadowboxing with the governor's rule book.

He lost, of course. As the ice congealed around Longyearbyen, he sold his provisions at a loss and took the last ship out. On the way to Norway, he planned ways to earn enough money to try again. Then he was drafted. Two years of shoveling snow for the greater glory of Norway.

But Ivar was stubborn. As soon as he was discharged, he started buying provisions. Instead of waiting until he reached Longyearbyen for clearance to trap, he took care of the paperwork in Norway. At least the bureaucrats in Oslo understood that Ivar knew as much about surviving in the high Arctic as their rule books. One man even told him that it was his own ass, and if he wanted to freeze it off, that was his problem.

And now, at the beginning of his fourth year here, he understood better why the governor had been so reluctant to turn an inexperienced youth loose in the Arctic. Hornsund can be an unforgiving place. At 77 degrees north latitude, less than 400 miles from the North Pole and over 100 air miles from the nearest town, Longyearbyen, Hornsund was no place for fools. The wind and cold were intense, the mountains swept clean of all except moss and lichen, rock and ice. The biggest tree on the island was an 8-inch-high birch.

A sudden barrage of noise rose above the sound of the engine. Ivar looked away from the land and back to the sea. Up ahead, several square miles of sea were churned silver. The dovekies were fishing.

They were amazing birds, like white-bellied bats, smaller than his hand, yet they dove deep into the cold sea in search of prey. And the noise those little birds made—a high, very rapid trill that poured out of them and was multiplied into an incredible cacophony.

Ivar shifted position almost unconsciously; he had been sitting on a hard, narrow plank for almost two hours. His muscles were stiff and his feet ached with cold as he flexed his toes inside his boots. Only an inch beneath his feet was water that never varied more than a few degrees from freezing. The cold that seeped through yellow hull and rubber soles could be driven out only by fire or exercise. As both of those were at least an hour away, he resigned himself to discomfort.

The northern shore slipped quietly astern, a pageant of mauve tundra, knife-edged gray mountains and gleaming ice. Ahead, the great stone pyramid of the Bird Mountain massif rose above the blue-green sea. At the base of sheer cliffs, a tiny peninsula crept out into the fjord. Ivar's cabin was still hidden on the far side of the peninsula, but he picked up the binoculars and stared ahead intently. He had prepared both cabins as well as he could against polar bears and storms, but tourists were another matter.

Even when they remembered to shut the door, they did not always leave empty-handed. Not that the tourists took much. By their standards

16

there was not much worth taking; a small mirror, an odd spoon, Norwegian flowers he had dried and nursed intact to Hornsund.

He could live without seeing his face and he could stir his coffee with a knife, but those dried flowers . . . in the long winter darkness when he hungered for sun, he had nothing else to recall summer's gentle fields.

Some of the tension left him when he finally saw the cabin—closed door, window shutter in place, no obvious damage. He beached the boat, grabbed his rifle and the roll of tar paper and trotted toward the cabin. He was still stiff and somewhat clumsy from cold, but he hurried anyway. He would not feel at ease until he had checked the cabin's interior.

The Bird Mountain cabin had begun as an overnight shack, hardly more secure or spacious than a one-man tent. During his second year in Hornsund, Ivar had rebuilt and expanded until a rough shack became a snug home. The cabin was still small, a 12-by-6-foot rectangle divided into two equal rooms, only one of which was heated by the stove.

The first room was used for storing provisions, fuel, guns and tools. The door, as all outer doors in snow country, opened inward. There was a hinged panel in its upper half. The small room had not been disturbed. He propped the tar paper on its shelf, put the rifle in its rack, then backed up to the center of the room in order to open the living-room door. Other than an arc for the door and a narrow passage from the outer door, the storeroom was completely full.

The living room had little more free space. Its 6-foot-square area was taken up by a bunk, table, washbasin, chair and stove. Except for one place beneath the window, the walls were covered with cabinets and shelves. A quick glance around reassured him that everything was as he had left it, except that the stove was rusty.

He oiled it with old blubber scraps, started the fire and fled back to the boat. The escape from the stench was only temporary; he had more supplies to bring up to the cabin. He unloaded the boat methodically, ammunition and perishables first, coal and cut wood last.

When he finished, he rolled a cigarette and leaned against a sunny cabin wall. But while his body was still, his mind was busy organizing what had to be done in the next few weeks. Rocks must be gathered for the fox traps and driftwood for his fires. If he waited too long, both driftwood and stones would freeze fast to the ground. Once gathered, the driftwood must be split into kindling. Main Cabin must be repaired while the weather held. The rest of Bird Mountain's supplies must be ferried up while the weather held. And he had to hunt geese and ducks before they left. Good weather would help for that. The huskies must have food, and only a fool hunted seal from an open rowboat in bad weather. The huskies' harness must be repaired, the homemade sled must be checked for damage and all the hundred other little things must be done that combined to mean survival.

His list was thick, his time was thin. And in the remaining weeks of Arctic afternoon, he could be sure of only one thing: the weather would change quickly, often and for the worse. Past experience told him he would use the boat only in good weather, hunt geese in changing weather, collect wood and stones in bad weather and repair harness in vile weather.

From habit, he looked at the mountaintops but saw no signs of coming storms. The mountains were nearly clear of clouds. The day was almost too perfect. It could not last. Either a hard wind or a dripping fog would descend soon. He hoped it would be fog, for with fog the sea was usually calm, usually safe for a man in a small boat. Usually.

Trills and screams and shrill calls of countless sea birds rose from Bird Mountain like mist off a lake. The racket did not wake Ivar; it was September now, late in the afternoon of the year-long Arctic day. Bird noises would be notable only if absent. But when the cloud cover broke and the sunlight changed from murky to transparent gold, Ivar stirred and awoke. His breath smoked in the cabin and he shivered when his bare feet touched the floor. He lit the fire in the converted oil drum which served as a stove. Nothing fancier was needed; the oil drum heated the 6-foot-square living area quite nicely.

He moved quickly to the window and looked out. When he saw that the clouds were withdrawing, thinning, almost gone, a feeling of relief warmed his body as much as the orange fire sizzling in the makeshift stove. For eighteen days the weather had been rotten; storms preceded and followed by high winds that made the fjord impassable for days at a time, then a day or two of decent weather in which he could travel, then bad weather again. Twice he had had to turn back from seal hunting and race for the nearest cabin. He must take a seal today, or the huskies would be eating his own food. That was a bad way to start his year.

His mind on the coming seal hunt, Ivar hurried through his breakfast, hurried out of the cabin, hurried to where his boat was beached high on the rocky shore. He braced himself against the boat and pushed. With grating reluctance, the yellow boat moved toward the sea.

He leaped into the boat. Under his steady rowing, it pulled out into the fjord and around Bird Mountain peninsula. Though pressed for time, he did not tire himself; he had a long day of rowing ahead. There was too much floating ice to use the motor today.

Out from Bird Mountain, around the peninsula, toward the closed end of Hornsund. The eastern end of the fjord was divided into two bays. Ivar called the northern bay Two Glacier Bay. The southern, Seven Glacier Bay, was larger and rimmed with 50-foot ice walls. Ringed seal were year-round residents of both bays; in fact, of all Hornsund. They were the most numerous seal in the Svalbards, and the staple diet of polar bears.

Ivar would prefer to take the much larger bearded seal; it represented four to six times as much blubber and flesh for the same amount of time, risk and killing as a ringed seal. Yet, like the polar bear, he would have to be satisfied with what the Arctic provided. Ringed seal were plentiful, therefore ringed seal were more likely to end up in his larder than their huge cousins.

He made fast time into Two Glacier Bay, rowing quietly, glancing over his shoulder from time to time to scan the rocks and floating ice and the two glaciers. A small peak divided the glaciers, thrusting a short peninsula out into the bay. The land was rough, but he had seen seals on the rocks before. Ice blocks, sculpted and worn by the summer sun, were also favorite hauling-out places.

Deftly, quietly, Ivar reversed his position in the boat, pushing rather than pulling on the oars. Still no seals in sight. The water, then. Perhaps the seals were not sunning today. Sometimes the hollow sound of ice chunks bumping the boat brought seals to investigate the strange, yellow-bottomed glacier calf. The curious seals approached underwater, then surfaced 20 feet away to stare with big eyes and spread whiskers at the strange upright animal who rode the wooden berg.

He searched each rock, each block of ice. No sleeping seals. At the end of three hours, rowing as quietly as the squeaky left rowlock would allow, all he had for his trouble were two very cold feet and eyes that watered from staring at shiny icebergs.

Ivar reversed his position again and rowed out of the bay, toward Seven Glacier. He rowed steadily about 20 yards off the face of Treskelen Peninsula, a thrust of rock that almost landlocked Seven Glacier Bay.

As he had expected, the portion of Seven Glacier in the lee of the peninsula was calm. Scattered throughout the calm part of the bay were at least two dozen good-sized bergs, some trapped against rocks that protruded from the bottom of the bay, others floating with a subtle rocking motion in the quiet eddy of the tides. The seals should be there, asleep on the low-floating ice.

Fifty feet away Ivar saw a nicely rounded ringed seal sunning itself on the only accessible rock in a mile of shoreline. The seal watched him with a mixture of alarm and curiosity, ducking its head toward the water as though it were going to flee, then hesitating for a quick look at the oddly shaped intruder.

The hesitation was fatal. It gave Ivar all the time he needed to lift the shotgun and trigger one quick shot that nearly lifted the seal off its rock. As the shot echoed in the bay, he dropped the gun and rowed as fast as he could toward the rock, praying that the carcass would not slide off into deep water. He knew that the seal had died instantly, or its reflexes would have thrown it into the bay. But a dead seal has no balance and the rock was humped up in the center. It was still early for the seal to float; once in water, the carcass could sink quickly.

By the time Ivar reached the rock, the carcass had started to slip down. Hurriedly he peeled off his gloves, reached into the icy water and groped for the seal's front flippers. His shoulder muscles bunched as he pulled the carcass free and guided it around to the stern. Now to get it aboard.

Ivar's fingers flexed, tightening over the slippery flippers. He took several slow breaths, then began to bob the seal up and down, up and down. With each bob the seal went a little deeper, rose a bit higher as it returned to the surface of the buoyant water. He worked and waited; timing was as important as strength. Once more . . . just a little higher . . . now!

With one smooth motion, Ivar lifted 200 slippery pounds of seal over the stern, along with several gallons of achingly cold water. But he did not mind the water. The boat could be bailed, the socks and boots could be dried and the dogs could eat. Ivar smiled, stretched the muscles in his back and arms, then began to bail.

If he could take just one bearded seal, he would not have to hunt again until the sea was frozen and the glaciers were quiet and there was enough snow that the dogs could drag their own meat up to the cabin.

He was farther from shore now, heading quietly for a line of small bergs that seemed to have grounded on a shallow shelf a mile from the front of a glacier. Ivar circled 200 yards in back of the grounded bergs, approaching them from the glacier side, the shadow side, stealing quietly along, watching the ice blocks and the water around them, slipping the oars cleanly into the water, stroking, slipping them out, lifting them high to clear the small wavelets before he silently returned the oars to the sea and stroked the boat forward.

The stalk was slow, wary and tiring. Ivar did not notice his fatigue; his whole mind was fastened on the hunt.

As he neared the line of ice, he slowed his strokes and edged into a narrow space between two bergs that reached 4 to 10 feet above waterline. Shipping the oars, he let the little boat drift for a moment, then moved to the bow to look down the lateral face of the line where seals should be.

There. Two bergs down, 400 feet away. A huge bearded seal was dozing in the sun, head pointed toward open water at the mouth of the bay.

Ivar inched backward and picked up the oars again. With a long backward stroke he pulled the boat out of the seal's line of sight. Spinning the boat quickly, he rowed along the shadow side of the line of bergs, aiming for the back of the iceberg adjacent to the sleeping seal. In the blue shadow of the ice, he again shipped the oars and silently moved to the bow, edging carefully around the stiffening carcass of the ringed seal.

The boat rocked slightly, kept rocking even though Ivar was still. The wind was on the move. It had grown bigger teeth, and more of them, but Ivar noticed only the balance of the rifle as he freed it from its sheath. Slowly, almost imperceptibly, the boat eased forward just enough to give Ivar a clear shot. The seal awoke, but it was too late; the bullet was already on its way, the rifle had already kicked against the coiled muscle of Ivar's shoulder. The big seal died even as its muscles tightened to propel it into the water. A second of shock so overwhelming as to be painless, and the seal's body stretched to its full length on the rocking ice.

A series of long oar strokes brought him quickly to the ice where the seal lay 3 feet above waterline.

The bow of the boat nudged against the ice below the seal's hummock. Dragging the bowline in one hand and a 10-foot length of rope in the other, Ivar leaped up onto the berg. The seal was huge, more than 800 pounds. Fortunately, the carcass was lying close to the edge of the shelf. Eight hundred pounds of dead seal was an almost immovable mass. As it was, he would have to butcher it at the water's edge when he got to the cabin, for there was no snow to help him slide the heavy seal across the rocky ground.

Almost unconsciously, he glanced at the sun's position, his always changing clock. It was late. Then he looked again and felt a chill move through his body. Far out beyond the peninsula, in the open waters of Hornsund, whitecaps leaped as though an invisible hand churned the sea. And behind the lines of whitecaps came the first sets of larger waves, 3 feet high now on the edge of the incoming tide, growing as he watched. He watched, time turning slowly around him, until the wind entered Seven Glacier Bay with a cold, harsh shout.

Quickly, he knelt beside the seal, whipped out the short-bladed sheath knife. He made two short slits in the seal's skin just forward of the rear flipper. Slipping the knife blade underneath the skin, he opened a channel between the two slits. He forced the rope through the channel, then tied the rope with a slipproof knot.

Ivar leaped back down into the boat, balancing easily, and secured the other end of the rope to a bolt hole in the sternpost. Then he swung back up on the ice shelf and began pushing and shoving the seal closer to the edge of the berg. With one last muscle-bunching heave, he tipped the balance. The seal slid over the edge of the berg and into the water. Ivar rode the rocking ice as he watched the seal sink, bob, then stabilize just beneath the surface, buoyed by the water and restrained by the line. If the wind got no worse, he could handle this 800-pound anchor.

He shoved off from the iceberg and rowed toward the open water off the peninsula. Time and again he had to veer off from the icebergs moving across the bay and the hollow thunks of smaller ice glancing off the boat followed his progress.

Each time he looked over his shoulder, the whitecaps had moved farther down the fjord; their leaping white lines were crossing the water where he would have to make his turn for Bird Mountain. Worse, the wind was shifting and getting stronger as it rode the back of the incoming tide. Even Treskelen's bony finger no longer sheltered Seven Glacier Bay. Waves rose in the formerly calm waters.

As he rowed, whitecaps moved into the bay. The wind no longer veered, but blew steady and hard from west-southwest, pushing everything down the fjord, into the bay and then against the ravaged glaciers. The bearded seal acted as a slightly buoyant anchor, dragging against the forward progress of the boat. And each wave that splashed over the gunwhale added to the weight of the boat and the ringed seal inside.

Twenty minutes passed, then forty; Ivar's progress was slow but measurable. Again and again, he looked over his right shoulder toward the open fjord, watching for clouds that might mean a sleet storm or one of the frequent, unpredictable squall lines that made living in the Arctic so interesting. But the sky stayed blue and empty. His bad luck seemed confined to the west-southwest wind.

He kept the bow of the boat on a diagonal line that would take him out of the mouth of the bay 220 yards beyond the rocky headland. There was no place to land on either side of the peninsula and he wanted no part of those unyielding rocks in broken seas.

After an hour's hard rowing, he stopped to bail. He was still a quarter mile short of his goal. As he bailed, he studied the conditions he would face when he left the relative shelter in Treskelen's lee. Even here, unruly waves had left ankle-deep water in the boat, and his feet were soaked inside the rubber boots. It would be worse out there.

He bailed quickly, emptied his boots over the side and flexed his toes to make sure they were still functional. He had lost all feeling in them.

When he turned to look at the seas he would pull into, the waves had grown—more than 3 feet now and running fast toward the ice cliffs of the seven glaciers. As he watched, the first of the ice blocks and bergs from glaciers farther up Hornsund hove into view off the tip of Treskelen, sailing majestically before the wind, so heavy that they barely rocked on the climbing waves.

Then Ivar saw the first of the real waves crash over the tip of the peninsula, shooting spray 10 feet into the air. He laid against the oars and began moving toward the turbulent gap.

The water became more and more choppy; small waves broached the gunwales time after time as he pulled away from Treskelen. He was still 80 yards short of the spot he had picked to turn into the wind when he saw the water ahead boil and buck up as though a whale had rolled over. He put both hands on the left oar and pulled, groaning, until boat and bearded seal were facing directly into the looming wave. The bow lifted slowly, lifted and kept on lifting as tons of blue-black water surged underneath the yellow keel. On top of the wave, Ivar looked anxiously over his shoulder. A diagonal heading was no longer possible; the wave had been a warning. He was closer to the headland than he cared to be, but the waves gave him no other choice.

The swell was now almost 4 feet high, with individual waves up to 5 or 6 feet and moving fast. As the boat sank into deep troughs, he lost sight of all except the dark heaving water. He had been at sea many times in a small boat, yet the loss of land always made him uneasy. At least with the bow into the wind, the boat was shipping less water. The ride would have been exhilarating, except for the fact that he was being pushed inexorably backwards into the bay, closer to the tossing icebergs that ground against towering glacier fronts.

Stroke. Stroke. Stroke. Not to make way, but to keep from losing it, and to keep the bow into the waves or be flipped like a coin. Stroke. Stroke. Stroke.

Time was meaningless, only the wind and sea and ice and the weight of the boat at the end of his straining arms were real.

The wind was at gale force now, yet the sky above was cobalt blue, untouched by clouds. The beauty of the clean sky was lost on Ivar. He had eyes only for icebergs and the black-rock peninsula which measured his progress. Each look told him he was losing way, moving backward toward the closed end of the bay, sliding closer to the flashing, floating mass of ice that broke in jagged waves across rocks and glacier fronts.

After an hour of rowing into the waves, he had been pushed more than a quarter mile down into the bay. Ivar was trapped inside an ice-and-rock bottle whose stopper was the wind. There was no way to get ashore, no place to land if he could. The water in the lee of Treskelen offered no refuge—that area was so chopped and churned that even a duck would have to fight to stay afloat. He was better off out in the bay, where the waves at least came from one direction.

Ivar worked over the oars, long rhythmic sweeps that used every muscle in his body. Underneath the gloves and calluses new blisters puffed and grew. His shoulders and back and thighs ached their protest, but he neither slowed nor broke rhythm. Lean and pull, lean and pull.

He could cut loose his sea anchor, the dead weight of the bearded seal. The more his body ached, the more seductive the idea became. But what a waste of meat, of blubber, of effort, of the seal's life. And there was no guarantee that cutting the seal loose would ensure his own safety. Besides, he still had a mile and a half of usable bay off the stern. After that, he would be into an icy marina filled with the grinding debris of the glacial scrapyard. He picked out a landmark, a jagged rock tooth on the side of Treskelen, a mile deeper into the bay. One mile. If he was pushed to that tooth he would cut the rope that held the bearded seal. Lean-pull. Lean-pull. Lean-pull.

Neither the rhythm nor the wind nor the pain varied. He could row another ten hours, easily, because he had no choice. All he had was an unbending will to survive.

Lean-PULL. Lean-PULL. Lean-PULL. Let the world shrink to a yellow boat and white ice and black waves. Time and pain had no color, no place in his shrunken world.

Wind-driven spray and breaking waves drenched him, slowly filling the boat with frigid water. He was forced to stop rowing and bail. When his numbed left hand refused to hold onto the bailing can, he wedged the can between his palms and bailed as fast as he could, stopping only to prevent the boat from sliding sideways into a wave. When he finished, he had lost a hundred yards to the tireless wind.

LEAN-PULL. LEAN-PULL. LEAN-PULL.

But at the end of two hundred wrenching strokes, he had regained less than half the lost distance. He returned to his former pace, his shrunken world, determined to hold station as long as he could. Every few strokes he checked his landmark. He was less than 300 yards above the jagged tooth and closing fast.

He looked over his shoulder, hoping to see an end to the marching whitecaps far out in the fjord. The horizon was somehow closer than he had expected. He stared intently, then realized that the sun had set while he fought the wind. There would be no real darkness, nothing more than a few hours of crimson light and shadows rising from the land. Very beautiful, if your life did not depend on judging distances accurately.

Ivar rowed, searching for a sign that the wind was diminishing with the light. What he saw was a tightly spaced flotilla of icebergs tossing into the bay. He would have to avoid them somehow, as he had avoided all the rest of the rolling ice. He needed time for that, time to see the danger, time to judge its angle of approach, time to ease the unwieldy boat onto a safe heading. But the draining light obscured icebergs until they were dangerously close, and Treskelen's jagged tooth was gaining on him.

Ivar rowed, eyes on the closing horizon where white ice rolled.

Too close.

Not enough time.

As a red-tipped wave drenched the boat, his knife swept across the taut rope which kept the bearded seal afloat.

Good-bye, my friend. I'm sorry.

The boat lurched, bucked up, then steadied under Ivar's hands. Strength seemed to rush back into his arms; the yellow boat seemed made of air rather than wood. The sensation would pass as his muscles adjusted to pulling less than half of the former load, but he was grateful for the mental lift the relative lightness gave him. He held the yellow prow into the waves and watched the approaching bergs, automatically gauging the best course through the shining ice forest.

He could go to his left, between the peninsula and the icebergs. It was the shortest way, but he might end up smashed all over Treskelen. To his right was open water, but he would be sideways to those huge waves. That left the middle—like trying to sneak carrion past a polar bear.

He began rowing in earnest, ignoring the water sloshing around his feet, the spray lashing across his face, the smaller pieces of ice that crunched against the boat. Normally he would have tried to miss any floating ice, but now he had eyes only for the massive bergs ahead. He strained into the red light, measuring distances and individual bergs. While he watched, several of the bergs wallowed eratically. Two of them flipped over, sending out fountains of spray and conflicting waves.

He marked the unstable icebergs; he would avoid them if he could. What he needed was big ice that would not turn turtle as he rowed by, big ice that was not too close to its neighbors.

Pulling hard on the left oar, he committed himself to a new heading, slightly off-center of the waves. He rowed quickly, lining the prow up with a gap in the two nearest icebergs. Both were big, fairly stable . . . he hoped.

At triple speed, Ivar shot through the opening, then wove through the next obstacles. Pause, right oar, climb the wave, look, stroke, left oar, stroke, wait . . . wait . . . PULL.

Behind him, two bergs touched in grinding caress, but Ivar barely noticed. The ice off his stern was of no interest; the ice in front of him was a shining enigma he must penetrate. There was one more narrow passage he must negotiate before he would be clear of Treskelen's reaching finger and the worst of the ice. The route to relative safety lay between one large and several smaller bergs. He could shave the big one or weave through the smaller ones. The small, nearly transparent bergs worried him. Most of them were visible only when a breaking wave limned them in foam. All of them were larger than his boat.

A triplet of big waves made Ivar's decision for him. The smaller bergs gnashed and gnawed among themselves like a pack of starving huskies. The large iceberg sailed silently on, impervious to the heaving sea.

He pulled on the right oar, veering toward the big berg. He had to pass far closer to the crenulated ice than he liked. He took a last sighting as the boat crested a wave, then began stroking the yellow prow through the gloaming chaos of ice. As the boat slid along the edge of the massive iceberg, he unconsciously held his breath, waiting to feel the oars wrenched from his hands or the crunch of hull slammed against immovable ice.

When the last of the iceberg's scarred length was astern, Ivar permitted himself a tiny feeling of relief. Though there was a lot of ice left in Hornsund, the worst was behind him. He had room to maneuver again. Now all he had to worry about was his own stamina. But that, unlike the weather, had never failed him.

Ivar rowed rhythmically, endlessly. He rowed against the tide and the wind and the waves and the ice, an automaton who knew only the metronome of lean-pull, lean-pull, lean-pull.

As the sun lifted above the horizon, round and red and rising into gold, Ivar wearily lined up his boat just off the shore of Bird Mountain. He held the boat stationary in the surging sea, choosing the right moment for a wild rush to shore.

The boat rose and fell as he waited for the right wave. He needed one big enough to carry him high up the rocky beach, but not so big as to wrench the boat out of his control.

Now.

He pulled hard on the oars, matching momentum with an incoming wave. In a blur of white power, the wave threw him toward the shore. At the first grate of beach meeting keel, he was over the side, bowline in hand. He staggered forward, pulling the boat up the rocky beach, using whatever help the dying wave could give him.

The last 30 feet were all his own, beyond the reach even of storm waves. Without stopping to measure his tiredness or relief, he dragged the stiff ringed seal out of the boat and up to the cabin.

EVENING

It was a fine, crystalline November day, with an icy edge to the wind. Long, thin clouds glowed gold and scarlet, like satin streamers flying above velvet shadow mountains. In six hours the colors would drain into blue and ebony and the silver of a rising moon. Six hours . . . so little light out of twenty-four, yet the light had such beauty that Ivar would not have traded those short hours for twelve of normal sunshine.

A small storm had moved through Friday, and swept the remainder of the summer birds out of Hornsund. The dovekies, sensing the shift in the weather, had fled all of an afternoon, shrieking their farewells into the wind. Now Hornsund would be quiet for six months, except for the wind and ice. He missed the little dovekies, but not too much. Their frenetic lives made the fjord ring with sound, but it had begun to wear—the incessant racket day and night, night and day. After they had gone, he found the silence not at all oppressive. In the Arctic twilight, his life and the hidden lives around him were being stripped to their essentials.

I'm not a god here. I can't make the wind blow or the snow fall. Sometimes I can't even make my huskies behave. But I'm the next thing to a god. I'm a man, alive, and no thanks to anyone else for it.

Ivar skied through midmorning twilight toward Fox Valley. He carried a hand ax, and the frames of two fox traps were strapped to the packboard on his back. Naika romped alongside, kicking snow dust over his skis. As he approached Fox River's sea outlet, he scanned the land carefully. Yesterday, on his way to set out the gill net beneath Fox Lake's new ice, he had spotted two more possible trap sites, small rocky knolls which the wind would keep free of snow. Today he would lay out the traps.

Naika did not share his working mood. She danced like a pup around him, chasing off toward heaps of rock and after shadows and anything else which offered the slightest excuse for a snow-plowing dash. Ptarmigan hollows and fox trails and the rest of the world of smells tormented and delighted her.

The temperature had dropped to zero, but the air was still. Ivar's and Naika's breath hung in front of them, drifting and finally dissipating into the thin, dry air.

When he approached the little peninsula which he had selected for one of the traps, he called to Naika, warning her to stay. The shy and crafty foxes would not venture onto the peninsula if Naika's scent were present.

Naika was used to the routine; she took the command to heart, sitting on her brown haunches, ears up and eyes alert as Ivar moved the 100 yards out onto the peninsula.

He surveyed the little tip of the peninsula for the best trap site, trying to guess how more snow would change the contours of the ground. Dropping the ax, he stripped off the pack and freed one of the traps.

The trap was simple, a 30-inch-square lattice of sawed lumber. He laid the trap flat on the chosen site and scouted around for conveniently sized rocks to put on top of the boards. He would not set the trap yet, though fox season had officially begun. He would wait two more weeks and be absolutely sure that whatever fox died in his trap would be wearing the full depth of its silky winter fur. If the fox were still in transition fur, the pelt would be worthless.

After his own fox season began, he would return to the traps, tip the square up on end, then complete the trap by adding a simple device Fredrik had taught him to make—a trigger stick that locked the two prop sticks together just tightly enough to support the trap and the 80 pounds of rock that would be piled on top of it. The bait, a ptarmigan head, was attached to the trigger. If that stick moved, the trap collapsed.

The weighted lattice would be poised on top of the trigger in such a way that a fox could not grab the bait unless the fox stood underneath the frame. Few foxes were quick enough to take the bait and avoid the falling trap. His traps had no middle ground: if the fox was trapped, it died instantly; if not, the fox was unscathed. No metal teeth grinding into a leg, driving its victim to a frenzy that ended in exhaustion and slow freezing death, or driving the fox to gnaw off its own leg and then face an even slower death by starvation or gangrene.

Close to the spot that he had chosen he saw a pile of rocks, shore stones and small boulders of exactly the type he needed.

The rocks were scattered, but still retained a ragged oval shape 5 feet long and 3 feet wide. At the edges of the pile were irregular smaller stones; the rocks toward the middle were the size of melons. He picked up several of the larger ones and cradled them in one arm while he reached for more. As he lifted the fifth rock, he uncovered a grayish white curve of bone. Gently he lifted a sixth stone, and gray curves became a smooth convex surface. The bone had once protected a man's brain, the blank hollows had once been eyes.

Carefully, he put the rocks he was holding aside and lifted several more away from the skull, shocked and yet intrigued. In silence he studied the skull and the bone fragments that had once anchored shoulder and chest muscles. The rib cage had sagged under the weight of time, but each portion of the skeleton could be identified.

He studied the skeleton for a long moment, seeking any sign that might explain the enigmatic grave. He had heard stories of whalers from the seventeenth and eighteenth centuries dying of scurvy or hunger or fear of months without light. Some of the men had been buried on desolate Svalbard shores, hundreds of miles from their homes in Thalwalkie or Odessa or Portsmouth or Hammerfest. It had been a teeming land then, rich with countless walrus and whales. But the whalers and hunters had pursued their prey—and themselves—into extinction. His eyes moved to the skull, weathered and gray.

At least he was not alone. Someone piled these rocks over his grave. That's more than I might expect.

But then, I am not going to die.

Gently, he replaced the rocks that shielded the skull. He straightened the smaller rocks that had formed the border of the grave, then quietly stood upright. He gathered his tools and traps and left without looking back. There were other, better places to trap. He propped the traps against a particularly high pile of rocks to be collected on his way back from the lake.

He resumed the climb up into the valley, where Fox Lake lay rigid beneath ice and shadow, surrounded by peaks of blazing scarlet and gold. He hiked across the rocky approach and down to the ice. Removing his skis, he stood them upright in the snow and walked carefully onto the ice.

The day before, he had chopped a series of holes through the 4-inch thickness of ice. Strung between the holes was a 100-foot gill net. The straight line of holes cut across the current flowing out of the lake into the river. He had no difficulty in finding his holes again; the chunks he had chipped out still littered the area, the only imperfection on the blue-black floor of ice.

He opened the first and last hole in the line and loosened the far end of the rope. Ivar stripped off his gloves and began pulling the net out of the water. Though the frigid cords made his hands ache, being bare-handed was better than facing the long hike home with soaked and frozen gloves.

He had pulled no more than 5 feet of net when the first fish hung up on the edge of the hole. A 6-pound Arctic charr, a salmonlike fish he had come to prize as a break from his diet of birds. The fish was tangled in the cords and as rigid as stone. In the icy black water, a fish that could not swim was very quickly frozen.

He untangled the frozen fish and threw it over beside his pack. He paused for a moment to breathe some warmth back into his hands; then he went back to pulling. Soon another, larger fish appeared, perhaps 8 pounds, heavy and thick.

He pulled out two more 10-pounders before he reached the end of the net. He stacked the four fish to one side, pulled on his gloves and slapped his hands against his shoulders as he walked to the farthest ice hole. After a few minutes of hauling on stiff rope, he had dragged the net beneath the ice again.

When he walked back to the pile of fish, Naika was also there . . . nose on her paws, about 1 millimeter away from a silver fin. She did not look up at his approach, but she did manage one tiny tail-tip wag by way of greeting. Obviously she could have demolished at least one fish while he had been occupied, but not so much as a tooth gouge marred the frozen beauty of the nearest charr.

When he spoke to her, the tip of her tail vibrated, but her eyes never left the fish. She watched until the last charr disappeared into his backpack. He shrugged into the pack, heavy and awkward with frozen fish. When he was ready, he looked around for Naika and saw her clear across the lake, playing hockey solitaire with a piece of ice as puck. He left, knowing she would follow.

Naika caught up with him when he stopped to put on his skis. The short light of day was already fading into crimson twilight as he worked his way down the path onto the shelf of land at the shore. He retrieved the trap frames left against the rocks, adding to his awkward burden.

He shuffled along the rough shoreline slowly. Naika ranged ahead, casting about a short blind canyon that opened onto the flatland ahead. Her low, penetrating growl snapped Ivar's eyes forward; the hairs on the back of his neck stirred, for that primal canine growl meant bear.

Naika quartered back and forth on a spot near the mouth of the little canyon, nose to the ground, alert and walking with springs in her legs. He dropped the trap frames, unslung the Mauser, and moved forward.

The first sign he saw was his own back trail, ski tracks shadowing the clear snow. But on top of his trail were the wide pad marks of a polar bear. Without wind to fill in the marks, there was no way of judging how old the tracks were.

He knelt and studied the ground where the bear's track overlaid his own. His scent and Naika's must have attracted the bear. It had crossed and recrossed their trail, making a mosaic of pad prints in the snow.

He backtracked the bear for 50 feet. The trail led from the shoreline but did not return. He studied the dark waters of the fjord and saw a large floe a mile or so out. The nomadic ice had brought him the first white bear of the season.

He returned to where the bear's tracks cut his own, then followed the large, long-clawed prints to the mouth of the blind canyon. He stared up into the cluttered chute but saw nothing. He made no move to follow the tracks; they led into an ambusher's paradise.

He turned away from the canyon. As he skied across the flatlands below Fox Valley, he measured the end of the Arctic day with eyes that missed nothing. The twilight was deeper now, the sky a cold cerulean bowl foreshadowing an endless frigid night. And into that night would come the heavy-bodied, light-footed bears. If he were to survive, he must walk even more lightly than the hungry white shadows.

NIGHT

The wind slammed the side of the cabin like a savage hand. It was early December and the wind screamed in harsh, continuous cacophony around the corners and past the windows of Main Cabin.

For three days he was shut up in the cabin, except for one bone-chilling outing to feed the huskies. He killed the crawling hours mending harness, washing clothes and laying them in the storeroom where the wash water froze and could be shattered off, whittling sticks for traps and talking to Naika. Halfway through the blizzard, the wind snapped the antenna he had rigged for his radio, and he lost the one-way company of Radio Luxembourg.

He slept as much as he could, and when he became totally bored, he made a month's supply of bread, kneading the dough furiously to loosen muscles tense with inactivity.

The third morning was much like the first two, with the wind wailing laments to the dark absence of dawn. He lay for half an hour in his bed, then decided that he had earned another raid on his store of books. He rolled out, lighted the lamp and fire, made a big breakfast and a full pot of coffee and sat down near the fire with the book he had nibbled at on and off through the storm. Scarlett and Rhett were locked in a mad embrace over his cooling oatmeal when he sensed that something had changed. He puzzled for a moment, then realized that the wind had died.

The chair grated loudly in the silence as he pushed back from the table and went to the door. The blizzard had blown the last twilight out of Hornsund, leaving behind an unbroken expanse of darkness and snow.

Ivar returned to the table and closed *Gone with the Wind*. After long days of enforced thumb-twiddling, he was eager to be out and doing. He pulled on his heavy clothes and gathered up his gear—a sackful of ptarmigan heads for trap bait, a shovel to dig the frames out of the snow, the Mauser and a box of shells. And Naika, of course.

The air was absolutely still as he pushed his skis along an arc toward the Fox Valley flatlands, where he had laid out his first trapline. The fresh snow, packed by the wind, squeaked beneath his weight. Overhead, stars glinted cold and hard against the bottomless sky. For an hour at midday, the stars would be lost in a faint wash of slate light, but for the rest of the day, the stars would be there, pinholes in the shroud of Arctic night.

He skied quickly, using body and poles in a rhythm that was as natural to him as walking. Naika worked to keep up and at the same time explore the nooks and holes along the trail. In the low spots, the snow was several feet deep, packed by the relentless winds. The high areas were almost bare. An intense cold fell from the brittle sky as man and dog moved across the snow, pushing the shapeless night before them.

The first trap was close to the cabin, surrounded by snow. He could see that the frame still hung poised on its prop. He looked back to make sure that Naika had not followed before he skied over to check the trap.

The snow had built up in small mounds around the wooden square, added girth to the outer edge of each rock on the trap but left the area under the trap relatively free of new snow. The bait was untouched. He did not change the bait, although wind and cold had dried the ptarmigan head. The less he handled the bait, the better the results. Even though he took the precaution of keeping a pair of gloves in a box of ptarmigan feathers and using only those gloves when working with trap or bait, foxes were notoriously quick to pick up even the most tenuous foreign scent. The trap was highly visible, close by a well-used fox trail. And fox curiosity was great; it would be a rare fox that overlooked this intrusion into its domain. Once the ptarmigan tidbit was scented, the trap should do its work, especially now, at the beginning of the season.

As he moved away from the unsprung trap and skied toward the next trap, he heard the sea ice creak as it sagged on the outgoing tide.

He checked his surroundings again. To the limit of his night vision, the snow lay in an undisturbed blanket. No movement, no tracks. He listened, breathing quietly through the cold that ached in his throat, heard no sound save the restive sea ice. But ice noise and night could conceal a multitude of living dangers.

He closed his eyes and held himself perfectly still, searching for the least indication that his unnamed senses had discovered what eyes and ears had missed. Nothing. No malaise, no thin, uneasy feeling of being watched by other life.

He opened his eyes and skied to the next trap, all senses alert. He knew he was most vulnerable checking traps alone in the darkness, when Naika's ears and exceptional nose were 100 yards distant. He was on his own, dependent on human senses that were no match for those of the polar bear. In the endless night, he had learned to rely on information that came to him from below the usual sensory level. Maybe it was the presence of other life within the sphere of his own life that warned him, or maybe it was a sound or scent so subtle that he perceived it only unconsciously. Whatever it was that triggered his awareness, he was grateful. It had saved his life many times.

The first trapline check was a long and fruitless one. The storms had flattened some of the traps; others had drifted so full of snow that he had to dig them out and relocate them on higher ground. Twelve wearying hours of darkness and digging and digging and darkness. By the time he had completed the circular trek, he was clumsy with cold and hunger. The billion stars overhead gave small light and less comfort—it was cold enough to freeze mercury, to say nothing of blood.

He skied forward eagerly, anticipating the rewards of Arctic labor, fire and hot food and coffee laced with Scotch.

For all his haste, he was alert. His eyes strained into the darkness, scanning rocks and sea ice, seeking bear sign. No movement, no danger yet. He stared around intently. The new snow magnified starlight, giving the land an eerie blue glow.

Silhouetted against the shimmering frozen surface of Fox Lake (left), Ivar chops holes for his ice-fishing line; at right, he pauses during a ski trek, faithful Naika at his side. Below, left, is Bird Mountain Cabin in summertime; at center, an inquisitive polar bear tests the wind; far right, Ivar takes the dog sled out on the sea ice.

Naika lagged behind. She had covered twice the distance he had, and she was tired. Her tail had drooped until it was level with her back. Suddenly she stopped, and her low growl curled down Ivar's spine. Bear.

He stopped immediately, slipped the rifle off his back. He knew that the bear was close, for Naika had caught its scent on the wind. But he had no idea where or how close. As he thumbed the safety off, he spoke softly to the vague dark blur that was Naika. She moved up beside him, staring into the night, head lifted a little to catch another scent. The bear must be out of sight, probably beyond the rocky rise 80 yards away. His eyes could not see the rise, but he had traveled this trail many times.

Naika was silent now, still sniffing the small breeze, and cocking her head from side to side, trying to locate a sound he could not hear. He stabbed his ski poles into the snow and knelt to undo the bindings on his boots. He worked with one hand, keeping the rifle ready in the other and watching the tiny circle of land he could see. No movement. Then he heard, far off, faint, the low sounds of a prowling bear. Naika answered, deep in her chest, uneasy yet excited. She loved the hunt, but she also understood its dangers.

Freed of the skis and poles, he shifted the rifle to his right hand and walked forward, calling very softly to Naika to follow. She trotted stiff-legged, head up.

Ivar circled toward the shoreward side of the rise, looking for tracks. He had to know where the bear was. Some bears avoided or ignored man, but the odds for either were not of an order to encourage carelessness. He had no desire to kill, only to know location, and if there were more than one bear. He paused, slowed his breathing, listened for another sound that would locate the bear. Nothing.

He advanced another ten steps and stopped again. This time he could hear low snuffling bear sounds. In his mind he could see the bear somewhere on the other side of the rise, aware of life approaching, head swaying on long supple neck, testing the air, waiting.

Naika growled again, but he made no move to silence her. If she could discourage or spook the bear, fine. Unless there was no choice, hunting polar bear in the polar night was plain stupid. Naika growled, loud and rumbling, a sound that released more adrenaline into Ivar's blood. If the bear was going to bolt, it would do so now.

But the bear stood its ground, out of sight, over the rise, wrapped in night. Then he heard the bear huff loudly. The fur along Naika's back rose like a black fan. She flowed to the base of the rise and stopped, a shapeless shadow among all the other shapeless rock shadows.

Ivar swore silently. He had no desire to take on a thousand pounds of aggressive bear when he could not see more than 12 feet ahead. He shifted the rifle to his left hand and pried a stone from the slope at his feet. The stone arced silently over the rise. Naika exploded into eager yaps and charged forward. He called her back, but her excitement drowned whatever small noises a retreating bear might make. He held his breath, hand over Naika's muzzle, listening with every sense of his body and mind.

Finally he heard the bear. He moved up the slope to hear better, but still could not be sure where the bear was. He had to know. The bear was between him and the only route to the cabin. The ice foot that was the trail was narrow, too narrow; it would be impossible either to avoid the bear or wait for it to wander off. The longer he waited, the colder he became. Soon he would not be able to depend on his body, his reflexes. His feet were numb, his bones sharp and cold with hunger.

Yet he waited, listening and hoping and motionless. The few squeaks and crunches he heard were inconclusive—the bear could be backing off or circling around or climbing the ridge. It was time to take the initiative.

He moved as quietly as he could up the remaining 10 yards to the top of the rise. When he breasted the small hill, the spot where the bear should have been was empty. He glanced right, toward the frozen fjord. Empty. A flicker of movement, no more, to his left.

He spun and faced the white bear less than 15 feet away, lunging from behind the boulder, cat-fast and deadly.

His shot was reflex. He snapped the Mauser forward at arm's length and pulled the trigger. The rifle barrel seemed to touch the point of the bear's shoulder as the muzzle flashed, and the 300-grain lead bullet slammed into bone and through the heart.

The impact of the shot lifted the bear off its right front paw and threw the animal sideways. The bear went down without a sound, rolling over and over down the unbroken snow slope.

Before the bear stopped rolling, Ivar whipped the rifle bolt and jacked in another round. The muzzle flash had blinded him for a few seconds. He held the rifle ready as his eyes began to readjust. Then he saw Naika snarling around the bear that lay bonelessly against a boulder.

As the last echoes of the single shot faded, he listened to the silence. Was there another bear? Was this one dead? No sound or movement but Naika circling the bear with low growls. Naika was not certain either.

He moved to his left along the crest of the rise, checking again the rocks where the bear had hidden. Even the quick glimpse he had of the lunging bear made him think it was a male, therefore probably alone. But

37

if the bear was a female, with a near-grown cub or even two, the threat was not ended with one death. Moving cautiously, breath quick and shallow, rifle halfway to his shoulder, he listened to the darkness.

He circled 50 feet to the left to examine the bear's tracks. The bear had been alone. The first wanderers of the dark usually were, but usually was not good enough when dealing with polar bears.

He doubled back on the slope to the motionless bear. Naika was still holding her distance, worrying the bear with growls and stiff-legged charges that stopped just short of the thick white fur.

With the threat of a second attack diminished, he decided to risk the loss of his night vision. From the pocket of his parka, he produced a flashlight. Holding it in one hand, but not switching it on, he approached the bear cautiously. He circled the bear at a distance of 10 feet, rifle trained on the long white neck.

Naika's growls increased as he walked up to the bear's head, partially buried by snow that had drifted in the lee of the rock. He switched on the light. The cold had sapped some of the strength from its beam, but the effect was still dazzling against the clean snow and pure white fur of the bear. The light picked up silver tones in the fur, gave it texture and depth. As he swept the beam across the bear, he spotted at once the small crimson entry wound, just forward of the massive shoulder. A fine shot, for reflexes—but then, the range had been point-blank.

The spot of light swept back up to the wedge-shaped head, where ebony eyes shone blankly. He extended the rifle barrel until it touched an unprotected eye. No movement, no flicker. The bear was indeed dead.

For the first time since he had heard Naika's primal growl, he began to relax. Using his teeth, he pulled off a glove and touched the silvery-white gleaming fur. Beneath his chilled fingers, the hairs felt cool. He worked his fingers into the pelt, seeking warmth. And there was warmth, but as he touched it he could sense it dissipating into the polar night.

Ivar stood and swept the beam of light along the bear. Male, rather small, probably no more than 700 pounds. The bear's fur had the fine white glow of health. The winter coat had filled in; there was no yellowing of age on the chest or along the legs. It was a good pelt, well worth the taking. No waste here, no regrets.

He snapped off the light and stepped back, savoring the understanding that his life had been at stake and he had won. Even as he weighed the experience, the rush of adrenaline was fading, diminishing, gone.

He had a lot to do and no adrenaline to help. The bear must be covered until he could return with the dogs to drag the carcass back to Main Cabin. If the bear were left unprotected, other bears might find and eat the carcass. In the long Arctic night, no source of protein was ignored.

Shouldering the rifle, he moved woodenly up the rise to get his shovel, calculating the hours between work and rest. He had been up since six; if he worked very quickly, he might be home by midnight.

After six hours of sleep, Ivar dragged himself out of the warm down womb and ate a fast breakfast. There had not been enough snow to do a proper job of covering the bear. Worse, a wind had come up as he slept. He had to get back before scavengers ruined the pelt.

When he appeared outside the cabin, harness in hand, the huskies went wild. Svarten did his best to keep order during the harnessing, but he could not be everywhere at once. Bumpsa and Grisen, normally affable, took a sudden and virulent dislike to being harnessed together. Ivar waded in and restored order with a few kicks and a multitude of curses. The huskies separated, unscathed.

The harness was another matter. That thirty-second tantrum had tied an unbelievable number of tight knots in the stiff leather. His invective soared as he tried to pick frozen knots apart with rapidly freezing fingers; he wished he had kicked Bumpsa and Grisen all the way around the cabin—twice.

Ivar knew that the only way to control a team of huskies was to convince the dogs that he was the meanest son of a bitch around. Huskies were not lapdogs. They would kill each other if he did not stop them.

He worried the last knot loose and put Svarten into the lead position. The harness was simple; a single trace connected to the sled, with dogs tied in staggered pairs on either side of the main line.

Svarten was clearly the leader. Surly was clearly the rear guard, where his long teeth and vile disposition encouraged any laggards to hold the pace. Naika was not harnessed. She ran loose behind the sled unless she was needed to help with an unusually heavy load.

Ivar gave a final check to the harness, his ski bindings and the gear strapped to the sled. When he slung his rifle over his back and picked up the towrope that trailed behind the sled, the huskies whined eagerly. He took a firm grip on the knotted end of the rope. His command to run was barely out of his mouth before Svarten leaped forward, yanking the rest of the huskies off their feet.

In seconds, the dogs were towing him and the nearly empty sled in a mad rush over the dark and frozen land.

For the first mile he did nothing more than hang on, knowing that there was nothing else he could do. The huskies were wild with their first run of the season. They would respond to nothing but their own pounding blood. The snow covered most rocks, but he still had to strain into the darkness, ready to swing out on the towrope to avoid boulders and bare spots. If he should get dumped now, the dogs would not stop for him. He hung on, knees flexed, cheeks burning, silent laughter curving his cold lips. Neither cold nor darkness nor hidden rocks could mar the sheer, rushing beauty of the huskies and the hissing skis.

At the end of the first mile, the team's all-out run settled into a steady, hard-pulling gallop. It was time to see if Svarten remembered his master's voice. Ivar yelled for Svarten to veer right. The big black dog responded promptly. Ivar called for a left turn. Svarten moved quickly to the left. Ivar was pleased, but he knew better than to press his luck by asking the team to stop. It would take a bit more running before the huskies would listen to such a ridiculous request. Better to give them their heads now, so they would not be fractious when he loaded the bear on the sled.

As they approached the rise, he waited for the dogs to show that they scented bear. When the team continued its ground-eating lope, he felt the beginnings of relief; the bear probably had not been disturbed. Just to be sure that there were no live bears downwind of the carcass, he let the dogs run before the wind for another half mile before he called out for Svarten to go left. Svarten immediately bore left, beginning a long arc across the flat coastal shelf as Ivar yelled encouragement from the end of the towrope.

Just as the dogs had half completed the turn and were facing out toward the fjord, a flicker of white flashed from behind a grounded iceberg close to shore. They had surprised a white fox on its scavenging rounds. Ivar saw the fox an instant before the huskies did and screamed for the team to stop, simultaneously kicking sideways and dragging against the towrope to emphasize his command. But Svarten had also seen the fox. The chase was joined.

Unfortunately, the fox was old and cunning, it knew that its chances of skirting around the team to the safety of shore were zero. The fox veered right, toward the fjord, running belly down away from the shore.

Ivar yelled repeatedly for the team to stop, but Svarten ignored the commands; the fresh smell of fox was irresistible. The big husky leaned right, pulling the team after the fox. Ivar was helpless to do anything more than hang onto the rope and scream curses at the headstrong leader. If Ivar turned loose of the towrope, the dogs might run unchecked for 10 to 15 miles. Svarten flattened out, working hard against the traces, running with great open strides that the other dogs strained to match. But the fox had the advantage. It became a white blur at the edge of vision, fading in and out of the darkness like a dream. The huskies ran on, still picking up speed, giving Ivar bare seconds to discover and avoid rocks leaping out of the darkness. He tried to keep loose, knees flexed, body ready to twist and weave as necessary.

Suddenly Svarten and the rest of the team dropped, the sled thumped loudly and Ivar was airborne over the 30-inch ridge that marked the last of the land and the first of the sea ice. He had known that the ridge would be there—the tide was ebbing—but there was no time to lean back and raise the tips of his skis. He landed hard enough to make his teeth ache, but he landed right side up.

The bay ice was thick, but it was far from safe. In every direction he could see vague shapes, the remains of summer icebergs frozen into the new ice. Knee-high, waist-high, head-high, they made an obstacle course that he had to negotiate at top speed in darkness. Without real hope of effect, he yelled at Svarten to stop.

He was still yelling when the fox faded through a narrow gap between two low icebergs. Svarten hit the opening flat out. Bumpsa and Grisen were forced up and over the bergs. Ivar hoped the sled would jam between the blocks of ice, forcing the dogs to stop, but Bumpsa's frantic scrambling had tipped the sled onto one runner; it was unceremoniously yanked through by the charging huskies. Ivar was jerked out of position, heading straight for an iceberg. He crouched and swung way out to the right, holding the towrope up to clear the top of the berg. He felt the outside edge of his left ski scrape and heard the thin song of wood against immobile ice. Close.

He breathed deeply and yelled until his throat was cold and hoarse, but he might as well have been shouting encouragement. The fox had faded into view again, a white cloud flying low in front of the silent, racing huskies. He opened his mouth to yell again, then heard something that froze the breath in his throat.

The sound seemed to come from far away, as though someone were slowly pulling nails from green lumber—new sea ice flexing as it gave beneath the combined weight of dogs and sled and man. The fox had led them onto thin ice disguised beneath a layer of snow.

Quickly Ivar swung out to the left, toward heavier ice and the safety of land, pulling and yelling at the team. But the huskies were too strong, the quarry too close. The team plunged on.

Ivar was helpless. If he let go, he would be stranded on the sagging ice.

Worse, he would doom the huskies. As long as he hung on, there was a chance that Svarten would respond. The huskies had run at top speed for more than 2 miles; they had to be winded. If only the fox would help out by doubling back toward shore. But what was acute danger for the heavy dogs was utter safety for the little Arctic fox, and the fox knew it.

The ice gave beneath Ivar's skis, stretching like an elastic sheet, humping up in subtle rises that became hillocks. He skied the flexing ice and abandoned the idea of stopping the dogs. Their only hope now was movement, never resting long enough for the ice to give way. And turn the team—he must turn the team.

His urgent command rang out over the ice, was swallowed up in darkness and groaning. He called again and yet again, called until either fatigue or training or the uneasy ice brought Svarten out of his single-minded pursuit of the white fox.

Svarten edged left, slowed, ice rippled and heaved. Svarten plunged forward, tightening the traces as he picked up speed again. Under the hoarse lash of Ivar's voice, the big husky kept the tired team running over the rubbery ice, running in a sweeping arc that pulled them toward shore. By degrees the ice stopped swaying and groaning, and finally Ivar was again dodging icebergs in the bay. When he saw the shore break, he called for Svarten to stop. Svarten did so immediately, a model of fatigued obedience. Cursing the dogs steadily, Ivar forced his cramped fingers to let go of the towrope. Svarten's head drooped; he did not understand the words, but the tone was scathing.

Ivar stood, flexing his hands to restore circulation, spewing imprecations until his breathing and adrenaline level returned to normal. He looked back over the bay of ice, but it was far too dark to spot the cause of all the trouble. He had a mental picture of the sly white fox sitting on its haunches, pink tongue quivering with silent laughter.

And as for you, you little bastard, if I trap you, I'll feed you to the dogs—pelt and all!

With a last dispirited curse, he pulled his mind back to the business at hand. There was still a bear to be dug out and levered aboard the sled and dragged back to the cabin. Then the entire trapline must be checked. Muttering softly, he helped the dogs pull the sled up over the ice lip onto shore. It was going to be a long day.

Ivar skied slowly along the shoreline east of Main Cabin. Behind him was a straight eleven hours of trapline work. Checking downed traps, knocking 80 pounds of rock off wooden boards, resetting triggers, piling

80 pounds of rock back onto tilted frames, watching piles slide off when the last rock was put into place, starting all over again. All but one of the traps was storm-downed; Ivar's packsack contained one lone fox.

Tomorrow he would shut down this trapline and reopen the wide, ragged circle of traps that started behind Main Cabin, curved along the lower edge of Fox Valley and out across the flatlands, then arced down and blended into the coastal trapline just below Fox River. Each day for seven days he would make the same twelve-hour circle. Then he would shut down that trapline and go back on the coast for another week.

He had between eighty and one hundred traps laid out and usually kept half of them open. Yet for all the movement from mountain to flatland to shoreline, he felt as though he were setting the same trap over and over and over again. In the dark, there was so little difference. The icy rocks and square frames and pale snow never varied. Only his body changed, more cold and tired with each dark stone, each dark trap, each dark hour.

But even more than fatigue, the long weeks of night dragged at him as he shuffled away from the last coastal trap. The stars gave some light, as did the crescent moon sliding down into the frozen sea, but the light was far too thin to feed eyes hungry for the colors of summer. The monotone wind matched the monochrome land, unvarying, uncaring, stultifying. Then an invisible bank of clouds condensed in the west, blotting out the moon and the polar stars. Landmarks and shapes and gradations of darkness all drowned in a tidal surge of featureless night.

His unease opened like a black flower, each petal a separate fear. He stopped suddenly, eyes straining to orient his body. There, that bulge of snow. Was it a rock close by or a hill further off? Was it a ptarmigan or a fox or a bear? Without perspective, there was no way to be sure. But did it matter? Did anything matter in this unreality?

Deliberately, he knelt and checked his ski bindings. The wind blew over his half-turned face, cut coldly across his eyes. The movement and pain reassured him; he was not dreaming, not caught in a shapeless nightmare from which there was no waking.

He stood and turned to face the wind. The rifle slung over his shoulder bumped his side. Another reality. He kicked the stock with his elbow, and the rifle moved again. With his left hand he reached up and touched the strap of the packsack over his other shoulder. The frozen fox, retrieved from a trap hours ago, rested lightly on his hip. He took a shallow breath, and the sound of air being drawn through nostrils crusted with ice calmed him. Still alive, still breathing.

Above the keening wind came the far-off explosion of two ice plates moving together on the force of the tide. The tidal flow was proof that the moon still existed and worked its ways upon the water. Again the far-off grinding crunch.

I exist, and the rest of the world exists. Nothing has changed but the light.

He had known the feeling of nonbeing before, many times, but each time its depth and cutting edge surprised him. During his first winter, it had struck him shortly after the sun set for the last time. He had been alone at Cabin Bay, working a one-man trapline while Fredrik stayed at Main Cabin with the dogs and the Fox Valley trapline.

The night malaise had struck deep and hard. Only his pride had kept him at Cabin Bay for endless days, skiing the traps and grappling with the fact of being totally alone. One night, in the dark cabin, he had cried with the realization that he was afraid and alone and there was little he could do about either. It had been a long, long time since he had last cried; the uncontrolled release of tension and anguish helped. He felt real again, if somewhat chagrined. The Arctic night had scoured him down to raw flesh, but he had found that flesh still existed.

Ivar stood for a while longer, letting the wind tug at his beard, measuring the loneliness that was the other face of freedom.

He knew that fear and the dark were corrosive, and that his own mind could be his worst enemy. But he was here and here he would stay until sunrise. He would endure because he had chosen to do so.

And because there was no other choice.

New Year's was followed by three weeks of wind and storm, trapline work and intense restlessness. The end of the long Arctic night was near, but the fact did not comfort him. Light was hanging just below the southeast horizon, two weeks to dawn. Just fourteen days. Just eternity.

Because the end of darkness was so close, he had unconsciously loosened his control over his tightly held emotions. Now they were racing ahead of him like a runaway team, pulling him in every direction. Almost three months with no more light than rare, cloudless hours dotted with tiny stars, and rarest of all, a full moon in a clear sky. Pale moon, paler stars, tiny lamps and flashlights and fires. Not enough. Not nearly enough. Cold and black and alone on the edge of the world.

He struggled against his writhing loneliness, knowing that it would vanish with the first touch of sunlight. But it was a difficult battle. Main Cabin's amenities no longer held his interest. Radio, guitar, books, even Scotch bored him. His mood was savage. Each day he made a small ritual of striking a square off the calendar, telling himself that was one less day in hell. Two weeks left, then twelve days, then ten.

When the countdown to light reached seven days, his restlessness won. The Main Cabin traplines had not yielded a single fox in ten days. The foxes were either smart or dead. He had no more skins to prepare except those of three bears frozen beneath the snow. He could not skin a frozen carcass; the bears would have to wait for the sun to thaw them. He had cleaned the cabin twice in one day. Bread was baked for a month. Harness was shining and supple. Rifles had been cleaned until they gleamed like antique pewter. He had melted enough ice to take a bath and wash his clothes. There was simply nothing left to do but wait for dawn, and waiting for dawn was a sure way to come down with terminal cabin fever.

It was time to go to Bird Mountain.

The dogs, including Naika, would stay at Main Cabin. If he took the team and found that the sea ice was impassable, he would have to turn back; the inland route was too rugged for the team.

He hacked off a generous amount of seal, better than three days' food for each dog, and chained Naika with the team. The meat would be gulped or hoarded, depending on each dog's temperament. Either way, the dogs were good for up to a week of waiting without hardship.

With the dogs taken care of, he attended to his own needs. A small supply of food, in case the cabin's stores had been raided by a bear. Pup tent, sleeping bag, ammunition, two very sharp knives, matches, primus stove, fuel, tobacco bag, extra socks, three chocolate bars, flashlight and extra batteries. And the Mauser, of course.

Everything but the rifle and knives went into the backpack, with no room left over. He eased the pack on, flexed his shoulder muscles to settle the load and picked up the Mauser. Although the rifle weighed 14 pounds, he accepted its weight as automatically as he accepted the weight of his own body. After a last check of the dogs, he set out on skis.

For the first time in weeks, the sky was partly clear and the wind was merely a minor-key moan over the frozen land. Starlight reflected by snow gave him a visibility of 15 feet. Even though he knew it was too soon, he kept on looking ahead, hoping to spot at least a faint paling of predawn in the east. Once his heart leaped at a silver glow spreading above the mountains, but in the next second he realized it was only the moon. Yet even that slender crescent added a few feet of visibility to his tiny world.

He shuffled east, reminding himself with every other step that this was indeed a different piece of ice, a different trail, a different destination.

Something new. But for all his self-lecturing, he felt like an ant on a treadmill. There were only so many ways ice could respond to wind and tide, and he had seen them all, too many times. Without light, certainty of progress was a matter of faith reinforced by experience.

When he arrived at Bird Mountain Cabin, it showed the scars of winter, plus long scratches down the wall where a prowling bear had casually raked claws across tar paper. A recent wind had dislodged the spring cache of dog food from the roof. The seal lay in the snow near the doorway. Bear tracks were all around it; the seal hide had long gouges but was otherwise intact. Apparently the bear preferred its dinners warm.

He considered heaving the carcass back onto the roof, then decided not to. The next bear probably might not be so fussy. He would rather have bears gnawing on the seal than gnawing on the cabin, or him.

The inside of the cabin was dark, cold and coated with hoarfrost. He swept out the frost before he lit the fire. The 6-foot-square living room warmed quickly.

Ivar shrugged out of his parka and put the rifle in the entryway-storeroom. The stove's heat would not penetrate that far, and the rifle would be safe from repeated cycles of heat and cold that could leave a destructive condensation of water and ice in the firing mechanism. Though he invariably cleaned his rifles at least once a week, he knew that no amount of care could compensate for alternating between fire and ice.

He warmed his fingers by the stove until they were supple again. After he had eaten an indifferent dinner of stew and coffee, he put on his parka and went back to the storeroom. He pulled open the hinged panel in the outer door, looked out, saw nothing. He picked up a hammer and a can of nails from a nearby shelf and renailed the tar paper on the outside of the cabin and the insulation on the inside. Where wind and claws had torn the tar paper, frost had got underneath the insulation, forcing it away from the wall. Nothing serious, but worth repairing.

Inside again, he sat in the lamplight for a few minutes, studying the 6-by-6-foot living space for other projects, and finally decided on a small shelf below the window, on the wall beside the stove, opposite the bunk. It was the only section of wall that was not already in use for storage. A fine place for tobacco, Scotch, seasonings, and whatever else would fit.

By the time the shelf was completed and completely full, he felt ready for sleep. The wind was picking up a little, just enough to make moaning noises through rocky passes and around cabin eaves.

He was keenly aware of his isolation. Not even Naika's alert brown eyes for company, no team to warn of bears, few supplies if a long storm settled in. All for an unnecessary trip, a sop to his savage cabin fever. The realization of unnecessary risks made him uneasy. In previous years he would have taken greater chances without a second thought. Now he took chances, then told himself what a damned fool he was.

He slept restlessly for an hour or more.

The strident sounds of splintering wood, screeching nails and shattering glass brought Ivar instantly awake. Only a polar bear could demolish the heavily shuttered window so quickly. And with the window gone, all the food smells of the cabin would pour out, spurring the bear's hunger.

Ivar thrust his hands above his head, groping for the tie cord. As he tugged at the cord, he heard the delicate, filelike sound of bear claws brushing down the nylon skin of the mummy bag. It took him less than a second to remember the knot and realize he was trapped.

A heavy weight fell on his chest and the sound of claws became less delicate. The bear had reached across the room and was testing the curious, unfleshlike covering of the wriggling bag. Adrenaline swept through Ivar's body, releasing a wave of strength. His arms went rigid, then slammed out against the bag, once, twice, and the tough nylon split away from his driving fists.

He flattened himself on the bunk, trying to avoid the bear's probing paw as he peeled the sleeping bag off his body and kicked free. He started to sit up, but his head crashed into what felt like a rock. Even as he realized that the rock was the polar bear's lower jaw, he threw himself flat again and scooted down the bunk on his back.

The sudden blow and the equally sudden appearance of Ivar's white undershirt where the dark mummy bag had been caused the bear to pull back slightly. Ivar was so close to the animal's massive head that he saw the bear's eyes widen with surprise, smelled the mixture of carnivore breath and spilled Scotch from the shattered bottle on the new shelf, felt the quick rush of air as the bear cleared its nostrils of the astringent alcohol scent. The bear's withdrawal sent a second bottle of Scotch flying over the stove. The room reeked of steaming, stinging Scotch, and the wind poured snow through the open window.

When the bear sneezed, Ivar came off the bunk in a tumbling rush. His bare feet came down on a pile of broken glass. He felt cutting edges and heard his curses over the bear's snarls. He threw himself back on the bunk, yanked pieces of glass out of his foot and hit the floor again.

The smell of blood encouraged the polar bear; its paw hissed by Ivar's body. Had he been standing, he would have been neatly gutted. He scrambled toward the door of the room without thinking, intent only on getting his rifle in the entryway-storeroom before the bear got more than a long neck and a longer arm into the tiny cabin.

The bear pushed hard against the groaning window frame and swiped again, lower this time. Ivar heard the whistle of claws an inch above his head. He hugged the floor and squirmed on. Then there was silence broken only by the creak of the door as he pushed it open and crawled into the storeroom.

He noticed the silence but not the minus-20 cold of the outer room as he stood up. He lifted the rifle from its rack, pushed a round into the chamber and slipped to the outer door. He listened. Nothing. He held his breath. Still no sound. Slowly, he eased open the hinged panel in the upper half of the door.

The bear's head and neck burst through the opening. Ivar jumped back, narrowly avoiding the open mouth and lethal teeth. Two steps and he was flat against the closed living-room door. The bear's hot breath bathed his stomach. No room to swing the door open and escape back into the living room, not even room to bring the rifle to his shoulder. The small space seemed filled with claws and teeth.

He raised the rifle over his head, wrapped his left hand around the barrel, hooked his right thumb through the trigger and slammed the muzzle down on top of the bear's weaving head. The flash of exploding power was like a knife across his eyes and the recoil slammed him against the wall. Blind, dazed and deafened, he tripped the rifle bolt and rammed home a new shell. When his eyes recovered, the bear was gone.

Ivar edged sideways down the row of shelves. He heard nothing, which meant the bear was either dead or waiting. At such close range it seemed impossible he had missed, but it was also impossible to rip a mummy bag like wet cardboard. He oozed up to the open panel and looked out.

The bear lay motionless a few feet away.

Ivar slid outside and checked the bear's eye for reflexes. The bear was quite dead. He laid his palm on the rough warmth of the white head and drew a slow breath, relishing the icy bite of air against his throat. He felt weightless, flying, incredibly and totally alive. Under pale starlight the land was exquisite, each fine detail utterly distinct, the frost tracery over tar paper, the pewter gleam of snow crystals, the timeless strength of wind, perfect beyond dreams.

With a sort of distant shock, he realized he was getting warm and sleepy; the snow was as inviting as a down quilt.

Back inside, Superman. You're freezing faster than that bear.

With glacial reluctance, he turned his back on the flawless moment and reentered the cabin. It seemed to take forever to build up the fire. Coal kept jumping out of his hands and rattling across the cabin. After the fire was going, he pulled on his pants and surveyed his damaged feet.

In the lamplight, a ragged red cut showed across the bottom of his right foot. He vaguely remembered pulling glass out of it earlier. The foot did not hurt, but that meant nothing—ice is a first-class anesthetic. When his foot warmed up, he would have a better idea of what damage the glass had done.

He turned the cut foot carefully in the light, trying to pick up glints from glass slivers that might still be embedded in the flesh. Finding nothing, he gave his left foot the same careful scrutiny. Random superficial cuts. Only a couple had drawn blood.

He boiled a pan of water on the stove, washed the cuts, poured Scotch over them and gritted his teeth, wishing that feeling had not returned quite so quickly. The right foot bled freely now, but pressure and bandages solved that problem. He bandaged the other foot, pulled on socks and boots and crunched through the glass to find a hammer and nails. He felt very lucky; none of the cuts had required stitches. Sewing himself up was his least favorite pastime.

The night had lost its fine edge of perfection, but he did not care. The moment of exhilaration was engraved on his soul. This bear had brought him as close to death as he had ever come. And as close to life.

After six more hours of sleep, he hurried through breakfast and cabin cleanup, including nailing tar paper over the broken window. In five hours, if the clouds were not too thick, he would be able to see some light in the eastern sky. It was illogical to hurry. The clouds would either lift or not. His rushing about would make no difference. But Ivar's hunger for light was not logical. His movements were electric with anticipation.

He made a final circuit of the cabin's exterior, noting that ivory gulls and foxes had already been at work on the polar-bear carcass. Then he strapped on his skis and went to close down his fox traps. A few hours work and one smoky blue fox. He stroked the lovely fur, then hurried back to the cabin for his packsack. He hitched himself to the heavy, frozen skin and moved down to the fjord ice.

Clouds were an invisible ceiling overhead, and the wind gusted erratically. The ice had brine slicks in some areas, slowing him down. After four hours he saw a star, then three, then hundreds scattered through rents in the cloud cover. The air was very cold and tipped with ice. Another storm in the making.

Half an hour later, just before noon, he stopped and drank from the small canteen he carried inside his parka. The water was chilly but well above freezing. As he tucked the canteen away again, he glanced overhead. The stars were very pale, almost invisible. The clouds were mounds of dark gray wool. He looked automatically over his shoulder, southeast. There, unmistakably, were the twin points of Hornsund Peak, silhouetted against the faintest wash of pale, pale blue light. As he watched, the horns sharpened, then faded again into darkness and clouds.

The afterimage glowed in his mind like a first kiss from a shy woman.

He leaned on his ski poles for a long moment, wondering if he had really seen that pale light, knowing he had, but hardly daring to believe. It had been so long since he had seen the mountains across the fjord that it was almost as if they existed only in his memory. But the mountains were real. He had seen them. The long night was ending.

He straightened above his ski poles and pushed over the fjord ice with easy, powerful strides.

MORNING

The hard, cold, blue-edged light of the middle March sun lay across Hornsund, casting narrow shadows around shore rocks and huge splinters of broken sea ice off the Main Cabin coastline. Ivar and the team moved across the flatland shelf and down a narrow break through the ice barrier built by tides and slashing storm waves.

Snow squeaked cleanly beneath sled runners as the team trotted across the sea ice to the first line of pressure ridges, tumbled blocks and jagged plates of ice thrust up like miniature, illogical mountains a quarter mile from shore. Svarten picked an easy passage through the obstacles, and with Ivar lifting and shoving on the back of the sled, they soon reached less jumbled sea ice.

For a week now, in the full and growing light, he and the huskies had been on the go, prowling Hornsund from Bird Mountain to Halfway Bowl. The traplines were shut down, for soon the foxes would begin seeking mates. From now until the snow and ice disappeared in the first warm winds of May or June or July, he would be constantly on the move, driving himself to exhaustion and his team to footsore, rib-showing thinness, racing up and down the fjord in search of the white bears.

But even in this frenetic season he stopped to savor the piercing turquoise of glacier fronts and the clear silver flow of sunlight down rugged mountainsides, and for a moment he knew a desire to share the wild beauty of the land. Then the team whimpered impatiently and he was racing off again, looking for creamy shadows moving over the radiant, blue-white ice.

If Ivar had been wealthy enough to live in Hornsund without hunting, he would have done so gladly. But few people have enough money to live without working. In order to pay for his fourth year in the Arctic, Ivar needed each of the ten bears the government allowed him to take, plus all the foxes he could trap. Next year he would also be allowed ten bears. The year after—none. No bears, no foxes, no seals, no geese or ducks, nothing but ptarmigan.

Yet Ivar did not fight the new laws. He respected the great white bears. He had lived with them and watched them, been hunted by them and hunted them in turn. Huge and graceful, savage and patient, to Ivar the bears were the essence of the high Arctic. But he did resent being forced out of his chosen home by thoughtless summer "hunters" who searched the sea with power boats and shot the helpless bears as they swam. Too often the bear sank before it could be retrieved. And even if the dead bear was brought aboard, a summer pelt was worthless for display. The easiest way for the government to end the abuse was to ban all bear hunting, even by men who lived alone in the Arctic and met the polar bear on its own terms.

Ivar rested the team for a moment and stood in the middle of the light-filled land. Wind blew curls of dry snow across the ice beyond the pressure ridges. He struck out toward the center of the fjord, looking for bear sign on the hard-packed surface of the sea ice. He had yet to see a bear this week, although he had seen plenty of tracks across the snow. Most of the tracks led eastward, down Hornsund toward the closed end of the fjord, across the island to the eastern coast of Spitsbergen.

He had discussed the bears' pattern of movement with scientists from the Polar Institute and with every old hunter he had ever met. The answer was always the same. Polar bears moved in a giant circle around Spitsbergen, coming down out of the northwest with the pack ice in spring, crossing or circling to the east coast, then following the ice highways and drifting pack ice north as the sun pushed back the cold. By summer the bears' wanderings had taken them to Northeast Land, the most northern of the Svalbard Islands, or onto the pack ice that circled the North Pole. In fall the bears moved south again, by land or by sea ice, following their own noses and an age-old urge out of the barren regions of winter to spots like Hornsund, where ringed seals denned up in spring to give birth.

On hunting trips like this one, Ivar worked out onto the ice, where he was most likely to find fresh bear sign. Most of the time polar bears kept to the ice or the shoreline, wherever travel was easiest. He preferred hunting on sea ice, for it gave him a better chance to spot the bears and to gauge their size from far away. He wanted every chance to avoid a confrontation with a bear that was not a prime male. The intense spring sunlight had allowed him to remount on the Mauser the telescopic sight, which doubled as a spyglass. Now he wanted every advantage he could get, both for himself and for the bear.

A mile offshore he spotted the faint indented trail of a bear on the move. The dogs scented bear. Svarten veered to intersect the tracks, stopping to put his nose into the pad depressions where the edges were serrated by claw gouges. As he caught the fullness of the bear's scent from the tracks, Svarten huffed softly. The fur on his ruff lifted and he raised his long black muzzle into the wind. The team moved restlessly.

Ivar quieted the huskies and knelt by the trail. The wind made judgments tricky, but the fine dusting of snow in the depressions indicated that the tracks were at most a few hours old. He straightened and lifted the rifle to his shoulder, scanning the horizon through the scope. No movement to the east, the direction in which the tracks led.

He knelt again and measured the tracks with his hands; nearly twice as long as his fingers and palm, and as wide as his hand placed sideways. A rather large bear, and alone. Probably a male on the prowl, or perhaps a very old female.

He scanned the horizon again. Nothing moved but wind-blown snow. He turned the team east and followed the bear's trail. The first bears of the spring migration were often fat and healthy, moving fast and easily across the roughest terrain.

As he had expected, the trail veered toward a shallow bay. He lost the tracks in a tumbled pile of glacier and sea ice. For a few minutes he cast around the edges of the pileup, but the iron-hard snow yielded no more tracks. If the bear kept on its former heading, it would end up in the mountains east of Main Cabin. The passes there were few and hair-raising, as he knew only too well.

Curious, he headed the team east, following the tracks. The huskies trotted easily, the sound of their passage drowned by the humming, moaning wind. Beneath the wind he became aware of a strange, very faint noise. He strained toward it, hardly believing his ears. A bear. Angry and rumbling and very far away, muffled by the wind.

He stopped the team and listened carefully. The sounds came again clearer but still faint, from somewhere on shore. He searched the rocks and flatlands for some sign of the bear. Nothing. Not even a track up the ice foot and onto the flatlands.

Again the sound, but so faint he could not pinpoint its source. He lifted the rifle to his shoulder and scanned the shoreline, where storm surf and tidal surges had sculpted fantastic ice shapes. Nothing. But he was not imagining things—Svarten had heard the bear, too. The husky's head was up, ears cocked to catch the sounds. Ivar held his breath and listened. And still he could not locate the origin of the low complaints.

He lowered the rifle and turned away from the shore for a moment. Sometimes the wind and rocky cliffs played games with sound, gathering a noise from behind and bouncing it back on itself. But there were no bears behind him. Nothing but ice.

He turned back toward the shore and slowly swept the ice foot with the scope, studying the flatlands behind. Nothing. He raised his eyes again, examining the base of the rugged mountain slopes. The wind paused for a moment and the sound came clearly. Higher, way up the mountain. There, tiny in the distance, a creamy blur on the blue-white snow. The bear was more than halfway up a steep, bowl-like depression in the mountainside, climbing, heading for a notch between two peaks and growling to itself at the difficulty of the path it had chosen.

The rifle scope brought the bear close enough to show the shuffling gait, the head down and swaying side to side as the bear walked across the hard-packed snow of the little bowl. A male, and a handsome beast, large even at this distance. His coat was so full it looked fluffy, altogether at odds with the tireless power of his shambling walk.

Ivar watched the bear for several minutes, laughing silently at the rumbling complaints that rose and fell in counterpoint to the wind. The bear went where he wished to go, then complained as he went, never quite sure why he had not chosen an easier trail. That was a bear Ivar could understand. The bear could have been only 80 yards away and his finger would have stayed off the trigger; there was something funny and fine about the solitary, muttering animal. He watched until the bear clawed his way to the top of the bowl and disappeared through the notch.

He had plenty of time to take bears, more than sixty days of the maddeningly beautiful spring, white and blue and glittering with light. It was the best time of the year. The mountains were carved out of crystal; every shadow had a lambent blue life of its own, and the horizon was a diamond line of ice punctuated by pale, blue-green glacier fronts. As he looked around, he felt a small ache inside his mind, a nameless, subtle sadness.

All winter you complain of the darkness, and when the light finally comes you're still not happy. What more do you want? What could be better than this?

You're changing. Last year it was enough to be young and alive and living in Hornsund.

The interior changing he felt was elusive. He left it where he had found it. He would live with it until he understood, then he would act.

Further up the fjord, he veered away from the land, toward long, ragged pressure ridges in the fjord ice. Seals sometimes gathered around the fractured ice, and where there were seals there might be bears.

As the wind whistled in from the fractured ice, he stopped the dogs and unslung his rifle to scan the pressure ridges. Three quarters of a mile away, partially hidden by an upthrust chunk of ice, he saw the dark oval shape of a ringed seal. The supply of seal meat at Main Cabin was a little low; soon the dogs should have bear to eat, but it would be foolish to pass up seal today in hope of bear tomorrow.

He began to maneuver into position. He found a spot where tidal pressure had thrown up a broad plate of ice and moved the team behind it. With the dogs tethered to a piece of ice and Naika tethered to the sled, he was free to begin a careful stalk.

He circled around pressure ridges, always keeping at least one ragged ice barrier between himself and the seal. As he stalked, the wind faded to an occasional icy sigh. He removed his skis and eased forward on foot.

After ten minutes, he calculated that he was less than 100 yards away from the seal. Cautiously, slowly, he crept up to the last, waist-high pressure ridge and peered over. The seal was gone; all that marked its passing was a small dark hole through shining ice.

He swore silently, wondering how he had given himself away. Of course, the seal might simply have gotten hungry and returned to the black water to fish. Perhaps it would surface again nearby, at another in the series of breathing holes that each seal maintained.

He scanned the ice through his rifle scope, but saw no fat dark forms on the ice. Then a vague suggestion of motion caught his eye 300 yards upwind, behind another, higher pressure ridge. Though he had seen nothing more than a subtle shift in color, a faint off-white against the blue-white of snow, he knew it had to be a bear.

Even before the thought registered consciously, he was crouched down and trotting toward the seal's breathing hole. The bear might have been stalking the seal, too. Though the seal had vanished beneath the ice, there was a good chance that the bear would move in to wait in ambush beside the hole. Two could play that game.

By the time Ivar flopped beside the breathing hole, the bear was still more than 200 yards off. Quietly, he unslung his rifle and waited.

But when he spotted the bear again, it was heading away. Nothing in its movements suggested hurry or fright; it was simply snuffling among the pressure ridges, hoping to smell its next meal. He watched the bear long enough to assure himself that it was male, above average size and beautifully furred. The wind held low and steady, blowing from the bear to him. He lay without moving, hoping that the bear would glance over and spot the dark, seal-like blot against the snow, an opportunity that no bear would pass up.

The bear continued on his course, out and away from Ivar. Ivar hesitated, then whistled through his teeth, a shrill rising sound that carried far over the ice. Through the scope he saw the bear's head turn. Ivar swung his feet up and down, imitating the motion of a seal's rear flippers. In an instant the bear shifted into hunting movements, low and sinuous and swift. With the controlled grace that always amazed Ivar, the white bear flowed behind a small pressure ridge and vanished.

He waited, knowing the bear would reappear. But where? Left? Right? He raised his eyes above the scope and waited. Though he doubted that the bear would come straight out of the wind, he checked the area ahead.

The bear materialized on the left, 100 yards away. There were no more pressure ridges, only random chunks and hummocks of ice. The bear would move more slowly now, stalking the dark seal-shape with the immense patience unique to predators.

With equal patience Ivar watched the stalk, admiring the consummate skill that allowed the bear to melt behind small ice humps and flow over open spaces. When there was nothing but flat ice left, the bear stretched low, slithering forward, a gliding white silence 50 yards away.

Ivar waited and watched. He could see the long, thick fur feathers behind the front legs fan out as the bear moved forward. Occasionally he caught a vague sigh, but if he had not known the bear was near, he would have assumed it was just the sound of windblown snow crystals.

Slowly, one muscle at a time, Ivar eased into firing position. His subtle movements froze the bear in place. Ivar could see the black shine of the eyes, but the black nose was lost behind a reaching paw.

The two hunters waited, motionless.

After a full minute the bear resumed his gliding stalk. Ivar waited and felt tension building. As long as the bear approached head on and flattened to the ice, Ivar's only target was the broad white forehead. He preferred a spine or heart shot. He could be sure of only one bullet; it had better be all he needed.

The polar bear was less than 30 yards away. A running bear could cover 30 yards in seconds.

Ivar waited, breathing slowly, shallowly. The bear was oozing closer with each breath and still Ivar's only target was the thick skull that could deflect an 8mm bullet. If the bear came much closer, even a heart shot might not kill quickly enough.

A subtle ripple of muscles beneath thick white fur signaled the potent ingathering of a bear about to charge. Ivar shifted the rifle barrel slightly to compensate for the scope setting of 100 yards. If he had had time, he could have counted each hair on the bear's forehead, but the ice seemed to explode as the bear surged forward.

Twenty-five yards—wait, not yet. Twenty—still only the forehead. Eighteen-sixteen-twelve-ten—skull swinging aside. Now!

As the rifle bucked against his shoulder, the bear slid in eerie slow motion that stopped only 20 feet away. The metallic click of the rifle bolt seemed as loud as the shot had been, louder than the echo rolling back from the mountains. But nothing was as loud as the enraged roar dying in the white bear's throat.

Ivar lifted his head from the scope, and his breath rushed out in a long sigh. Too close. Without taking eyes or rifle off the inert bear, he pulled himself slowly upright. Standing, he could see a small scarlet circle spreading slowly, high up on the neck. He started to move closer, but his legs responded sluggishly; unlike a seal, he was not equipped to lie motionless on ice. He stumbled slightly and looked down for better footing. Almost instantly, he returned his attention to the bear.

The black eyes were open. He could not remember if that was a change. Without getting closer he inspected the bear again. His hunter's sixth sense was alert, though he knew that no animal could survive a spine shot from 20 feet.

No flickering eyelids, no twitch of muscle, nothing. Yet the stain of blood on the neck seemed larger. Some residual life must remain, pumping bright blood over white fur, heart beating, blood flowing, time slowing. With dreamlike disinterest, Ivar watched as the bear surged upright, front claws gouging, diamond ice chips flying and the world a long, deep growl. Reflex, not thought, brought the rifle up and triggered a second shot into the bear's heaving shoulder, but reflex would have been too slow had not the hindquarters given way, transforming a fluid lunge into a futile slide.

Even as he leaped backward, Ivar tripped a third shell into the chamber. The bear was quiet again—and less than 10 feet away. With the rifle trained on the near shoulder, Ivar circled around the white form, waiting for any further sign of life. He came up from the rear, reached out with rifle barrel and prodded the flank. No twitch. Rifle barrel on the head, he moved forward again, watched the vacant, half-closed eye. No flicker of reflex, even when cold metal touched naked eye. The bear was dead.

With his eyes, Ivar measured the bear. He was a big animal, more than 9 feet from nose to tail. The pelt was superb, heavy and white, and the long fur behind the front legs lifted gently in the wind.

Crouching, Ivar inspected the two wounds. He was disappointed that he had needed two shots—and disturbed that he had taken so long to get off the second one. The first shot had been a fraction too high. It had missed severing the spinal cord, but the shock wave of the bullet's passage must have damaged the nerves controlling the rear legs. Were it not for that, the bear would have finished his leap and killed him as easily as a careless seal. Just a quarter inch either way would have meant the bear's instant death at the first shot or Ivar's before the second.

The days of April were running away from him. More than three weeks were gone already. His work was largely finished; all but the frozen bears had been scraped, and the pelts were curing in salt. He had taken nine bears and passed up many times that number. He was a little worried about taking the tenth bear; he could not count on time and ice enough for more than one last hunt.

The morning light never left Hornsund now. The sun made a daily, sweeping elipse above the mountains, pouring white light over the icy fjord. Where rock pockets caught the sun and reflected it, the temperature nudged within a few degrees of thawing. As he looked at the glistening land around Main Cabin he sensed that the flawless crystal spring would all too soon melt into summer.

The realization brought sadness. He loved this time of year better than any other—the quality of the light, the pristine snow, the magnificent austerity of ice and sky and polished mountain peaks. Life went into the Arctic's primal crucible and came out changed, refined, melded into a seamless whole, and spring was the time of realization.

He sat motionlessly beside the cabin window, ice-blue eyes brooding over the shining land. Then his chair grated in the quiet room as he rose and pulled on a jacket. He had promised himself a fresh ptarmigan dinner; staring out the window would not get it. Gathering the heavy Mauser and the light .22, he walked out into the sun-filled world.

Ivar skied over the crusty snow behind Main Cabin, heading for Ptarmigan Slope. In late spring and summer, sea birds swarmed over the talus slope, building or burrowing nests to raise their young. The breeding multitudes drove the ptarmigan inland, but left a thin layer of droppings that fed the grass. When the transient birds left, the ptarmigan returned to bulge their crops with nourishing seeds.

Before he reached the top of the slope, several dinners were assured; five fat ptarmigan rested in his rucksack. There were many more of the round white birds in sight, moving on feathered feet among the rocks and ice, but he did not shoot them. He had what he needed; now he could relax and enjoy the chuckling, feeding ptarmigan that looked more like animated snowballs than proper birds.

He searched along the ridge top until he found a rock that was flat and free of ice. The cold wind sighed up the slope, blowing just hard enough to make him glad to button his jacket again. He rolled a cigarette and surveyed the land beneath him.

The fjord was still a silver swath of ice except toward the middle, where tidal surges had forced small leads through it, spilling frigid salt water onto the snow. The narrow, blue-black fingers were harbingers of the breakup. Five weeks, maybe a little bit more, and the governor's trim ship would enter Hornsund.

The tortured groans of sea ice rose up the slope. The tide was turning, water flowing out from beneath broad plates of ice, narrow leads closing, ice grinding as it adjusted to the changing sea.

He looked away from the sea, down to where Main Cabin was a rectangular box no bigger than his hand. The dogs were tiny black dots against the snow.

He sat for long minutes, until he became aware of the numbing cold seeping into his body from the slope. Summer might be coming, but it was not here yet. Time to get moving.

An hour later, Ivar was almost at the bottom of the slope when the wind carried up the sounds of an aroused pack of huskies. That crescendo of rage could only mean a bear was very close to them.

He covered the distance to Main Cabin in record time. When he came around the corner of the cabin, rifle ready, he saw the huskies straining at the ends of their long chains, silent except for an occasional deep snarl. Naika stood among them, fur erect and teeth bared, wild as a wolf.

The bear was nowhere to be seen. Only tracks remained, making a wide, ragged circle around the huskies.

He praised and quieted the dogs as he followed the tracks around them. Obviously the bear had looked the dogs over, decided they were more fight than food and left. But it could not be far off, and its tracks were large enough to make his blood quicken.

He skied alongside the crisp tracks. Naika moved after him, still wild. The trail went over the ice foot and out onto the fjord. He scanned the ice until he spotted the white bear going away, heading out toward distant ranks of pressure ridges where less fierce meals lay sunning on the ice. It was too late in the season to pass up a prime male. The range was extreme, even for the long-barreled Mauser, but it was the best shot he would get.

He knelt, steadied the rifle and gently squeezed off a shot. The bear seemed to stumble, then broke into a gallop, apparently unhurt. A second and third shot only kicked up chips of ice behind the bear, urging him to a faster speed. Ivar thought he had missed all three shots until he saw through the scope a red sheen of blood on the ice. The bear was wounded, though he seemed to run with undiminished strength.

Ivar turned and skied back toward the cabin. He tossed the rucksack full of ptarmigan into the storeroom, traded jacket for heavy parka, slammed the .22 into its rack, then grabbed Naika and chained her next to Svarten. With the Mauser slung across his back, he skied off in pursuit of the wounded bear.

The swish of his skis was punctuated by the rhythmic thunk of ski poles digging in for purchase and speed. The bear's tracks made a long, shallow, west-southwest curve, heading out to the center of the fjord.

Bright patches of red appeared along the trail. He was surprised by the amount of bloody snow. At this rate the bear would be dead by the time he reached the first line of pressure ridges. But as Ivar continued skiing along the trail, he saw that the space between the large prints did not diminish; the bear continued to travel at a long gallop in spite of the quantities of blood left along the trail.

Ivar's eyes checked the ice ceaselessly, hoping to catch a glimpse of the bear. There was nothing ahead but that first pressure ridge, and he was far out into the fjord. He recalled the center of the fjord as he had seen it from the top of Ptarmigan Slope, narrow black leads and blue-black shimmer of salt-water puddles on top of unstable ice. But the ice beneath his skis seemed secure and the wounded bear could not run forever.

At the end of an hour, the length of the bear's strides seemed to have shortened. Straight ahead were rumpled lines of pressure ridges. He leaned on his ski poles and rested, taking quick, shallow breaths, studying the ice ahead. The bear must be close to finished, if not already dead behind the pressure ridges. Where wind had scoured through snow, the ice plates under his skis showed signs of having been broken up and pushed back together recently. Yet the ice sounded and felt solid. The tracks and spots of blood were a clear trail, leading up and over a notch between two crumpled, upthrust ice plates.

He hesitated, then unslung his rifle and skied as far as he could into the jungle of jagged ice.

When his skis hampered more than they helped, he took them off and jammed them upright into a shallow snowdrift. Cautiously he pulled himself up to the top of a rough, slanting line of ice and stared ahead. The tracks continued, threading through ice obstacles. Then, 400 yards off in a flat area between two ridge lines, he saw the bear. He was moving at a fast walk, but there was a heaviness to the gait that told of weakness.

Ivar slid down the far side of the ice block and jogged along the trail, hoping to get within range, slowing only to scramble over thrusting ice. He passed the area of flat ice, but the bear was out of sight. He trotted on.

Huge, crumpled plates of sea ice tilted steeply where they had ridden over each other to form yet another wide span of pressure ridges. He was nearly a mile away from his skis, deep into an area of recently fractured ice. Shadows lay everywhere, glowing blue patterns against blinding white snow. Ragged ice blocks rose above his head, burning silver in the afternoon sun. Wind moaned around him, blowing stronger than an hour ago, coming in from the Arctic Ocean, driving an increasing swell beneath the ice. To the northwest, storm clouds thickened the horizon.

He measured the weather signs and kept up his steady jog. The bear had to be tiring rapidly.

Another half hour of scrambling and jogging brought him to an opening, a flat snow meadow surrounded by ice peaks. Thirty feet away, the bear was stretched out on the snow. At the sound of Ivar's approach, he surged to his feet.

Ivar raised the rifle, and a single shot echoed over the ice. The bear slid back onto the snow. With cautious steps, Ivar circled the animal, watching for movement. When there was none he nudged the nearer eye with his rifle. No response. With a last look around for other bears attracted by fresh death, he pulled his skinning knife and knelt.

As he worked quickly, hands exposed to the deep cold, he found himself looking up more often than usual. His instincts prickled across his consciousness uneasily. By the time the bear was half skinned, the subtle warnings became urgent demands. He dropped his skinning knife next to his mittens, grabbed the Mauser and scaled the nearest block of ice to look around.

He saw a 60-foot slash of open water between himself and Hornsund's north shore, and knew a long moment when his strength drained away.

Too wide. Too cold. Is death warm?

No, LIFE is warm. Move, damn you. RUN!

Even as his mind shied away from the knowledge that he was stranded on breaking pack ice, his body was sliding down the other side of the ice block and running east, running and measuring the widening, zigzag lead. He only looked back once, and what he saw made him run faster; the lead had doubled in size. He ran on, ignoring the icy air stabbing into his lungs when shallow breaths no longer gave his body enough oxygen. He ran until the black lead narrowed to 20 feet.

Ahead the lead fanned out again.

Without stopping for thought or breath or fear, he flung his rifle across the open water. Before the rifle landed on the far side, he was swimming in the freezing sea. Three strokes took him across, booted feet kicking, bare hands reaching for purchase on the 3-foot-high ice plate. His unfeeling hand slipped, fumbled, then held long enough for a desperate pull to lift him up and out of the water.

Part of him was surprised that he felt no stunning cold. The rest of him knew nothing but a driving need to be off the breaking ice. He slung the rifle over his back and ran, beating his hands against shoulders and thighs, trying to force blood into fingers he could no longer feel. He ran and saw ice cracking off his frozen clothes, ice shifting beneath his feet, black leads opening all around him.

He ran, leaping across black water from floe to floe, balancing, running, beating white hands on icy clothes, running with a pounding heart toward a shoreline that was more than two hours away. Behind him came the wavering shrieks of ice shearing, long groans of pressure ridges falling away, endless grinding of ice disintegrating. He ran until he tripped and his palms flared into sudden pain as they broke his fall. He smiled grimly as he staggered to his feet, smiled because palms that hurt were still alive.

At some point he realized that he had cut across his own tracks and had automatically veered to follow them.

He clawed up yet another pressure ridge and skidded down a ragged plate of ice. A few feet away stood his skis, dark exclamation points in the endless white. He reached, but felt nothing as his hands knocked the skis aside. He breathed on his hands and felt nothing. He fumbled with the bindings and knew it was hopeless.

He turned his back on the skis and the breaking ice and the distant storm and ran, ran until he could not remember a time when he had not fled over shifting ice, leaped over sudden black water.

He ran without looking up from his outgoing trail, beating his nerveless hands against his shoulders, running until his beard was a thick white crust of exhaled breath, miles and hours of running until he could run no longer and his tears were ice on his cheeks.

And then he looked up and saw his cabin, warm brown against the blue shadowed snow.

Home and fire and life just ahead; just a few more steps and he was no longer running but leaning against the door, gasping and fumbling at the latch with rigid fingers until it swung inward, spilling him into the cabin. He must start the fire, start it in spite of hands that could not hold onto skis, much less matches.

He kicked the stove doors open and reached for the small box of matches on the shelf. Before he realized that he had touched it, the box flew off the shelf onto the floor. He must have them.

He knelt in front of the stove and reached carefully for the elusive box. Using one hand as a weight to hold the box in place, he tapped at the end with unfeeling fingers until the box flew open and matches fanned out across the floor. But when he tried to pick up a match, his fingers were as useless as claws.

With an inarticulate cry of frustration, he beat his useless hands on his knees again and again and again. And felt nothing.

He went back to work on the matches. In time he discovered that he could pick up a match if he pushed the outer edges of his palms together like a clumsy vise. He carefully lifted the matchbox between his palms and wedged it between his knees. He squeezed down over the nearest match, worked the red head down, and swept it across the striking surface of the box. The match flared to life.

With agonizing care he guided the tiny flame into the stove. The match landed in fine kindling, a tiny point of light in the dark stove. He held his breath for fear that the least draft would snuff out the vulnerable flame. A thin piece of kindling darkened, charred, then grew tiny points of blue flame. The pale tongues of light wavered, spread, burned red and orange and then gloriously gold. The flames leaped incandescent.

Warmth spread across his face like a rising sun. He stayed motionless, kneeling in front of the stove, his eyes reflecting the miracle of fire.

He watched the flames for long moments, then rose and paced the cabin, arms flailing, trying to force blood into white fingers. When the room warmed enough, he struggled out of his wet clothes and rubbed himself as dry as his unfeeling fingers would allow. He pulled on warm clothes and resumed walking, beating his hands against his body every second step. He tried not to think about what would happen if his fingers were frozen beyond healing, the insidious gangrene that would spread and spread and be stopped only by self-amputation.

Once he felt a faint tingling sensation, as though a feather had brushed over the back of his fingers. With growing hope he strode around the room, swinging his arms to force blood into his fingers, hands thumping against his shoulders.

With infinite slowness the tingling spread, became a subtle pulse of warmth. Gradually a feeling of heat crept across fingers that throbbed and throbbed and finally burst into pain.

With a last hard pull, Ivar settled the bear hide over the sawhorse he had set up just outside of Main Cabin. He leaned over and moved his knife across the skin, scraping away bits of blubber. For three weeks he had roamed the fjord, looking for polar bears on the thinning ice, his fingers throbbing with cold. The weeks had been swift and beautiful and empty of white bear—until last night, when his huskies had burst into savage snarls beneath the midnight sun. Another bear that had been determined to eat huskies had now become a heavy white pelt underneath his flashing knife.

After a while he stopped, flexed his fingers and looked toward the little bay just beyond the cabin. The ice was white and gray and sagging beneath the weight of a thousand hours of sunlight. Shallow pools and brine slicks glimmered through the crumbling cover of snow. Further out, near the center of the fjord, a ribbon of open water shone blue-black between wide white borders of ice. Soon the bay would break up. The fan would spread and widen with each tide, sweeping ice before it, opening leads and channels until waves once again surged the length of the fjord, and a ship would come, riding the backs of swells from the distant sea.

Ivar watched, and knew his year-long day had ended.

DORIS DAY
HER OWN
STORY

A condensation of the book by
A. E. HOTCHNER

CHAPTER 1

After twenty-seven years of band singing, radio, nightclub appearances, recording, movie and television acting, my public image is unshakably that of America's wholesome virgin, the girl next door, carefree and brimming with happiness.

And what are some of the sweet, virginal roles I have played on the silver screen? I was slugged and raped by Jimmy Cagney, battled the Ku Klux Klan with Ginger Rogers and Ronald Reagan, was terrorized by Hitchcock kidnappers, stalked by a murderous Rex Harrison, was the long-suffering wife of alcoholic baseball pitcher Ronald Reagan, and became so hysterical with fear of Louis Jourdan that the movie had to be shut down while I recovered.

Well, then, it's my carefree personal life that has given me this image. At ten years of age I discovered that my father was having an affair with the mother of my best friend. Divorce followed. At thirteen, I was in an auto that was hit by a train, and that abruptly ended my promising career as a dancer—and threatened to make me a cripple for life. I was married at seventeen to a psychopathic sadist. When my third husband died, a man I had been married to for seventeen years, I discovered that not only had he secretly contrived to wipe out the millions I had earned, but he left me with a debt of a half-million dollars.

And to complete those virgin credentials: I've had one child of my own and a couple of dozen movie and television children.

But nothing seems to daunt the persistent image of me as the unsullied sunshine girl. So there must be something I give off that accounts for this disparity between who I am and who I appear to be. It is the real-life Doris Kappelhoff from Cincinnati who is going to be the subject of this book.

No holds barred, no pandering to the public image. This is the life I lived, distorted only by the vicissitudes of memory.

I was named by my mother in honor of her favorite movie actress, Doris Kenyon, a silent-screen star of that year, 1924. My parents lived at Greenlawn and Jonathan streets in a red-brick, two-family house in Evanston, a moderate-income Cincinnati suburb. I was born in that house, attended by a good German midwife as my two brothers had been before me.

My father, William, was a music teacher—primarily piano—and choral master, while my mother, Alma Sophia, was a true hausfrau. Both my parents were born in Cincinnati but their parents were German immigrants. My mother's father came from Berlin when he refused to join the German army on the grounds that he didn't believe in military activity. He came to Cincinnati, where there was a large German community, and he opened a pretzel factory—the heavy, thick pretzels that are soft and covered with salt. My grandmother and all their many children, including my mother, worked in the pretzel factory, and my mother's brothers sold the pretzels on street corners all over Cincinnati. With the profits from his pretzel factory, my grandfather bought a building, the downstairs of which he converted into a big bakery and dining room. The family lived in the apartments above the bakery.

I don't know much about my father's parents, but as for my own parents, from my earliest memory of the relationship that existed between them, I knew it was an ill-matched, ill-fated marriage. No two people were ever more opposite. My mother is very barrelhouse, loves to yak it up, loves parties, and the more people around, the better.

My father was an introverted, quiet man who loved classics and adored listening to opera. As a boy he shunned sports and other boyhood distractions, using all his spare time to practice. At sixteen he was an organist for a Catholic church. By the time he married my mother he was a well-established teacher of piano and violin, and a respected choral master. His base of operations was the St. Mark's Catholic Church, which was our church. I was raised a Catholic, and I went to Catholic schools, but I'd have to say that the Catholic side of me never took. I found the Latin, which of course I didn't understand, very boring, and so was all the ritual. I went to church on Sundays with my mother, but I was a child who liked to ask questions and the church preferred dogma to giving answers.

When my father separated from my mother, and then when they got divorced, it became a scandal when it was revealed that my father had been running around with my mother's best friend. I was eleven at the time. Although my father was a rigid man, remote and ungiving, his leaving was an enormous loss to me. I loved him and he had a profound influence on me. But I could no longer fantasize that the happy marriage I wanted for my parents was going to happen. This was my big dream as a girl—that my parents would have a happy marriage and that I would someday have a happy marriage too. It was the only real ambition I ever had—not to be a dancer or Hollywood star, but to be a housewife in a good marriage. Unfortunately, it was a dream that would elude me just as surely as it had eluded my mother.

After the divorce I saw my father once a week, on Wednesday afternoons. When I came home from school he would be sitting in his car in front of the house, waiting for my brother Paul and me. He would invariably take us to his sister's for dinner and bring us right back. That's all we ever did. My father said very little to me; I don't think he ever mentioned the divorce, or asked about my problems, but I never expected him to. He had always been so closed, so inhibited, I did not expect him suddenly to be different.

After a while he married the woman for whom he had left my mother, but by then I was singing with a band and not visiting on Wednesdays anymore. My father, in his fashion, did not tell me about the marriage, which, I heard, worked out very well for him for a time. But, tragically, she died of cancer. For a time my father was alone, but then his life changed, changed more drastically than the life of any man I have ever known. He was a rigid man who had been so set in his ways and views, so unyielding, so bigoted—Italians were wops and dagos, blacks were niggers or coons; Jews were always kikes. But something happened later on that turned my father around, to an amazing degree, and the telling is best left for later on.

My mother never went with anyone after my father left. There were men who were interested in her, but she was not interested in them. As I got older, I made many an effort to get her to go out, but after an hour she'd be back home, complaining about a headache. My mother's lack of interest in developing a new life for herself had an enormous advantage for me, of course, since she could devote all her time to me, not only in my growing years, but afterward, too, when my own marriages collapsed.

Even though my father had not been home very much, I missed him terribly after he separated from my mother. I missed hearing the piano of his students, the loud arias emanating from the Victrola. And now when I came home from school, it was quiet and empty, for my mother had taken a job in the Evanston Bakery.

A saving grace for me was my dancing. I had taken my first dancing lessons in kindergarten and now had a regular dance act with a twelve-year-old boy named Jerry Doherty, whom I had met at dancing school. We'd sing a chorus of a song and then go into our tap routine. And we went all over Cincinnati to perform—church affairs, Odd Fellow temples, Elks lodges, Masonic temples, and other boring places. We were paid a few dollars for our performances, just about enough to cover our expenses.

The dance team of Doris & Jerry scored a resounding success by winning the grand prize of five hundred dollars in a big city-wide amateur contest run by one of the department stores. My mother and Jerry's mother discussed what they should do with our five-hundred-dollar windfall. They asked us if we'd like to spend it on a trip to Hollywood, where the nationally famous dance school Fanchon & Marco was located. We saved our money all that winter.

We set out in July with my mother driving, stopping at inexpensive motels along the way. At the conservative pace my mother drove, it took us almost a week to get there. We rented a little apartment for four weeks, and we all four stayed there, taking turns on who slept in the bedroom and who slept on the Murphy-in-a-Door that folded out of the wall in the living room. All of our meals were cooked in the closet-sized kitchen.

At Fanchon & Marco our teacher was Louis De Pron, who had danced in films and whose name I had seen in credits on musicals. He liked our dancing and right away Jerry and I were sent to perform at events in and around Hollywood. By the time our four weeks were up we had received such encouragement from Fanchon & Marco, and we had all become so enamored of Hollywood, that my mother and Jerry's mother decided to move to Hollywood for good. The plan was to go back to Cincinnati, rent our apartments, say our good-byes, and move to the Coast.

On Friday, October 13, 1937, a good-bye party was given for us by friends who lived in a little town about twenty-five miles out of Cincinnati. While I was there, I received a phone call from my boyfriend, Larry Doherty, the brother of my dancing partner. He was with two of our friends, Albert Schroeder and Marion Bonekamp, and they wanted to pick me up and go nearby for a hamburger and shake.

It was a cold, rainy night. The steamy car windows were all closed, the radio going full blast. We were driving rather slowly, talking. There was a flash of a locomotive's light, a moment when I became aware of its black, looming hulk, but no sound, no warning, a crossing with no lights or signs, just the giant presence hurtling at us, a split moment of our screams, then crashing into us, not once but twice as we were struck again by a freight car in back of the locomotive.

Soon people were running to our assistance. Albert, bleeding heavily, was helped from the front seat. I pushed his seat forward and started to get out to see if I could help Marion, who was still pinioned in the shattered windshield. I collapsed. My right leg wouldn't support me. I probed along my leg and discovered sharp ends of shattered bones protruding from my leg. Then I fainted in the gutter.

My mother was in my room at Mercy Hospital when I regained consciousness. When I looked up and saw her, I started to cry. "What about my dancing?" I asked her. "What do the doctors say?"

CHAPTER 2

The X-rays showed that I had a double compound fracture, and there were shattered bone fragments that had to be fitted back into place. A steel pin was inserted in the bone and a cast encased my leg from my thigh to my toes. But despite the long and complex surgery, the doctors were optimistic about my being able to regain normal use of my leg; they were not optimistic, however, about my ability ever to dance again.

My mother was able to induce the people to whom we had rented our apartment to return it to us, so it was there that I went when I was finally released from the hospital. Jerry Doherty and his mother had visited me the day after the accident, and when he found out that I would be on crutches and in a wheelchair for at least four months, he realized that his Hollywood dream was fractured as badly as my leg. As it turned out, he never did have a career. He finished high school and became a milkman.

I tried going back to school on crutches but it was just too difficult. My mother couldn't take me, since she was working, and I had to take three streetcars to get there.

My mother finally agreed that until my leg got completely well, I should stay out of school. Little did we know how long that would be. As it turned out, that second year of high school was the last formal education I was to receive.

It was not long after I began my convalescence that we moved to Price Hill. My uncle Charley had retired from the bakery business, sold the family bakery, and built a beautiful home in Sailor Park. But retirement was driving him crazy, so he bought a tavern in Price Hill and went into business. My mother agreed to take over the kitchen for him to provide such tavern staples as roast beef and chili, and Uncle Charley provided an apartment for us that was upstairs from the tavern.

As for me, I couldn't have asked for a better place to convalesce. The jukebox was going all the time, and whenever I got hungry I just scooted down the stairs on my fanny, holding my crutches above my head, and helped myself in the kitchen. Looking back on that period, I ask myself whether I was depressed and whether I brooded about my fate—after all, dancing had been the biggest thing in my life. But I think I'm being honest when I say that I did not moan over what had happened. It is my nature to accept events as they happen and adjust to them. By sheer coincidence, a song was written for a picture I made twenty years later, "Que Sera, Sera," which precisely stated my philosophy, a philosophy which has not been dented over the years by the arrows of misfortune. Whatever will be, will be, and I have made the best of it.

My leg had finally started to mend, and the doctor was beginning to talk about removing the heavy cast, when, in one impetuous moment, I undid everything. My mother had put a recording of "Tea for Two" on the Victrola, a song that is the tap dancer's national anthem. I responded to its call by standing on my crutches and moving my good foot in a kind of tap-shuffle to the music.

"Now, be careful what you're doing," my mother warned.

But too late—one of my crutches slipped on the edge of the throw rug and I did a complete flip and landed on my busted leg. This time the prognosis was really bad. All the partially knitted bones had been broken, with some further damage, and I was condemned to stay in my cast and on crutches for at least another year.

To distract me from my idleness my mother decided to give me singing lessons. Through an acquaintance of hers who was a song plugger, my mother came up with a voice teacher by the name of Grace Raine. If I had to name one person who had the greatest effect on the career that was in store for me, that person would be Grace Raine. She lived in a second-floor apartment which I reached by going up backward sitting on my fanny. (I never did learn how to master stairs on crutches.) A gentle, smiling woman, she led me over to the piano, which was covered with sheet music. I picked out something. Grace sat down at the piano and played it, and I sang for her.

After three lessons, she told my mother, "Doris has tremendous potential. I'd like her to come three times a week."

"I'm sorry," my mother said, "but I can only afford once a week." The lessons were only five dollars but that's all my mother could afford.

"All right," Grace said. "The other two lessons are on me."

Those first weeks with Grace Raine were tremendously exciting. My mother didn't own a piano but I've never needed musical accompaniment to practice. I cannot read music but, after glancing at a piece of sheet music, I can usually sing it correctly first time through.

Grace Raine really taught me virtually everything I ever learned about singing. Of course, no one can teach you to sing—either you are naturally endowed or you are not—but you can be taught how to make the most of whatever your natural talent is. Grace taught me the importance of singing the lyrics correctly. "When you sing the words to this song," she'd say, in that sweet, gentle way of hers, "imagine that you're singing to one person, just one, a very special person, and that you're singing it in that someone's ear. Don't just belt out a song, because that's impersonal, just putting it up for grabs. Remember that when you're singing a lyric it's really like playing a scene, and you can make it mean something to you. How many times have you heard marvelous singers with beautiful tone quality whose song means nothing to you because it doesn't mean anything to them?"

I worked very hard on projecting lyrics, *feeling* them, putting them within the framework of some imagined scene that fitted the song. It was this early work on lyrics, I'm convinced, that later helped me make the transition from band singing to movie acting.

Grace Raine had been, for many years, the voice coach at radio station WLW, and she was very well-connected with the music people at all the stations; one of her contacts was with Andre Carlin, who ran a local radio show called "Carlin's Carnival." Carlin was a small-time Major Bowes, who had a two-hour Saturday-morning program that featured students from the Cincinnati schools who wanted to perform. There was a piano player in the studio who would play any sheet music you gave him, and Mr. Carlin would tell a little about each performer—where he lived, went to school, his teacher's name—before he did his stuff. Grace arranged for me to sing on the show so she could hear how I sounded on radio.

The song I chose to sing was "Day After Day," a song that was destined to play an important part in my life. The studio audience was mostly composed of relatives of the performers. Grace stayed at home and listened to me. She later told me that she thought I had an attractive radio voice but that I needed to work on my delivery. Painstakingly, she taught me all the tricks of radio singing, which were to prove of such great value over the years. For instance, when I sang a word like "people," she showed me how to turn my head to the side so the double *p*'s would not pop.

Grace's husband was a song plugger and he got me my next job at a Chinese restaurant in downtown Cincinnati that was looking for a girl singer on Saturday nights. I was only fifteen, but I said I was eighteen and no one seemed to question it.

Over the ensuing months, my singing lessons, weekend appearances at the Shanghai Inn, and rather regular unpaid stints on "Carlin's Carnival" helped keep me distracted from my slow-mending leg. And so did Tiny, the little black and tan who was my constant companion during these long tedious months of convalescence. It was the start of what was to be for me a lifelong love affair with dogs.

As for Tiny, who was indeed the sunshine of my life, he was destined to hurt me in a way that I would feel for the rest of my life. Not through any fault of his own, God knows—but through my own fault, really. Twice a day I would take Tiny for a walk. He invariably walked alongside me as my crutches carried me along the sidewalk. I never used a leash with him because he was so well trained in staying close beside me, and also because a leash might have become entangled with my crutches. But there came this day when we were walking along as on all other days when, for absolutely no reason that I know, Tiny dashed away from me and out into the street. I screamed at him but of course I couldn't dash after him. There was a screech of brakes, and a sickening thud that I can hear to this day. I hobbled out to him where he lay inert on the street. I dropped my crutches and picked him up. What had been so vital and animated a moment before was now a still form in my arms. I leaned my face against his lifeless cheek and cried my heart out. By letting him run free, I had betrayed him.

It was a searing, indelible experience. I cried for days. My loneliness was intolerable. And so was my guilt. I could not stop running what had occurred through my mind. From then on, and to this very day, I would berate anyone I saw with a dog who was not on a leash. If I now find a dog running free, I will corral it; and if it has a tag, I will deliver it to its owner along with a blistering lecture about unleashed dogs that he will not soon forget. But as for Tiny, all I could do was bury him and grieve for him. It certainly made the rest of my convalescence much harder to take.

Finally, eighteen months after the accident, I was given permission to trade in my crutches for a cane. And just about that time, Grace Raine received a phone call from a band leader friend of hers named Barney Rapp, who had heard me sing on "Carlin's Carnival." Barney Rapp and his New Englanders were a good, small-time band that traveled around the country playing smaller hotels. He had decided to settle down in Cincinnati and start a club, and he was looking for a girl vocalist to replace his wife, who had always been his singer but who was pregnant now and permanently retiring. Barney Rapp told Grace that he liked what he had heard of my voice on the radio and he wondered if I would like to try out with his band.

I got the job and the band manager fixed my salary at twenty-five dollars a week, which was not quite enough to cover my expenses. It wasn't until I had been working for Barney for a long time that I discovered that my salary was fifty a week and that the manager had been ripping off half of it for himself. That incident should have forewarned me of the many rip-offs during my big-band, movie, and television careers that were to follow. I suppose from the very beginning I was just too naïve and trusting in a business that attracts predators.

I worked for Barney Rapp six nights a week, from early evening to two in the morning. After the first few days, Barney had a talk with me about my name.

"Doris, I want to put your name on our marquee and in the ads we're running, but Kappelhoff is just too much of a name. Now my name was originally Rappaport; why don't we change yours to Kapps."

"No," I said, "Doris Kapps. No, that's pretty awful."

"Well, what about your mother's maiden name?"

"Welz."

"Doris Welz—not bad."

"No, but not good."

"Well, what about naming you after the song you sing that everybody likes so much—'Day After Day'? Doris Day."

"I'm not crazy about it."

"Why? Doris Day—it has a nice lilt to it."

"It sounds like a headliner at the Gaiety Burlesque House. It sounds phony."

"Well, think about it. I think it's just right. Has a nice fresh sound to it—like the dawn of a new day."

I tried Doris Day out on my relatives and they all liked it, and since I couldn't come up with anything else, Barney put it on the marquee. But I never did like it. Still don't. I think it's a phony name. As a matter of fact, over the years many of my friends didn't feel that Doris Day suited me, and gave me names of their own invention. Billy De Wolfe christened me Clara Bixby—with the result that many of my friends now call me Clara instead of Doris. Rock Hudson calls me Eunice (I call him Ernie because he's certainly no Rock), Gordon MacRae and others call me Do-Do, and lately one of my friends has taken to calling me Suzie Creamcheese. I like them all better than Doris Day.

It was a long drive from where we lived in Price Hill to The Sign of the Drum. My mother had to drive me there and then come back at two in the morning to pick me up. It was, of course, very hard on her and after a week or so she asked me if there wasn't someone in the band who lived near us with whom I could hitch a ride. I found out that one of the trombonists, Al Jorden, lived in Price Hill. He was a tall, slender, attractive man who had not spoken two words to me. He was an extraordinary trombone player, one of the best musicians in the band. I asked him if he would mind giving me a lift.

"You have to go right by my door to get here," I told him, "and I'll gladly help pay for the gasoline if you'd let me drive with you."

I could see he was not too thrilled. "I'll tell you, Doris," he said, "I have to be here a quarter to seven for the theme, and the one thing that will make a guy late every time is a girl vocalist."

"Al," I said, "I promise, listen, you don't know me, I'm an *on-the-mark* girl. . . ."

"Well, I don't know. . . ."

"Listen, you give the horn one honk and if I'm not right out of the door and into the car, you take off and that'll be the end of it."

With great reluctance, Al agreed to my experiment. I was never late, not once, but the arrangement had other complications. To begin with, Al had one of the glummest personalities I ever ran into. In the beginning, I would get in the car and we would drive all the way there with him not saying a word and looking straight ahead. That eventually improved somewhat, thanks to my efforts, but what didn't improve was his general irascibility.

We continued like this all through the winter until Barney announced that we would all have to take a two-week vacation without pay while he brought in an out-of-town band. The first day of that enforced vacation, I was out when the phone rang and my mother answered. It was Al Jorden. "Tell Doris I'll call her later," he said. "I wanted to know if she'd like to have dinner and see a movie tonight."

When I got home and my mother told me about Al's invitation, I broke up laughing. "Come on, stop teasing me," I said. "What did he want?"

My mother insisted that that's what he had said. "Why, he's got a steady girl," I said, "and besides, the way he treats me, why would he want to be with me on his first free evening? Anyway, he's a creep and I wouldn't go if they were giving away gold nuggets at the movie."

"Well, I don't think he's so bad. Nice-looking. Just the right age. You don't have to get involved with him, just go out and see a movie—you work all the time and you deserve an evening out on the town."

"I don't deserve him with his bad disposition. I should say not!"

By the time Al called, my mother had talked me into going out with him, and the surprise was that Al Jorden as a date bore no resemblance to the surly Al Jorden who was my chauffeur. He was amusing and relaxed and I had a really good time. I was baffled by the fact that a man who had been so consistently dreadful to me could have changed so completely. This Jekyll-Hyde switch from grump to charmer should have forewarned me about Al Jorden, but when he asked me to go boating with him the following day, I innocently said yes.

Al invited the band's drummer, Wilbur Shook, and his wife, Virginia, to come along with us. Al owned a sixteen-foot speedboat that was one of the fastest boats on the Ohio River. Also plying the Ohio that Sunday was the *Island Queen*. The *Queen* carried fifteen hundred people or more, and was powered by a big paddle wheel on her stern. This wheel churned up a mountainous wake, with high waves rolling out from the wheel. Al decided to give us a big thrill by zooming along in back of the *Queen* and riding that wake, crisscrossing into the churning waves.

We were screaming at him, drenched with spray, but he kept getting closer to the *Queen*'s paddle wheel, and as he got closer we struck a wave as high as a house, and the next thing I knew I had been pitched in the muddy water and Al's speedboat was burbling its way to the bottom.

Finally, we were rescued by a boat manned by Jerry Hurter, who was a reporter for the Cincinnati *Times Star*. The next day our mishap was front-page in the newspaper. Looking back on it, it's hard to explain why, in the face of his erratic and rather spooky behavior, I continued to date Al. I suppose that to a sixteen-year-old, there was something glamorous about this twenty-three-year-old's behavior. He called me constantly and we went out every night. He was mostly on good behavior, but he did become angrily jealous whenever I so much as spoke to another man. At the time I thought his jealousy was flattering. Too late I was to discover that it was a pathologic jealousy that almost destroyed me.

Another signpost about Al that I should not have ignored, but did, involved an incident that occurred at his house. Al had been hurt in a motorcycle accident, and my mother and I went to pay him a visit. This was the first time I had met his mother. After we had been in the house for ten minutes or so, Al's mother managed to get me off by myself. "I think I should make something very clear to you," she said, looking right at me with eyes that burned, "and that is that Albert is never going to get married. He has promised never to leave me and his father, and I think it's only fair that you know that."

"We're just dating, Mrs. Jorden—that's all."

"Yes, well, I know how girls get once they get their hands on an attractive man like Albert, and I thought it was only fair to let you know that Albert will never be serious about you or anyone else."

As I later told my mother, I didn't feel that she had anything against me—she probably made the same speech many times before to girls Al had gone with. I asked myself, What kind of mother talks like that about her son? I should have asked, What kind of son allows it?

Al received a telegram from the drummer Gene Krupa, who was leaving Benny Goodman to organize his own band in New York; he wanted Al for the trombone section. It was a great opportunity to break into the big time, but I was heartbroken. He sent me his itinerary as he traveled the country playing one-night stands, and I would write to him every day. He wrote to me and telephoned quite often. I was back singing with Barney Rapp and meeting new people, but I only cared about Al. He wrote marvelous letters which underscored that old saw about absence making the heart grow fonder. I think that if Al had not gone off our relationship would have lost its steam, but as it was, I only had eyes for my absentee boyfriend.

The Sign of the Drum limped along for a while, but Barney finally folded it and decided he'd be better off going back to playing band dates. We played about four one-nighters a week, often traveling fifty or a hundred miles for a night's work. The pay was a little better but the work was a darn sight harder. A hundred miles in a broken-down band bus, singing for six or seven hours, then a hundred bumpy miles back to Cincinnati, was not an easy night's work. Bob Crosby was looking for a vocalist, and Grace Raine suggested that I go up to Chicago to audition for the job. Bob Crosby and his Bobcats! I had never really thought about singing beyond the Cincinnati city limits. I really had no ambition about my singing, and never tried to create opportunities, but neither was I ever loath to embrace one if it came my way.

The Raines drove me to Chicago, and we went directly to the Blackhawk, where Bob Crosby was playing. Crosby's Sunday afternoon jam session was already in progress. Grace had arranged in advance what I was to sing but my only memory of that afternoon was the way the band improvised as I sang. Back at our table Crosby's business manager, Gil Rodin, joined us and offered me the job at seventy-five dollars a week.

I joined the band right then and there. My mother brought my clothes and belongings to Chicago and stayed with me. Later she traveled with me when she could, but when we went on a one-nighter tour on the Crosby bus, I had to travel alone. My mother was uneasy about her sixteen-year-old being thrown to the wolves, but actually I never had a hard time with any of the men in the band. I was their kid sister. They knew that I was completely devoted to a boyfriend who was traveling with another band—Al had left Krupa for Jimmy Dorsey—and they used to tease me unmercifully about my postal love affair.

The next band I joined was that of Les Brown. We played some set dates, but the big money was on the road, and when our New York engagement ended, Les handed me our itinerary—three months of nothing but one-nighters! Living on a band bus was by now part of my being. When you're with the same people all the time, there's nothing much to talk about, so life aboard the bus was reading and sleeping—mostly the latter. It was too bumpy to write but I'd daydream about Al, who always had a letter waiting for me at the next stop. Al wrote wonderful love letters—how was I to know that this was a side of him that was split from his "other" personality? If only this hadn't been a paper romance, if only we had had a normal courting period, I am sure that Al and I would have parted company. But as it was, every letter made me miss him more. There was no doubt, from his letters, that he loved me intensely—but what I couldn't tell was what an overly possessive, destructive love it was.

The next time we played New York, Jimmy Dorsey's band happened to be there at the same time, and Al and I got to see each other. All we had was the fragmented time between shows, and late at night when the last shows were over. But we did get to stay together every night, and on the fourth or fifth night, Al presented me with an engagement ring. We only had a week together in New York, but by the time our bands took off for the road again, we had agreed to get married as soon as we could.

As it turned out, "soon" was not very soon. Les took us on a long tour, months of one-nighters, which culminated in a month-long engagement at Michael Todd's Theatre Café in Chicago. It was there that Al telephoned me. Jimmy Dorsey had a long engagement in New York and Al wanted me to quit Les Brown and come to New York to get married. I couldn't say yes fast enough.

Les was shocked when I told him what I was going to do. "You're young, Doris," he said, "just beginning what is going to be a glorious career, and now you want to ruin your life. It'd be a crying shame for a girl with your potential to throw it all away on a guy like Jorden. He's a good musician but he's not any prize as a husband."

Nothing Les said could dissuade me. From the time I was a little girl, my only true ambition in life was to get married and tend house and have a family. Singing was just something to do until that time came, and now it was here.

So I quit the band and went back to Cincinnati to pack my things before joining Al in New York. My mother was after me for days to change my mind. "Nobody likes Al Jorden, not Les or anybody else. But that's not the point. Here you are just starting out and getting somewhere after all that struggle, and now you're not giving yourself a chance. What's the hurry?"

When she finally realized that it was hopeless to try to dissuade me, my mother helped me prepare a wedding costume, and then she drove me to New York. Al and I got married between shows in City Hall. One of the guys in the band and his wife came along as witnesses. There was a hotel directly across from the stage entrance to The Strand, where the band was playing, and Al had a little reception there in a small room. Our wedding guests were the boys in the band and some of their wives.

Al had rented a two-room apartment for us at the Whitby, a Times Square place across from the Martin Beck Theatre, off Eighth Avenue, that featured seedy, furnished accommodations. Most of the band men who had wives visiting used to stay there because the apartments had little kitchens and they were inexpensive. My mother returned to Cincinnati the afternoon of the wedding.

As for my life as a band wife, Les Brown had not exaggerated how difficult it would be. Wives didn't hang around the band, so most nights I just waited at the apartment, knitting or writing letters or visiting with the other wives until Al got home, which was usually around two in the morning. Since that's when we would eat, I had to stay up to do the cooking. It would be three or four when we got to bed, and by the time we got up the following day, there wasn't much time until Al had to go back to work.

But the real difficulty for me was not band-wife boredom but the shocking revelation of the kind of man I had married. What had been represented to me as love emerged as a pathologic jealousy that was destined to make a nightmare out of the next few years of my life. I do not mean that Al didn't love me—I think he did, and in the beginning I certainly loved him; but Al's love was destructive, a fire of uncontrollable jealousy that eventually burned out my feelings for him.

This dark side of Al's makeup showed itself immediately. On the second day of our marriage, I was to meet him at The Strand at the dinner break. Just inside the stage door there was a little waiting room with benches. On one side of this waiting room were the steps that led down to the orchestra pit; on the other side of the room were steps that led upstairs to the dressing rooms. These were open stairs that you could look through and see the landings above. On the first landing, just above the waiting room, was a combination office and dressing room that was shared by the band's manager, Billy Burton, and Jimmy Dorsey. On this day I was sitting in the waiting room as the show was ending and Billy Burton looked down through the open steps and saw me waiting there.

"Doris—hi!" he called out. "Listen, can you come up for a minute? I have something for you—a wedding present."

I jumped up. "Oh, how lovely!" I started running up the steps to the dressing room just as the musicians began coming up the lower steps from the pit. I went into the dressing room and Billy handed me a big package, beautifully wrapped.

Inside was a beautiful leather makeup case, completely fitted. I was just about to tell Billy how thrilled I was with it when the door slammed open and there stood my husband of two days. His face was absolutely white. His eyes seemed to extrude from their sockets.

Billy didn't know what to say. He finally said, "We . . . we thought . . . as a wedding gift . . . you know, traveling and all, Doris might like a case like—"

"I'm sure she will," Al snapped, then he grabbed my arm, just below my arm pit. "We'll be going," he said, tightening his grip. Al steered me down the steps and out on the sidewalk. I was frantic to find out what was wrong. I kept asking him but he wouldn't say a word. For the first time in my life, I really felt afraid of someone.

The minute we walked into our apartment, he spun me around and hit me again and again, knocking me into the furniture and against the wall. All the while he was yelling at me, in uncontrollable rage, shrieking at me. "You tramp, you no-good little whore, you call that a wife, running up those stairs so all the men could take a good look up your skirt! You thought I wouldn't notice it—do you think I'm blind? You timed it just right, didn't you, you little two-bit bitch! Well, you ever do it again, I'll kill you! You're my wife now, and you better behave like one!"

I finally collapsed on the floor, with him standing over me with his fists clenched. A minute or so later, I heard sounds coming from Al. I looked up. His body was slumped, and he was sobbing. He lowered himself to the floor beside me and held me against his crying face. "Oh, please forgive me, please," he sobbed. "I love you too much. I shouldn't have hit you.

I'm sorry. Please forgive me. I just can't stand the thought of anyone else looking at you. Can you forgive me?"

I tried to believe that this was a singular outburst that would never be repeated. For the most part, Al was loving and humorous and enjoyable to be with. Sexually, we got along fine. I admired him as a musician. And I loved him. But it didn't take long before his psychotic jealousy again broke out, in endless incidents, with the scene of contrition repeating itself. He was sure he'd be better and not to worry about it.

But he wasn't better. In fact, it got worse. The tension of not knowing what I might say or do that would set off one of his attacks became an unbearable burden. In fact, I most certainly would have left him soon after the marriage if I hadn't become pregnant. It happened in the second month. I didn't know how Al would take the news. To my surprise he wept. I hoped in joy and not in sorrow. He didn't say anything, he just wept. As for me, after the initial shock of finding out I was so soon pregnant, I was suffused with joy. My dream of marriage and children was being fulfilled, and even though the husband had brutalized the dream, I suppose I hoped, optimist that I am, that my pregnancy would make him less jealous. But that was a rational hope, and Al was an irrational man.

It would not have been so bad if Al had been away on one-nighters, but when a band has as big a name as Dorsey's, it could pick and choose its dates and Jimmy preferred playing long hotel engagements in big cities, especially New York, where he lived. Shortly after I had told Al about being pregnant, he came home with the name of an abortionist recommended by someone in the band. I was appalled. Now I knew Al's tears had been anything but tears of joy.

"I'm not going to give my baby to some grimy abortionist," I said.

"We're too young to have kids," Al said. "You won't be able to travel, you'll have to spend all your time with the kid. Listen, let's just get rid of this one and then we can have one we really want later on."

"No, Al. No dirty abortionist is going to get his hands on me! Now that's the end of it!"

Al knew I meant it and that was the end of his attempt to get me to an abortionist, but it had succeeded in draining off any good feelings I might have had about having my baby.

I soon realized that I should not be having this baby under the conditions into which it would be born. I was indeed terribly young, and Al certainly would be a rotten father. But there formed in me a desire to somehow get through my pregnancy with Al and then leave him as soon as the baby was born. So my plan was to stick it out until I had the baby, and then go back to Cincinnati to live with my mother and get a job. But as it turned out, sticking it out proved to be almost beyond my endurance.

In the third month of my pregnancy, Dorsey booked an engagement in Chicago and Al decided that we should stop and visit in Cincinnati on the way. We stayed at his parents' house, which was not too far from my mother's apartment. This was only the second time I had laid eyes on Al's mother, who was just as withdrawn and unfriendly as she had been the time before. But I had a joyful visit with my mother, who spotted that I was pregnant the minute I walked in. I was glad that she had been so intuitive about me, because Al had forbidden me to tell anyone.

That evening Al and I went to my uncle's tavern, where all my relatives and friends showed up to see me. We all had a good time, Al included, I thought. The gathering broke up around midnight, but Al and I were no sooner in the car than I knew he was bugged. He was furious because my mother knew I was pregnant and my aunt and uncle and others had happily drunk to the impending event.

"I didn't tell her, she just took one look at me and knew."

"You're lying! Don't lie to me! You told her. After I told you that no one was—"

"Oh, Al, what difference does it make?"

By the time the car arrived at the house I was upset and frightened because he was on the verge of violence. At all costs I wanted to avoid an outburst in this house where his parents were. But he hustled me up the steps to the front door, grabbed my arm in that terrible grip of his, and started to push me into the house.

I wrenched away from him and ran up the steps and into our bedroom, which was on the second floor. A second later he burst into the room, locked the door in back of him, and then started hitting me, pushing me, knocking me over the furniture. The racket awakened his parents. His father pounded on the door and shouted at us to open up. Finally, mercifully, Al went over and opened the door.

"Albert, what in the hell is going on in here?" his father demanded. Al went out in the hall where his mother and father were and I closed the door and locked it. I sat down on the bed, crying hysterically, feeling the hurts and pains of where he had struck me. Outside, I heard the men go down the steps. Then there was a knock on the door and his mother asked if she could come in. I went over and opened the door.

She came in and looked at me; I couldn't stop crying. "What on earth was going on here?" she asked. "All that racket—what will the neighbors think?

"Your son was hitting me, that's what happened," I said. "It's not the first time and I think you should know it."

She looked at me more intently. Then she said, "Well, from the looks of you he didn't hit you very hard."

I jumped up from the bed. "Get out of this room," I said, starting to push her.

I pushed her into the hall and locked the door behind her. I sat down, trembling, a captive in this strange house. All I could think of was somehow getting to the corner to catch a streetcar that would take me to my mother's. But there wouldn't be a streetcar now until morning and somehow I'd have to last through the night here. Al came to the door but I wouldn't let him in. His father, a really decent man, wanted to talk to me but I said no, I didn't want to talk to anybody. Finally, I heard doors closing down the hall and then it was quiet. I sat there for the rest of the night, alert, fearing some other evil in that house.

At daybreak I tiptoed out and down the stairs and let myself quietly out of the house. I didn't tell my mother the whole story, just what had happened the night before. She was appalled and urged me to leave Al then and there. But I explained that I did not want to burden anyone, that I had never borrowed a dime, and I told her about my plan to come back to Cincinnati as soon as the baby was born. We didn't have much time to discuss it because Al showed up. He was contrite and apologetic and gave his usual speech about loving me too much. At times like this he could be very appealing, and I think my mother felt rather sorry for him. But before we left, I made secret arrangements with my mother. I would have the baby in New York, where my mother would join me. Then, the first time Al went on the road with the band, we would hightail it back to Cincinnati and I would start divorce proceedings.

I really don't know how I got through those nine months, for there were more rages, more beatings.

My mother was staying with me at the Whitby on February 7, 1942, when, at midnight, my water broke. Al was playing in Buffalo. Before he left, I told him that I thought I would go back to Cincinnati with my mother after I had the baby since I could no longer travel with him and didn't want to stay at the Whitby with the baby alone.

I was in labor for twelve hours, but at high noon, February 8, I produced an eight-pound, one-ounce boy whom I named Terry, since Terry had been a favorite name of mine ever since I started to read "Terry and the Pirates" as a little girl. I had previously discussed it with Al, who didn't care about the name one way or the other.

When I returned to the Whitby with the baby, I impatiently bided my time until Al was to leave with the band for a string of one-nighters. Then back to Cincinnati I would go, finally escaping from Al Jorden. My mother had already alerted a lawyer to be prepared to start divorce proceedings immediately. But Al was not to be handled so easily. In the midst of our preparation to depart, Al walked into the apartment and announced that he had quit the band and was going back to Cincinnati with us. I was stunned.

My mother had found a little home for us (at the time she thought it would be for me and the baby and herself) not far from my uncle's tavern, that was directly across from a pretty neighborhood park. When Al found out about the house, he gave my mother the down payment she had made and took over the mortgage for himself. All my well-laid plans were suddenly defeated and here I was again, trapped with him. He immediately got jobs playing with local bands and with a band on radio—with his kind of musicianship, he found work easily.

But I was no longer as isolated and insecure as I had been in New York. My aunt Marie lived right next door to our house and with her alongside me, I had resolved not to absorb any more of Al's abuse. For the first few weeks he was on good behavior, but after a few minor outbursts, he came in late one night and threw one of his black, yelling tantrums.

The next day when Al came home from work he couldn't get in. I had had the locks changed and all his things were in his bags on the porch. I was next door at my aunt's. Al banged on the door and shouted my name, but after a few minutes, to my surprise, he picked up his bags and left.

"How will you get along?" my aunt asked.

"Why, I'll get a job," I said. All my life I have known that I could work at whatever I wanted whenever I wanted. This is really not conceit—I just feel secure in what I know I can do.

The very next day after Al left, I made an appointment with the radio station WLW, was hired by them and within no time I had several sponsored shows. My first show was for MGM, "The Lion's Roar," advertising MGM movies. It was a fifteen-minute show, five times a week. I'd chat with the announcer about whatever MGM movie was in release, and sing a couple of songs with the studio band. I also did a beer show on weekends, and then I became the vocalist on "Moon River," which was the biggest radio show out of WLW.

On those nights when I did "Moon River" I often had dinner in restaurants with friends. Wherever I went, Al Jorden was invariably there, sitting at a table across the room, staring at me, making me apprehensive and uncomfortable. He would never come up to my table or talk to me, just sit there in the restaurant staring at me, watching my every move, not taking his eyes off me.

One night when I got home Al's car was parked in front of the house. He called me over, and reluctantly, I got in the car with him. I could feel myself trembling. Al was quite subdued. He said he had had a long time now to think about things and he really felt that if I took him back we could have a good life together and be a happy family. He said how much he needed me and missed me, and how much he wanted his baby son. It was really quite touching, what he had to say, but I had been through this too many times now for it to have any effect.

"I'm sorry, Al," I said, "but the feelings I once had for you are dead and gone. There's no way to resurrect them. I don't love you anymore, and without love it just wouldn't work. There's nothing to talk about—the good feelings are gone, and its all over."

Before I left, I agreed that he could come to see the baby once in a while, and occasionally take him out for an afternoon at his mother's. I was plenty apprehensive about that, but I knew it would have to be part of the legal arrangement anyway. As I started to get out of the car, he put his hand on my arm. I looked at him. His face was full of pain and he was near tears. I thought to myself, No, I am through comforting you. I felt a curious kind of revulsion. The pain was his and his alone, and I would have nothing to do with it. I looked away from him and got out of the car and quickly went into the house.

Al did come to see the baby a few times, and once or twice he took Terry to his mother's house to visit, but it was not long afterward that he left Cincinnati to go into the service. He was sent to the Great Lakes Naval Station, where he was made a member of the splendid service band they had there.

Les Brown called and tried to get me to rejoin his band. He had heard me singing on "Moon River" and he was elated to find out that I was divorcing Al Jorden. My mother was all in favor of my going back with Les. I had taken the house back from Al and the mortgage was a heavy monthly burden. So when Les called me for the third time I met up with him in Columbus. It was musically very exciting.

Les was constantly putting new material into our repertoire. We would rehearse these new songs and arrangements late at night when we finished playing; I memorized the lyrics the following day on the bus.

We were playing the Pennsylvania Hotel in Newark, New Jersey, when, at a late-night rehearsal, Les gave me the sheet music for a new song that he had helped compose, "Sentimental Journey." The band went through it and I scanned the lyrics as they played. I felt a distinct rise in my scalp. I always feel a rise in my scalp or on the backs of my wrists when something is special, whether it be song or man. I stepped to the microphone, and on the second run-through I sang the lyrics. I loved the song, I loved singing it, and we all thought it was going to be a big hit.

Les introduced "Sentimental Journey" the following night. I started to sing the lyrics and by the end of the first eight bars the couples had stopped dancing and were just standing there listening. It was an overwhelming success. A short time later, we recorded it on the Okey label and it became my first hit record.

I had other hit records with Les, like "My Dreams Are Getting Better All the Time," but none rivaled the success of "Sentimental Journey." I was usually pretty good at guessing which new songs would be hits, but I also had some notable misses. When the composers first played "Que Sera, Sera" for me, I thought it was a nice, simple little child's song that would never get out of the nursery.

Whoever planned Les's tour was a sadist—we played Canada in the dead of winter and Florida in August, but whenever we had a stand of a week or more, I'd bring Terry and my mother there, whatever the weather. Terry was almost two by now and into everything.

But Terry was as lovable as he was mischievous and the men in the band and their wives were always helping to look after him, taking him to the park or the zoo. Despite the little troubles he caused, he was a joy.

I had not heard from Al since he left to join the Navy. But when the band rolled into Chicago for an engagement at the College Inn and we checked into the Sherman Hotel, the phone rang and there he was on the line. I decided to go out to dinner with him, and afterward we came back to the hotel and talked. Al was making his last desperate pitch to get me back, and I was determined, once and for all, to convince him that my feelings for him were dead and gone, and that we should never see each other again. Some of the things he said were very touching; he pleaded with me to come back to him, that he had no life without me.

Finally, when he had talked himself out and the early dawn light was in the windows and he knew that his cause was hopeless, Al put his face in his hands and wept. Out of compassion, I wept too. He slept with me.

He wrote to me several times after that, and finally I wrote to him and told him in as final terms as I could that there was no hope that I would ever have any feelings for him again. I urged him to make a new life for himself, just as I was trying to make for myself.

That did it. I never heard from him again. Not too long afterward, I heard he had gotten married to a woman from around the Great Lakes area, a woman who had a child. After his discharge he moved back to Cincinnati.

CHAPTER 3

You would think that after my experience with Al Jorden I would never have anything to do with a musician again, but I did. This time, however, I learned once and for all that I could not make beautiful music with a musician.

I had been with Les Brown for several months before I "noticed" the lead alto sax and he "noticed" me. George Weidler was tall, slim, dark, with deep-brown eyes, a moustache, soft-spoken—a quiet man and very gentle. Just the opposite of Al.

In no time at all I fell in love with George and we saw each other every day and slept together every night. The way I felt about love then was different from the way I feel about love now. I have come to realize that there is loving someone and there is being in love and the difference is that one involves physical love and one doesn't. There are men I love whom I've no desire to go to bed with. On the other hand, a dynamite sexual relation may not have anything to do with love. A strong physical reaction can addle your senses, but it can also wear off as quickly as it sprouted, and suddenly you are saying to yourself, "I can't be in love with him, I don't even like him! I don't like the way he thinks and we don't really have all that much to say to each other. I like him in bed—my heart flutters when I see him and all those experiences I'm having in bed with him are super—but how can I be in love with him if I don't like him?"

But I wasn't wise enough to make this distinction way back then in my late teens, so within a year George and I were married. A native Californian, George longed for the warm climate of Los Angeles and decided to leave the band. I gave Les notice but promised to stay on until he found a replacement. Poor Les, again he tried to talk me out of marriage. He pointed out that I would have a tough time finding adequate work in Los Angeles. He also felt that I should give myself more time to recover from Al Jorden. But I had decided to strike out on my own as a singer without band attachment. An agent named Al Levy, who was associated with the Century Artists agency, had been coming to the Pennsylvania Hotel and he had been urging me to try to make a career for myself. But I was not much interested in that, as I've never been fixed on a career—I was interested only to the extent that I could go to California to be with George. I planned to stop in Cincinnati on the way to get Terry. George had seen little Terry and had not seemed to respond to him one way or the other, but I felt that he would accept him once we all started living together.

But it was not to be as easy as that. The war had just ended and there was a severe housing shortage in Los Angeles. Months passed while George hunted for a place to live, and finally all he could come up with was a trailer in a place called the Midway Trailer Camp. Of course I wasn't able to bring Terry as planned.

I still had the responsibility of supporting my mother and Terry—George didn't have much money and I wouldn't have taken it from him if he had. I made the rounds and wound up as vocalist on "The Sweeny and March Radio Show"—Bob Sweeny and Hal March, who were comics at that time on a local CBS station.

Al Levy came around quite often, to tell me of things he hoped would open up for me, and to discuss my "potential," which he thought was fantastic. I remember one time he came by the trailer in that big, black, four-door Cadillac of his, and as usual began telling George and me what a big star I was going to be. "Al," I said, "I'm not interested."

"You're not interested? How can you be not interested?"

"Oh, Al, of all the people for you to latch onto as agent I'm the worst. I'm just not ambitious. I'm not interested in being somebody because I feel I already am. I'm the somebody I want to be. Just cozy here in this trailer."

Al turned to George. "George, listen, do something—your wife has got to stop talking like that." George got a funny look on his face.

Despite Al Levy's enthusiasm, his attempts to get me going in Hollywood were fruitless. Months passed with only local radio work available to me. Al introduced me to his partners at Century Artists, Dick Dorso and Marty Melcher, who agreed that I was on the threshold of something big, but during the passing months I never got over that threshold.

The one definite offer that finally did materialize was to appear for a month in New York at Billy Reed's Little Club, a new spot that was just opening its doors. I didn't want to leave George but I would be getting four times what I'd been earning in Hollywood—and we were badly strapped for money. I talked it over with George, who urged me to go. It was only a month, he reasoned, and it would be good money and good exposure. And on the way I could stop and see Terry. That decided it.

I did not have much time to enjoy my success at the Little Club, because a couple of days after I opened I received a letter from George that devastated me. Married only eight months, and here was this letter telling me that he thought we should put an end to it. He said it wasn't right for me to be stuck in the trailer and living that kind of life. "You are going to be a huge success," he told me, "Al says so and I believe it. You are going to be a star and I'm never going to be anything more than just a side man in a band. You're going to outgrow me and sooner or later the imbalance will destroy our relationship—so rather than wait until that happens I think we should break up right now. It's easier. We haven't yet put much into our marriage. We won't have lost very much."

The letter shattered me. I tried to reach him at the trailer but he had moved out. I phoned around but no one knew where he had gone. Finally, toward the end of my month at Billy's, I contacted George through his mother. I told him I was coming back and he agreed to meet the train when it arrived in Pasadena, so that we could sit down face-to-face and talk about what had happened.

We talked for hours, but nothing I said changed his mind. Finally, when it was late and we were all talked out, we wènt to bed and made love and I could not doubt his strong desire for me. But I guess his desire not to be Mr. Doris Day was even stronger, for in the morning we parted, and I knew it would be final.

I walked to the nearest bus stop and sat down on the waiting bench. The optimist in me rummaged among the debris of my ruins and found nothing of comfort. My second marriage, after eight months, was over. I had only a few dollars in my purse. I had no prospects other than going back to New York to pick up a second month's work at the Little Club. And then?

But there were a few things I had to do before I could leave Hollywood, like selling the trailer. George had gone out on the road with Stan Kenton and it was up to me to dispose of our mobile love nest. I needed my share of the proceeds to get back East. Al Levy did what he could to help me and try to cheer me up.

The evening of the third day Al phoned to say he had sold the trailer at a good price. "Now," he said, "there's a nice party tonight and I'd like to take you."

"Thanks, Al," I said, "but I'm really not up to going to a party."

"I'll pick you up at eight and that's that!"

The party was at Jule Styne's house on Elm Drive in Beverly Hills, and most of the people at the party were entertainers—musicians and singers.

There was good food and lots to drink and an air of jollity and good fellowship. I was glad I had come, until Jule Styne and Sammy Cahn and all
of their friends started to get up and perform, one after the other; I began
to get uneasy. Oh, God, I thought, I hope they don't ask me to stand up
there and sing.

They did. When I tried to beg off, Sammy Cahn put his arm around me
and guided me firmly over to the piano. I had no alternative but to sing.
Before the evening was over, Jule, Sammy, and Al got me in a corner.
They explained that Jule and Sammy had written the score for a musical,
Romance on the High Seas, that was ready to go before the cameras at
Warner Brothers, under the direction of a famous director, Michael Curtiz. They had written the score for Judy Garland, but the deal with her
had fallen through. Then Betty Hutton had been set to play the lead, but
they had just found out that she was pregnant and there was a frantic
search on to find someone to replace her. How would I like to come to
Warners in the morning and audition for the part?

"Well, I'm leaving in a day or so—"

"You're leaving!"

"And you see, I'm a singer—I don't know a thing about acting."

"Leave her to me," Al promised. "I'll have her there in the morning."

I really had a fine time doing my screen test but, being a realist, that afternoon I booked a reservation for Cincinnati and phoned my mother to
tell her when I'd be there. It would probably be weeks before Curtiz made
a decision on the part, and if he was looking for a Betty Hutton type for
the role, I sure wasn't it.

Late the following afternoon, I was in my room packing when the
phone rang. It was Al calling. The part was mine.

CHAPTER 4

A t the start of the picture, I began taking lessons from the Warners
acting coach, Sophie Rosenstein. But Curtiz soon put a stop to that.
"Doris, I tell you about acting," he said. "Some people, the lessons are
very good for them. But I tell you about you—you have very strong individual personality. No matter what you do on screen, no matter what
kind of part you play, it will always be you. What I mean is, the Doris Day
will always shine through the part. This will make you big important star.
You listen to me. Is very rare thing. You look Gable acting, Gary Cooper,

Carole Lombard, they are playing different part but always is the same strong personality coming through. But you take other actors, maybe better actors, who become the character they are playing and lose all of themselves. They can be fantastic but big stars, never. Because there is not that personality, always there, that the audience identify with. Always there is Humphrey Bogart himself coming through every part he play. So with you. Is unique. That's why I don't want you to take lessons. You have a natural thing there in you, should no one ever disturb. You listen to me, Doris. Is very rare thing. Do not disturb."

From the first take onward, I never had any trepidation about what I was called on to do. Movie acting came to me with greater ease and naturalness than anything else I had ever done. Often before a take, despite all the pictures he had made, Jack Carson, jittery and on edge, would show me his hands, wet with nervous perspiration; I never had a qualm.

During the making of the film, Jack Carson began taking me out. He was divorced and lived in a beautiful home in Longridge out in the Valley. A couple who once worked with him in vaudeville lived there and took care of the house for him. Jack was a very sweet, considerate man whom I liked very much, but I wasn't in love with him. I spent a lot of time at his place and often stayed there with him, but Jack was a closed man who couldn't communicate. He was amusing and we got along very well, but I was just out of a marriage where there had been no communication and I wasn't about to repeat that mistake.

Perhaps Jack was in love with me. I don't know. He was basically a lonely man who drank too much. When he became too serious about us, I eased away from him and eventually stopped going with him. But I have fond memories of Jack, of how much fun we had at parties where he was comical and entertaining—but then when we got back to his place, he would often sit with a brandy bottle, the party spirit gone, lapsing into a kind of quiet sadness. My second and third pictures were also made with Jack, but after that we fell out of touch. Some years later, after a long and painful illness, he died of cancer.

Romance on the High Seas turned out very well. However, when I saw it, I was terribly disappointed. I hated the way I looked, especially my heavily pancaked face. I'm a casual person and I wear very little make-up and I let the freckles fall where they may. But there I was, a pancaked, lacquered Hollywood purse made out of a Cincinnati sow's ear!

But the one thing that really pleased me about my new career was the organized life. The chaotic, nighttime life of big-band singing just wasn't my dish. Now I went home at six and had the evening to myself.

One evening the phone rang and it was George Weidler. He asked me whether I'd like to have dinner and I unhesitatingly said yes. I was feeling positive again and I knew I could see George without getting upset. Or getting involved. *My Dream Is Yours* was about to get under way. I was looking for a little house where I could bring Terry and my mother. My social life was just fine—besides Jack Carson, and the usual constant attention of Al Levy, I had also been regularly dating Hal March, who was an amusing man and a good friend.

George never looked better. We were really happy to see each other again. We drove to a place on the beach to have dinner, and it seemed to me that George was much more open and communicative than he had been when we lived together. He seemed much more at peace with himself. I told him so.

The following day, George said, "You know, you've been saying I've changed and you've asked me about it. Well, I've found a way of life."

"What are you talking about?"

"I'm studying a religion." He handed me a small book. It was *Science and Health with Key to the Scriptures,* by Mary Baker Eddy.

"Why, that's the woman who doesn't believe in doctors!" I gasped. My Cincinnati upbringing had taught me that she was a sort of witch and that Christian Science was some kind of crazy ritual which caused you to end up sick and dying because you were forbidden to see a doctor. My first thought was, Oh, my God, if George is into this then that's the end of him. But then I thought, No, there must be something to it, because look how he has changed; how impressed I am with these qualities I see in him now that weren't there before.

So I said I'd like to look at the book.

I spent all that evening reading Mrs. Eddy's book. "There is no life, truth, intelligence, nor substance in matter," I read. "All is infinite Mind and its infinite manifestation, for God is All-in-all. Spirit is immortal Truth; matter is mortal error. Spirit is the real and eternal; matter is the unreal and temporal. Spirit is God, and man is His image and likeness. Therefore man is not material; he is spiritual."

They were words of gleaming light that I did not fully understand, but they were to become beacons that would lead me to a spirituality of my own. A spirituality that would sustain me through some very dark times in the years ahead.

The only sad thing that happened during this period was that I had to give up my dear friend and agent, Al Levy. He had fallen in love with me, and had begun to spy on me—in the lobby, at the studio, even in restau-

rants where I'd be having dinner with a date. Finally, I went to his partners at Century Artists, Dick Dorso and Marty Melcher, and I told them
why it was impossible for me to continue a client-agent relationship with
Al. They said the situation was going to solve itself since Al was being sent
to New York to run their office there, and Marty would become my
agent. Marty Melcher was then married to Patty Andrews of the Andrews
Sisters. I had seen him on occasion and found him to be a bright, affable
man who seemed organized and competent.

George was traveling with the Stan Kenton band but I saw him quite
often on his frequent returns to Los Angeles, where the band was based.
We liked each other and had a fine time together and George began to
talk about how our relationship had changed. "We could have now what
we couldn't achieve before," he said.

For me, however, although there was still a strong physical attraction
and I enjoyed sleeping with George, I no longer had the kind of feelings
toward him that would have made for a marriage. Something was over. "I
really think that we should stay just as we are," I told him. "No reason we
can't go on seeing each other. We enjoy that. You're traveling and I'm
busy with my work. Soon my child will be here with me. I like you,
George—maybe I still love you, but I don't think we have the makings of
a marriage anymore."

CHAPTER 5

During *Romance on the High Seas,* I had become good friends with
my hairdresser at the studio, and she suggested that it would be
more pleasant for me to leave my hotel room and go to live with her and
her husband while I was looking for a house. By coincidence, her house
was located directly in back of Marty Melcher's house. She and I often
went over to Marty's to play volleyball on Sunday mornings, but although
I saw a lot of Marty, it was strictly business. He had negotiated my movie
and record salaries up to around two thousand a week, and he was a very
sympathetic listener during those long stretches when I felt lonely and depressed. My career was going well, of course, but I brooded about my two
failed marriages, and I still didn't have Terry with me.

I wanted a solid home for him, though I knew that a home without a
man in it who was a good husband for me, and a good substitute father
for Terry, would not be very solid. And I also knew that none of the men I

was seeing at the time could be taken seriously. So by myself I bought a house at Toluca Lake for $28,000, furniture and all, and for the first time since his birth, I had a home in which to live with Terry. Marty helped me with the purchase and all the problems of moving in, and he took an immediate shine to Terry, who was a freckle-nosed, outgoing, ebullient little boy. For eight years Terry had led a rather nomadic life, but now, finally, we had a home of our own where we would likely stay put for a long time.

Warners required a lot of publicity appearances, which in my case consisted primarily of late-night visits to disk jockeys to promote songs from my pictures; Marty would take me to the radio stations, and afterward, when he took me home, we would often sit in the car and talk for hours. Rather, I talked (about my busted marriages, my growing involvement with Christian Science, about whatever was bothering me that day) and he listened.

One such night, I was holding forth as usual.

"The fact is, Marty, I'm a failure."

"A failure? Why, you're at the beginning of a great career."

"I'm not talking about that. I've failed at the only thing that matters to me—being a good wife, having a happy marriage—"

"Now, Doris, you've got to stop getting on yourself about those marriages of yours. You're young, you're on your way, give yourself time, you'll meet someone and everything will fall in place. The trouble with you is, you think you're the only person in the world who's had a marriage flop. Well, it's not so—it's just not so. There are an awful lot of people in your boat."

He was right about that. I really did regard myself as a unique failure in the land of milk and marriage.

"Well, let me tell you something," Marty went on. "I'm having a pretty rough time in my own marriage. It's been going downhill for a long time. Patty and I just aren't getting along anymore."

"Oh, I'm sorry to hear that, Marty. You always seem so—well you know, all right when you're together."

"Well, as you know, you can't judge a marriage by what's out in the open."

He never mentioned his marriage again, but it wasn't long afterward that he moved out of his house and took an apartment by himself. At the time a lot of people jumped to the conclusion that his leaving Patty was motivated by an affair he was having with me. Not so. There was absolutely nothing between us when Marty left Patty. But I heard that Patty was very angry for a while, and that Al Levy became convinced that I had been having a secret affair with Marty and that was why I had turned Al aside when he confessed his love for me.

After his separation Marty and I did start to see each other regularly. Marty had no children with Patty, and the more he was around the house, the more he became involved with Terry, who responded to him whole-heartedly. Marty was a tall (6 feet, 3 inches), well-built man with brown hair, gentle brown eyes, even features, and a good smile with good teeth. His easygoing, amusing manner enchanted Terry, who obviously saw in Marty the father figure he had never known. Terry called Marty his "manager," figuring, I guess, that what was good enough for me was good enough for him. Marty, on the other hand, seemed to find in Terry the child he had wanted but never had with Patty.

Marty became a constant visitor to the house. My mother liked him, Terry adored him, I found him to be an amusing companion who gave the house some substance when he was around. Our involvement was gradual, a slow-gathering, amiable relationship which kind of snuck up on me. When we started sleeping together, it was good and satisfying— not overwhelming, but I guess I didn't want to be overwhelmed by a relationship anymore. I stopped seeing other men. I can't honestly say I was in love with Marty, because I had become very suspicious of love, of what it really was, of what it really demanded. I knew that if love was what there had been between Al Jorden and me I certainly didn't want any more of that. I suppose it was the low-key, undemanding nature of the relationship with Marty that attracted me to him as much as anything else.

Marty was Jewish. He came from an Orthodox Jewish family, New England background, father a shopkeeper, marginal existence. Marty was not a religious person, in the sense that he went to the synagogue or even observed Jewish holidays. But my deepening interest in Christian Science aroused his curiosity and he began to read some of the Mary Baker Eddy books which I had assembled. He seemed to be even more enthusiastic than I had been when the power of her words first struck me. He began going to meetings with me, and we spent a lot of time reading aloud to each other and discussing the meaning of what we read. We both stopped smoking and drinking, which Christian Science demands, and we both felt better for it. Not just physically better, which we did, of course, but spiritually better for clearing our senses of those artificial stimuli, and letting the natural stimulus of ideas take their place.

I have no recollection of when or how the subject of getting married came up—Marty once said that Terry suggested it. But on April 3, 1951, my twenty-seventh birthday, we were married at the Burbank City Hall by Justice of the Peace Leonard Hammer. After a motor trip to the Grand Canyon we returned to the Toluca Lake house; shortly afterward my mother found a small apartment for herself nearby. I seemed to have found the solid, serene life I had been seeking. And for many years that illusion persisted. I say "illusion" because I lived with Marty Melcher for seventeen years, until the day he died in 1968, but not until then did I discover that this man who had slept with me, adopted my son, managed my career and business life, was indeed an enigma. He may have been a charlatan, he may simply have been a dupe, but he was certainly secretly venal and devious. But that day in 1951 when we returned from our wedding trip, Terry excitedly running to the car, I thought he was the answer I had prayed for.

CHAPTER 6

The ultimate yardstick of achievement in Hollywood has been the annual poll of the theater owners of America. To be voted by them into the top ten is to enter the celluloid sanctum sanctorum. Shortly after my marriage, I got a call one morning from Bob Thomas of the Associated Press, telling me I had made the hallowed ten. At this point I had made only nine pictures, and Thomas complimented me on so remarkable an achievement after so relatively few movies.

In 1953 I made one of my favorite musicals, *Calamity Jane,* not realizing that on its completion I would be starting the run of Calamity Doris. There were no storm warnings. I had just completed a routine but charming period musical with Gordon MacRae, *By the Light of the Silvery Moon.* Marty had left Century Artists and was devoting himself full-time to managing my affairs and a music company which we had established to handle not only my songs and records but general music publishing as well. Terry was reveling in his new and complete home life. Marty had legally adopted him in 1952, when he was ten, and Terry was proud to be Terry Melcher. My mother was well settled and happy with her life and newfound friends. My brother, Paul, had moved out to Los Angeles with his wife and children and gone to work for our company, which we called Arwin Productions. My earnings were now in the neighborhood of five thousand a week; I was near the top in both movie and music polls.

But that's when I became unstuck and fell apart.

Calamity Jane was a demanding picture but no more so than a few others I had done. I loved portraying Calamity Jane, who was a rambunctious, pistol-packing prairie girl. I can't say that the physical high jinks of jumping on horses, bars, wagons, and belligerent men or doing pratfalls in muddy streams seemed to be particularly exhausting while I was doing the picture. I had a great working relation with my costar, Howard Keel, and absolutely first-rate songs to sing, one of which, "Secret Love," became my third million-plus recording and won that year's Academy Award.

The picture was a rousing success, but shortly after finishing my work on it I began to have trouble breathing. I couldn't take a full breath, short gasps were all I could manage. The days and weeks that followed were a hideous nightmare. Not only was I plagued by this inability to breathe, but I also began experiencing terrible heart palpitations. Next, I discovered a small lump in my left breast.

I tried to keep it all from Marty. The only person in whom I confided, was my Christian Science Practitioner, Martin Broones, who was the husband of that marvelous English comedienne Charlotte Greenwood, also a devout Christian Scientist. He was a warm, sensible, compassionate man with whom I had become great friends. He had never dealt with anyone with a breathing problem like mine, but he felt that he could help me overcome my physical problems by concentrating on certain fundamental precepts in *Science and Health,* which contains Mrs. Eddy's fundamental truths. " 'The cause of all disease is mental,' " Mr. Broones read aloud, and I closed my eyes in concentration. " 'A mortal fear, a mistaken belief or conviction of the necessity and power of ill-health; also a fear that Mind is helpless to defend the life of man and incompetent to control it. Without this ignorant human belief, any circumstance is of itself powerless to produce suffering. It is latent belief in disease, as well as the fear of disease, which associates sickness with certain circumstances and causes the two to appear conjoined, even as poetry and music are reproduced in union by human memory. Disease has no intelligence. Unwittingly you sentence yourself to suffer. The understanding of this will enable you to commute this self-sentence, and meet every circumstance with truth. Disease is less than mind, and Mind can control it.' "

But not *my* mind. At night I lay in bed beside Marty, sleepless, my heart pounding, my eyes riveted on the ceiling, monitoring every gasping breath as I repeated and repeated Mrs. Eddy's words—to no avail. Of course, by now I had told Marty about my maladies, and often he would wake in the night and read to me from *Science and Health.* Contrary to popular belief, Christian Science does permit a visit to a doctor if the person, after conscientious effort, cannot rid himself of the mental condition that is causing his physical problems. But I am a disciplined person who abides by the rules. If I were indeed a true Christian Scientist, then I should be steadfast and stick with it. I was being put to the test, I felt, and I wanted to measure up. And Marty, having embraced Christian Science even more avidly than I, certainly shared my point of view.

I became a virtual recluse, not going out of the house for days on end. The starting date was approaching for a new picture at Warners, *Lucky Me,* with Robert Cummings and Phil Silvers, but I postponed all my pre-production meetings, such as costume fittings. I didn't speak to my friends and I canceled all recording dates, interviews, and other publicity activities. My only concern was survival. I lost weight rapidly. My depression was so numbing that often I stayed in bed from morning till night.

I don't know who made the decision to call the doctor, but one day Dr. Hearn, who lived nearby, was there. As he examined me I rattled off my ailments.

"Look, Dr. Hearn," I said, "I don't want you to try to spare my feelings. I know I'm dying so you may as well level with me."

"Doris," he said, "I'm going to give it to you straight—you're hyperventilating."

"I'm . . . what?"

"Overbreathing."

"Well, that doesn't sound very serious."

"It isn't."

"You mean all these months, this absolute hell, and all I am is breathing too much?"

"Did you do a film recently?"

"I'm always doing a film recently."

"Were you tired?"

"I was exhausted."

"That's when it started. A very common affliction among people who are high-strung, exhausted—it's a nervous condition that can be brought on by stress, overwork, being overly tired, or being anxious. The tendency is to breathe too much, take too much oxygen into the body, and expend too much carbon dioxide. That makes you short of breath, which induces you to try to breathe in even more oxygen, and when finally you get too much oxygen into you, and too little carbon dioxide, you faint."

Marty came in with a small brown paper bag. Dr. Hearn gathered the mouth of the bag into a small opening and handed it to me. "Now put your lips on this," he said, "and start to breathe in and out, don't take your lips away, just breathe in the air you breathe into the bag. That way you'll get some carbon dioxide into you."

I did as he instructed and after a while I began to feel a little better. He gave me a sedative. "I've reserved a room at St. Joseph's Hospital for you," he said. "We've got to put you back together again."

"What about the lump in my breast?"

"I think it's benign but we've got to make sure."

"When shall I check in?"

"Now."

"You mean . . . but it's three o'clock in the morning."

"They're open."

Dr. Hearn was right about my physical condition; after two days of tests, they found nothing wrong with me; the lump in my breast proved to be benign, and the cyst was removed with simple minor surgery. I felt somewhat relieved, but I was still a nervous wreck. Dr. Hearn came in with Marty for a consultation.

"You have been so worried—so full of fear and anxiety—for such a long period," Dr. Hearn said, "that your nerves are shattered. I've suggested to Mr. Melcher that we bring in a neuropsychiatric specialist to treat you—to talk to you."

I readily consented, and the next day when Dr. Karl von Hagen came into my hospital room I burst into tears. I finally pulled myself together and started to tell him about my life. I thought that that's what I was supposed to do. I went back to my failed marriages, and then to my childhood, the divorce of my parents. Eventually he stopped me. "I'm not really that kind of doctor," he said. "I don't want you to go into those previous events in your life. You are terribly nervous and I want you to concentrate on your recent fears and anxieties which have induced this nervousness. Now I want you to tell me everything that bothers you about your health, so that we can discuss it fully. If your heart starts palpitating, I'll tell you why. If your vision seems cloudy, I'll explain it to you. It's all nerves. In each instance, I want you to understand the connection. I want you to keep a diary of every physical manifestation that bothers you, and we'll go into them every day."

"But that's really not much different from what I was trying to do through Christian Science—make my mind overcome its fear so that it wouldn't impose bad reactions in my body."

"Yes, in a sense, that's true."

"But I wasn't able to do it. What makes you think you can succeed where Mrs. Eddy has failed? Or, I should say, where I failed Mrs. Eddy?"

"Well, we're going to use some physical medicine, like sedatives, and we're going to deal *specifically* with your physical problems. Christian Science is a *general* application of the philosophy of the dominance of mind over matter. Medical approach is the *specific* application of knowledge to a specific bodily malfunction. We have given you a very thorough physical checkup. These tests show there is absolutely nothing wrong with you. And yet you suffer. You have told me about your inability to breathe properly, your heart palpitations, the occasional blurriness of your vision when you move your eyes, the prickly feeling in your right arm, the recurring headaches, your occasional inability to swallow, and the way at times your left leg twitches uncontrollably. All these, plus the fear related to discovering that lump in your breast, have added fear upon fear about what is happening to you. And these accumulating, escalating fears have made a massive assault upon your nerves. Well, the nerves are like rubber bands. They have great resiliency, but pulled too far and too often they begin to lose that resiliency, and that is what has happened to you. As we alleviate fear, we will little by little restore that resiliency—but it won't happen overnight. We have a lot of ground to cover."

The doctor gave me a note pad on which I was to keep track of every physical thing that bothered me, along with what I was thinking as it bothered me. He allowed me to go home but put me on a strict program of rehabilitation. No newspapers or news programs. No telephone calls. No entertaining—the fewer people I saw, the better. As much quiet and tranquility in the house as possible. No discussion about work. As little talk as possible, because talking caused overbreathing. As much reading as possible, but only "positive" books that were uplifting. I was forbidden to read any movie scripts. Dr. von Hagen put me on a regimen of swimming three times a day, with particular emphasis on the dead man's float. He said swimming was a complete relaxant that affected the whole body, and that the dead man's float was one of the best ways to remove tension from the body.

During Dr. von Hagen's daily visits, as I went over my diary with him, I began to have the feeling that I was getting on top of my problems. The thing that seemed to help me the most was the dead man's float. I could literally feel the tension drain out of me into the warm water of the pool. Afterward I felt less depressed, less bleak, less set upon by afflictions.

During those weeks of recuperation, I leaned heavily on *Science and Health.* "Oh! Thou hast heard my prayer; And I am blest! This is Thy high behest:—Thou here, and *everywhere.*" That had such power for me.

Not "Oh, please hear my prayer! Help me!" but "Thou hast heard my prayer and I am blest." An accomplished fact. Not praying to a God somewhere out there or up there or wherever. In other words, there's no duality. Everything is one. So you don't have to go anywhere or pray to anything but just go inside yourself, for that is where God is.

During my convalescence, I came to see that no matter what you achieve you really can't take credit for any of it. God, the Creator, whatever you want to call Him, has put you here to fulfill a function, everything in you predestined, and you perform as ordained and that's all there is to it. I found a sense of religion as a result of my indoctrination into Christian Science. I feel that God is my very being and God is the life of everything around me. So I don't have to seek God. He's right here. I don't pray. I just realize God.

CHAPTER 7

Liberation from Warner Brothers when my contract with them expired brought with it, for the first time, the right to say no—but I found that in some ways my newfound freedom made life more difficult, not easier. For now a great variety of scripts were offered to me and I had to make judgments that I had never had to make before.

One of the scripts that intrigued me was a dramatization of the life of Ruth Etting, the torch singer of the Twenties who got her start through gangland connections. The picture, called *Love Me Or Leave Me,* had a veteran producer, Joe Pasternak, a first-rate script by Isobelle Lennart, a very competent director, Charles Vidor, and Jimmy Cagney already cast in the role of Marty Snyder, "the Gimp"—a small-time hood who devoted his life and fierce ambition to furthering Ruth Etting's career. Etting was an important singer of her day, and the relationship between her and the crippled, hard-driving Snyder was an unusual and compelling one, but Ruth Etting was a kept woman who clawed her way up from seamy Chicago nightclubs to the Ziegfeld Follies, and I wondered whether audiences would believe me in a part like that.

I had several discussions with Joe Pasternak about the part which would require me to drink, to wear scant, sexy costumes, to string along a man I didn't love in order to further my career. There was a vulgarity about Ruth Etting that I didn't want to play.

"That's just the point," Pasternak said. "It will be in the playing—that's why I want you for the part. You will play Ruth Etting in a way that will give her some dignity, that will play away from the vulgarity. Besides, there's great music that will do a lot to affect the characterization."

It was a great score, all right, but I think what finally induced me to do the picture was the opportunity of performing with Cagney in a role that was marvelously detailed, combative, involved; the Gimp was a difficult and demanding role that would bring out all of Jimmy's fire, and the prospect of performing with him at the top of his form was my primary reason for doing the picture.

The only unpleasant aspect of *Love Me Or Leave Me* was some of the fan reaction I received. I was deluged with mail attacking me for drinking, for playing a lewd woman, for the scant costumes I wore in the nightclub scenes. I suppose many Christian Scientists were disappointed and in some cases angry that I, a Christian Scientist, was up there on the screen drinking and smoking. What's involved in this kind of protest is the movie realism that made me hesitate to play the role in the first place. On the screen I am not Doris Day playing a part, I *am* that part. They may call me Ruth Etting in the movie but to the audience I am Doris Day and I shouldn't be doing those dreadful things on the screen. I answered every piece of mail, explaining this as best I could, for I feel a performer has the same responsibility to his public that a politician has to the electorate. It was a beautifully made picture about which I had no regrets, but I cared very much about people who were disturbed by my characterization. It was a picture that could not have been made at Warners, where musicals were done as quickly and cheaply as possible. The time, money, and expertise that MGM devoted to the film were what gave it its look of quality. My first adventure in the free world was certainly a rewarding one.

There is one other aspect to *Love Me Or Leave Me* that didn't really register with me until some years later, and that is the parallel, in some respects, between Marty Snyder and Marty Melcher—and I don't just mean the coincidence of their names. I will go into this later on, when I discuss my relationship with Marty as it developed over the years; I didn't realize in 1955 how much Ruth Etting and I had in common.

Alfred Hitchcock redeemed a six-year-old promise to me with *The Man Who Knew Too Much*. I was as tentative about doing it as I had been about *Love Me Or Leave Me* but for a totally different reason. Hitchcock was going to film most of the picture in London and Marrakesh. I had never been out of the United States, and with my uneasiness about air travel being what it was and is, I thought maybe I'd pass up this Hitchcock for the next one. Between my first and second pictures at Warners, I toured with Bob Hope's radio troupe, and it was these tours through impenetrable winter weather that had spooked me off the airplane.

Marty would have none of my protests. "Now, Doris, this is a fine picture that you want to do with Hitchcock and Jimmy Stewart and you simply can't back out just because you have to travel. You're not going alone—I'll be with you and we'll take Terry and we'll all go by train and boat. It will be *fun*."

There was a song-writing team under contract at Paramount, Livingston and Evans, to whom Hitchcock had assigned the task of composing a song for me to sing as a lullaby to my little son in the picture. One afternoon when I was in Wardrobe having a fitting, Ray Evans came in and asked me whether I'd like to hear the new song for the picture, which had just been approved by Hitchcock. We went to their music studio, where they played "Que Sera, Sera" for me. I thought it was fine for the spot in the picture where it was needed, but later, when I saw Marty, I expressed my disappointment that it did not have a broader appeal.

"What do you mean?" Marty asked.

"Well, it's a kiddie song. It's sweet, and perfect for where I sing it in the film, but I was hoping it would be more than that. You know—'whatever will be, will be'—that's not really my kind of lyric."

"I think you're dead wrong. Hitchcock and I both think it's going to be a big hit. You'll see."

Of course, I've never been wronger about anything than I was about "Que Sera." I recorded it for Columbia and for the movie album and it became the most popular of all my songs. Also, although I did not know Jay Livingston or Ray Evans, they had by pure chance hit upon a philosophy in "Que Sera" that was my theme song. Whatever will be, will be.

CHAPTER 8

E ver since my release from Warner Brothers, Marty had been trying to find a property he could produce on his own; *Julie* was what he turned up with. It was a heavily dramatic script in which I played an airline hostess who was bedeviled by a rabidly jealous husband. I didn't want to do it. It wasn't a bad script, but playing the part of a woman victimized by a jealous husband washed back the reality of the insane jealousy of Al Jordan, the bizarre jealousy of Al Levy, and George Weidler's jealousy of my career. I had had more than enough real jealousy to contend with in my life. I didn't want to act in a film in which I played a woman whose husband was so jealous of her he was trying to kill her. That kind of sick film never has appealed to me and I told Marty so.

"That's the trouble with you, Doris," he said, "you just want to keep doing the same thing."

"Now that's not true, Marty. I've just done a dramatic picture for Hitchcock, and *Love Me Or Leave Me* before that."

"They had music. This will be different. A straight dramatic role. You'll be great in it."

"Look, Marty, the part doesn't appeal to me—"

"I've got a great deal all set with MGM—a budget of one million six with a fifty-fifty split of the profits. Everything is set to go. I've even got Jerry Rosenthal looking into a tax shelter for us."

"Well, you should have shown me the script before you went so far—"

"Don't you think I know a good script when I see one?" Marty was beginning to lose his temper.

"Marty, take it easy, I didn't say it wasn't a good script—"

"Then stop worrying. This is Oscar material. Would I put you into something I didn't *know* was going to be a big hit?"

"It's just the part, Marty—a jealous husband trying to kill—"

"And would MGM set me up to produce the film if they didn't believe in it?"

"I'm not saying it won't do well at the box office—"

"Then what more can you ask? Just do this one for me and the next one we'll get you a nice, easy musical."

This discussion lasted for the better part of two days but finally, as I always did with Marty, I gave in, albeit reluctantly. The Jerry Rosenthal whom Marty mentioned was a lawyer whose offices adjoined that of Arwin Productions, our company. (Marty made up the name and I have no idea what "Arwin" refers to.) Rosenthal worked very closely with Marty on deals, contracts, and tax matters; at that time he was considered *the* Hollywood specialist on tax shelters. He had an impressive list of clients.

Julie was a terrible ordeal, from start to finish—not the movie itself as much as the events that surrounded it.

Almost all of *Julie* was shot on location in Carmel, which is a lovely resort town on the coast a little south of San Francisco. My costar was Louis Jourdan, whom I liked very much. An amiable man, very gentle, very much interested in the people around him; we had a good rapport and I found talking with him a joy. I think that Frenchmen are much better at conversation than Americans. They *like* to talk. They are reflective and responsive. I don't know why the "strong, silent" American specimen is held in such esteem. Louis and I had long talks about our problems, about life in Hollywood, about Paris, about our children, about Life in the larger sense. We would take long walks on the beautiful Carmel beach, chatting by the hour. There was nothing between us, but Marty became very jealous of Louis. He suspected we were having an affair but he was also jealous of how much I enjoyed our walks and talks. Marty and I had a compatible relationship but Marty was not a conversationalist. He liked to talk about pictures and albums and grosses, the usual Hollywood conversation, and he liked to discuss our Christian Science lessons, but he never really talked about us.

But he should have talked about us, for our relationship was changing. Marty's relationship with Terry, which had been so good at first, was also changing. As Terry got older, Marty's easygoing manner turned increasingly more tyrannical. And up there in Carmel, as producer of the picture, he was also showing a tyrannical side of himself. I can frankly say that I enjoyed being with Louis much more than with Marty. Of course Marty sensed this, and that too was part of his jealousy. But what irony, that during the making of this picture about a jealous husband, I should be beset with a real-life one.

We were about two weeks into the picture when another upsetting event occurred: I began to hemorrhage. Marty suggested that we call our practitioner, Martin Broones.

But the hemorrhaging got worse. I was losing quite a lot of blood, and there was a constant, rather intense stabbing pain in my abdomen. I spoke to Broones every day but it didn't affect the hemorrhaging. I begged Marty to let me go back to Los Angeles, but I was in virtually every scene and it meant shutting down the film. Marty wouldn't hear of it. "You're not *concentrating*, that's all that's wrong with you," he said. "Instead of thinking about running to a doctor, you should be working on your lessons and conquering whatever is causing the bleeding."

"But, Marty, there's this pain, and I feel so darn weak."

"All mental. In between setups, instead of spending your time gabbing with that Frenchman, you should lie down in your trailer and study *Science and Health*. You are what you think you are. You can think yourself well, and you know it. You better get hold of yourself or next thing you know you'll be hyperventilating."

Somehow, despite the bleeding, the pain, the loss of energy and weight, I got through the picture. Marty had been concerned about me—I don't want to give the impression that he wasn't. But the day I returned from Carmel, I drove straight to the office of my gynecologist, Dr. Willard Crosley. He poked around on my belly a few times and said, "You have an endometriotic tumor growing into your intestines. It's quite bad. We've got to get it out—*immediately.*"

"Can you tell me if it's malignant?"

"Most likely not. But even if benign it can cause a lot of damage."

The operation at Glendale Memorial lasted four hours. It was not only a hysterectomy, but my intestines had to be surgically rebuilt to repair the damage the giant tumor had done to them.

I was in the hospital for ten days, which was recuperative procedure then, and while I lay there, it dawned on me that I had lost the possibility of having another child. My life had been too crowded for childbearing, but I had intermittently thought about how I had been deprived of Terry's very young years and how nice it would be to have a baby that could be with me all the time. I was only thirty-two and although we never really discussed it, I felt Marty would have adored the experience of fatherhood. Well, that was gone now, and thinking about that—the finality of it—threw me into a terrible depression. I burst out crying at the strangest times, and continued to do so long after I was out of the hospital.

As I said, the making of *Julie* was something of an ordeal.

But after my recovery some sunny events helped dispel the gloom. First and foremost was the fact that we bought a new house on North Crescent Drive in Beverly Hills, the home I now live in. It was a single story house, and even though it cost around $150,000 it was rather modest by Beverly Hills standards. What I liked most about the house was the enormous, graceful old sycamore tree whose branches formed a canopy over the house and patio. (I have a deep feeling about trees, akin to my feeling about dogs, but what I'd like to be in my next life is a bird.)

I really enjoyed working on the interior decoration for the house. I used lots of prints and yellows to brighten the new house and give it a warm look. I chose comfortable, conservative furniture. I wanted to remodel the living-room, but Marty would not let me spend money on such projects. I had just signed a recording contract with Columbia Records for $1,050,000, the biggest contract of its time, but Marty wouldn't spend money on a new ceiling.

"We need all our surplus money for Rosenthal's investment program" was Marty's explanation. "Without tax shelters we'll be turning over everything we earn to the government." Oh, how I wish I had put it all in my ceilings!

Because *Julie* was Marty's debut as a producer, I consented to participate in an all-out razzle-dazzle premiere—something I had always tried to
avoid. MGM's plan was to open the picture in Cincinnati with a week of
hoopla leading up to a gala premiere in the downtown Albee. I hadn't
been back to Cincinnati in all those years, so it was the good old tried-
and-true formula of hometown girl returning in cinematic glory to be
hailed by the proud natives. Governor Frank J. Lausche issued a procla-
mation making October 8-11 "Doris Day Week" throughout the state of
Ohio, and the mayor of Cincinnati was poised to give me a key to the city.
There was to be an endless round of civic functions and banquets.

There was a big crowd waiting to greet me at the Cincinnati railroad
station when our train pulled in. Marty, Terry, and Warren Cowen, who
handled my public relations and was a good friend besides, were on
board, as well as a retinue of MGM wardrobe mistresses, photographers,
press agents, and executives. In these times of movie austerity it's hard to
imagine the opulence with which premieres were then staged.

I was standing in the little vestibule of our car, waiting to get off the
train, when a man's face appeared in the window. The man waved and
smiled at me. He looked familiar, a face I had known but couldn't place.
After I got off the train and had met the various local dignitaries who were
there to greet me, I felt a hand on my arm and turned to face again the
man I had seen in the window. Tears came to the man's eyes, and at that
moment I realized it was my father. We embraced. He wept quite openly.
He was gray now and had less hair and had put on some weight.

"How nice that you came to greet me," I said. "That's really nice."

"I'm so happy to see you," he said.

"I'm sorry that when you appeared in the window . . ."

"Oh, it's been many, many years and people change."

There was a great crush of people and it was difficult to talk. "Would
you like to come to the hotel and have breakfast in the morning?" I asked.

"I'd love to."

"We're at the Plaza. Come around nine-thirty, ten o'clock. That will
give us an hour before my first interview."

When I went to bed that night, I thought about my father. I had heard
from a relative that his second wife had died of cancer. And another relative had written that my father had bought some property in the black
ghetto as an investment. It seemed ironical that a man so bigoted about
the blacks should buy black property as an investment; but he was probably exploiting them, as many white absentee owners do, and if so, that
would go snug with his prejudice.

Thirteen-year-old Doris Kappelhoff and her partner, Jerry Doherty (left), were on their way to Hollywood fame when an accident cut short her dancing career; instead, the renamed Doris Day became a band vocalist—the trombonist in the picture at left, below, is Al Jorden, her first husband. Below, the young mother finds time between band travels for son Terry.

Wearing the heavy Warner Bros. pancake makeup and lacquered hair she abhorred, Doris appeared with Jack Carson in her first film, Romance on the High Seas. *James Cagney was her co-star in her best film,* Love Me or Leave Me *(below).*

She had not danced since the accident, but Gene Nelson got her started again (above, in Lullaby of Broadway). Below, Doris and James Stewart heed Alfred Hitchcock's advice on location in Marrakesh for The Man Who Knew Too Much.

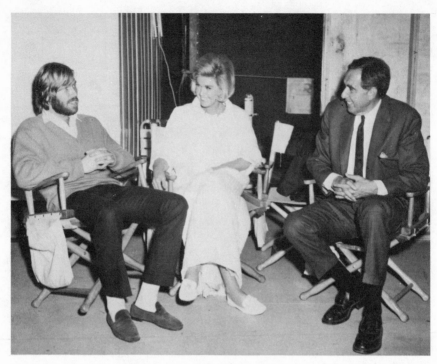

A rare moment of family happiness—Doris takes a break from shooting with son Terry and her third husband, Marty Melcher (right). Below, the star enjoys frolicking with one of her beloved dogs on the terrace of her California home.

But I was certainly very glad he had come to the train. In the brief glimpse I had of him, it seemed to me that his whole aspect had changed. There was a warmth and softness about him that seemed to belie my childhood memory of him. When he had lived with us, it would have been inconceivable for him to have shed a tear. Now he had wept openly and unashamedly, and his tears had touched me very much.

When my father appeared at the hotel the following morning, he was nervous and ill at ease, but Marty had a friendly, loose quality about him that soon made my father relax. But it was difficult to have a decent talk because the phone was already busy ringing. I did manage to ask him about his teaching and choral groups.

"I've given that up," he said.

"Well, what do you do? You're not retired, are you?"

Before he could answer, I was called to the phone. When I returned, my father said, "Listen, Doris, I see how busy you are. Why don't you and Marty come to my place—I'd love to show it to you. I'd like you to meet my friends. Do you think you'll have time?"

"Oh, sure. We'll *make* time, but we can't do it till the end of the day, after all the interviews."

"That's fine."

My father wrote down the address and gave it to Marty. I was dumbfounded at my father's having given up his life of music. "Well, you said he bought a big apartment building in the black section," Marty said, "with a bar and grill. You'd be surprised how much income a place like that generates."

Around five o'clock that afternoon, in a big, black MGM Cadillac, liveried chauffeur at the wheel, Marty, Warren Cowen, and I drove to the address my father had given us. It was in the heart of the black ghetto that the driver pulled up in front of a bar and grill. The sidewalk and street were crowded. Bunting was strung across the face of the bar, and a small, hand-lettered sign above the door said "WELCOME DORIS." My father came out to greet us and to lead us into the bar, his bar, of which he was obviously proud. It was a charming German bar with beautiful wood in back of the bar itself, beveled mirrors, and beer steins all arranged in neat rows. He had obviously told all the neighborhood that I was coming. The jukebox had nothing but Doris Day recordings, which played all the time we were there.

The only word to describe that crowd and that evening is "joyous." The people there were really glad I had come and they obviously had a wonderful kind of affection for and rapport with my father, who worked behind the bar with two assistants, a black man who helped him with drinks, and a lovely black lady who handled the grill.

"What a wonderful place you have," I said, "and oh, how they love you!"

"It's mutual," he said.

"But how did it happen?"

"Quite by accident. I had bought this property as an investment but had nothing to do with it, until one evening I got a call that the man who was running the bar had taken ill. I came down and took over the bar myself, and I tell you, Doris, it was an instant love affair with the people here. We just seemed to understand each other. From that day on, I've been here every night and loved every minute of it. In fact . . . I'd like you to meet Luvenia."

He led me over to the woman who was making the sandwiches, and introduced us. Her full name was Luvenia Williams and she had one of the sweetest smiles I ever saw.

"We're going to be married, Luvenia and I," my father said. I was totally at a loss for words. I simply smiled at her and shook her hands, and—well, as always when I am moved by something, tears came to my eyes. I had drunk a lot of beer by then, and I felt totally enveloped by the warm glow of the beer, the loving, joyful people, and the beautiful change that had come over my father. People were constantly getting up on chairs and proposing a toast to me and we would clink glasses all around and down some beer.

In the car going back to the hotel, no one said a word. We enjoyed the euphoria. I sat back and closed my eyes and thought about how much hate and prejudice there had been in my father, and how now he had come all the way around to loving and marrying a black woman. And I thought about how happy he was with all those blacks who were truly his friends.

I did not see my father again during the *Julie* week, but several years later, when my mother, Marty, and I were on our way to New York, we stopped in Cincinnati to visit relatives. I telephoned my father, who I had not heard from since my *Julie* visit, and invited him to come to see us. I told him my mother was with me. He said he would drop by.

When he pulled up to the door, he had his wife and another black woman in the car with him. I was watching him through my aunt's living-room window. My heart sank at the prospect of the confrontation that was about to take place. But my father left the women in the car and came to the door by himself. I greeted him at the door and brought him into the living room. He said hello to my mother but he was very cool toward her and did not look at her or say anything further to her. They hadn't seen each other for twenty years and I had thought that there would at least be a kind of civility. But there wasn't. My mother stayed in the room for only a few minutes, then excused herself and left. My aunt and uncle sat with us but the conversation was very strained. Through the living-room window we could all see the two women sitting in the car, but neither my aunt nor my uncle invited my father to bring in his wife. I didn't know what to do. I was dying to invite the women to come in, but this wasn't my house, and there was so much terrible prejudice on the street that if they did come in, my aunt and uncle were sure to suffer for it at the hands of their neighbors.

So I did nothing. My father did not stay very long. When I took him to the door and said good-bye, I came out on the porch and waved to the two women in the car. They waved back and I stood there until the car drove away. I don't know if my father felt humiliated. I would think that he did. Afterward I wished I had gone down to the car and spoken to the women. That wouldn't have compromised my aunt and uncle and it would have eased my father's departure. I regretted not having done that. Instead, I just stood there at a safe distance on the porch and watched them go. It was the last time I saw my father.

Nor did I ever hear from him again. When he died, I sent flowers to his funeral but I did not go. I never go to funerals. I mourn the passing of someone dear in my own private way. I don't approve of public grief.

I have never heard from my father's widow. I don't know where she is. But I hope that he had some happy years with her.

CHAPTER 9

I previously indicated that my relationship with Marty had begun to change. In the beginning we had a compatibility that seemed solid enough. Our son, Terry, our movie-music company, our new house in Beverly Hills, our religion, a lovely little house we bought on the Malibu beach, some very good friends, going to Dodger ball games—all those things fed our mutual enjoyment of life. And we had a good sex life too.

But eventually many of these very things that we had enjoyed together became problems for us. One of the most troublesome areas was in connection with my work and earnings, and how Marty was handling them.

Marty's working arrangement with the lawyer, Jerry Rosenthal, became an increasingly dominant force, and irritant, in my life. As my earnings increased, Marty and Rosenthal increased my investments in oil wells, cattle, and big hotels. I felt I had no business in any of these high-risk ventures. Marty was constantly bringing home new investment papers for me to sign in connection with big-capital projects he had gotten into with Rosenthal, when what he should have been doing was producing the films I was making. But after *Julie*, Marty devised a producing arrangement much more to his liking. He let others produce the pictures, giving himself credit as coproducer or executive producer and putting himself in the budget for a fifty-thousand-dollar fee. Whether because he lacked confidence in his ability or because he wanted a more leisurely life, the fact was that Marty was happiest when his day consisted of going to his club for lunch, briefly visiting the set where I was working, and then spending the rest of the afternoon playing tennis at the Beverly Hills Tennis Club. He didn't like vacations or any other distraction that took him away from this Hollywood.

Marty was much more gregarious than I, and in the evenings he wanted to go to the many parties, home screenings, and premieres to which we were invited. But I was invariably tired from a tough day's work at the studio, which had usually started at five or six in the morning. I used to urge Marty to go without me, but he'd say that we were only invited because of me and that they certainly didn't want him if I wasn't along.

That always irritated me. "Now, that's really stupid, Marty," I'd say, "putting yourself down like that. You're fun at parties and they love having you for yourself."

But nothing I could say had any real effect on his reticence. Perhaps that was one of the reasons he was so intent on making a great fortune out of what I earned—to prove himself, what he could do on his own, as Marty Melcher. But I'm inclined to think, on the basis of the startling revelations which turned up after his death, that his fondness for money, his drive to amass it, was something that existed apart from me. It has been said by some people who knew Marty rather well that he was attracted to Patty Andrews because of her money, and that he quickly left her for me when he became aware of the size of my potential earnings. I really don't know about that, but it was certainly a fact that Marty had an enormous concern about money, a concern about not spending it and a concern about making as much of it as possible.

Of course, Marty had no money of his own, so he could nourish his hunger to be very, very rich only by using the money I earned. The fact that I have little interest in money per se suited his purposes very well. But as I became aware of what Marty, through Rosenthal, was doing with my money, I became increasingly concerned.

What I wanted to do with the money I was earning was to buy paintings I liked, some lovely antiques for the house, and land that I was interested in, especially in the Valley in the area now called Woodland Hills. But Marty wouldn't allow any expenditure except as authorized by Rosenthal. I bought a little painting, a Vlaminck snow scene, for four hundred dollars and Marty made me return it. "We need every cent for Rosenthal's program," he said, "and Rosenthal doesn't approve of paintings." I was earning a million dollars on a picture and I couldn't buy a four-hundred-dollar painting!

I did arrange a couple of confrontations with Rosenthal to protest his investments, but his explanation of what he was doing and how it would benefit me as a tax shelter was too technical for my comprehension. And despite my occasional uneasiness and protestation, I did agree with Marty when he said that either you trust a husband or you don't. Although I didn't like being in oil wells and hotels, there was no question that I did trust Marty. Moreover, I don't want to give the impression that there weren't many good things about our marriage. I enjoyed Marty, his sense of humor, his warm concern about my well-being, our mutual love of our house at the beach. We had bought the house despite Rosenthal's objections, and Marty and I adored our weekends there. Marty loved to putter around, and I like nothing better than to scrub, clean, polish, and shine. When we weren't cleaning and puttering, we took long walks along that beautiful beach with our poodles, and those were some of the nicest hours I ever spent.

As Marty gradually changed in his relation to me, so he changed too with Terry. As Terry got older and began to have a life of his own, Marty seemed either incapable of understanding this natural development or unwilling to allow it. As a result, Marty became more and more of a strict disciplinarian. The camaraderie that they had enjoyed began to dissolve into orders and resentments and punishments.

Terry was a high-spirited, mischievous boy, but a loving, amusing boy, not difficult to handle. Early on Marty had convinced me that it would be best for the family if he was the one who dealt with Terry, so that there would be a single person in authority, and since I was working six days a week and preparing every Sunday for the week ahead, it was only natural for Marty to become the united parental front. That was certainly a mistake. I know now that there is no such thing as a formula for dealing with children within the home. I should have had an equal voice. As it was, Marty made the decision to take Terry out of the Christian Science school where he was going and send him to a military school in Beverly Hills where he would be boarded. We lived in Toluca Lake then, and Marty objected to the friends Terry had made on our street. They were just high-spirited boys like Terry—and I recall they broke a streetlamp and that was the incident that set Marty off. Hooliganism, Marty called it. Of all the boys in the world, Terry was the last one to be sent to a military school, and I tried to convince Marty of that, but he wouldn't listen.

CHAPTER 10

It has been my good fortune that, at those times in my life when tragedy has struck, I have had to work. I think there is nothing worse for the grieving spirit of someone who has suffered death or disaster than to withdraw into her own shadows and cut herself off from all possibility of rehabilitating her morale. Life must go on, and it is only through the society of the living that one can overcome the despair that a death inflicts.

My brother, Paul, whom I adored, a lovely, gentle, amusing man, died suddenly, finally overtaken by a baseball injury of his youth. The drugs he had been taking all those years had kept his seizures under control, but apparently the drugs were not able to withstand this fatal attack. I felt his death very deeply, and I know I would have been laid low by it if I had not been committed to start on a picture with Clark Gable.

I had just finished *The Pajama Game*, which had been an arduous assignment and would have taken a few months off if the opportunity to perform with Gable in *Teacher's Pet* hadn't presented itself. Gable was called the King and for good reason—no actor I ever performed with had such public appeal. He was as masculine as any man I've ever known, and as much a little boy as a grown man could be—it was this combination that had such a devastating effect on women.

When Clark came on the set in the morning, I could actually feel the magnetic force of his personality. He dressed in marvelous tweeds, which obviously had belonged to him for a long time, or in leather, and he wore heavy, thick-soled oxblood brogues that were always shined. He had very big hands, and a thick, large-boned physique that gave him great dimension. There was something very affirmative about him, and a directness that suggested great inner strength.

But there was nothing of the King about his personality. Just the opposite. Utter simplicity. Uncomplicated. Gable, like Cagney, steered clear of the Hollywood social whirl. He lived with his wife, Kay, out in Encino in the farmhouse where he had lived with Carole Lombard. Gable's close friend was his makeup man; they had been friends for years. At the end of a day's shooting, Gable would go to his dressing room and have a drink of Scotch with his makeup man, sometimes joined also by his stand-in. They'd shoot the breeze for a while, then Clark would head home. That was the only staff Gable had—those two men. Quite a contrast to Sinatra, who also has a kind of royal status in the entertainment world but only moves behind a phalanx of bodyguards.

In 1958 and 1959 I made a couple of pictures that did not do well at the box office. *Tunnel of Love* with Richard Widmark, and *It Happened to Jane* with Jack Lemmon. The former had a poor script that I didn't want to do but Marty had already signed me for; the latter, which Marty also contracted for, should have done all right, it was pert and funny, but whether it was the insipid title or something else, it just didn't make it. Marty became terribly concerned over these box-office failures. I had dropped out of the top ten, which meant nothing to me but everything to Marty, primarily because it would have an effect on my earnings. I pointed out to Marty that if he hadn't hustled me into doing these films, if he had waited, I might have found good scripts that would have produced better results.

But actually, as I look back, there was more to it than that. I had been making films for a dozen years by then, primarily films of nostalgia, costume musicals, films depicting wholesome families. There had been a few notable exceptions, of course, but a "Doris Day movie" had come to mean a very specific kind of sunny, nostalgic, sexless, wholesome film. America had undergone great change in the Fifties, the Korean War being one of the main influences, but the Doris Day movie remained a stable commodity.

It was against this background, then, that I read a script submitted to me by a producer named Ross Hunter. The plot, for 1959, was quite sexy, and even involved a climactic scene in which the leading man grabbed me from bed and carried me, in my pajamas, down an elevator, through the lobby, and out onto the street. Clearly, not the kind of part I had ever played before.

Hunter convinced me that I was God's gift to this part, and he also persuaded Rock Hudson, who had never performed in a comedy (his latest role had been in *Giant*), to play opposite me. Marty enrolled himself as

119

coproducer and tried to get Ross to call the picture *The Way the Wind Blows,* which happened to be the title of a song Marty was about to publish, but in the end Ross stayed with the original title, *Pillow Talk.*

I had never met Rock Hudson before, but the very first day on the set I discovered we had a performing rapport that was remarkable. We played our scenes together as if we had once lived them. Every day on the set was a picnic—sometimes too much of a picnic, in that we took turns at breaking each other up. Rock was sexy in the part, but not lascivious; bemused, but not overbearing; tough, but not rough.

There was one other element that added to the effectiveness of the film—the casting of Tony Randall in the second male lead. Tony, Rock, and I were made for each other and it was hard to tell sometimes where life left off and make-believe began. We were destined to make two more pictures together, *Lover Come Back* and *Send Me No Flowers,* which did not quite equal the success of *Pillow Talk* but which did very well indeed.

I was surprised at being nominated for an Academy Award for my performance in *Pillow Talk,* and even more surprised to find that by the end of that year I had shot up to number one at the box office. For the next several years, besides the films with Rock and Tony, I did pictures in the *Pillow Talk* vein with James Garner (*Thrill of It All* and *Move Over Darling*) and Cary Grant (*A Touch of Mink*). I had the same kinship with Jimmy that I had with Rock—truly a blessing to have had two such talented, amusing, darling men to work with, men with whom I have had enduring friendships. I really love Rock and Jimmy.

CHAPTER 11

I have previously mentioned the change in my relations with Marty, but now the marriage actually started to unravel. I loved him, I continued to love him until the day he died, but I was no longer in love with him. For me, being *in* love is an essential ingredient of marriage.

The confrontation about our marriage occurred the day Marty, in a fit of anger, struck Terry. It provoked one of my rare outbursts of anger, for I deeply feel that no one has the right to hit another living thing, human or animal. Being a nonviolent person, I almost never raise my voice, but that day I really screamed at Marty. I told him that I had had enough brutality in my first marriage to last me a lifetime, and that I didn't want to go on living with him.

It was a propitious time to break up. Marty was about to go on the road with a play he was producing, *The Perfect Setup,* so I asked him to move out altogether. Too many things had gone wrong with our marriage, and this altercation with Terry had simply triggered the inevitable.

One of the things that had gone wrong was that in many ways Marty had changed from being a husband to trying to be a father figure. He was becoming more and more rigid and dictatorial, trying to make me into a child. He was *telling* me to do things, rather than discussing them with me. And when I showed any resistance, he'd have a temper tantrum. He never hit me, but there were times when his anger became so uncontrollable, his face wild with rage, that he would smash his fist repeatedly against a wall. I didn't want this ugliness in my life. I felt I had earned the right to have a peaceful and harmonious home life. I worked hard, with very little respite, and I did not want to put up with anger and turmoil.

Also our sex life had deteriorated. In the beginning it was fine but in recent years it had become meaningless. Good sex requires that each person be aware of the other, a mutually shared experience, but Marty had lost that ability and desire to create the kind of flow that is so vital to making love; his patience had become very limited and he was satisfied simply to gratify himself. But I'm not one of those women who can fake it. I know that a lot of women do. Many women have confided things to me about their sex lives with their husbands. How they fake a reaction to their husbands when they approach them for their once-a-week Saturday-night sex act. Some of them can barely stand the thought of having to face those Saturday nights. They pretend sleepiness, headaches, whatever; they much prefer those pretenses, they say, to pretending orgasms. Well, that's not for me. I have never faked a reaction to anything and I wasn't about to begin with sex.

It was to be a trial separation, but the day after Marty left I knew that, for me, it was permanent. His departure gave me a sense of freedom; I realized I had been smothered by him and the sense of being on my own released a certain tension which I had had for a long time. In the years I had been married to Marty, I felt I had grown as a person—in my work, in my religious convictions, in knowing myself, in asking questions and seeking answers. There comes a time when a marriage must be terminated. Nothing is forever. It isn't so much a matter of getting tired of someone as it is a question of whether a relation has sustained itself, whether it's growing, moving *toward* something. The past is fine for a scrapbook, a photo album, but the memory of how things were contributes nothing to how they are or will be.

I think it's a terrible handicap when husband and wife are involved in the same profession. When we first married, I thought it nice to work together, but I came to realize how much better it would be if my husband had a career of his own and we could talk about his work as well as mine, and have a circle of his acquaintances, instead of being confined to the narrowness of my work and movie people. I came to realize too that I really wanted my husband to be the star of the family. A strong man. All the things that Marty and I had to deal with should have been left to an agent and kept out of the home.

I had become contemptuous of Marty's uncontrollable anger, his insistence on keeping me constantly at work, his treatment of Terry, his dependence on my career, and even his attitude toward Christian Science. He was an avid convert who always had C.S. books around him, and unfailingly did his daily lesson before going to work. He involved himself with the Malibu church and was one of the ushers on Sunday morning. But then, despite all these manifestations of his devoutness, he would sleep through the service. That irritated me. I'd nudge him awake. "Now look, Marty," I used to say to him, "if I intended to sleep through the service I wouldn't go. But by God if I go to a service then I make sure I hear every word. I'm going to get something out of it or I don't go. Now, why do you go? Why don't you stay home and sleep? You're bored. You're obviously bored. You lose track of what the readers are saying and then you fall asleep."

"You're right, I do lose track . . ."

"That's because you don't concentrate, and then when you lose track you get bored."

"Yes, that's what happens. I force myself to go on Sunday because it's right that I go."

"No, no, it's wrong that you go if that's why you go. You should go because of what you get from going, not because it's a duty."

"I like to be there. That's enough for me."

This rigid adherence to the doctrines of a religion that he didn't really understand or try to understand would eventually have dire consequences for Marty. At the time, all it did was to make me a little contemptuous of him, because his attitude toward Christian Science was uncomfortably near the old, too familiar attitude fostered by the Roman Catholic church which I had long ago rejected.

After Marty's departure I got to thinking about how difficult it is for both partners to be happy in a marriage. If I had to do it again, I would never marry a man without first having lived with him. If I had lived with

Al Jorden, I'm sure I would have never married him, and since one is much more careful in an affair it's quite likely I wouldn't have had a child with him. I had had an affair with George Weidler but if I had actually *lived* with him, I don't think we would have gotten married. I don't know about Marty. There were so many things between us that were good, they might still have won out in the balance. But the point is, I would have much more clearly known the nature of the man I was marrying. If I had a young daughter who came to me with plans to marry a young man with whom she was in love, I would strongly urge her first to have an affair with him. I think it is sad for a young woman, barely out of her teens (and sometimes in her teens), to turn off her life, so to speak, because she has fallen in love. For when young marrieds have a baby, the woman must give up a good part of those years that should have been devoted to her own growth, enrichment, and education. I'm not saying for a minute that a baby is not an enriching and rewarding experience—what I'm saying is that it has so much more meaning when it comes somewhat later on, after the woman has had a fair chance to enjoy the freedom of her very young years.

Marty and I had one of the shortest separations on record. After a few weeks on the road, *The Perfect Setup*, somewhat less than perfect, opened on Broadway and lasted one night. A short time later, Marty phoned and asked if he could see me.

He was pale and subdued. I attributed his appearance to the dismal failure of his play. I was wrong.

"I had to see you," he said, "because I've just had a long conference with Rosenthal about us."

"Meaning what?"

"Well, I explained about how we were separated and how you wanted to get started on a divorce."

"I don't want Rosenthal for my lawyer."

"All right, but that isn't what's involved here. What's involved is that there's no way we can part company."

"What are you talking about?"

"All our investments, Doris. All our capital is tied up in joint ventures that require loans and reinvestments. Rosenthal showed me that it is impossible to divide up the kinds of things we own, like oil wells. And we don't own them outright. It's very complicated. All I can tell you, I can *assure* you, if we split up we will lose everything." Marty became quite agitated and there were tears in his eyes. "All your hard work, Do-Do, and you'd wind up with hardly anything. I can't do that to you. Isn't there *some* way we can stay together? We do get along, in many ways. And I promise to . . . well, try to, you know, make it work . . . ."

I got up and walked out to the patio, trying to assimilate what Marty had told me. I would check Rosenthal's dire pronouncement with financial people I knew, but I had a feeling that if we were stretched out as far as Marty indicated, that we would indeed be ruined if we got divorced. I was very moved by the pathetic figure of Marty still sitting in the living room, trying to choke back his tears. As I have said, in many ways I still loved Marty and I certainly did not want anyone I loved to suffer. I walked around the swimming pool and thought about all this before going back to talk to Marty.

"I'll tell you, Marty. You can come back and we can save our investments but there are some things we've got to talk about and clear up. We've never talked about how it is between us but now we've got to if you come back to live here. I'm talking about our sex life. I've reached the point, Marty, where I can't have sex with you anymore. I don't have anyone else; it's just that I don't feel anything for you in that way any longer. I like you in a lot of other ways, but I'm not the type that pretends, you know that. You know I'm honest about how I feel and I've got to be honest about this."

Marty looked at me as if he didn't understand. I expected him to say something but he just looked at me.

"You say we have to stay together for financial reasons," I said. "All right, but then it has to be on my terms. From now on, what you do is your own business. I don't want to know about it and I only hope you'll be discreet."

"And you?" Marty finally managed to say.

"If I'm not really in love I just don't think about it. I'm not interested in sex just for sex. Back when it was good between us, I loved it. Well, that's gone. But I'm not looking for anything. You don't have to worry about me. You've got me working so damn hard there's not time for it anyway."

The newspapers headlined our reconciliation, and when Marty returned he brought me a diamond ring, a large four- or five-carat solitaire. It had a flaw in it big enough to see with the naked eye. But flaw or no flaws, I'm not a big diamond lady. I like antique jewelry, but big rocks leave me as cold as they are. When I see Liz Taylor with those boulders hanging from her neck I get nauseated. All I can think of are how many dog shelters those diamonds could buy.

The arrangement with Marty worked out better than I had expected. It was a strange relationship, in that despite the ground rules, we enjoyed each other's company. We adored going to the Dodger games, where we sat in a special section next to the visitors' bench, where many of our friends—Cary Grant, Dyan Cannon, David Janssen, Milton Berle, Nat "King" Cole, to name a few—also had boxes. For a couple of seasons we also went to most of the Laker basketball games. We had great times at our beach house, where we had long Sunday brunches with friends like Ernie and Edie Kovacs, Jack Lemmon and his wife, Shirley MacLaine, Richard Quine, Danny and Rosie Thomas, Tony Randall and his wife, Ross Hunter, Gower and Marge Champion, Gordon and Sheila MacRae, Jean and Dino Martin, and Warren Cowen, who was then married to Barbara Rush.

For five years our arrangement worked perfectly all right for Marty and me. If Marty had "outside interests," he kept them discreetly to himself and I was never aware of them. As for me, as I predicted, my body followed my heart, and since I wasn't in love with anyone, I had no interest in sex.

But in the press, my sex life was something else again. I was Lady Bountiful of the Sheets. Some of the best fiction of the Sixties was written about my amorous adventures with an assortment of lovers who could have only been chosen by a berserk random sampler.

My most consistently reported affair was with Maury Wills, the Dodger shortstop, who at that time had captured everyone's fancy with his base stealing. What seemed to have caught the gossip columnists' fancy was the fact that Wills and his wife were reported to be getting a divorce at just about the same time Marty moved out of our house. Since I had been going to most of the Dodger games, and of course, Marty and I knew many of the ballplayers, it was easy to stir all that together and come up with the conclusion that Maury Wills and I were having an affair. The only times I had seen Maury were at the games or at an occasional party. I never once saw Maury when Marty wasn't present and we certainly never saw each other alone anywhere. I don't know if some Dodger publicity man helped stir up those rumors, which persisted for a long time.

After Marty and I stopped going to the Dodger games (baseball seemed to be getting slower and slower and frankly we got bored) and transferred out interest to basketball, the columnists transferred my affair from Maury Wills to the Lakers' star forward, Elgin Baylor. Marty and I had become friendly with the owner of the Lakers who invited us to several parties where we met the players and their wives. That was the extent of my acquaintance with Baylor, but not in the press.

My most recently reported fling is the zaniest of all. My son, Terry, phoned me recently from New York, where he had gone on business.

"Hey, Mom," he said, "guess who you're having a hot love affair with."

"Am I having a hot love affair?"

"You sure are! And wait till you hear who it is."

"Who?"

"Sly."

"Sly who?"

"Sly—you remember Sly, Sly and the Family Stone. He came by my house that day."

Terry produces albums for RCA, and musician friends often drop by his house. I was visiting him recently when in came a young black man who was dressed in one of the most bizarre costumes I ever saw. That was Sly. He told me that "Que Sera" had always been a favorite song of his, and that he wanted to do an offbeat version of it in his new album. He proceeded to sit down at the piano and sing it for me as he planned to record it. The whole visit lasted maybe fifteen minutes. I never saw him again. Terry read me some of the reportage about Sly and me from an assortment of magazines and newspapers and I had to marvel again at the inventiveness of the press.

Of course, it occurred to me that one basis for these rumors could well have been the fact that my father married a black woman. Like father, like daughter. Mind you, I have no feeling about white or black—I believe I could just as easily fall in love with a black man as I could with a white man; my problem is, I don't fall in love easily.

But my media affairs were by no means limited to black men. At one time or another I was reported to be sexing around with Jerry West, Pancho Gonzales, Glen Campbell, Frank Sinatra, and, would you believe it?— Jimmy Hoffa! Variety was certainly the spice of my life.

The Jerry West rumor started because we talked on the sidewalk one day when I was on my bicycle and Jerry was taking some things to the cleaners. The Gonzales rumor came out of the fact that he would occasionally hit the ball with me at the Los Angeles Tennis Club, and on two or three occasions Marty and I had dinner with Pancho and his wife. At the time of the Glen Campbell rumors, extensively reported, I had never even met him and knew him only as a voice on his records. But there were heavy items about us everywhere.

By pouring cold water on all these rumored romances, I don't want to give the impression that I was completely celibate. There was a time, when I was doing my television show, that I did have an exciting and fulfilling affair that lasted over a year—I'll go into that later. It was a beautifully kept secret that the press never got wind of.

I must confess that there were times over the course of those five "arranged" years with Marty when every once in a while I did have a crush on a leading man in one of my pictures. In the course of the many weeks it took to make a picture, there was sometimes an intensity and intimacy that developed that I responded to. There were times in the playing of romantic scenes, which often had to be shot over and over again, when my leading man would clearly react to me and I to him. Had we both been free, it's possible that something would have come of it, but since we weren't, our "affairs" were as make-believe as the film we were making.

CHAPTER 12

In the early Sixties, the comedies I made with Rock Hudson and James Garner, plus a big MGM musical, *Jumbo*, produced an era of high earnings and, for five consecutive years, a continuance of my number-one rating at the box office. But later in the Sixties, Marty began to bring me scripts which I disliked and wanted to turn down; but to my growing consternation, I was forced to accept them because he had already signed me to contracts to do them.

These movies were *Do Not Disturb, Caprice, Ballad of Josie,* and *Where Were You When the Lights Went Out?* There were good actors like Rod Taylor, Richard Harris, and Peter Graves cast in them, but these poor men were the pearls before the swine of these scripts. I particularly recall the day Marty, with his usual nonselective enthusiasm, handed me the script for *Caprice.* That evening, when Marty returned from the tennis club, we had a discussion that went something like this:

"Marty, I read the script—all I can say is, thank God I don't have to make movies like that anymore."

"You're wrong, Doris, *wrong,* and you'll realize it when you see how it turns out. Now, I'll tell you who we've got—Richard Harris—"

"Wait a minute, Marty! Hold it! What are you trying to tell me?"

"Doris, we've made a deal and there's no sense getting all steamed up about it."

That did it. I blew my stack. "*You* made a deal—you and Rosenthal, that it? Well, you and Rosenthal don't have to get in front of the camera and try to make something out of terrible stuff like this! I know that you and your friends are only interested in making money, but I don't give a damn about money. I never see any of it and I don't have the time to use any of it even if I knew what to do with it—which I don't. When are you going to stop chasing money for the sake of money?"

"That's not fair. I'm doing it for your sake and you know it. How many superstars out here wind up with nothing because they didn't handle their money right when they were making it big? Well, I'm trying that for you—us. You keep putting Rosenthal down, but he's a genius and what he's doing for you, you should write him a thank-you note every day."

"What he's doing for me is getting me into a lot of terrible movies and putting me into hotels and oil wells and all kinds of things I know nothing about."

"Then why raise such a fuss about them?"

"Because I don't trust Rosenthal, that's why."

"Do you trust me?"

"Yes, of course I do."

"So when I tell you that Rosenthal has made some of the most brilliant investments for you, that they are paying off like you can't believe—"

"Then why do you keep pouring my money into them? All these rotten scripts, one right on top of the other—"

"That's the nature of this kind of investment. You keep pyramiding your capital—"

"I'd like to pyramid a couple of good movies."

"This is a good move, believe me."

"If *Caprice* is your idea of a good script, God help my investments."

The movies went from bad to worse, and I quickly tumbled off the box-office perch.

But *With Six You Get Egg Roll*, the last movie I made, it finally seemed to me, Marty had come up with a pleasant, funny family film and I urged him to produce it himself.

One day my makeup man said to me, "I've been noticing how thin Marty is getting—is he dieting?"

"No," I said, "he isn't dieting and I don't know why on earth he's getting so thin." That afternoon I mentioned to Marty that everyone was beginning to notice how thin he was. He said yes, he was losing weight but it was nothing to worry about. I suggested he go to a doctor for a checkup.

"Why? I feel fine," he said testily. "Don't bother me—I'm fine."

The day the picture ended, Marty picked me up at the studio and complained on the way home that he seemed to be getting a bad cold and felt wobbly. When he got home, he undressed and went to bed. In all the years I had been married to Marty, he had never taken to a sickbed. I tried to get him to talk about how he felt, but he would only say that he had the flu, that he certainly didn't need a doctor, and that it was just a matter of putting Christian Science to work.

For three months Marty stayed in bed. He developed chronic diarrhea; nothing stayed in his stomach; the color slowly drained away from his face until he finally turned gray. I tried every which way to get a doctor in the house, but Marty got terribly agitated and I dropped it.

Marty constantly studied his *Science and Health* and desperately wanted to see Martin Broones, but all this time he was on a lecture tour. Marty talked to him on the phone every day, and I overheard Mr. Broones telling Marty which page and which lines to concentrate on.

Marty would allow no one to be in the house except my mother and our housekeeper, Katie. Some nights I would sit in the little darkened study by myself and cry all night long. I was so weak from worry, from not being able to eat, from the frustration of watching Marty slip away from life without letting me help him, I didn't have the strength in my arms to comb my hair. I thought he had cancer and I feared that every day that passed might be worsening his condition. I turned to Mary Baker Eddy for help, but found none. All I knew was the black taste of despair.

Terry was the only outside person that Marty saw, and then infrequently. Terry too tried to persuade Marty to get medical help, but Terry got no further than I had. Finally, on one of Terry's visits, he brought Dick Dorso into the room without asking Marty's permission. Dick had been Marty's partner in the Century Artists Agency, and he was a man whom Marty respected and liked. It was Dick who finally forced Marty into letting a doctor examine him—and even then the only doctor that Marty would accept was a man he used to play tennis with.

This doctor, whose name I don't recall, came right over and spent a half-hour alone with Marty. When he emerged from the bedroom he told me he was calling in a heart specialist. I was amazed. "Didn't you know that Marty has an enlarged heart?" the doctor asked. Of course, I didn't. He said it was a condition Marty had had for a long time.

The specialist came and ordered Marty into a hospital immediately. The doctor explained to me that Marty was suffering from an inflammation of the heart muscles. I felt a sense of relief that it wasn't the cancer I had feared. "That can be treated, can't it?" I asked.

"Two months ago, quite effectively—now, well, we have a much more difficult job on our hands."

I spent every day and night at the hospital, from eight in the morning until midnight. Marty didn't talk much; he was completely listless, an air of resignation or defeat about him, but he liked for me to be there in his room with him.

One afternoon a particularly lavish display of flowers arrived. The nurse handed me the card.

"They're from *your* friend, Jerry Rosenthal," I said.

The nurse started to arrange the flowers in a vase. Marty stared out the window. Then he turned and looked at me, and his eyes were different than I had ever seen them before.

"Please take those flowers out of here," Marty said to the nurse. She hesitated. "And keep them out of here," Marty said.

I went over and sat down on the floor in front of the chair in which Marty was sitting. I put my arms on his legs and looked up at him. "Marty, when you get out of here, we have to have a talk about Rosenthal," I said. "The time has come, don't you think?"

He took one of my hands in his and nodded his head affirmatively.

He turned his head and looked out of the window, then for quite some time kept my hand firmly pressed between his. After a while he said, "We have to go away and really have a good time." He continued to look out the hospital window. "These last few months. I kept thinking about you and how you've worked so hard. When we have gone away, it's always to do with your working. Now you've got to go away to have fun."

"But work is fun for me. If I hadn't enjoyed it, I wouldn't have done it. I don't regret working."

"I know. But you haven't had the fun you should have had."

"Well, when you get well and get of here, before we take a vacation or do anything, Rosenthal is the first thing on the agenda, okay?"

Marty looked at me in agreement, squeezed my hand, then released it. "I think I'll get in bed," he said.

I helped him into bed. He was so thin I could feel the bone through the flesh on his arm. I pulled the covers over him and he dropped off to sleep almost immediately. I pulled down the shade and left the room.

Early the following morning I received a call from the hospital, asking me to come as soon as I could. Marty was in a deep coma. I looked at the clock—ten to seven. I phoned Terry, who said he would come right away to pick me up. While I was waiting for Terry, I phoned Marty's brother, Jack, who lived in San Francisco, and told him to go right to the hospital.

At the hospital, the doctor told me that Marty's heart condition was tied in with a cerebral condition, and that they were now into emergency procedures which included a tracheotomy. Numb with despair, I went to the little waiting room down the corridor while Terry went downstairs to await Jack's arrival. When Jack arrived, he and Terry immediately went into Marty's room. The doctor had asked me not to go in, until he gave permission. Terry and Jack stayed in the room for only a few minutes. They told me not to go in. They said that Marty was all open with tubes, that he was in deep coma, and that the room was busy with medical personnel. The doctor had asked Terry to take me home, and had promised to send for me as soon as it was the right time for me to come. I was rather reluctant to leave, but both Terry and Jack insisted.

Four o'clock the following morning, the phone rang. Marty was dead. I could not bring myself to tell anyone. Not just then. I walked out on the patio that adjoins my bedroom, the night air heavy with the scent of flowers in their hanging baskets. I hadn't lost a husband, because he hadn't been that in the past past few years, but I had lost a man I had loved for seventeen years. He had done everything for me. And with me. Made every decision. Had total control of everything I had. At this moment of his death, in my aloneness, he was my father, and I was a ten-year-old child. And I loved him very much.

CHAPTER 13

Marty's death was the one thing that happened in my life that I really handled badly. I had lived closely with Marty for seventeen years; he had done everything for me; and we were together much more than the average couple. As a consequence, his abrupt departure left a terrible void in the conduct of my life. The earth had opened and he had fallen through and I was totally alone.

I couldn't talk to anybody on the phone. I saw only a few very close friends who came to the house, for that's all I could manage. I had lost the center of my being. I could not even turn to Christian Science, which had always been my support, for C.S. does not embrace death (hence there is nothing to grieve); God is love and God's love should replace your grief. It didn't work that way for me—when I am filled with grieving tears, I shed them. It was during this period that I turned from Christian Science as my religion. I still devoutly believe in much of what Mrs. Eddy preached, and I would always make her revelations a part of my life, but I no longer wanted to be a member of a formal church; I did not want to call myself anything. I wanted to have my own personal religion, one suited precisely to my own spiritual emotions. I don't honestly know how much this judgment was affected by Marty's too stubborn adherence to Christian Science at a time when he should have been seeing a doctor. Perhaps I felt some kind of subconscious guilt for having brought Christian Science into Marty's life. I just don't know. It was a long period of scrambled emotions for me, and anything was possible.

The year following Marty's death I bitterly rejected the whole concept of there being a God. I could not explain to myself why, if there were a compassionate God, he should have taken Marty from me. I stopped thinking about religion. I stopped reading those books which had always given me strength. In my grief I rejected what they taught. All that had sustained me before was as dead as Marty.

But my feelings about Marty began to be assaulted by a series of revelations that occurred soon after his death. The first of these revelations happened when I forced myself to open the door of his room and go inside. I was very moved by the impact of his familiar belongings, but when I went into his dressing room I received a severe jolt from what I found on a bureau—two completed television scripts for a "Doris Day Show"!

Marty had often discussed television with me—I had been approached many times to do a series—but I had always said I wasn't interested, that I'd much rather stick with movies. Marty, though, felt that films were running toward explicit sex and that television was a much better medium for my kind of movie. He also felt that the whole theater concept of entertainment was finished.

But I had been quite emphatic about how I felt. "The whole nature of television is wrong for me," I had said. "The constant pressure of having to shoot an entire script in a few days is not for me. Under no circumstances do I want to do television."

Now here, on top of his dresser, were two shooting scripts for what looked like a series that was all ready to go. I asked Terry to investigate for me. But whether I was committed or not, that Marty had gone this far in the face of my emphatic opposition came as a shock.

I received a much greater shock a few days later. It was Terry who had to bring me most of these shocking disclosures. It was on the evening when Terry had said that he was going to come by the house around dinnertime. Terry had been appointed administrator of the estate, and he had said he would drop in after an afternoon appointment he had scheduled with Rosenthal on some estate matters. But Terry didn't show up. I was somewhat concerned because Terry usually called when he was not coming. I finally gave up on him and went to bed.

It was quite late when my mother came into my room to tell me that

Terry had arrived with Dick Dorso and they were in the den waiting to see me. "I think something's wrong," my mother said. I put on my robe and went into the den and sat down in a chair facing the two of them. Terry came over to me and hugged me, just held me for the longest time. He didn't say a word. Just held me and held me and I started to cry.

Finally, he sat down directly in front of me and talked to me in a low voice. "After I saw Rosenthal this afternoon, I phoned Dick and asked him if he'd drive around with me for a while. That's what we've been doing, for hours now—just driving around."

"Why?" I asked.

"So I could screw up my courage to the point where I could come in this house and tell you what I've got to tell you."

"What can be so terrible?"

"The day after Dad died, a check arrived for sixty thousand dollars. One of your film checks which came to me as executor of the estate. Rosenthal called and said, 'Son, endorse it and send it right over to me. I have to have it right away.' I said, 'I don't know what I'm signing, Mr. Rosenthal. That's my mother's check for sixty thousand dollars and I have to know where it's going.' Rosenthal said, 'Now, son, don't you trust me? You know that I handled all financial affairs for your father.' I said, 'I'm sorry, Mr. Rosenthal, but since I'm the executor, I'll have to find out things for myself.'"

Terry looked down at his hands for a few moments before he went on. "Mom, these past four days, I've had a showdown with Rosenthal, and the bad news is—you don't have anything. Not a penny. The hotels are bankrupt, all the oil wells are dry, and there aren't any cattle. Nothing, Mom, and what's even worse, you have a lot of debts—like around four hundred and fifty thousand dollars. Most of it is taxes. They have to be paid. You may have to sell this house."

I stopped crying. I don't shed tears over money things. "But where has it all gone?"

"It will take a lot of digging to find that out. Right now I've got to concentrate on getting rid of Rosenthal, and then to get someone to take the whole thing apart to find out what really happened."

"Twenty years of hard work—all those films," Dick Dorso said, shaking his head, "and nothing to show for it. Christ!"

Only one thing seemed important for me at that moment. "Do you think—was Marty in on this with Rosenthal? I mean, did Marty know it was all gone—or was Rosenthal just using him?"

"I don't know, Mom."

I was finding it difficult to assimilate this additional tragedy. I had not slept for too many nights, and I did not have enough energy to mount a reaction. "I've got to know," I said. "More than anything, I've got to know about Marty."

"Well," Terry said, "it won't be easy. I went to Dad's office this morning, and there was nothing there—all the file cabinets were empty. His desk was cleaned out."

"What? When did he find time to do that?"

"He didn't. It just so happened that Don Genson was looking out of his office window on the morning after Dad died, when he saw a Bekins moving van pull up. The Bekins men carried a steady stream of cardboard packing boxes out of the office. Of course, that entrance also serves Rosenthal's offices but you can bet that that's what happened to Dad's files."

"What does Rosenthal say?"

"He claims it was a shipment that had nothing to do with Dad's office. But we have no proof . . . just as we have no proof about the will."

"What about the will?"

"There isn't any. We've opened the safety-deposit box, looked all through the office—no will."

"But Marty was frantic about people having wills. He used to lecture everybody about having a will. Did you ask Rosenthal if he ever drew one up for Marty?"

"Says he didn't. Most likely went the way of those files."

"We've got to pay those debts, Terry. I've never owed anyone in my life and I'm not going to start now. If we have to sell the house, then sell it."

"But you've got to live somewhere—"

"Sure, but not in an expensive house when I'm in debt. I'll rent a place somewhere."

"Everything that could be borrowed against has been used. Rosenthal and Dad even borrowed against your record contract."

"You mean albums I haven't even done yet?"

"Yes, they've already taken the money for them. And the money's all spent."

I had to get away from the house. A coldness had settled into my bones, cold despair, and I felt desperately that I had to go where there was heat. I rented a house in Palm Springs and drove there with my mother, my brother-in-law, Jack, and my dear friend Barbara Lamston. It was a lovely house, on the grounds of the golf course, with a broad, sweeping view of the desert and the mountains.

Before I had left, Terry had brought me the doleful news that Marty had indeed signed my name to a contract for a television series, and that he had received a large advance, ostensibly for preproduction costs, which had long since been spent by Rosenthal. To make matters worse, I had to start work in six weeks.

When I first arrived in Palm Springs, I was a vegetable. I could do little more than sit in a chair and stare at the desert and the distant mountains. I swam a little, but mostly I sat zombielike in the sun, grateful that I could feel the desert heat warming my insides. But regeneration, I found, was a long, arduous process.

I knew I only had a few weeks to get myself in good enough shape to begin the television series to which I had been committed. Of course, there was no possibility that I could get myself in a good mental state in so short a time, but I hoped that physically I would have regenerated myself to the point where I could get to the set each day. At the end of a month I was swimming twenty laps and taking long, vigorous walks. But mentally I had made very little progress.

I had spent long hours thinking about death, and about Marty. Who was Marty Melcher? That was the question that constantly thrust itself at me. How could I have lived with a man for seventeen years and not know who he was? I kept hearing his voice: "We have oil wells that are gushing so much that we don't know how to handle them." "Do you know how long it would take me to explain this contract to you? I'm your husband—don't you trust me?" "Now, how can you ask those things about Jerry Rosenthal? He's your friend and my friend and the best damn lawyer in L.A. Do you know how much money he's made for his clients? Well, he's doing the same for you. It's hard to tell how much we actually have, that's how it's pyramiding."

Marty was certainly a fool, to have been duped to this degree by a man who had mismanaged my life's earnings, twenty million or so, to the point of wipe-out. I could try to understand Marty's being a fool. He was a fool to tie up with Rosenthal, a fool not to see through him. But was he devious? Was he in league with Rosenthal? Did he knowingly plunder and siphon off and manipulate what I had placed in his care with trust? Did Marty know there was no oil in many of those wells? That the hotels were a disaster? That the cattle ranches had no cattle? Was he duped by Rosenthal's fake reports or was Marty a part of Rosenthal's operation, taking advantage of my trust in him with lies and connivances? Who was this man I had lived with all those years—fool or thief or both? The answer would have to come from those who knew him and saw him with some perspective. From people who never really expressed themselves about

Marty until after his death. The more I thought about it, the more it seemed to me that Marty had suffered a peculiar death—death by resignation—which could have been caused by guilt over what he discovered had been done to me, or anguish when he knew that what he had been doing was about to be found out.

CHAPTER 14

It was bad enough that I had been forced into television against my will, but what made it doubly repulsive was the nature of the setting that had been chosen for my weekly series. A farm. A widow with two little kids living on a farm. With Grandpa, naturally. Whatever reputation I had made in films it certainly wasn't bucolic.

But I was too enervated that first year really to care. I looked upon my ability to get from my bed to the set and back to my bed again as an end in itself and something of a miracle. I should have worked on the scripts but I didn't have the energy or the desire. I simply didn't care. When there had been such deep sorrow and upset in my life, how important was a script? My resignation to mediocrity was strange, since by nature I am a perfectionist and I am normally concerned about every aspect of a role I am performing. But I would sometimes stop right in the middle of shooting a supposedly happy or funny scene and burst out crying. For that entire season, I was prey to my erratic emotions. I had lost three things: my husband, my life's savings, and my freedom—for television was much more rigid and confining than Warner Brothers ever was.

One hot afternoon in August 1969, the summer after Marty died, I was swimming in my pool when a bulletin came over the radio. A bizarre, multiple cult murder had occurred at the home of the Polish movie director Roman Polanski. He was away, but one of the victims was his beautiful actress wife, Sharon Tate, in her eighth month of pregnancy. The bulletin gave the address of the house: 10050 Cielo Drive.

I stopped swimming. "That address," I said to my mother, who was sitting poolside, "that's where Terry used to live."

"Are you sure?"

"Yes, of course. My God, all those people were murdered in his house."

Thus began one of the most frightening periods of my life—fright for Terry rather than myself, for those were the Manson murders; and later on, when Manson and his followers were identified, it was believed that Manson had sent his killers to that house looking for Terry.

Since Marty's death, Terry had been having as bad a time as I. As administrator he was saddled with the responsibility of investigating my financial plight and of trying to find some way for me to function without going into bankruptcy. He was with lawyers day and night. As a result of all this legal activity, Terry had to give up his own career in music. He also had to find new lawyers and accountants and work with them in an attempt to reconstitute my affairs. And Terry also had the problem of his own finances. As a producer of albums since he was twenty-one, Terry had made a considerable amount of money, all of which Marty had induced him to turn over to Rosenthal. Of course, Terry's money had gone the way of mine and he was now as broke as I was.

Besides all that, Terry was executive producer of my new television series. He tried to supervise it but he simply did not have any time to give to it, which was an additionally frustrating thing for him.

Now came the Manson-murder involvement on top of all this. Terry had moved out of the house on Cielo Drive the previous December. My house on the beach was unoccupied. I simply couldn't go there after Marty died. So with reluctance Terry gave up the house on Cielo Drive, where he had been living with Candice Bergen, and they moved into my beach house to protect it.

Of course, I had been to the Cielo Drive house many times. It was a charming little French farmhouse with two bedrooms, a big stone fireplace in the rustic living room, and a loft that was reached by ladder. There was a well outside the front door, with an old oaken bucket, and cats were everywhere. Terry loved that little house and I was sorry to see him give it up for the beach. I tried to talk him out of it but he said that he had discussed it with Candy and they both felt that the beach house had to be protected.

Now, eight months later, five young people lay brutally murdered in and around that house, and the irony of it was that Terry was no longer living at the beach. In his efforts to raise money to pay off my debts, Terry had recently sold the beach house and rented a place off Sunset Boulevard. He had also, after several lovely years together, come to a parting of the ways with Candy. This too was a result of the aftermath of Marty's death, for Terry told me that he still loved Candy, and she loved him, but the pressures of his life were such that he felt he was cracking up and that it would be better for him to be alone. Terry felt that Candy was someone to look after, to care for, and Terry said he was no longer able to do that.

It seemed that life for both of us had become just one casualty after another.

Of course, when news of the Cielo Drive killings first broke, the killers' identities were unknown; it was not until November, three months later, that the full impact of Terry's involvement with the murders became evident. The way I learned of it was when Terry came by one evening and led me into the den for a "closed" talk.

Two detectives had come to see him that day, he told me, to report that a young girl named Susan Atkins, who was in jail on another matter, had confided to a cell mate details about the Cielo Drive murders which identified the killers. According to this girl, Susan, who identified herself as one of these killers, the mastermind behind these murders was a man named Charles Manson, and the culprits were all members of his nomadic "family."

"You know Charles Manson, don't you?" the detectives had asked.

"Yes, I've met him a couple of times."

"Well, we hate to tell you this," the detectives had said, "but from what Susan Atkins says we have good reason to believe that when they went to the Cielo Drive house that night, they were looking for you."

"You mean, they had come to kill *me*?"

"Yes, and when they didn't find you, they simply went ahead and butchered everyone they did find."

"But why would they want to kill me? I've never done anything to Manson, or any of these people. I treated Manson very well."

"Who knows? When you're dealing with crazies you can't look for logical explanations."

"Now I don't want you to get alarmed," Terry had said, "but the detectives think—and this is just pure precaution—that we ought to have a couple of guards around us until this whole thing is finished and over."

"Why? I don't understand." "Well, you can imagine what kind of people would commit mass murder like this. Absolute crazies. So if they came for me once, they may still want me. And you, as my mother—if what they want is some kind of notoriety—well, who knows?"

"My God, Terry—you mean the detectives think they may try to kill both of us?"

"No—it's just for protection. For all we know they may never give me another thought." There was absolutely no conviction in his voice. Terry was frightened, for me as well as himself. I thought, Oh, God, what he has been through since his stepfather died, and now this! He's only a kid in his twenties. How will he bear it? And for that matter, how will I?

Terry said that although the detectives had recommended protection, they unfortunately could not furnish police bodyguards because we were not technically linked to crimes. That meant we would have to furnish our own bodyguards, which is what Terry did. From that day until the end of the trial, a period of over a year, Terry had a private bodyguard at all times, and I had a guard who patrolled my house around the clock.

The black shadow of these people hung over our lives for more than a year. I think it's best that Terry himself describe his encounters with Manson and his followers, and what happened after the murders and during the trial.

Terry Melcher

In the summer of 1968, a few months after Marty's death, I met Charles Manson. I had hired a friend of mine, Gregg Jakobson, to scout potential recording talent for me, and one of the people he wanted me to hear was this fellow Manson, who lived in a commune on a deserted movie ranch way out in the Valley.

When Jakobson and I arrived at the ranch, Manson was sitting in a chair in front of a defunct saloon on a simulated Western street, sound asleep. Gregg woke him and he led us along a path to a gulley where there were about forty people, sitting in a circle around a campfire site. Of these, five or six were men, and all the rest were girls. There were tents pitched all around. Several of the girls were holding babies. Gregg had urged me to come because he thought the setup was interesting on a kind of cultural level as well as musical, and that it might make a television special.

Manson was very anxious that I hear all his songs. My arrival was a big event in their lives because I was on the board of the Monterey Pop Foundation; I had been one of the producers of the original Monterey Festival that had made stars out of a lot of unknown people like Jimi Hendrix, Otis Redding, Janis Joplin, and The Who. So in Manson's eyes I was a talent discoverer with a big track record and he was very anxious to impress me.

Unfortunately, the music was below-average nothing, and as far as I was concerned, Manson was like every other starving, hippie songwriter. After an hour or so, the audition ended and I said the usual noncommital things—sounded pretty good, nice blend of voices, did he belong to any guilds or unions. When Manson pressured me about how I liked his music, I suddenly remembered a friend of mine who had an interest in Indian tribal music and who had a specially equipped truck for recording it. I said I'd like to return with my friend in about a week. I was fascinated with the communal aspect of Manson's tribe and I did think that something might work out for television along those lines. I don't recall how the subject of money came up, but before I left I gave Manson fifty dollars, which was all the cash I had on me.

I went back to the ranch about ten days later with my friend Michael Deasy, who, in addition to owning the recording van I mentioned, was one of the best, highest-priced guitarists of his day. I didn't stay very long, but Deasy went back several times by himself and recorded a lot of their stuff. That's the last time I saw Manson, until two years later, in court, when I testified for the prosecution.

About a year after that last visit to the ranch, two detectives came to my door one evening and asked me if I knew anyone who wanted to kill me. I said no, I didn't. "You're familiar with those murders that were committed in the house on Cielo Drive where you used to live?"

"Sure." For the past two months that's all anyone talked about. I hadn't been in the house since I moved out, but I had presumed that the murders had had something to do with the weird films Polanski had made, and the equally weird people who were hanging around that house. I knew they had been making a lot of homemade sadomasochistic-porno movies there with quite a few recognizable Hollywood faces in them. The reason I knew was that I had gone out with a girl named Michelle Phillips, one of the Mamas and the Papas, whose ex-husband, John Phillips, was the leader of the group. Michelle told me she and John had had dinner one night, to discuss maybe getting back together and afterward he had taken her up to visit the Polanskis in my old house. Michelle said that when they arrived there, everyone in the house was busy filming an orgy and that Sharon Tate was part of it. This was just one of the stories I had heard about what went on in my former house.

"Well," the detective said, "we've got a girl in custody who's spilling the whole thing. You know a guy named Manson? And a group that used to hang out with him at the Spahn Ranch? Well, the night they killed all those people—they came there looking for you. This girl says Manson wanted you to record him but you didn't and he was mad at you. We've picked up some of Manson's people, but there's still a lot of them running around loose. So we've come here to warn you that you'd better get yourself some bodyguards with guns—and for your mother. You're dealing with some genuine crazies and there's no telling what they might do."

From then on the cops were at me all the time. Mostly to show me pictures that they wanted me to try to identify. And because I was Doris

Day's son, the newspapers and magazines really went to town on my alleged involvement in the killings. There was one account of how I was into dope with Manson, and we had had a falling out over that. Several times I was grilled by the police about some of the babies in the Manson camp. The cops said that five or six of the Manson girls claimed that Manson had set me up with them and that I was the father of their babies. Not all the rumors were about me. There was one to the effect that Jay Sebring had lured some of Manson's girls into one of the sado-porno movies they were making and had whipped them and beat them up for the camera, and that that's why Sebring and all the others at the house had been killed.

While all this was going on, I was suffering from a monumental guilt feeling that I was the one who was responsible for all those killings, since it was I they had been looking for. While all the Manson fracas was going on, I was also (1) meeting with lawyers every day in my battle with Rosenthal, (2) trying to help my mother with her television show, (3) trying to do my own recording work, and (4) trying to deal with the glut of guilts Marty had left me as his legacy when he went to that big numbered account in the sky. He had made me feel guilty for having made money ("It's too easy for you, you made it too fast"), guilty because I hadn't starved, guilty because I had talent, guilty because I had survived him. It was all too much. Just too much.

One day I simply cracked under the load. I went to a psychiatrist two hours a day and unloaded on him. He gave me some tranquilizers. And I was crazy for a while.

I cut off everything. I got someone to answer the phone and to cook and I shut out the world. For two years. I pressed the down button and went all the way to the bottom. Russian vodka and those tranquilizers. Plenty of time to think, and the more I thought, the blacker everything got. I began to put the blame on my mother, to resent her—a real buildup of hostility.

I resented the role I had assigned myself with my mother. I had worked hard on turning her mind around and getting her interested in her television show. But as she responded to this and began to look happier, I got to thinking, goddamn it, she's going along fine now, whereas all I do is sit in lawyers' offices and in court for three months and it's only the beginning. Then when the Manson thing broke on top of that—well, I was really feeling used and abused.

But what I brooded about most was Marty, trying to square the reality of finding out the truth about him with the image I had lived with. For a few weeks after his death I went to this office every day to wind up the business. There were phone calls from ladies in town who wondered what they were going to do about their rent. Marty, the sanctimonious usher. I don't know how much my mother knew about all that. We never discussed it. It really wasn't all that important. What was important was discovering his hypocrisy, his lack of values, understanding his shallow rigidity. He was the kind of parent who is proud to see his kid make it if the kid makes it exactly as he outlines it—if the kid doesn't, then no matter what success the kid has, it's much worse than failure.

As far as the Manson thing was concerned, I found out at one point that Manson knew I had moved to the Malibu beach house. That he had, in fact, stolen a telescope from the deck of the Malibu house, presumably to let me know he knew my whereabouts. But then why didn't he knock on the door, if he wanted to get in touch with me? None of it made much sense. Susan Atkins, one of the murderers, had told her attorney on tape, "The reason Charlie picked that house was to instill fear into Terry Melcher because Terry had given us his word on a few things and never came through with them." I have no idea to what she was referring. I made no representations to them about anything. But facts and logic don't mean much when you're dealing with minds like these.

It didn't mean much that Manson and four of his followers, who slaughtered Sharon Tate and others, were in jail. Manson had a legion of devoted henchmen who were at large. And they were totally capable of carrying out their leader's wishes wherever he was. I cite all this to explain why I hired round-the-clock bodyguards for my mother and myself.

At the trial I was not cross-examined; Manson's attorney said that Manson had no ill feelings toward me. But what did that mean? Manson and his people killed for love as well as other things. And the fact that Manson was sentenced to life imprisonment also didn't do much to promote my peace of mind, for according to California law he will be eligible for parole in 1978.

So I stayed in my house and avoided everyone. In a sense, I had given up on myself. My heart was full of bitterness and fear, and it looked like it was going to permanently stay that way.

There's no doubt that what happened to Terry was much harder on me than Marty's death and all those shocking postmortem revelations. Terry collapsed under the weight of all the problems that had been imposed on him, and in an act of self-preservation he shut himself off from everything and everyone. I myself rarely saw him and I couldn't get him on the phone. He became a recluse, and his refuge was alcohol and pills. He couldn't face anything.

I had hoped for a turning point in Terry's life, some God-given intervention that would set him back on his course, but I had not anticipated the kind of brutal intervention that actually occurred.

The call came at night from the Hemet Valley Hospital. Terry had had a motorcycle accident. He was in critical condition.

There was little I could do but wait outside the intensive-care room. I was told that Terry had gone for a ride on his motorcycle, negotiated a turn badly, and had rammed head-on into a car. The impact had catapulted Terry high into the air; he had landed on his feet, shattering both legs, as glass shatters, and inflicting other injuries.

The day following the accident, Terry developed a high, persistent fever and a deep infection. Embolisms had also developed, dangerous blood clots that put his life in jeopardy. The doctors put me on notice that quite possibly both legs might have to be amputated.

It took two weeks to dissolve the emoblisms and contain the infections that had threatened his legs. With those two afflictions eliminated, Dr. Howard Lieberman moved Terry to a private room and went to work on his shattered legs.

The bones of both of Terry's legs contained thirty-seven fractures. Dr. Lieberman's method was to reconstruct those bones and align the broken pieces without performing surgery. To accomplish this, he would sit Terry on the side of the bed, with his legs dangling down, and pull on them. Obviously, this caused excruciating pain. After a series of tugs and pulls, Dr. Lieberman would wheel Terry into X ray and study the bone alignment; then he would sit him on the bed again, and pull and yank the legs some more to correct whatever he had seen in the X rays.

Slowly but surely over the ensuing weeks, using this process, the bone fragments began to fall into place. Finally, under a general anesthetic, Dr. Lieberman prepared Terry's legs for plaster casts, but at no time during this long process was surgery involved. Just pulling and observing.

Shortly after Terry was removed from intensive care, he was visited by the chief of mental therapy, Dr. Charles Head, to see if there was anything he could do for Terry. Terry told him no, that he really had it all together and it would be better for the doctor to spend his time with the people who really needed him.

"Well, that's really rare," Dr Head said, "flat on your back, both legs smashed up, a long hospitalization and recuperation staring you in the face, and you feel really on top of everything?"

"Yes, I'm okay, no problems."

"That's great, but if you ever feel like talking, just call me."

A few days later, at three o'clock in the morning, Terry called Dr. Head. I wasn't at the hospital that day—I usually stayed for three or four days in Hemet at the Ramona Inn, and the other days of the week back in Beverly Hills. Dr. Head dressed and drove to the hospital; Terry had fallen apart. His brave front had deserted him and he desperately needed someone to talk to. That's how Charles Head, a really remarkable man, came into our lives. I say "our" because I too began to see Dr. Head professionally, and until recently I had an appointment with him on the day when he made his weekly visit to his office in Los Angeles. Both Terry and I, in our relationship to each other and in our ability to handle the problems that have beset us during the past five years, have benefited enormously from having this professional help. Friends help, religion helps, but a psychologist with his trained perspective uniquely augments whatever else you've got going for you. Or haven't got going for you.

What Chuck Head did for Terry and me was to free us toward each other as we had never been before. By the time Terry was ready to leave the hospital, we had completely overcome the strain that had developed between us after Marty's death. It had taken the horror of that motorcycle accident to achieve this, to rescue Terry from the pit of booze and pills into which he had fallen. As a result of the accident, he had *needed* me for the first time, and I had eagerly responded to that need. As I said previously, out of such disasters in my life there has always emerged a new positive force, something attained, something learned, albeit at a stiff price. Terry's accident was an awful ordeal but the relationship that Terry and I have now, which dates from that accident, is rare and fulfilling and surely one of the most sustaining parts of my life.

During the weeks that I kept vigil over Terry, my religious feelings, which had deserted me after Marty's death, began to return. But they were changed. One of the new forces which came into my religious thinking was Joel Goldsmith, whose background was Christian Science but who had evolved his own religious philosophy in a series of powerful books. During very tough times, passages from his books have sustained and uplifted me. Sometimes when I wake in the night, sleepless and disturbed, I put one of Joel Goldsmith's lectures on my tape machine and I find marvelous solace in what he says and how he says it.

In addition to Joel Goldsmith, I have found metaphysical sustenance in the writings and preachings of Kathryn Kuhlman, a truly remarkable, Christlike woman. Her book, *I Believe in Miracles*, has been a source of inspiration to me, as have her appearances on television. Seeing her in person at her shrine, as I have a few times, has intensified my feelings about her and what she preaches.

When Terry finally got out of the hospital, six months later, I fixed up my guesthouse for him. Confined as he was, first to a wheelchair and then to a walker, I made the guesthouse, which is on the far side of my patio, as easy for him to live in as possible. When I had to be at the studio, either my mother or my housekeeper was on hand to take care of Terry. Ironically, this long period of convalescence was the first time that Nana, Terry, and I had lived together amicably as a family under the same roof. It took four months, casts on both legs, for Terry's legs to mend and grow strong, but it was also a time during which our family ties also grew strong. Terry and I established a real mother-son relationship. Although he was thirty years old, it was the first time I had really taken care of him.

The day Terry left to go to live in his own place again, I was happy to see him strong enough to be on his own, but sad to see him leave the guesthouse. I had watched my son fight his way through a terrible ordeal, with courage, intelligence, and a loving heart, and I was proud of him. I didn't tell him that, because it would have embarrassed him, but when he left we had a farewell drink, and although he was only moving ten minutes away, I wept a few tears. I'm sure that told him everything.

CHAPTER   15

A nyone who knows anything about me knows how involved I am with dogs. The dogs I live with are just as much my family as are my mother and son. During the bleak, difficult years since Marty's death, my canine family has been a source of joy and strength to me. I have found that when you are deeply troubled, there are things you get from the silent, devoted companionship of a dog that you get from no other source.

In a way I never got over what happened to Tiny, the little black and tan, who, when I was on crutches, was hit by a car and died in my arms. It was totally my fault for walking him without a leash, and I've had a lingering sense of guilt about his death all my life. To this day, if I see a dog in the street, I will hop out of my car, stop traffic, and try to lure the poor little thing into my car so that I can take him home (if he has a collar with identification) or turn him over to Actors and Others for Animals, which will try to locate his owner or, failing that, find a home for him.

My passion for and understanding of dogs are really directly attributable to two remarkable books which I read as a girl—*Letters to Strongheart* and *Kinship with All Life*, both written by a man named J. Allen Boone. The books are primarily about a German shepherd named Strongheart, who was a big movie dog long before Rin-Tin-Tin came on the scene. Boone lived alone with Strongheart for a long period of time, during which Boone, intrigued with the unusual and uncanny powers of the dog, began to experiment with ways and means of communicating with him, but not using the ordinary master-dog method.

In *Kinship with All Life*, Boone taught me the difference between training a dog and educating one. Trained dogs, Boone points out, are relatively easy to turn out. All that's needed is a certain amount of bluff and bluster, and things that can be used for threatening and rewarding purposes. Educating a dog, though, demands keen intelligence, integrity, imagination, and a gentle touch—mentally, vocally, and physically.

Boone found ways to communicate with Strongheart during the long silences they shared, and it was those revelations that had such a profound effect on me. Boone relates how he freed himself of prejudices and purified his thinking to the point at which Strongheart was truly able to share precious dog wisdom with Boone, "wonderful secrets having to do with the great dog art of living abundantly and happily in the present tense regardless of circumstances." Boone found that after establishing a strong rapport with Strongheart, he was able to establish a mental two-way bridge between them, over which it was possible for Boone's thoughts freely to cross into Strongheart's thinking areas and for the dog's thoughts just as freely to cross over into his.

I realize that, summarized like this, Boone's account seems rather irrational, but I can assure you that with the details and documentation in the book it is all very rational indeed. In fact, it is this attitude toward communicating that I brought to my relations with my own dogs, with extraordinary results. I do indeed communicate with my dogs but not in the usual dog owner's manner of talking down to them in a way that smacks of baby talk.

What I have learned is that dogs are here on earth to teach us. They have taught me how to be serenely patient, and they have taught me about love—fundamental love, such as Jesus taught. No matter how abusive or inconsiderate its owner has been, a dog will turn his other cheek and continue to love him. And loyalty—I have never found in a human being loyalty that is comparable to a dog's loyalty. And yet people buy a dog as they buy a plant, and they treat him like a plant after they get him.

They buy him from pet shops and backyard breeders without checking on the dog's condition. They breed the dog because they think it would be cute to have puppies. They haven't the slightest interest in or concept of the spiritual qualities of the dogs they buy.

My dogs are completely tuned in on my moves and moods. When I start to put on my bathing suit, they immediately rush around and get their pool toys. When I start to get ready to go for a bike ride, they go off to their quiet corners and settle down, for they know I never take them with me when I'm on my bicycle. When they are in the car with me and I'm going over a familiar route—for instance, to and from the studio when I'm working—if I deviate so much as one block from the regular route they will react nervously and anxiously until I get back on familiar roads. When I wake depressed and not wanting to communicate, they keep their distance. When I wake feeling good, they are on the bed saying good morning. They too have their moods of depression, of joy, of feeling antagonistic, and I respect their moods as much as they respect mine. If I cry, they all nestle around me and lick my tears and give me their paws and try to cheer me up.

Mr. Boone says, "Had someone come upon the dog and me sitting quietly shoulder to shoulder in some picturesque outdoor location, and had our observer been told in all seriousness that we were exchanging stimulating points of view with each other through the medium of silent talk, he would probably have found it exceedingly difficult to believe. But had he cared to become one of us, had he been sufficiently flexible and receptive for such an experience, he could have joined in with us and shared in the simple universal language we were using, that language which moves without the need for sound from heart to heart."

From heart to heart. That is precisely how my dogs and I communicate. And that is how my dogs communicate with each other. I think it is wrong for anyone to own a single dog, thereby denying him the pleasure and fulfillment of having a dog friend to talk to. I feel strongly that no animal should be deprived of one of his own kind for companionship. I also feel that all dog owners should have their animals spayed and neutered. The world's dog population has long since passed the explosion point. We have a serious food shortage and it relates to dogs as well as to humans. The old shibboleth that every female dog "deserves" to have one litter is nonsense. Spayed females who have never had a litter are just as happy and often healthier than females who have given birth a time or two. Backyard breeding in order to earn money is one of the worst offenses. Pet stores that sell puppies should be outlawed. If you knew as much as our organizations knows about the health of many of these pet-store puppies, I'm sure you would readily agree. I realize, of course, that there must be some breeding to sustain a reasonable dog population, but even the reputable breeders have to take their sights off the almighty buck and look at the overall picture.

There are so many homeless, deserving dog waifs in pounds and shelters around the country that it is a crime that people who want nice companions for their children pass them up because they are so obsessed with having a pedigreed dog. My dogs were all strays, rejects, most of whom would have been put to sleep if I had not rescued them.

Obviously, I could not continue befriending every stray orphan who came my way. So I have turned my compassion and energy toward the Actors and Others for Animals organization. But personnel and finances limit the scope of what we can do. We raised substantial amounts at our annual bazaar and other fund-raising events, but all of it goes out as fast as it comes in, for emergencies, spaying and neutering, and housing strays and unwanted animals. Scarcely a day passes that someone does not call about or come by with some poor little creature who needs care and attention and a place to live. They break my heart. So beautiful and vulnerable, and alone. Totally dependent upon a human being, who, if he takes the orphan to his heart, will become just as dependent on the dog for those unique qualities that only a dog can bring into your life.

CHAPTER 16

During the fourth year of my television show, I fell in love—completely, unexpectedly in love. For four years I had been so immersed in the traumas of Marty's death and Terry's near-death, and in the demands of turning out my weekly television shows, that I had forgotten that the love part of me even existed. That's why it was such a shock when it happened—and how fast it happened!

It all began when, by chance, I ran into an actor I knew from having once worked on a film with him. He had a supporting role in that film, so we hadn't had many scenes together. He lived in the East but I had occasionally bumped into him when he was in Hollywood for a picture. There had been nothing at all between us; we were acquaintances, not even friends.

On this occasion, when we met, he had come to Hollywood to make a movie-of-the-week for television. He invited me to dinner, and before the evening was over I had fallen head over heels in love with him. Who can explain it? I had been so uneager to see him that when I came home from the studio that day I had wanted to cancel our date, but I didn't know where to reach him. Then, a few hours later, the earth was trembling under my chair at the restaurant.

I don't have much insight into why I fall in love or even what love is. I only know that a curious, mysterious reaction sets off inside me, like some mechanism that is tripped and starts to function with no way to turn it off. I do know that when it happens, it totally consumes me. I want to be with that person every minute of every day. I want to sleep with him and eat with him and talk with him and breathe the air he breathes. My eyes are blinded to his faults. He is letter-perfect. He has weaknesses but I only see his strengths. I am engulfed with a physical desire for him, but that is just one of three things which must work for me if I am to be completely in love. The other two are spiritual rapport and absolute honesty.

This man I fell in love with was totally different from the men I had known before him. He wasn't a father figure, as Marty had been, a guardian telling me what to do and when to do it and what not to do. He was as interested in metaphysics as I was and we had a wonderful time talking and exploring each other's minds.

Our affair lasted for over a year, for, as luck would have it, the movie he made became a television series on which he had a regular weekly part. So during the day we were both busy at our respective studios and every night we shared the sweet excitement of being together. He was married to a woman he no longer loved but to whom he stayed married for the sake of his three children. I didn't care whether he was married or not. I have no qualms about the other person's marital life. He was an adult, a forceful man, and if he had honest feelings for me, that's all I asked of him. Sometimes he wanted to talk about his marriage, and we discussed that, the talk on a few occasions revolving about his indecision about leaving his wife. I didn't try to exert any pressure about that, for having had three marriages that turned out as badly as mine did, I was in no way thinking about getting married again. I don't know what I would have said if he had left his wife and proposed to me. Thank God I never had to make that decision.

By that I mean he neither left his wife nor proposed to me. It was a perfectly marvelous year for me. It was a time in my life when I badly needed to be uplifted, and uplift me it did. When we met, he was feeling depressed and unhappy about his marriage, and I brought as much into his life as he brought into mine. We helped each other enormously.

When the season was over and his series wasn't renewed, he went back East and I never saw him again. We had had a little disagreement before he left but that really had no effect on our parting. I realized after he left that I did not love him in an enduring way, but that he had brought something important into my life at a time when I sorely needed it. But as it turned out, he was a man who passed through my life without leaving a trace of himself.

CHAPTER 17

On March 4, 1974, after five long years of investigation and preparation (not to mention enormous legal fees), we finally brought Jerome Rosenthal to trial in the Superior Court of California. It was a trial destined to last for one hundred days, with twelve attorneys participating, at a cost of $250,000. It was my great good fortune to have an extraordinary lawyer representing me, Robert Winslow, a soft-spoken, gentle man who was as dedicated to nailing Rosenthal as Terry and I were. Bob Winslow did virtually nothing else for five years than stalk Rosenthal.

At stake in the trial was the possible recovery of some of my money that had been dissipated by Rosenthal in his oil and hotel ventures. I was told he had no visible assets, but there were six malpractice insurance companies involved and there was the possibility of recovering several millions of dollars from them.

But in all honesty, I was as much interested in the justice of bringing Rosenthal to his knees as I was in the money itself. And Terry's hatred of Rosenthal had risen to the point at which he was positively obsessed by nailing Rosenthal to the jailhouse door.

And there was something else. I was still baffled and deeply troubled by Marty's role in all this. I had never stopped wondering if he had been a villain or a dupe. It was my hope that the trial might throw some light on exactly what happened between Marty and Rosenthal. Terry had received a phone call from Kirk Douglas, who said that many years ago he had phoned Marty to tell him that he, Kirk, had fired Rosenthal as his lawyer because he had discovered that Rosenthal was squandering his investments in questionable deals that smacked of double-dealing. At that time Kirk and his wife, Anne, were good friends of ours whom we saw all the time. Marty never told me about that call, but I do remember that just about that time Marty came to me and said, "I don't think we should see Anne and Kirk anymore. Kirk's done something—well, let's just say he's no friend of yours. Take my word for it. I'd rather not talk about it." As a result we didn't see them anymore. But if Marty had listened to Kirk and fired Rosenthal, most of my money would have been saved. Why didn't he? Why had Marty reacted as he did?

Terry had also discovered that Marty had paid the accounting firm of Price-Waterhouse the sum of $25,000 to investigate Rosenthal's investments and accounting practices as they related to me. Their report was entirely negative and advised immediate termination of Rosenthal's position with me. Marty paid the $25,000 fee but completely ignored the report. Why?

By far the worst Rosenthal-related incident involved the beautiful actress Dorothy Dandridge, who killed herself a few years ago, shortly after her agent had called to tell her that he had checked on certain investments which her lawyer, Jerome Rosenthal, had made for her, and had discovered that she was penniless. Of course, she had no money to sue Rosenthal; not very long afterward she had committed suicide.

So the start of that trial, as you can see, had great psychological meaning for me. It was an opportunity to exorcise something that had been gnawing at me for many years. I looked to God for the prevailment of justice, hoping that it had been preordained in the order of things for me to triumph over this man who had brought such evil into my life and the lives of so many others.

The case was tried before Judge Lester E. Olson, without a jury. Judge Olson, it seemed to me, was strict, fair, amiable, and very knowledgeable. During the trial seventy boxes of files, containing tens of thousands of papers, almost 2,500 exhibits in all, were introduced into evidence, but Judge Olson seemed to handle it all pretty effortlessly, and to stay abreast of what was in the boxes. He also remained unflappable in the face of some weird maneuvering on the part of Rosenthal and his lawyers.

I particularly enjoyed the moment during the trial when Rosenthal had finished testifying about a meeting which he said he had had with me in his office on May 11, 1956. Rosenthal spent two and a half hours on the witness stand, telling the court how he had informed me on that day of everything he was doing with my money—thereby proving that he was open and aboveboard with me. Bob Winslow's cross-examination consisted of showing Rosenthal his own office diary for that day, which showed that I had been in his office for twenty-five minutes. "Mr. Rosenthal," Judge Olson said, "it took you two and a half hours to tell us what you allegedly told Doris Day. How did you manage to cram all that into twenty-five minutes?"

In his oral opinion on the case Judge Olson found against Rosenthal, citing attorney-client conflicts of interest; failure to provide financial, legal and investment advice; kickbacks, negligence, tax fraud, inaccurate financial statements and failure to keep proper records among other, more specific, things.

The total damages given me were $22,835,646. It was the largest amount ever awarded in a civil suit in California.

It was over, and the forces of evil had been put to rout.

CHAPTER 18

I had a dream recently that I was at a wedding. The marriage ceremony was just ending, and I was desolate. I had a terrible crush on the groom and I kept saying to myself, Why is he getting married? Oh, he's so darling, why is he getting married? Why is he doing this to me?

Of course, dreaming about marriage is quite understandable. I do think about marrying again, and Terry talks to me about it quite often. We're not at all like mother-son; we're more like contemporaries who are really good friends. He calls me up and says, "What are you doing? Come on up—I've got a great fire going, we'll open a bottle of wine and talk."

One of his favorite subjects to talk about is why I don't go out more. He'd love to see me happily coupled, if not married. But I tell him that if somebody calls, and I don't feel that seeing the fellow has a prayer of going anywhere (I can always tell that much about a man), then I don't go out simply for the sake of going out. I'd rather read. I love being in my house. I'll know when it's the right man, and when it is, I will respond to it for all it's worth. But I really don't feel that I have to run around to a lot of cocktail parties on a looking mission. I enjoy my life as it is.

"Now, listen, Mom," Terry said, the last time we had one of these talks, "let's face it—you are really a terrific-looking woman. You're very healthy and desirable with a terrific body. You're *young*, you really are. All my friends think that."

"Well, that's adorable of you to lay those compliments on me," I said, "but I'm just very funny about whom I go out with. My time is precious to me and I don't want to waste it. I'm just very selective that's all. Not that I think I'm such hot stuff, but everybody has the right to be selective."

"Sure. Right. But you can't really know a guy unless you see him a few times—"

"I'll know him the *minute* I see him. He'll show up. I'm sure of that. So why should I go out looking for him? I'm in no hurry. But that doesn't mean that I wouldn't love to be married."

There's no doubt that life has more meaning when you have someone to share things with. I don't think God made us to walk around by ourselves. I'm lucky to have loved and been loved in my life, so I know what I'm looking forward to. I think about the men and women in this world who have never experienced real love. Both married and unmarried. And I pity them for what they've missed out on.

"So, who is this guy?" Terry asks. "This dude who will walk in and cause you to faint?"

"Well, he is someone who will turn me on sexually, but he's also someone who is as turned on by listening to Joel Goldsmith tapes and reading his books as I am. Someone who does not want to gossip about who did what to whom, or what the grosses of anything were, or any of that. He's someone who wants to learn as much about life as I do. Maybe he'll be a surgeon, gray at the temples, who would like to settle down on a big old New England farm. Oh, how I'd love that. No neighbors for miles around. Lots of room for eleven dogs to run and play. Where I could rake leaves and shovel snow and pluck rock-hard apples out of the barrel on the back porch. I'd sell everything and be out of Beverly Hills in a week."

"Well," Terry said, "I'd hate to lose you to the East, but bon voyage!"

What bothers me about falling in love is how impermanent it can be. In the beginning of all three of my marriages, I thought I was deeply and forever in love—but look what happened. But as I've said before, it was predestined that it work out that way. I think the Al Jorden period gave me tremendous strength and a depth of emotions from which I later drew in my acting and singing.

Looking back, I'd say the train accident was designed to turn me away from dancing and to start me toward a singing career. The one really positive value in my marriage to Al Jorden was the birth of my son. George Weidler was part of the plan in that his desertion gave me a sense of self-sufficiency, of a new inner strength.

And Marty's death—well, to be honest about it, had he lived I would have been totally wiped out. He and Rosenthal would have dissipated my five years of television earnings just as they dissipated everything else. I would have lost my house—everything. In the scheme of things, Marty had to die in order for me to survive.

I know that I am often thought of as a Pollyanna, but I'm much too realistic to qualify as a Pollyanna. However, I have overcome a lot, and I have developed an inner strength on which I can rely. It has nothing to do with me. It's simply built into me and nobody can ever take it from me. I don't care about "success" in the conventional sense of my ratings or earnings. The success I care about is in knowing how to deal with situations, in not allowing anything in my life to get out of hand. I know I can handle almost anything they throw at me; to me that is real success.

I know how I want to live. I know what's good for me. I know what brings me joy. I know what has value and what doesn't. That doesn't mean that there aren't some nights when life seems bleak and I cry myself to sleep. Okay, I'll say to mayself, I'll give them tonight, but tomorrow is mine. Life has to be up and down—if it isn't down once in a while how would I know what up is? So I don't pretend. When I'm miserable, I tell everybody I come in contact with. I never try to put on a happy face. I deal with it. I try to understand why. I fight my way out of it. And when I'm happy everybody knows about that too. So many people stop themselves from feeling good—that's so hard for me to understand. They can't even accept a compliment. God, when I feel good I do pirouettes! If you squelch an emotion inside yourself, how does it get out? Where does it go! I'll tell you where—it shrivels up and dies inside you, but I don't think the human body is equipped for burials.

No, I let it all hang out and I suppose that outgoing quality accounts for some of the reactions I get from people who have seen me perform. I really love how most people are with me. God knows I'm not one of the awesome beauties, like Elizabeth Taylor, who epitomize the words "movie star." What I am is the truck driver's delight. People on the street always call me Doris. That's just the way I want it. We are family, my audience and I, and that's why I especially liked performing in a series that brought me into the living room every week. I think that's where I belong, as one of the family.

In one of the episodes on my television series I had a scene in which I wore a bridal gown. I received a letter from a young lady who said, "When you wore that little wedding gown on your television show, it absolutely made me cry. I'm going to be married in five months and I want a gown like that so badly—can you please tell me what store the gown came from so I can buy one like it? I want to look like you looked."

My costumer and my fitter went to work on the gown to make it even more attractive. Then they got yards of tulle and they made a beautiful headpiece decorated with lilies of the valley and little orange blossoms.

We sent it off to the girl who had written, with all my good wishes for her marriage. Months later, the dress long forgotten, I received a lovely letter from the girl, together with a picture of herself at her wedding in my make-believe wedding dress. So pretty. So radiant with happiness. So much the bride. It was very touching, and I shed a few tears of happiness for that sweet, anonymous girl. I thought to myself, that's what it's all about, isn't it?

There was another wedding in my life a short time later—my son's. He married a lovely girl named Melissa, at the Spanish-style home of some friends of his in Rancho Santa Fe. It was an informal, festive event, and while we were all waiting for Melissa, who was upstairs being nervous, I began to ruminate about Terry, standing there with his best man, looking so handsome, waiting for his nervous bride. I thought about what a splendid young man he had turned into, and how much I liked him. I hoped that this adventure into marriage would be a happy one.

Melissa made her entrance, beautiful, nervous, looking lovingly at Terry, and as they took their places in front of the little improvised altar, a thought darted across my mind—we should have had a double ceremony! If only I had found someone. That would have been fun. It would really have been a kick.

EDITORS' NOTE: On April 14, 1976, Doris Day, fifty-two, was married to Barry D. Comden, forty-one, a Beverly Hills restaurateur, in a private ceremony at a friend's house in Carmel, California; it was her fourth marriage, his second.

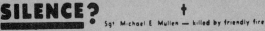

A SILENT message to fathers and mothers of Iowa.

We have been dying for nine, long, miserable years in Vietnam in an undeclared war...how many more lives do you wish to sacrifice because of your

SILENCE?

Sgt Michael E Mullen — killed by friendly fire

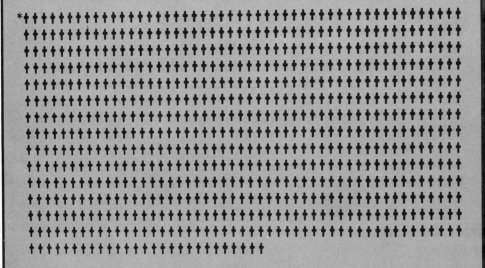

*These 714 crosses represent the 714 Iowans who have died in Vietnam.

In memory of Vietnam War Dead whom our son joined on February 17, 1970...and to those awaiting the acceptable sacrifice in 1970...

From an advertisement in the Des Moines Register April 12, sponsored by Mr. and Mrs. Gene Mullen, La Porte City, Iowa.

FRIENDLY FIRE

A condensation of the book by
C. D. B. BRYAN

CHAPTER   1

September 3, 1969, his last night of leave, Michael Eugene Mullen, who was to have been the fifth generation of his family to till the same fields, worked until ten o'clock on his family's 120-acre farm five miles west of La Porte City in Black Hawk County, Iowa. He remained down in the lower 80 acres upon his father's old plum-red tractor ripping out brush and dead trees, bulldozing the trash into the dry streambed of Miller's Creek, clearing and filling in the land so it could be used as pasture.

By midnight, when his father, Gene Mullen, had returned from working the late shift at the huge John Deere tractor plant in Waterloo, Michael had completed his packing and was still awake talking to his younger brother, John, behind the closed door of the bedroom they shared. Peg Mullen, Michael's mother, and Mary and Patricia, his two younger sisters, were asleep, so Gene made himself a cup of instant coffee and sat alone at the kitchen table, listening to the muted voices of his sons. Then he stood up and knocked on their bedroom door. Michael opened it.

"Would you like anything from the kitchen, Michael? A beer?"

Michael finished locking up his metal tackle box. It held his arrowhead collection, special letters, snapshots, the corporal stripes he'd earned at Fort Benning, addresses, insurance papers.

"No, no thanks, Dad," Michael said. He carefully taped the key to the lid and slid the tackle box onto the top shelf of his closet.

Gene, still standing in the doorway, could not look away from Michael's uniform hanging on the back of the open closet door.

"Mikey?"

"Yes?"

"Be careful?"

Michael smiled at his father. "I will, Dad. I will."

The center of Waterloo is about fifteen miles northwest of the Mullens' farm, and the airport is another few miles beyond that on the other side of town. They drove past the big new shopping center on Route 218 with the Hy-Vee Market, the Sears and J. C. Penney stores. Gene said something about how fast all that area was changing, and Michael agreed.

They passed the Robo-Wash and Burger King, Donutland and the Cadillac Bowling Lanes, and soon they were caught up in Waterloo traffic. They cleared the city, and beyond were the flatlands and railroad tracks they had to cross before reaching the airport.

Michael wouldn't let his father help him with the barracks bags, insisting it would be easier for him to carry them both himself. The Mullens entered the terminal building a little after nine. They took seats in the small, near-empty waiting room and stared out the large window at the vacant airfield.

When Michael's plane landed, he and his family rose.

"Look," Michael told them, "don't stick around for the plane to leave. You don't have to wait."

"We'll wait," his mother announced firmly.

"No, please," Michael insisted, "I'll be all right." He went to Mary and Patricia and told them good-bye, that they shouldn't wait around, that they should tell John there'd be a lot more work now that he was going. And Patricia and Mary each had a moment to themselves with Michael, a chance to tell him to take care of himself, to be careful, that they would pray for him, miss him, that they loved him and would write letters all the time and would send him things, anything, all he had to do was tell them what he needed. Michael kissed them each, and they moved away because it was their parents' turn.

Gene fingered a small bronze medallion the size of a twenty-five cent piece that hung from a chain around his neck. The medal, depicting the Virgin Mary, had been struck in commemoration of the first Catholic missionaries who went into China. The inscription around it was in Chinese. The medallion had been given Gene thirty-five years earlier by a Chinese student he had befriended when they were undergraduates together at Marquette University in Milwaukee. Gene had worn it ever since. He lifted its chain from around his neck and handed it to his son, saying, "Mikey, I've tried to give you everything. . . ." Gene's voice broke, and he took a deep breath and began again: "Tried to do everything that a father could do. . . ."

Michael looked down at the medallion, chestnut-colored with age.

"I wore this medal through the Second World War," Gene was saying.

"It protected me, and so I give you this . . . I give you. . . ." He could say no more. Gene looked at his son, half in pride, half in agony, his throat too tight to speak.

"I'll wear it," Michael said. He loosened his black Army tie and unbuttoned the collar button of his khaki shirt. He draped the medal and chain around his neck, carefully centered it with the dog tags on his chest and buttoned his shirt back over it. Michael then turned to his mother and hugged her.

"Mom," Michael said, "don't worry yourself now, okay?" He squeezed her hand lightly. "It will all be over March first, okay?"

He gently pulled his hand from hers, picked up his barracks bags and turned away. Peg unconsciously pressed the hand he'd been holding to her lips. She watched her son walk past the cafeteria toward the doors that would lead to his plane. Michael stopped in the narrow passageway, dropped his barracks bags and turned back for one last look at his family. But as they started toward him, he quickly lifted his bags and hurried out the door.

Mary and Patricia cried quietly on the drive back to the farm. Peg could see that Gene was gripping the steering wheel so tightly his knuckles were white. When they were once again on the other side of Waterloo, back on Route 218 past the Robo-Wash and Burger King heading toward their farm, Peg resolved to cheer everybody up by telling them what Michael had said just before boarding the plane.

"Why March first?" Gene asked her.

"I don't know," Peg said. "He just told me not to worry. That it would all be over then."

On March 1, 1970, Michael Eugene Mullen, age twenty-five, was returned to the Waterloo Airport in a U.S. Army issue silver-gray casket.

The following November, his mother was under FBI surveillance.

CHAPTER 2

When the telephone rang in the parish office of the Sacred Heart Catholic Church off Poplar Street in La Porte City a little after nine o'clock on Saturday morning, February 21, 1970, the thin, stooped late-middle-aged country priest assumed it was just another mother whose child, sick with a midwinter cold, would be unable to attend catechism classes that day. He unhurriedly walked to his desk and, lifting the receiver, was surprised to hear an unfamiliar male voice ask for him by name.

"Father Otto Shimon?"

"Yes-s-s?"

"Father Shimon, this is Master Sergeant Fitzgerald. I'm with Fifth Army Headquarters. . . . Do you have an O. E. Mullen in your parish?"

"Yes-s-s, Gene Mullen's in my parish." The priest did not like this sergeant's tone; he sounded altogether too businesslike. "As a matter of fact, Sergeant, the Mullens have always been very good members. . . ."

"May I see you this morning, sir?"

"Me? This morning, Sergeant? . . . Fitzgerald, you said it was?"

"Fitzgerald, that's right."

"A fine old Irish-Catholic name," Father Shimon said, still trying to be congenial, still fighting down the apprehension rising within him. "You are, I presume, Catholic?"

"No, sir, Episcopalian," Fitzgerald said. "Please, Father Shimon, it's important I see you this morning. As soon as possible."

"About Gene Mullen?" Father Shimon asked, his lips suddenly dry. "Is there something, ah-h-h, wrong?"

That morning the sun had finally broken through the flat pearl-gray overcast that had been brooding over the Mullens' farm. Although the temperature hovered near freezing, the week-long Arctic winds had ceased, and at last it again felt warm enough to be outside.

Gene Mullen walked back from the mailbox to the house. As he climbed the stairs into the kitchen, he called out, "Letter from Mikey." He dropped the bills, the Des Moines *Register* and the second-class mail on the kitchen table and tore open the envelope. Peg wiped her hands on a dish towel and put a kettle of water on to boil."

"What's he say?" she asked. "When did he write it?"

Gene glanced at the top of the letter. "Dated the thirteenth," he said. "Let's see now, 'Dear Mom and Dad: Will be on the bunker line about two more days, then back out into the field.'"

"Ugh!" Peg groaned. "That means more search and destroy."

"No, it doesn't," Gene said. "He's been doing company sweeps like he wrote in the other letter."

"Same thing," Peg said.

"No, it isn't," Gene insisted. "A company sweep is—"

Peg waved her hand impatiently. "Go on with the letter."

"All right, all right. He says, 'Glad that all is well—weather here been rather good. Have decided not to take R&R if I can get a drop. So 'til later, hang loose.'"

"That's it?"

"That's it," Gene said. He passed the letter across the table.

Peg read through it quickly. "Oh, see," she said, "he's decided for sure to ask for an early drop. You remember the letter before last Michael said he was writing the University of Missouri to get the papers."

Michael hoped to be released early from Vietnam so that he could be readmitted to the Agricultural School. Peg and Gene discussed for a moment what they thought his chances were; Michael himself had written that he felt they were very good. The only part of his letter that bothered them was that he would again be going into the field, that he wouldn't be in the relative safety of the fire base bunker line anymore. Still, in one of his first letters, Michael had written that he was in "probably one of the better places over here," a comparatively quiet part of Vietnam.

"So he might be coming home in June," Gene said.

"Looks that way," Peg said, "knock wood."

Gene finished his coffee and stood up "Well, Mother," he said, "I guess I might as well try to fix the television antenna for you."

The windblown television antenna was attached to a post near the east side of the farmhouse. Gene was just coming around that east corner, blowing hot breath on his fingertips and trying to remember where he had last put the light wrench he would need, when, out of the corner of his eye, he noticed two automobiles turning into his driveway.

Gene thought he recognized the first car, believed the parish priest, Father Shimon, had one like it, but that second car. . . . Gene read the black letters painted on the Chevrolet's olive-drab door: U.S. ARMY—FOR OFFICIAL USE ONLY. Gene's chest tightened, and he stood still while the priest and the sergeant stepped out of their cars and slammed shut the doors. Gene watched them walking toward him as if in slow motion. Not until the priest forced himself to look up did Gene recognize the fright, the despair, the agony within his eyes, then very quietly Gene asked, "Is my boy dead?"

"I can't tell you here," Father Shimon said, his hand fluttering up toward Gene's shoulder. "Come into the house with us . . . please?"

Gene spun away before the priest's pale fingers could touch him.

Peg Mullen hurried out of the sewing room in time to glimpse the Army uniform entering the kitchen. She found Gene standing with his back to the sink, clutching the counter behind him, the Army sergeant halted just to the side of the doorway. Father Shimon, between them, had removed his glasses to wipe away the steam. Peg started to move toward her husband but had to turn away. Never had she seen such terrible devastation in his face, so raw a wound. She looked next at the sergeant, who avoided her eyes by glancing at the priest whose job it was to tell them. But Father Shimon would not stop wiping his glasses.

Peg scowled at the Army sergeant and said, "Is my son Michael dead?" She glared at him with such utter contempt that the sergeant flinched. "The Army doesn't come to tell parents that their sons are wounded!" Peg said. "You know the Army comes only when they're *dead!*"

The sergeant turned to the priest, waiting for Father Shimon to break the news, to speak. But the priest was incapable of talking.

Very slowly, deliberately, almost threateningly, Gene Mullen pushed himself away from the sink and moved toward the two men. "Now I want to know the truth!" he told them. "Is . . . my . . . boy . . . dead?"

Sergeant Fitzgerald looked at the priest, then back at Gene: "Yes."

And, "Yes-s-s-s," Father Shimon said, too, as if he had been holding his breath all this time. "Yes, Gene, yes, Peg, I'm sorry, yes-s-s-s."

Gene sagged as if hit. He looked at Peg and she at him. "Why?" he said to no one in particular. "Why?"

Peg had moved to the kitchen table and stood now gripping the wooden rung of a chairback until she felt herself under enough control to speak. Then she asked the sergeant how Michael had been killed.

Sergeant Fitzgerald sorted through some papers and pulled one out. "I only know the official casualty message given me by Fifth Army Headquarters this morning over the phone."

"Read it," Peg said.

The sergeant lifted the paper to the light. "It states that 'Sergeant (E-5) Michael Eugene Mullen, US 54 93—' so on, 'died while at a night defensive position when artillery fire from friendly forces landed in the area.'" Sergeant Fitzgerald's hand dropped. "I'm sorry . . . I really am very sorry, Mr. and Mrs. Mullen. . . ." He put the paper away and began buttoning up his trench coat as if to leave. "Generally, at this time," he said, "families of cas ualties prefer to be alone with their priests—"

"Sit down," Peg said quietly. "We're going to talk about this message, this, official casualty report."

Gene watched the sergeant leaf back through the papers, start to say, "Mrs. Mullen, I only—"

"Sergeant," Gene ordered, "read that thing again."

Fitzgerald cleared his throat and re-read the message. He looked up from the paper. "That's all it says . . . really."

"We're going to talk about this message," Peg said. "I want you to explain it to me. This word, what do you mean by 'friendly'?"

"It merely means that it wasn't enemy artillery," the sergeant said. "Your son was killed by friendly fire."

"Friendly fire? *Friendly fire?*" Peg repeated incredulously.

Sergeant Fitzgerald shrugged lamely. "It means any artillery from forces not the enemy."

"*Not* the enemy! *Goddamn you!*" Peg cried, beating the chairback with her fists in frustration. "You couldn't even give him the decency of being killed by the enemy!" She glared at the sergeant. "These 'friendly forces not the enemy,' how come the word 'American' isn't used?"

"Because it wasn't 'American,'" the sergeant said.

"And why wasn't the word 'accidental' there?"

"Because, Mrs. Mullen, it wasn't an accident."

"Wait a minute," Peg warned ominously.

The sergeant began talking about the accidental shelling at Bien Hoa.

"We know all about Bien Hoa," Peg snapped.

"Well," Fitzgerald said, "this is how and where your son was killed."

"You don't know very much! Michael wasn't anywhere near Bien Hoa. My son was three, four hundred miles from there!"

"Good God," Sergeant Fitzgerald said, "it must have happened all over Vietnam that night." He sat down at the kitchen table. "You understand how it could have happened," he said. "The Vietcong infiltrated these South Vietnamese artillery units, got onto their radio channels and called in the wrong artillery coordinates so that when the ARVN artillery fired, they hit Americans." Sergeant Fitzgerald apologized for not having any more information than was contained in the official casualty message and added he did not want to say positively that this was what had happened to Michael, but the Vietcong had infiltrated ARVN radio channels in the past, and this is what might have happened to their son's unit.

Sergeant Fitzgerald next explained that the Mullens had the right to request a special escort to accompany Michael's body back from Vietnam. If they had some friend of Michael's in mind, someone whom they would like to have return with Michael's remains, they should let him know.

"Well, it's so soon, so sudden . . ." Peg said. "Michael had so many friends, I really don't know. . . ."

"There's no need to decide now," Sergeant Fitzgerald said. "Either myself or another survivors' assistance officer will call you tomorrow. Now," the sergeant said, "what funeral home do you want your son's body delivered to?"

Peg and Gene looked at each other speechlessly.

"Well, we don't know," Peg said. . . . "We really don't know yet."

"How long will it be before Michael . . . Michael's body returns?" Gene asked.

"Just as soon as they have a plane full," Sergeant Fitzgerald said.

Peg said, "I know it won't be long then."

"One more thing, Sergeant," Gene asked. "When will Michael's death be announced on the news?"

"After I notify Fort Leonard Wood that I've seen you, they'll release it. That should be about two hours from now."

"Two hours!" Peg protested. "You can't! You've got to give us time to tell our children. Our daughters are away at college, and we can't let them hear about it on the radio. You've got to hold back the news."

"Can't you call them?" Sergeant Fitzgerald asked. "You'll have at least two hours."

"They'll be in classes," Peg said. "I won't be able to reach them until tonight. Can't you wait?"

"I'm sorry, Mrs. Mullen, I'm only a sergeant. I can't tell the Army what to do."

"I can!" Peg said angrily. "I'm not afraid of the Army or the Pentagon. If you won't do anything about it, then I'll . . . I'll call Senator Hughes in Washington. He'll help."

"Look, Mrs. Mullen," Sergeant Fitzgerald said, "you don't have to do that. I'll tell Fifth Army you want them to wait. They won't release the news until you give them the go-ahead."

The Mullens' friends and neighbors, stunned by word of Michael's death, began arriving at the farm a few hours later. The men wearing faded bib overalls, ankle-high work boots, day-glo orange earflapped vinyl caps, their weathered faces creased with sorrow, approached Gene shyly. They touched him on the shoulder, laid their calloused hands across his back. Their wives, in woolen slacks and heavy hand-knit cardigans, brought baskets of food, stews and casseroles, and pots of coffee.

Gene would be explaining to the latest arrival that the family knew only that Michael had been killed by the South Vietnamese artillery, that the Vietcong had somehow made the artillery fire on his platoon's position and that Michael had been killed two days ago.

"But, Gene," the man would say, "I didn't see nothing in the paper about it. Where'd it say anything about American boys being killed by South *Veet*-namese artillery?"

"You heard about the shelling at Bien Hoa?" Gene asked. "How a lot of American boys got killed and wounded at Bien Hoa? Well, see, it happened all over Vietnam that night."

"I sure am sorry, Gene. It seems the whole world is coming apart. It gets so a man just doesn't want to read or know about anything anymore."

"You got to care," Gene said. "You got to keep caring."

Patricia Mullen had been met by a friend of Peg's in Iowa City and reached the farm late that afternoon. Like her mother's, Patricia's reaction to Michael's death was a cold and bitter rage. Only three days before she had written their Senator, Harold Hughes, pleading with him to get her brother out of combat, that it was such a waste to let "Michael's mind be destroyed." Senator Hughes had replied the same day to explain the process by which Michael could request an out-of-combat assignment. Patricia had received the Senator's letter that morning.

Peg's sister, Isabel Strathman, and her husband, Gerald Strathman, arrived at the farm next. Gerald Strathman, an Army Air Corps bombardier during World War II, had taken part in the raids on the Ploesti oilfields.

Peg's brother, Bill Goodyear, arrived early that evening. He had driven to the farm directly from Omaha. Bill Goodyear had served in the Army during World War II and had helped build the Burma Road.

Mary Mullen, then nineteen years old and a freshman at Rockhurst, had been picked up in Kansas City by Peg's other sister, Louise Petersen, and Mike Kitt, the Petersens' son-in-law. Herman Petersen, Peg's brother-in-law, had fought through the Battle of the Bulge. Mary and the Petersens would not arrive until late that night.

Howard Goodyear, Peg's older brother, was driving in from Pittsburgh and could not reach the farm before Sunday afternoon. Now an executive with Alcoa, Howard had been the radio operator-medic on the weather plane which had preceded the *Enola Gay* to Hiroshima. As part of its mission Howard Goodyear's B-29 had to fly over Hiroshima to report the effects of the first atomic bomb.

At two-thirty in the morning, while the Mullens were still waiting for their daughter Mary and the Petersens, Peg started writing down all the information she had learned from her conversation with Sergeant Fitzgerald. She wasn't sure yet why she was doing it, but she felt a need to commit the details to paper. Gene got up from the kitchen table to check on John, who was awake, lying with his arms folded behind his head, staring up at the ceiling.

"Johnny," Gene asked quietly, "are you all right?"

167

"I'm okay, Dad. . . ." John turned to his father standing in the door-way. "You know, Dad? Mikey's got it made."

"What do you mean?"

"I mean he's in heaven now. He doesn't have to worry about what's go-ing to happen to him next."

Gene stood looking down at Michael's empty bed, then back at John, and because he knew he was going to cry, Gene hurried out through the kitchen past Peg and on into the darkened living room, where he sank into a chair and buried his face in his hands.

CHAPTER 3

A t 7:45 P.M. on Sunday March 1, the ninth day since the Mullens had learned of their son's death, the Ozark Airlines flight carrying Mi-chael's casket touched down at the far end of the Waterloo runway. The airplane braked, reversed its thrust, shuddered, slowed, braked some more and taxied in toward the terminal.

Peg was not there to see it. She simply could not make herself drive out to the airport where six months earlier Michael had kissed her good-bye and told her not to worry, saying, "Come on now, Mom, please? It'll all be over March first." It was March 1, and it was all over.

Gene Mullen, his son John and daughter Mary went with Sergeant Fitzgerald to meet the plane. The four of them stood by the picture win-dow looking out at the nearly deserted airfield. As the airliner braked to a stop and shut down its engines, Gene Mullen asked Sergeant Fitzgerald what had impressed him most about Vietnam.

Without turning from the window, Fitzgerald said, "The corruption."

Tom Hurley, requested by the Mullens to be Michael's escort, was the last passenger to leave the plane. As the Mullens crowded forward to watch, Hurley walked down the boarding steps and stood next to the freight bay, watching while Michael's casket, covered by an American flag, was slid onto a baggage cart. The cart backed away from the plane, turned and gently lowered and guided Michael's casket into the hearse. Only when the hearse's back doors were closed did Hurley enter the ter-minal to embrace his own waiting family.

The Hurleys departed together, and the Mullens and Sergeant Fitz-gerald followed the hearse to Waterloo. Michael's casket was taken inside the Loomis Funeral Home, and Tom Loomis, the director, asked Gene to wait in the vestibule while the casket was opened. Sergeant Fitzgerald followed Loomis, and Gene, Mary and John stayed behind. They sat silently, patiently in the vestibule wondering whether they could be certain it was Michael, worried that his body would have been so shattered by the artillery shell's explosion that they might never be able to know. After about twenty minutes Tom Loomis called down to Gene that he could now view the body. Gene rose and glanced, stricken, at his children.

"We'll be all right, Dad. You go ahead," John said. Mary gave her father's hand a gentle squeeze. "We'll come up after a while."

Gene Mullen nodded and slowly turned away. He took a few steps and paused at the doorway of the funeral parlor's viewing room. The casket was in a far corner, and he forced himself to raise his eyes to look at it. The casket's lid was up, and Gene noticed Tom Loomis standing somberly to one side. Feeling apprehensive and ill, Gene walked forward until he could see a uniformed body inside. Despairingly, haltingly, he took another step. And another. Then Gene stopped, looked reluctantly at the face and quickly away.

It was Michael, his son. There was no question about it.

Gene Mullen steeled himself, made himself move right next to the coffin, close enough to touch the cold hands so carefully folded across his son's chest. Gene examined the military tunic, the strangeness of its brass buttons, the uniform jacket's lapels with the brass infantry and U.S. insignia, the black Army tie, the starched khaki collar's points, the throat, the lower jaw, the still blue lips, the mustache—the *mustache?* When had he grown a mustache? But there was something else that bothered Gene. He just sensed there was something wrong. Suddenly he realized there wasn't a mark on his son.

Gene looked up at the funeral director in bewilderment, then back down. He noticed that Michael's face was a little puffy, his neck seemed swollen, but if it weren't for the uniform, there would be no sign that Michael had been in a war at all. In exasperation and puzzlement, Gene removed his glasses and wiped his hands across his eyes.

"Something wrong, Gene?" the funeral director asked.

"But, Tom, he was supposed to have been killed by *artillery!*"

"When we lifted the body up out of the casket—we had to," Loomis explained, "because it had settled into it a little—I couldn't feel any broken bones or abrasions. . . ."

"Do you think he could have been killed by the concussion?"

"I couldn't say," Loomis said. The funeral director leaned forward and traced his finger beneath Michael's khaki shirt collar. "There's some tape along here," he said, "but that's where they embalmed him."

Gene looked again at his son. For some reason Michael's coal black hair (which even when he had left was already thickly flecked with white) had now become a strange and alien brown. He noticed that his son's complexion, which had always been dark, almost mahogany-colored, seemed gray and chalky. But Michael's hair and complexion were the only things that seemed wrong, and Gene kept asking himself how could Michael have been killed by an artillery burst, an explosion of burning jagged chunks of shrapnel, and still be perfectly whole? The more Gene tried to understand it, the more agitated and suspicious he became until finally, unable to tolerate it any longer, he asked the funeral director where Sergeant Fitzgerald had gone.

"I'm right here, Mr. Mullen," Fitzgerald said. The sergeant had been standing out of the way at the back of the room. He now came forward.

Gene scowled at the sergeant. "Now I want to know *how*-my-son-*died*! I want a death certificate. I want a death certificate stating how my son was killed!"

The sergeant began leafing through an accordian-pleated manila file folder. "I don't have a death certificate, Mr. Mullen. All I have is the original message I read to you . . . that and the notes I made when I received the information over the phone. That's this, here. . . ." Sergeant Fitzgerald resignedly handed Gene a piece of white typing paper upon which he'd handwritten the message: "Sgt. Michael E. Mullen, son of Oscar Eugene and Margaret Mullen, RFD #3, La Porte City, Iowa. Killed 18 Feb 70 near the village of Chu Lai. Nonbattle."

Gene studied the page for a long moment, and then, in a howl that compressed all the rage and confusion and pain he felt into one anguished question, he asked, "What does this mean: '*Nonbattle*?'"

"It means a casualty not the result of action by hostile forces," Sergeant Fitzgerald replied.

When Gene Mullen returned to the farm that night, Peg's first question was: "Is it Michael?"

"Yes," he said and dashed the one desperate remaining hope she had been nurturing all along.

The day after Michael's funeral, back at their farm, Peg was reading the letter that had arrived that day from Vietnam:

Dear Mr. and Mrs. Mullen:
It is with deepest sorrow that I extend to you the sympathy of the men of the 1st

Battalion, 6th Infantry, for the loss of your son, Michael.

On the early morning of February 18, 1970, Michael's unit was located in their night defensive position near the village of Tu Chanh, approximately 13 miles south of Tam Ky City, in Quant Tin Province, Republic of Vietnam. At 2:50 AM, the unit was adjusting artillery to provide a predetermined range of fire in the event of enemy contact. During the testing, Michael received a fatal missile wound when an artillery round fell short of its intended target and detonated near his position. May you gain some consolation in knowing that Michael was not subjected to any prolonged suffering.

I sincerely hope that the knowledge that Michael was an exemplary soldier who gave his life assisting his fellowman and in the service of his country will comfort you in this hour of great sorrow.

A memorial service was conducted for your son. Michael's comrades joined me in rendering military honors and final tribute to him. You were in our thoughts and prayers at that time also.

The sincere sympathy of this unit is extended to you in your bereavement.

> Sincerely yours,
> s/H. NORMAN SCHWARZKOPF
> LTC, Infantry
> Commanding

The second paragraph was the only one that interested Peg. The others were mere formalities. She picked up a ball-point pen and carefully read that paragraph again, this time underlining key words: "Tu Chanh . . . 13 . . . Tam Ky . . . Quant Tim . . ." and then, after a pause, she underlined "prolonged."

What did that mean? It could mean that Michael had suffered from anywhere from a few seconds to fifteen minutes or more. Peg abruptly pushed herself away from the kitchen table and walked to the bookcase in the living room. She searched until she found one of her children's paperback pocket dictionaries.

> Prolong, vb1. to lengthen in time: continue (a meeting)
> 2. to lengthen in extent or range (a line)
> syn: protract, extend, elongate

She returned to the letter and tried the sentence again. Michael was not subjected to any *lengthened in time* suffering . . . subjected to any *continued* suffering . . . any *protracted suffering* . . . *extended* suffering, *elongated* suffering. . . . She covered her eyes with her hands. *But he had suffered nevertheless.*

"Near the village of Tu Chanh approximately 13 miles south of Tam Ky City in Quang Tin Province, Republic of Vietnam."

Peg's Hammond map of "VIETNAM and Neighboring Countries" showed Tam Ky about twenty miles north of Chu Lai.

Chu Lai was where Michael got his haircut; it was where he had been when he had telephoned his mother.

"Michael's unit was located in their night defensive position," the letter stated. ". . . At 2:50 AM, the unit was adjusting artillery to provide a predetermined range of fire in the event of enemy contact. . . ." Peg read those two lines again: "Michael's unit was located. . . . The unit was adjusting artillery. . . ." It could only mean that Michael's unit was adjusting the artillery. In other words, someone in Michael's own outfit had called in the artillery that had killed her son. Why? And why at two-fifty—nearly three o'clock in the morning? It didn't make sense unless they were under attack. And yet they said Michael was a nonbattle casualty. The letter clearly implied that the unit hadn't been under attack, that the artillery was called for "in the event of enemy contact." There was nothing in the letter about Vietcong infiltrating radio channels, no mention of the artillery having been from a South Vietnamese unit. In fact, as Peg studied that paragraph, she became more and more suspicious.

Why had Michael's unit, which was not under attack, asked for artillery to be fired over its position at three o'clock in the morning?

How could the one shell have "detonated near his position," have exploded next to Michael and have left him virtually unmarked except for a small hole in his back the size of a pen top or . . . or a bullet?

Why, if Michael's unit had called in the artillery, wasn't he in a foxhole? Why hadn't he been wearing his flak jacket?

Why had the shell fallen short?

Why had the only letter received by the Mullens from anyone even remotely connected with their son been from the battalion commander? Why had they not heard from his company commander? His platoon leader? Why had she not heard from anyone in Michael's unit? He had been dead more than two weeks. Hadn't Michael had any friends?

Peg looked at the letter again. "Approximately 13 miles south of Tam Ky City. . . ." There was something familiar about "Tam Ky." Michael had mentioned it in a letter somewhere. Peg went to the box in which she kept all of Michael's correspondence. Perhaps, she felt, if she read all his letters again very carefully, she might discover some clue she had overlooked, some hint as to what really might have happened to her son.

The following morning Peg Mullen wrote Martin Culpepper, a young man from Waterloo that Michael had mentioned in one of his letters having met in Vietnam, and asked him to help find out what had happened to her son. That same morning a letter arrived from Major General Kenneth G. Wickham, the Army Adjutant General:

I have the honor to inform you that your son has been awarded posthumously the Bronze Star Medal and the Good Conduct Medal.

Prior to death, Michael had been awarded the National Defense Service Medal, Vietnam Service Medal, Vietnam Campaign Medal, Combat Infantryman Badge, the Marksman Badge with rifle, automatic rifle, and machine gun bars.

Arrangements are being made to have these awards presented to you in the near future by a representative of the Commanding General, Fifth United States Army.

My continued sympathy is with you.

"What do you think of the Army suddenly offering us medals?" Peg asked Gene. "That Good Conduct Medal, I mean *really!*"

"It's only a piece of ribbon." Gene shrugged. "We used to laugh about getting them during the war."

"*Posthumously?* Why would they award Michael a Good Conduct Medal after he was dead? It's as though they were giving it to him for not—for not complaining about what they did to him!"

Gene reread the list of medals. "Well, these others, the National Defense Medal, the Vietnam medals, he got those for just being in the Army, for being in Vietnam. But the Bronze Star"—Gene brushed his hand through his silver hair—"that's supposed to be for bravery."

"That doesn't make sense either," Peg said. "Mikey said he'd only ever even seen the enemy, what? Three times? I'll tell you why I think they gave him the Bronze Star. It's because he *died!* I'm sure of it."

The Mullens refused their son's medals.

The next week's mail brought letters of consolation from the commanding general of Michael's American Division, Lloyd B. Ramsey, and from Stanley R. Resor, the Secretary of the Army. The Mullens read them searching for a sign that their son's sacrifice had had some meaning. "We sincerely hope that your burden may be lightened by the knowledge that Michael was a model soldier," Major General Ramsey wrote, "whose actions and conduct brought credit to himself, the Division and the United States Army. . . . Michael was an exemplary soldier whose ability, spirit and dedication to the service earned for him the respect of his associates and superiors alike. . . . We share your burden and we pray that you will find consolation in the sympathy of your friends, your family and your faith."

Secretary of the Army Resor wrote, "We are proud of his military accomplishments and grateful to him for his contribution to our Nation's strength."

Peg tossed both letters onto the kitchen table pile she reserved for "official mail." The letters landed in such a way that Major General Ramsey's overlapped Lieutenant Colonel Schwarzkopf's just enough to display the date "2 Mar 1970" stamped on both. The rubber stamp infuriated her; it was, to Peg, as if some anonymous Army bureaucrat had simply decided, "Okay, on March 2, send all these letters out." Suddenly she noticed something even more disturbing: the "1970" on the two rubber stamps printed just a hair lower than the "2 Mar" and both "Mars" seemed to tilt slightly to the left. Of course, Peg realized, the Army purchased rubber date stamps by the thousands, but was it mere coincidence that the battalion's rubber stamp and the division's contained identical flaws? The more likely explanation, she felt, was that the two letters had originated from the same office. The correspondence had been coordinated for but one reason: the Army had something to hide.

Peg had cause to be skeptical. During the week Michael was killed, seven other Iowans died in Vietnam. If Iowa's eight casualties were about average for the losses from the other forty-nine states, it would indicate that at least 400 Americans died that week in Vietnam. Peg already knew that one planeload of bodies had landed in Oakland on Monday and two more landed Tuesday the week Michael's body arrived. The planes carried 75 bodies each. And yet the official casualty figure released for that entire week listed only 88 Americans killed in Vietnam.

When Peg called the parents of that week's seven other Iowa casualties, she discovered the majority of them, too, had been told their sons were "nonbattle" casualties. But not until she learned that the weekly casualty figure reported on the evening television news was for those killed in action only did Peg begin to suspect why the nonbattle casualties were so high. Nonbattle casualties, such as Michael, weren't counted, and she wondered just how many other so-called nonbattle casualties there might have been. (Correspondents covering the Vietnam War in 1970 were already aware that the Army was classifying as nonbattle casualties any soldier who died in the hospital as a result of wounds.) Peg was convinced the Army was deliberately disguising the number of casualties suffered to prevent the American people from learning their true losses in the war.

That evening the Waterloo Daily *Courier* published a letter critical of the poor turnout given a Vietnam veteran who had come to Waterloo to give a booster talk on the war. The lady accused her fellow citizens of lacking patriotism. Peg's furious reply appeared on Sunday, March 15, under the heading "Parents of G.I. Killed in Viet—'Immoral War'":

Please get down and pray for the boys in Vietnam and for the boys and girls who are not waving the flag in defiance of this cruel and immoral war.

Our boy was buried on March 3 in a beautiful, Christian, "nonmilitary" funeral. We have been criticized because we did not have a military funeral and our decision was made on the fact that the Army took our boy (who was a chemist and not a soldier), trained him to kill, sent him to Vietnam and on February 21st, they told us, he was killed by friendly forces—accidentally, we will never believe.

Do you realize how many thousands of American boys have been lost in this manner—denied the decency of being killed by the enemy? These boys' deaths are listed as "nonbattle"—are they included in the casualty lists? Do we know how many bodies come back to Oakland each week—does the number of deaths tie in with the casualty lists? Think about this. Please. . . . "Think." . . . "Read." . . . "Study." . . . Evaluate this war.

                                                        Mr. and Mrs. Gene Mullen

On Wednesday, March 18, three days after their letter appeared, Nick Lamberto, a feature writer for the Des Moines *Register*, telephoned wanting to know why Peg had questioned the casualty lists. She explained how Michael had been on a search and destroy mission, was at a night defensive position when the artillery shell had killed him and "wasn't considered a battle casualty, so he wasn't counted."

Because of Peg's letter, a *Register* researcher had gone through the newspaper files and compared the Pentagon's casualty count against the newspaper's own. As of March 1, Lamberto told Peg, the Pentagon listed 532 Iowans killed in Vietnam. According to the researcher, the *Register* files indicated the Pentagon figure was 129 casualties short.

CHAPTER 4

The morning after Nick Lamberto's telephone call, Peg Mullen returned from the mailbox with a letter from Martin Culpepper in Vietnam. Culpepper's letter was the first the Mullens had received from anyone who had served in Charlie Company with their son. Michael had been dead a month, and they still had not heard from any members of Michael's platoon or from the ROTC lieutenant he had mentioned in his letter or his company commander. Peg had written the Pentagon complaining, "It's just too damned bad that we can't find out who lived and died with our son. There's no communication and I firmly believe my son had at least *one* friend in Vietnam." The Pentagon never answered.

Through Culpepper Peg discovered for the first time that six or seven other soldiers had been wounded and one other young man had been killed:

It was an air burst, it hit in between your son's bunker and another bunker. The round burst in the air when it hit a tree in between the foxholes. This was about 2:15 AM on Feb 18 before daylight. It was a short round that killed him. Meaning the round didn't travel the distance it was supposed to travel. He was not killed by enemy forces, but by an accident.

Culpepper explained that DTs (defensive targets) were set up in advance in "an area or place where they call in artillery for support in case you are attacked. From this area they can direct it to any place they want." One line of Culpepper's particularly intrigued Peg: "They normally shot about 200 to 300 meters away from you, they used to do this almost every night until the accident." They *used* to, but they stopped. Two killed, six or seven wounded, never anything in the newspaper about it, no investigation, no communication with anyone but Culpepper—whom Peg had discovered only by chance—and after that accident the Army didn't fire DTs again. Why not?

The obvious reason, Peg believed, was that what had happened was so wrong, so inexcusable the Army didn't want anybody to find out about it. That is why no one had been permitted to write, why the newspaper stories had been blacked out, and why the letters from the battalion and division commander had been coordinated. In a postscript to his three-page hand-written letter Culpepper added, "If the army's story is different please let me know." Clearly Culpepper would not be surprised to learn that the Army had lied. His letter closed:

Even though the Lord has taken him away from you, we both will carry the memory of him in our hearts. The loss is great and nothing can replace him, but I hope the Lord will find peace in your heart. I would appreciate it if you would read in the New Testament, I Thessalonians, Chapter 4. The sixteenth through the eighteenth verse and may it comfort your heart.

Love,

Martin L. Culpepper

Peg wondered whether Culpepper had found some passage in the Bible which would provide her with even more information, something which he dared not write openly but instead could only hint at.

Peg located the section in their family Bible.

16. For the Lord himself shall descend from heaven with a shout, with the voice of the archangel, and with the trump of God: and the dead in Christ shall rise first;
17. Then we which are alive and remain shall be caught up together with them in the clouds, to meet the Lord in the air; and so shall we ever be with the Lord.
18. Wherefore comfort one another with these words.

She studied the three verses for a few minutes, then gave up. Except for the "descend from heaven with a shout," which *might* have referred to the artillery shell, there didn't seem to be anything she could interpret as a code.

On Tuesday, March 17, the death certificate demanded by the Mullens arrived. The document, a standard DA form 10-249, forwarded from the U.S. Army Mortuary at Danang, was dated 18 February 1970, and below the statement "I have viewed the remains of the deceased and death occurred at the time indicated from the causes as stated above" was the signature of John S. Schechter, MD, Captain, Co D. 23D Medical Bn. The certificate listed Mr. and Mrs. Oscar *T.* Mullen as next of kin; the mode of death, "accident"; the interval between onset and death, "unknown"; and the cause of death ("enter only one cause per line"), "missile wound of chest." The space reserved for "circumstances surrounding death due to external causes" was blank, as was the space indicating whether or not an autopsy had been performed. Although the date and hour of death, *0250 hrs 18 Feb 70*, and the map coordinates for the place of death, *BT 3660 15* (the hillside overlooking the village of Tu Chanh), confirmed the information given them in Lieutenant Colonel Schwarzkopf's letter, the death certificate did nothing to allay the Mullens' suspicions.

Why was the space reserved for "circumstances surrounding death" blank? Michael, the Mullens had been told, was killed when an artillery round fell short. Why, if Michael had not been "subjected to any prolonged suffering" was the "interval between onset and death" unknown? Most disturbing of all, however, was the question why, if Michael's only wound according to Tom Loomis, the funeral director, had been that small hole in his back near his right kidney, did Captain Schechter list Michael's cause of death a "missile wound of *chest*?" The Mullens wrote back requesting a complete medical report on their son's death.

Two days later the Mullens received notification from First Lieutenant

Arthur A. Belefonte of the U.S. Army Personal Property Depot in Saigon that Michael's posessions had been collected and sent and would reach them soon. Enclosed was a USARV form 438 inventory of Michael's belongings. Nowhere on the list was the $200 dollar camera sent Michael by his uncle Howard Goodyear. Although the inventory did list a "watch, Seiko without band," neither watch nor camera was ever returned.

The simple cardboard carton reached Waterloo on Saturday morning, March 21. A friend who worked in the post office voluntarily drove the package to the farm himself. He refused Peg's offer of a cup of coffee, explaining that he had to return to work, but Gene and Peg knew he understood they would want to be alone.

The carton lay on the kitchen table between Michael's parents. Neither moved toward it until finally Peg pushed it over to Gene and said, "You do it. Go on."

Gene carefully untied the package's knotted strings, then slowly, almost reverently, removed the top. They began to sift through the empty, folded clothing, 2 Shirts, khaki; 1 Cap, Garrison; 1 Necktie; 1 Pair of gloves. They found the fingernail file and clippers they had joked about (Michael had always kept himself so immaculate that his parents had speculated he would even clean his fingernails in the jungle); Michael's shaving kit with his worn, soft-bristled toothbrush inside; a pair of sunglasses; 1 Belt, web with buckle; 1 Coin purse with 2 souvenir U.S. pennies; 1 Insignia, U.S. brass; 1 Nameplate, plastic; a hairbrush which someone had cleaned; Michael's prayerbook, sweat-stained and bent to the contours of his hip. There were three rosaries; one was simply string tied in knots for each of the ten prayers. Gene decided he would give that one to Johnny; the other two to Patricia and Mary.

Peg was silently sorting through the papers, the driver's licenses, addresses, receipts, the two photographs of his former girl friend Caroline Roby. She pulled out the 1 Pair of shoes, dress oxfords and put them aside, and then she lifted up a small bronze-colored religious medallion hanging from a chain. "Oh-h, Gene. . . ."

It was the medal Gene had given Michael at the airport. He took it from Peg and gently, tenderly, sadly lowered it around his neck again.

A letter from Creighton W. Abrams, the commanding general of the United States Military Assistance Command in Vietnam, arrived the following week. Peg sat holding it in both hands: "It is my hope that you will find a measure of solace in knowing your son gave his life for a noble cause, the defense of liberty in the free world. Rest assured that we who remain here in Vietnam will continue our efforts to bring peace to this troubled land so that your son's sacrifice will not have been in vain." Peg crumpled the paper in a rage; then, because she thought Gene might like to read it, she carefully smoothed out the page again.

Peg had mailed Michael's letters to the Des Moines *Register*, and the editors decided to run them in their Easter Sunday edition. On March 27, Good Friday, a *Register* editorial headed "Why? And for What?" devoted to Michael's letters concluded:

He was in a night defensive position when artillery fire from friendly forces landed in the area and killed him.

Why? and For what? his parents still ask.

So far some 41,000 Americans and 102,000 "friendlies" have been killed in this futile war. These are not statistics, they are individual human beings—sons and husbands and brothers.

Nick Lamberto, the *Register* reporter who had earlier interviewed Peg about her Waterloo *Courier* letter questioning the casualty figures, telephoned shortly after Peg returned from the stone carver. She complained that only "the cream of the crop" were sent to Vietnam, that "if you got a girl in trouble, or were too fat, or too thin, you didn't have to go." She spoke to Lamberto for about fifteen minutes, and it wasn't until she had hung up the telephone and cooled off that she began to worry about what she had said. By the time Gene returned from John Deere she had telephoned her sister Louise, who lived next door to Lamberto in Des Moines, to find out more about him.

"Lamberto's going to kill me, Gene," Peg said that night. "He really is. I didn't find out until this afternoon that he was a hawk on the war."

"What can he do to you?" Gene asked.

"I just think he's going to print things that will cause me trouble." Peg thought for a moment, "Maybe I'll drive to Des Moines tomorrow and see if I can talk to him in person." Peg did meet with Lamberto and asked if he would delete a couple of statements.

"Lamberto just laughed at me," she reported back to Gene. "And when I left, he said, 'Well, have faith, hope and charity, Peg Mullen.'"

Michael's letters and Lamberto's interview appeared in the *Register* on Easter Sunday. Lamberto's piece began: "A distraught mother, bitter over the death of her son in South Vietnam, has vowed to use his insurance money 'to save the boys still over there.'"

By this time the Mullens had received the bulk of Michael's insurance policies. The $10,000 U.S. Army policy had been split four ways: $2,500 each to Gene, Peg, Caroline Roby and the Don Bosco High School. In addition, Michael carried a $10,000 policy with the Knights of Columbus (Gene Mullen later tried to invoke the double indemnity clause since the Army had ruled Michael's death "accidental." He did not collect) and $980 from a $1,000 policy with the Federal Life Insurance Company.

The Mullens had also received the money Michael had withdrawn and converted to traveler's checks five days before he was killed and a U.S. Army check for $2,014.20, a gratuity payment representing six months' projected salary to defray the cost of his funeral. It was this gratuity pay and not, as Lamberto reported, the insurance money which the Mullens had decided to utilize in their fight against the war. Lamberto wrote that Peg had vowed to use $5,000 "to ferret out the truth about the war. I have no organized plan," he quoted her as saying, "but I'm writing letters and making phone calls, telling our story." Lamberto then reprinted the majority of Peg's letter to the Waterloo paper but added two sections based on his telephone interview one of which Peg denies ever having said: "They accuse us of a massacre at My Lai. That's a farce. Our boys had a right to kill those people. How many Americans have been killed by 'local' citizens over there?"

The other passage was the one Peg had tried to have him delete, the part where she had spoken of the boys who had gotten girls into trouble or were too fat to be sent to Vietnam.

Monday, March 30, the day after Michael's letter and Lamberto's article appeared, two local television stations, KCRG-TV of Cedar Rapids and KWWL-TV of Waterloo, arrived at the Mullens' farm to interview them. Gene and Peg were good material: angry, articulate, emotional and defiantly opposed to the war. At a time when the American Midwest was the bastion of the Silent Majority and the only real opposition to the war existed among the draft-age young and their college professors, the Mullens represented a newsworthy exception. And, the Mullens were quick to recognize they could take advantage of the media, too.

The television reporters had come only because of the interviews and letters which had already appeared in print. Peg and Gene realized that the newspapers therefore provided the cheapest and most effective platform from which other, broader outlets such as radio and television coverage became accessible. Gene now began to consider the possibility of purchasing newspaper space through an advertisement.

On April 1 Peg joined a group of Iowa antiwar activists on a plane trip around Iowa to publicize and campaign for the passage of the Hatfield-

McGovern amendment (609), cosponsored by Iowa's Senator Harold Hughes, which attempted to set a definite time limit on American presence in Vietnam. That same day, in Vietnam, the Communists launched their spring offensive. By the end of that week American forces had suffered their heaviest losses in seven months.

On Monday, April 3, Peg mimeographed the following letter to the many who had written to express support or to say they also had lost sons or husbands in Vietnam.

Dear Friends:

We wish it were possible to answer each letter personally, but it can't be done at this time. We'll try later. We have too much work to do in carrying on our protest—each hour that is lost haunts us.

Michael's story has also appeared in the Kansas City *Times* and the Columbia *Missourian.* We have someone taking it to the St. Louis *Globe-Democrat* and the Milwaukee *Sentinel.* If any of you have contacts with large newspapers such as Omaha, Minneapolis, etc., please let us know.

We feel that letter writing to Washington is a waste of time. I have done it for years and all of you seem to have been pouring out your anguish to Congress and to the President and it is like knocking your head against a stone wall. The only response I get is from Senator Hughes and he is certainly behind all of us.

We apologize to those parents who feel we played up the plight of the college graduates. . . . We felt we could not tell your story, only the one we know best, ours! Please tell YOUR story of the fine 19 or 20 year old boy you lost—only you can tell it. It costs no money . . . the news media want to donate their facilities.

We need your ideas—not your money—and thanks so much.

s/Mr. and Mrs. Gene Mullen

Now when the Mullens drove into La Porte, they noticed people avoided them, ducked into stores when they saw Peg or Gene on the street. The townspeople knew the Mullens would want to talk only about the war. Even John, their only child who still lived at home, was finding it increasingly difficult to be around his parents. No longer able to bear hearing them go on and on about the war, he began giving one excuse after another to get out of the house.

One night in the middle of the first week of April Gene was sitting at the kitchen table making little marks on a yellow pad. He and Peg had been discussing their advertisement again. "How many Iowa deaths have there been now?" he asked.

"Altogether? Since the beginning of the war?" Peg thought for a moment. "I suppose somewhere around seven hundred by now. At least that many, don't you think?"

Gene did not answer. He continued to doodle on the pad. Suddenly he said, *"Crosses!"*

"What?"

"A full page of crosses!" Gene said excitedly. "Think of it! Just crosses, a cross for every boy who died in Vietnam. A page full, a half page, whatever we can afford."

The Mullens' half-page Des Moines *Register* advertisement appeared on April 12, 1970, on page five of the first news section, and exploded habitually taciturn Sunday breakfast table conversations throughout the state. There was a half-inch-high banner black headline:

A SILENT message to fathers and mothers of Iowa:

And below, in slightly smaller but still boldface type:

We have been dying for nine, long, miserable years in Vietnam in an undeclared war . . . how many more lives do you wish to sacrifice because of your SILENCE?

Two inches to the right of the "SILENCE?" was a small black cross and beneath it, the epitaph "Sgt. Michael E. Mullen—killed by friendly fire."

Then came the crosses. Fourteen rows containing forty-nine crosses each, a fifteenth row with twenty-seven and space left open for more.

"These 714 crosses," a legend explained, "represent the 714 Iowans who have died in Vietnam."

Near the bottom-left-hand corner of the page was printed: *"In memory of Vietnam War Dead whom our son joined on February 17, 1970 . . . and to those awaiting the acceptable sacrifice in 1970. . . ."* On the opposite side appeared the credit: "Sponsored by Mr. and Mrs. Gene Mullen, La Porte City, Iowa."

That Sunday morning Peg had attended the five o'clock mass at Father Shimon's Sacred Heart Church. Gene Mullen awoke at seven, carried the newspaper into the house and left it opened to the advertisement for Peg to see upon her return. She took a quick, satisfied look, asked Gene to wake her if there was any response and went to bed. Peg got less than an hour's sleep.

Iowans were already busy telephoning neighbors, friends, relatives. College students were calling their parents; fathers were arguing with sons. The Mullens' telephone began ringing at eight o'clock and never let up. United Press International interviewed the Mullens at nine. At ten a Des Moines television station newscaster complained he had been trying to reach Peg all morning but had had so many incoming calls himself about their advertisement he hadn't been able to get an outside line.

The Mullens were overwhelmed by the response to their advertisement. Virtually every Iowa radio and television station featured it on their evening news. The UPI interview was carried by wire service newspapers throughout the country. Local television stations again sent reporters to the Mullens' farm. Television network commentator Paul Harvey, using the *Register* page as a backdrop, told how the Army's gratuity check had paid for the Mullens' antiwar protest and how the Iowa farm family's anger expressed his own growing dissatisfaction with the war.

Peg learned from Culpepper that publication of Michael's letters and the Lamberto interview in the *Register* had reached Vietnam. "I've just come from Bayonet to the field," Culpepper wrote Peg. "In the rear they told me about your articles. I'm glad to see that your son told how it was and you had it published so the public can see what goes on over here. I'm glad that you stand up for us boys in Vietnam." Culpepper also told Peg that if anyone asked where she was getting her information from, she should "tell them about me. They can't do anything. It might get me out of the field."

Peg was enormously gratified by Culpepper's letter. He had provided vindication for the antagonisms her outspokenness had generated. She was "stand[ing] up for us boys in Vietnam." She was even more encouraged when she subsequently learned that soldiers who had seen their advertisement were writing back for fifty more copies at a time. The Mullens' antiwar protest was being tacked up on orderly room walls all over South Vietnam.

The next time Peg Mullen heard from Martin Culpepper she had to read his letter twice to make sure she had understood it properly: anyone from Michael's old unit could be court-martialed for writing the Mullens. Any correspondence with the Mullens had to be copied and a duplicate retained by the Army. "Anything sent to you," Culpepper wrote, "can be censored as we are in a war zone." Culpepper had misspelled "censored" and someone, with a handwriting quite different, had crossed out Culpepper's misspelling and corrected it. Peg felt the entire tone of his letter was so different from Culpepper's previous ones she was sure it had been dictated—and dictated by whoever had corrected the spelling, presumably the censor. No one had ever opened or censored letters to the Mullens before; it was, to Peg, an indication of a new policy—a policy in response to the Des Moines *Register* interview, her letters and the advertisement confirming that the Army's attitude was that the Mullens, too, were the enemy.

Obsessed by her conviction that she and her family were the targets of a conspiracy on the part of the United States Army to prevent them from learning the details of their son's death, Peg fought back harder. She sought more proof that the military and the Nixon administration were deliberately preventing the American public from knowing the truth about the war. She had been able to locate Fred Wilson, Michael's friend from NCO school, who was now with an infantry company in Vietnam. Wilson wrote Peg about Ed Gardiner, a young man who had gone through NCO school with Michael: "He is with a reconnaissance unit in the 3/22 working around Tay Ninh. He has been crossing the border into Cambodia since early April, when the 'Administration' was saying no U.S. troops were in Cambodia." Wilson also noted that lately the list of casualties "Killed as a Result of Hostile Action" and "Died not as a Result of Hostile Action" carried by the *Army Times* were of about equal length and that in the 4th Infantry Division "more people are being killed in accidents than by the enemy."

Two weeks earlier Peg had castigated Iowa Senator Jack Miller for letting ten weeks pass since Michael's death without any expression of sympathy. "You always find time to vote in the Senate in favor of those issues which condemned our sons to death in Vietnam," Peg wrote, "how is it you are unable to find time to write these dead soldiers' grieving parents?"

The Senator's reply arrived one week after a letter from the Army Finance Center announcing the deduction of nine days' pay from Michael's final paycheck for excess leave taken.

Dear Mrs. Mullen:

Replying to your letter of May 5th, I naturally extend my deepest sympathy to you over the loss of your son. I have written a good many letters of sympathy—not only to people like you, but to parents and wives of our prisoners of war. Also, you should know that many Members of Congress have shared some tragedies and concerns of people like you. Our son-in-law flew over 120 combat missions in Vietnam, and fortunately returned.

It has been my observation that, with few exceptions, the persons bearing the real burden of this war—the men who have been doing the fighting, the wounded, their wives and parents—have been the least complaining of anyone over this tragic war.

I regret that you are one of the exceptions.

Very truly yours,
s/Jack Miller

Peg was convinced that the high casualties Charlie Company was suffering were entirely Lieutenant Colonel Schwarzkopf's fault. She recalled Michael's letter written late that previous October: "We are supposed to have the BN Co. out here sometime this week—kind of a laugh, for they live in a dream world! They have to have figures and nobody knows what is a VC or a plain ignorant villager, at least in this area." And Culpepper in one of his earlier letters mentioned that Charlie Company had been "harassed a little bit and it wasn't much fun" during Michael's last stand-down. Peg wrote Schwarzkopf an angry condemnation of the Army in Vietnam, his harassment of Michael during the stand-down and swore her determination to avenge her son's death. She explained how she had taken Michael's gratuity pay and spent it on the antiwar advertisement (which she enclosed along with excerpts from Michael's letters). She wrote that neither she nor Gene would rest until they learned who was responsible for Michael's loss. Although Peg did not accuse Schwarzkopf specifically, she left no doubt that she felt he was at least partially to blame not only for Michael's death but also for the high rate of casualties incurred by his battalion since.

What Peg did not realize was that Schwarzkopf had not taken command of the battalion until December. The battalion shortly thereafter received a new brigade commander as well: Colonel Joseph Clemons, whose unhappy assignment in a previous conflict, that of a young infantry lieutenant during the waning interminable peace negotiations of the Korean War, had been portrayed by Gregory Peck in the movie made from Brigadier General S.L.A. Marshall's book *Pork Chop Hill.* Shortly after Michael was killed, Colonel Clemons shifted Schwarzkopf's battalion out of the "Rocket Pocket" and sent them south to relieve the 5th Battalion of the 46th Infantry in the Batangan Peninsula. The new area of operations (AO) was a fifteen-by-twenty-five-square-kilometer section of the peninsula which included My Lai. The Batangan Peninsula had been notorious since the French Indochina colonial wars for its booby traps and overlapping minefields. Colonel Clemons had decided to rotate Schwartzkopf's 1st Battalion of the 6th Infantry with the 5th of the 46th because that battalion's men had become so leery, their morale so shattered by the minefields and booby traps, the brigade commander no longer felt the 5/46th was effective.

Lieutenant Colonel Schwarzkopf requested and received from the 5/46th an overlay depicting the minefields in his new Batangan Peninsula AO. When the overlay was unrolled and positioned on his map, Schwarzkopf, whose previous tour with the Vietnamese Airborne had taken him all across South Vietnam in 1965, would later remark that the Batangan Peninsula was the worst experience he had ever been through in his life. It was an entirely different sort of AO from the one in which Michael had been killed. The battalion's whole *modus operandi* changed. The primary enemy was no longer ambushes; it was minefields and booby traps. "It was terrifying to me," Schwarzkopf said about the Batangan Peninsula, "and I know it was terrifying to the men."

On May 28 Bravo Company of Schwarzkopf's battalion became trapped in a minefield, and Schwarzkopf himself was wounded.

CHAPTER 5

Early in May, the same week American troops were ordered into Cambodia, the Des Moines *Register* reported a group of Iowa clergy and laymen planned to travel to the Capitol to lobby in support of the Hatfield-McGovern amendment. The group called themselves CALCAV, an acronym for Clergy and Laymen Concerned About Vietnam. A couple of days after the *Register* article, a man telephoned Peg that if she were willing to join the CALCAV group, he would pay her expenses to Washington. Peg did not know the man and declined, saying she did not think she was "the type clergymen would want along."

The man urged Peg to reconsider, but when she seemed adamant, he told her, "If you should change your mind, my offer still stands."

During the next week, nothing whatsoever occurred to diminish Peg's suspicion that the military was deliberately falsifying the casualty counts. And when letters from soldiers spoke of deceptions and censorship and urged her to continue to "stand up for us boys in Vietnam," Peg knew she had to go to Washington, that she could not avoid going. She telephoned the CALCAV group's organizers in Iowa City and asked if she might join them. The group eagerly begged Peg to come. They had been worried that there would be too many college-age participants and that the seriousness of their purpose would be diminished if their image was that of just another college protest group. "To tell you the truth, Mrs. Mullen," the spokesman told her, "we want all the middle-aged people we can get."

Peg laughed. "Well, thanks. I guess."

She telephoned the man who had volunteered to pay her fare and said she would accept his offer, but she wouldn't fly. She would travel to Washington by bus. "God bless you, Peg," the man said. He sent her $50.

186

Peg was still packing when Gene returned from feeding the hogs. He stood watching her until Peg looked up from her suitcase and asked, "You don't mind my going, do you?"

"Peg, you have to go."

"Johnny's all packed, and we'll meet Patricia in Iowa City. You'll mail those letters for me?"

"You know I will."

Even in the midst of her preparations Peg could not forget her correspondence. Repeatedly she would interrupt her packing, her discussion of the trip to remind Gene that the letters were to be sent registered mail and not to forget to request a receipt. Almost as often as she mentioned the letters she expressed concern that Gene should take care of himself. "I've put some meat loaf in the freezer for you. Take it out before you leave for Deere's."

And Gene, proud of Peg as well as anxious about her, urged her to take care of herself.

"Oh, I will." She smiled. "Patricia and John will see to that."

Finally, as Peg was about to leave, Gene hugged her and told her, 'Give 'em hell."

In Washington the morning they arrived they met first with the Moratorium Committee at the Mayflower Hotel, and Peg writhed while the Moratorium spokesman instructed the CALCAV group on how to lobby. Peg did not like anyone to tell her how to do anything. She was impatient to get inside those Senators' offices so she could tell them what she thought. After the meeting she hurried to the Senate Office Building ahead of the others. Their meeting with Senator Hughes was scheduled for one o'clock. Peg simply roamed the halls, killing time. She passed one open door and peered inside. The office was filled with Rath Ham advertisements and canned hams. Rath Hams was in Waterloo. Peg walked in and asked, "Whose office is this?"

A secretary looked up, "It's Senator Miller's of Iowa."

"Well," Peg said, "I should have known I guess."

"Are you with the CALCAV group?" the secretary asked.

"I sure am."

"May I ask who you are?"

"I'm Peg Mullen."

There was an audible groan among the office staff which the secretary ignored. "Your organization asked for a meeting with the Senator, but at the time we were unable to make any definite plans. However, you can tell them now that we will be able to see you all at three."

"That's fine," Peg said. "We've a meeting a few minutes from now with Senator Hughes."

"Oh, well, then, we'll arrange for the meeting to take place in the same hearing room."

The CALCAV's meeting with Senator Hughes lasted an hour and a half. Since the group knew that Hughes, as one of the cosponsors, obviously favored the Hatfield-McGovern amendment, the discussion moved to other topics before the Senator excused himself saying he had to return to his work. Peg and the others had a few minutes to wait until Senator Miller was to join them. Before he arrived, his secretary entered and, walking directly to Peg, asked whether she would like to meet Miller.

Peg, embarrassed to have been singled out, explained that she had met the Senator the year before. "If the Senator wants to meet anybody," Peg said, "I think he should be introduced to the young man who arranged the trip. He's sitting right up over there."

As the secretary went forward to meet the CALCAV organizer, an attractive middle-aged woman drifted into the hearing room and sat down beside Peg. They struck up a conversation, and the woman explained she was originally from Iowa but lived now in Virginia. They were still talking when Miller's secretary suddenly returned, took Peg by the arm and pulled her up to the front of the hearing room.

"Senator Miller?" the secretary said. "I want you to meet Peg Mullen."

Both Peg and the Senator were embarrassed. His face turned red and Peg's even redder. When she shook his hand, he gave her a limp, deadfish handshake before turning away.

Unlike the meeting with Senator Hughes, the meeting with Senator Miller was filled with challenges and accusations. Peg told Miller she thought Congress should simply end the war immediately. "We should bring all the troops home bang! Right now! There's no need to stay another hour, another day or lose another life."

Senator Miller glared at Peg. "You're a dreamer, Mrs. Mullen!" he said. "You live in a dreamworld with your theory on ending this war!"

"So do you, Senator," Peg replied.

"Well, Mrs. Mullen, your theory is an obsession with you," Senator Miller said angrily. "It would never work; it can't work. It won't work."

Peg shrugged and tuned the Senator out.

Afterward Peg telephoned Gene to tell him what had happened since she had left the farm.

"I got the casualty list from Senator Fulbright's office," Gene told her, "the one for the week Michael died. Michael's name wasn't on it."

"*Wasn't* on it? Are you sure?" Peg asked.

"Of course I'm sure."

They spoke for a while about others missing from that list—casualties which might have resulted from South Vietnamese artillery firing upon American forces. While they were getting in touch with families whose sons had died on February 18, they learned four helicopters had been shot down with at least thirty men on board that same day and that there were at least five sites where mysterious shellings had occurred. But when it was confirmed that Michael had been killed by American, not ARVN, artillery, they had quit their search. Peg told Gene she would try to see Senator Fulbright the following morning.

She spoke instead with James Lowenstein, Fulbright's military liaison aide, and told him the casualty list sent her had been incomplete.

"What do you mean 'incomplete'?" Lowenstein asked.

"I mean," Peg said, pausing deliberately, "our . . . son's . . . name . . . isn't . . . on . . . it! I know something fishy's going on. Isn't there some way I could speak directly to whoever makes up these casualty lists? I can't believe my son's death wouldn't be recorded somewhere," Peg said. "And if it isn't, then how many others have there been like him? How many boys have never been counted?"

Lowenstein seemed hesitant to contact the Pentagon any further about the casualty lists, so Peg suggested she would call them herself. A young man with the CALCAV group telephoned the Pentagon for her and was able to arrange a briefing for the following afternoon.

Although the young CALCAV member had arranged the briefing for twenty members of the CALCAV group, twice that number showed up. To Peg's outrage, just within the front entrance a display booth had been set up to "sell" the Cambodian war. The rear projection screen showed American GIs chopping through the jungle and breaking open crates of captured supplies while a brisk and hearty narrator described how successful the operation was. Patricia, standing next to her mother, said, "They're neglecting to show one thing: the American boys dying there. There aren't any pictures of dead bodies."

The briefing room appeared familiar. It was the same one, Peg thought, they used for their briefings on TV. Since the seats were nearly filled, she perched on an oak table near the back. A man asked her if she wouldn't like them to bring her a chair, but she declined. Then she leaned toward a colonel standing next to her and asked whether the three men on the podium would be delivering the briefing. The colonel said they would and identified them as Daniel Z. Henkin, an Assistant Secretary of Defense for Public Affairs; Jerry W. Friedheim, Henkin's deputy assistant; and then-Brigadier General Daniel "Chappie" James, Jr., USAF, the senior military officer in Henkin's office and chief of information at the Pentagon.

"And what is your name, sir?" Peg asked.

"I'm Lieutenant Colonel Giorgi, Air Force."

Assistant Secretary Henkin commenced with a discussion of the Cambodian operation. Peg had the feeling she had heard it all before, that it was, in effect, the same justification delivered by the President on TV. Henkin showed the same maps, the same photographs, the same rationale. Peg listened wearily to the same promises of success. Throughout Henkin's talk Peg had the sensation that the CALCAV group was being photographed, that the briefing was being taped. Although no evidence was in sight, she learned that others in her group had had the same reaction. At Henkin's conclusion he asked if there were any questions. Peg's hand shot into the air. "Why didn't you tell us we've been in Cambodia for weeks, for months before Nixon went on television and said we were?"

"How do you know we were?" Henkin asked.

"Because every mother who had a son there was written by her boy that he was in Cambodia. I found out because when something like this happens, these people will write or call me. I heard from mothers whose sons"—Peg shuffled through some papers—"whose sons were with the 198th Brigade of the Americal, the 25th Infantry, the Marines—"

"Ma'am?" Henkin interrupted.

"The 5th Infantry, the 47th, the 1st Air Cav, the 11th Armored—"

"Yes, ma'am," Henkin said, "and what is your question?"

"My question, Mr. Henkin, is do you *deny* that American boys were in Cambodia for weeks or months before the President said they were?"

"No, you're right," Henkin said. "American troops were there."

"I don't know why we're even talking about Cambodia at all," Peg continued. "My son lived and died in 'Eye' Corps, First Corps. You people have been fighting a war there for almost ten years now and you haven't accomplished a thing! You still can't go a mile from the beach without getting your head blown off! So what are you worrying about Cambodia for? Why don't you clean up 'Eye' Corps first?"

"You seem to be quite well informed about the war," Henkin said. "Next question, please."

For about two hours the Iowans questioned the Pentagon briefers. Each member of the group had some special area of interest, some aspect of the Southeast Asian war which he had studied. Peg leaned over to the Air Force lieutenant colonel by her side and asked him to supply her with that week's casualty list in Vietnam. "I haven't had a chance to read this morning's paper," Peg said, "but I know the figures are released today."

Lieutenant Colonel Giorgi leaned back and asked a man in civilian clothes sitting behind Peg if releasing that information would be all right. Peg was already suspicious of the civilian's function. Throughout the briefing he had been taking notes, and several times Peg had caught him pointing to one member of the CALCAV group or another so that Henkin would know who to let talk. When one of the Iowans would get out of hand, it had been the civilian who would signal Henkin to cut the questioner off. Peg turned to look at the man and their eyes met. He appraised Peg coolly, then nodded. Lieutenant Colonel Giorgi excused himself and left the room.

Several minutes later Giorgi returned and told Peg that the number of men killed that week in Vietnam was 125.

"Is that *all* who died, Colonel?" Peg asked. "I want the total number of people who died there, *not* just the number that you publish."

Lieutenant Colonel Giorgi again leaned back to the man in civilian clothes and a moment later left the room a second time. When he returned, he whispered to Peg that the figure would be twenty-five more. Peg's hand shot back up. "I have a question," she said.

Henkin recognized her, saying, "May I ask you something first? Are you a newspaperwoman?"

"No, sir," Peg laughed. "I'm only a simple farmer's wife. As a matter of fact, we finished planting the corn just before I came down here."

Henkin looked embarrassed and asked what her question had been.

"There's something I want to know about these casualty lists," Peg said. "Who isn't telling the truth? Is it your office? Or is it the press who isn't telling us each week how many died in Vietnam?"

"I'm not sure I understand what you mean," Henkin said.

"Here's what I mean," Peg said coldly, "I just asked this gentleman sitting next to me, Colonel Giorgi, how many died this week and he gave me two different figures. First he said one hundred and twenty-five died. A few minutes later he came back and added twenty-five more. This is what I mean. As far as the public is concerned, one hundred twenty-five died, but," Peg said, "one hundred and fifty mothers and fathers know their sons died! This is what I just . . . can't . . . stand! I happen to be the mother of one of those boys you didn't count!"

Lieutenant Colonel Giorgi suggested Peg accompany him to his office and he would try to straighten her out.

"No," Peg said. "I don't want to go to anybody's office. I want to know who's telling us these lies?"

"Won't you please come, Mrs. Mullen?" Giorgi asked. He was joined by another younger man in civilian clothes. "We can take you directly to the office where these casualty lists are compiled. Any question you might have, all the information will be right there on hand."

Peg relented and was led down more Pentagon corridors until she was halted before a door which opened into a huge tan room, a room so large Peg believed her entire La Porte City farmhouse might have fitted inside.

The open space in the middle of the room was filled by long oak tables lined up end to end like flatcars spanning the entire length of the room. On the tops of these tables papers had been stacked so tightly that practically no wood showed. When Peg stepped closer to see what these papers might be, she suddenly realized to her horror that each paper was a casualty list, and she sagged back against the doorframe for support. She could not even count how many tables there were. She saw only that the room was filled with tables, the tables filled with casualty lists, the single-spaced casualty lists filled with dead boys' names.

"Colonel, please," she said, holding up her hand. "Please, I don't want to see any more." She hurried past him out the door.

"Mrs. Mullen," he called after her, and caught up with her in corridor, "Mrs. Mullen? What did you really want to know?"

Peg leaned back against the corridor wall. "I wanted to know. . . . I wanted to know why you lied to Senator Fulbright. Why you sent him half a list instead of a whole one?"

"Mrs. Mullen," Giorgi said unhappily, "I still don't understand. I don't know what you want. What you mean."

"All right, Colonel," Peg said wearily. "I want you to send me the names of all the boys who died the week of February 15, 1970, in Vietnam. I want the names and that's all I want—except to get out of here."

Later that night Peg Mullen and her children boarded their bus for the twenty-two-hour drive to Iowa. She arrived back at her farm late Friday.

On Saturday, June 13, Peg heard from the Air Force lieutenant colonel who had taken her to the Pentagon casualty room.

"I am sorry to say that nowhere is there a list of U.S. casualties which is kept by the date," Giorgi wrote. "Your request is the only one to develop such a listing for the week [your son died]."

Lieutenant Colonel Giorgi did, however, enclose a "List of Casualties Incurred by U.S. Military Personnel in connection with the Conflict in Vietnam by Home State of Record." The document listed those Iowans who had died in Vietnam between January 1 and April 30, 1970. Twenty-seven Army men, four Marines, and one sailor had been killed in action. Six soldiers and one sailor were nonbattle casualties.

The following week a letter arrived from Lieutenant Colonel H. Norman Schwarzkopf in Vietnam. The letter, written in response to Peg's angry blast of three weeks before, told the Mullens nothing at all. Its whole tone was strange, guarded, impersonal: "I sincerely hope that I can be of some assistance in answering your questions. . . ." That was the sort of line one expected from a salesclerk in response to some shopper's query. "Michael's platoon leader was in a defensive position approximately eight to ten feet away from him. . . . The Company Commander, the Company First Sergeant, and the Battalion Chaplain were also located within thirty feet of Michael's position. . . ." No names. Just their titles. Why weren't the Mullens told who these people were? To Peg the answer was obvious: if she knew their names, she could write them. "Unfortunately, United States Army, Vietnam policy," Schwarzkopf's letter continued, "does not allow me to release the names of its servicemen," a convenient policy, Peg felt, should the Army have something to hide.

Schwarzkopf's response to Peg's outrage at Michael's harassment during his final stand-down read as if it had been copied from some training circular: "It is the policy of this command to utilize stand-downs for training and relaxation," to "maintain the health and welfare of our men," to "maintain the proficiency and skill of each soldier. . . ." What sort of man would write such an insensitive, detached letter to grieving parents? What sort of man would write a letter such as this at all unless he had something to hide? The Mullens were now convinced more than ever that Schwarzkopf had been instrumental in both the death of their son and the subsequent cover-up.

Imagine what the Mullens would have felt had they known that the two letters they had thus far received signed by H. Norman Schwarzkopf had not, in fact, been written by him at all.

On Wednesday, June 24, 1970, the United States Senate by a vote of 81 to 10 repealed the Gulf of Tonkin Resolution. The Senate's August 7, 1964, passage of the resolution provided the sole legal basis for the Vietnam War's escalation and the inevitable acceptance by American forces of the major burden of the ground, sea and air war in Southeast Asia, which resulted in the death of Michael Mullen and, by the end of June, 1970, more than 50,000 other Americans as well. The repeal of the resolution was backed by the Nixon administration, which stated it did not need the Resolution to justify current U.S. involvement in Vietnam.

The next morning Peg received a letter from Martin Culpepper, whom she had written after her trip to Washington.

It was very interesting to read about your trip to D.C. with some ralliers who think the same about the war here. The army couldn't answer your questions or all of them anyhow. For them to do so is to quote "break your back." The truth is they can only beat around the so long but I pray it's not too long or late for our sake.

Peg read the last sentence again: "The army couldn't answer your questions . . . for to do so is to 'break your back.' The truth is they can only beat around the so long," the *what* so long? Culpepper had omitted a word. "Beat around the *bush*?" "Around the *truth*?" Was he saying that if the Army told Peg the truth, it would break her back? Her spirit? Was Culpepper not telling Peg what had really happened? She wondered whether she was being overly suspicious, or had Culpepper been trying to hint at something? She recalled having told him some of the questions her CALCAV group had asked about the secret treaties, the border crossings, the secret operations and bombings. That line about the Army's being unable to answer her questions, was he referring to her questions about Michael or those asked at the Pentagon? It was infuriating not knowing what Culpepper really meant and frustrating, too, getting just one little nugget of information at a time.

She also heard from Lieutenant Colonel Giorgi in that same day's mail. His letter, in response to Peg's request for more information on how the casualty reporting system worked, was a celebration of Pentagonese:

As I have mentioned to you in my previous letter to you the casualty lists are available in alphabetical order and alphabetically by state. We do not maintain lists by those who were casualties on a specific date. To get such a list would require an extraordinary amount of time and personnel resources which are not available.

However, I am sending you the official casualty release of February 25, 26, and 27, as you requested. As I discussed with you these lists do not necessarily indicate that those are names of U.S. servicemen who died the previous week or on a specific date. Quite possibly some died the previous week but you cannot determine if this is the case by reading the release. The attached explanation will clarify this point.

There followed a typed single-spaced "Procedure for Reporting U.S. Casualties in Southeast Asia," which filled one-half of a sheet of regular office typewriter paper.

The number of casualties as they are reported, is expressed as a cumulative number beginning in January, 1961. At the end of each week the previous cumulative number is subtracted from the new cumulative number and the difference is referred to as the number reported for the week. This statistical process permits us to make necessary changes; such as, from non-hostile to hostile, missing to died-while-missing, etc., and still preserve the accuracy of the published totals. Everyone of the dead, missing, and captured are on our lists, with date of casualty. Note that the weekly number represents the number reported during that week and will almost always contain reports of a few whose date of casualty was earlier.

There are two principal reasons for this: One, some men are initially reported as missing and as evidence is later received are changed to dead although the date of death is established as the date they were reported as missing. Secondly, in some instances the circumstances are such that a determination as to cause of casualty cannot immediately be made and the report would then usually be classified as non-hostile and later changed, if necessary, according to information in the final report. Some of these cases take quite a while.

The foregoing is to explain why we would find in the list of names of those reported as having died during any week some who would have an official date of death which was earlier. Conversely, some who actually died during the week in question could not be reported until later.

Several points should be made about Giorgi's letter and the enclosed casualty reporting procedure. His assertion that "to get such a list [of casualties on a specific date] would require an extraordinary amount of time and personnel resources" was probably correct. Since, however, lists were available by alphabetical order and alphabetically by state, and since "everyone of the dead, missing, and captured are on our lists, with date of casualty," there is a means by which a computer search by date could have been made—were the military to have wanted such a thing done. The computer might not have been programmed to provide such information, and the creation of a new program is what might have taken the time and personnel resources.

Secondly, the procedures Giorgi outlined permit considerable flexibility in reporting the actual number of casualties. Heavy losses on any given week could be delayed in filing and thereby spread out over a series of weeks, hidden away, or at least dispersed so that no one state adjutant need become overly alarmed by having to report a large number of area casualties at one time.

Thirdly, as the procedure document points out, in those instances where "the cause of casualty cannot immediately be made," that casualty would "usually be classified as non-hostile." Why? Nonbattle casualties were not included in the casualty count given on the evening news. This policy, therefore, facilitated keeping the "reported" casualties as low as possible. By the end of June, 1970, the actual casualty figure for the Vietnam War was 42,754 deaths as a result of hostile action, 8,122 deaths from "non-hostile" causes.

CHAPTER 6

Patricia Mullen and Alan Hulting were married at the St. Thomas More Church in Iowa City on August 28, 1970. A small coffee and cake reception was held following the ceremony at the University of Iowa's Student Union cafeteria where Patricia had worked, and afterward about seventy-five persons drove back to the Mullens' farm for a buffet dinner. Alan Hulting, sweltering in his tuxedo, found himself at one point trapped by an intoxicated friend of the Mullens' in their basement recreation room. When the man finally turned to Alan and asked, "By the way, who are you?" Alan replied, "I'm the groom," and went back upstairs to find his bride. Patricia was in the living room worriedly watching her father corner one guest after another to talk about the war.

When it was time for Alan and Patricia to leave, Gene and Peg followed the young couple out to their car. Gene held the door for his daughter and kissed her lightly on the cheek. Patricia got in, and Gene and Peg walked beside the automobile as Alan slowly maneuvered out of the Mullens' driveway and turned onto the dirt road. When Patricia twisted in the front seat to wave out the back window at her parents, she saw they had continued across the dirt road to the mailbox. Patricia sadly realized that whatever little reprieve her wedding might have provided her parents, it was now over. The "cease-fire" had ended, and her parents' private, lonely war with the United States government had resumed.

The Mullens' obsessive correspondence, their bitterness, their inability to talk or think about anything but the war, their utter impatience with any divergent points of view are symptoms of their continuing belief that a conspiracy existed to prevent them from discovering the details of their son's death. The letter they brought back from the mailbox as Patricia and Alan drove away had been forwarded to them by Senator Jacob K. Javits of New York.

Javits had redirected his copy of Peg's registered special delivery letter to each Senator to the Pentagon, where Major Thomas F. McMorrow, a General Staff officer in the Chief of Legislative Liaison Office, was assigned the task of providing answers. McMorrow's point-by-point response was mailed to Javits on August 20.

McMorrow confirmed that Michael's "death was caused by a missile wound to the chest which was the result of an artillery round which exploded when it hit a tree in his company area." But because McMorrow then added, "He died before he could be removed to a medical facility," the Mullens now wondered if Michael had not been killed instantly as they had been told and instead had lingered, suffering for an unspecified amount of time. McMorrow's letter continued: "Accordingly, the only medical record available is the Certificate of Death which was completed at the mortuary, signed by a medical officer and a mortician. A copy of this document, which confirms the cause of death, is enclosed."

The enclosure was the same DA form 10-249 the Mullens had received that previous March 17 listing the mode of death as "accident," the interval between onset and death as "unknown" and the cause of death "missile wound of chest." The Mullens still questioned how it was possible for their son to have been killed by artillery and be perfectly whole—except for the small puncture above his right kidney Tom Loomis at the funeral home had discovered in preparing the body for burial. Why did the Army insist the wound was in Michael's chest? Michael, they believed, had been asleep when the shell hit. They knew their son usually slept on his left side. Loomis' placement of the wound made the most sense. Because of this confusion, the Mullens had requested a complete medical report. It was never sent because no such report ever existed.

"On 22 February the Chief of Support Services, Department of the Army, sent a message to Private Mullen's father. . . ." McMorrow's listing of their son as a "private," not "sergeant," was the sort of needless error which so infuriated the Mullens. The telegram containing information on the return of Michael's body also mistakenly listed his rank as "private." The indifference to the details of their son's life suggested to the Mullens an equal indifference to the details of Michael's death.

The remainder of McMorrow's letter dealt with specifics: the problem the Army had had in securing the special escort requested by the Mullens, the Army's attempts to locate Michael's missing camera, the procedures the Mullens should follow to file their claim. Then a brief section was devoted to the itemization of Michael's final paycheck including the deduction for unearned leave.

Payment of the sum of $97.46, reflecting net unpaid pay and allowances, has been held in abeyance of the Finance Center pending receipt of the claim form signed by Mr. Mullen. That sum reflects a careful determination of remaining monies due him as beneficiary.

Gene and Peg never did sign the claim form; to have signed it would have meant they accepted the Army's right to deduct nine days' leave from Michael's final pay.

Iowa's summer had given way to fall by the time the Mullens heard from Major McMorrow again. McMorrow's second letter, written to Senator Harold Hughes in response to the Senator's request for information, was, like Javits' letter, forwarded to the Mullens in La Porte.

McMorrow repeated the previous details of Michael's death, but then continued:

Added information from the overseas command revealed that the artillery fire had been requested by the forward observer assigned to that company from the supporting artillery unit. It should be noted that an assigned forward observer for a company habitually lives and works with the supported unit at all times.

At the time of Sergeant Mullen's death, the forward observer was within the overall defensive area and was preparing to adjust fire on four specific locations. This is a standard precautionary measure, even though there was no contact with the enemy at the time. The preparatory action assures the rapid and accurate delivery of artillery fire at predetermined locations in the event of an enemy attack without requirement for the adjustment of fire during the attack itself. It is confirmed that the unit firing was a platoon of a U.S. Army artillery battery.

The Army, for the first time, had admitted an American forward observer had called in the artillery which had killed Michael Mullen. Peg realized that the one young man who could answer all their questions would be that forward observer—but, of course, the Mullens did not know his name. Remembering Lieutenant Colonel H. Norman Schwarzkopf's second letter—"Unfortunately, United States Army, Vietnam policy does not allow me to release the names of its servicemen"—Peg knew she'd never learn the name through the Army. McMorrow's letter continued: "Michael was not the acting platoon sergeant at the time of the incident, but he had previously performed in that capacity since he was a ranking enlisted man."

McMorrow's allegation was in direct refutation of Culpepper's letter of March 16: "Your son was acting platoon sergeant at that time. He was a soldier like us all, but he was fair to everyone because he believed in right." The Mullens thought if Michael had been the acting platoon sergeant, he would have been due more pay, but more than the denial of extra pay the Mullens resented the Army's repudiation of the accolade, the honor of the higher rank.

At the time of the accident, his platoon leader was in a defensive position approximately eight to ten feet from him. Other members of the unit within the immediate area included the company commander, the company first sergeant, and the battalion chaplain, who were located within 30 feet of Sergeant Mullen's position.

Peg read that paragraph twice. At first she wasn't even sure what bothered her about it. It wasn't simply the lack of names; it was something more. Then she recalled the description in Lieutenant Colonel Schwarzkopf's second letter and searched through her papers until she found it:

When the tragic incident occurred [Schwarzkopf had written] Michael's platoon leader was in a defensive position approximately eight to ten feet away from him. Other members of the unit were within the immediate area. The Company Commander, the Company First Sergeant, and the Battalion Chaplain were also located within thirty feet of Michael's position.

The almost exact duplication of the wording was more than coincidence, Peg felt; certainly the descriptions had been coordinated, but whether or not the similarities provided concrete evidence of a cover-up conspiracy, Peg couldn't be sure.

Every incident in which our personnel are fired upon by friendly forces is thoroughly investigated so that any warranted corrective action may be taken to preclude any recurrence. The loss of life of an Army member under such circumstances is a matter of deep concern to all commanders and is a source of untold grief to all those immediately involved.

Peg seized upon that first sentence. In May Senator Fulbright had forwarded to Peg Daniel Henkin's letter on how nonbattle casualties are listed. In that letter the Mullens had learned the accident was termed a "misadventure." Henkin had also written, "I am informed that each instance where Americans have been killed by friendly artillery fire is investigated." McMorrow's letter confirmed this fact. Somewhere, therefore, a report of such an investigation must exist. If Peg could read it, she would know exactly what had happened to her son.

McMorrow's next paragraph was in response to the Mullens' demand to know why no one was permitted to write them and why they had not heard from any of the other officers in Michael's unit:

Under established procedures the commander of a deceased or missing member's unit of assignment, the chaplain servicing that unit, or the installation commander will write a letter of sympathy to the next of kin and to his parents if they are not the designated next of kin. In accordance with the policy of the 1st Battalion, 6th Infantry, the battalion commander sent letters of sympathy in behalf of the battalion. In addition to the letter of sympathy, the battalion commander forwarded a letter dated 10 June 1970 to Mrs. Mullen in response to an inquiry he had received from her.

There is no censorship of mail from Vietnam. A serviceman who wants to communicate with the next of kin of a deceased comrade is not prevented from doing so; he is often encouraged. However, the member is under no obligation to correspond, and the extent of his communication is a matter of personal choice.

The Mullens did not believe this. They had Culpepper's letter of May 9: "Today we were informed of rights in the army. If any people have written to you in mail, the future is in jeopardy. . . . For they can be court-marshalled for mutiny and undermining the army. Don't publish any article of such writing for it would bring harm to people and their future. Anything sent to you can be censored as we are in a war zone." Lieutenant Colonel Schwarzkopf himself later confirmed that Division had written the letters sent out under his signatures and that he had not been permitted to answer the Mullens' letters, although he had wished to.

McMorrow then defended the Army's classification of Michael as a nonbattle casualty: "It has been definitely established that Sergeant Mullen's death was not directly related to hostile action, nor was the presence of the enemy a contributing factor. Therefore, his death was correctly classified as non-hostile."

The Mullens still smarted over that judgment. Michael, they knew, had been going out on a combat mission. With increasing bitterness and irritation, Peg Mullen read on:

At all levels the Army is keenly aware of the human feelings that are involved. Individuals designated to act as official representatives of the Army are carefully selected for their ability to perform this difficult task with tact and understanding. In view of the seriousness of allegations that Master Sergeant Waldo T. Fitzgerald made certain comments, a full report was requested from the Commanding General Fifth U.S. Army.

Information received indicates that when the parents saw the notifier in uniform accompanied by a Catholic priest, they immediately sensed the purpose of the visit and became very emotional. Approximately one-half hour later, when they were sufficiently composed, Sergeant Fitzgerald read the official casualty message he had received by telephone. It stated only that Sergeant Mullen died at a night defensive position when artillery fire from friendly forces landed in the area.

During the conversation that followed, Mrs. Mullen recalled a radio broadcast reporting the shelling of friendly patrols by personnel of the Army of the Republic of Vietnam (ARVN), and it was noted by the family that Michael's unit may have been one of those allegedly so shelled. Reverend Otto B. Shimon, the priest who was present, says Sergeant Fitzgerald mentioned that the enemy may have gotten into friendly communication channels and caused the friendly unit to fire on the patrol, but he gave this only as a possibility.

Sergeant Fitzgerald states that he did not at any time say, suggest, or imply that Sergeant Mullen or any base camp mentioned on the radio had been deliberately shelled by ARVN forces. This statement is confirmed by Father Shimon. In his opinion Sergeant Fitzgerald was in control of his feelings and performed a diffi-cult task as well as could be expected under trying conditions.

I realize how deeply Mr. and Mrs. Mullen have been hurt and how lasting will be their sorrow. It is most unfortunate that misunderstandings added to their dis-tress. Michael was a brave and dedicated soldier, and my deepest sympathy is with all the members of the Mullen family in their great loss.

"Of course," Peg told Gene that night after he had read McMorrow's letter, too, "it's just between whether I'm crazy or Sergeant Fitzgerald is. I know I didn't make it up! I can see him standing there with his back to me and he was ready to go, remember? And I said, 'Sit down!' I said, 'We're going to talk about this wire. What do you mean by "friendly"? How is it the word "American" isn't there?' And he said, 'Because it wasn't American fire.' I know I didn't make that up!"

Gene nodded. "And when you asked the sergeant why the word 'acci-dent' wasn't in there, he said, 'Because it was no accident.'"

"Another thing," Peg continued, "I'm sure they'd been talking about the Bien Hoa shelling at Fifth Army when this message about Michael came through. Someone probably said, 'What's this deal about "friendly fire"?' And another person said, 'Well, that's probably another deal like Bien Hoa.' That's the way I think it all came about—and the whole Bien Hoa story about Michael being killed by ARVN artillery was printed in the Des Moines paper. Why didn't Sergeant Fitzgerald deny it then? He was here several times, and I told that same Bien Hoa story over and over again in those next few days to anybody who would listen, and he never once made any effort to correct me. I was so damned mad I told every-body who came the same story, and Fitzgerald or that captain—"

"Captain Pringle."

"That's right, Pringle. They were here. They never made any effort to correct me."

"What are you gonna do about that investigation report?" Gene asked. "Do you think they'll ever let us see it?"

Peg shrugged. "I'm going to write General Ramsey and tell him to send it to us. I don't know what else we can do."

Several weeks passed, and then, to the Mullens' astonishment, a telegram from General Ramsey's adjutant was forwarded by the Veterans Hospital in Iowa City saying that the artillery investigation report was on file at Long Binh and a copy would be sent them. The Mullens waited.

The report was never sent.

In early October, while Peg and Gene were listening to the morning news about the Vietnam War, there was a knock at their kitchen door.

"I'll get it, Mother," Gene said. He walked down the back steps and peered through the storm door. A young black man looked at him from the other side. Gene opened the door and said, "Yes? Can I help you?"

"Mr. Mullen? Mr. Gene Mullen?" the young man said.

"Yes, that's right."

"I'm Martin Culpepper."

Gene took Martin's hand in both of his and squeezed it in joy. He whirled around and shouted up the stairway, "Mother? Mother? It's Martin! Martin Culpepper. He's back from Vietnam!"

"For heaven's sakes, Gene," Peg called back, "don't just stand there, let Martin come on in!"

Martin Luther Culpepper was then twenty-one years old. He had been born in Mississippi, but three months later his family had moved to Waterloo, Iowa, where his father, the Reverend G. L. Culpepper, took a job with the Rath Packing Company and became the pastor of the New Zion Baptist Church. Martin attended local schools and, upon receiving his high school diploma, he too went to work for Rath. At night Martin attended the Hawkeye Institute of Technology, where he was learning welding with the hope that his skill would keep him out of the Army. It didn't. He was drafted six months later at the age of nineteen. Like Michael, Martin was sent to Fort Polk, Louisiana, for basic and advanced infantry training. He arrived in Vietnam a week after Michael Mullen.

Culpepper was pleased to be assigned to Charlie Company. He had been told that more Iowans were there and that "if things got hot, Charlie Company had the most dependable people. They didn't get rattled." That is how, he told the Mullens, he came to be with their son on that steep, wooded hilltop on that terrible night five months later when Michael Mullen died.

"All right now, Martin," Gene said, hitching his chair up to the kitchen table so that he and Culpepper could sit close. "We want to know what happened. Who was responsible that night? Who called in the shot? *Who-killed-our-boy?*"

Peg had a pad of paper and pencil and was prepared to take notes. "We want you to tell it like it really is, Martin. Give us their names," Peg said. "What were you doing that night? There was no enemy around. Why were you in the mountains? Why did they call in artillery? Start at the beginning, and tell us everything."

"Well, we heard it might have been any one of three things," Culpepper said. "We were told that the gun was the same gun that had killed some guys in Bravo Company a couple of months before—"

"The same gun!" Peg said. "There was something wrong with it?"

"We heard something about a gun that always fired low," Culpepper said. "We also heard that the officer in charge of the guns was drunk, or that the guys firing were drunk and—"

Gene's fist slammed the table in rage. "Who was drunk? WHO WAS DRUNK and killed my boy?"

"I don't know who it was, Mr. Mullen. Nobody ever told us any names."

"You heard the officer was drunk, am I right?" Gene asked.

"Well, we heard that, yes. But we also heard there was something wrong with the gun."

"Martin, you said it could have been any one of three reasons," Peg said. "What was the third?"

"There was a rumor that someone back on the hill they were firing from had failed to correct for the height of our hill," Culpepper said. "When the lifers came out the next day, they tried to get us to say it had been Vietcong."

"Was there a lot of drugs around?" Gene asked.

Culpepper looked uncomfortable. "While I was there, they called us in the Third Platoon a bunch of dope addicts, pot heads, acid freaks—you name it. But we weren't really. We smoked, sure. At one time everybody in the platoon had smoked pot except the lieutenant."

"Did Michael?" Peg asked.

"Smoke? No, no. Mike never smoked," Culpepper said. "I didn't know Mike all that well—I knew him, you understand, but we were in different platoons. I liked him. He was just a regular guy, calm and quiet. He didn't do too many things to excess. He didn't gamble or anything like the normal guys did. Everybody on payday—well, somebody would get out the dice, they'd scrape some place out on the ground, get out the money and the dice. Mike would come around and watch once in a while, but he didn't gamble. There was one kid nicknamed Perfect—everybody had nicknames." Culpepper smiled. "There was Perfect and Razzle-Dazzle and the Prince. . . . Nobody ever calls you by your full or last name. You get a nickname, and everybody sort of adopts it. Everybody called me Pep, for instance, or Pepper. . . ."

"Did Mike have a nickname?" Gene asked.

Culpepper thought for a moment. "No, I don't think so. Everybody just called him Mike."

"Martin?" Peg said. "What was it like the night Michael was killed?"

For the rest of the day the Mullens' kitchen became that jungle hilltop in Vietnam. The more Martin Culpepper spoke, the less he seemed aware of his surroundings. Culpepper wasn't just talking about what had happened that terrible night; he was *there*. As Peg and Gene watched uneasily, Culpepper stormed about the table, hacking and chopping at the imagined dense jungle growth. The Mullens could only try to visualize what the young man still so clearly saw: helicopters swooping down for a combat assault, shark-faced Cobra gunships circling beyond their kitchen window, a white phosphorus artillery marking round exploding with a soft, plushy *foop!* above their stove. Flares popped high in the night sky illuminating the wounded, who lay groaning and bleeding about the Mullens' yard.

Throughout it all Peg was taking notes.

"Did you know about the boy who went berserk?" Culpepper asked.

Gene looked at Peg, who shook her head.

"His name was Polk," Culpepper said. "He was a black private in the First Platoon. He was asleep between Mike and Leroy Hamilton when they died. Polk wasn't even touched. He went crazy that night."

"What happened to him?" Peg asked.

"He's in jail at Leavenworth," Culpepper said. "Court-martialed."

"Polk, black private, went berserk," Peg wrote in her notebook. *"Court-martialed. Leavenworth."*

"Mike was always looking out for Polk," Culpepper was saying. "Whenever Polk got in an argument, Mike would try to calm him down, say something like, 'Man, you're here. We're all here. We can't do anything about it.' Mike and Sergeant Gregory would try to talk to him sensible. But the other guys in the First Platoon wouldn't have much to do with Polk. They said he was a troublemaker."

"Friend of Mike's," Peg added to her notes. And on the line below she wrote, "Sgt. Gregory, 1st Platoon."

"We need names, Martin," Gene said. "We want to know who was with our son." Peg's list began to grow:

General Lloyd Ramsey, Commanding General, Americal Division
Colonel Joseph Clemons, 198th Infantry Brigade Commander
Lieutenant Colonel H. Norman Schwarzkopf, 1/6th Battalion Commander
Captain (—) Cameron, Company Commander, Charlie Company
Lieutenant (—) Rocamora (sp?), Forward Observer w/Charlie Co.
Lieutenant (—) Joslin, Platoon Leader, 1st Plt. Mike's.
Sgt. Webb, 3rd Platoon, now in Des Moines,
Russell Schumacher, 3rd Plt. Still in Vietnam. Iowa boy.
Albert Gaynor, 3rd Plt. Back in States. Still in Army.
Abe Aikins, Black medic. Probably back in States.
Prince (nickname?), 1st Platoon. Wounded. Lost leg, maybe two.
Polk, Black Private, went berserk. Court-martialed. Leavenworth. Friend of
    Mike's.
Sgt. Gregory, 1st Platoon

"Did you know that our platoon and Mike's platoon traded positions that night?" Culpepper asked. "We were originally supposed to set up on their side of the hill."

"Whose decision was that?" Gene asked. "Schwarzkopf's?"

"No, it was the lieutenant's," Culpepper said. He told them how the 3rd Platoon had already dropped their equipment off and begun digging in when the order came to switch positions. The 1st Platoon was emplaced on the south side of the hilltop, and the 3rd Platoon to the north where there was a cliff. "I was set up right on the edge of it," Culpepper said. "It was about eighty feet straight down."

"Martin, what was Schwarzkopf really like?" Peg asked.

"He was a real gung-ho sort of man. He just wanted to get promoted."

"How old a man is he?" Peg asked.

"Thirty-two, thirty-three."

"Another thing, Martin," Gene said. "Why did they fire the artillery so late?"

"They told everybody as soon as we were dug in to put on their steel pots because they were going to fire the DTs. That's when everybody started making smart cracks about the helmets: 'They aren't any good no-how.' 'What good do they do? Don't stop nothing.' Things like that. That would have been about five-thirty, six o'clock, somewhere in there. It wasn't dark yet, I remember.

"They said Rocamora was going to call them in," Culpepper continued. "And everybody was to get into their foxholes in case the arty wasn't right. But they didn't fire them. They called the DTs off. We all know the DTs were for our protection. As Schwarzkopf told us, 'If they want to get to you, let them come through a ring of steel.' . . . *Ring of steel!*" Culpepper laughed, shaking his head. "All this gung-ho stuff they used to feed us!"

"But, Martin," Gene asked again, "why did they fire the DTs so late?"

"I don't know," Culpepper admitted. He explained how the artillery investigators had arrived on the hill the following morning. They had looked at where the shell had hit and asked if the men were sure it hadn't been a Vietcong mortar round. "Everybody just started cussin' at them," Culpepper told the Mullens. "Someone said, 'It wasn't no mortar round,' real quietlike. 'You know what it was! You know who fired it!' Finally they ordered us to be quiet, to return to our side of the perimeter. But even as we were walking back, we heard the artillery experts saying things like, 'Well, it could have been an ARVN round. . . .'"

"*An* ARVN *round?*" Peg asked, glancing at Gene. Could the original message, the Bien Hoa story, have been true after all?

"We know it wasn't the South Vietnamese," Culpepper was saying. "Those lifers were going around. 'Well, we have to examine all the possibilities,' they said. 'It may not have been an error. It could have been the enemy.' We know it wasn't."

The moment Culpepper left that evening, Peg threw a quick dinner together for Gene, swept the kitchen table top clean, and sat down to write Russell Schumacher, an Iowa boy, who was still with Charlie Company in Vietnam. He would tell her the truth. Hank Webb, according to Culpepper, was back in Des Moines—Webb had formed a sniper unit along with two other men so that he could move separately from the company. He carried an accurized M-14 with a telescopic sight and, Culpepper told the Mullens, was wounded a third time before being rotated out—Webb would, however, probably know Albert Gaynor's address. So Peg now had the names of three other young men who had been on that hill the night Michael was killed. She had specific questions to ask them and, for the first time, could expect to receive specific answers. Peg heard first from Russell Schumacher:

Yes I remember the night of February 18th when your son was killed. I was on guard talking with Albert Gaynor at his foxhole. I think Al & I were talking about how close they were firing defensive targets, "DTs." I was telling Al how funny it was to fire them at all much less at around 2:30. Then the 5th artillary round came in & hit in the trees near your sons hole. We knew it was in the perimeter and seconds later we heard guys in pain. . . . Your son died in a few minutes after he was hit. He probably never woke up to feel any pain. Leroy Hamilton died very shortly after being hit, too. It was a bad night that sure none of the guys that were there will ever forget.

The next morning the lifers came out to investigate. I think they said that morning that the officer in charge of the artillary mite have been drunk. Then later a roomer was it was the same gun that killed a guy—maybe two—in another company earlier this year. . . . Then later we were told that someone mite not have figured out the elevations of the hill the artillary gun was on and the hill we were on right. How ever it happened there was no reason at all to be firing artillery at that time in the morning. There was no fresh signs of enemy around.

When death comes its allmost to much for ones heart. I think your very brave in checking into your sons death. I truly hope you can help GIs out by learning the truth.

Maybe when the army & leaders find out that people care about the soldiers safety they will care. Many of the guys who knew Mike and know what you're trying to do believe you're right.

Do what you can and may God give you a hand.

During the first week in November the Mullens visited Hank Webb in Des Moines. Webb repeated the rumors Culpepper and Schumacher had mentioned: a faulty gun, the men were drunk, or the elevation had been incorrectly figured. But, he added, he didn't think the forward observer, Lieutenant Rocamora, had called in the shots. Webb explained to the Mullens while his parents sat listening that Rocamora wasn't a lifer and had no great loyalty to the Regular Army. Rocamora always alerted the men when the DTs were to be fired. If Rocamora had called in the artillery and not alerted the men, the men would have blamed him. "They would have made it so uncomfortable for Rocamora," Webb said, "he wouldn't have wanted to remain with the company."

"Did he stay?" Gene asked.

"Oh, sure," Webb said. "Everyone liked him. When the shell hit, there wasn't any warning. I thought it was an attack. I can remember sweeping, just throwing the men into their foxholes!"

Like Michael, Webb had been an acting platoon sergeant. He had been in the 3rd Platoon along with Culpepper, Gaynor and Schumacher. Polk, however, had been in Michael's 1st Platoon.

Schumacher wrote that he remembered Polk: "He had been afraid and quite a troublesome guy before. I think he had bad nerves for one thing. On the night your son died, Polk was sleeping right next to him. That really got to his mind. I could see how he cracked up. He was almost in shock that night."

Webb, that afternoon in Des Moines, told the Mullens Polk had "gone crazy." Some of the men from Webb's platoon had had to knock Polk out, restrain him, before he could be loaded onto a helicopter and flown out.

Gaynor, however, wrote:

As to your question about Pvt. Polk, it seems there's some sort of mix up. As far as I know nothing happened that night with Polk. I'm not sure, but I heard nothing of it. To my knowledge he was sentenced because of incidents a few days following the night of the 18th. Possibly the 20th or 21st. There were charges brought against him for a number of things. Hitting an officer and a non-commissioned officer, firing his weapon at civilians, and some other things which I do not know. Anything related to the night in question, I'm not aware of.

Gaynor had rotated out of Vietnam and was then stationed at Fort Hood, Texas. His letter was the most explicit the Mullens received:

As I remember that night we were set up in a night defensive perimeter, which was located on a ridge line quite a few miles from Chu Lai. We dug foxholes as usual and set up for the night. Each platoon having its own sector of the perimeter. At about 8:30 PM we were informed over the radio that D.T.'s were going to be shot out in the next five minutes. . . . Most of the men in the company usually felt quite uneasy about the firing of these because they thought it was possible something could go wrong and somebody could get hurt. This is one of the reasons we were usually informed shortly before they were fired. So if some of the men wanted to get into their foxholes, they could do so. Some of the men did, but no artillery came. Finally it seemed that they were going to cancel the D.T.'s that night. Then about 3 AM, or some time around there, they started firing them. I know, because I was on guard that night. They fired some on our left and right which were a safe distance away. A safe distance is usually about 600 meters away.

They fire two rounds for each D.T. One round is a white phosphorus which explodes in the air and gives off white smoke. This is to make sure of the exact location where the round is to hit because the next round is H.E. (High Explosive) which is an extremely destructive round. The third set of D.T.'s was the one that hit inside the perimeter. A white phosphorus was fired first. It went directly over the middle of the perimeter. I heard it explode and saw the white smoke. It looked to me like it was in the right spot. A bit close possibly. Then the next round came in, this is the H.E. It sounded so close I hit the ground. I heard the explosion and I remember thinking to myself it sounded awfully close. That round hit 50 yards inside our perimeter. You already know the rest. Mike and another man were killed, 6 others were wounded.

In your letter you said you were told Lt. Rocamora called in the artillery at 2:50 AM. Personally, I can't believe that. Of course I never asked him. But looking at it from my point of view it would seem foolish of him to do such a thing. Especially since most of the men liked to be warned before it came and at 3:00 AM in the morning everybody would be asleep except for the guards. I was on guard, as I said before, and no for-warning was given.

We were told that it was the artillery people's fault. They told us that some officer and some sargent were being held responsible. There were rumors going round about the people firing the artillery being drunk and some sort of neglect was evident. Neglect isn't uncommon in Vietnam. This wasn't the last instance of it. There was much, much more to come in the following months.

I don't know if Hank Webb told you, but at one time we wrote a letter to you about the February 18 incident and some of the conditions afterward. It was signed by about 60 men in the company. That letter was never mailed because the Company Commander got word of it. We were threatened with reprisals and also he said that our mail could be censored. The letter was destroyed. When your in the army you don't have quite the freedom civilians have.

Mrs. Mullen, I think you are doing the right thing. If more people were as concerned as you are about the war, possibly something could be done.

Over and over again the Mullens had been told that Michael was killed because an artillery round had fallen short. Both Peg and Gene would have understood and might even have been able to accept that this was what had happened to their son were it not for the Army's unwillingness to provide them with the details as to why it had happened. It was obvious to the Mullens that it wasn't *what* had happened, but how it happened that the Army was so determined to hide.

The Mullens were now certain an American artillery unit had, for no apparent reason, suddenly and without warning, commenced firing over Charlie Company's night defensive perimeter at approximately three o'clock in the morning, taking Charlie Company by surprise. None of the men Peg had communicated with believed that the artillery had been requested by Rocamora, the company's forward observer. There was no reason for the artillery to have been fired at that hour; there were no signs of enemy activity around. One of the artillery shells fell short, detonated when it hit a tree above the company perimeter and killed Leroy Hamilton and Michael Mullen and wounded six others.

The Mullens were also now certain they knew why: the men back at the guns were drunk.

Peg was invited to be a guest speaker at the November 15 Black Hawk County Moratorium. She accepted and had her first brush with the FBI.

From the moment she stepped out of her car until she returned home Peg Mullen was photographed. No matter whom she stood next to or spoke with her picture was taken. At least eight men with cameras were among the protesters, and the thought of FBI agents photographing a peaceful gathering of American citizens was so repugnant, so absolutely *foreign* to Peg that when it was time for her to speak she was shaking with rage. She was outraged that she, Peg Mullen, whose own son had given his life in support of his government's war, should be considered a potential subversive by the very government which had killed him.

Peg rose before the protesters and related step by step what had happened to her son in Vietnam, how he had been "killed by some drunken officer shooting off an artillery gun." She told how the Army's first reports had placed their son 400 miles from where he had actually died, how they had lied, led them to believe that Michael had been killed by South Vietnamese, not American, artillery. She explained how Michael was a "nonbattle casualty and, therefore, not counted," how the young men he had served with had been threatened with court-martial and reprisals if they attempted to write. She described how callously and insensitively the Army and Congress had treated her family from the moment they were notified of their son's death and her outrage at the deduction of nine days' leave from his final pay. She expressed her utter contempt with the White House for having included the President's Vietnamization speeches in a letter of condolence at a time when the family still believed their son had been killed by the South Vietnamese. She told of the letters she had received from young men who admitted to being in Cambodia a month before the President announced they were, and looking directly into the closest upturned camera lens, she said, "We are tired of President Nixon's lies! We were good members of the Silent Majority, but we cannot remain silent any longer. We are determined to speak out, to expose the government's lies. All across America there are mothers and fathers, young men and women, *good Americans,* who feel the same way we do about this immoral war! We have come here today, all of us, to make our opposition known. We are not afraid." She vowed to continue her battle in behalf of the 44,000 killed in combat and the 9,000 nonbattle deaths like her son.

CHAPTER 7

On April 12, 1971, a Monday, I drove up the dirt road to meet Peg and Gene Mullen for the first time.

The editor of the magazine with which I first discussed the possibility of doing an article on the Mullens asked if I thought Peg Mullen might be "deranged." He did not ask this because he felt Peg's protesting of her son's death was a symptom of any derangement, but rather out of concern for her health. If she were deranged, then any exploitation of her grief could only contribute to whatever imbalance she might have. And it was precisely the exploitation of her grief upon which any article would have to depend.

And yet when I first telephoned Peg Mullen, introduced myself and explained what it was I wanted to do, she was willing to have me come. In fact, I was a little startled and dismayed by how eagerly she had invited me. I left for Iowa two days later.

I turned into the Mullens' farm a little after twelve noon. I parked my car by the shed in which rested the old plum-red tractor Michael had used to pull out the tree stumps his last night of leave. Peg Mullen, wearing slacks and a yellow short-sleeved sweat shirt with a SLIPPERY WHEN WET traffic sign printed in black on its front, met me at the farmhouse door. We had barely introduced ourselves when she said, "Michael would have just died if he had seen this lawn!" We both winced slightly. The hogs had broken through the fence the night before and rooted up the spring rain-softened yard. The late March snows had melted away from the fields, but there was still snow in the ditches on either side of the section line roads. Since Gene was out in the lower field with his son John, Peg brought me into the kitchen and offered me lunch and coffee, apologizing for the papers covering the kitchen table.

A little later Gene Mullen came up the back stairs followed by John. Impatient to get on with it, Gene sat at the kitchen table, swept some papers aside with his arm, gestured for me to pull my chair closer, took one of my yellow pads and a pen and started right in.

"One boy was on guard here," he said. He drew an oval on the legal pad and placed a small circle near one edge. "Each platoon had their guard. Schumacher, he was Third Platoon." He circled Schumacher's position again. "Culpepper was in the Third Platoon. Platoon Sergeant Webb was Third Platoon. . . ." Gene drew two more circles.

"Gaynor was Third Platoon," Peg said. "We've heard only from Third Platoon boys."

"And Abe Aikins, the medic, was stationed here." He drew another circle. "We have letters from all these boys. We can tie it all in. Wherever you set up a defensive perimeter, your forward observer radios back to your artillery unit to get your coordinates in case of an enemy attack. The boys tell us they fired a little around eight o'clock."

"There's a conflict in their stories there," Peg said. "One boy says they never fired at all. That they called off the artillery and didn't test it that night. Two of the boys said they did fire artillery around eight o'clock and finished. But the shot that killed them came in at two-thirty, and nobody believes it was called in."

"It wasn't called in," Gene stated flatly.

"We're searching for this Lieutenant Rocamora because he was the forward observer who would have requested the artillery."

"Now whenever you have artillery," Gene said, "you can fire from this point here. . . ." He made an x on the yellow pad below and to one side of the oval "hill." "Or from this point here," Gene continued, marking another x above and to the other side of the "hill."

"It's against the Army Code to fire over a group," Peg explained. "But this is what they did. They were firing over the boys' heads evidently."

"The shell came in, and it killed Michael, here." Gene drew an x within the oval. "Leroy Hamilton, here." He marked an x near Michael's. "And a colored boy name of Polk, Private Polk from Detroit, was right between them and wasn't even scarred. There were seven boys wounded in the First Platoon. We know of a boy name of Prince who lost his leg—"

"—We're trying to locate him, too."

"—and this boy Polk went berserk. He tried to kill the artillery forward observer for calling in the shot. They handcuffed him. And that morning when the choppers came in to pick up the dead and wounded Charlie Company was moved over to another ridge for the boys to cool off. Sergeant Webb, who lives down to Des Moines, was guarding this boy Polk, but Polk got loose and took a machine gun and started spraying some Vietnamese working in a rice paddy. He also evidently struck a couple officers. So a helicopter came in and picked Polk up. They gave him a shot of sedatives that almost killed him. When they got back to Chu Lai, they had twenty-seven charges against Polk. Now here's his letter."

Polk's letter, dated four days earlier, had a Fort Leavenworth, Kansas, return address.

Dear Mrs. Gene:

I received your letter today. I must say that your letter brought back some sad memory. Yes I was in Michael platoon, He was my platoon sergeant at the time of his Death.

You might have been told this, but I'll like to tell you again. I was with your son at the time of his Death. Michael Died in his sleep, he never woke up. Before his Death him and I became very close friend. I was the only Black in our Squad, and I can honestly say I had heard the word Nigger enough to last me a life time. You see I could talk with Michael, he didn't care if you was Black or White. He was a good guy and we both had a Great Deal of Respect for each other.

You know I almost went to jail the night of the Accident. I was trying to get to our Fire Direction Officer. Today I still believe he call the rounds in short. Anyway the guys in the Company keep me away from him.

You might like to know, if you don't already know, the reason why I'm in jail. Well it started right after Michael Died. I was out in the field when this E-5 call me a Nigger, I came close to shooting him. But I was talk out of it buy the Officer in our Company. I was treated unfair because of my color. People dislike me in the Company with out full knowledge of the type of person I was. I was Prejudg the day I got into Co. C., 1/6, 198th. Your son Michael, and Prince, and a few other Blacks who names I can no longer remember, were the only People in the Company I could communicate with. Well, on the 26th of Feb 1971 I woke up in the hospital with a concussion and a contusion on the side of my face. They said I shot some Friendly Vietnamese and hit a Lt. (Officer) and a E-6. All the while I was in the field and saw the Death of your son I was Depress. I often have Dream about that night, and sometimes I can't sleep for thinking about them guys and how young they were. Please excuse me, but you are the first person I have talk with fully about that night and it Feel Good To Do So.

I have been lock up for 14 months and I'm tired of this. All I want is to get out of jail and see my Family. I haven't seen them in 16 month. I'll be so glad to see them (smile). I guess I'll have to wait until June 1, 1972. I wish you could Be of some help to me, Mrs. Gene, but you see I don't know what to ask you. If you could stop by and visit me I would like that Very Much. Oh yes! I try to get your address in March 1970 to write you to tell you how Sorry I was. But they wouldn't give me your address.

Well, until I hear from you may God blessing be with you and your family.

Sincerely yours,
s/Willard

"The clue to everything is Private Polk at Leavenworth," Peg said when she saw I'd finished the letter. "We asked him to send us the name of Prince, the white boy who Culpepper told us had lost a leg that night— they didn't think he would live, but he did. We want to meet Prince because he was in the First Platoon. . . . The thing is, I don't know whether we are just suspicious characters or whatever, but right away we didn't believe what we were told And this whole story we were first told by the service officer about the ARVN artillery, we repeated it, of course. So when the boys in Vietnam read about us in the newspaper, how I'd said Michael had been killed by South Vietnamese artillery, that's when we found out the truth. They wrote back that Michael had been killed by *our* artillery. That there had been investigations made."

Gene said, "We have asked for the artillery log. You see a record of every shot fired has to be kept for one year. We wrote Senator Fulbright—"

"He and Senator Hughes are trying to get it for us."

"We want to know if that shot was scheduled, who called it in. That information has to be in the artillery log." Gene sorted through some papers and pushed one to me. "Read this. It's my son's death certificate."

Before I had a chance to finish it, Gene said, "Michael did *not* have a missile wound in the chest. He was lying on his left side. He used to sleep on his left side." Gene pushed himself back from the table and stood up. "The wound was right through here," he said, pointing at his right kidney. "The undertaker told us that. The shock I got when we opened the casket and there wasn't a mark on him! I'll never forget it. Never!"

"We have to get in touch with Private Polk," Peg said, "and through him Prince."

"Once you do," I said, "what do you plan to do with the information? What's next?"

"We're waiting for one letter, to find one man," Gene answered, "Lieutenant Rocamora."

"We don't believe Rocamora called in the round that killed Michael," Peg said. "We want Rocamora to tell us he didn't call it in. Mike's death was investigated the following day, as we've said. But we've never been sent the results of that investigation, even though they promised us they would. Several of the boys we've been in touch with indicated that either the officer and the men on the gun were drunk—"

"Or they think it was an old gun," Gene said. "Or that someone else called in the target coordinates wrong."

"But assuming you found out the worst," I said, "that the artillery forward observer was drunk or that the battery commander and his men back at the guns were drunk and had been firing off shells as a lark and one of them exploded and killed Michael. What are you going to do?"

Without a moment's hesitation Peg replied, "We're going to demand about five hundred thousand dollars."

"Michael was in the citizens' army," Gene said.

"His potential, even with just the degree he had at the time he went to Vietnam, was from thirty to forty thousand dollars a year in his field. We don't want the money for ourselves," Peg said. "But we think they destroyed somebody with a terrific future for no reason."

"We know *something* happened there that night," Gene said, "and we know they're trying to cover it up."

"The fact that it was never a news item," Peg said. "We feel that with the one platoon being practically wiped out, the two men killed and seven wounded, that alone would have been a news release."

"If Mike died on the streets of LaPorte City," Gene said, "if some drunk had run over him, that would have been manslaughter, and there would have been a trial."

I spent five days with the Mullens that April out on their farm, for the most part listening to them talk about Michael.

After our last session Peg said, "You won't forget about us, will you?"

"No," I smiled. "I certainly won't do that."

I began gathering up my notebooks, pads, pens, the tape cassettes. Peg handed me a pen I'd overlooked and followed Gene and me to my car. Gene held open the door. "What are you going to do now?" he asked.

"I guess, the same as the two of you," I said. "I'm going to try to find out what happened to your son."

CHAPTER 8

In late July Gene telephoned me and excitedly said, "Listen, I've got an ending for your book!"

"Where are you?" I asked.

"We're in Washington, D.C. At the American Friends Office. We're driving up your way tomorrow. May we stop by and see you?"

"Of course," I said, "but what's up?"

"I've gotta run. Peg's got us a cab so I can't say much yet except that I've found him! I've found the man who killed my boy! I located Schwarzkopf," Gene crowed. "We're going to see him this afternoon!"

Two mornings later I met the Mullens at their motel, then drove them out to my house. Several times at breakfast and during the drive they had started to tell me about their meeting with Lieutenant Colonel Schwarzkopf, and each time I begged them to hold off until we could be isolated from interruptions and I could take proper notes. When we finally did begin, I discovered that by having made them wait I had unwittingly created an artificial atmosphere in which they seemed to feel themselves "testifying" before some judge. Peg took notes from her pocketbook and spread them out on the low table before her as if she were playing solitaire. Gene, his hands clasped together, fingers intertwined, sat across from her and leaned forward, eager to speak.

Colonel Alan Thompson, a Pentagon officer, located Schwarzkopf for the family. Peg had turned to the Pentagon on June 14 to see if she could obtain a copy of Charlie Company's morning report for the day Michael was killed. The report would have listed every man in Michael's platoon. Colonel Thompson found Schwarzkopf was assigned to Fort Myer, Virginia. The Mullens had not had time to visit Schwarzkopf then, but when they had returned to Washington in late July, they went directly to Fort Myer. There they learned Schwarzkopf had been transferred to Fort McNair, and at Fort McNair they were told Schwarzkopf was at the Walter Reed Army Medical Center on a year's convalescent leave.

"I called the hospital," Gene said, "and they told me that Colonel Schwarzkopf had been moved to Ward One, Orthopedic. I called there, and Colonel Schwarzkopf answered the phone. I said, 'This is Mr. Mullen. I'm calling about an incident that happened to your battalion, the One-over-Sixth of the Hundred and Ninety-eighth in Corps One on February 18 at two-thirty in the morning.'

"Colonel Schwarzkopf said, 'Do you mean that artillery incident?'

"I said 'Yes, that artillery incident.'

"'Mr. Mullen,' he said, 'I can tell you about that artillery incident.'

"I said, 'Colonel, I know more about that artillery incident than you think I do. I've been looking for you for a year and a half. I consider you the man who killed my son. I am going to take you to federal court.'"

"The colonel said, 'I wish you would take me to federal court. It would prove me innocent. I would like to talk to you.'

"'Colonel,' I said, 'I would like to talk to you, too, but how can I?'

"'Is your time pressing?' he asked. 'Why don't you come out to the hospital to visit me? I want to talk to you.' He repeated approximately four times, 'I want to talk to you.' So we made an appointment to see him at about five o'clock at his wish—very much his wish," Gene added. "And that's when we telephoned you. We took a cab out to Walter Reed and found Ward One very easily. There were six other patients in the ward, all officers. As I stood in the doorway and looked into the room, I noticed an officer in uniform sitting on the left side of Colonel Schwarzkopf's bed and on the right side, an empty chair. I walked in, and I said, 'Lieutenant Colonel Schwarzkopf?'

"He said, 'Yes.'

"I had expected a tall, thin man with the appearance of a West Point officer," Gene said, "but I was amazed at what I saw. I saw a round-faced, blond, overgrown, boyish-looking man of about thirty-five years of age. He had a cast on, a full body cast. He was not in pain. But he was in discomfort. All during our conversation he was very restless due to the cast.

"I said, 'I'm Mr. Mullen.'

"He said, 'I am pleased to meet you.'

"I did not shake his hand.

"Schwarzkopf acknowledged me and my wife, and then he introduced us to this Major Knap. Now he never told us who this Major Knap was or what his business was there. But from the way he had positioned his chair at the opposite side of the bed, it was obvious it had been prearranged."

"Gene," I interrupted, "could you tell Knap's branch of the service?"

"I don't know," Gene said. "Frankly, I wasn't interested. He was Army, that's all I know." He looked over at Peg, but she didn't know either. "Anyway, I said, 'Colonel, I would like to talk to you.'

"'I would like to talk to you, too,' the colonel said. 'We could go to a private room if you like. I can be moved.'

"'No, that isn't necessary.' I said. I went over to the wall and brought another chair for Peg, and we sat down. I was approximately a foot and a half from Schwarzkopf's face at all times, so I could hear and see his expression as we talked. Peg's and my chair were on the right side of the bed. This Major Knap was on the left in a position to view both Colonel Schwarzkopf and ourselves and to hear us. We sat down and I said, 'Now, Colonel, you can tell your story of what happened.'"

Gene wiped his mouth with the back of his hand. "He proceeded to tell us that on the night Michael was killed he, Schwarzkopf, was not with Charlie Company; he was instead on Hill Four Ten, the same hill as the supporting artillery. He told us, 'When the incident happened, I was notified by Captain Tom Cameron, Charlie Company's commander. I immediately ran down to the artillery unit and told them to stop firing, to lock their guns. I wanted those guns locked because this was the second incident that had happened to my battalion in thirty days! The first time it happened, the colonel in charge of the artillery unit said it was a once-in-a-lifetime fluke and—'"

"That was the Bravo Company incident," Peg interrupted. It was the first time she had spoken since Gene started telling me their story. Gene looked at Peg as if waiting for her to say something more, but when she remained silent, he continued.

"We don't know how many were wounded then, but the boys told us to ask Schwarzkopf about the time thirty-two men in Bravo Company got hurt. . . . Anyway, after Schwarzkopf ordered the guns locked, he said, he went to Michael's hill the next morning. I said, 'Yes, about ten minutes to eight.'

"Schwarzkopf turned and looked at me. He said, 'I went down with another officer—'

"I interrupted him again," Gene said. "'Colonel,' I said, 'there were four of you. You and three other officers were at the scene at that time.'

"He looked me in the eye and said, 'Yes, Mr. Mullen, you are correct. There were three other officers, but,' Schwarzkopf said, 'I want you to know I was not part of the investigating committee.'

"I said, 'No, we know that,'" Gene continued. "'They came out at approximately twelve o'clock noon in a Sloop helicopter, and they consisted of the artillery, plus some liaison officers between the infantry and the artillery, the investigating artillery team from 'Eye' Corps artillery.'

"And Schwarzkopf said, 'Yes, you are correct.'

"I then said, 'The rumors tell us, sir, that three things could have happened: the men were drinking, or the guns were off target, or the wrong coordinates were called in. Now,' I said, 'what did you find when you got there?'"

"Well, he replied that the guns were perfect," Peg said. "They had told Schwarzkopf after the Bravo Company incident that they blamed it on the gun. That is why he demanded the guns be locked. He told us, 'I could have killed Colonel Kuprin when he stepped off that helicopter because this was the second incident his artillery outfit had perpetrated on my battalion.' Kuprin was the artillery commander," Peg explained. "And, see, the boys told us it was the same gun that had done it before and the gun had not been repaired. Schwarzkopf, however, insisted the guns were okay. So I said, 'Colonel, I'm just going to ask you one thing: *Were the men drinking?* And he looked me right in the eye and said, 'Yes, Mrs. Mullen, the men had been drinking beer.'"

"See?" Gene said.

I asked Peg if the colonel had stated or implied that the men were drunk.

"No, only that they had been drinking beer. He seemed to want me to know that. I was kind of surprised he said yes because I don't think they should have been drinking. And then," Peg said, looking down at her notes, "Colonel Schwarzkopf told us, 'I think you should talk to Colonel Valentin Kuprin. He was the artillery battalion commander. He's in the Washington area and assigned to the Pentagon.' So that night, when we went back to the motel we called Kuprin. I told him who I was and said, 'Your name was given us by Lieutenant Colonel Schwarzkopf, and I would like you to identify the artillery officer who was reprimanded.'"

Kuprin did not remember the young lieutenant's name. According to

Peg, the former artillery battalion commander said, "The gunnery officer neglected to take into account the height of the trees. He failed to use his judgment and he was reprimanded. The procedure was corrected the next day." Kuprin also told the Mullens that he did not believe Lieutenant Rocamora had called in the artillery. Rocamora's radio operator had been on duty at the time; Rocamora was asleep.

"Okay," Peg said, referring again to her notes, "I then asked Kuprin about the rumors that the artillery officers had been drinking beer. He denied it. I told him that's what Colonel Schwarzkopf had said. Kuprin said, 'I'll take care of Norman.' I told him Schwarzkopf had said it was about time corrections were made because he 'had had it.' And Kuprin asked, 'Do you think the artillery just runs around with pistols shooting at people?' He said, 'Artillery isn't one hundred percent accurate. When we shoot four hundred rounds a night, we're going to kill a few people we shouldn't.' Kuprin said he had offered to remove Rocamora from Charlie Company after this incident, but Rocamora elected to stay with his assignment. He liked Charlie Company, and they liked him. And, well, my feeling is that if Rocamora *had* called in that artillery and *hadn't* alerted the boys, he wouldn't have been allowed to stay there. For his sake. That's why the boys were so upset: they didn't have a chance! When I told Kuprin of Hank Webb's comment about thinking it was an attack and sweeping people into their foxholes, Kuprin said, 'Well, if you call a six-inch sleeping trench a foxhole, then it's no wonder they died!' "

"Peg," I said, "the boys wrote they had dug foxholes, didn't they?"

"Everybody dug a foxhole that night," she said. "A foxhole and a sleeping position. But they were in their sleeping positions when the shell hit."

"Can I use one of your pieces of paper?" Gene asked. He started to draw as he spoke: "Now, there was a group here, one, two, three, four, with a guard. And then there was Michael . . . Polk . . . Hamilton . . . another one here and a guard. The first Platoon was here, Second Platoon in the middle, the Third Platoon was over here. Webb and Culpepper were Third Platoon . . . Culpepper had just got off guard at two o'clock and he was changing positions with Schumacher. Schumacher was saying, 'The artillery's coming in closer,' and then, all of a sudden he says to Culpepper, 'My God, they're walking them right in on us! They're trying to kill us!' " Gene drew an asterisk with little lines radiating out from its center. "Right here was a high knoll. There was a tree here. This is Hill Seventy-six because in the court-martial of Private Polk that's how it's referred to. And Hill Four Ten was back over here." Gene drew a series of elevation lines on the other side of his drawing. "The shell came right over this way"—Gene's finger followed the arc from the top of Hill 410 to the asterisk he had drawn before "—hit the tree here and"—Gene gestured as if flicking water from his fingers—"came down. It killed Michael, Leroy Hamilton and wounded six or seven others."

Gene and Peg both fell silent. I suggested we break for lunch.

We spoke for quite a while that afternoon about what had happened that night on the hill where Michael died. Had the artillery been firing all night long or not? Why was it senior noncommissioned officers did not go out into the field? Why had a plea of temporary insanity never been entered in Willard Polk's case? Mightn't the explosion that night have been considered "mitigating circumstances" especially since the men on either side of Polk had been killed? But over and over again the conversation would return to Lieutenant Colonel Schwarzkopf, and finally, I asked the Mullens if their own attitude toward him had changed.

They were both silent until Peg, very hesitatingly, said, "Yes, my attitude has changed. . . . I mean, finding him there in that body cast, I thought, 'Well, the Lord has taken care of you. . . .'" She paused again, then blurted, "I guess I really don't know how I feel about him. I'd learned to hate him after hearing the boys talk. But he told us he was hated because he insisted on discipline, on taking the proper precautions. And I couldn't help thinking, if only Michael had had his flak jacket on that night, he wouldn't have died. . . . Schwarzkopf, you know, repeatedly told us what a fine man Michael was. He said over and over again did we realize what a tremendous soldier our son had been, the rapport he had had with his men and so forth. He kept saying this to me. . . ."

"And, too, Mother," Gene said, "the letter he wrote us about Michael's death was very sympathetic. At the time, we thought he was laying it on a bit thick. The only thing he didn't tell us was that Rocamora was asleep. He told us as much as the investigation could have, and well, he didn't think we'd look any further."

"Who would?" Peg asked.

"What are you going to do now?" I asked.

"We'll find Rocamora. We think now he's in Hawaii," Gene said. "You see I have an undying faith. Everything we've looked for we've found out. It only takes time. Can you imagine all the information we've picked up? Just two people? And it's all authentic! It can be documented. Where in the world could two people like us do what we've done? It's not only through our efforts. At times, at certain moments we've been led some place and the story opens up. We move somewhere else, and something more opens up. The last thing we need to do is find Rocamora and," Gene said, slapping his knees, "I think we're going to find him."

"Say you do find him, Gene," I said, "what do you hope to learn?"

"How Michael died," Peg answered.

"Who . . . killed . . . our . . . son!" Gene said.

Why? What good would it do? I liked the Mullens very much. I felt terribly sorry for them—it was impossible not to. But no matter how much affection and sympathy I felt for them, I could not accept that their confrontation with Lieutenant Colonel H. Norman Schwarzkopf had, as recounted by them, really taken place. I did not doubt that they had located the colonel, spoken to him face-to-face, or that he had answered their questions as best he could. I suspected only that Peg and Gene had become, like the United States government which so enraged them, no longer able to listen to what they didn't want to hear.

I was especially disturbed by the realization that the Mullens' attitude was partly my fault. Gene himself had indicated as much just two days before when he had telephoned me so excitedly and said, "I've got an ending for your book!"

That anticipated sweet revenge must have seemed the perfect ending indeed, one which the Mullens could almost set in type themselves: GOLD STAR PARENTS BRING SON'S MURDERER TO HIS KNEES.

But of course, Schwarzkopf *hadn't* killed their son. And I worried about to what awful lengths the Mullens might drive themselves to achieve their next "perfect ending" for me. The Mullens had already demonstrated a surprisingly sophisticated awareness of the impact media exposure might have. The enormous attention they had received as a result of their first antiwar advertisement could not help having seemed heady stuff indeed. National prominence once achieved—no matter how momentary and elusive—creates a craving for ever more attention. Inevitably the different media, television especially, not only report news but inspire, influence, feed upon and demand ever more news. The temptation to create "perfect endings" was the corruption I wanted the Mullens spared. The only way I could achieve this was by finding out for them exactly what had happened to their son. I believed I already knew. I believed, also, that they knew, too. Colonel Valentin Kuprin, the artillery battalion commander, had told them. It had not, however, been what they had wanted to hear.

I told Peg I would go talk with Lieutenant Colonel Schwarzkopf myself. She said, "I'll bet you ten dollars he won't even see you."

I spent two days with Lieutenant Colonel Schwarzkopf during the first week of October. He had been released from the Walter Reed Army Medical Center and was recuperating at his home in Annandale, Virginia, with his wife, Brenda, a former TWA stewardess, and their then two-year-old daughter, Cindy. I had written the colonel asking if I might speak with him, and he had promptly urged me to come. I rang his doorbell, and as I waited, I recalled Gene's description of Schwarzkopf as a "round-faced, blond, overgrown, boyish-looking man." There was nothing boyish about the man who answered the door. Schwarzkopf is big, solid, over six feet tall, and weighs maybe 220 pounds. He still wore a cast starting at his hips which rode high over his shoulders like football shoulder pads. His brown-blond hair was short, but not crew-cut, and his expression—like his handshake and greeting—was open and friendly.

I asked him if he would mind my using a tape recorder, and he replied he wouldn't mind at all; in fact, he added, he intended to use one himself. He explained he had called the Pentagon to make sure the interview would be all right, and the Pentagon had placed no restrictions on him whatsoever. They had suggested, however, he use his own tape recorder to ensure that his answers would not be distorted or lifted out of context.

As we took our places on opposite sides of the dining-room table, I explained that I had heard the Mullens' version of their conversation, and I was interested in hearing his. I asked, to begin with, how Gene Mullen had introduced himself on the telephone.

"Okay," Schwarzkopf said, tilting back in his chair, "I'll recite it to you exactly: I was notified I had a phone call, and they had to bring the phone to my bed. I was then in a body cast that went all the way down to my knees, so I couldn't move. I picked up the telephone, and this voice at the other end said, 'Is this Colonel Schwarzkopf?'

"I said, 'Yes.'

"He said, 'Were you the commanding officer of the First Battalion of the Sixth Infantry in February, 1970?'

"I said, 'Yes, I was.'

"The voice on the other end said, 'Does the name Michael Mullen mean anything to you?'

"'I recall the name,' I said, 'but right now I can't specifically place it. . . .' See," Schwarzkopf explained, "it had been almost two years since the occurrence of this thing. Mr. Mullen then said, 'Does an incident that took place on the eighteenth of February—' and he went into so many miles north of Quang Ni at such-and-such—'mean anything to you?'

"I said, 'No, I'm sorry, but based on what you've given me I can't recall exactly—wait, are you talking about an incident where some men were killed by friendly artillery fire?'

"He said, 'Yes, I am.'

"I said, 'Yes, I recall that.'

"And he said, 'Well, I want to inform you that we are bringing charges against you in federal district court for suppressing the facts of the investigation into the death of my son.'"

The colonel's chair legs banged forward on the floor. "'Mr. Mullen,' I said, 'look, I think there's a misunderstanding here. I was in no way responsible for the investigation into the death of your son.' Mr. Mullen was very emotional, and I said, 'But I don't think we're going to get anything accomplished talking to each other over the phone. Can you come out to Walter Reed and see me? He said he could, and I said, 'Fine. Come on out. Let's sit down and talk about this thing. You look at me, and I'll look at you and we'll talk this thing through.'"

"Colonel Schwarzkopf," I said, "did Gene Mullen ever accuse you of having killed his son? Did he say, 'I've been looking for you for a year and a half. I consider you the man who killed my son, and I'm taking you to federal court.'?"

"No." Colonel Schwarzkopf shook his head. "Nothing like that. What I told you is almost verbatim. I remember it because it came as such a shot out of the blue: 'I want to tell you that we are taking you to federal court—' He didn't say 'for killing my son.' He said, 'for covering up the facts of the investigation.'

"I knew I wanted to talk to the Mullens," Schwarzkopf said, "but I also knew I wanted a witness there. I didn't want to get off in a closed room someplace, talk with them, and then have them turn around and say, 'He told us this or that.' I wanted somebody there to know what I said. I also wanted some advice on whether I'd be out of line talking to them at all. So I called up the JAG [Judge Advocate General, the legal branch of the Army] section at Walter Reed and asked them to send somebody down. I just wanted to ask a few questions about what I should do. Major Knap came down. We had just about decided that sure, I could talk to them, I could tell them anything they wanted to know when the Mullens walked in through the door. At that time I thought only Mr. Mullen was coming. I had no idea Mrs. Mullen was along. I think they were rather surprised by my condition, my cast. I reached out to shake hands with them, to introduce myself when they came up to my bed, and it was very apparent that Gene Mullen was very reluctant to even shake my hand. I was concerned because I wasn't sure what their emotional state was. I was lying in bed. There was a bed on my right, five beds on my left with guys in traction, and I wasn't sure if because of the Mullens' emotional state it was going to degenerate into them shouting and screaming at me or what. So I asked if they would like to go to a private room, and they said, 'No, we'll talk to you right here.' In fact, Gene Mullen said, 'We want to talk to you, and we want you to have a witness here to hear what is being said, too.'

"I said, 'Fine. Major Knap is present.' I asked Knap to stay. I wanted to talk to them because, well, I felt I could help. Here was a family obviously very upset about their son's death, who obviously had some false information, false ideas about how and why their son had died. I felt if I could give them the circumstances of their son's death, tell them exactly what happened right down the line, if they could look me in the eye and see that I was telling them the truth, then they would feel they had finally gotten the straight story about the entire thing and that this would somehow set their minds at ease. I wanted to show them that their son's battalion commander wasn't a Nazi, wasn't an arch-right-wing military conservative. That I was a human being who felt like they felt, who had cared about their son. I wanted to make it very clear to them that nobody was more upset about Michael's death than I was. I was furious when it happened!" Schwarzkopf said. "Particularly since I'd had another artillery incident from the same artillery battalion only a month before. I was so damned mad when the brigade commander landed with the artillery battalion commander at my position the following morning I couldn't even speak to the guy."

"Was this the artillery battalion commander Colonel Kuprin?" I asked.

"Right."

"Did you tell the Mullens, 'I could have killed Colonel Kuprin'?"

"I may have," Schwarzkopf admitted. "Like I said, I was furious! But don't get me wrong," he quickly added. "It wasn't because I blamed Kuprin directly as the man responsible, but it was as if my unit had done something terrible, caused casualties in someone else's unit. The unit commander is responsible for everything his unit does or fails to do. I was tremendously emotionally upset about that whole incident, and as I told the Mullens, nobody was more upset than I was."

"What was the Mullens' response to that?" I asked.

"The whole conversation had started off in a rather accusatory fashion," Schwarzkopf replied. "Questions like: 'Why did you do this?' 'Why did you do that?' 'Why did you cover up the circumstances of my son's death in your investigation?' I proceeded to explain that, first," he said, tapping his cast, "I did not, in fact, conduct the investigation. Any time there is a friendly artillery incident, the friendly artillery investigates it. And second, it's all disinterested parties who are involved in the investigation. Therefore, I had nothing to do with the investigation whatsoever! Still, when I tried to explain how upset I was by Michael's death, Mrs. Mullen then asked me, 'Well, when you flew out in your little helicopter, wasn't your first statement, "Gee, it looks like the Vietcong did this!"?' I explained again I didn't conduct the investigation, that the artillery investigators were, in fact, the ones who flew in in the small helicopter. What happened was this: Colonel Clemons, the brigade commander, picked me up in his big helicopter as soon as he could get to my position. Kuprin was with him at the time. We next flew to Charlie Company's position— that would have been at about eight in the morning. Charlie Company had had to cut a landing zone large enough for our big helicopter to come in. We then flew back out prior to the artillery investigators' arrival." Schwarzkopf paused. "As I was explaining all this to the Mullens, the more we talked, the more I recalled the circumstances of the entire thing. I remembered then that someone later in Charlie Company had said that in fact, one of the artillery investigators had gotten out of the small helicopter and his first reaction was that it hadn't been done by American artillery at all, but by the VC. The point is, however, the lieutenant colonel Mrs. Mullen was referring to, the one who flew in in the small helicopter, wasn't me at all. It was the lieutenant colonel in charge of the investigation. He had been assigned by the division."

"About what time do you think they arrived?"

"About ten in the morning would be my rough guess."

I asked Lieutenant Colonel Schwarzkopf how far he had been from Charlie Company when the shell hit. About two or three kilometers, he said. Why then if the artillery round had killed the two men and wounded six others at nearly three in the morning, had he then not been able to come to Charlie Company until five hours later?

"I couldn't," he said. "No helicopters were available. Generally I never had a helicopter at night. No one had a helicopter at night. No battalion commander, no brigade commander, no anyone—Med-evac got to them. Med-evac will fly in all weather conditions any time, any place, anywhere, under any circumstances. But that night the Med-evac pilot had a tremendously difficult time even finding them. There was a thick fog, Charlie Company was down in the valley firing all sorts of flares and everything else." He took a sheet of yellow paper. "You had huge mountains on one side, very high mountains on the other"—Schwarzkopf drew two ellipses—"it was almost a river valley. A very narrow one." He penciled in a thin line meandering between the two ellipses. "But seated on the left, on the south side of the river, was another piece of high ground that rose in the middle of the valley. Charlie Company was on top of that." He put an x on top of the small hill. "I was sitting on the mountain over here. It was Hill Four Ten."

"And that was where the artillery had been placed?"

"That's right," he said. "But let me explain this because it's one of the ironies of these things happening."

The maximum range of a 105mm artillery piece, the colonel told me, was approximately 12,500 meters. The artillery which would normally have supported Charlie Company was located at "Fat City" (the division artillery base camp over Chu Lai), and for this operation the guns would have been firing at their extreme range. The greater the range, the less accurate the artillery. Schwarzkopf, wanting to ensure that Charlie Company would be covered adequately, asked that the supporting artillery be moved forward. Colonel Joseph Clemons, the brigade commander, approved Schwarzkopf's request, and ordered Colonel Valentin Kuprin, the artillery battalion commander, to displace a battery (minus) of 105mm howitzers to a position from which Charlie Company's operation would be well within range. Kuprin had the responsibility to select that spot from which the artillery would be fired, and he chose to place the guns on Hill 410.

"Frankly, I would have picked Hill Four Ten too," Schwarzkopf said. "Hill Four Ten was the only location that far out where the guns could have been placed. There was another hill, Hill Seven Oh Seven but we're talking in meters now, and that would have placed the guns over twenty-three hundred feet high."

Was it essential the guns be placed in a position from which they would have to fire over Charlie Company's heads?

Nobody at that time could have predicted the artillery either would or would not have had to fire over Charlie Company's position, the colonel explained. If Charlie Company had set up on the north slope of the hill or on the southern side, rather than the crest, it would not have happened. But where the company commander establishes his night defensive perimeter is totally that commander's responsibility and prerogative. "In any case," Schwarzkopf added, "it's even more significant that Hill Four Ten had been used many, many times in the past for similar operations, and there had never been any incident whatsoever or any unsafeness involved. Therefore, I think it was not only the logical choice to put the artillery there, but the *only* choice."

Why, if the defensive targets had been called in earlier and if the artillery had announced its intention to commence firing Charlie Company's DTs at about eight that evening, had they then not fired but instead rescheduled the DTs for almost three the following morning?

"All artillery firing is done on priorities," he said. "Obviously a contact mission takes first priority. Say an infantry company over here is calling for DTs and the artillery unit is firing them when suddenly another unit over there is involved in a big fire fight. The priority of all the artillery units is going to shift to that unit that's under fire, in contact with the enemy. Here's how this thing works. . . ."

Schwarzkopf explained how a company commander, upon moving into a defensive position, attempts to determine the most likely routes an enemy might use to attack him. He had his artillery forward observer select targets that would place artillery fire upon those most likely spots. Each unit might select as many as twenty DTs, and with any given number of units requesting DTs and other units engaged in fire fights which took priority, a unit's DTs would not be fired until firing time was available. "Sometimes," he said, "this is very late. In Charlie Company's case it was very, very late. The night Michael Mullen was killed the artillery firing was interrupted and not resumed until five hours later."

Why did the round that killed Michael fall short?

Lieutanant Colonel Schwarzkopf shook his head. "It was fate. As I said, Charlie Company was sitting on a ridge between two mountains in what amounted to a valley. The artillery was to their north side on top of a hill and the defensive target the guns at this particular time were firing was a DT to the south side of the ridge Charlie Company was sitting on. The artillery fired the first round—the white phosphorus [WP] marking round that is supposed to burst fifty meters above the spot you want the high explosive [HE] round to hit. The WP round did, in fact, burst fifty meters above that spot. Then, naturally, to make the HE round land in the right spot, you would have to depress the tube of the gun to make the round land lower. The calculations of what data to be placed on the gun to lower the tube to account for this fifty meters of airspace are all done back at the fire direction center [FDC]. The FDC is supposed to take into account the mask clearance of the hill along the line of fire and the tree heights on top of the land. In other words, you've got to make sure you're not only going to clear the ground but where the trees stick up from the ground, too. Well, evidently"—the colonel paused—"in this case, this was not done. When the next HE round was fired, as it passed over the ridge to land on the other side, it hit a tree quite a ways up. A tree right over Charlie Company's position. . . ." Lieutenant Colonel Schwarzkopf let his breath out slowly.

And that's how Michael Mullen was killed. Just as Colonel Kuprin had told the Mullens, just as had been hinted at in correspondence with members of Charlie Company: someone back at the fire direction center had failed to take into account the height of the trees on Charlie Company's hilltop night defensive perimeter.

Two details remained to be cleared up: Who called in the artillery round? Were the men drinking?

Lieutenant Colonel Schwarzkopf wasn't sure who had requested the artillery. The forward observer team consists of three men: a forward observer, his reconnaissance sergeant and a radio operator. Each of them is qualified to call in artillery and make corrections. Schwarzkopf believed the DTs had been radioed in late that afternoon by Lieutenant Rocamora. It was clear, however, that it didn't matter who had requested the artillery since whoever it was, he had provided the correct target coordinates. That the artillery had not fired its DTs until three that morning had nothing to do with the forward observer team; the delay was solely the responsibility of the artillery. They had fired only when firing time had come available. As for the drinking:

"General Ramsey, the commanding general of the Americal Division, had a policy when I first got to the division that there could be beer on fire bases and in the field," Schwarzkopf said, "but he had a serious incident in the Hundred and Ninety-sixth Brigade. I think it was in one of their stand-down areas that a man got drunk. General Ramsey then put out the policy that there was to be no more beer in the field period. I assume it was enforced by everyone. I enforced it in my battalion. And on this particular mission the artillery came out and set up in position on Hill Four Ten, and the next morning—not at the time, but the morning following Michael's death—when I went down to the guns to try to conduct my own semiformal investigation into what had happened, I looked down and there was a whole bunch of fresh beer cans. As I told the Mullens, it was obvious that they had been drinking beer. I doubt, however, that this fact is even contained in the investigation. Why? *Because the error was not on the guns.* Again, the error that caused Michael's death was made back at the fire direction center. So it was not a question of anybody on the guns drinking or anything else. The aiming of the guns was in no way a contributing factor to Michael's death. I'll say this again because it's important: everything that was set on the guns was, in fact, exactly what had been relayed to the guns over the radio by the FDC. The target coordinates radioed by the forward observer with Charlie Company were the correct coordinates. Now, I'm sure the reason why there was no mention in the investigation about the drinking was because it wasn't drunkenness. The division commander's policy was no beer in the field, so don't mention the beer and don't make waves. But waves were made. Colonel Clemons was out there, he knew they had been drinking beer, and he raised holy hell with Kuprin about it. Heads were chopped. Corrective action was taken but not through the investigation simply because the beer was in no way a contributing factor to Michael Mullen's death."

"You mentioned an artillery incident a month before in which artillery fire from an American unit landed on, I believe, Bravo Company?"

"That was in a different place," Schwarzkopf said. "It was Bravo Company. They were in a place called Dragon Valley, and there had been a great deal of contact out there. I can't recall if DTs were being fired or whether it was an enemy probe, but in any case the rounds fell short—incidently, no one was killed in the Bravo Company incident. There were some wounded. They conducted an investigation and found that on one of the guns there was a faulty elevating mechanism. It's a screw-type device, a bunch of teeth and a screw that turned to raise or lower the tube, and there had been a slippage in the teeth. As a result, the tube had dropped down to a lower angle than it should have been, and this is why the rounds fell short. Frankly, as an infantry battalion commander, I couldn't care less what caused it. My primary concern was to insure that it didn't happen again! And that is why, naturally, when the same guns that had an artillery firing incident on one of my units exactly one month later has another, I'm furious!"

"When you said, just now, 'the same guns,' did you mean—"

"It wasn't the same gun." Schwarzkopf quickly corrected me. "What I meant was that they were guns from the same unit, Division artillery."

At the interview's conclusion Lieutenant Colonel Schwarzkopf insisted on driving me back into Washington where I had reserved a hotel room. He said he needed the air, and maybe it would help him sleep. Because of his cast, he said, he was never able to sleep more than a few hours at a time. I asked him about his wound. He was in a cast, it turned out, not because of anything that had happened in Vietnam but rather because the accumulated strain and pounding his back had taken over the years had been aggravated by parachute landings. The Army decided an operation might alleviate some of the pressure on his lower spine. He would be free of the cast, he told me, in another couple of months.

During the drive I asked him about his correspondence with the Mullens and whether Peg had sent him Michael's letters.

"The only letter I ever got was from *Mrs.* Mullen. It arrived in May, as I recall, shortly after I was wounded. She told me she had taken his gratuity pay and spent it to buy a newspaper advertisement. I think she sent me a copy of the ad and excerpts from his letters and that was about it. . . ." He thought for a moment, then said, "I was very upset by the tone of her letter. I wanted to write an answer. I contacted Division and was told I shouldn't, that I should forward the letter to Division instead, and they would handle it from there. And so, of course, that was my guide."

"You mean the two letters the Mullens received from you weren't written by you at all? Why wouldn't the Division want you to answer?"

"I don't think it was a question of not wanting me to answer," he said. "I think it was because it involved friendly fire casualties—in fact, any casualties at all."

He explained how it was the Division's policy in situations involving casualties to have the Headquarters write and coordinate all letters sent to next of kin. The purpose for this policy was to ensure that no conflicting details were given, thereby sparing families the sort of anguish varying versions might cause.

The result, in the Mullens' case, however, was clearly the opposite. It was precisely the conflicting evidence, plus an implicit policy of information control, that started the Mullens out on their search to learn what had happened to their son.

I asked the colonel what he would have written the Mullens had the Division not intervened.

"Oh, God, I don't know," he said. "I probably would have tried to give them as much detail on what exactly happened as I could. And I probably would have tried to convey to them my personal feeling of . . . of, I guess, horror that this did happen. . . ."

We were both silent. I could not reconcile the discrepancies between what the Mullens had told me Schwarzkopf had said and his version of what he had said. I tried to imagine Gene leaning over the colonel, their faces inches apart, and how Schwarzkopf would have reacted to Gene's constant correcting him on details and Gene's comment at one point about his having "lost thirty-two men from your stupidity of marching them through a minefield."

We were in the old Georgetown part of Washington when I turned to the colonel and asked, "When the Mullens visited you in the hospital, who did most of the talking?"

"Mrs. Mullen did," he said.

"She did? Peg did?"

"As a matter of fact, I was very concerned for Mr. Mullen. At times he was very emotional and would become so choked up he was almost incoherent. Why? You sound surprised."

"I am. That isn't the impression I got at all."

"What did they tell you?" he asked.

"I guess it wasn't so much what they said as how they said it. The 'Colonel Schwarzkopf' they told me about just doesn't seem like you at all."

A couple of weeks later I telephoned Lieutenant Colonel Schwarzkopf and said I was sending him the transcript of our conversation. I also told him I would be enclosing a transcript of the Mullens' talk with me, adding that I wasn't doing him any favor by doing so. I explained, however, with his help I hoped somehow to reconstruct the conversation he had had with them at Walter Reed and write it as it had occurred.

About a week later—this would have been around the beginning of November—Lieutenant Colonel Schwarzkopf mailed me two cassette tapes. On them he explained it was difficult for him to write because of the cast and, if I didn't mind, he would rather speak into the tape as though we were together again. The first long section answered specific questions I had added to the margin of our transcript or enlarged upon areas he felt needed clarification or qualified statements which, in print, he felt might have carried too strong an emphasis. Wherever applicable, I simply inserted these comments in the text. He next turned his attention to the Mullen transcript saying, "You were absolutely right when you said you weren't doing me any favors by sending me this interview.

"Frankly, my immediate reaction was one of anger and shock—even after many days of reading and rereading it, of trying to assume a dispassionate viewpoint on this entire thing, I still find myself somewhat disturbed when I see their comments here. I am going to try to approach this as best I can from an unemotional standpoint, but this sheds an entirely different light on the Mullens from what I had before.

"They have quoted liberally out of context, extracted certain words I said and ignored the meaning of everything else I've said in my talks with them. They've made assumptions that I felt a certain way when I said something. Then somehow turned it into words supposedly stated.

"Obviously they have taken my interview and twisted it to substantiate or justify whatever strange idea it is that they have—and, frankly, what their idea is I really don't know—but it upsets me that I did not accomplish what I set out to do by talking to them in the first place. I wanted to tell them the straight story of what happened to their son, to somehow set their minds at ease. Instead, all I've evidently accomplished is added fuel to their fire."

Schwarzkopf, as best he could, discussed the sequence of topics raised during their conversation. He apologized for occasional vagueness but explained he had had no idea at the time he met with the Mullens that he would be later asked to reconstruct the conversation in detail. "It was particularly difficult," he added, "because it was an emotional moment for me, and like I said, it was obviously an emotional moment for the Mullens." Then, directly referring to the transcript, he said, "All right, where Gene Mullen said, 'Now he never told us who Major Knap was or what his business was there, but from the way he had positioned his chair at the opposite side of the bed, it was obvious it had been prearranged,' well, this is absolutely ridiculous! I explained to you before who Knap was and what he was doing there. I guess what I'm trying to point out is . . . is . . . the intent. That attitude with which the Mullens approached this interview is what has upset me more than anything else. The obvious looking for trouble, for something not the truth but which would substantiate their feelings. That statement, 'it was obvious it had been prearranged,' is typical of their evident approach to the whole thing."

The colonel paused, and I could hear a page turn. "Okay, another thing," he said. "This comment of Gene Mullen's about the minefield. Well, you know me well enough, I think, to realize that a comment such as 'You lost thirty-two men from your stupidity of marching them through a minefield' is a little bit of bravado on his part. I wouldn't have tolerated that for one minute from anyone no matter how conciliatory I was trying to be toward them. The subject was brought up, and we discussed it, but he certainly didn't approach it in that fashion. They also said that an 'officer suckered [me] down' into that area. In the first place, nobody called me in. Nobody on the ground ever calls his battalion commander and says, 'You must come down here and land.' A battalion commander does what he wants to do. It's his battalion! And secondly, no officer could have suckered me down because when I landed, there were *no officers there.* That was one of the big reasons why I went into that area to take care of Bravo Company. The one officer who was with them—a real fine young man—had been wounded and had to be evac'd out. The first sergeant had also been wounded, which upset me very much because he, too, was a fine man. So without, with this lack of real leaders I had confidence in, I felt I had to get in there and get things squared away.

"And here where he says, 'The company first sergeant was out there that night, and it was the first time he was out in the field in I don't know how long.' And she says, 'They have to go out.' 'By the book,' he says. And she says, 'Every three months or so.'

"Well, this thing about the first sergeant was ridiculous," Schwarzkopf said. "You're aware of the administrative duties that a first sergeant has in a company, the paperwork that goes with the job. But Colonel Joe Clemons decided that because first sergeants had had so much valuable experience and because we were so short of experienced NCOs, their place was in the field. He put out a directive stating that the first sergeant of every rifle company spend a minimum of fifty percent of their time in the field with their unit. It was just that simple. I concurred wholeheartedly and enforced it in my battalion. Frankly, in Charlie Company's case, there was a personality clash between the first sergeant and the executive officer. So, any time the XO was back in the rear, the first sergeant intentionally went out to the field—and one of the reasons was to get away from Charlie Company's executive officer. . . ."

The colonel paused, and I could hear him turning more pages on the transcript. "Okay," he said, "where Mrs. Mullen makes the comment 'All the boys said it was the only time they remember all the officers being there. And even Schwarzkopf—it was the first time he was in action with them on the ground.' Again, that's incorrect.

"I made it a point to be with every single one of my units every single day. I was constantly in and out. One of the reasons, as I explained to you before, why I didn't stay with one company all the time was that I didn't want to harass that one company commander. But secondly, I had a responsibility for four rifle companies on the ground, a mortar company, a reconnaissance platoon, and my rear, any one of which was or might have been in a dangerous area. Therefore, I went everywhere. And, all right, I wasn't even with Charlie Company on the ground that night. I was back on Hill Four Ten with the artillery because I had two rifle companies out there . . . but why am I going into such detail on this?

"For a very simple reason," Schwarzkopf said. "The Mullens just don't have the facts! Or if they do have the facts, they choose to ignore them. What really bothers me is that they are so convinced that they are so right. And they're so loaded with wrong information.

"I'm not sure any of this has any bearing on your book—I don't know whether it does or not. It's just that I'm sure every time the Mullens get up and issue public statements, nobody can get up and rebut them.

"I felt a—I still feel a great deal of compassion for the Mullens. I do. It's a terrible tragedy that they lost their son—it's a terrible tragedy that so many women have lost sons—but although I feel sorry for the Mullens, I think the biggest tragedy is their mental state at this time.

"I now feel the Mullens have been told over and over again exactly what happened to Michael, but unfortunately, they're not willing to believe it. They're not willing to accept it. They still apparently think everyone is wrong except them. Somehow they have adopted the very role they are condemning in the rest of us."

The tape ran silent for about ten seconds. When the colonel spoke again, his voice was discouraged, tired, a little sad.

"I'll just finish off by saying it's a terrible thing that happened to Michael Mullen . . . a terrible, *terrible* tragedy. He was a very fine noncommissioned officer. Very well thought of by the men in his company. He was intelligent. He had brains and common sense. Michael was a leader. And that's why his death had such an impact on Charlie Company. Michael was one of those individuals who stand out. He was a very fine young man, and his death was a tremendous loss. It's terrible that any young man should lose his life in such a violent way. And I guess that is what your book is about. But it's an even more terrible thing that has happened to the Mullens themselves."

CHAPTER 10

A lmost exactly a year after I had first met Gene and Peg Mullen at their Black Hawk County, Iowa, farm I drove back through La Porte City to talk to them again. I had not seen the Mullens for nine months, not since the day we spent discussing their meeting with Lieutenant Colonel H. Norman Schwarzkopf.

We had not talked long before Peg asked, "Was Michael, or was he not, the platoon sergeant? Now this you've learned."

"He was not," I said.

"Why not?"

"Because a new sergeant came into Charlie Company who had a higher rank. He was with the company one or two days the night Michael was killed, and he was wounded, too."

"Who was he?" Peg asked.

"His name was Wetsel. He was a staff sergeant. Michael was an acting platoon sergeant, but it was only temporary."

"We know that," Gene said curtly.

"Because Michael didn't want to be platoon sergeant," Peg said. "Why was Michael made a platoon sergeant to begin with?"

I explained that Michael's previous platoon sergeant had rotated home. While Charlie Company was awaiting the replacement, Michael, as ranking sergeant in the 1st Platoon, was appointed acting platoon sergeant. Michael was a sergeant (E-5) with three stripes. When Wetsel, a staff sergeant (E-6) with three stripes and one rocker, arrived in the company, he became the 1st Platoon's platoon sergeant. "Look, I don't know whether this is the proper time or not. It's up to you. But if you'd like, I can cover with you all the information I've been able to learn and—"

"Oh, I don't know whether that's necessary or not," Peg said, looking distressed.

"It's up to you," I said.

"Michael was hit between the shoulder blades, wasn't he?" she asked.

"Yes, a piece of shrapnel entered his back and pierced his heart. He died right away. In his sleep. There's no question about that."

"Yes," Peg said. "They all told us that."

"But what I meant, Peg," I said, "is that I can give you the background of the operation he was involved in, what their mission was if you want to know any of this, what it was like. . . ."

"There's something I want to know," Gene said. "Something that has always bugged me: *Why was it covered up?*"

"That was the thing," Peg said. "Why wasn't it ever in the news?"

"In our telegram from that general," Gene said, turning to Peg, "you have that telegram, don't you? The general told us that the incident had been investigated and the investigation was on record at the Logistics Center at . . . at. . . ."

"Long Binh," Peg said.

"Long Binh, that's right," Gene continued. "And he said it would be released to us immediately. But it never was!"

"First of all, Gene," I said, "I don't believe the incident was deliberately covered up. I don't believe that there was ever a conspiracy to prevent you from learning what had happened to Michael. The details given you in that first letter from the battalion commander dated March second which you received the day after Michael's funeral were, in fact, correct. The reason why you were never sent the results of the investigation was that the report was classified 'For Official Use Only,' a very minor security classification, but one which would nevertheless prevent it from being released to civilians without a 'Need-to-Know.' It doesn't matter that you are Michael's parents. Secondly, the investigation would obviously contain hypotheses on what might have happened, and these hypotheses might be open to misinterpretation, depending on the point of view of the reader. If, for example, the report mentioned that a lieutenant back at Hill Four Ten with the guns was asleep at the time of the incident, you might still believe that if he had been awake, Michael would have been spared. I don't know if I've made myself clear, but the reason why the report was not sent was to spare you more anguish."

"I don't buy that," Gene said flatly. "No, I don't buy that. The simple reason why the report was not sent was because this was the second artillery incident to have happened in twenty-one days."

"Did Schwarzkopf mention that to you?" Peg asked me.

"Yes, we talked about it."

"Schwarzkopf did tell you about that?" Gene asked, clearly surprised. "It was actually the third incident that had happened in a little over a month with this same unit. That's why they tried to hush it up."

"There wasn't a third incident," I said. "The previous incident, the one in which some men from Bravo Company were wounded—none, incidentally, were killed—the cause of that accident was a faulty artillery piece. There were teeth missing on the elevating gear, and when the tube was raised, the mechanism indicated a higher elevation than was actually on the guns because of the slippage caused by the missing teeth. As a result, when the artillery piece was fired, the round fell short. In Michael's case, however, the guns were fine. The round fell short because a lieutenant back at the Fire Direction Center had failed to take into account the height of the trees on top of the hill where Charlie Company had set up."

"What happened to that lieutenant?" Peg asked.

"He was given an official reprimand."

"Yeah, see, Schwarzkopf said he would have had him court-martialed," Gene said.

"What about the boys who were drinking?" Peg asked.

I explained how the drinking had not made any difference because the error was not on the guns. The men had done exactly what they were told to do. The investigation confirmed that the target information was exactly what had been forwarded from the Fire Direction Center.

"Okay now," Gene said. "Who called in the DTs?"

For the next couple of hours I answered the Mullens' questions as best

I could: Who asked for the DTs at that time of night? Who adjusted the artillery? How could someone correct the artillery if he couldn't see where the shell hit? Why were the DTs postponed? If the artillery wasn't firing for Charlie Company, then why did the boys write they heard artillery firing all night long? I explained how Charlie Company was not the only infantry company operating in that area that night, that Delta Company was to their northwest and had requested DTs as well. I told them about the artillery's priorities which would cause fire to be shifted if a unit made contact. And Peg asked me why the boys who wrote were threatened with court-martials.

I tried to explain that if the boys had written, they would have directly disobeyed the order from Americal Division Headquarters stating that all communication with next of kin was to emanate from Division to ensure that parents were not given conflicting facts and accusations.

"We didn't get any facts!" Peg protested.

"In other words," Gene said, "they only give out the facts they want the parents to know. To fit the story."

"But there wan't any story," I said.

"So that's why the platoon wasn't allowed to write us," Peg said. "I see now. It has to be covered up."

"It wasn't covered up, Peg," I said. "What you were told was true." I went back through my notes until I found a copy of that first letter sent over Schwarzkopf's signature. I read the second paragraph to them. Michael's unit was in their night defensive position where the letter says they were. The unit was 'adjusting artillery to provide a predetermined range of fire in the event of enemy contact.' Michael did receive 'a fatal missile wound when an artillery round fell short of its intended target and detonated near his position.' Admittedly you were told the barest minimum, but what you were told was the truth."

"Well," Gene said, "Schwarzkopf has destined his life for the Regular Army. But he's all through because of—"

"Because of his back," Peg said.

"His back has healed," I said. "He's out of the cast now."

"Listen, this so-called event they went out on," Gene said, and he began rapping the kitchen table top for emphasis, "was Schwarzkopf's [bam!] own [bam!] planned [bam!] adventure! He thought there were some Vietcong out there and this was the first [bam!] time [bam!] that Schwarzkopf had ever been out on a search and destroy mission. The first time the chaplain had been out. That the company clerk had been out. The first sergeant. Did Schwarzkopf tell you that?"

"Gene, it wasn't the first time Schwarzkopf had been out. Or the chaplain. I don't think the company clerk was with them that night, but I'm not sure. I do know that the first sergeant went out any time the executive officer came in. There was a conflict betw—"

"Schwarzkopf used to come out in his helicopter," Gene interrupted.

"He'd never stayed out all night on a mission with them, had he?" Peg asked.

"He wasn't on the hill with Charlie Company," I said. "He was on another hill, Hill Four Ten, with the artillery unit."

"When I told Schwarzkopf, when he sat there in that hospital bed with that other colonel, Colonel Knap, who was sitting there with him. . . ." Gene paused, then asked, "Did he tell you about Knap?"

"Yes, he was a major in the Judge Advocate General," I said. "He was a lawyer."

"Why'd he want a lawyer there?" Gene asked.

"For a witness," I said. "He had first asked Knap to come so that he, Schwarzkopf, could ask him some questions. But when you said you wanted a witness there, too, he asked Knap to stay."

"In other words, he was afraid I was going to get a little bit violent?"

"I think he was concerned for your sake and his own, as well as the other men in the ward."

"Why was he concerned for my sake?" Gene asked indignantly.

"Because it was so obviously an emotional situation," I said. "He wasn't sure how you were going to react and he had asked Knap down initially to advise him. You had said you were bringing charges against him in federal court, remember, so Schwarzkopf asked Knap what it all meant and was it all right for him to talk to you."

"He'd had time to plan," Gene said. "When I looked at him out at Walter Reed, I saw a defeated officer of the United States Army. I don't care what *anybody* says, he's got a guilt complex."

"But, Gene, he didn't kill Michael. You know that. What should he feel guilty about?"

"Because he was hungry!" Gene answered angrily. "He wanted to be a brigadier general at thirty-five. He made that brag, and we can get the boys to prove it to you!"

"Oh-h," Peg said uncertainly, "I'm not sure whether we can or not." She pushed herself away from the sink and sat down with us at the kitchen table. "One thing I want to know," she said. "What was the company out there for? There wasn't anything in that area, was there?"

"They went out for two reasons," I said. "Their primary mission was to provide security against rocket attacks on the Americal Division head-quarters at Chu Lai. On this particular mission, however, Division intelligence had had some 'unidentified radio intercepts.' They had picked up Vietnamese talking on radios where there weren't supposed to be any Vietnamese operating. So Charlie and Delta companies from Schwarz-kopf's battalion were sent in to make contact. But they didn't find any."

"You know damn well they couldn't find any Vietnamese radio!" Gene said.

"They were looking for the North Vietnamese troops using the radios," I explained.

"The whole incident was Schwarzkopf's stairway to a brigadier general," Gene shrugged.

"No, Gene, let me try to correct you on this because you've mentioned it again and again. Schwarzkopf was a lieutenant colonel. He still had to be promoted to full colonel before he could make brigadier general—"

"He could make that in sixty days!" Gene scoffed.

"Gene, no one has made colonel in sixty days since the Army Air Corps days of World War II," I said. "We can talk about this some more if you'd like, but we'll just keep going around in circles and end up with my having to defend the military, the government, the system or whatever, and this is not what I came back out here to Iowa to do." I sat there for a moment looking at them. Gene was angry with me; Peg was clearly upset. "I thought if I could find out the truth for you," I said, "if I could learn what had happened to Michael, how he had died, what had caused the shell to explode over his position. . . ."

The Mullens' expressions did not change.

"I guess," I said, "I don't know what you want from me anymore."

"What we want from *you?*" Gene said indignantly. "The whole thing is this: when you came out here, you wanted something from *us!*"

"What do you mean?" I asked, surprised. "What do you think I wanted from you?"

"You wanted a story," Peg said.

"You wanted the story, and you wanted the truth," Gene said.

They were right, of course.

The following morning, March 1, 1972, was the second anniversary of Michael's burial. A gentle rain had fallen during the night, and before dawn the temperature had suddenly dropped to fifteen degrees below zero. The roads were covered with a thin sheet of ice, the usual five-minute trip from La Porte City to the Mullens' took twenty minutes.

Gene was asleep when I arrived, but Peg was up and gave me coffee.

"Peg," I said, "I don't think there is an appropriate time to ask this question, but I want to get it over with. Yesterday you mentioned being asked to speak by a women's club and someone else asked you to help organize the peace vigil here in La Porte—"

"They almost had to drag people off the street to get enough people in this town to maintain a twenty-four-hour vigil," Peg said. "I found that very difficult to understand."

"I want to continue with this question for a moment," I said. "You're known now by the newspapers, the local television stations. You're often asked to comment on the news. Presidential candidates call from Washington asking your endorsement. Has achieving this 'celebrity' status in any way disturbed you?"

Peg paused for a moment. "Well, yes. It does disturb me, I think. I mean it disturbs me because of why it happened. It came about because Michael died."

"Do people think you're cashing in on Michael's death?"

"Well," Peg said, rubbing her brow, "you wonder about it. I suppose many people do think this way, and I guess you can't help it. I have this fear of being used by groups—except groups like the American Friends. They're the one group I have faith in in the whole country. Oh, look who's up!"

Gene lumbered sleepily into the kitchen, as the telephone rang and Peg went to answer it. He sipped his coffee, then asked me, "Are you going with me to visit Michael's grave this morning?"

"I'd like to very much."

We could hear Peg trying to comfort whoever it was on the telephone.

"Listen to her," Gene said. "That's the kind of phone call we get all the time."

Peg was reading off a list of telephone numbers the caller should try: Senator Harold Hughes' office, the Senator's military liaison adviser, a lawyer who specialized in military cases. Peg was saying don't worry, don't cry, everything was going to be all right. A few minutes later she hung up the telephone and slumped down at the kitchen table.

"Who was it?" Gene asked.

"A widow with six children." Peg sighed. "Her oldest son was a helicopter gunner in Vietnam. God knows how, but he survived. He's back at Fort Hood now, and this is the third time this year he's gone AWOL to come home. He was worried because his mother hasn't been real well. She telephoned to ask what she could do to help him, so he wouldn't have to go back into the stockade. Then when she got to crying, I thought, *Oh, God, that poor woman.* She told me, 'They got my one boy, but they'll never get the other.' " Peg rubbed her eyes wearily. "Here's the thing, here's what really gets me: How can I do anything for these people? How can I help them?"

"You already have," I answered. "You gave her the names and phone numbers of people to call. That's all she wanted. There was nothing but quicksand beneath her feet when she telephoned, and all of a sudden, Peg, there you were: solid as a rock."

Peg looked over at her husband. He had buried his face in his hands. "No, Gene!" she scolded. "Don't you start!"

Gene could not help himself. He was crying, and the tears coursed down his cheeks. He turned to me, his eyes glistening. "Are we crazy?" he asked. *"Are we?"*

I shook my head, not sure of my voice.

"How *long* can we do this?" he asked.

"A lady came out here who had lost her son fifteen years ago!" Peg said. "She sat there and talked about him for four, for four . . . hours. . . ." Her voice faltered, and she, too, began to cry. "And I thought, *My God, am I going to be doing this for the rest of my life?*"

"I *love* my country," Gene said. "It hurts me to see what's happening. I don't understand it."

"The thing that gets me is that I'm still angry!" Peg said. "How in the hell can you live a lifetime of being angry? How can you?" She was struggling for self-control. "I just think I have to be mad about Michael's death because . . . because it was *obscene!* I have to be angry, but how . . . how do—oh, God!" Peg cried, burying her face in her arms. Gene walked around the kitchen table to comfort her, placed a gentle hand on Peg's shoulder. He stood there crying also, uncertain what to say or do, Peg rubbed her eyes against her sleeve, then, looking up, patted Gene's hand and forced herself to smile.

"Why don't both of you get out of here?" she asked. "I'll clean up the breakfast dishes while you two visit Michael's grave."

THE
ROCKEFELLERS

AN AMERICAN DYNASTY

A condensation of the book by

PETER COLLIER and DAVID HOROWITZ

*Four generations of Rockefellers:
Junior, Senior, Nelson holding Rodman,
first male of the Cousins' generation.*

THE FATHER

In the early years of the twentieth century, when the Protestant church was united in its crusade to save the heathen world, the Congregationalists worked hard to conscript their share of Christian soldiers for assignment to the dark lands where the climactic battles between good and evil were to be fought. It was an expensive war, and under normal circumstances a group of the church's ministers meeting in Boston in early 1905 might have reacted to the announcement of a $100,000 donation to its Board of Foreign Missions with a prayer of rejoicing and perhaps a spontaneous chorus of the Doxology. But when they found that this great gift was from the purse of John D. Rockefeller, angry murmuring filled the room. One of the ministers rushed to the podium to demand that the Congregationalist elders return the gift of "tainted money" at once.

"Is this clean money? Can any man, can any institution, knowing its origins, touch it without being defiled?" the Reverend Washington Gladden—the most eminent Congregationalist in the land—had asked. On every side, wealth had been accumulated "by methods as heartless, as cynically iniquitous as any that were employed by the Roman plunderers or robber barons of the Dark Ages. In the cool brutality with which properties are wrecked, securities destroyed, and people by the hundreds robbed of their little, all to build up the fortunes of the multi-millionaires, we have an appalling revelation of the kind of monster that a human being may become."

The controversy eventually spread from the small rented hall in downtown Boston to the whole nation. Newspapers were flooded with opinions on the mixed blessings of accepting the offering. The term "tainted money" entered the vocabulary of the common man. ("Sure it's tainted," went a vaudeville routine of the day. " 'Taint yours, and 'taint mine.") Yet few of the many Americans who pleaded with the Congregationalists to reclaim the $100,000 in the service of the Lord went so far as to suggest that the soul of the donor might also be saved. For John D. Rockefeller was the most unrepentant sinner of the day. Senator Robert LaFollette called him "the greatest criminal of the age." If there had been any lingering doubts about this strange, secret man with impassive eyes and a cruel slash of a mouth, Ida Tarbell's recently published *History of the Standard Oil Company* was enough to convince anyone that the name Rockefeller was a synonym for unbridled ruthlessness and power.

Of all the men Theodore Roosevelt indicted as "malefactors of great wealth," John D. Rockefeller was indeed the wealthiest. At the time of the "tainted money" controversy, his fortune amounted to $200 million; it would coast effortlessly, of its own velocity, to the $1 billion mark within a few years. (The sum staggered the imagination; one astute Christian calculated that it was more than would have been in Adam's bank account if he had deposited $500 every day since his precipitous exit from the Garden.) Yet in other ways Rockefeller was far different from the other great robber barons who had terrorized the land for the previous twenty years. A pillar of the Baptist church since his youth, Rockefeller's tithes had already approached $100 million by 1905, and he was even then devoting his attention to creating the widest-ranging system of philanthropy the world had yet known. A loyal husband and devoted father, his courtly manner had disarmed many a government lawyer and made him wonder if this man was indeed not more sinned against than sinning.

Withal it was Rockefeller—confessed plodder and conservative—whom the public identified as the symbol of a heartless economic system seated firmly in the saddle and riding mankind. Whatever his private personality, the John D. Rockefeller they knew had invented a new form of economic power—the corporate trust—for a nation whose very lifeblood was business. And the menace he had come to exemplify was not that of the pirate operating outside the social norm, but of the unjust and uncontrollable power inherent in the norm itself. He was, in some sense, the system carried to its logical and unchecked extreme—the competitor who utterly destroys the competition. It was no accident that the era called the Gilded Age chose John D. Rockefeller to be its representative American.

Unlike the other robber barons, who had come to accept and even revel in their outlaw status, making no bones about what they were up to and defying society to stop them, Rockefeller remained always convinced that he had been as much the Christian gentleman in business as in his private life. And the strong feeling that he had been unjustly maligned coupled with the equally strong desire for vindication would become important traits in the life of the family he sired.

The 66-year-old Rockefeller would live for another 32 years, becoming in a sense the only survivor of that heroic and lawless age. Long after the Congregationalist hierarchy had admitted with chagrin that they themselves had solicited the tainted contribution their ministers had assumed, was the oil man's guilty effort to sneak through the eye of the needle, long after that and other controversies had been forgotten, Rockefeller would live on, surrounded by a newfound respect and power his philanthropy had won for him. Long after the others who had risen in the great industrial wars of the nineteenth century were gone, the Fifth Avenue mansions where they had lived like dissolute Renaissance princes having passed to other hands and their fortunes scattered, Rockefeller's name and power would be carried into the future by a dynasty without peer as an enduring institution of American life.

The making of the great Standard Oil fortune was an accident. It was as if a door had stood open for a brief historical moment and Rockefeller, who just happened to be passing by, managed to squeeze in before it closed. Never before had it been possible for an individual to build the organization he built—it would never be possible again. It was the random collision of a man with an opportunity. To a lesser degree, the same could be said of the other great concentrations of wealth that occurred at this time. Only later would justifying the accidental and investing it with the magnificence of predestination become important, the job of the publicists and "kept" biographers all the robber barons hired.

Rockefeller was born on July 8, 1839, in a modest box-shaped house ringed by apple trees and flanked by two barns, a hard two hours' drive by buggy over the rutted roads leading from the small hamlet of Richford. His father had paid $631 cash for the 160-acre farm. William Avery Rockefeller stood out among the sinewy, taciturn farmers who had been left behind in this part of western New York after the flood of emigration led west along the Erie.

John D. Rockefeller would later discover that his father's primary occupation was that of pitchman and con artist. Cut from the same mold as the legendary P. T. Barnum, he was far from chagrined by his secret life. In fact, he seemed to revel in his petty larcenies. When he visited Indian reservations with his buggy full of goods for sale, William Rockefeller pretended to be deaf and dumb, he admitted to a friend, because he believed the Indians took this to be a sign of supernatural power. But there was not that much money to be made flimflamming the Iroquois in upstate New York, and so he found a more promising career in patent medicines. He journeyed for hundreds of miles to camp meetings, passing out handbills that read: "Dr. William A. Rockefeller, the Celebrated Cancer Specialist, Here for one Day Only. All Cases of Cancer Cured unless too far gone and then they can be greatly benefited." He sold bottles of his elixir and gave consultations for the princely sum of twenty-five dollars, a good two months' wages at the time.

If younger brother William came to resemble the father in his robust physique and expansive good nature, John did not. Early photographs show a narrow, almost expressionless face, eyes that were hooded and impassive, and a mouth accustomed to silence. The hair was parted so far to the left that his head seemed almost lopsided. It was the face of his mother, Eliza, who had named her firstborn son after her father, a prosperous New York farmer named John Davison. A thin, hatchet-faced woman with flaming red hair and equally stark blue eyes, Eliza Rockefeller was different from her genial, meandering husband in almost every way. (They were opposites with a strong attraction, however, and had married quickly in 1836 after a brief courtship.) As William Avery was roving the countryside, she was doing her best to normalize her six children's youth, protecting them from the rumors that swirled constantly around the family, filling in for the peculiar man she had married in an uncharacteristic fit of passion.

His mother's influence was moral, strict, severe with harsh Scottish piety. Her Calvinist maxims filled her oldest son's mind, and he would recollect them all through his life. One would be particularly appropriate to his career: "Willful waste makes woeful want." Long after her death he recalled an instance in which his mother switched him for an offense he had not committed. In the middle of the punishment, after he had finally convinced her of his innocence, she said, "Never mind, we have started in on this whipping, and it will do for the next time." Yet she was predictable, rational even in anger. And however much he might have been secretly attracted to his bold and amoral father, his mother's way would be his way. He would always remember her plight: a humiliated, abandoned woman spoken of in backfence gossip, who spent long nights alone in a rocking chair staring into the fire, with a Bible on her lap and a corncob pipe in her mouth.

After piling his family and their possessions into a westbound train and settling them in Cleveland in 1853 so that he could be closer to the "marks" flooding into the West by covered wagon, William Rockefeller appeared less and less often. Eliza received an occasional letter between visits and knew of an address out west where he could be reached in an emergency. But she went to her death in 1889 a grass widow. For years after, though, the elder Rockefeller would drop in unannounced at the elegant Cleveland estate of his famous son. He would alight from the streetcar as he had from his buggy in the old days, bringing a .22 rifle or some other present for John D. Rockefeller, Jr., and trinkets for his sisters. The grandson had warm memories of the old man. As he recalled years later: "He was a great storyteller. He played the violin too, holding it down on his waist instead of tucking it under his chin." But then, after playing with his grandchildren for a few days and occasionally borrowing money from his son, he would vanish as suddenly as he had come.

The Cleveland John D. settled in at the age of fourteen was like a seafaring town. At the lakefront, white-sailed ships headed for harbor with passengers and cargo. There were side-wheelers and even some screw-propeller-driven ships built in local yards. The docks were crowded and dirty, worked by husky stevedores, and ruled from afar by local merchants. Rockefeller often strayed there after school to watch commerce taking place, usually standing alone and observing the bustle. One day he fell into step with a schoolmate who asked, "John, what do you want to be when you grow up?"

Without hesitation young Rockefeller spoke up, "I want to be worth a hundred thousand dollars, and I'm going to be, too."

He had few friends in Cleveland's Central High School, where his mournful countenance won him the nickname "the Deacon," although he did form a lasting bond with classmate Mark Hanna, later to be a U.S. senator, presidential kingmaker, and political fixer for the Standard Oil trust. Graduating in 1855, Rockefeller decided to go into business instead of to college. For several weeks he walked the streets of Cleveland looking for work, determined to take not just any job, but *the* job that would prepare him for his great expectations. He had set his sights high. "I went to railroads, banks, wholesale merchants," he recalled later. "I did not go to any small establishments. . . . I was after something big."

On September 26 he was hired as a clerk accountant by Hewitt and Tuttle, commission merchants and produce shippers dealing in grain and other commodities. This date became a red-letter day on his personal calendar, and he always celebrated it thereafter as a sort of second birthday.

On his Pocantico estate along the Hudson, September 26 was the day that a special flag was run up the pole. Once, well into his sixties, while driving through Cleveland on a *voyage sentimental* he passed the site where he had first reported for work. Suddenly he jumped up in the open carriage and shouted, "Look! Look at that rectangular building. I commenced my career there at four dollars a week." He got the driver to stop so he could take a misty-eyed silent walk around the much changed building.

Discipline, order, and a close reckoning of debits and credits would be the code of his life. The only surviving relic from his youth is Ledger A, the commonplace book he kept during his first years on his own. In an exact and spidery hand, he wrote down, day by day and to the penny, the income and expenses, the saving and investment, the business and benefactions of his life. Besides the modest $1 for a week's room and board, there might be 75 cents for the Mite Society and 5 cents for Sunday school at the Erie Street Baptist Church, or 10 cents for the poor and 10 cents for foreign missions. The church was his only recreation, almost his only connection with the world outside the commission merchant trade. The total of the gifts he made was almost invariably 10 percent of his $3.50 weekly income. Other than grudging purchases of clothing, there was little else besides this disciplined giving. Ledger A was as close to keeping a diary as Rockefeller ever got; the figures recorded there were his autobiography.

By 1858 he was earning $600 a year. He knew his worth to the company to the exact penny and asked for a raise to $800. When Hewitt and Tuttle equivocated, Rockefeller began to look for a new job. He had previously made the acquaintance of Maurice Clark, an Englishman twelve years his senior, who was a clerk in another commission firm in Cleveland. Together they decided to start their own commission merchant business. In its first year, the firm of Clark & Rockefeller netted a tidy $4,000 profit on a gross business of $450,000, and a year later the profits had risen to $17,000. The partners had been fortunate in beginning their enterprise in the upswing of the business cycle. But even greater good fortune was in store for them.

The Civil War, which had begun in April, 1861, caused unparalleled grief for millions of Americans, but a chosen few—the Morgans, Armours, and Vanderbilts—made overnight fortunes from it, and a whole new business class made an audacious entrance on the American scene. While Rockefeller's bonanza was not quite as dramatic as some, it was impressive nonetheless. As war orders came pouring in to the firm, commodity prices rose sharply. The rising price levels made success a matter of methodical planning, attention to detail, and a relentless pressure for the hard bargain—tasks to which Rockefeller was singularly well suited.

His younger brother Frank managed to get to the front and suffer two wounds. "I wanted to go in the army and do my part," John D. explained long afterward. "But it was simply out of the question. There was no one to take my place. We were in a new business, and if I had not stayed it must have stopped—and with so many dependent on it."

An event that had impressed Cleveland businessmen almost as much as the outbreak of war was the successful drilling of the first oil well by Edwin Drake two years earlier. Titusville, Pennsylvania, lay beside a wide stream called Oil Creek because of the black film on its surface. For years people had known of the oil on local streams, and though early settlers had condemned it as a nuisance, the Indians had valued it as a medicine. By the time Rockefeller joined Hewitt and Tuttle, oil bottled in small vials was an important part of the pharmacopoeia of his father and other frontier doctors. It had also been established as the cheapest, most efficient, and longest lasting of illuminants, so that in 1859 Colonel Drake's Titusville well set off a stampede into the area, which soon became known as the Oil Regions.

Overnight, as wells were brought in, tiny settlements along the basin grew into thriving cities. It was an invasion like the one John Sutter's discovery had touched off in California a decade earlier: wildcatters, entrepreneurs, and the whole demimonde that their big spending supported. With their heavy whips shaking out over their teams, the hard-bargaining teamsters were the masters of the region. They carted the oil out of the fields to be refined, first in Pittsburgh and New York, and then in refineries that sprang up in Cleveland, some of them just blocks away from the prospering firm of Clark & Rockefeller. The junior partner was impressed by the bonanza and, along with other Cleveland businessmen, considered making an investment in oil. But he knew that the *real* money would be made not at the pump but in the middleman stages of haulage and refining. He knew as well that transportation was still too quixotic and refining processes were not yet sufficiently developed. Rockefeller thus decided to stick with consignments of meat and grain for the time being.

Four years after the Titusville oil strike, a momentous event occurred at the Cleveland junction. The Atlantic and Great Western Railroad line ran its first trains into the city to connect with the Erie and give Cleveland a direct communication to New York, also providing a broad-gauge line into the heart of the Oil Regions. One refinery after another sprang up along its tracks in the city. In 1863 the Atlantic and Great Western carried more than 1.5 million barrels of petroleum and at once became the principal oil carrier in the nation. In turn, Cleveland became one of the emerging capitals of oil.

It was also in 1863 that Samuel Andrews, an acquaintance of Maurice Clark, came to the partners with a proposition to go into the refining business. Rockefeller also knew Andrews, whom he had met at the Erie Street Baptist Chruch, but the 23-year-old John D. was still skeptical. He had enough money saved to hazard a $4,000 speculative investment as the silent partner in the new firm of Andrews, Clark and Company, but he made it clear that for him the oil venture was subsidiary to the grain business, which had proved itself time and time again in recent years as a reliable, if not spectacular, enterprise.

Sprouting thick reddish-brown mutton chops and dressing in black broadcloth suits that were often shiny with wear, Rockefeller had reached that time of life and level of prosperity where he could think about a family. And in March 1864 he became engaged to Laura Celestia Spelman, a pretty young Cleveland woman from a strong political and religious background whom he had known in high school.

John appreciated the enlargement of his life that she represented, but was hardly thunderstruck by love. He pursued Cettie (as Laura was known) with the same dogged determination that had already made him one of Cleveland's leading businessmen. By this point in his life he had long since run through the pages of Ledger A and begun Ledger B. No more were the items concerned with a few cents here and there for the Mite Society and other small charities. The figures were in dollars. Under the heading of "Sundry Expenses" he told the story of his courtship: 50 cents a week spent for several weeks on courting bouquets; $1.75 rental one weekend for a hansom cab to drive the couple and their chaperone down to the Rocky River. The wedding ring cost $15.75. On September 8, 1864, he found time for the following entry: "Married at 2 o'clock P.M. to Miss L. C. Spelman by Reverend D. Wolcott assisted by Rev. Paige at the residence of her parents."

Having accomplished marriage, he returned his full attention to business. By 1864 dozens of oil refineries had sprung up in Cleveland, and more appeared with each passing month. At first, Rockefeller worried that this was another fad that would pass and spent his days shaking his head distastefully at the clumsily made barrels leaking sticky crude on to the floors of his warehouse. Yet he soon realized that the oil was not going to dry up. He began to transfer his attention from the commission business to refining, spending more and more of his time at the Andrews,

Clark and Company headquarters on a site just outside the city.

There was a natural division of labor among the partners. Andrews had a fine competence in the early technology of oil and took care of the mechanics; the genial Clark made deals with the Oil Regions producers for the crude and with the teamsters for shipment; Rockefeller took care of finance and sales. Business procedures in the new industry were still primitive and there was much inefficiency. Always alert to any tendency to willful waste, Rockefeller was in his element and lost no time in asserting himself. Instead of continuing to be dependent on the obstreperous teamsters for deliveries of crude, Andrews, Clark and Company soon had its own force of wagons. Instead of buying barrels of indifferent quality from others, Rockefeller bought up stands of strong white oak and set up his own cooperage. The bright blue barrels it turned out would soon be the hated symbol of Standard Oil's ominipresence, but for now Rockefeller was satisfied with the fact that they cost 96 cents apiece instead of the $2.50 his firm had previously paid.

Early in 1865 the thriving firm of Andrews, Clark and Company was split by dissension. Rockefeller, the formerly silent but now most enthusiastic partner, had become increasingly annoyed with Clark's timid attitude toward expansion. The firm was $100,000 in debt, but Rockefeller wanted to extend the operation further and take advantage of the booming market. An impasse resulted, and it was mutually agreed to sell the business to the highest bidder.

The auction was held on February 2, 1865, with Rockefeller representing Andrews and himself against Clark. Clark began the bidding at $500, which Rockefeller raised to $1,000. The price went up and up, to $40,000, to $50,000, and then to $60,000. Gradually, with both sides unyielding, it crept up to $70,000. There was a long silence.

"Seventy-two thousand," said Maurice Clark in desperation.

"Seventy-two thousand five hundred," Rockefeller replied.

Clark threw up his hands: "The business is yours."

Although only twenty-six years old, Rockefeller already had good enough standing in Cleveland's financial community to be able to borrow the purchase price. He took control of the business—rechristened Rockefeller and Andrews—on the crest of an oil boom that was making Cleveland rich, and at the apex of the great Civil War business bonanza that would introduce the word "millionaire" into the vocabulary of Americans. Rockefeller and Andrews was already the largest refinery in Cleveland. He convinced his brother William to come into the business and sent him to New York to handle the export trade, which accounted for

two-thirds of the sales of Cleveland oil. It was about this time that a startled bystander watched one day as Rockefeller, thinking himself alone in
his office, jumped up in the air, clicked his heels together, and repeated to
himself, "I'm bound to be rich! Bound to be rich! *Bound to be rich!*"

If the other robber barons, with their mistresses, excesses of body and
spirit, and artistic booty imported from the Old World, made Rockefeller
seem a dull and predictable man, it was simply that he poured his passion
and genius into his work, into the creation of Standard Oil, instead of his
life. The development of the great trust would in retrospect seem the result of an almost unbelievably cunning plan; it would establish
Rockefeller as an industrial Napoleon. Yet, while his amazing sin-
glemindedness did help Rockefeller build the company, a good part of the
Standard Oil epic involved his uncanny ability to be in the right place at
the right time and always to have his "bowl right side up." He later admitted as much to a would-be biographer who was looking for a more stirring
genesis. "None of us," he said, "ever dreamed of the magnitude of what
became the later expansion."

He was looking for new men to become his lieutenants in the firm. In
1867 a new name was added to the enterprise, which then became Rockefeller, Andrews, and Flagler. Henry M. Flagler, who would one day retire from Standard Oil a multimillionaire and devote his old age to developing Florida's virgin coastline into an American Riviera, became one of
Rockefeller's few real friends, in or out of business. Their desks were in
the same office. Before long, they would move into homes a few blocks
from each other on Euclid Avenue, attend the Erie Street Baptist Church
together, and walk to the office each morning in earnest conversation
about the day's plans. "It was a friendship," as Rockefeller later wrote,
"founded on business, which Mr. Flagler used to say was a good deal better than a business founded on friendship, and my experience leads me to
agree with him."

The people Flagler was best at dealing with were the railroad men. It
was a talent Rockefeller prized because of the significance of the freight
problem. In the first days of the oil boom, there had been a natural community of interest between the producers and the men who brought the
oil to market. The teamsters may have driven a hard bargain with the well
owners, but in the end each shared the other's interest in maximum production. No such common bond, however, linked the producers with the
railroads. The railroads preferred a steady, high-level movement of oil;
what they faced was widely fluctuating supply, the result of disorganized

production in the highly competitive fields, where rushes of overproduction would come one week and shortages the next. To the railroad interests, this meant costly irregularities in the demand for cars, locomotives, and yard space. In this situation, the key element was the middleman who could organize the flow of oil from the fields and establish a steady and high freight volume to conform to the railroads' needs. The natural candidate for the task was the larger refiner. Accordingly, even as Rockefeller was using the large chunks of capital at his command to expand his refining capacity, he also set Flagler to the task of cornering the available tank cars and containers for the shipment of oil. Soon competitors seeking to transport their oil discovered that the railroads on which they had always depended had no tank cars for them because Rockefeller, Andrews, and Flagler had leased every available car.

Sometime late in 1867, Flagler visited General James Devereux, the new vice-president of the Lake Shore Railroad, and told him that Rockefeller, Andrews, and Flagler would stop shipping by canal and guarantee sixty carloads of oil per day to his railroad in return for a large rebate on freight charges. The official freight rate was 42 cents a barrel on crude from the Oil Regions to Cleveland and $2 on the refined oil from Cleveland to the eastern seaboard. As Devereux later testified before government investigators, the Lake Shore gave Flagler secret new rates of 35 cents and $1.30. When other Cleveland refiners heard of the rebate, they protested. The Lake Shore agreed with them that it was indeed an advantage and said that they too could have a rebate if they would also make a comparable freight guarantee.

The word "rebate" quickly became one of the most hated in the oil man's lexicon. Rockefeller's competitors didn't have to recognize that the term came from the French *rabattre* to know its meaning was "to beat down." The rate advantages Rockefeller received were a powerful addition to his already formidable arsenal. It was like the humorist Artemus Ward had said: "Them as has, gits."

Parlaying his freight advantages with loans and new investors, Rockefeller formed a new company on January 10, 1870, with a capitalization of $1 million. Its name was Standard Oil.

Eighteen seventy was a depression year. Total freight-car loadings were falling, and the heads of the mighty but hard-pressed railroads began to seek better solutions to their problems than the free market afforded. Why suffer the ravages of a competitive situation that was costing them money, they asked, when they could pool their resources with the largest refiners and plot out their own prosperity? They conceived a plan. It bore the innocuous name of the South Improvement Company.

The chief architect was Tom Scott, former Assistant Secretary of War to Abraham Lincoln and now president of the Pennsylvania Railroad. One of the items of business that Tom Scott had for the 1870 Pennsylvania legislature (which he and others in Pennsylvania's emerging business elite brazenly manipulated) was the chartering of a new kind of corporation, a holding company, which would allow its owners to control stock in companies both in and outside the state. The charter was so broad and vaguely defined as to permit the company's owners to conduct any business they wanted, in whatever manner they chose.

What they did choose was simplicity itself. The railroads would combine with the largest refiners in each major refining center to plan the flow of oil for their mutual benefit. Freight rates would rise, but the rebate to members of the scheme would more than compensate them. Those who refused to join the cartel would be driven to the wall. Participating refiners would not only receive rebates on their own shipments but "drawbacks" on the shipments of nonmembers as well.

Throughout the winter of 1871 the scheme went forward in absolute secrecy, with Rockefeller and other large refiners frequently journeying to New York to hold clandestine summit meetings with Scott, William H. Vanderbilt, Jay Gould, and the other railroad bosses. The promoters in each area decided which refineries they wanted in on the scheme and circulated an oath that prospective participants were forced to sign before learning the particulars of the plan.

Rockefeller saw the plan as a way of eliminating the Standard's annoying competitiors in Cleveland. They had two alternatives—collapse their businesses into his in return for stock, or go it alone and be bankrupted by the rebate system. Starting with his largest competitors and working downward, he would make an appointment to see a rival and then with his usual civility explain how the plan would work to the benefit of all. The offer could be refused only by those who valued principles more than economic survival. To add leverage to the already crushing advantage of the secret rebates and "drawbacks," Rockefeller had offered the executives of Cleveland's leading banks stock in the Standard; thus independent refiners who held out would have a hard time financing their lonely uphill battles.

Isaac Hewitt, Rockefeller's former employer, who had since become a partner in the large refinery of Alexander, Scofield and Company, was urged to commit himself to the scheme and to take stock in the Standard.

When he questioned the plan, Rockefeller shrugged him off cryptically: "I have ways of making money that you know nothing of." Others who were reluctant to join because they were already doing a good business were shown a hint of the iron fist underneath the velvet glove Rockefeller habitually wore. Frank Rockefeller, by then a partner in a competing firm, was told by his brother: "We have a combination with the railroads. We are going to buy out all the refiners in Cleveland."

The cabal went along smoothly for almost two months. When word accidentally leaked out revealing the nature of the South Improvement Company, there was immediate panic in the Oil Regions; all-night meetings, torchlight parades, angry petitions carried to legislators, and threatening telegrams to railroad presidents. It was not only the creation of a combination that outraged the producers; they too had tried to form associations in order to keep prices of crude high. It was rather the cold and calculating nature of the plot, the combination of the strong against the weak, and most of all the use of the loathsome "drawback" that aroused them. As Ida Tarbell later wrote: "The rebate system was considered illegal and unjust, but men were more or less accustomed to it. The drawback on other people's shipments was a new device, and it threw the Oil Regions into a frenzy of rage."

Until this time, the name of Rockefeller had been unknown outside a small circle in Cleveland. Almost overnight, it became identified with infamy. For the duration of the conflict, the *Oil City Derrick* printed the names of the conspirators in a black-bordered box on the front page of each edition; notable among them was John D. Rockefeller. It was the first of many public battles Rockefeller would fight, the first time that words like "octopus" and "anaconda" would be used to describe the organization built by his methodical talent.

Yet, at the height of the South Improvement furor, Rockefeller displayed that characteristic inner discipline and iron self-confidence, the unflagging belief in his own rectitude, which he would always possess under fire. As he said later: "It was right. I knew it as a matter of conscience. It was right between me and God." When his wife Cettie worried that public outcry might endanger his life, he wrote her reassuringly. This event was a Rubicon for Rockefeller, and forever afterward when he relived its crossing he would remain utterly convinced that he had not erred. Late in life, he told W. O. Inglis, who had been commissioned to write his life story: "The procedure was without precedent. We find here the strongest and most prosperous concern in the business . . . turning to its less fortunate competitors . . . and saying to them, 'We will stand in for the risks and hazards of the refining business. . . . Come with us, and we will do you good. We will undertake to save you from the wrecks of the refining business.'" What other men saw as villainous self-interest, he regarded as Christian charity.

Unhappily for Rockefeller, the stiff-necked people in the Oil Regions persisted in their inability to understand his benevolence. Producers and refiners united; they clamored and threatened and agitated until the railroads finally backed down. Even imperious Jay Gould of the Erie was forced to cable his surrender, claiming that he had gone along with the South Improvement Company only because he was forced to by the other promoters. As a gesture of peace, the railroads signed new contracts with the producers to end the South Improvement Company and equalize the shipping rates for all parties. The Pennsylvania legislature rushed through a bill repealing the South Improvement Company's charter. The oil men formed a Producers' Protection Association, raised a million dollars to support the refiners in the Oil Regions, and pledged to send no crude to the Standard Oil Company.

It looked as though Rockefeller and his angel of mercy had suffered a major defeat. But as the euphoria dissipated and people in the Oil Regions looked around, they were stunned to realize that the Standard now had Cleveland's refining capacity in its hip pocket. In the three-month blitzkrieg, Rockefeller had managed to buy up all but three of his twenty-five competitors in the city. It was as Mark Twain said of the Sandwich Islanders: the missionaries had been so successful in their efforts that the natives' vices no longer existed in name—only in fact.

In the years following this coup, he could easily have relaxed. The Standard was thriving, with one-quarter of the refining capacity of the entire country. He himself was a prosperous citizen of Cleveland, rich even beyond his dreams, and raising a growing family in a rambling 700-acre country estate he had bought in Forest Hill on the outskirts of Cleveland. Yet he pushed ahead, driven by a passion for completeness.

In May 1872, with the smoke from the South Improvement battle hardly cleared, Rockefeller—together with W. G. Warden, head of the Atlantic Refinery, Philadelphia's largest; Charles Lockhart of Lockhart, Frew and Company, the biggest refinery in Pittsburgh; and several other of the large refiners who had been in on the scheme—went on a pilgrimage to the Oil Regions. They came to shake hands with those who, like themselves, had become "prisoners of a misunderstanding" and to get their cooperation in a new association of refiners, called the Pittsburgh Plan, which would be open to anyone who wanted in.

It was hoped that the refiners of the Oil Regions would bury unpleasant memories and agree that the problems of overproduction and cutthroat competition could be solved only through such a central association. Rockefeller did manage to make one important convert in the person of John Archbold, the cunning independent who had led the refiners' opposition to the South Improvement Company and who one day would head the Standard itself. Otherwise there was only antagonism. Although themselves separated by economic interest, the Oil Regions' refiners and producers were united by a common xenophobia concerning Rockefeller and Cleveland that was stronger than economic laws.

During a meeting held to discuss the plan, an independent refiner, finishing a fiery speech against the Standard, glanced over at Rockefeller, who had been sitting impassively in a rocking chair, just as John D.'s hands fell away from shading his eyes. "He took me all in, saw just how much fight he could expect from me, and then up went his hands and back and forth went his chair."

Having seen the voluntary association spurned, Rockefeller returned to Cleveland with the calm knowledge that there must be war to bring the Oil Regions to their knees. The producers had never worried him. He had taken their measure and found them self-indulgent and weak. They wanted premium prices for their crude, but could not discipline themselves enough to combine to restrain production. Their repeated attempts to form protective associations invariably fell apart when anyone approached a few of their number with a large enough order. In this way Rockefeller himself had easily beaten the producers' boycott against the Standard in the aftermath of the South Improvement scheme.

Unlike the producers, however, the Oil Creek refiners were a force to be reckoned with. (It was about this time that observers noted the appearance of a map indicating all the Oil Regions' refineries on the wall of Rockefeller's office.) Their output of 10,000 barrels a day was close to his own in Cleveland, equal to the combined capacity of the seaboard refineries, and some 4,000 barrels a day greater than that of Pittsburgh. Furthermore, the refineries in the Oil Regions had pipelines running the crude from the well to their doorstep, while he had to have his shipped by rail to Cleveland, and then, after refinement, on to the seaboard. Rockefeller knew he must begin his campaign by squeezing the railroads to eliminate the advantages of geography that his opponents enjoyed.

The monopoly he had won in Cleveland had given him an even greater hold over the railroads who depended on his freight. By playing them off against each other, he was able to secure freight agreements that would eliminate the Oil Regions' advantage while increasing his own control over the freight market and the shippers. Formerly, the Oil Regions had paid $1.50 a barrel to ship direct to the coast while he paid $2, in addition to a 40-cent-a-barrel charge on crude from the Oil Regions to Cleveland; henceforth all refiners would pay the same amount to the coast, $2 a barrel, and Rockefeller would get a rebate on the charges he paid to bring crude into Cleveland.

But this was only part of his offensive. In something anticipating the Appalachian gatherings of latter-day syndicate chieftains, Rockefeller and Flagler arranged a meeting with their counterparts, W. G. Warden and Charles Lockhart. Sitting in the sun of Saratoga (later called "that Mecca of schemers" by Ida Tarbell), Rockefeller spoke in his thin, reedy voice, assuring the others that the only way to head off constant fighting and uncertainty in the refining business was to come together in one organization. The Standard, because of its size and the advantages it commanded with the railroads, was of course the ideal candidate. The other men were, naturally, skeptical. Rockefeller invited them to come to Cleveland and inspect the books of Standard Oil. They did and came away believers. Both men traded their refineries and equipment for stock in the Standard.

Almost simultaneously, the Charles Pratt Company of New York came into the Standard fold, bringing the considerable daring of Henry H. Rogers, who was later also the friend and patron of Mark Twain. These firms at first did not make public their new status as part of the Standard combine, for Rockefeller wanted them to buy up as much of their own local competition as they could before the outlines of his plan became known. Along with John Archbold's newly formed Acme Refining Company in the Oil Regions, the firms proceeded to act as stalking horses for the Standard, purchasing competitors in their own name.

When he began his campaign, the Standard was flanked by 15 refineries in New York, 12 in Philadelphia, 22 in Pittsburgh, and 27 in the Oil Regions. When he finished, there was only the Standard. The shape of the emerging monopoly in oil became apparent only after it was almost a *fait accompli,* and Rockefeller had already reached a stage in his plot where neither the public outcry of refiners or producers, nor even the actions of legislatures, could stop him. In the Oil Regions the refiners tried to wrest from the railroads some acknowledgment that as common carriers they had certain public responsibilities, but it was not forthcoming; nor could they secure redress in the form of regulatory laws that would check the Standard's momentum and preserve what was left of the competitive market. For the legislatures also had been bought by the Standard's largesse. As the socialist scholar Henry Demarest Lloyd later said in *Wealth Against Commonwealth,* the first great broadside against Rockefeller: "The Standard had done everything to the Pennsylvania legislature except refine it."

By 1877 the Standard had no competition in the Oil Regions, Philadelphia, or Pittsburgh. Only in New York was there a small pocket of resistance left among scattered independent refiners. In April 1878 Flagler wrote an acquaintance that the total refining capacity in the United States was 36 million barrels a year, and of this the Standard produced 33 million. By 1880 Rockefeller refined 95 percent of the oil produced in the nation. Not since the early days of the New World when the Crown gave out monopolies had an enterprise cornered a market so completely.

CHAPTER 2

On a chilly day in the winter of 1874, John D. Rockefeller burst into his office and grabbed Flagler by the sleeve. With tears rimming his eyes, he told his only close friend the good news: Cettie had finally given birth to a son. There had been four girls; now there was a male heir, John D. Rockefeller, Jr. Mr. Junior (as the boy would be known from the time he was a teenager) and sisters Bessie, Alta, and Edith (another, Alice, died in infancy) would have few childhood memories of Standard Oil. Once in a while they visited their father at the huge plant on the edge of town, but most of their memories of their increasingly famous father were of more relaxed moments. They saw him in a way no one else did and would always remember the simple joy he took in doing things like driving the fine team of matched horses at breakneck speed over Cleveland's bridle paths; dog-paddling around a lake in the summer months, his face held high out of the water and a straw hat on his head; ice-skating with geometric precision for a few minutes in high hat and frock coat before leaving for work in the winter.

Not long before the birth of his son, Rockefeller had celebrated his prosperity by purchasing a large brick townhouse on Cleveland's increasingly fashionable Euclid Avenue. It was also shortly before young John's birth that Rockefeller had acquired Forest Hill, 79 heavily wooded acres on the outskirts of town which he added to until it was a 700-acre estate. He loved it there. The Rockefeller children grew up unaware they belonged to the richest family in Cleveland. They kept to themselves. All four did chores to earn spending money; all kept their small replicas of Ledger A; all burned with indignation when they began to understand that the world condemned as a heartless monster the father they worshiped. The John D. Rockefeller they knew was incapable of the crimes attributed to him.

Yet this private Rockefeller was not the same man who commanded the great Standard leviathan that now surfaced after swallowing up or terrorizing the smaller fish. Within the company, he was a benign tyrant, and the corporation bore the imprint of his personality. He was constantly on the prowl around the several Standard units, looking things over, dropping in unannounced on young bookkeepers, running a practiced eye over their ledgers, and perhaps whipping out the notebook he carried in his breast pocket to jot down small economies to be passed on to the workmen. On one occasion he was inspecting one of the plants where kerosene was placed in cans for shipment abroad. For a moment he watched the five-gallon tins being constructed, and then he found out from one of the workers that forty drops of solder were used on each. After observing a moment longer, Rockefeller said, "Have you ever tried thirty-eight? No? Would you mind having some sealed with thirty-eight and letting me know?" Although some of the cans sealed with thirty-eight drops leaked, none did when thirty-nine drops were used, and in the future this became the specification in the Standard factory. Late in life, when asked about these economies, Rockefeller would smile broadly and say, "A fortune. That's what we saved. A fortune."

Under the existing laws, Standard Oil of Ohio's expansion was menaced because it could not take possession of manufacturing facilities outside the state and operate them. To find a way out of this dilemma and to continue his untiring effort to integrate the national market, Rockefeller turned to Samuel C. T. Dodd, a gifted attorney and one of the first to devote himself solely to a single corporate client. The trust agreement Dodd authored was signed early in 1882. It provided for the transfer of all outstanding Standard stock to nine trustees, including John D. and William Rockefeller, Flagler, and Archbold. In return the stockholders received trust certificates in hundred-dollar blocks. The trustees were empowered to dissolve participating corporations and begin setting up others—Standard of New York, Standard of New Jersey, and so on—in each state. The new organization had no name or charter. It was just a trust—the common-law concept describing the relationship between parties when one held property for the benefit of another. But in the emerging world of modern finance the major benefits it provided were to those seeking to build monopolies. One of the first governmental agencies to investigate Dodd's brainchild, a New York senate committee of 1888, would call the Standard trust "the type of a system which has spread like a disease through the commercial system of this country."

The Standard trust encompassed forty corporations, of which fourteen were wholly owned. Its very complexity set up a maze of legal structures that successfully rendered its workings impervious to public investigation and exposure. Under the trust arrangement, it was never clear who owned what or who was responsible for which actions. The problem it presented to the analyst was ontological. As Ida Tarbell later wrote: "You could argue its existence from its effects, but you could never prove it."

The trust took up headquarters in New York, where Rockefeller regretfully moved his family, leaving deep roots in the soil of Forest Hill and in the foundations of the Erie Street Baptist Church. He learned to become a New Yorker, buying a fashionable Fifth Avenue town house and going daily to work at the new corporate offices at 26 Broadway, soon to become the most infamous business address in the world. Yet in some sense Rockefeller never changed from the provincial businessman. He joined another Baptist church, refusing to move up in class to a more respectable denomination. "Most Americans when they accumulate money climb the golden ramparts of the nearest Episcopal Church," H. L. Mencken was to write. "But the Rockefellers cling to the primeval rain-God of the American hinterland and show no sign of being ashamed of him." John D. arrived at the office as unobtrusively as any clerk. His secretary, George Rogers, later said, "I never knew anyone to enter an office as quietly as Mr. Rockefeller. He seemed almost to have a coat of invisibility." Rogers also remembered that his employer often jotted down notes in pencil on his left cuff during the trip downtown.

Every day he sat down to lunch at 26 Broadway with the proconsuls of the great Standard empire. There was William Rockefeller, good-natured and placid, with two sons who would marry two of banker James Stillman's daughters in a dynastic alliance whose descendants, the Stillman Rockefellers, controlled the First National City Bank that one day would contend for supremacy of the financial world with their cousins' Chase Manhattan. There was Henry H. Rogers, called "Hell Hound" by people on Wall Street because of the spectacularly lethal swoops he made into the market as a private investor; Flagler, a proven warrior in the Standard battles; John Archbold, who, after making a pledge to the teetotaling

Rockefeller to control his drinking problem, had risen steadily in the Standard hierarchy and was to achieve unwanted notoriety later as its "Great Corruptionist." There was Oliver Payne, treasurer of the Standard, whose father, Henry B. Payne, would become a U.S. senator from Ohio and make common cause with the powerful Mark Hanna. Rockefeller himself sat demurely beside Charles Pratt, to whom he had surrendered the head of the table because he was the oldest of the group. He listened calmly as the others discussed, only occasionally injecting his opinions. The "Standard Oil Gang" comprised the most potent array of executive talent yet gathered in one organization.

It was more than thirty years since he had begun his career, and Rockefeller was the central figure of the most spectacular success story in business history. The Standard was indisputably the most powerful industrial organization in the nation, and the most visible symbol of growing American might abroad. But for Rockefeller personally the price had been heavy; he had become identified with all the excesses the Standard had committed in its rise to power; hatred clung to him like iron filings to a magnet. He tried to dissociate himself from some of the onerous charges against the corporation by insisting that figures like Henry Rogers and John Archbold, the Standard hatchet men, were free agents acting for themselves and beyond his control. Yet this was one case where the country believed, as Emerson had said, that the institution was only the lengthened shadow of the man. Rockefeller had pursued his leviathan with complete dedication. But now he found himself lashed to its back as inextricably as Ahab, and in equal danger of being taken down for good.

Years later, when his image had benefited from the cosmetic surgery provided by the skillful hands of public relations men and three decades of association with philanthropy, Rockefeller would see it as just a problem of communication. He speculated on how different things might have been if the Standard had just "called the reporters in" (as he claimed to have wanted to do) and told its side of things in the aftermath of the South Improvement scheme.

It was not only before the tribunal of public opinion that Rockefeller was tried. By the turn of the century, the trust found itself subjected to one official investigation after another. At first, the Standard executives saw these inquisitions simply as nuisances to be treated with contempt. Archbold, Rogers, and other leading figures in the corporation perjured themselves freely under examination, knowing that the records of the trust were encompassed by a maze of secrecy and legal deception so thick it would not yield to investigation.

Publicly Rockefeller remained imperturbable. But privately the burden began to take its toll. "You know," he later told an acquaintance, "for years I was crucified." By the 1890s, he clearly had reached a crossroads in a life that until then had room for neither doubt nor reflection. He had come a long way from the youthful days when the mere thought of great wealth had made him click his heels in delight. He had accumulated a great fortune—more than a hundred millions. But now, as his days were absorbed in the endless orchestration of his income and expenses, of investments and charities, of corporate strategy and legal defense, it became questionable whether he had mastered the money or the money had mastered him.

Over the years he had steadily increased his share of the corporation, and as the great Standard money machine pumped its way toward the twentieth century, fantastic dividends poured into Rockefeller's hands. He tried to dispose of them in investments but it had become literally impossible for him to keep pace with himself.

Under the accumulating pressures, the body that he had pushed so remorselessly for the past forty years finally rebelled. Letters between Rockefeller and his wife during this period tell of sleepless nights. He began to suffer from serious digestive disorders, and his doctor insisted that he retreat from his cares. The tall figure with the dignified and composed features who had stridden confidently through the wars on America's corporate frontiers in the seventies and eighties underwent a sudden change; almost overnight the people who visited Rockefeller came away shocked by his stooped and careworn demeanor. Bearing whatever look was in vogue—first muttonchops, then a brush moustache and sideburns, and finally a more modest moustache, his face had been somehow nondescript. Now people who had not really noticed his appearance before suddenly found themselves aware of how he looked. His face had become deeply lined; he had put on weight, sagging at the midsection. He was ravaged by a nervous disease—generalized alopecia—which left him without any hair on his body, and in the first noticeable vanity of an otherwise spartan life, he began to worry about his baldness, hiding it first with a grotesque black skullcap and later with a series of illfitting white wigs, each of them slightly different in length so that he could imitate a natural growth of hair over a two-week period.

Slowly, John D. Rockefeller began to relax his grip on the affairs of Standard Oil. In 1896 he stopped going to 26 Broadway every day. The following year, he stopped going at all, making John Archbold his regent in the corporation and staying in daily contact by direct wire to his home.

The legendary attention and energy was now applied to such tasks as landscaping the new estate located in Pocantico Hills on a spectacular range overlooking the Hudson. With that perfectionism that once charted his campaigns across the undiscovered country of corporate America, he plotted the seventy miles of road to be built over his estate, moved in several tons of topsoil so that breathtaking formal gardens could be planted, and arranged the views to his liking by moving trees around as an interior decorator would move chairs. He moved into Kikjuit (Dutch for "the lookout"), a magnificent Georgian mansion his son had persuaded him to build. In all, the Pocantico estate was (as a Broadway wit of later years wisecracked) an example of what God could have done if He'd only had the money. On the sculpted greens of the golf course he built there, Rockefeller's attention more and more drifted from oil rates and competitors' prices to his scores for nine holes, which he whittled down as persistently as he had the drops of solder that sealed up the Standard's tins.

If his life had ended here or if he had spent the rest of his days clipping the coupons he had accumulated, the Rockefeller who followed him would probably have been no different from any of the other descendants of the great robber baron industrialists. But in his leisure, the master of Standard Oil began thinking about the creation of another kind of institution, one that would find a more receptive place in the public heart than had his great trust. He had made his money; now he would put it to work to make sure his heirs did not face the same hatred he had in his life. Almost imperceptibly, he began to change the habit of the monopolist for that of the philanthropist. Slowly, the grand acquisitor began the metamorphosis that would transform him into a benefactor of mankind.

CHAPTER 3

As a student of the scriptures, Rockefeller was aware of the verse from 1 Peter: "Charity shall cover a multitude of sins." Yet unlike Gould, Fisk, and some of the others, he had not conveniently managed to discover charity late in life and then frenetically begun endowing schools and hospitals to salve a guilty conscience and burnish a darkened reputation. For him, the tithe had always been part of his continuing commitment to Eliza Rockefeller's Baptist religion.

Giving was a Christian duty to be taken care of without a flourish. Yet as he grew older, Rockefeller began to have the semimystical feeling that he had been especially selected as the frail vessel for the great fortune. He startled a reporter during a rare interview in 1905 by blurting out: "God gave me my money." As the statement began to raise eyebrows, he elaborated: "I believe the power to make money is a gift from God . . . to be developed and used to the best of our ability for the good of mankind. Having been endowed with the gift I possess, I believe it is my duty to make money and still more money and to use the money I make for the good of my fellow man according to the dictates of my conscience."

The prophet who set the tone for philanthropy, however, was a man wholly outside the church, an atheist and ardent disciple of Social Darwinism named Andrew Carnegie.

By his own stunning disbursement of one of the greatest fortunes in history, Carnegie made sure the public was interested in the way the princes of industry used their money. In Carnegie's charities, there was always a large element of self-advertisement, for which at least one aristocratic acquaintance criticized him: "Never before in the history of plutocratic America had any one man purchased by mere money so much social advertising and flattery. He would have given millions to Greece had she labelled the Parthenon 'Carnegopolis.'"

Rockefeller's benefactions followed a less flamboyant course. He had given millions to the Baptists. But this had been in piecemeal donations. By the late 1880s, with all the talk of the rich man's burden in the air, the church elders felt emboldened to ask him to make a large "investment" in a great center of Baptist learning. Some favored a new university on the East Coast, but others urged Rockefeller to rebuild the University of Chicago, which Stephen Douglas had founded in 1856 as the Morgan Park Theological Seminary. This institution, they argued, could be made to rise again as a powerful mother school for the handful of rundown Baptist colleges in the West and could exercise a powerful religious influence over the new states being rapidly carved out of the frontier. In 1887 Rockefeller gave $600,000 to begin this great work.

Rockefeller became absorbed in the university's reconstruction and direction. In some sense it was a vexing tax on his already over-burdened time, but he never regretted his involvement. When he came to the 1896 convocation, it was one of the first times his public appearance had been greeted by cheers instead of hostile curiosity.

Yet the problem remained of how to organize his philanthropy into the "scientific giving" Carnegie had been first to realize was important. The field of philanthropy seemed as much a jungle as the world of industry he had spent forty years trying to tame. Everywhere he went he was deluged with appeals for gifts and help. He received begging letters by the bushel at 26 Broadway. It was as if there were an elemental struggle between two estates of men—those with money and those trying to get it from them. Finding a solution became a matter of survival. As the unique man who would finally solve Rockefeller's problems for him later wrote: "Neither in the privacy of his home, nor at the table, nor in the aisles of his church, nor during business hours, nor anywhere else was he secure from insistent appeal. . . . He was constantly hunted, stalked, and hounded almost like a wild animal."

The author of these words was the Reverend Frederick T. Gates, who was destined to be a pivotal figure in Rockefeller's future. Having first met and been impressed by the dynamic Gates during the often trying negotiations with the Baptist national hierarchy that finally led him to underwrite the University of Chicago, Rockefeller, in March of 1891, asked the 38-year-old minister to call on him at 26 Broadway. As he was led into the spartan office, Rockefeller motioned him to a chair. "I am in trouble, Mr. Gates," he began with uncharacteristic directness. "The pressure of these appeals for gifts has become too great for endurance."

Three months later, when Frederick T. Gates began doing business as Mr. Rockefeller's chief almoner, it could not have been foreseen that this represented a first step in making the Rockefellers an American institution; that the small office Gates began work in would one day take up three floors in a Rockefeller Center skyscraper and employ over two hundred people whose daily work would consist only of servicing the Rockefeller dynasty; or that the minister himself would be the first in a long line of dedicated and talented people who would be full-time retainers to the Rockefeller family.

Rockefeller soon saw that Gates's business acumen might well be useful in another area where he also sorely needed help, that of his personal finances. These had become chaotic during the past few years, when he had been devoting every waking minute to steering the trust from one crisis to another. He was indeed being victimized by the sheer velocity of his income. In the ten-year period from 1885 to 1896, his share of the dividends of the trust alone totalled some $40 million. (Ironically, his total fortune, which amounted to some $200 million at the time of his "retirement" in 1896, would increase with the advent of the internal combustion engine until it reached the $1 billion mark in 1913, quadrupling during his years of inactivity.)

In 1893, after receiving a few of Gates's shrewd and observant memorandums on his investigations, Rockefeller asked the minister to take up an office at 26 Broadway and combine management of the philanthropies and personal investments under one hand. Gates was overjoyed.

For the time being at least, Rockefeller was as concerned with giving as he was with getting. He knew that the decisions he must make about the great fortune would be as momentous as any he had ever made about the giant trust. He had Frederick Gates to remind him of the dangers of inaction. "Your fortune is rolling up, rolling up like an avalanche! You must distribute it faster than it grows! If you do not, it will crush you, and your children, and your children's children."

Gates had more in mind than simply giving away money, even large amounts, to individuals and organizations requesting help. When he mused about the future of philanthropy, it was with an evangelical fervor. He dreamed of great charitable trusts that would equal in impact the trust Samuel Dodd had created for Rockefeller. They would be corporate philanthropies that would "rationalize" the world of giving the way the Standard had the world of oil. Gates began by inducing Rockefeller in 1901 to create the first institution to bear his name, the Rockefeller Institute for Medical Research, which half a century later his grandson David would transform into Rockefeller University.

Gates might have succeeded ably as one of Rockefeller's lieutenants in Standard Oil if he had come along thirty years earlier. The minister understood those principles of monopoly that had allowed his employer to organize the oil industry, and he proposed to apply them to philanthropy. At Gates's urging, Rockefeller wrote Carnegie inviting him to become a trustee of his next great philanthropy, the General Education Board, incorporated in 1903.

From its inception, the GEB had been an illustration of the principle of monopoly, choosing Negro education in the South as its subject. Its influence there was soon unrivaled, and the General Education Board next broadened its focus to include the rest of the country. In 1905 Rockefeller added $10 million to the initial endowment of the GEB, along with a letter specifying that the income had to be used "to promote a comprehensive system of higher education in the United States."

The GEB next combined the Rockefeller Medical Institute's interest in medicine with its own interest in education in a campaign that was to revolutionize the whole system of professional medical training. The less than two dozen beneficiaries of the $45 million ultimately made available for medical education included Johns Hopkins, Yale, the University of Chicago, Columbia, and Harvard. They would henceforth be the standard-setting institutions for the field.

Rockefeller was pleased at the good works of Gates's charities, pleased that they seemed to soften the harsh public opinion that had followed him remorselessly since the South Improvement plan and that they offered an area where his delicate and skittish son, John D. Rockefeller, Jr., could take hold.

In 1910 the great institution that would embody the world mission of the Rockefeller wealth was created when Rockefeller signed over to three trustees—Gates, Mr. Junior, and Harold McCormick, his son-in-law and heir to the International Harvester fortune—$50 million worth of Standard Oil securities for the initial funding of the $100 million Rockefeller Foundation.

Within a few years after its establishment, the Foundation had in fact become the international presence Gates had foreseen in his early dreams, involving itself in a variety of relief and educational campaigns at home and abroad. Not long after its creation, Gates was writing proudly to an associate that they had been fortunate to be "engaged in an exacting, stupendous enterprise pregnant with measureless destinies."

Thoreau once observed that "philanthropy is almost the only virtue which is sufficiently appreciated by mankind." Americans were indeed impressed by the great Rockefeller charities. Their advent happened to come at a time when the wave of hatred had crested. In the iron law of the pendulum's swing, there began a slow reversal of the public's reaction to the Rockefeller name, a reshaping of opinion that seemed spontaneous but in its own way was an impressive labor. The most crucial step was the decision to abandon the policy of silence that the Standard had always pursued, a policy nicely summarized in a maxim of Rockefeller's personal attorney, Starr J. Murphy: "Uncover no surface unnecessarily."

In 1907 the company hired a former journalist, Joseph I. C. Clarke, to be its publicity agent. Given an office staff of three and complete access to the Standard's files and executives, Clarke went right to work. As he later said in his autobiography, "I followed my plan of going into the open for the Company. When a paper made an attack on the Standard Oil I hunted up the facts, stated them briefly, had the local Standard Oil agent call on the editor and demand that he should print it. It worked wonderfully. Standard Oil emerged from the sub-cellar."

Imperceptibly a change began to occur, especially after 1913, when the masterful Ivy Lee took over the job of beautifying Rockefeller's public image. Lee didn't have to be schooled in his art. He never announced the large sums with which Rockefeller occasionally increased the endowments of the foundations, fearing it would appear egocentric. Instead he arranged for the recipients of Rockefeller bounty to make grateful announcements. Lee planted feature stories of the aging billionaire's trips to church, his relations with neighbors, his golf games. His idea was to promote, in a low-keyed way, a new view of Rockefeller the human being.

For others, old age might be a time when an autumnal spirit of reconciliation replaced the passions of youth, but for Rockefeller, who had never allowed himself such passions, it was just another passage from one stage of a self always under control to another. He was known to cry only twice—once when returning to the breakfast table after learning of his wife's death, and the other time when hearing—incorrectly as it worked out—that the upstate New York farmhouse where he had been born was being raised on jacks for transport to Coney Island. He went to his first stage entertainment—a Weber and Fields musicale—but was not impressed enough to go again. He remained what he had always been—a businessman. Each morning Rockefeller retired for two hours to a private office at Kikjuit, the manor house at his Pocantico estate, to buy and sell stocks over the telephone. It was business, but also a type of diversion—a form of shadow boxing that reminded him of the great fights of the old days.

Rockefeller had had one great passion—the Standard—and once he stopped his involvement with this institution that had so consumed his life, he was like a salmon at the end of spawn, content to remain in the shallows, confident that he had fulfilled his destiny. Now, as he grew older, he allowed himself the eccentricities befitting one who had weathered the storm of public resentment and become a sort of national resource, a name to be used in jokes and the lyrics of popular songs as a harmless synonym for great wealth.

There was the matter of giving out coins, for example—at first nickels, and then nickels for children and dimes for adults. In part this was a public relations ploy, sprung from the fertile imagination of Ivy Lee. But Rockefeller took to it with enthusiasm. Of the estimated thirty thousand shiny new dimes he gave out in later years, most were accompanied with the sort of admonition that might well have fallen from his own mother's lips: "A dime for the bank, a penny to spend." Wherever he went, people waited with palms up, clamoring for one of the coins as if in hopes that some of the genius of the giver would rub off on them.

He had homes in New York, Florida, and Seal Harbor, Maine. He built a retreat in Lakewood, New Jersey, called "Golf House," where he pursued the passion of his old age. But after the old Forest Hill estate in

Cleveland burned down in 1917, Pocantico remained his true love. He had come there first in 1893 after his brother William had bought a small piece of property near the Sleepy Hollow area of the Ichabod Crane legend. He came to love this area. His sons and grandsons might have large, international aspirations, but after his retirement, spiritually he never strayed from Pocantico.

He seemed to shrink with the passing years and, by the time he reached his nineties, weighed less than a hundred pounds. His thin face had become the texture of an old brown parchment manuscript, as brittle as the Dead Sea Scrolls and so seamed that the mouth and eyes appeared held in place by a carefully constructed network of tiny scars. He ate like a bird, taking a mouthful of food from each of several dishes set before him. He became a vestige from a former age, given a kind of grace by the sheer number of the years he had accumulated. He became an eccentric figure, "riding" a bicycle by balancing on the seat and having a valet push him with one hand and hold a parasol over him with the other. He played golf every day, even if it meant calling out a small army of servants to shovel several inches of snow off the course, and even when he was in his late eighties could hit a ball over one hundred yards off the tee. Whatever the weather, Rockefeller would ready himself for his daily automobile ride by donning a paper vest, aviatorlike goggles, and a duster cap whose flaps hung down the sides of his face like a hound's ears. Each year he would appear before the whirring newsreel cameras on the day of his birth, tipping his straw hat, smiling, and occasionally delivering a sober message, preserved by Pathe talking newsreels, which captured him murmuring almost inaudibly through an old man's shrunken lips, "God bless Standard Oil, God bless us all."

THE SON

CHAPTER 4

In the winter of 1874, John D. Rockefeller, Sr., was at the midpoint of his career. Twelve years earlier he had begun the firm of Clark & Rockefeller; twelve years ahead lay the creation of the great Standard trust. On January 29, the good fortune that had followed him through his life touched him once again when Cettie was delivered of a son.

Years later, Edith Rockefeller would refer to her brother, John D.

Rockefeller, Jr., not without an undertone of jealousy, as the "Crown Prince." Yet the title related more to his position as bearer of the name and fortune than to any special privileges accorded him, for his childhood was far from pampered. A short, somewhat sickly child with a Spelman's square jaw, large mouth, and vulnerable eyes, Mr. Junior (the nickname came from his precocious insistence that there could be only *one* John D. Rockefeller) grew up shy and serious, and usually alone. No playmates came to the Euclid Avenue home; his walks through the woods around the family estate at Forest Hill were solitary except at those times when the gatekeeper's son could be conscripted as a companion. There were long hours at church, but they did little to relieve his loneliness, since the congregation, as he said in an unguarded moment, "was made up of lower middle class people whom we didn't find particularly congenial."

The family was his only resource, and his growth was inward toward it. He saw his father as the kind of hero out of whom legends are made. The elder Rockefeller was just then at the peak of his manhood, a figure to stay forever in a boy's imagination—tall and purposeful, with blue eyes that looked as if they could freeze steel, and full, reddish whiskers. If others saw the thin mouth as cruel, at home it was often turned up in laughter. Later in life, reminiscing warmly about his father, Junior said, "He was one of us. He taught us to swim, row, skate, and drive horses. . . . At Forest Hill he loved to make footpaths through the woods and when we learned to bicycle we used to ride these paths in the moonlight."

Such tantalizing moments of intimacy were memorable mainly because they occurred so infrequently. As Junior grew up, his father was more and more occupied with the wars of conquest he fought as the head of Standard Oil. It was not that he enjoyed time spent away from wife and family; on the contrary, home and family for him were bastions against the world. Once, on a trip that kept him in New York longer than he liked, he wrote back forlornly to Cettie in Cleveland: "I feel more than ever . . . the world is full of Sham, Flattery and Deception; our home is a haven of rest and freedom." Yet the empire he was building demanded his fullest energy and attention.

During these frequent absences, his son's only role was as the harem male in the matriarchy that made up the Rockefeller household. There was Grandmother Eliza, thin and severe and as fond of her successful son as she was sensitive about her own absent husband. There was Grandmother Spelman, who had come to live with her son-in-law after her husband's death. There were his sisters: Bessie, Alta, and Edith, eight, three, and two years older than he. They were his playmates and mentors.

But of all the women who made up his daily life, his mother was by far the most influential. The small, frail woman with a remarkably strong will moved through his days like a divinity, concentrating her intellect and energies (her son later recalled) on "exemplifying the life of Christ." Her gentle discipline was theological—and irresistible. Coercion was unnecessary. When someone told the elder Rockefeller that his two finest accomplishments were the Institute for Medical Research and his son, he answered, "The boy's mother must be given credit for the last."

Every morning there were breakfast table prayers, each member of the family reading in turn from the Bible. Friday was prayer meeting night. On Sunday, Mrs. Rockefeller held the "Home Talks," for which she made notes as thoughts came to her during the week. At these chats each of the children was asked to concentrate on one sin, discuss it with her, pray with her over it, and resolve to conquer it the following week.

The sisters, especially the spirited Edith, whose divorce from Harold McCormick and flamboyant affairs with male secretaries would be a mighty burden to her father and brother, may have entertained furtive thoughts of rebellion; but it is unlikely that Junior ever did. As he grew up and began to practice handwriting in his copybooks, one of the homey maxims he copied hundreds of times in neat Spencerian script seemed to summarize what he had learned from life thus far: "He who conquers self is the greatest victor." The heirs of the other nineteenth-century fortunes might prepare for a lifetime of amusement and pleasure, but John D. Rockefeller, Jr., was meant for larger things. He had been given custody of the family name and therefore of its honor. It was his duty to see that the world knew his father as he did—as a great man. He didn't believe the muckraking exposés, yet the feelings of guilt his father managed to escape descended to the boy in double measure.

He worked hard to keep the money at bay. His father helped him, insisting that the fortune had been put in their custody by the Lord and was a special trust not to be wasted. He showed Junior how to keep accounts in a ledger book that mimicked his own Ledger A. It was one thing to keep such accounts if you were an eighteen-year-old bookkeeper setting out to make your way in the world, however, and quite another if you were the crown prince to the throne of Standard Oil. Junior must have suspected that his entries were a parody of his father's: "Practicing the violin at $.05 per hour; Drinking hot water at $.05 per glass; Killing flies at $.02 per fly."

After 1884 New York was the Rockefellers' legal residence although Cleveland, especially Forest Hill, always remained home in a sentimental sense. The family took up membership in the Fifth Avenue Baptist Church, John D. becoming a deacon and trustee and Cettie Rockefeller teaching Sunday school with such meticulous dedication that she marked a "C" in the margins of her rollbook beside the names of the lucky children she thought to be Christians and therefore saved.

Junior's secular education had been in the hands of tutors, but now his mother decided that it was time for him to go to school. He attended the New York School of Languages for a year and then, at the age of sixteen, enrolled in the fashionable Cutler School. There followed two years at the Browning School. By 1893 he was ready for college. Although nearly twenty years old, he was, as he admitted later, "shy, ill-adjusted, and not very robust."

Junior toyed with the idea of going to Yale but became discouraged on hearing that a "fast set" of students established the tone of that school. After consulting with family friend William Rainey Harper, the man his father had installed as president of the University of Chicago, he decided a smaller college would be more in keeping with a person of his own conservative nature and outlook, and selected Brown. He arrived in Providence very much the naïf. He couldn't dance and didn't want to; he thought the center on a football field was called "the middle." He was 5 feet 6 inches and weighed 127 pounds, and his square-jawed face, habitually pinched in the forehead and serious, made him seem less like a carefree underclassman than a sanctimonious young vicar.

He set up housekeeping in a suite of rooms at Slater Hall, the newest dormitory on campus, and amused his new roommates by immediately sitting down to hem his own dish towels. But whatever else he was or wasn't, he was not insincere, and for the first time in his life he began to make friends. He wrote home enthusiastically after his first week to tell his family that the freshman class had already had a spirited prayer meeting, which augured well for the four years ahead, and added that Grandmother Spelman, with her racial sympathies, would be "interested to know that there are three colored men in the class."

In his second year at Brown he turned twenty-one, and the long arm of the family reached from New York to Providence to mark the occasion by reminding him that great things were expected of him. Among notes of congratulation was one from his mother, who told him: "You can celebrate your birthday in no better way . . . than by such earnest work as I know you are giving for God and the saving of the souls of your fellow students." His father sent him a check for twenty-one dollars, in lieu of candles to mark off the years, and a brief note which said in part: "I cannot tell you how much happiness we all have in you, and how much we are looking forward to and relying on you in the future."

College was in some sense a normalizing experience, momentarily blocking out the future that loomed ahead. For the first time and probably the only time in his life, he did the things other young men his age did. He dated girls, went to football games, and attended dances; the summer before his senior year, he grew a neat beard and made a bicycle tour of Europe with a friend. Yet he also persevered in the rituals by which he conserved and controlled money, earning a reputation as something of an eccentric. His fellow students were amused to see the heir to one of the greatest fortunes in the country acting like a scholarship student, trimming frayed edges on his cuffs or standing in rapt concentration over a tea kettle steaming two stuck postage stamps apart. A standing joke at Brown was that by the time young Rockefeller had finished auditing a dinner check, someone else in the party would have paid the bill.

His last year at Brown, Junior decided to host a dance to pay back all those who had been hospitable to him. He needed a chaperone and wrote his mother about the problem: "It would give me the greatest pleasure to have you receive upon such an occasion, but feeling as you do about such things it would, I suppose, be quite out of the question." Cettie Rockefeller asked her husband about Junior's request, wondering if perhaps they might not make the counter offer of a musicale, and thus, "set a standard of enjoyment better than the dance." But her son insisted, and she reluctantly agreed to appear in evening dress to greet some four hundred of his guests at a rented hall. On the night of the event, however, she was suddenly stricken by a headache, the final recourse of the Victorian lady, and did not leave her hotel room. Attired in tails and white gloves, John D. Rockefeller, Sr., stood solemnly in the receiving line by himself.

By graduation, Junior had rid himself of many of the parochial attitudes with which he had entered Brown. He had become a good enough student to win a Phi Beta Kappa key; the rigorous Spelman morality was now tempered somewhat by a philosophy more in keeping with his father's pragmatic cast of mind. As Junior wrote his Grandmother Spelman, "My ideas and opinions change, I find, in many ways. I would stickle less for the letter of the law now, more for the spirit."

As the interlude at Brown ended, the future began once again to lean heavily on Junior. By this time his father was under such heavy attack that even his iron constitution had broken, and he had seemingly lost his health. Later in life an associate asked him if he had ever considered the ministry, for which he seemed perhaps better suited. Junior answered,

"Absolutely not. My one thought from the time I was a boy was to help my father. I knew from the beginning I was going into his office."

CHAPTER 5

In 1897, thousands of young men of good family took a last, nostalgic look at the ivied walls and Gothic arches where they had spent their college years and went out to take their places in the bustling world of business. It was a heady moment for the forces of finance and industry in America. In the presidential campaign of the previous year, Mark Hanna, John D. Rockefeller's old schoolmate, had engineered the victory of the gold standard and of "class money" over "mass money," opening the door to a vast boom for American business. Huge corporations were born overnight, and watered stock flowed like Niagara over the frenetic exchanges as fortunes were won and lost and the center of gravity of American industry shifted inexorably to Wall Street, where the captains of finance ruled the securities market. It was the money men's version of the frontier epic, the Era of Frenzied Finance.

If 26 Broadway was one of the most fabled financial storm centers of the period, for Junior the romance was missing. The son of John D. Rockefeller could not prove himself in the usual ways: his arrival at this famous address was not an achievement, but an inevitability. With no other alternative, he dutifully journeyed to the office, where he found a heavy oak rolltop desk set aside for him in the small, sparsely furnished room on the ninth floor in which the Rockefellers' private affairs were handled. There he joined George Rogers, his father's personal secretary; a clerk named Charles O. Heydt; Mrs. Tuttle, the telegrapher who also had the job of answering the hate mail; and a contingent of bookkeepers. Presiding over the whole operation was the august Federick T. Gates.

Gates's energies were too undisciplined and his passions too much on the surface for Junior to be comfortable with him. But Junior respected Gates and understood that he was to be his mentor; he settled down to an apprenticeship in the family business under the former minister's guidance. After learning the office routine, Junior began taking long trips with Gates to visit Rockefeller investments scattered all over the country.

These early days were not happy ones for Junior. He had two strong personalities to deal with—Gates and his father—and no way to define himself. "From the day I entered my father's office until the day of his death," he recalled, "my one desire was to help him in every way in my power. I was always as glad to black his shoes, to pack his bags . . . as I later was to represent him in various of his interests, business and philanthropic." But even his one romantic indulgence—to see himself as a paladin bent on removing the stain from the family escutcheon—was balked. It was too large a job, and he did not know how to begin it.

If Junior had ever secretly dreamed of following in his father's giant footsteps, he had a rude awakening when given his first considerable sum of money to invest. Since first coming into the office, he had borrowed money from his father (at 6 percent a year) to invest in a margin account for himself and Alta, with the profits jointly shared. After a few modest successes, Junior met an investor named David Lamar. Lamar managed to persuade him he had secret information concerning certain important developments that would soon dramatically increase the value of the stock of the U.S. Leather Company. With an eagerness that betrayed an anxiety to prove his commercial worth, Junior invested heavily. Once committed, he bought all the U.S. Leather stock he could get. It was only later that he realized he had been gulled. Lamar (who subsequently became known as the "Wolf of Wall Street") himself owned the stock he had touted and had been unloading it on the rising market that Rockefeller's impetuous buying had created.

Junior's losses amounted to more than a million dollars. He went to his father to confess what had happened. Looking back at him with his impassive eyes, the old man (whom the office staff had begun to call "Mr. Senior") said simply, "All right, John. Don't worry, I will see you through." If anything, the lack of criticism made the pill harder to swallow. A few days later, Junior wrote his father in a paroxysm of contrition: "My one thought and purpose since I came into the office has been to relieve you in every way possible of the burdens which you have carried so long. To realize now that instead of doing that I have been . . . instrumental in adding to your burdens is bitter and humiliating."

If Junior's early years at 26 Broadway were marked by fits and starts and emotional crises, there were also moments that would later be seen as turning points. One of them occurred in 1901, when his first and only serious love affair reached a climax.

He met Miss Abby Greene Aldrich at a Brown dance he had attended seven years earlier. The daughter of Senator Nelson Aldrich of Rhode Island, she was a pleasant-looking young woman with a long nose, prominent chin, and luxuriant hair in love curls. If not as attractive as other young ladies he had met, she nonetheless made the best of her good features and was the sort of woman who would be called handsome when she reached middle age. More important, she was outgoing, graceful, and cultured—all qualities that Junior lacked.

Although not as wealthy as the Rockefellers, the Aldriches were a powerful family and had an undeniable legitimacy. Nelson Aldrich was descended from a Bay Colony family on his father's side and from Roger Williams on his mother's; his wife could trace her ancestry back to a Brewster who had come to the New World aboard the *Mayflower.*

The marriage took place in October 1901 at Warwick. For his guests, the elder Rockefeller reserved several suites of rooms at the Narragansett Hotel. He chartered two steamers to take them across to the island, where streetcars conveyed them to the estate. "For several days past," went the *Times* account of the reception, "every boat and train from New York, Washington, Newport and other cities has brought its quota of guests prominent in social and political circles in the country." Over one thousand guests were present, and to the mild annoyance of the Rockefeller entourage, champagne was served.

The newspaper headlines blazed "Beauty Weds Wealth," and reporters tried to follow the couple on their honeymoon, but Junior managed to escape with his bride to Pocantico, which his parents had vacated to ensure their privacy. It was an interlude of long walks in the white frosts of early morning and the fiery autumn colors of the afternoon. The romance consummated there would, in a true sense, last forever. There had been only one discordant note in their first idyllic days together: when Junior had commanded his bride to keep a close account of daily expenses, in the Rockefeller manner, she had flatly refused.

After their honeymoon, the newlyweds moved in with Junior's parents at 4 West 54th Street until the home they had rented across the street at 13 West 54th was vacant. Soon after moving in, they began to fill it with children. Their firstborn, Abby (1903), was their only daughter; then came the five sons who were destined to play so great a role in the next generation: John D. 3rd (1906), Nelson (1908), Laurance (1910), Winthrop (1912), and David (1915). By the time Laurance was born, the family had moved into the town house Junior had built next door to his father's house. Number 10 West 54th, where the children would spend their youth and adolescence, was one of the largest private residences in Manhattan at the time, its nine stories including a nursery, a gymnasium, and spacious quarters for servants and employees. The growing family alternated between 54th Street and Abeynton Lodge, the old house that had come with Pocantico and sat within shouting distance of Kikjuit.

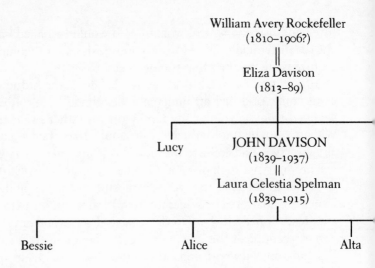

William Avery Rockefeller
(1810–1906?)
‖
Eliza Davison
(1813–89)

Lucy · JOHN DAVISON
(1839–1937)
‖
Laura Celestia Spelman
(1839–1915)

Bessie · Alice · Alta

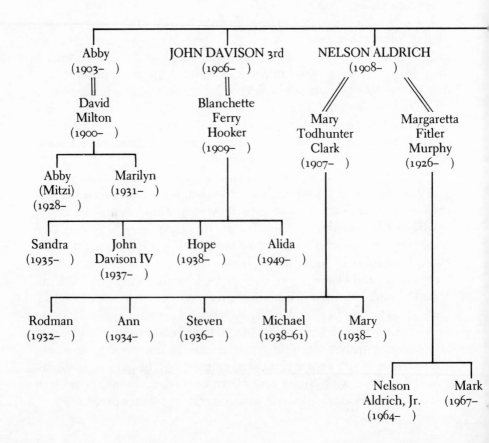

Abby
(1903–)
‖
David
Milton
(1900–)

JOHN DAVISON 3rd
(1906–)
‖
Blanchette
Ferry
Hooker
(1909–)

NELSON ALDRICH
(1908–)
⫽
Mary
Todhunter
Clark
(1907–)

Margaretta
Fitler
Murphy
(1926–)

Abby
(Mitzi)
(1928–)

Marilyn
(1931–)

Sandra
(1935–)

John
Davison IV
(1937–)

Hope
(1938–)

Alida
(1949–)

Rodman
(1932–)

Ann
(1934–)

Steven
(1936–)

Michael
(1938–61)

Mary
(1938–)

Nelson
Aldrich, Jr.
(1964–)

Mark
(1967–

The Rockefellers

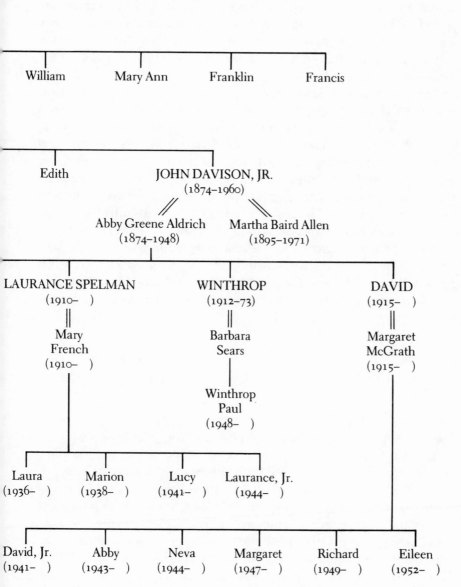

William   Mary Ann   Franklin   Francis

Edith   JOHN DAVISON, JR.
(1874–1960)

Abby Greene Aldrich   Martha Baird Allen
(1874–1948)   (1895–1971)

LAURANCE SPELMAN   WINTHROP   DAVID
(1910–)   (1912–73)   (1915–)

Mary   Barbara   Margaret
French   Sears   McGrath
(1910–)   (1915–)

Winthrop
Paul
(1948–)

Laura   Marion   Lucy   Laurance, Jr.
(1936–)   (1938–)   (1941–)   (1944–)

David, Jr.   Abby   Neva   Margaret   Richard   Eileen
(1941–)   (1943–)   (1944–)   (1947–)   (1949–)   (1952–)

Abby Aldrich Rockefeller soon became active in the cultural and social life of New York. She had become a partisan of the modernism pounding at the gates of the tradition-bound art establishment shortly after the celebrated Armory show of 1913. She had collected the Old Masters that appealed to her husband's taste but began to buy more contemporary works, as she said, to have artifacts her children would "be interested in and want to live with." In 1929 she became one of the founders of the Museum of Modern Art, to which the family ultimately donated all its property on West 54th Street. But for Junior, she was more than a society matron enhancing the prestige of the Rockefeller family. She was the one person with whom he could be himself, indiscriminately revealing weakness and strength, momentarily relinquishing the awesome control that had governed his public and private existence for the first twenty-five years of his life. Junior hated to be away from her; when he was, he wrote back impassioned love letters graphically describing the ways in which he longed for her. Toward the end of his own life, when Abby had been dead for many years and he was going through his private papers for the family archives, he came across these letters, which Abby had saved. After rereading them and discussing the matter with an associate who was helping him sort through the papers, he decided that some of the correspondence should be burned because of passages that were so intensely private, and so passionately real.

CHAPTER 6

At the turn of the century, when many of the great figures who had reshaped American industry were beginning to pass on, the attention being paid to the transfer of their fortunes was as great as if they had been titled nobles. It was expected that most inheritors would simply waste the money. The famous John W. Gates, whose raids on the stock market and daring gambles in the steel industry had earned him the sobriquet "Bet-a-million" Gates, left his fortune to a son whose excesses so delighted the public that the newspapers dubbed him "Spend-a-Million" Gates. No one thought Junior would become a prodigal, but there was curiosity about what he would do with the great Standard Oil fortune. In 1905 Hearst's *Cosmopolitan* published a symposium titled "What Will He Do With It?" The lead article began:

No little interest is centered upon the world's greatest fortune, that of Mr. John D. Rockefeller. The fortune will in the course of years be inherited by the Son, Mr. John D. Rockefeller Jr. It is needless to say that the power of the money covers so vast a territory that a man inheriting such a fortune has it within his power to revolutionize the world . . . or use it so evilly as to retard civilization for a quarter of a century.

Yet these were questions for others to ask. For the time being at least, Junior would be happy simply to take hold at 26 Broadway and pull his own weight there. Marriage and a family of his own had helped stabilize any doubts he had about his mission. Moreover, there had been signs that he had become more comfortable in his father's office even before he had put the question to Miss Aldrich.

Junior's upbringing had taught him to do his duty, but it had also filled him with yearnings that succeeding in business could not satisfy. Given the sort of person he was, it was only natural that he should feel more at ease working in the philanthropic foundations the Reverend Gates was building than in corporations like Standard Oil. The one represented virgin territory; the other would always have a certain taint.

The elder Rockefeller was neither interested in the details of Gates's philanthropic schemes, nor especially informed about the issues in question. His emotional remoteness from organized benevolence—prodigious though his financial investment would be—created an opportunity toward which Junior was inexorably drawn. "Gates was the brilliant dreamer and creator," he recalled later. "I was the salesman—the go-between with Father at the opportune moment." By picking a strategic time when the elder Rockefeller was "in a relaxed mood"—after dinner or out for a drive—Junior was able to secure his approval of ideas "which others couldn't have secured because the moment wasn't right."

Over the next twelve years, the father would invest $446,719,371.22 (a true Rockefeller reckoning) in four vast corporate philanthropies, the Institute for Medical Research, the General Education Board, the Rockefeller Foundation, and the Laura Spelman Rockefeller Memorial Fund. In the process, he would endow Junior with "businesses" in which, rather than merely occupying a seat on a board, he could take an active role in management—businesses worthy of the Rockefeller heir that could also serve the son's fervent wish to restore honor to his father's name.

As he became associated with the foundations and the millions of dollars they dispersed, Junior's image started to change. He became a celebrity. But to continue as a front man for business would equivocate his efforts as a philanthropist. He knew he had to choose once and for all between business and charity, and there was no doubt in his mind about which of the two endeavors was more promising.

After discussions with his father, he resigned as vice-president of Standard Oil and U.S. Steel. The other directorships were soon to follow. One of the few companies he kept an association with was a relatively innocuous coal-mining operation out west—Colorado Fuel and Iron.

The company was a prime example of what the liberal press would later call "industrial absolutism." The miners' low wages (about $1.68 a day) were paid in scrip redeemable only at company stores charging extortionate prices. The miners usually lived in small two-room shacks provided by the company at exorbitant rents, and from which they could be evicted on a three-day notice. More than $20,000 a year was spent by the company to maintain a force of detectives, mine guards, and spies whose job it was to keep the camps quarantined from the virulence of unionism.

Colorado Fuel and Iron's political power helped the operators make sure that even the primitive mine safety standards of the time were not enforced; the result was, predictably, an epidemic of accidental deaths and injuries to the workers. In this emotionally charged atmosphere, the United Mine Workers provided a focus for the dissatisfaction and anger in the camps.

On September 23, 1913, some 9,000 miners and their families—close to 70 percent of the working force—walked out of the mining camps. They settled into tent colonies the UMW had set up for them near the small, nearly anonymous mining towns of the area. One of them was called Ludlow. What previously had been regarded as isolated incidents between the company detectives and miners now turned into military skirmishes, lasting through the bitter winter months. And on the morning of April 20, 1914, the labor war that had already cost dozens of lives came to a bloody climax.

A company of state militia that had repeatedly clashed with strikers took up a position on a rise overlooking the tents of Ludlow. The chill wind whipped at laundry drying stiffly on the clotheslines and curled the smoke climbing out of stovepipes poked through the tent tops. The strikers stared suspiciously at the men above them. Just after daybreak, a shot rang out from an unknown source, and the jittery militiamen responded by opening fire from their Hotchkiss guns, beginning a battle that would last all day.

As their tents, punctured with bullets, caught fire, the strikers retreated to positions in cellars dug under the floorboards. By nightfall, the scene was one of complete devastation. There were forty dead and countless wounded. But the worst was to come. Next morning, as the people of Ludlow emerged from under ground and walked through the smoldering colony counting their losses, they discovered the bodies of two women and eleven children who had suffocated in a cellar when the tent above them had burned. The outrage had found its symbol, and as news of it spread, other colonies of strikers began an offensive against the mine operators, seizing towns and attacking company outposts within a 250-mile radius of Ludlow. President Woodrow Wilson ordered federal troops into the area to end what threatened to become an all-out war.

In the early days of the strike, Junior had been busy with other crises, such as the Wilson administration's apparent intention to push anti-trust legislation through Congress. Gradually, he became nervous about events in Colorado and began following the dispatches from Denver with more than usual concern; soon most of his time at 26 Broadway was consumed by the strike and its violence. Even before the miners had walked out, he faced pressure from as high as the White House to use his influence to settle the conflict.

In March, just a month before the Ludlow Massacre, Junior was called to testify before the House Committee on Mines and Mining. "Do you not think you might have paid some attention to these bloody strike conditions out in Colorado, where you have one thousand employees in whose welfare you seem not to have taken any deep personal interest?" the chairman asked.

"I have done what I regard as the very best thing in the interest of those employees and the large investment I represent," Junior replied evasively.

The chairman continued to press him: "But the killing of people and the shooting of the children—has not that been of enough importance to you for you to communicate with other directors and see if something might be done to end that sort of thing?"

In answer, Junior said that it was not a local but a national issue that was at stake, as to whether workers would be allowed to work under any conditions that they might choose.

"You are willing," the chairman shot back, "to let these killings take place rather than to go there and do something to settle conditions?"

Junior answered that he expected to stand by the officers at all costs.

"And you will do that if it costs all your property and kills all your employees?"

"It is a great principle," Junior replied.

Some criticized him for his uncompromising stand, but Junior's parents were elated; his father made him a gift of 10,000 shares of Colorado

Fuel and Iron stock. Junior felt stronger than ever in his views. The only miscalculation he made, in fact, was in the impact Ludlow would have on public opinion. Yet this was a crucial mistake, and soon after news of the massacre had flashed around the country, the hatred that stalked him was equal to anything his father had ever faced.

It was clear that Ludlow threatened to become the albatross around Junior's neck for the rest of his life. Even if he could have tolerated the image he saw in the mirror of public opinion, he realized that his patient work to create goodwill and respect for the Rockefeller name was now in jeopardy.

Junior began looking for new advisers and new advice—not only to make possible his escape from the guilt for Ludlow but to provide him with indispensable strategies for building and maintaining an institutional network that would propel the Rockefeller dynasty into the twentieth century.

By late August 1914 much of the criticism caused by the strike had died down; CF&I production was almost back to normal as a result of scab labor and the gradual return of the starving and terrorized miners to their jobs. Junior's personal metamorphosis into a pioneer in industrial relations began with a pilgrimage to Ludlow and other points of interest in the Colorado coal fields in September 1915.

The climax of the two-week visit came when Junior was a guest of honor at an evening social in the camp at Cameron. After standing up in the schoolhouse and giving a short talk to the workers and their families, he suprised everyone by suggesting that the floor be cleared for a dance. The orchestra struck up a fox-trot, and Junior, asking the superintendent's wife to do him the honor, began to circle the floor with stiff formality. Later he announced the Industrial Representatives Plan, a scheme that invented the "company union" which, before it was outlawed by the Wagner Act of 1935, was to prove an invaluable instrument for management in blunting the great union drives of the period.

Ludlow was both a terrifying experience for Junior and an exhilarating one. Long after the massacre had slipped into the vast forgetfulness of American history, he called it "one of the most important things that ever happened to the family," a statement he would later repeat to his grandchildren. It marked that moment when the Rockefeller family entered the twentieth century and, even more, marked Junior's personal liberation from the past. By handling the crisis, he won his spurs; family leadership passed to him and his associates. He was on the course that would make him a national figure in his own right.

CHAPTER 7

Junior was soon in control of a constellation of cultural and economic institutions whose reach was international and whose power was unrivaled in American life. He breakfasted with Presidents and was accepted in circles where his father's name had been anathema. He had a plan for the future. If he could be said to lack anything, it was, ironically, financial independence. Over forty years old, he was still dependent on the old man's periodic generosity.

The question of finances might ultimately have created problems between him and his father if it were not for a law passed in 1916 whereby the federal government dramatically increased its inheritance taxes to 10 percent on estates of more than $5 million; the following year, it increased the rate to 25 percent on estates of $10 million or more. It was then, without ever formally indicating exactly what he was doing or why, that the elder Rockefeller started making his fortune over to his son. First came a huge block of Jersey Standard, Socony Mobil (Standard of New York), Standard of Indiana, and the other splintered companies of the great trust dissolved by the federal government in 1911. Then came the industrial properties he and Gates had worked for thirty years to assemble. In all, the transfer took more than four years; but by 1921 it was complete. The amount placed in Junior's hands was close to $500 million. It was about the amount his father had already given away, leaving the old man only $20 million to amuse himself with in the stock market.

Although the transfer of the huge fortune was legally complete and final, in another sense it was an optical illusion. Junior had the money, yet in a larger sense it would always belong to the man who had accumulated it; the power it brought in the financial marketplace would remain his, as would the glory in the philanthropies it built. Junior had gained nothing for himself. His father had said that the money was a gift from God; Junior had no choice but to believe it was so. He himself was only the trustee, dispensing the money in ways he assumed his father—if the old man had been interested in such things—would have approved.

Twelve years after the transfer was complete, when Junior was on his way to becoming one of the most admired men in the world because of his wide-ranging philanthropies, he wrote a letter to his father in which he indicated that his feeling of stewardship had not changed:

In all these years of effort and striving, your own life and example have ever been to me the most powerful and stimulating influence. What you have done for humanity and business on a vast scale had impressed me profoundly. To have been a silent partner with you in carrying out these great constructive purposes and benefactions has been the supreme delight of my life.

The conception entailed a curious reversal. If either of them was a "silent partner" in the thirty-odd years of their collaboration, it was the elder Rockefeller, who had never attended a meeting of the foundations, who had expressed only a passing interest in his son's impressive achievements, and who had played a subsidiary role in family affairs from the time he "retired" from 26 Broadway. In describing himself with this phrase, Junior was unconsciously passing a poignant judgment on his life. It was as close as his finely controlled character came to recognizing the awesome suppression of self his life of service had entailed.

The unconditional reverence in which he held his father had the inevitable effect of establishing a distance between them. "Neither Father nor I," Junior later recalled, "had the temperament which gives itself freely. We talked about whatever we had to talk over—never discursively." It is difficult to imagine what the older man, wise in the world's ways and suspicious of the flattering phrase, made of the stream of effusive letters that regularly flowed to him from the pen of his middle-aged son, who though financially independent still thanked him for the most trivial convenience or gesture.

In 1920, for example, when the 46-year-old Junior was receiving the last pieces of his great legacy, he wrote:

For your Christmas check of $1,000 I send you most cordial thanks. Not only for this further and beautiful gift would I express my appreciation, but for all the wonderful gifts you have made me this past year, and for those recurring gifts which add so much to the comfort and convenience of our family life and are nonetheless gratefully received by reason of their being so continous. I refer to the use of electricity in the city, the horses and carriage in the country, and the participation with you in the enjoyment of the farm produce, the flowers and plants from the greenhouse, the occupancy of Abeynton Lodge, and the many services rendered to our family.

Junior's attitude toward his father was all the more striking given the fact that the old man became capable of bewildering eccentricity as he entered his nineties. Controlling every conversation he could and ignoring those he didn't control, he held forth in the ornate dining room at Kikjuit as the host of large dinner parties at which he himself hardly ate at all. In these years, as Raymond Fosdick later admitted in a private letter, he often "greatly embarrassed his children, particularly John Junior." Yet this was something Junior himself was never able to admit. The father was always seen through a child's eyes: a figure too powerful to criticize, too revered to suspect of succumbing to senility.

In 1932, when Senior was in his ninety-second year and Junior was fifty-eight, the son could still be wounded by a gesture that might have been better dismissed as an old man's momentary humor. Senior had complained one evening to Thomas M. Debevoise, Junior's personal attorney and close adviser, that he felt his son owed him something in the neighborhood of $3,500,000 to make "an equitable adjustment" between them in the matter of expenses for maintaining the family office during the previous ten years. Told of the claim, a stunned and heartsick Junior wrote Debevoise the following morning:

In all the years of my business association with Father, I have sought in matters both small and large to be scrupulously conscientious and just. . . . I cannot concede that anything has been done on my part which is inequitable and which now makes appropriate a readjustment for the past. For my own self respect, for the sake of my standing with my wife and children, I cannot for a moment recognize or seem to recognize any such claim or the existence upon which such a claim can justly be made.

Having drawn his line of defense, Junior turned to the "other side of the picture" and came as close to baring his soul as he ever would:

Never once in my life that I can recall have I asked Father for a single cent. He has been generous to me beyond anything that has ever been known. The vast sums he has given me, I have sought to use in ways which he would approve, having in mind his own broad philanthropies. . . . I did not seek nor choose to be the recipient of great wealth, with the staggering responsibilities inevitably coupled with its marvellous opportunities. It has not meant the greatest happiness. From my earliest years I have had but one thought and desire, namely to be helpful to Father in every way in my power. This I have striven all my life to be. I have ever been proud to lay the credit for things accomplished at his feet, where alone it belonged. I have gloried in the greatness of his unparalleled achievements in industry and his world wide services to humanity. I have never sought anything for myself. I have striven always to serve his interests. Perhaps you can understand, then, how deeply wounded I have been by the criticism which Father's request implies. Nothing in my life has hurt me as much.

The old man, however, had forgotten about the matter long before his son set signature to this letter. It is not known if Debevoise told John D. how deeply wounded Junior had been. The issue disappeared as suddenly as it had come, never again entering the almost daily exchange of letters between the two men that continued until Senior's death. John D. went on playing golf; Junior went on building the Rockefeller myth that sprang from his father but somehow did not include him.

When Junior first came to work for his father, the office had been a one-man show presided over by the venerable figure the clerks called "Pop" behind his back. But Frederick Gates had long since ceased to be influential in the Rockefeller's personal affairs (although he remained, until his death in 1923, a powerful presence in the corporate philanthropies his genius had inspired). Gates had deeply mistrusted experts, feeling that they inevitably put their own bureaucratic interests ahead of their principal's welfare. Time and again he had warned Junior against them, once going so far as to predict that in the future the Rockefellers might well find themselves in Lemuel Gulliver's predicament: tied down and controlled by scores of Lilliputian advisers.

But Junior was comforted by bureaucratic structure. It was a nice solution to the problem of insulating oneself while at the same time retaining the ability to intervene. Thus a new classification was born in the Rockefeller Office: the Associate. Junior had already accumulated Lieutenants; he now gave them a kind of official status and began to forge them into the nucleus of an organization that would be a major force in his own life and would continue to serve his children and grandchildren as well. His habit was to lunch daily with these advisers, when he was in town, to discuss the Rockefeller family's diverse affairs. It was reminiscent of his father's meetings with his Standard executives; and in their own way, the individuals Junior collected would have a power transcending even that of the Standard Oil Gang of the past. Rockefeller Associates would move with ease between service to the family and service in local and national government. Their network would extend across the whole range of Rockefeller interests, from oil and banking, through foreign policy and education, religion and medicine, politics and art. They would worry about succession within the Office, and be constantly on the lookout for other well-connected people who could be brought into the organization to augment its power. They would be the thread out of which the dynasty would be spun. Junior's Associates would institutionalize the Rockefellers as an enduring feature of American life in the way that Senior's aides had institutionalized Standard Oil.

The full development of the Office to a staff of several hundred took decades. It began modestly with aides Junior had inherited from the Gates regime. One was Charles O. Heydt, who had been hired in 1897, the same year Junior came down from Brown, and whose interest was in real estate development. Another was Bertram Cutler, who entered the service of the Rockefellers in 1901 as a bookkeeper and developed such expertise as a financial adviser that, after Gates's departure, he was able to take over management of all the family's investments. In the fifty-one years he served the Rockefellers, Cutler would come to be known on Wall Street as "the man who votes the Rockefeller stock."

Junior was soon filling pivotal roles in the Office with people his own age who owed their allegiance only to him. When Starr J. Murphy died in 1921, the crucial post of family legal adviser was left open for three years until Junior finally decided on Thomas M. Debevoise, an old fraternity brother. Debevoise was different from the cultured, conservative Murphy in that he had no ideology and never confused his interests with the Rockefellers'.

As the first years of Junior's leadership passed, the Office came to function more and more like a business. Decisions that had once been made according to Gates's and Senior's individual quirks and interests were now made through established channels. The foundations had their own administrators; in making his personal charitable gifts, Junior came to rely heavily on what became known in the office as the "philanthropic unit." It was headed by Arthur Packard, a former field secretary to the World Peace Foundation. Packard hired a team whose sole duty would be investigating possible recipients for Rockefeller charity. Organizations from developing fields as diverse as civil rights and birth control would pass under Packard's glance, as he decided whether they were responsible and potentially significant enough for Rockefeller support. Under his leadership, giving was soon integrated into the smooth operation of the Office and its routines, allowing Junior to master the art of spending money as well as his father had mastered the art of making it.

In 1923 the Reverend Dr. William Goodwin, professor of sacred literature at William and Mary College and sometime chairman of the school's endowment fund, met Rockefeller at a Phi Beta Kappa meeting he was attending in his capacity as chairman of the fund-raising committee. For years, Goodwin had cherished a private dream of restoring the slightly shabby, worn-out little town of Williamsburg, three centuries earlier the cultural and political epicenter of the Virginia Dynasty, which had played a major role in the creation of the Republic. That evening, Goodwin broached the subject to Junior, astutely sensing that a Rockefeller might have more than a passing interest in being associated with a project to create a national shrine to the birth of American democracy.

Junior was politely encouraging, yet declined to get involved at that time. Then in 1926 Goodwin received word that Junior and Abby were to motor through Williamsburg on their way back from a trip south, and he decided to try again. He arranged to give them a guided tour of "old" Williamsburg with special emphasis on the buildings still standing from the colonial period. At this time Goodwin gave the Rockefellers sketches he had made showing what a restored city might look like. He was heartened when Junior agreed to take the sketches back to New York with him.

When one of the few remaining old brick buildings in the town—a public house immortalized by a reference in Boswell's *Life of Johnson*—came on the market, Junior agreed to buy it. He signed his telegram telling Goodwin the good news, "David's Father" (after his last-born son), later adopting the pseudonym "Mr. David" to use in land purchases, for fear knowledge of Rockefeller involvement would send prices skyrocketing. Working under the strict secrecy Junior demanded, Goodwin began to buy up a large portion of the old town. It was only after a year of secret purchases that Junior told Goodwin he was now prepared to go ahead with the plans as originally presented and to restore the entire city. It was another year before Goodwin was able to announce the name of the patron and the intention of the project to a crowded hall of Williamsburg citizens, who greeted the announcement with a spontaneous ovation.

At first it was assumed that Williamsburg would be an antiquity that would draw modest numbers of people: the old inns and ordinaries were rebuilt to accommodate visitors. But they were always booked; Williamsburg was on the verge of financial success. It became Junior's favorite philanthropy. He brought his family there for at least two months a year for the rest of his life, staying at Basset Hall, the most elegant manor house in the city, which he had reserved for his private use. From his front yard, he could look out onto eighteenth-century America and see how his $50 million investment was progressing.

Junior felt comfortable when surrounded with re-created antiquity. The same was true of art. He had never allowed himself to become a compulsive collector like Frick and some of his father's other contemporaries. Yet he did have personal weaknesses, especially for Chinese porcelains. Just as he kept himself abreast of even the most mundane details of the Williamsburg purchases, going over floor plans and old maps of the city with great care, so he spent countless hours minutely inspecting each new porcelain before and after its acquisition, having it photographed and then cataloguing it himself. Later, as Abby began to improve the walls of their town house with Italian primitives and Goyas, Junior struggled to keep up. He educated himself to the point that he felt comfortable with paintings of the Mannerist school, but even as he did so, there was a certain kind of art entering the top-floor museum (formerly the children's playroom) of his 54th Street house that he did not like at all. These were the modern works which Abby ordered and paid for with her own Aldrich inheritance—the O'Keefes and Bellowses, the Braques and Picassos.

These canvases presented a challenge to Junior's sensibility which he never quite managed to handle. "I am interested in beauty," he once said, "and by and large I do not find beauty in modern art. I find instead a desire for self-expression." It was the sort of indulgence he had never allowed himself, and it upset him enough so that late in life, when his son Nelson (by then the foremost Rockefeller in the art world) asked Junior to sit for the Italian sculptor Marini and showed him photos of his work, Junior wrote back: "As much as I hate not to do anything one of you children ask me to do, I would not be happy to go down in posterity or to be represented in the manner shown by the photographs."

Yet uncomfortable as he was with the uncontrolled individuality in the paintings Abby collected, Junior deferred graciously to her on this matter, suffering through dinners with Matisse and other artists who barely concealed their contempt for him, and finally donating $5 million to help his wife become a co-founder of the Museum of Modern Art in 1927. After his children had grown and left home and he and Abby had moved to a smaller apartment on Fifth Avenue, he even made the property on West 54th Street available for the outdoor gardens of what was always referred to in the family as "Mother's Museum."

A project far closer to Junior's own heart was the Cloisters, a museum of Romanesque arches, Gothic sculpture, and medieval tapestries. As in Williamsburg, Junior was here an investor in another man's vision—this time an eccentric artist named George Grey Barnard, who would later be described as "one of the most romantic and rugged collectors of our time," and whose lack of funds had compelled him to comb the ruined abbeys and churches of Europe personally to discover his treasures. Junior bought the Barnard Cloisters for the Metropolitan Museum of Art and arranged for their transfer from the small museum Barnard had opened on 190th Street to Fort Tryon Park, on the upper west side of Manhattan, which he had purchased earlier. In 1935 he began the construction of a monasterylike building to house Barnard's dazzling collection. Completed in impeccable taste by 1938, it was surrounded by lovely gardens that gave it the atmosphere of a refuge. As a perfect finishing touch, Junior donated the famous Unicorn Tapestries that had adorned the walls of his town house.

The impulse to build enclaves of quiet harmony was a deep-seated one in Junior, and the interest in cultural conservation led naturally to the conservation of nature. The 3,500-acre estate at Pocantico, which Junior had been primarily responsible for building, itself had been an experiment in conservation. And when Junior bought his vacation home at Seal Harbor, he found that former Harvard President Charles W. Eliot, Edsel Ford, and his other affluent neighbors there were concerned that Mount Desert Island would be altered by tourists and traffic brought by the automobile. Junior took on the major role in their attempt to preserve the area. By 1916 he had helped assemble some five thousand acres, which was given to the federal government for the first national park in the eastern states.

Had his activities gone no farther than this, it might have been said that the creation of Acadia National Park was merely a way of isolating and protecting his retreat at Seal Harbor (Junior continued to buy up Mount Desert land and give it to the park, including a long narrow strip running to the ocean, which, in effect, completed the barrier around his mansion, called the Eyrie). In fact, it was only the beginning of a major Rockefeller involvement in the growing field of conservation.

In 1924 Junior journeyed west for an extensive sightseeing trip with Abby and the three older boys of his growing family, John D. 3rd, Nelson, and Laurance. They went first through New Mexico and·Colorado, and then made plans to stop at Yellowstone, the jewel of the fledgling National Park Service that had been created in 1916. The superintendent of Yellowstone, Horace Albright, was cabled from Washington to expect a visit from Mr. Rockefeller, Jr., who would be traveling under the alias of Mr. Davison. When Albright met the Rockefellers at the railhead, he found that Junior had already arranged to have a chauffeured limousine on hand and had a timetable drawn up for their visit. Albright was further surprised when Rockefeller ordered his boys to run over and help the depot's one black porter unload all the passengers' baggage. Then he and Abby and the doctor traveling with them drove off to the lodge with Albright, leaving his sons to catch the bus.

For the next three days, Junior traveled through Yellowstone and then headed north for his next stop at Glacier National Park, where he and the boys went on a two-week pack trip up into the mountains. Returning to New York, he wrote Albright to say that he had had a good time, but was distressed by the amount of debris that had gathered along the rough roads through Yellowstone. He asked how much it would take to clean it up, and after receiving a figure from Albright, sent him a check.

Two years later, Junior returned to Yellowstone, bringing Laurance and the two younger boys, Winthrop and David. This time Junior allowed Albright to give them a tour, and the superintendent arranged an itinerary that took them to the magnificent Jackson Hole area in the Grand Tetons. He purposely led the Rockefeller party past a number of dilapidated ranches and cabins cluttering the landscape and told the curious Junior that he feared the scenic drive might further degenerate under the impact of roadside stands and billboards about to move into the area. Albright concluded the tour by taking the party up to a rim high in the Tetons for a breathtaking view looking down at the Snake River winding through the Jackson Hole Valley. Albright remarked, seemingly in passing, that the piecemeal speculation and commercialization then taking place was a sad fate for such a beautiful area, and that it had always been his dream to find a way to save it.

That winter Junior asked Albright to come to New York to present plans for preserving the area. The superintendent thought he meant the area along the drive and was prepared to tell Rockefeller it would cost $250,000 to buy up these lands. In New York, however, he found that Junior had it in mind to buy up all of the Jackson Hole Valley Albright had showed him from the top of the rim. Rockefeller said, "I'm only interested in *ideal* projects. You showed me an ideal." And he told the stunned Albright to work out the details.

On the second trip west, Junior had also stopped in northern California, where he was met by members of the Save-the-Redwoods League, who took him on a motorcade through the redwood forest to Eureka and then Crescent City. Junior agreed to make the first of contributions that would eventually amount to over $2 million in the cause that culminated in Redwood National Park. Later Junior would give money to such conservation projects as the Big Trees in the Sierra Nevada and the Great Smoky Mountains National Park in Tennessee. Men he worked with in building these monuments soon found their careers accelerated into the high reaches of the Interior Department. Albright became head of the fledging National Park Service, working to solidify the Rockefellers' identification with the conservation movement.

Whether the field was conservation or education, foreign policy formulation or medical research, public administration or the collection of fine art, Junior was coming to occupy a unique place in the most prestigious and influential of the nation's institutions. Other wealthy families were setting up foundations and making bequests—it was an activity that would intensify with the advent of New Deal tax laws—but most of the large gifts went to museums or hospitals, or to a remembered alma mater, while the smaller ones were based on fleeting personal whim or an irrecoverable impulse of *noblesse oblige*. With Junior it was different. Such impulsive generosity as had managed to sneak through the cracks of the bleak Baptist ethos of his upbringing was banned as inefficient and potentially dangerous. Giving for him was a profession, a vocation, a *métier*. Always on the lookout for new fields in which to make charitable investments, he pursued the spending of the prodigious sum he had been given with the same solemn industry his father had marshaled while in command of his great trust. Junior too seeded the growth of subsidiary enterprises, and soon the philanthropic empire he had assembled was in its own way as impressive a creation as Standard Oil.

As early as 1910, under the influence of Gates and John R. Mott, he had been struck by how much effort the competing Protestant denominations spent in sectarian squabbles, and how this weakened the missionary effort abroad. After World War I, he became deeply involved in the Interchurch World Movement, which was based both on the optimism engendered by the victory in Europe (if a united effort could defeat the Kaiser, why not heathenism?) and on a practical feeling that another crusade was needed to bring the warring factions of Christianity together. The formation of the Federal Council of Churches in 1908 had given the ecumenical movement a preliminary organizational form, and Junior was among those who thought the hour had come to launch the movement in the rest of the world.

Junior gave himself to the Interchurch World Movement, both financially and administratively, contributing more than $1 million to the movement's initial operating budget of $40 million and exhausting himself in a national speaking tour. He had not reckoned on the cynicism of the various denominations, which used the movement as a fund-raising pitch to bring in nearly $200 million for their own coffers although they contributed less than $2 million of it to the crusade itself. Soon the organization was bankrupt, and Junior was raising money not to send legions of Christian soldiers around the world but simply to discharge the movement's debts. After this, Junior took a more cautious approach to ecumenism, although he continued to fund on a more modest scale agencies such as the Federal Council of Churches.

All of these strands came together in the early thirties to make Junior the most important financier of liberal and ecumenical Protestantism and a rallying point in the demands for change inside the church. In this cause he was as usual greatly influenced by friends and Associates, including Charles Evans Hughes, a leading layman of the Park Avenue (former Fifth Avenue) Baptist Church, the Reverends Buttrick and Gates from the charitable trusts, John Mott, and even Ivy Lee. All were partisans of modernism in the church, endorsing the "progressive" trends that were transforming the life of the country: the centralization of administrative units, the growth of scientific ideas and technology, the internationalization of American influence and power. They wanted the church to relate to those tendencies in a positive way, and thereby retain its effectiveness as a cohesive social force in American life. Arrayed against them were the fundamentalists, responsive to the small-town conservatism of rural America and clinging to the old doctrines and the old ways.

These conflicts had broken in a storm about the head of one of the rising young clerics of the time, the Reverend Harry Emerson Fosdick, pastor of the Old First Presbyterian Church at 11th Street and Fifth Avenue. Fosdick had begun as a conciliator, not a warrior, and when he rose in the pulpit to deliver his sermon "Shall the Fundamentalists Win?" it was little more than a plea for tolerance for the liberals under assault.

"There might have been no unusual result" of the sermon, Fosdick later observed, "if it had not been for Ivy Lee." Taken by Fosdick's pragmatic liberalism, Lee promptly printed the sermon in pamphlet form, changing its title and adding subheadings and a flattering introduction. He then began distributing it to a nationwide clientele. The attack that followed made headline news and called forth "an explosion of ill-will [in Fosdick's words] that went the limit of truculence." When the smoke cleared, Fosdick had resigned from the First Presbyterian.

As Fosdick was about to leave his pastorate, he received an invitation to lunch with Junior. The two men already knew each other, and after the young clergyman arrived at the new Rockefeller town house on Park Avenue, Junior wasted no time in offering him the ministry of his own Park Avenue Baptist Church, whose pastor was scheduled to retire soon. The only surprise was Fosdick's refusal. When Junior asked him why, he replied bluntly: "Because you are too wealthy, and I do not want to be known as the pastor of the richest man in the country."

There was a long silence, and then Junior drawled: "I like your frankness, but do you think that more people will criticize you on account of my wealth than will criticize me on account of your theology?"

In the end, the Park Avenue congregation removed the two final obstacles that had stood in the way of Fosdick's taking the job when it relaxed its insistence on baptism by immersion and agreed to move to a less swank area. After Junior provided $26 million toward the construction of a new interdenominational church on Riverside Drive in Morningside Heights, Fosdick agreed to accept the calling, which was now the most influential pastorate in the country and the one that would be largely responsible for the victory of the Protestant liberals.

On October 5, 1930, six thousand people gathered for the opening service in the massive Gothic edifice of the Riverside Church, whose effort to bridge the gap between traditional and modern architecture was derisively styled "neo-eclectic" by its critics. The building itself was located a block away from the northern boundary of New York's leading university, Columbia (an institution that had been the recipient of numerous large Rockefeller gifts) and adjacent to Barnard College (to which Senior had given money half a century earlier, and in recognition of which Cettie had been put on the first board of trustees). Across Claremont Avenue, which bounded Riverside Church on the east, was the Union Theological Seminary, whose site Junior had helped to choose and whose 1922 endowment drive he had launched with a $1,083,333 gift, amounting to a quarter of its goal. Already one of the foremost divinity schools in the land, whose faculty would boast such formidable voices of modern Protestantism as Reinhold Niebuhr, Henry Pitney Van Dusen, and John C. Bennett, the Seminary's influence was to be greatly enhanced by its proximity to Riverside Drive and the other institutions the Rockefellers had helped to locate there.

By the time of his death, Junior had contributed nearly $75 million to these developments, including $23 million to the Sealantic Fund (the foundation for his religious charities) "to strengthen and develop Protestant theological education" for more mortar in the edifice of the Protestant establishment he, more than any other individual, had made possible.

CHAPTER 8

By the early 1930s Junior's success was undeniable, yet it had been purchased at a high price. His letters from the previous decade show a man terrified of sickness and often exhausted almost beyond his endurance. In 1922 he had excruciating headaches that none of the doctors he visited could cure. He spent three weeks at a Michigan sanatorium, where he took a battery of tests and was finally told that his problem was "auto-intoxication" brought on by strain.

It was inevitable, given who he was. His father had learned how to unbend, relaxing in the methodical exertion of the golf course and the whimsy of dinner table conversation. Junior did not have the old man's rejuvenating wit and irony. He was always looking to the next project, searching for new ways to push the dynasty he was building one step farther, hoping to accumulate yet a greater degree of public regard and personal influence and honor for the Rockefeller name. His quest centered on his father, yet in the last analysis he was his mother's son and unconsciously condemned unearned joy as a sign of unworthiness. Abby knew this tendency well and struggled against it most of their life together.

He was an odd little man, filled with contradictions. If he had been asked what exactly he thought he had accomplished with the millions he dispensed, he might have said that he had tried to bring men and nations closer together, consolidate important but disorganized social fields, and build the sort of landmarks that great numbers of people could enjoy and learn from. In some of these ambitions he had succeeded. But underneath the altruism, his philanthropy had a shrewdly practical side in which good works interfaced smoothly with power and a sense of the control that could come from intimate involvement in the social movements his growing band of Associates forecast would be important in coming years. His approach to giving was businesslike. This was only fitting, for while he had found it convenient to sever his public ties with business after Ludlow, he never lost sight of the importance of the business process.

Publicly he tried to convey the impression that making money was no concern of his. As he once said to a reporter from the New York *Tribune,* "What do I want with more money, or what does Father want with more? Nearly all my time and nearly all the time that my father gives to financial affairs is devoted to studying how best and wisely to distribute the money accumulated." But privately he never relinquished his obligation to manage and preserve the family fortune. In fact, his life was like the parable of the loaves and fishes, for even while he was giving away vast amounts of money, he was taking steps to make sure that his five sons would have something like the sum his father had put in his custody.

On the Black Thursday of October 24, 1929, the first precipitous plunge of the Great Crash sent stock prices tumbling downwards. At the offices of J. P. Morgan & Company at 23 Wall Street, the heads of the nation's leading banks gathered in a well-publicized effort to restore confidence, recalling the drama twenty-two years earlier when the senior Morgan had stopped the Panic of 1907. Nearby, at 15 Broad, Ivy Lee was on the phone, urging Junior to consider the benefits of a public utterance from the ninety-year-old Rockefeller patriarch at this historical moment.

Senior was drawn with reluctance into the turmoil that younger and less prudent generations had wrought. But to please his son, he finally agreed to read a press release prepared by Ivy Lee. In it, the figure that had once been the scourge of the American economy took the posture of its Ecclesiastes. "These are days when many are discouraged," he said in the quavering voice that had not been heard in public for a decade. "In the ninety years of my life, depressions have come and gone. Prosperity has always returned, and will again." He added: "Believing that the fundamental conditions of the country are sound, my son and I have been purchasing sound common stocks for some days." (Many must have appreciated Eddie Cantor's rejoinder: "Sure, who else had any money left?")

Senior's pronouncement on the nation's soundness had never been intended as considered economic analysis, but only to show once again that the Rockefellers were bullish on America. Subsequently, the symbolism of the decision to erect Rockefeller Center in the wake of the stock market disaster seemed unmistakable. It was an epic sign of faith in the American future despite the darkness of the present moment.

In time, Ivy Lee would succeed in making the project seem almost a privately funded public works program. Yet it didn't begin that way. In fact, it had been initiated in 1928, at a time when the economy was spiraling upward in what seemed like a never-ending boom. The Metropolitan Opera Company, deciding on the need to move from its old quarters, had opened negotiations with Columbia to lease the area the university owned between 49th and 50th Streets and bordered by Fifth and Sixth Avenues. Junior had been introduced to the project by Otto Kahn, and after consulation with "five real estate experts," all of whom pronounced it "good business," committed himself to a $3.3 million 24-year lease.

Then came the crash. The opera company pulled out, and Junior was faced with the collapse of his scheme and the loss of $3 million a year until the economic indicators turned upward. His decision at this point reflected the same practical sense shown earlier when, complimented by Fosdick on his courage, he replied: "Often a man gets into a situation where there's just one thing to do. There is no alternative. He wants to run, but there is no place to run to. So he goes ahead on the only course that's open and people call it courage." With no place to run to, he would use his immense resources to build his own commercial development.

The economic situation made the financing difficult, even for a Rockefeller. The buildings alone would cost an estimated $120 million, $45 million of which came from a loan by the Metropolitan Life Insurance Company on Junior's personal guarantee, and the rest of which he raised himself despite the staggering losses it involved. One day Junior came into the offices of Wallace Harrison, chief architect for the Center and the man who got RCA as a prime tenant. Noting that Rockefeller looked downcast, Harrison asked him what was wrong. Junior replied that he had just been forced to sell some Standard of New York stock at $2 a share. Yet bit by bit the project began to rise. In 1933 the RCA Building was opened and Junior celebrated by moving the Rockefeller Family Office from the Standard Oil Building at 26 Broadway to the 56th floor of 30 Rockefeller Plaza. The office was now Room 5600.

While it was widely felt that Junior's decision to go ahead with the development showed spunk, some thought it seemed odd a philanthropist should devote such resources to construction. Yet Junior had always been obsessed with building. Williamsburg, the Cloisters, the restoration of Versailles—his favorite works had all involved construction, a kind of progress he could see and measure as it occurred day by day. It was a way of leaving his mark on the world. Each new structure he raised bespoke his worth in concrete and steel, and he was never so happy as when going over blueprints and talking to workers on one of his construction sites.

If the philanthropist in him saw Rockefeller Center as an opportunity to do something for the city, the real estate promoter in him realized that it had a good chance for success. From the beginning of negotiations he had insisted on a commercial quotient for the project. After Ivy Lee first told him about the opera company's negotiations with Columbia University and sold him on the project, Junior had gotten the plans changed so that the part of the property not used for the opera house could be developed for commercial purposes.

When the Depression deepened and the opera company was forced out of the project, Junior decided to go it alone on a grand scale; from that point on, there was no longer any ambiguity about the purpose of the development. As its board of directors resolved: "From now on the development should be based upon a commercial center as beautiful as possible consistent with the maximum income that can be developed."

It was in 1937, when the great monument was nearing completion, that John D. Rockefeller, Sr., finally passed from the scene. His spirit never failed him, but as he entered the middle of his ninth decade he became aware of just how frail his body was. "I'm like your bike when you're coasting downhill," he once told his grandson Laurance. "I can coast just so far and nothing much can be done about it." Living to be one hundred was the goal he had set for himself, but there were laws that even a Rockefeller had to obey. Early on the morning of Sunday, May 23, Junior was sent for by his father's physician. His agitated arrival woke the servants, who huddled in the kitchen wondering what was going on upstairs. At four A.M. the old man lapsed into a coma; an hour later he was gone.

The next day Abby wrote her sister:

I think you might say he died in his sleep. So really it was a wonderful ending. At times both John and I rather feared that he might become bedridden and might be uncomfortable, but as it was he motored 40 miles on the Friday before he died and sat in the garden comfortably for four hours on Saturday, and missed his morning prayers only on Sunday morning. So it was a remarkable record.

On May 25, funeral services were conducted at Pocantico by the Reverend Harry Emerson Fosdick. Two of Junior's sons, Nelson and Winthrop, had been in Latin America when the news reached them, and they traveled for forty-eight hours straight to be home when their grandfather was laid to rest. The descendants of William Rockefeller were present, along with the families of John D.'s original partners in the trust, and a few old friends he had made in his years of retirement. After the service, the workers of Pocantico filed through the big house, hats in hand, for a last look at the Laird of Kijkuit. At six-thirty that evening Junior and his five young sons boarded the two private railway cars that were part of a funeral train carrying the body home. On May 27 John D. Rockefeller was back in Cleveland, where he had begun the great adventure three-quarters of a century earlier. As he was lowered into place between his mother and his wife in the plot he had purchased decades earlier, the offices and shops of Standard Oil and its affiliates across the country and all over the world ceased work for five minutes, as the employees paused to honor the man who had once been loathed but was now admired as a benefactor of mankind.

Two years later, with his father dead but far from forgotten, John D. Rockefeller, Jr., put on a hard hat and heavy workmen's gloves, and with the strain of concentration showing in his forehead, drove the last rivet into Rockefeller Center. He was sixty-five years old. He had many years of life left to him, yet in some sense what he had set out to achieve was done. The voice of the people speaking through Ida Tarbell, Frank Walsh, and all the others had once indicted his father's fortune; Junior had tried to show that the wealth was only entrusted to his family to invest in the well-being of mankind. They had said that the name Rockefeller was synonymous with irresponsible power and privilege; Junior had tried to prove that it was the embodiment of responsibility and obligation. As he stepped back from the girder and handed over the rivet gun amid a burst of applause, he was not only a personal success in a way that had somehow not seemed possible forty years earlier; he was also the author of a myth regarding the Rockefeller family that strained upward in the same way as the structures rising in awesome spires above him. Rockefeller Center was the capstone of a life, Junior's *summa*. Yet his real achievement would prove to be the children waiting in the wings.

THE BROTHERS

CHAPTER 9

From the beginning, things were easier for Junior's children than they had been for Junior himself. When Mrs. David Gardiner, matron of a socially prominent New York family, forbade her son to play with the five Rockefeller boys, commenting, "No child of mine will play with the grandchildren of a gangster," it was looked upon as a tasteless, even comic faux pas. The Rockefellers had long since been accepted into the exclusive ranks of American society. They were not only received by the Right People, they were themselves people to know. Mrs. Rockefeller, Jr., was one of the few ladies in town who could go to a party at the William Vanderbilts one night and attend Mrs. Cornelius Vanderbilt's soirée the next, and still manage to maintain neutrality in the bitter social war between the two branches of that family.

While he understood that it was necessary for his children to grow up with the "proper" connections, Junior also knew that they must not be too conspicuously identified with the upper classes. Such people were not as adaptable to the changing conditions in American society as he wanted his boys to be. Moreover, he worried about the effect moving exclusively in "high" society would have on their characters. All around were examples of other inheritors of the great fortunes floundering in a sea of options, caricatures of the idle rich without purpose or motive who squandered their fortunes on what H. L. Mencken called the two principal occupations of the wealthy—polo and polygamy—and in the end became little more than stock figures in the melodramas of the tabloid press.

While the world may not have known what exactly went on behind the walls of the estates where the Du Ponts, Astors, Vanderbilts, and others lived, lurid details of divorce and debauchery nonetheless somehow managed to filter out into the morning papers. Junior intended to keep the Rockefellers' private lives private. And he succeeded. People knew only what he wanted them to: that John D. was now retired and somewhat eccentric, shuffling from one magnificent home to another with the alternation of the seasons, and appearing publicly only for a round of golf or to give out an endless supply of dimes; that his son was involved in the most ambitious philanthropies ever conceived; that there were six children in the third generation. Their names and birth dates were all that appeared in the newspapers until 1922, when it was recorded that Nelson had accidentally shot himself in the leg with an air rifle.

It was not that people didn't try to penetrate the genteel curtain Junior had drawn around the family. Scarcely a week went by that the guards at Pocantico didn't catch some reporter or photographer trying to scale the fences to find out the inside story. None ever succeeded; if they had, they would probably have been surprised to find that while Junior and his children made frequent trips to the estate, they did not live there.

Junior realized that he had suffered from growing up in a sheltered, almost hermetically sealed atmosphere and did not want to repeat the mistake. At any rate, his affairs placed him in New York City, and there the family lived in the huge nine-story town house at 10 West 54th. It was just a short walk to Central Park, where the six children went unrecognized to play every day after school in the company of French governesses (inevitably called "Mademoiselle"), nurses, or male companions hired from the Union Theological Seminary.

Many motifs of their father's upbringing were repeated in their own, but the austerity of the boyhood at the old Forest Hill estate in Cleveland, where he shared one bicycle with his sisters and wore their hand-me-downs, was not one of them. Although not surfeited with possessions, Junior's children had what they wanted. Yet, like their father, they earned their spending money—by killing flies for pennies, shining shoes, hoeing the garden. Like Junior, they kept accounts, having been shown grandfather's Ledger A and allowed to study its yellowing, brittle pages and faded ink entries as if it were a church incunabulum. "I was always so afraid that money would spoil my children," Junior later said, "and I wanted them to know its values and not waste it or throw it away on things that weren't worthwhile." Any child with an unaccounted-for item in his ledger at the end of the week was fined five cents; those keeping accurate accounts received a five-cent bonus.

It took a while for the fact that they were Rockefellers to make an impression on them. They lived in their own world, playing with each other on the top floor of the 54th Street house. They spent their summers at Seal Harbor and played with the children of the Edsel Fords, the Eliots, and other prominent families who had, with their father, gotten Mount Desert Island designated a national park to protect its misty beauty and their own secluded refuges. Surrounded by lush gardens of annuals that were changed several times a year, Oriental statuary, and carefully manicured lawns, their father's house looked like a huge inn and was a stone's throw from the shoreline where they learned to sail, venturing out into the Atlantic in their small boat. On these family vacations in Maine, each of the children had his own personal governess; occasionally, Junior and Abby would escape to go for walks alone, stopping at Rest House, the spacious "cabin" deep in the woods behind the Eyrie, where they ate blueberries and bread and butter and, after finishing their snacks, happily went about the unfamiliar task of doing their own dishes.

The children were fond of Seal Harbor, but it was nothing like Pocantico, the rambling 3,400-acre estate where they spent weekends and shorter vacations. The house they grew up in, Abeynton Lodge, was within hailing distance of the Big House, Kikjuit. Standing on a rise that commanded the hillside and looked down to the woods and the flowing Hudson tide, the stately Georgian mansion dwarfed the wrinkled old man they formally addressed as Grandfather. Yet they understood that it was more his monument than his home, the centerpiece of the estate that was richly landscaped with eighteenth-century tiered gardens of ornamental shrubs and immense flowerbeds, with orange trees from France, larch from Scotland, yew from England, with stone fountains feeding the sunken brook paved with colored stones, and a nine-hole golf course encircling the whole.

Junior had a playhouse built for Babs (as daughter Abby was called to distinguish her from her mother)—four furnished rooms the size of a small apartment—so that she would have a place to go when the girls from the town of Pocantico Hills came to play with her. But when people spoke of *the* Playhouse, they meant the two-story gymnasium with its indoor swimming pool, indoor and outdoor tennis courts, indoor basketball and squash courts, and billiard room and bowling alleys, which he had built for his boys. It was here they played as children and entertained as teenagers, often having up to fifty of their friends in for parties, the music produced by bands that Junior brought up from New York and the chaperones provided by Abby.

Pocantico was ten times larger than Monaco, five times the size of Central Park. It cost $50,000 a year just to maintain the Big House, $500,000 for the entire property. The boys could go to the stone stables and have the riding master take them out on the trails; they could check out one of the fleet of electric cars that sailed silently around the grounds of the 250-acre "park" that lay at the core of the estate. The place had an intentional magnificence, the other side of the coin from the austerity of keeping accounts and doing chores. It was as if their father were showing them the rewards that hard work and bearing up under the pressures of being a Rockefeller could earn them. It was a way of teaching them, without ever needing to say it directly, that if they learned to control their wealth, they could discreetly enjoy it.

If the estate was in part a teaching device, Junior's children would always remember the simple joys more than the lessons: playing cards with Abby and eating hand-turned ice cream on humid July afternoons; going with the groundskeepers every spring to hunt for newborn animals in the forest surrounding their home; killing copperheads and turning them in to their grandfather's steward for the 25-cent bounty. When they got to be ten or twelve, all the boys got "red bugs"—four-seated buckboards with red wooden-slat sides that were powered by Smith motors. They drove "to town" to see friends in the tiny hamlet of Pocantico Hills. In wintertime, a mechanic from Tarrytown came to the estate and replaced the wheels with spiked runners so they could negotiate the icy roads. When they were teenagers, the groundsmen regularly rescued and then shooed away young women who had become entangled climbing the six-foot fence around the estate in hopes of getting inside where some young Rockefeller would see, fall in love with, and marry them.

But the most special thing about the estate was the fact that Grandfather lived there. They knew that they were not his favorites. In his impenetrable way, he seemed to prefer Fowler McCormick, the only son of his renegade daughter Edith. Yet he liked them well enough and saw far more of them than any of his other grandchildren. Living with his housekeeper and valet in the mansion that was too large for him, he constantly amazed them by how different he was from their father. Each one of the boys remembered playing tag with the surprisingly spry old man.

Sunday afternoons were state occasions. The brothers were required to dress in their Eton collars, dark coats, and pin-striped pants for dinner at Grandfather's house. They would remember him best at the head of the table, his white wig slightly askew with the cloth backing visible at the part, his lashless eyes darting from one face to another as he picked at his food and mimicked people they all knew, in his slow, ironic drawl. He occasionally seemed to embarrass their father, but Junior's reverence toward this parchment-faced old man told them he was no fool. If they were different, they learned early in life, it was not because they were rich, but because they were of Grandfather's blood.

Junior's children had been born during the hardest period of his life, punctuating the moments of the family's greatest crises—Ida Tarbell's muckraking attack on Standard Oil, dissolution of the trust, Ludlow. By the time they were teenagers, the conflict had begun to subside, leaving their father more time to spend with them, more time to prepare them for what he liked to call "the large affairs that have fallen to us." He enjoyed the role of teacher. He tried to make sure to see them at least during breakfast, which occurred precisely at seven forty-five, leading them in prayer and examining them about their schoolwork and opinions. He catechized them on their accounts and insisted that they avoid the crime of waste by turning out lights and eating all the food on their plates. When they were at Pocantico, they went on long walks in which he taught them the names and growth patterns of the native trees; the boys knew he carried chunks of maple sugar in his pocket and that he would hand them out only as a reward for reaching their final destination.

He insisted that they sit respectfully at church on Sundays and occasionally lectured them on the special trust being a Rockefeller entailed. Wednesday nights were given over to "domestic education," with the children in charge of the kitchen, each one preparing a different course in the evening meal. This was to chasten them out of any high opinions they might have of themselves.

Yet while Junior could be a conscientious father, it was hard for him to be an affectionate one. His was a character that rationed emotion carefully. He was often under great pressure and his children grew used to seeing him sick in bed with colds or blinding headaches. He was easily annoyed by their boisterousness and somewhat at a loss as to how to deal with them. He left that to his wife. Abby was the center of the real intimacy in the Rockefeller household, and she recognized that they were all a strain on her husband. "Your father is so wonderfully thoughtful himself," she once wrote in a letter to one of her sons, "and so considerate to all the people with whom he comes in contact that I am sure he must occasionally find the rest of us somewhat difficult. Perhaps there is too much Aldrich in us and not enough Rockefeller."

The Aldrich quality Abby had brought to the family was new and vigorous, as Laura Spelman's contribution had been before her. Yet in this case, it was not a sense of humanitarian duty, but rather a spontaneity and exuberance lacking in her husband and his forebears. Abby's "zest for life" was something people would always comment on, along with her taste for floppy hats. It was part of her family's heritage.

Noting that the family prayers her husband prescribed for the children to learn were an ordeal, Abby copied out Bible verses on cardboard flash cards so they would be easier to memorize. When interviewed about his philosophy of child rearing, Junior might make pronouncements such as this: "For the rich, as for families of modest means, family rearing presents the same problems with the same solutions—insistence on set studies . . . and the basic necessity of moral example through inculcation of religious habit." Yet largely through Abby's intercessions, the ban against tennis and other entertainments on Sunday was lifted, and a reign of domestic liberality unknown in either of the two previous Rockefeller generations was established.

Junior often tended to see the children, especially the five boys, as a unit. In his mind, they represented the next Rockefeller generation, which would inherit not only what was left of the great fortune, but also the complex financial and philanthropic apparatus he was building to deal with it. But to Abby, they were individuals growing up with problems and quirks that would last a lifetime. Babs was out of place in this man's world. It was not that she wasn't valued; on the contrary, Junior's tender feelings for her are clear in a letter she wrote him during her early teens when away from home: "I certainly miss you very much, specially in the morning when you used to come and sit on the tub and rub my hands and say nice things to me." But Babs's gender was against her: in the due course of things she would marry and have children. This was the logic of her role, but it meant she would no longer be a Rockefeller.

John D. 3rd, or "Johnny," seemed somewhat stunned by the name he bore, his long face always frowning in puzzlement and his lean frame given to sudden jerky and self-deprecatory movements; he took after his father, and Abby often hurt his feelings by jokingly calling him "demi-John." There was Nelson, with Abby's own square jaw and Aldrich energy. He was always interested in outdoing his other brothers and only rarely did he fail.

Laurance was frail and often ill, but he was the only one of the children with a sense of irony. He became Nelson's accomplice in all things; his sharp features and self-deprecating laugh reminded some of the first John D. In contrast, Winthrop, pudgy and moon-faced, was good-natured, awkward, and easily goaded; his brothers sensed he was the weak link in the family and picked on him constantly. David was still in velvet knee pants and brocaded shirts when the others seemed grown-up. He had a kind of serenity and self-confidence they lacked; secure in the role of the baby of the family, he didn't need to struggle so hard for advantage. Pocantico employees remembered him wandering solitarily around the estate with a butterfly net or a straw basket filled with roses he'd picked for his mother.

They made shifting alliances, the strong bond between Nelson and Laurance and a treaty for mutual defense between Winthrop and David the only ones that would ripen into permanent relationships. The family situation was filled with ambiguities, and they wrestled for precedence and power. Babs, Johnny, and Laurance were clearly Rockefellers, colder than the others in temperament and taking most seriously their father's strictures about responsibility. Nelson, Winthrop, and David were Aldriches, both in body type and character, hardier, warmer, and more experimental than the others, and favored by their mother.

Babs, who had been sent to the conservative Miss Chapin's School for Girls, was the most rebellious of the children. Despite the affection between her and Junior, she carried on a running struggle for many years with her father, which intensified after her graduation in 1921, when she became the first Rockefeller in three generations (except Eliza, with her corncob pipe) to smoke openly and take an occasional drink. Once she fell asleep with a cigarette in her hand and set a mattress afire. Growing into an extremely attractive young woman, she adopted the flapper dresses, cloche hats, and feverish hedonism of the Jazz Age, spending the year after her coming-out going to parties and dinners, coming in late and sleeping until noon so that she could begin again the next night.

She was courted by a young attorney named David Milton. He was tall, blond, athletic, and came from a good family with a summer home in the Pocantico area. He had a red Stutz roadster and shared Babs's passion for fast driving. They would roar over the paths of Pocantico, parking to carry out their romance beyond their parents' view, but ignoring nearby workers (as one commented later) "as so many sticks of furniture." They married in 1922, much to the dismay of local scandal-mongers, in whose diet they had become a staple item.

John 3rd followed his father's footsteps to Browning School and finished at Loomis, a boarding school in Connecticut. It was while there that he received a letter from his mother, who was worried he would inherit his father's saturnine disposition along with his name, entreating him to go to dances. "I got your very discouraging letter on Monday," he answered. "I can't say that I feel very enthusiastic at present about going to that dance. . . . It seems to be your one ambition to get me to go to dances. I suppose I *will* go if you want me to." In his schooling, as in other things, John 3rd was marked off from his younger brothers, who were able to participate in an interesting educational experiment.

Lincoln School was the brainchild of Abraham Flexner, longtime family Associate whose brother, Simon, was head of the Rockefeller Institute for Medical Research. For years Flexner had operated a successful private school in his hometown of Louisville, running it without examinations or report cards and with a curriculum stripped of the old classics and in tune with twentieth-century progressivism. Many of Flexner's students would end up at Harvard, and there come to impress President Charles W. Eliot. In 1914, when both Eliot and Flexner were trustees of the General Education Board, which had become concerned that American high schools were both "slow and ineffective," they decided to resurrect aspects of the Louisville experiment in a demonstration high school that would provide a laboratory for the kind of education that was, in Flexner's words, "adapted to the needs of modern living."

In 1917, the GEB established Lincoln School in collaboration with Columbia Teachers College. Located in a large building at 123rd Street and Amsterdam Avenue, it was, from the beginning, a model of Deweyite pragmatism. Latin and Greek were banished and rote memory in the study of history was deemphasized; units of study about modern culture were instituted, drawing from the new initiatives of social science. Lincoln School took a flexible attitude toward the students, allowing them to learn at their own speed and without conventional forms of coercion. For the sake of the educational experiment and because of the philosophy of the Rockefellers and other wealthy patrons, it brought in a sprinkling of poor and minority students through scholarships. When Lincoln opened its doors in 1917, there were 23 of the best graduates of Teachers College ready to instruct the 116 students.

The Rockefeller boys would set out early in the morning for school. During the first few years, they walked or roller-skated up Fifth Avenue until they tired, at which point they would get into the back seat of the limousine Junior had ordered to crawl along beside them. Their mother would call for them at three o'clock in an electric car called a "hatbox" because of its high square shape. When they got older, they all drove in Nelson's hiccuping old Ford roadster. A classmate, Mrs. Linda Storrow, recalls: "Everybody in the school knew they were Rockefellers, but after a while forgot about it. They just became part of the total atmosphere. Nelson, especially, was always clasping people and laughing with them. He was terribly popular, always running for class chairman and winning. All the girls thought he was terribly handsome and had crushes on him."

In 1929 the press was allowed to meet one of Mr. Junior's sons for the first time. It was the oldest boy, John D. 3rd, recently graduated from college and ready to carry on a family tradition by going to work for his father. Tall, thin, slightly gangling, he blushed easily and had that square-jawed innocence that Charles Lindbergh and Gary Cooper would soon popularize as the face of the archetypal American hero. After watching him go through his first question-and-answer session, the reporter for *Outlook* magazine wrote: "Here, if there ever was one, is plutocratic America's opportunity to have a Prince of Wales. The young Rockefeller is no mere rich man's son; he is the sign and symbol of a vast fortune carried into the third generation. His is a proud dynasty which he must administer wisely and hand on intact. . . . He will have more money than anyone can visualize. Whether he will have much fun is another matter."

This was exactly the problem. "Mr. John," as he would be called around his father's office, had consented to go to dances to please his mother, but he had never allowed himself to enjoy them. Princeton's Class of '29, in an act of supreme whimsy had voted him Most Likely to Succeed, but he had never really felt at ease in the school Scott Fitzgerald, "Bunny" Wilson, and their friends had made into an academy of the Jazz Age. Despite his family's wealth and connections, he had felt provincial, hampered by his name the way another might have been by hands that were too large. Acquaintances delighted in telling of the time he had tried to cash a check at a store near campus, only to have the proprietor glance at the signature, sigh in disgust, and then tack it up with the J. P. Morgans, Abe Lincolns, and other forgeries decorating the wall above his cash register, leaving John 3rd beet red with embarrassment.

JDR3 (the abbreviation he picked out for himself) was also afflicted with an almost painful naïveté. A few years after his graduation, he married Blanchette Ferry Hooker (whose mother was heiress to the Ferry seed fortune and whose father was a distinguished engineer who became president of the Hooker Electro-chemical Company). "Hookie," as she had been known at Miss Chapin's School for Girls and then Vassar, was an immensely attractive woman ("a cool, pale beauty with a regally poised head that gives her the look of a Despiau sculpture," one writer later said); when she stepped off the boat from their Bermuda honeymoon with her husband, reporters asked them what the high point of the trip had been, and the blushing young Rockefeller blurted out, "Well, there was the honeymoon part."

The great difference between Junior and his sons was that he had grown up with a single overriding purpose in mind—to help his father. He had succeeded well enough so that his own boys had no comparable quest to undertake. But the family's affairs had grown to vast proportions in the last thirty years. Although he had no master plan for fitting them into these affairs, Junior did expect his sons to become involved with him. He decided that his eldest and most compliant son had the temperament to take on the family philanthropies. By 1931, JDR3 had become a trustee for the Foundation, the General Education Board, the Institute, and others—in all, thirty-three different boards or committees.

Forty-three years later, sitting under a Charles Eastman portrait of the first John D. in his oak-paneled office on the 56th floor of the RCA Building in Rockefeller Center, JDR3 recalled these early days with an irony that masks a lingering (but unadmitted) bitterness. "My father had the idea that his sons would follow the same pattern he had. My brothers and I would do what was useful for him. I got involved in a considerable number of his activities. I came in young into all these established institutions where I worked among older and more capable people. It was all intensely interesting and worthwhile, but I was in a position where it was all done for me, where I couldn't make a mistake of my own. I was chairman of a personnel search committee here, and chairman of a finance committee there. I was on everything with father, boards and committees, I think, which ranged from the Rockefeller Foundation to the Seal Harbor Tennis Committee—and my job there was to find the pro each year. That shows you the range of my opportunity."

The lessons in JDR3's experience were not lost on his younger brothers. They saw the same fate awaiting them—to have their lives parceled out in bits and pieces as they submitted their ambitions to the requirements of an institutional role. Yet to rebel, at least for JDR3, was unthinkable. If you were the Prince of Wales, you simply did not recoil from ceremony or worry about a career to fit your interests. You just waited to be put on the throne.

Most people assumed that the major drama of the third generation, therefore, would be how well JDR3 would do with the power his father had doled out to him and how far he would advance the family's affairs. But those who were close to the Rockefellers realized that the first son did not have a unique vision of the family's role and destiny to support his hereditary claim to leadership. The drama of the third generation would be the overthrow of primogeniture and JDR3's relegation to a position of secondary importance in the generation of brothers.

There was no overt struggle for power: everything had been decided by the order of birth and the caprice of the genetic code. As Howard Knowles, a longtime family employee, recalled: "John was removed and aloof. You felt he was always trying to draw back. He was very shy and he'd slide right by you without saying a word if he could. Now Nelson, on the other hand—he would come into the room and slap you on the back and ask how you were doing. He was different. And he muscled John out by the sheer force of his personality, without even trying."

From the beginning, Nelson felt he was marked for something special. He had been given the name of his maternal grandfather, Nelson Aldrich, whom he didn't remember except in the stories of the senator's political prowess his mother told. He regarded it as even more of a portent that he had been born on the birthday of John D. Rockefeller, Sr. He was always aware of this dual tradition. Later he said: "The example of my grandfathers made me feel a terrific challenge. . . . Grandfather Rockefeller was a leader of men. Grandfather Aldrich was completely different, a great man with the people." Unlike John D. 3rd, Nelson didn't try to understand the tradition that had produced him; he simply embraced it, joyously and without doubt.

Originally Nelson had hoped to follow JDR3 to Princeton, but his grades were so poor that for a time it was not clear if he would be able to get into any of the "good" schools. Although he had to do remedial work with tutors, his self-confidence was never shaken. (He once admitted to a friend, "You know, I don't have a very high I.Q." The friend asked why he thought so and Nelson replied cheerfully, "Because I took one of those tests and found out.") He "buckled down" in his final year at Lincoln School and managed to get into Dartmouth, where he worked hard enough to overcome what he later understood was an undiagnosed case of dyslexia (he transposed words and phrases when reading) to become Phi Beta Kappa. He was interested in facts rather than ideas, and showed a tendency to subject every concept to a pragmatic test, almost as if he wanted to be sure it had a market value before accepting it.

Nelson was a paradox: of all the brothers, he was most in touch with his impulses and desires and least affected by the guilt that seemed as much a part of being a Rockefeller as the money. But this freedom did not lead him to strike off on his own. On the contrary, he was quick to defend the family. When it came time to select a topic for his senior thesis in economics, he chose to write a defense of his grandfather's creation of Standard Oil. The old man was amused to hear about the project, but declined Nelson's request for a formal interview. All that was past history to him, and he had never really agreed with Junior's attempt to make a heroic enterprise out of something that had been, in its own way, just a business. But Junior was pleased by Nelson's interest, regarding it as a vindication of his own attempts to foster loyalty toward the family. When Nelson had reported his American history teacher's position on the founding of the Standard, Junior had called it "a warped and erroneous view" and arranged for W. O. Inglis to appear before the class with "the truth." In the matter of the thesis, he sent Nelson the unpublished manuscript about Senior that Ivy Lee had commissioned Inglis to distill from a series of conversations with the old man. Nelson was not curious about the critiques written by Tarbell and the other muckrakers, but he avidly devoured the Inglis manuscript and wrote home after finishing it: "I don't know when anything has interested me more. . . . For the first time I felt that I really knew Grandfather a little—got a glimpse of the power and grandeur of his life."

As he neared graduation, the question of exactly where he would fit into the family's affairs became increasingly bothersome. He declared himself indirectly in a letter written to his parents just before graduation: "Just to work my way up in a business that another man has built, stepping from the shoes of one to those of another, making a few minor changes here and there and then, finally, perhaps at the age of sixty, getting to the top where I would have real control for a few years. No, that isn't my idea of living a real life."

But this decision was put off for the time being by one that loomed even larger. In between his junior and senior years, Nelson, along with his brother Laurance, had gone on Sir Wilfred Grenfell's expedition to Antarctica. On the way home, worries about his future were entwined with thoughts about Mary Todhunter Clark, a girl he had met at Seal Harbor years earlier and dated ever since. For his first three years at Dartmouth, "Tod" was only one of many girl friends. But now, with graduation approaching, he decided to "get serious." He wrote his mother, "You know, I'm beginning to think that I really am in love with Tod, whatever being in love means. She is the only girl I know who measures up anywhere nearly to you. . . ." By early fall in his senior year, despite his father's urgent advice to wait, he had gotten himself engaged.

Junior was irate at what he saw as yet another sign of impetuousness in Nelson. As for the girl herself, however, he and Abby both liked her. A tall brunette with a long aristocratic face, Mary Clark had grown up on a Philadelphia estate given to her ancestors by King George III. After attending the exclusive Foxcroft School in Virginia, she had gone to Paris for a year to be "finished." An intelligent woman with a good sense of humor, she looked equally at ease in a riding habit or a formal evening gown. She had impeccable manners and an icy sense of dignity that would, in time, grow almost regal as she stoically suffered the scandal of her husband's extramarital affairs and the decision to seek a divorce.

Abby eventually soothed Junior into accepting the engagement; the match itself was not unlike their own marriage in that it brought the family a socially elevating contact. In the winter of 1929, Junior sent the couple to see Senior at his winter home in Florida, and the old man indicated his approval of his future granddaughter-in-law by playing a ritual round of golf with her. When Nelson married Tod in an elegant Philadelphia wedding after his graduation in 1930, Junior informed Senior that twenty thousand dollars, the same amount he had given Babs when she married, would be sufficient as a wedding gift. ("I am confident they would lay the sum away in some safe investment as a nest egg," he wrote.) Junior's own present to them was a trip around the world.

It was the sort of grand tour only a U.S. Ambassador at Large or a Rockefeller could have taken. The ports of call were exotic—Honolulu, Tokyo, Seoul, Peking, Java, Sumatra, and Bali among them. When, after an absence of nearly nine months, they returned to New York and moved into an apartment on Fifth Avenue, Junior hoped that Nelson would be ready to settle down and apply himself to family tasks as his older brother was doing. But if anything, the people he had met and the sights he had seen only inflamed Nelson's ambition to begin some great task of his own.

A few months later, in the summer of 1931, when he did go to work at 26 Broadway, he found his worst fears confirmed. Things proceeded there according to the slow, steady rhythms his father had perfected over forty years. Everywhere Nelson turned, he found his ambitions blocked by the monolithic caution practiced by Junior's advisers.

In 1932, Nelson's first child, Rodman Clark Rockefeller, was born and the four Rockefeller generations posed for a historic photograph. (Babs had already had two girls, "Mitzi" and Marilyn, but the appearance of heiresses did not call for a dynastic photo.) Despite his pride at fathering the first male heir of the next age, however, Nelson continued to chafe under the regimen at 26 Broadway. Finally, he began to spin out of his father's orbit. Defying Junior's expressed wish that he conserve and focus his energies on projects whose importance they agreed upon, Nelson accepted an invitation to become a trustee of the Metropolitan Museum of Art. (He already had taken on an active role in the Museum of Modern Art.) "My justification for spending the time which I do in this work," he wrote his father, "is that I feel . . . that the aesthetic side of a person's life is almost as important as his spiritual development or his physical well-being. And finally, as I said before, I feel that the contacts which such a position offers are not to be disregarded. I am sorry to go against your feelings in the matter, but I hope you can see my point of view."

Nelson never really quit working at his father's office. He just gravitated to other projects. In 1932 he and a couple of friends formed a firm they called Turck and Company, which was an odd combination of brokerage and the rental of office space. Nelson showed a sharp entrepreneurial eye and a willingness to trade on the family connections that did not please Junior. (It worked this way: if Turck and Company found a certain cement firm that wanted to expand its operations, for instance, it would arrange a loan from the Chase Bank and a contract for some part of the work at Rockefeller Center; in return, the cement company would agree to rent office space at the Center; Turck and Company would receive a brokerage commission for its efforts.) Soon Nelson bought out his partners, changed the name of the company to Special Work, Inc., and limited the operations to renting space in Rockefeller Center.

Finally, however, he was forced to admit that the family alone possessed the institutions that could give him the kind of power he wanted. The turning point came late in 1933, after he had just returned from Mexico City on a trip to acquire paintings for the Museum of Modern Art. On his return, he wrote his father a letter admitting he had been "in a state of flux as far as my ideas and theories are concerned," and promising he had "just emerged into a new period." It was a letter that showed he was willing to adopt the long view to attain his objectives:

The purpose of this letter is to tell you that . . . I hope that I will be able to be of distinctly more assistance to you. I don't think the time spent outside the office has been wasted, for I am much richer in experience now than I was two years ago and therefore should be able to make myself correspondingly more useful. For the immediate future, my plan is to become more familiar with all the phases of your real estate interests and to avail myself of every opportunity to get acquainted with your oil, coal, and banking interests. Of course, if there are special problems which I can handle or help you with, I will be only too glad to do what I can.

To summarize, I might say that I simply want you to know by this letter that I am back in the fold as far as my interests are concerned and that from now on my desire will be to be of as much help as I can with my limited experience. . . .

One element of his rapprochement with his father was selfish: the recognition that by helping develop the family's influence, he would also enhance his own importance. But it went deeper than that. Although different from his father in other things, he was similar in feeling that the family was on the threshold of accumulating the sort of power no other group had ever wielded in American life. Like Junior, he felt the Rockefellers had a manifest destiny and that it was his duty to further it.

In December 1934, Junior wrote each of his sons a letter to inform them that he was settling most of what was left of his fortune on them in the form of trusts composed primarily of Standard Oil stock and amounting to about $40 million dollars each. In parceling out the fortune, Junior had acted more hurriedly than he would otherwise have liked because of the New Deal's new inheritance tax, which would have laid claim to more than 70 percent of his estate if he were to die without having so disposed of it. The year 1934 was also the year that the new Securities and Exchange Act required individuals owning 10 percent or more of a corporation's stock to report the extent of their holdings. With the setting up of the "'34 Trusts" (as they would be called), Junior had disposed of enough of his Standard of New Jersey and Standard of California stock so that he did not have to report under the act.

If the timing had been dictated by external circumstances, the transmission of the fortune from one generation to the next would have come in any case. It marked a fateful moment for the Rockefeller dynasty, and the brothers knew it as well as Junior. It seemed to spur Nelson in particular to even greater efforts. He had been a director of Rockefeller Center since first coming to work, when headquarters was still 26 Broadway, but now he threw himself furiously into the campaign to rent its space in the Depression market. He became the Center's public relations man and seemed to enjoy giving what a *New Yorker* writer described as "graceful little speeches in the manner of a particularly successful high school basketball coach" to commemorate the openings of its buildings and plazas. The fact that by 1938 the Center could see its way through the dismal economy to a time when it would not only break even but make money was due largely to Nelson's efforts. As a reward, Junior made him Rockefeller Center's president.

It was the same with whatever institution he entered. Drawing on seemingly inexhaustible energy, he was able to apply himself to several different enterprises at once, and manage to make them intersect, however contradictory they might seem. At the same time he was becoming deeply involved in the family's affairs at Rockefeller Center, he was also moving into the avant-garde of the modern art movement. The latter was a natural development, for, by the time he was a college freshman, he fully shared his mother's obsession with modern art. On his honeymoon trip around the world, he collected the first object (a Sumatran knife handle in the shape of a shrunken head) in what would become the best primitive art collection in the country. Shortly after his return to New York, his mother had arranged for him to go on the Museum of Modern Art's Junior Advisory Committee. In the period when he was trying to make it outside the Family Office (and perhaps in reaction to his father's well-known aversion to modernism), he had become deeply involved in MOMA, mastering the infighting that took place there and getting himself elected to the board of trustees in 1932. (He would later say, "I learned my politics at the Museum of Modern Art.") With Abby looking after his art career from her position as one of MOMA's founding mothers, Nelson became treasurer in 1935 and was elected president four years later.

If some of the trustees distrusted his aesthetics, winced when he referred to the permanent collection as "the stuff downstairs," and were annoyed when he brought in time-and-motion specialists to study the museum's operation, they had to admire the way he raised memberships and broadened MOMA's base of support. In 1939, when the museum moved into its permanent home on 54th Street (the very building site another example of Rockefeller largesse), the grand opening was marked by a nationally broadcast radio speech by Franklin D. Roosevelt. There followed a speech by Nelson A. Rockefeller, whose words rather pointedly failed to make clear that MOMA had been in existence for a decade and had had previous presidents.

The business of art and the art of business would often merge into a single act as Nelson traveled to international conferences and came home laden with treasures. In 1937, when he went on his first trip to Peru, his chartered twin-engine plane was so bloated with artifacts on his return that it was barely able to negotiate the steep mountain passes of the Andes. Three years later, when he visited Mexico's President Cardenas to talk of expropriated Standard Oil properties, he presented himself not as "El Principe de Gasolina" (as some members of the Mexican press were calling him) but as the president of the Museum of Modern Art, on a trip to arrange a show in New York that would portray the early cultural history of Mexico.

Nelson's was a uniquely integrated life. It was inevitable that he would sooner or later be attracted to the powerful oil companies with which the family maintained discreet ties. In 1934, upon reentering the family fold, he had taken the advice of Debevoise and gone to work for the Chase Bank as a way of getting acquainted with its operations and understanding how it fit into his father's other interests. But the only part of the Chase that really interested Nelson was the foreign department and its relations with international politics and the oil companies. His father had refused to answer correspondence dealing with the Standard and had done everything in his power to foster the illusion that, except in times of extraordinary moral crisis, the Rockefellers were simply stockholders with no special influence. Yet Nelson remembered how the presidents of the various Standard companies had stopped by the 54th Street house for long talks with Junior. His father had been anything but ambiguous in the opinions he expressed during these private meetings, and he himself had no qualms at all about using the family's connections and its leverage.

While doing his apprenticeship in the Chase, he became close to Joseph Rovensky, who, as head of the bank's foreign department, knew the leading figures in the international cartels controlling raw materials markets. The talk of the international oil set attending the parties Nelson hosted in London and Paris was the fabulous oil fields of Lake Maracaibo, which almost overnight had made Venezuela the biggest producer of oil in the world after the United States. Over a hundred companies had vied with each other for Venezuelan crude, but in the end only three controlled 99 percent of it: Standard of New Jersey which owned a 49 percent share; Shell, 36 percent; and Gulf's Mene Grande subsidiary, 14 percent. The biggest Venezuelan producer by far was the Creole Petroleum Company, the crown jewel in the Jersey system. It was to this company that Nelson was drawn. Asking his father to exchange some of the Standard shares that had been put in his trust fund for enough Creole shares to make him a significant stockholder, he arranged to have himself put on the board of directors.

The year was 1935, a turning point not only for Nelson Rockefeller, but also for Creole and the other companies that controlled Venezuela's oil wealth, for in mid-December Juan Vicente Gómez, dictator since 1908, died. The Gómez regime had been one of the cruelest and most corrupt in Latin American history. While the Venezuelans suffered, however, the foreign oil companies had grown rich. During the oil boom of the twenties, when the rights to the Maracaibo Basin were opened up, Gómez had given foreign companies everything they asked and was paid handsomely for his service. At his death, oil amounted to 99 percent of Venezuela's exports. Yet some 70 percent of the country was illiterate, 60 percent lived in houses of straw and sticks with dirt floors, and only 32 percent of the entire Venezuelan population was employed.

After the dictator's death, the oil men in whose circles Nelson was now moving were alarmed at the tough petroleum reform laws the new government passed to mollify the forces of nationalist outrage and social unrest that had been bottled up during the Gómez decades. But they were far more worried about the fact that the entire hemisphere seemed increasingly inflamed by the politics they associated with Communism. In 1937 the rebel Bolivian regime nationalized the Standard Oil properties there; the following year, Mexico's Cardenas government, acting on the program of Marxist labor leaders, announced the expropriation of foreign oil interests.

Nelson Rockefeller was in the middle of this ferment, intrigued by the oil business and understanding intuitively the role it was destined to play in international power politics. In the spring of 1937 he embarked on a twenty-nation tour of Latin America climaxed by a journey up Venezuela's Orinoco River in a Standard Oil company yacht. His party included Rovensky, Standard executive Jay Crane, his wife Tod, and his brother Winthrop (who was also becoming interested in oil). After touring the Creole Company properties and visiting Caracas—where at two parties he met Gómez's successor, General Lopez Contreras, his entire cabinet, and the governors of four Venezuelan states—an exhilarated Nelson reported home to his parents that "unless something unforeseen happens, it looks as if this would turn out to be one of the soundest . . . countries in the world—and there's certainly plenty of oil here."

The trip marked the moment when Nelson found that "something big" he had been looking for. Returning from Caracas, he began a crash course in Spanish at Berlitz, and only those who didn't know him well suspected that this was another of his momentary enthusiasms. He was serious about Latin America. He tried to convey his sense of crisis and opportunity to a meeting of executives of the Jersey company. He urged upon them a more active policy of social responsibility, pointing out that the corporation held property only by the will of the people and the laws of its governments. If the corporation didn't recognize its social responsibilities, he said, "they will take away our ownership."

One of the chief cries heard against the oil companies in the years following Gómez's death was that the oil boom had made Venezuela a one-product economy, wrecking agriculture and inflating prices and thus ruining domestic industry. All factions in the country agreed that economic diversification was necessary to lessen the dependence on oil production. To demonstrate the path such diversification might take became Nelson's next crusade.

Gathering together a group of friends and business associates in 1940, he formed the *Compañía de Fomento Venezolano* (Venezuelan Development Company). He raised $3 million in initial capital, a third coming from his family, a third from Venezuelan partners, and a third from the oil companies. (Nelson had gone to Jersey Standard with this idea of developing the Venezuelan economy, and they had agreed to an investment of $300,000 if he could secure equal commitments from Gulf and Shell, which he surprsied them by doing.)

The first effort was a huge resort hotel, the Avila. As the *Compañía's* pilot project, it took much of Nelson's time. He made quick trips to Venezuela himself and shuttled as many as five aides back and forth between New York and Caracas to oversee its progress. In the summer of 1940, Robert Bottome, whom Nelson had recruited from the Rockefeller Center rental department, wrote back suggesting that they consider other investments to go along with the hotel. But with war approaching, Nelson wanted to know if such investments would be safe, whatever the possible outcome. He sent Carl Spaeth to Caracas to evaluate the situation. "To postpone such programs as ours until after the war," Spaeth wrote back, "is to lose an excellent opportunity to get in a substantial position in advance of German commercial interests, which will certainly come here in great numbers, supported by substantial subsidies in the event that Germany wins the war."

It was the sort of *Realpolitik* that appealed to someone who was in many ways more fearful of the Communists' inflaming nationalist passions in Latin America than the hemispheric consequences of a possible German victory in Europe. Yet the approaching war had clearly created a new set of circumstances in the hemisphere, and Nelson's ambitions pointed him in the direction of Washington. About the same time that he was founding the *Compañía*, he brought together a number of people, most of them his own age and with similar views, whom he had met since making his first South American tour. The regular briefings they held about the state of things in Latin America, and plans to cope with them, resembled a war council.

Twenty years older than anyone else, "Uncle Joe" Rovensky was the *éminence grise* of the group. He was an insider's insider when it came to the economic affairs of nations, and when Nelson later went to Washington to join the Roosevelt administration, Rovensky went along with him. Jay Crane of Jersey Standard was also in the Rockefeller study group, as was Wallace Harrison, the tall laconic New Englander who had gained attention while still a young man by becoming the leading architect of Rockefeller Center. Finally, there was Beardsley Ruml, the large florid-faced Czech economist who had been brought into the family's orbit years earlier. The group met first at his place in Greenwich Village and later at Nelson's Fifth Avenue apartment. As the world crisis deepened, their discussions began to focus on the outlines for a hemispheric policy consistent with Nelson's ideas. By late spring 1940, Ruml had distilled their thinking into a sort of white paper called "Hemisphere Economic Policy," outlining ways of increasing U.S. investments in Latin America and preventing the Nazis from winning a diplomatic war there with the same lightning speed their armies were displaying in Europe.

On the evening of June 14, 1940, Nelson appeared at the White House with the three-page memorandum and delivered it to Roosevelt's right-hand man, Harry Hopkins. Less than a month later, on July 8, Nelson was celebrating his thirty-second birthday with his family and close friends when the telephone rang with a long-distance call from Washington. It was James Forrestal, special assistant to President Roosevelt, asking about a job: could Nelson come to Washington to talk further? The following evening Nelson dined with Forrestal in the garden of the F Street Club. When offered the newly created post of Coordinator of Inter-American Affairs, Rockefeller asked for a few days to think it over. Then he immediately boarded a plane for Salt Lake City to ask permission from the Republican presidential standard-bearer, Wendell Willkie, who was on the campaign trail in a candidacy the Rockefeller family was heavily backing. But he knew before he hung up what his answer would be—not only because (as Willkie would tell him) accepting the post was his patriotic duty, but because he himself had proposed the idea of creating such a position in his talk with Harry Hopkins barely a month earlier.

CHAPTER 10

L aurance Spelman Rockefeller had been Nelson's buddy as a child and would continue to be as a man. Yet by the time Forrestal called from Washington, Laurance had begun to grow out of his brother's shadow, a tall and dignified young man with a promising career of his own. If he was socially adept, it was not because he shared Nelson's easy familiarity. He was incapable of that kind of self promotion. For him, being with people was a pleasurable game of give-and-take in which he enjoyed parrying attempts to penetrate his defenses. He would be the brother most sensitive to the conflict between the role of Rockefeller and the private person it menaced. His quiet agnosticism in regard to the family was similar to that which had manifested itself when he was a teenager and felt constrained to confess to doubts about God while the other brothers simply accepted the form of their father's religious views, even though its content was beyond them. More than the rest of them, Laurance was a freethinker.

He followed John 3rd to Princeton, where he too was named Most Likely to Succeed. He majored in philosophy, taking every course available in the department. His bachelor's thesis was entitled "The Concept of Value and Its Relation to Ethics." Later in his life, however, when his career was swinging him into the public light, Laurance's interest in Immanuel Kant gave way to Norman Vincent Peale *(The Power of Positive Thinking* became a favored guide) as he—the brother most sensitive to the moral problems inherent in his position—tried to make difficulties disappear by an act of will.

By the time Laurance was graduated from college, his two older brothers had already become young men of affairs. Of all the brothers, he was most interested in the outdoors, having fallen under the spell of Horace Albright on the 1924 trip to Yellowstone. A memorable camping trip through the western states the summer after his junior year heightened his interest. But while the budding field of conservation may have been an acceptable philanthropy, it was not something strong enough to support a Rockefeller career, at least not then.

Partly because his mother thought it would be nice to have a lawyer in the family, he enrolled at Harvard Law School. But he never really got going. In the middle of his first semester, he fell ill. Abby had worried over his frailty as a child, and in his last year at Princeton he had been so sick from German measles that she had taken him home for a time. To save his eyes, they would sit in a darkened room while she read aloud to him from his texts to help prepare for his final exams. But this time he had pneumonia, and she took him out of law school and sent him to Florida to spend the winter months with his grandfather.

He returned to Harvard in 1934 and finished the year. The difficulty he had passing his finals convinced him that he was no longer interested in the law. That same year, he decided to marry Mary French, sister of Nelson's roommate at Dartmouth and a descendant of Vermont's Billings family, founders of the Northern Pacific Railroad.

Setting up housekeeping in New York (later they would acquire the mansion in Mary's family seat at Woodstock, Vermont), Laurance began working in Room 5600. He did a few months' apprenticeship in the Chase and then went on the board of Rockefeller Center. But as he later said, he was looking for something that was "non-competitive with the family interests, and thus with no built-in anti-climax."

Laurance had become interested in the contemporary Scandinavian furniture that had become *de rigueur* in the mid-1930s, and as his first enterprise, he joined with architects Wallace Harrison and Harmon Goldstone in 1937 to form an import and sales company called New Furniture, Inc. Within weeks of Senior's death, Laurance had purchased his grandfather's seat on the stock exchange. The established companies he saw traded there interested him less than the fledgling enterprises he could help by applying some of the force available in the family name and connections. Intrigued by the chic existential implications of the term, Laurance began to call himself a "venture capitalist."

The first of the new technologies he backed was aeronautics. In 1938 he was invited to participate in a syndicate that was being formed by Kuhn, Loeb to back one of Laurance's boyhood heroes, Captain Eddie Rickenbacker. The World War I flying ace wanted to buy Eastern Airlines (a company he had run and made successful) from General Motors and needed $3.5 million to do it. The Kuhn, Loeb syndicate raised the capital, including a modest $10,000 from Laurence. Hard-driving and energetic, Rickenbacker intrigued Laurance, who increased his investment in Eastern over the next few years, availing himself of stock splits and options until he was the largest individual stockholder and a primary influence on the board of directors.

Meanwhile, in 1939, another ambitious, self-confident young entrepreneur contacted him. A slender, energetic Scot from Arkansas, James S. McDonnell, had been working for years as chief engineer for the Glenn L. Martin Corporation. But with war on the horizon, he had decided to form his own company and build airplanes of his own design. Renting an office above the American Airlines hangar at the St. Louis municipal airport, he hired fifteen engineers and turned them loose designing a new pursuit plane while he went off looking for backers for the company and buyers for the product.

Laurance first listened to McDonnell as a courtesy to a fellow Princeton man. But he became interested in McDonnell's proposition—not only because he was tooling up for production at a time when fighter planes would be obviously needed, but even more because of McDonnell's interest in aircraft powered by jet propulsion. Laurance made an investment of $10,000 and cast about for ways of helping the enterprise get off the ground by securing government contracts for it.

Aside from Nelson's eagerness to get into the action in Washington, the coming war seemed far away from the Rockefellers. This unique family looks almost idyllic in the formal photographs from the period in which six smiling children surround proud parents. But beneath this surface were the categories that make up all families—victors, survivors, and victims. Later, some of John 3rd's children would claim that their father's growth as an individual had been stunted by the hold Junior had on him; and Babs's daughters would feel a shadow had been cast over her life by Abby's open preference for the boys. But these wounds were minor in comparison with Winthrop's. Abby had realized his vulnerability but had been too removed from the daily events of his childhood to be able to do anything about it. As a boy, his good nature and naïveté, as well as his fits of crying and petulance, had been viewed by the other brothers as signs of weakness. They took advantage of him and punished him for being different. It often seemed that only by hurting him were they able to establish the powerful unity of purpose they displayed for the next half-century.

In some sense, the problems he faced were those of any middle child. Bullied by Nelson and Laurance from above and outshone from below by the precocious David, he was squeezed out of any psychological space in the family he might have claimed as his own. The problem, once begun, seemed to feed itself: the more he was abused, the more difficult he became; the more difficult he became, the more justified the abuse seemed. Soon he began to see himself as an outsider, someone who did not fit into the family. One childhood impression that was branded into his memory, he later confided to an aide, was that of going to bed every night looking up at the shadows cast on the bedroom wall by moonlight streaming in through the railings his father had workmen place over the windows. The bars were meant to keep trespassers out, but Winthrop assumed that they were intended to keep him in.

He became the "black sheep" of the family. He wanted desperately (almost pathetically, some family friends felt) to succeed on his father's terms. But by the time he was a teenager, his brothers already occupied the range of alternatives, from gamely struggling to live up to the awesome Rockefeller tradition to eagerly embracing it. It appeared that the only way Winthrop could distinguish himself was by failure.

At Lincoln School he was affable and got along well with the children who were not his brothers, but his academic performance was abysmal. Junior assumed it was because he needed a more authoritarian environment and shipped him off to boarding school at Loomis. When Winthrop managed to finish his final year there, Abby wrote her sister Lucy in relief, "Thank fortune, he is really graduated!" After a summer's hard work with a tutor and his father's intercession, he also managed to get into Yale. But outside his father's field of vision, he began to slip. He let his account book go untended for weeks at a time, panicking in the middle of his freshman year when it came time to show Junior his ledger in order to get the following semester's allowance. Once, the situation became so bad that he thought of stealing money from another student in order to balance his books; to avoid a major crisis with his father, he begged a large loan from Babs. It took him three years to repay her.

He entered in the Class of '35. After a couple of disastrous semesters, he had succeeded only in being pushed back to the Class of '36. About the only thing he felt he learned, when he surveyed his college career several years afterward, was to smoke and drink. The latter had taken some work. At first he couldn't take more than three drinks without getting violently ill. But as he reminisced sadly, "Unfortunately, I later got over that." He told his mother and father it was pointless for him to continue. They agreed. As he left New Haven for the last time, he was troubled but not unhappy. "Easygoing" and "good natured" were the terms most often used by contemporaries to describe him, although such virtues did not seem to recommend him to his family.

With his smooth, regular features and vulnerable eyes, Winthrop had grown into the best-looking of all the Rockefeller boys. (When he sprouted a military moustache in the army, some women would say he looked like a baby-faced Clark Gable.) He was also the biggest; 6 feet 3 inches and 225 pounds. He seemed almost embarrassed by his size, by the unmobilized mass he represented, and he agreed with his father that it would be well not to try to squeeze his bulk into an office just yet. Instead, Junior arranged for him to go to work for the Humble Refining Company, Standard's giant crude subsidiary in Texas.

Winthrop spent most of 1936 in the Texas oil fields, working as a "boll weevil," an apprentice roughneck. He was the first of the brothers to mingle with the public. He always acquitted himself well, and by the end of his year in the fields he had worked at every phase of oil production (geophysics crews, roustabouts, refining, pipe laying). His co-workers liked and respected him, calling him "Rock." Winthrop had been attracted to this world where a man, whatever his name, was measured by how quickly and how well he dug postholes. He always regarded this year as the best of his life.

Yet succeeding as a laborer did not offer a permanent solution for him. However much he liked the work, he knew it was only a prelude to the job awaiting him in New York; however close he got to ordinary people, he felt himself irresistibly drawn back into the vortex of the family. After his year with Humble was over, Junior recalled him and installed him as a trainee in the Chase Bank, while keeping an eye open for a position in one of the oil companies in which he had influence. In 1937, after returning from Nelson's trip up the Orinoco and the tour of Venezuelan oil fields, Winthrop took a job in the foreign trade department of Socony-Vacuum and assumed a share of the family's philanthropic obligations by becoming a vice-chairman of the Greater New York Fund. He was trying to be part of the family team, but it was hard to win their respect. At twenty-five, most of them still called him "Winny," and Nelson, who knew how much he loathed the childhood nickname, still introduced him as "my little brother, Wissy-Wissy."

The United States was poised on the terrible expectancy of world war, and many young men, waiting to know what would happen, stalled in planning their future. But Winthrop's sea of opportunity was vaster than most, and he seemed especially adrift. His father was so bothered by rumors of his drinking and by the frequency with which Jimmy Fidler and other gossip columnists placed him at the El Morocco and other nightspots, that he was almost relieved when his most troublesome son enlisted as a private in the infantry in 1941.

If Winthrop was the most unaffected of the Rockefeller boys, his younger brother, David, was the most serious, the one who was conscious of the birthright from the beginning. (Years later, his daughter Peggy would say, "Uncle John doesn't seem comfortable in the role. My father is *very* comfortable. If he has any conflicts about it at all, they don't show.") In his caution and formality, he greatly resembled his father. Yet with David, reserve was not a manifestation of insecurity, but of insularity. He was the last child of the family, the baby. The solipsisms of his childhood would become part of an unshakable self-confidence as he grew older.

As a boy, David was fat and ungainly. At Lincoln he was not particularly popular. A classmate of the Rockefeller boys, Mrs. Louise Marr, recalled that everyone liked Nelson, Laurance, and Winthrop. "David was younger, and he was always boasting about his money, and boasting about where he had been, about having gone to Europe and how much money his family had. So, from a high school girl's angle, he was a pain in the neck."

By the time he graduated from Harvard in 1936, David was a large young man but no longer fat. "Fleshy" was the word that came to mind. He had a long vulpine nose sticking out of a pleasant face.

David went to London that fall to enroll in the London School of Economics and found himself invited to the kind of cocktail parties usually reserved for diplomats and high-ranking civil servants. He met the family of Ambassador Joseph Kennedy and dated his daughter Kathleen. He spent several hours a week working in the London branch of the Chase. Finishing his studies in London, David returned to the University of Chicago to take a Ph.D. in 1938.

He returned to New York in 1940 and soon thereafter married Margaret McGrath. At this point—just before Nelson got the telephone call from Forrestal—it was David of all the brothers who was thought to have the potential for a political career. He was steady and analytical and had spoken out publicly on issues of the day when at college, even though he knew that in doing so he would inevitably have to defend his family.

CHAPTER 11

For the Brothers, World War II was, as Virginia Woolf had said of a prior conflict, a step over the past. By 1942 they were mobilized. JDR3 had joined the navy and moved to Washington. Laurance was also stationed there as a naval lieutenant, in a job overseeing fighter production and development. David, who enlisted just after Pearl Harbor, emerged from Officer Candidate School, served in intelligence in North Africa for two years, and then went to Paris as assistant military attaché. Winthrop was the only brother to make his way up to officer by progressing through the ranks. He enjoyed the democratic spirit of the infantry, as he had of the oil fields, saw action in the Pacific, and was slightly wounded at Okinawa. Nelson was in fact much closer to the war than the others, although he spent it as a civilian—arriving in Washington in 1940 as coordinator of the Office of Inter-American Affairs and later serving as Assistant Secretary of State for Latin American Affairs.

The war years provided the Brothers a release from the discipline of their father and a time for mid-course steering corrections in the trajectory of their lives. Nelson, the only one who might have retraced his grand-father's path to a career in oil, discovered that for better or worse his quest would be for political power in Washington. John 3rd, out of his father's grasp for the first time in his life, was now ready, as he said, "to find my real interests." Laurance had discovered ways to blend his talent for making money with an interest in the new technologies that had become so important in armaments and defense. David had seen that the best of his many alternatives was to join the Chase Bank. Only Winthrop was still uncommitted. His future mistakes, however, would not be the peccadilloes of a young man, but the errors of an adult. He had definitely come of age. When the war began, they were still Mr. Rockefeller's boys; when it was over, they were the Rockefeller Brothers.

They came home filled with confidence—in their generation's ability to manage the world and in their own ability to take control of the family from their father. In 1940, just before America entered the war, they had united to form the Rockefeller Brothers Fund to handle their personal philanthropy. In its articles of incorporation was a statement of purpose that sounded more like the preamble of a constitutional document:

We, the undersigned, being brothers and having interests and objectives in common, have joined together in our desire to continue the tradition of public service and fearless leadership established by our grandfather and carried forward and extended by our parents. In uniting our efforts and coordinating our activities, we hope to be more effective in aiding in the preservation and development of the republic form of government and the private enterprise system which in our opinion have been fundamental factors in making the United States a powerful nation of free people. . . . In line with those convictions, we are prepared to subordinate personal or individual interests as and when necessary for the sake of accomplishing our broader objectives. We propose to use our individual abilities and those material resources which are at our disposal to further these objectives. By acting together with a common purpose, we will be in a stronger position not only to promote our common interests, but also to foster our individual interests.

Pearl Harbor had partially forestalled them from this enterprise, but now, six years later, they came back to the offices on the 56th floor of the RCA Building to take up where they had left off.

"This was a fresh period," John 3rd later said. "We all came together and decided there should be a reallocation of assignments." Nelson was allotted responsibility for Rockefeller Center; John, for the Foundation; Laurence took the family's conservation interests; Winthrop became involved in the Urban League and Colonial Williamsburg; and David went onto the board of the Institute for Medical Research (soon to be renamed

Rockefeller University) and took on responsibility for Riverside Church.

It was something less than a Platonic harmony of the spheres. Underneath the surface of cooperative unity and absolute propriety that the Rockefellers would manage to preserve even at times when tensions were high between them, there was conflict and a struggle for precedence among the sons, and a chafing desire to be free of their father's authority. As usual, Nelson was the center of it. He was used to Washington, where one could get as far as his capacity for political maneuvering would take him—though he himself had been forced out of government in August 1945 following a dispute with the new Truman administration. He was not pleased to return to a situation dominated by a more restrictive order, particularly one that didn't adapt to the changes he had gone through in the past five years. Almost immediately he was acting with an abandon and disregard for proprieties that caused some of the old antagonisms between him and his father to flare up.

Nelson had been appointed by Mayor O'Dwyer to a committee attempting to persuade the United Nations Organization to locate permanently in New York. Initial hopes of getting delegates to accept the old World's Fair grounds in Flushing Meadow had collapsed. Now it seemed that Philadelphia and even San Francisco had better chances of becoming the new world organization's permanent home. Nelson had impulsively offered the Rockefeller Center Theater as a meeting place for the General Assembly, a gesture that had been picked up by the press. But his father, annoyed at not being consulted and unwilling to break a lease with the Center's tenants, vetoed the idea, forcing his annoyed and embarrassed son to retract the offer.

The U.N. delegates had set December 11, 1946, as the deadline for the decision. Nelson had been in Mexico with Frank Jamieson attending the inauguration of President Alemán. When *New York Times* editor James Reston told Jamieson that he felt the delegates still preferred New York if the proper site could be found, Nelson decided to fly home to make one last attempt. On the morning of December 10, he was in Room 5600 brainstorming with his close aides Jamieson, Harrison, and Lockwood and his brother Laurance. Pocantico came up as a possible site. Nelson quickly ordered maps and got on the phone to begin cajoling his absent brothers into agreeing with the plan to give up all or part of the family lands in Tarrytown. One by one they did, John 3rd with great reluctance and David only after asking plaintively, "Couldn't I just give money instead?" He even got an anguished OK from Junior, but then the site selection committee indicated that Westchester County was too far away.

It was that evening, just hours before the U.N. decision was to be made, that Wally Harrison suggested a seventeen-acre tract that the flamboyant real estate man William Zeckendorf was developing along the East River between 42nd and 49th Streets, called "X City." Harrison (who was to be the principal architect) figured that Zeckendorf would be willing to sell for $8.5 million. If the deal could be concluded, it would also have the added advantage of wiping out a potentially serious rival to Rockefeller Center, which even then was only 60 percent occupied, and of upgrading the whole midtown area.

With spirits raised considerably, Nelson put through a call to his father, who offered personally to donate the entire amount. "Why Pa, that's most generous!" Nelson exclaimed. Even before he hung up the phone, he had dispatched Harrison to find Zeckendorf, whom he located at the Monte Carlo nightclub, where the deal was concluded.

Two mornings later, after the East River site had been formally accepted by the U.N. delegates, Junior breakfasted with Nelson and signed the papers. As Nelson was about to dash off to deliver them to Senator Warren Austin, chief of the U.S. delegation, his father reached up, grabbed his coat, and said rather gently, "Will this make up for the Center Theater?" Observing the scene, Frank Jamieson wasn't sure until afterward that Nelson had realized what his father meant, so excited was he about finalizing the deal. He embraced his father around the shoulders and then left for the meeting with Austin. It ended well, but the episode had helped convince him that he would be cramped until the centers and symbols of family power had passed over to him and his brothers. It was not something to be done overnight. But it had to be done.

This was not Nelson's feeling alone, but was shared by all the Brothers. As Lindsley Kimball, an aide Junior had brought into the Office in 1940, recalls, "The brothers felt that they *had* to get out from under the shadow of their father. It was a necessity. I remember once when Winthrop came to me with tears streaming down his face and said, 'Oh, how I wish I could do *something* on my own.' The father was a tough man. A couple of brothers had what amounted to awe for him—they wouldn't go near him if they could help it."

As the nerve center controlling the family's financial and philanthropic investments, the Office was a logical place to start the assault. As early as 1933, on the occasion of his decision to devote himself to the family, Nelson had commissioned a consulting firm to do a study of its functions and to survey and tabulate its activities, because (as he had written his father) "The Rockefeller family is entering upon the third stage of its development, a period which will afford further great opportunities for serving society, but during which the unity of the family is going to be seriously tried."

As the Brothers returned from the war, Nelson in particular took up the old scheme to divide authority. The Brothers brought new ideas with them, along with an impatience with their elders they wouldn't have dared show before the war. Not having a close emotional relationship with his sons, Junior was somewhat bewildered by it all. His old-guard Associates were more than bewildered; they saw the Brothers as a threat to the whole way of performing this complex and unique service that they had perfected over the years, and thus anathema to the interests of the man and the mission they had always served. In their view, the Brothers generally and Nelson in particular would make the Office a circus and a business all at once, cheapening the stately quality of its operations.

The conflict revolved around Debevoise. He had become old and set in his ways. He saw the boys as chaos; they saw him as an old fogy. Called "the Prime Minister," he was determined that there would be no departures from the standard operating procedures established over the years. The boys felt that the Office had to be bent into a more contemporary posture to accommodate the postwar world and their own individual preference. Nelson knew that by controlling the allegiance of the family *consiglieri,* he would control the family, and he began a campaign to replace Debevoise.

For a time the conflict simmered, but by 1947 it had broken into the open. Nelson wanted to hire John Lockwood (who had become in effect his personal lawyer) as the official legal counsel for the entire family. Knowing that his time had come but feeling a responsibility to the rest of the old guard, Debevoise tried to have Vanderbilt Webb, who had been involved in the Office since 1939, named as his replacement. The resulting struggle for power was carried out at an almost elegant level, the discussions couched in so genteel a code that some lower-level employees never knew what was happening. It was the sort of thing Nelson had mastered during his years in Washington. By the time the smoke had cleared, Lockwood was appointed the principal attorney for the family, Webb was out except for special assignments, and Debevoise's status had been limited to that of an emeritus advising Junior personally.

Once Debevoise had been replaced, resistance to the Brothers collapsed. Packard, Cutler, and the others in the old regime were more willing to divide their loyalty between father and sons and acquiesce in the inevitable dynastic process. In return, the Brothers made it clear that they had no intention of purging Room 5600, but would be content to let the old guard stay on until they reached retirement age. Although technically still their father's guests (he never charged them rent or asked them to share in the Office's considerable expenses), the Brothers began to create mini-offices of their own, bringing in personal associates with whom they replaced Junior's staff as they died or retired.

Next came Rockefeller Center. After lengthy negotiations, Nelson convinced his father that the time had come to transfer the stock in the Center to him and his brothers. A multimillion-dollar gamble in the thirties, the Center had now turned the corner and was New York's most imposing and valuable real estate, its market value rising with each surge of the postwar construction boom that had overtaken midtown Manhattan in the wake of the U.N. project. Not only did controlling it give them a significant voice in the affairs of the city, but it also provided dozens of high-paid jobs in which they could (and did) place people whom they wanted to keep in a holding pattern around them. Nelson knew it would be his generation's most significant asset and persuaded his father to "sell" the Center to the '34 Trusts he had set up for the Brothers.

For a man considered by his sons to be aloof and authoritarian, Junior capitulated to the demands of their manhood more easily than they expected. The only time he really bridled at their takeover was when it came to Pocantico itself. New houses had been raised on the estate and there was already a new and growing generation—the fourth—of Rockefeller children playing in its woods; but it was still as quiet and remote as it had been when Junior talked his father into buying it half a century earlier.

Since then, he had expanded the estate's borders by buying up any piece of nearby land that happened to come on the market. He had moved into the Big House after Senior's death, assuming the role of the Laird of Kikjuit. His children moved into homes that seemed to mirror the character and interrelationships of the third generation. After their marriage, Babs and David Milton had moved into the Saportas place (so named for an eccentric old man who had originally built it and later sold it to Junior). It was a large house of native stone with an 1812 sundial set into the rose gardens. It was tucked romantically into the thick woods, but Babs had felt too far away from her parents living in the "park" area of the estate, and had commissioned a house to be built nearer her father. The Miltons moved there in 1939.

JDR3 built a slate-roofed French château two miles from Kikjuit on a long, rolling stretch of pastureland near the town of Mt. Pleasant in 1940. But if this seemed a desire to escape the pressures of the role by living apart from the patriarch who embodied it, two of his younger brothers reacted quite the reverse, moving into the spiritual center of the estate. After his marriage, Nelson claimed Hawes House, an old Dutch colonial with deep gashes on the door that according to local legend, had been made by the sabers of Hessian soldiers during the Revolution. Laurance built a contemporary building in white brick, which he called Kent House, a stone's throw from Nelson. David, however, with the thrift that might be expected of one whose Ph.D. thesis was about waste, bought Babs's newly built house after her divorce in 1943 and began calling it Hudson Pines. Winthrop never got around to building a permanent home at Pocantico, but periodically lived in Breuer House, an ultramodern structure in wood and glass designed by Marcel Breuer.

Whatever other residences the Brothers had (and most of them eventually had three or four), they were encouraged to settle at Pocantico. Now Nelson was proposing that the Brothers take legal title to Pocantico, as they had to Rockefeller Center, and it didn't sit well. After lengthy discussions, in 1950 Nelson finally convinced Junior to form Hills Realty, a holding company for the family lands, including Pocantico. In the beginning, Junior was the only stockholder. But by 1952, Nelson was pushing him to sell his interest in Hills Realty to the Brothers. He sent a memo to his father pointing out that "the sale of the stock to the brothers would in no way change Father's relation to his or their use of the property during his life." Later in the year, Junior finally gave in, agreeing to sell his stock in the Hills company to his sons, subject to his life tenure. The price they paid for 245 acres and buildings would have shocked real estate specialists: $311,000 for an area worth ten or twenty times that. With a major philanthropy and all the centers of family power in their possession, the Brothers were now ready to strike out on their own.

CHAPTER 12

Both as individuals and as a group, the Rockefeller Brothers seemed to embody the best in the tradition of America's great and powerful families. Presenting a front that was wholesome and enthusiastic, yet dedicated and involved, they were an argument on behalf of *noblesse oblige.* They were *responsible* wealth and power; the group portraits taken of them in the early 1950s show five knights in three-piece suits ready to sally forth to act for the "well-being of mankind."

Yet there were certain things the photographs didn't show. One of them, quite literally, was Babs. As a woman, she was not expected to achieve much more than a happy marriage, which was the one thing that seemed completely out of her grasp. By 1942 the workmen and servants at Pocantico, always the first to know what was going on, had noticed that her husband, David Milton, was absent from their home for increasingly long periods of time. By the next year, he had stopped coming altogether, and the couple made their separation official. After the divorce and sale of the Pocantico house to her brother David, Babs moved to Long Island, marrying Irving Pardee, the next of her three husbands. When asked why she came to the estate so seldom, she would answer that its bittersweet memories overwhelmed her.

Junior was upset by Babs's troubles, but he had already seen the difficulties of a strong-willed yet aimless woman in his sister Edith. In some sense, he was prepared to be disappointed in his daughter. Winthrop's falling off was a far more serious problem.

Aside from the fact that his hair was beginning to thin and he was still scarred from burn wounds suffered when a kamikaze plane struck the ship he was on during the Okinawa invasion, Winthrop had come back from the war much the same as when he had left. In certain ways, he was like the rest of them—conservative, well-mannered, Republican.

Yet in other ways he was different. He could not take hold of an event or opportunity and bend it to his purpose the way his brothers could. After coming home from active duty, he had proposed to Secretary of War Robert Patterson that he should do a study of veterans' problems. Patterson OK'd the project, and for the first half of 1946, Winthrop toured the United States by automobile studying how men who had given the best years of their lives were welcomed back to their hometowns. In the report he forwarded to the Pentagon at the end of the year, he concluded that the GI bill was just "an effort to buy veterans off with cash" and suggested that what was needed was for each community to have citizens' committees to work out the veterans' problems on an individual basis. He offered to put up the first million dollars for such a project out of his own pocket. But President Truman, who had just gotten rid of one Rockefeller, was not anxious to appoint another to an important policy post and turned thumbs down on it.

Nelson might have found a way to bull the project through on his own, but Winthrop just gave up. He went back to New York and took up his old job at Socony-Vacuum. Even after they gave up on other hopes for him, his parents believed he could succeed in business, specifically in the oil business, and had tried to groom him for such a career. Before the war, he had been in the Foreign Department. As liaison officer for the Near East, he had toured Iran as a consultant for the Anglo-Iranian Oil Company and had been in Egypt looking over oil properties when Hitler invaded Poland. But on his return, Socony gave him a less glamorous position in the Production Department. It was a desk job and he embraced it with scant enthusiasm. He was on the outer edge of the upheavals remaking the family, although he accepted the obligations thrust on him by his father. Yet there was a sleepwalking quality to his work; it was as if he were being fitted for clothes he could never wear. His aging mother had seen what was happening and was alarmed by it. In 1947 she wrote her sister Lucy, "I think Winthrop is still going through a stage in which . . . he is a little bit afraid the family will try to manage him."

He picked up his nightlife where he had left off before the war. He dated actress Mary Martin frequently enough for gossip columnists to speculate that they would marry. Seeing the family name bandied about in such a way annoyed Junior and increased the distance between him and his only wayward son.

Winthrop began to drink heavily and acquired hangers-on in New York's café society. ("He was an awfully nice guy," a close family friend recalls, "but you'd have to say that he was pretty much a confirmed alcoholic by the time he was thirty-five.") Then, in 1948, he married a buxom blonde named Barbara ("Bobo") Sears at fourteen minutes after midnight on Valentine's Day morning. The marriage took place at the Florida home of Mrs. Winston Guest. The previous afternoon, the toast of Palm Beach's winter society, including the Duke and Duchess of Windsor, had given a champagne reception for the couple. Laurance was the family's representative at the wedding. Junior and Abby were conspicuous in their absence.

When news of the "playboy" Rockefeller's marriage flashed over the wire services, the papers scrambled to find out just who this Bobo Sears was. Cholly Knickerbocker haughtily informed his readers that she was Mrs. Barbara Paul Sears of the Philadelphia Main Line Sears. But she was in fact Jievute Paulekiute, who had been born to Lithuanian immigrant parents in a coal patch near Noblestown, Pennsylvania. Starstruck as a young woman, she had taken the more glamorous first name of Eva, shortened her last name to Paul, and begun angling for a screen career. She had been named Miss Lithuania in a Chicago beauty contest when she was seventeen and gotten bit parts on the stage, managing to win the lead role in a road company production of *Tobacco Road*. In 1945 she married Richard Sears, a proper Bostonian who became third secretary at the American Embassy in Paris. Even after divorcing him, she clung to some of his social prejudices. "Actually I was surprised to find the Rockefellers included in the *Social Register*," she had replied to a reporter's question about how it felt to have made a "Cinderella" marriage. "The Sears family considered them merchants."

In September, when the couple had their first and only child, Winthrop Paul, *The New York Times* marked his birth without noting also that the marriage was barely seven months old. Yet even before the child came, the Cinderella marriage was nearing its midnight hour. Within a year, the couple separated. Bobo took their young son and moved in with her mother in the Midwest. She decided on divorce, and her attorney held out for a huge $6 million settlement.

The Rockefeller brothers rallied around Winthrop, lending him money for the divorce settlement and temporarily taking title to his share of Pocantico and other holdings so that Bobo could not claim them as community property. Yet they were all aware that he had made a fool of himself and disgraced the whole family. Nobody had to say it; there was no other conclusion to draw. For Winthrop himself, it was the climactic incident in his life, showing once and for all that there was no way for him to succeed in the fast-paced milieu of his father and brothers. He quit his job at Socony and gradually began cutting ties with the world he had grown up in. He drank heavily, his eyes showing yellow and his large frame buoyed by a look of bloat.

Early in 1953 he went to Arkansas, partly because of the state's ninety-day residency requirement for divorce but also to visit Frank Newell, an old army buddy who lived there. Newell took him around the state and introduced him to some of the leading people of Little Rock. He found the area pleasantly provincial, and it occurred to him that while he had been one of five in New York, he could easily be one in a million in Arkansas. After several trips back and forth between Little Rock and Manhattan, he decided to move to Arkansas for good, not realizing that once he had left the family his father would stand like the archangel barring his return with a flaming sword.

He had gone south in defeat, but he did not take up a monastic life. One of his first acts was to buy some 927 acres of prime land on top of heavily wooded, craggy Petit Jean Mountain near the backwoods Arkansas town of Morrilton. He hired an army of workmen to clear the trees and literally shear off the mountain top to make room for the massive farm he called Winrock and which some would see as an attempt to

337

re-create Pocantico. Winthrop invested $2 million in the estate, creating long, rolling lawns and carving an airfield into the wooded valley from which he would be able to take off in his Falcon Jet and be in Little Rock in five minutes. He built two lakes, which he named Lake Abby and Lake Lucy, after his mother and aunt. He brought in breeding stock of the celebrated Santa Gertrudis cattle that would soon make his ranch famous among cattle buyers.

Within a few years, Winrock Farm was the first wonder of Arkansas. It attracted over 50,000 visitors a year, most of them citizens of the second poorest state in the nation who came to gawk at all the marvels of the place, including a $31,000 stud bull named Rock. Winthrop began to play a role in the civic life of the state, donating several million dollars to establish a demonstration school that would show what might be done with the state's abysmal educational system, and to build a medical clinic. As he told a reporter, he liked the state because "what you do here shows up in a hurry. You can see the results."

In 1956, after he had been appointed head of the Arkansas Industrial Development Commission, observers speculated that he might have a good political future if he were to reregister as a Democrat. The same year he married a pretty divorcée named Jeannette Edris, daughter of a theater-chain operator. He seemed happy: it was as if he had found his *métier* as the "hillbilly Rockefeller." Once, when taking a group of Eastern newspaper men on a tour of Winrock, he stopped to gesture down at the broad valley visible from the height of Petit Jean Mountain and said, "This is my show. It doesn't have anything to do with any Rockefeller family project."

CHAPTER 13

By the mid-1950s, the United States was locked into its global crusade and the Rockefeller family was established as an important resource in the life of the nation. If it was not quite the "Rockefeller conspiracy" some charged, it did have the appearance of careful organization. Through its connections with the Chase Bank and the Standard Oil companies, and its association with such great Wall Street investment and law firms as Kuhn, Loeb; Lazard Frères; Debevoise, Plimpton; and Milbank, Tweed, the family had its fingers on the pulse of the country's industrial and financial heartlines. Through the Rockefeller Foundation, the

Council on Foreign Relations, and the Republican party, it was connected to the highest directorates of national policy. Whenever members of the power elite gathered to make the crucial decisions of the postwar period, one or two of the key individuals would inevitably be drawn from the executive levels of the institutions with which the family was deeply involved. Men like John J. McCloy, C. Douglas Dillon, James Forrestal, Robert Patterson, Robert A. Lovett, the Dulles brothers, and Winthrop Aldrich were never elected to office, but wielded a power that was in many ways greater and more sustained than that of the elected officials they served. While they shaped the contours of America's postwar strategy, the policy technicians who would succeed them—individuals like W. W. Rostow, Zbigniew Brzezinski, and Henry Kissinger—were busily working their way up through the complex of international institutes and think tanks the Rockefeller Foundation had helped create.

JDR3 had come home from wartime Washington still lean and square-jawed, although his brown hair had thinned to a widow's peak and the onset of middle age had scoured away some of the naïveté that had been so noticeable in the first years after his graduation from college. He still slouched slightly to reduce his height and make himself inconspicuous, yet he seemed less apologetic about himself than he had in the past. It was as if the modest job he had had, shuffling military papers and writing reports, had offered him an important opportunity to inventory his character. He would never have Nelson's ability to win people over by grabbing them and sharing a joke, he now understood, but if his habitual seriousness could be proposed as sincerity, it might serve him just as well in the long run.

He had never really had a chance to declare himself before the war, but had passively (almost somnambulistically, some friends of the family thought) accepted all the responsibilities thrust upon him, the mundane with the momentous. One of his closest associates says bluntly, "John was in the padded cell from 1927 to the war." When he returned, he did not intend to be straitjacketed again.

JDR3 envied Nelson's ability to unify his life so that the public and private man were welded together. Before the war, he had tried to achieve this synthesis, but always found that the one was duty-bound to do certain things the other wanted desperately to avoid. Now he decided just to accept this schizophrenia and try to make the most of it. In the partial seclusion of the rambling château he had built at Pocantico, he began to construct the emotional base he had never had as a child because of his father's high expectations and his younger brothers' effervescence. In some sense, the family he and Blanchette raised at Fieldwood Farm (a daughter, Sandra, followed by the son called "Jay," and two more daughters, Hope and Alida) was an alternative to *the* family. He built a more ceremonial residence at 1 Beekman Place in New York, where he could play the Rockefeller in the life's work he now began to seek.

It started with Asia. Originally, he had been interested in that part of the world because his father was interested in it and because he knew his father wanted him to be interested in it. Yet it had something of its own that attracted him. In 1929 he had gone to Kyoto and wandered through the temples and shrines of carved and gilded wood and sat in the ornamental gardens talking to some of the old rulers who now held court in exile in this religious center of old Japan.

In the navy, JDR3 began to see the Orient less as a family charity and more as an area vital to the balance of power. He had started in the Navy Bureau of Personnel, but had been transferred first to a job with the committee coordinating the efforts of the Departments of War, Navy, and State, and then to a position as Special Assistant on Far Eastern Affairs to Navy Undersecretary Artemus Gates.

In the summer of 1949, as the Russians exploded their first atomic bomb and the armies of Mao Tse-tung began their final sweep toward Peking, Secretary of State Acheson appointed a three-man committee to tour Asia on a fact-finding mission. Headed by Philip Jessup of the State Department and including Raymond Fosdick (now president of the Rockefeller Foundation) and Everett Case, a director of the Institute for Pacific Relations, the team stopped off in Saigon to bestow official recognition on the Emperor Bao Dai, whom the French had just installed as a puppet to oppose Ho Chi Minh. On returning to the United States, the team submitted its findings to a round table of China experts convened at the State Department to recommend policy toward the Chinese Communists. JDR3 was among the select group of "China hands" present.

The issue was whether to put maximum pressure on the new regime in an effort to promote its collapse (but thereby driving it also into the arms of Russia) or to maintain diplomatic and trade links with the mainland in an effort to encourage the forces of nationalism and wean Peking from Moscow's camp. In the discussions on these questions, JDR3 participated very little; but when he did, it was to come down on the hard side: "On U.S. trade with China," he offered at one point,

my own reaction is that it should be terminated. It seems to me that the fastest way to contain communism is to discredit it in the eyes of the people of China. It

340

seems to me that if the economy worsens, that this will arouse opposition to it, and as I see it, the opposition is essential if new leadership is to develop in China.

It was, as he added, "a negative approach to the problem in China and I dislike very much negative approaches," but it was the consensus view of the men who gathered with him in the Council on Foreign Relations, and whom JDR3 regarded as peers. The round-table group was more disparate, more academic, and less socially distinguished. Their lack of enthusiasm for the hard line disturbed JDR3, and after returning to New York, he wrote a follow-up letter to Phillip Jessup, who had chaired the meeting. He noted that there seemed to be pretty general agreement that even if China was not actually controlled from Moscow, its thinking and ideology were "in tune" with the Kremlin. The "big question" that remained was, Is China different? JDR3 was concerned that many of the experts at the round-table seemed to think so. "Much of the discussion at our conference was on the basis, it seemed to me, that China is different. Is this assumption justified today, when totalitarian regimes have such effective methods of control as the secret police and the tommy gun?"

If this was not the most subtle view of the factors determining China's destiny, it was to be the prevailing one for the next two decades. With the isolation and encirclement of Mao forming the backbone of U.S. Asian policy, the pivot of Washington's strategy in the Far East fixed on Japan. The time had come to negotiate a peace treaty so that the Japanese could become partners in America's Asian security system. To make the move bipartisan, Dean Acheson assigned John Foster Dulles, Dewey's foreign policy adviser, to negotiate the treaty. Dulles asked JDR3 to come along.

Petty and insensitive, Dulles would never inspire a deep sense of loyalty among most of his colleagues. Yet something like an affectionate relationship sprang up between him and JDR3. They had known each other for years, moving in the same small social world of New York's most exclusive clubs, associations, and boards of directors. Dulles had been a trustee of the Rockefeller Foundation since 1935, and after he was appointed chairman of the board in 1950, he and JDR3 saw a good deal of each other, frequently meeting in Dulles's apartment over matters like the selection of a new president. (In 1952, they would decide to give the post to Dean Rusk, who, with the Democrats out of power, was then unemployed.) Dulles may have distrusted Nelson, but he took a liking to John. Possibly he saw a potential for development in the most repressed of all the Rockefeller Brothers; he certainly realized that such a person could be useful in negotiations where a cultural and philanthropic association with the Orient would be a rare asset.

The 1951 mission to Japan was a turning point for JDR3. Although he went to Japan as a sort of ornament for the mission, JDR3 had been assured by Dulles that his efforts would play an important role in future U.S.-Japanese relations. The view that cultural relations were an important aspect of diplomacy had become increasingly standard in foreign policy councils since Nelson's pioneering efforts in the coordinator's office. JDR3 assembled a small staff of his own and spent several weeks in Japan talking to political and cultural leaders all over the country. Then he came home and worked on his report along with a team of experts Dulles had gotten for him on loan from the State Department. The 88-page document proposed the creation of a cultural bridge across the Pacific: exchange of university students and professors, the establishment of Japanese-American cultural centers in the United States and Japan, and a continuing exchange of leaders between the two countries.

The mission to Japan was, as JDR3 now says of it, "a major step in my independence and a major step outside the family orbit." Self and family—the Dulles mission helped solve both problems. For it emboldened JDR3 to begin a series of projects on his own, all of them informed with the spirit of an American mission in Asia to make the Pacific a breakwater against the Communist tide through efforts in the social and cultural realms.

By providing this outlet and direction, JDR3 had an alternative to working in Room 5600 and running constantly into Nelson. For, although the tension never became public, this was a time when antagonisms were hard to contain, let alone avoid. The contact that the Brothers did have in the Brothers Fund, for instance, showed these tendencies. JDR3, as the brother publicly identified as a philanthropist, had been the Fund's president since its creation. But Nelson dominated its activities. As Donald McLean remembers, "Nelson was a big bully. He was fast on his feet and Johnny wasn't, so it turned out that all of Nelson's ideas were picked up and not so many of Johnny's. When the Fund's meetings were over, the staff would be out there working on hot tickets for Nelson, but nobody was moving merchandise for John."

Nonetheless, as the 1950s ground to a conclusion, JDR3 had achieved a kind of liberation from his family—not so much from the myth, which he continued to uphold, but from the fact. He traced it back to Dulles. And when he appeared at the former Secretary of State's funeral as one of twenty-three honorary pallbearers, he was not just someone lending his symbolic name in tribute to the dead statesman but a public personality with achievements and identity of his own.

Before the war Laurance Rockefeller's path had seemed less definite than any of his brothers'. But the time he served in the Navy gave him an insight into investment opportunities that would be in the "national interest" as well as in his own. He had spent most of the war overseeing patrol plane assembly lines on the West Coast for the Bureau of Aeronautics. Then, a few month before Hiroshima, he was transferred to the Fighter Desk. He used this vantage point to help enterprises like the McDonnell Company, which he had become involved with before the war. When J. S. McDonnell had heard that Laurance was conferring with Navy Secretary James Forrestal about a job overseeing production of naval aircraft, he wrote urging him to put in a good word about their joint venture. "Our company likes competition," his letter stated, "but during the emergency, we can service the Navy with the least waste of man hours, if the Navy could tell us person to person what new design of airplane they need most."

Laurance may already have known about Forrestal's intention to get a commitment from Congress for postwar armaments while the war was still providing emotional leverage, but even if not, he had seen airplanes and other weapons on the drawing boards capable of revolutionizing not only warfare but the economy and possibly society itself. In order to have the sort of "preparedness" the military brass was pushing for, the government could not wait for research and development to occur spontaneously. It would have to underwrite the costs and support the wartime mobilization on an ongoing basis into the postwar world.

He had set an explorer's foot on that virgin ground President Eisenhower would later name the military-industrial complex, and it left an impression on him. Like Nelson, whose lead he continued to follow, he made the transition from the World War to the cold war almost without taking time to discover that peace had broken out. ("I've never really demoblized," he later commented to a *Time* correspondent who asked about his peacetime contacts with the Navy.)

Investments in young corporations with strategic potential soon followed—Piasecki Helicopter and then Reaction Motors, a New Jersey company involved in classified research on liquid fuel rocketry. It had fine engineering capabilities, but poor administration. Laurance purchased 21 percent of the company for $500,000 and sent his aides in to strengthen its managerial core. He also picked up a 20 percent interest in Marquardt Aircraft, which built ramjets; a 27 percent interest in Wallace

Aviation, which built jet engine blades; a 30 percent interest in Flight Refueling; 24 percent of Airborne Instruments Laboratory; and 24 percent of Aircraft Radio, which specialized in electronic quipment.

To see his investments through what he called their "ten-year risk cycle," he assembled a group of employees to watch over his ventures and make them pay off. Laurance's associates were different from the employees the other Brothers had brought into Room 5600. They did not concern themselves with family policy or even with the personal career of their employer. They were money men, technicians who looked after Laurance's investments (as well as other family holdings) as his eyes and ears, bringing proposals for involvement in what they called "new horizons products"—the new technology ranging from optics to the computer science nurtured by fallout from the defense industry.

He benefited enormously from his contacts in government and finance, yet Laurance still prided himself on being the sort of man who could have made it even if he hadn't been named Rockefeller. And while he generally seemed to feel less of what he called the "missionary impulse" than his two older brothers (the extravagance of the family's rhetoric about itself, in fact, seemed to embarrass him), he was involved in the dialogue about the direction the third Rockefeller generation should take. As in other things, he supported Nelson's view that the family should try to expand its influence; and he felt that the best contribution he could make would be financial—not only because the fortune had diminished from the time when Junior first began to disperse it ("We just don't have money the way people used to have," Laurance once remarked with half-serious irony), but also because he felt that the technological advances of the postwar period would mean new centers of power with which the Rockefellers had to connect themselves if they were not to become a second-rate family.

Business, family, and mission had appeared to converge for Laurance in 1945 with the formation of Rockefeller Brothers, Inc. Although the New York *Daily News* greeted the announcement of the new enterprise with one of its trademark headlines ("Rock Mob Incorporates"), it described itself as a "a holding company for ideas" and as "an attempt to achieve social and economic progress as well as a fair profit," with each brother investing an equal share of the $1.5 million initial capitalization.

Yet in Laurence's project, the crusading aspect was subordinated. Randolph Marston, one of his aides, wrote an executive of the Chase Bank: "This is just to give you an idea of the fields of investment currently of interest to the Rockefeller Brothers Company. The primary interest is in

344

matters of aeronautical or air transport industries; other items of interest [include] industrial developments in foreign countries close to raw materials sources, particularly where there is an opportunity to produce something of real social benefit." For Laurance, the company never distinguished itself from his other venture capital projects.

Rockefeller Brothers, Inc., was only the first of several vehicles that Laurance would create over the years in order to guarantee that the family participated in new and potentially important business enterprises. Although modest in scope, this development was actually a significant change in the identity of the family. In Junior's time, the financial aspect of the office had been carefully controlled, reflecting his recognition that making money was a dangerous occupation for a Rockefeller. (The ritual emphasis on "fair" profit and social benefits in the public relations of RBI and other business projects in which the brothers engaged was a partial homage to this fact.) In the old days, the investments had been handled conservatively and discreetly; when a man like Bertram Cutler sat on a board representing Rockefeller interests, it was almost always a defensive maneuver designed to protect an old investment rather than to extend a new one. Laurance, however, had managed to place the financial concern at the core of the office, where it had been in his grandfather's day.

JDR3, who saw philanthropy getting shunted to the background, did not really approve of this new emphasis, and Winthrop, as he became more deeply mired in his personal problems and withdrew to Arkansas, ceased to participate very actively in RBI ventures. But Laurance had long ago understood that the momentum of the third Rockefeller generation would have to come from a triangulation of his interests and abilities with those of Nelson and David. Neither of them had any qualms about the fact the Family Office was undergoing a subtle change of character that would make it into an efficient money-making machine. Less involved in public affairs than the other Brothers, Laurance came to be the one in charge of Room 5600.

In his first decade and a half of venture capitalism, Laurance parlayed a $9 million investment into $40 million. While an increase of capital four and a half times was more than respectable, he could not help reflecting on the fact that the much larger amount he had left in the blocs of conservative Socony Oil stocks had increased three times in the same period without any effort at all on his part. If, on the other hand, he attempted to measure his achievement by the fact that a high percentage of his investments were successful—that he had, as he said often, a ".900 batting average"—he came up against the awareness that what might be a gamble for an ordinary man could easily become a sure thing when a Rockefeller exerted the force of his name, his connections, and his capital on it.

Laurance had thus reached a climax in his career. As a Rockefeller, he couldn't afford to go out aggressively and make a lot of money or reach for vast corporate influence. But as a member of the third generation of a public dynasty, he couldn't be totally happy in his accustomed position behind the scenes. By the end of this ten-year cycle, he began to move away from business in search of a field that would offer a better footing to build the public personality that every son of John D. Rockefeller, Jr., had to have.

It was natural that he should look to conservation. He had grown up more interested in the outdoors than his brothers, more aware of his father's contributions to the National Park Service as well. The men who were his father's chief advisers in the conservation matters, Horace Albright and Fairfield Osborn (son of the New York Zoological Society's Henry Fairfield Osborn, "Fair" was the author of the influential book *Our Plundered Planet* and considered the leading conservationist of his day), were his mentors as well. He would later tell his children that these two men, along with Captain Eddie Rickenbacker, had a greater influence on his career than anyone else.

In 1947 Laurance had become head of Jackson Hole Preserve, Inc., the foundation his father had established to pursue his conservation interests; the same year he helped Fairfield Osborn start the Conservation Foundation, soon to be one of the most prestigious organizations in the field. At the time, his involvement was limited because his own interests and the nation's had intersected in his venture capital investments. While it appeared that conservation was a good philanthropy (like his work as a trustee of the Sloan-Kettering Memorial Cancer Clinic), it did not seem important enough to warrant more than his passing interest.

At the beginning of the fifties, however, conservation had been dramatically elevated in the scale of national interests. Nelson had warned of the future importance of the resources of the Third World countries. ("Of the critical and strategic materials upon which armaments depend, they supply three-quarters of all United States imports.") Now his words were being echoed in the highest councils of state. In 1951, Truman appointed a blue-ribbon presidential Commission on Materials Policy under the chairmanship of CBS head William Paley to study the country's present and future needs, not ruling out the possibility of war, and to make recommendations for policy. Along with Horace Albright, Nelson appeared before the commission to testify on the crisis.

The commission report, published in June 1952, as *Resources for Freedom*, began with a question: "Has the United States of America the material means to sustain its civilization?" Much of the five-volume work was a detailed inventory of each strategic resource located in the underdeveloped countries, which, in the words of the report, offered the best solution to the U. S. problem because they were blessed with "rich and relatively undeveloped natural resources often far in excess of their prospective needs." At home, the study called for an opening of the U.S. resources and federal lands to private industry, inveighing against "the hairshirt concept of conservation which makes it synonymous with hoarding. A sound concept of conservation, in view of this commission, is one which equates it with efficient management—efficient use of manpower and materials; a positive concept compatible with growth and high consumption in place of abstinence and retrenchment."

Laurance and his associates were enthusiastic about the conclusions of *Resources for Freedom*—by adding a national security component to the field of conservation, it had made it worthy of attention—and they joined the chorus of those who made the control of raw materials sources seem like a necessary preparation for Armageddon.

As a Rockefeller, Laurance could not help having great peripheral vision, seeing as simultaneous developments what others would regard as unconnected incidents. For him, each venture led logically to the rest; one field merged with its opposite. When he heard that the Caneel Bay Plantation, an exclusive resort on St. John (most unspoiled of the U.S. Virgin Islands), was available, he bought it for $600,000 and immediately began purchasing the lands surrounding it. As in his father's decision decades earlier to protect his pristine Seal Harbor retreat by donating lands that became the nucleus of Acadia National Park, Laurence's decision to buy up the properties surrounding his resort was both a philanthropic gesture that would make the beautiful St. John one of the jewels of the national park system and a pragmatic means of protecting an investment. By 1955, his Jackson Hole Preserve, Inc., had spent over $2 million assembling nearly 6,000 acres, which Laurance then turned over to the Department of the Interior. The Virgin Islands National Park was unveiled the following year in ceremonies that coincided neatly with the formal opening of the refitted Caneel Bay Plantation resort.

In addition to its aesthetic dimension and its social and financial possibilities, however, the revitalized field of conservation filled a personal need. For years Laurance had been comfortable in the anonymity that

347

allowed him to work behind the financial scenes. He had been successful, but not in the same way as his brothers. For the first time in his life, he felt the itch for the kind of achievement that would bring public recognition. This impulse had something to do with a biological clock—his fiftieth year was in sight—but it was even more the result of membership in a family that had come to depend on a certain annual quota of complimentary inches in *The New York Times* to indicate it was doing right.

Laurance was not inclined to reject a flattery that so coincided with his desire to play a public role as a "citizen-conservationist." By 1958, his *curriculum vitae* was weighted toward his new career. He was a commissioner of the Palisades Park, a director of the Hudson River Conservation Society, and a trustee of the Conservation Foundation and the New York Zoological Society, as well as a director of Resources for the Future. His baptism into the world of official studies and commissions came this same year, when President Eisenhower selected him for his first important government post, head of the Outdoor Recreation Resources and Review Commission, which was to determine the nation's recreation needs to the year 2000. With this, the Rockefeller brother who had once humorously referred to his lack of a public voice by calling himself "the Harpo Marx of the family," was in a position to make a serious bid for fame.

CHAPTER 15

For the first ten years of his career, he followed the same morning ritual as other rising young executives—a quick series of calisthenics, a light breakfast of toast, bacon, and coffee, and then the brisk walk from his four-story red brick town house on the upper east side to the Lexington Avenue subway. Tall, looking heavier than he actually was, he would have been easily recognizable to other junior executives riding the IRT—not by name perhaps, but by such symbols of office as the bulging attache case, the *Wall Street Journal* tucked under his arm, and the unvarying uniform of dark suit, white shirt with a suspicion of starch at the collar, and shined (but not shiny) wing-tip shoes. With the long nose poking outward, the round face was the sort that might have had a jester's good humor if it had belonged to another man. But it was the face of David Rockefeller, commercial banker, whose philosophy of life was summed up in a comment to his oldest son: "Whatever you do, if you do it hard enough you'll enjoy it. The important thing is to work and work hard."

David had done just that, beginning his career (as Junior proudly noted) "at the bottom." In 1946, while his brothers were vying for position in the Family Office, he began work in the foreign department of the Chase as an assistant manager, lowest of the junior executive positions. Two years later, as a second vice-president, he was in charge of the bank's business in Latin America, opening branches in Cuba, Puerto Rico, and Panama, and starting an influential financial quarterly, *Latin American Highlights*. By 1952, he was one of six senior vice-presidents of the Chase (although not yet a director like his brother Laurance, who was the only man under fifty on the board).

In 1955 he became executive vice-president, and a year later received his most important promotion—to the vice-chairmanship of the Chase board. In addition to its other advantages, this position meant a full-time chauffeured limousine and the end to subway rides at rush hour. He could have bought such service anytime he wanted it, of course, but David had learned the unwritten law that unearned luxury was damaging to one's career, if not one's self-image.

It was a swift rise for a man barely forty years old, really more the grooming of an heir apparent than a Horatio Alger success story; still, it was not so swift that it could be said to have occurred *only* because of nepotism. With his youth, intelligence, and his Ph.D. in economics, David was exactly the sort of man (regardless of his name) that banks look for. While he did not plan to subject himself to the whole tedious process of rising through the ranks, he knew that he would never have the authority he wanted if he appeared to be merely the owner's son, and so he made sure to pay his dues, for others' benefit if not for his own. He had worked patiently in all the major areas of the bank (except for the relatively arcane world of trusts), including such unexciting departments as economic research and customer relations. Even though his own interests were strongly centered in international banking, he spent time organizing a metropolitan department and pushed for an expansion into branch banking. The Chase had previously ignored such innovation, concentrating instead on corporate and foreign business. In the intense competition for the saver's dollar that characterized the postwar banking world, the Chase had fallen from first to third position, disadvantaged by the fact that all but two of its twenty-eight branches were in Manhattan. Deciding to solve the problem through merger, it set its sights on the Bank of the Manhattan Company, only fifteenth in size but strongly represented by branches in the other boroughs of the city. John J. McCloy, who handled the Rockefeller account at Milbank, Tweed and became chairman of the

Chase board in 1953 when Winthrop Aldrich was appointed U.S. ambassador to England, used all his legal skill to bring the merger off, and by 1955 the new Chase Manhattan was the largest bank in the country.

David was only one of four executive vice-presidents in the newly merged institution, yet there was no doubt as to his future. "Among the top men," commented *Business Week* at the time of the merger, "it is David Rockefeller who is heir apparent." Some of his colleagues may have seen that his almost perpetual smile had an element of the clenched jaw, but most simply accepted him as an inevitability. He accented the distance that naturally separated him from others by standing behind a polite yet awesome reserve that led one co-worker to refer to him as "the phlegmatic forty-year-old." He did not have Nelson's ability to simulate warmth and familiarity ("No one, and I mean *no one,* calls David Rockefeller 'Rocky,'" a Chase exec once admonished a newsman who had committed this unforgivable gaffe), yet he shared his older brother's Aldrich metabolism that allowed him to work all day, come home and change clothes, and then spend almost every evening in the entertaining that made him such an important asset to the bank.

Sometimes his activities stretched the working day to eighteen hours. Yet no one pushed harder for the jammed routine than David himself. In rising to power at the bank, he had come to see himfelf as a "self-made man." Even his wife, Peggy, most critical and independent of all the Rockefeller wives, brought their children up to feel that they were different from their cousins because their father was the only Rockefeller who "had a profession."

As he grew older, David reminded family friends more and more of his father. He was methodical, orderly, reasonable, less excited by exercises of the imagination than by facts and blueprints. And there was something almost Victorian in his willful desire to leave the verities unchallenged. Although he eventually became a leading figure in the Museum of Modern Art (his involvement began when he asked MOMA President Alfred Barr to decorate his town house with some paintings that would provide an "esthetically stimulating" environment for his children), and would eventually assemble one of the finest collections of post-Impressionist paintings in the world, David's early interest was in collecting Chinese porcelains like those he had seen Junior spend hours admiring, arranging, and cataloguing at his Park Avenue apartment. He had also inherited his father's interest in real estate and building, and in seeing his will exemplified in the changes he could make on the face of a city. Unencumbered by qualms about his role or doubts about the family mission, in time he would become the complete Rockefeller.

In the general division of responsibility that ensued when Junior turned over to his sons the institutions he had built and the interests he had developed, David's combination of seriousness and competence made him the logical brother to take on the chairmanship of the Institute for Medical Research, perhaps the family's proudest creation. In 1950 he became its president, and in 1953 he surrendered that position to become chairman of the board. The office of president was filled by Detlev Bronk.

Under Bronk's leadership and with David's backing, a reorganization of the Institute was begun at once, transforming it to a graduate university and scientific research center. (Its official name was changed to Rockefeller University in 1965). Specializing in advanced scientific research, it quickly became one of the half-dozen most prestigious and influential scientific institutions in the country, with a roster of Nobel prize winners on its faculty second only to those of Harvard and the University of California at Berkeley.

Of all the brothers, it was also David who took an active, if businesslike, interest in his father's investment in the institutions clustered on Morningside Heights. As early as 1946, he had become involved in discussions of the Morningside neighborhood, which was more and more dividing itself into two communities. Up on the Heights were the institutions of civilization and culture, their imposing architectures dominated by the Gothic bell tower of Riverside Church; below, in a belt known as the "Valley," were the residential dwellings of sixty thousand people, ugly, rapidly deteriorating structures packed with six and eight persons to a room. Socially and economically, the Valley was an expanding outer edge of Spanish Harlem.

The directors of International House decided to commission a study of the problem by William Munnecke, a University of Chicago urbanologist David, himself a university trustee, had brought to their attention. Munnecke's report called for a "total approach" on the part of the surrounding institutions to rehabilitate the area. In February 1947, David hosted a planning dinner. Attending were those who had been identified for years with his family's activities in the city, including Harry Emerson Fosdick of Riverside Church and Wally Harrison, along with representatives of the other Morningside institutions. Out of this gathering Morningside Heights, Inc., was formed, with David (who contributed $104,000 to help in the launching) as its president. His mandate was to put through an unprecedented scheme of "urban renewal," the first attempt to "remake" a major community in the United States.

351

The city agreed to condemn ten acres of "blight," inhabited by some 3,000 families, while Morningside Heights, Inc., raised $15 million to tear down the condemned dwellings and replace them with a modern apartment complex that would stand as a buffer against further incursions from the surrounding ghetto. The program was not universally applauded. It soon became clear that only one thousand families would be accommodated in the new apartments, and since these were to be middle-income units, few of the dispossessed would qualify. Despite efforts to take the edge off local resentment by involving the community in decisions that had already been made and by finding housing elsewhere for those forced to move, there was bitter opposition to the plan. A Save-Our-Homes Committee organized neighborhood resistance, and in a tumultuous town meeting, David was forced to brave hecklers and protesters in defending the project and himself. Eventually, the Morningside renewers prevailed. In 1954, the year that demolition began, Columbia celebrated its bicentennial, and the university gave David an honorary degree with a citation describing him as "relentlessly dedicated."

To some degree, the Morningside project was an attempt on David's part to protect the family investment in the area. Over the years, Junior had donated more than $50 million to Riverside Church, Union Theological Seminary, and International House alone. But it was also the logical extension of a banker's-eye view of a city as the sum of its businesses and institutions.

As David's rise at the bank brought him increased distinction in the financial community, his interest in urban redevelopment shifted to the plight of the financial district, whose future seemed doubtful by the mid-1950s. Though the Wall Street area had been the scene of the city's first skyscraper boom in the first quarter of the century, little major construction had been undertaken there since the Depression. And as the downtown area settled into a kind of regal decay, the midtown area experienced a real estate boom of imposing proportions. The Chase itself was at a crossroad, having so outgrown its headquarters at 18 Pine Street that its administration had to be scattered over eight separate buildings.

Its executives knew that if they decided to move the bank uptown, they might well set off a stampede that would make the financial district a ghost town. They knew, too, as David's top aide, Warren Lindquist, said, that the area was "the heart pump of the capital blood that sustains the free world," and re-creating it elsewhere in the city was hardly feasible. The Chase's $40 million in real estate investments in the area also convinced its management to make every effort to rehabilitate the district.

The task ahead was formidable: suitable building sites had to be found, old offices sold, leases renegotiated, and all under the most difficult market conditions because of the uncertainty about the area's future. To undertake such an entrepreneurial feat, David called in William Zeckendorf, whose imaginative assembling of the U.N. site had shown him to be just the man for what he himself would later refer to as "the Wall Street Maneuver."

While Zeckendorf was busy assembling the core of the new "Wall Street," David was forming the Downtown Lower Manhattan Association (DLMA), which brought together the big financial institutions of the area to plan for its development. The most audacious element in the DLMA's plan was the creation of a World Trade Center, twin 110-story skyscrapers that would occupy sixteen of the most valuable acres in the world. It would be David's reprise on Rockefeller Center. "A World Trade Center seems logical," he explained simply, "and it seems logical to have it near the banks that service the bulk of United States foreign trade."

As in the case of Morningside Heights, the Trade Center was to be raised on land occupied by small businesses and some low-income housing; residents and shop owners joined to take the matter to court, charging that the project was designed less to stimulate trade than to elevate the values of property owned by the Chase and others in the lower Manhattan area. If David was invulnerable to such criticism, it was because he believed he was acting in the same spirit of public concern that had always motivated his father. If what was good for the city was also good for his bank so much the better.

As he sat in his vice-chairman's office in the soon to be vacated Chase headquarters at 18 Pine, David could contemplate a grand future for the bank, and the financial community and nation of which it was part. The Chase was an overarching presence in the economic life of the United States—indeed, of the world. Alongside David on the board sat directors of more than one hundred of the largest corporations and financial institutions of the country.

Within the family, David's leadership of the Chase made the offices he maintained in Room 5600 and at the bank the hub of the Rockefellers' economic power and influence. The network of the family's interests and those of the Chase were intertwined through trusts on deposit, through the Standard Oil companies it serviced, and, outside the bank, through the offices of Milbank, Tweed. The resources of the Chase, including its army of analysts, were always available to the financial men in the Family Office, and when Laurance sent his associates into the aerospace companies he invested in, they could usually count on a generous line of credit from the big bank to help in their efforts to turn the companies around.

By the end of the decade, David had emerged as a banker-statesman in a class by himself. Jetting from continent to continent in the family's fifteen-seat Caravelle, he negotiated with monarchs and ministers with a cachet normally possessed only by high-ranking diplomats. He had a card file at the Chase with twenty thousand names of people he knew in high places around the world, and whom he thought of as "personal friends." He was all the things that such a man was supposed to be: fluent in three European languages; a wine connoisseur with part interest in a vineyard in France and, in his Pocantico home, a renowned temperature-controlled cellar sealed with a bank-vault door; a yachtsman with three 40-foot boats he sailed off the Maine coast from his elegant Seal Harbor estate; possessor of a major collection of Impressionist and post-Impressionist paintings; and enough of a gourmet to walk casually through a wall of French paratroopers during the Algerian crisis to get to a favorite Paris restaurant. His six children would have glimpses of the private person in uncharacteristic moments, as when he invited such intimacies as joining him in the bathtub; but for them, as for the world, he was primarily a banker and a Rockefeller.

In 1960 the New York *Post* suggested David as the ideal fusion candidate for Mayor. David's interest was piqued, yet he was not really tempted because he knew he was already able to achieve political ends (be it remodeling New York City or making foreign policy) without the necessity of submitting to the political process. Not yet forty-five, he knew he could soon expect to be president of the Chase and chairman of its board. There was the possibility of taking a high appointive post to cap his career later, he told intimates, but for now he could serve himself and his family best by staying in the institution that was the cornerstone of their power.

CHAPTER 16

N elson was pleased by the achievements of David and his other brothers, if for no other reason than that they were like jewels surrounding his own career and setting it off to better advantage. In 1950 he had returned to Washington to chair Truman's International Development Advisory Board and between April 1953 and December 1955 he had held top positions in the new Eisenhower administration. But when he left

Washington for the third time, he felt that he would never return as Secretary of State, as he had once hoped. He had burned too many bridges for even a Rockefeller to repair. Nor was he the sort of man to mend fences or, like Dulles, to spend half a career in intrigue and humbling maneuvers within the Republican party to achieve a high policy-making position. He returned to New York, therefore, at a crossroad in his life. It was as his friend and adviser A. A. Berle, Jr.,, noted in his diary after a telephone conversation with Rockefeller on April 4, 1956: "With Nelson . . . the question is what to do with his life; and with the most magnificent 'do-it-yourself' kit ever provided; only it has no plans or suggestions."

While making up his mind, Nelson resumed his old position of influence in family institutions as president of Rockefeller Center and again became a presence in the Family Office. Along with the Brothers' careers, the office had grown to the point where, in 1956, there were more than one hundred employees in the major departments of taxes, accounting, investments, public relations, and philanthropy. The Office now handled every aspect of the family's life—from paying the small army of gardeners and groundskeepers in charge of Pocantico and the other estates, to scheduling travel on the family's three airplanes. Unofficially it was "Room 5600," although it had long since expanded beyond the 56th floor to parts of the floors above and below.

The Rockefeller Brothers Fund (or "RBF," as it had become known in the family's burgeoning system of acronyms) had also expanded in size and influence. In the growing bureaucracy of the Office, it had become the premier institution of the third generation, and Nelson also settled into its presidency. The Fund was the perfect place for him. Under JDR3's administration, it had not developed any strong identity that would restrict him when he sought to make it conform to his purposes. And unlike the Rockefeller Foundation, it had not become an independent foundation with an independent board of trustees. It existed to serve the Rockefeller Brothers, and its philanthropy was still conceived primarily as advancing the specific causes associated with their personal careers and interests.

From the moment in 1956 when he replaced his older brother as its president, Nelson proceeded to transform the Fund into a personal instrument reflecting his new realization that the kind of power he aspired to could come only through an electoral mandate. It was not a new idea. As early as 1949, it had been suggested that he run for mayor of New York. (One of his aides responded, "He doesn't want to be Mayor, he wants to be Pope.") Seven years later, Republican leaders had actively considered him as a possible candidate for the Senate seat being vacated by Irving Ives. But Nelson had made up his mind that he was going to run for the governorship, a stepping-stone Al Smith, FDR, and Tom Dewey had used before him in their bids for the presidency—the only goal worthy of his ambition.

The gubernatorial elections were not to be held until 1958. In the interim, the Rockefeller Brothers Fund was a perfect vehicle to keep Nelson's name before the public. By far the most ambitious effort he undertook was assembling the Rockefeller Panel Studies, an enterprise that brought the four Brothers together for a climactic show of their joint ability to influence national policy. When, three years later, the studies were completed and published under the title *Prospect for America,* the directors had spent over a million dollars in gathering nearly a hundred of the most illustrious and influential names in America for the project. It may have originated in a sense of pique at having been shunned by the Eisenhower administration, a determination to go ahead and create a personal manifesto for a Rockefeller party. But by the time six panels had produced their reports, the recommendations would be incorporated into both party platforms in the 1960 presidential elections and would exert a profound influence on the course of America's military policies and domestic affairs over the next troubled decade.

The entire Special Studies Project reflected Nelson's apocalyptic vision of the cold war. ("At issue is nothing less than the future of America and the freedom of the world," he announced in the preamble to the final report.) But international security was the object of his keenest interest. The Panel II report could be easily interpreted as a point-by-point rejection of the Eisenhower defense policies and, particularly, of the administration's efforts to impose budgetary limits on military spending. "When the security of the United States and of the free world is at stake," Panel II declared in one of its most memorable passages, "cost cannot be the basic consideration." In a direct challenge to the President's military prestige, Panel II charged that present defense spending was "insufficient to maintain even our current force levels" and recommended "successive additions on the order of $3 billion each year for the next several fiscal years." Pressing priorities included missile development and antimissiles, the expansion of conventional mobile units "essential for limited war," and the initiation of a national civil defense program of fallout shelters to prepare the country for all-out nuclear war.

By the spring of 1958, Nelson had come to a familiar point in his projects where, having gotten something going, he began to lose interest and was content to turn things over to others. With most of the panel reports either published or close to publication, he stepped down, leaving Laurance, as the new chairman of the Special Studies Project and president of the RBF, to finish up the details. As for himself, he was now ready to declare his candidacy for governor and turn his full attention to the electoral struggle ahead.

At first he met with unexpected resistance. Some members of the family, notably JDR3, sensed a great difference between public service, as exemplified by sitting on commissions and accepting appointive posts, and the aggressive pursuit of office through public combat that would revive old antagonisms. The impulse to shield the family from publicity was shared to a degree by David, and by the female members of the family, who had no direct voice in the councils of Room 5600. But for Nelson these were qualms not worth considering.

Nineteen fifty-eight, the experts agreed, was going to be a "Democratic year." Tom Dewey told Nelson to forget it. Even Frank Jamieson, who had been guiding Rockefeller toward a political career for more than fifteen years, agreed that he should bide his time. Yet, ironically, the incumbent governor, Averell Harriman, helped make up Nelson's mind. Having noted ironically in 1957 that the Republican chances were so dim they ought to try a long shot "like Nelson Rockefeller," he also appointed him head of a bipartisan state commission, delegated to resolve a dispute between the parties over reapportionment. The Commission on a Constitutional Convention (its published findings ran to seventeen volumes) allowed Nelson to travel around the state talking to local political leaders and becoming associated in the voters' minds with state problems.

His identification with the New Deal and with massive federal spending did not make him a favorite of upstate New Yorkers. Yet potential primary opposition to Rockefeller, never strong to begin with, was demoralized by the prospects of battling Rockefeller money and by gloomy predictions of a Democratic landslide. In August, when the Republican state convention met, no other name was entered against him.

When he went upstate before conservative audiences, Rockefeller hammered away at the Harriman administration's deficit spending. But the Democratic stronghold of New York City provided a milieu that drew out the many facets of his political personality. There he campaigned as a liberal, drawing on the connections and alliances his family had established in three generations of living and giving. Negroes were reminded that the Rockefellers had funded Spelman College, built the Paul Laurence Dunbar apartments, and kept the Urban League alive. Jews knew that the Rockefellers had been generous in purchasing Israel bonds and had contributed to Jewish philanthropies. Union members were made conscious of the high regard their leaders had for Nelson. The average person was surrounded by the family's building projects—Rockefeller Center, the Cloisters, and the Museum of Modern Art, the massive Lincoln Center project JDR3 had helped begin, and David's ambitious plans for the restoration of the downtown area.

Nelson did not impress anybody by his ability as a platform speaker. From the beginning, the professionals on his staff had cringed when he began to read prepared remarks, his dyslexia causing him to stumble over words, invert phrases, and look generally puzzled as he tried to decipher the paper in front of him. (Eventually he would partially overcome this difficulty by memorizing key sections of his speeches.) Yet he had an asset that overcame all this—the ability to participate in politics as a contact sport. The excitement of the crowds he plunged recklessly into was not in thinking him a common man, but in the fact that he was willing to drop the posture of a frigid aristocrat and, for a moment at least, act like one of them. It was a special charisma, drawn out of the name. They liked to see him and touch him. He knew they liked it and played it to the hilt.

He was the perfect candidate for New York City's multiple personalities. He campaigned through Harlem on a flatbed truck with Count Basie sitting at the piano beside him; he spoke to Puerto Rican audiences in Spanish that was by now fairly fluent; his already nasal voice developed a more pronounced plebeian twang when he spoke to workers on the job. The issues of the campaign became secondary when Nelson arrived at a crowd gathered by his advance men and treated it to the spectacle of a Rockefeller donning beanies, twirling Hula-Hoops, eating any kind of ethnic food in sight.

As in the old days at the coordinator's office, he drove himself remorselessly, getting at most six hours' sleep a night as he toured nearly 8,500 miles throughout the state and made more than 100 formal speeches. Jamieson, to make sure Rockefeller's odyssey was fully covered, organized what for its time was an innovative media campaign: he assigned a television crew to accompany Nelson and hand out film of some aspect of the day's campaigning each afternoon to local television stations that might not have been able to cover it themselves.

Another Democrat might have used Rockefeller's wealth against him, but Harriman too was the scion of a robber baron fortune and spent as much as the Rockefellers in what the papers billed as "the millionaires' sweepstakes." The govenor tried unsuccessfully to make the election a referendum on the Eisenhower administration, but Nelson stayed on the offensive. By the end of the campaign Harriman's tall patrician figure was wilted by fatigue and his gaunt features sagged in defeat. Nelson appeared even more youthful and vigorous by comparison.

It was still early on the evening of November 5 when the governor appeared at the Biltmore ballroom to make a concession speech. Just blocks away, Nelson was pushing through crowds and flashing the toothy grin that pulled his eyes into slits. Surrounded by his wife Tod and his favorite son, Michael, he surged forward to claim victory. History was present a few weeks later when, on New Year's Eve, he paid homage to the tradition that had produced him by taking the oath of office with his right hand resting on his Great-Grandmother Eliza's Bible.

It was hard to tell, so completely had he perfected the suppression of emotion, but no one was more profoundly moved by Nelson's swearing in than his father. Now eighty-five years old and growing feeble in body if not in mind, Mr. Junior was proud of all his sons—less specifically for what they had accomplished, perhaps, than for the way their success vindicated his own efforts as a parent. In 1955, after reading a collective portrait of the boys that had recently appeared in *Fortune,* he wrote them a joint letter (as he often did on important occasions). "What you are doing for the well being of mankind throughout the world is breathtaking," he said. "How proud I am of the contribution you are making to your day and generation, of the wise, intelligent, unassuming way in which you are making it, and above all, of the kind of men you are! To our family have come unprecedented opportunities. With the opportunities have come equally great responsibilities. Magnificently and modestly you boys are measuring up to those opportunities and responsibilities."

When they first came back from the war and began taking over the Office and other institutions he had built, Junior had been disturbed, feeling once again that he really didn't know his sons and hoping that *their* associates would help explain them to him. In effect, they were telling him that youth must be served and that he had to stand back even though he felt in the prime of his life. They rejected advisers like Debevoise, who had served him long and faithfully, and began changing the nature of the family's identity, doing things that were foreign to him and ignoring others he thought were important. He could have stopped them; yet the fact that they should *want* to shoulder the responsibility, he knew, was the fulfillment of the hopes he and Abby had had when raising them.

He had tried to step gracefully into the background, not leaving the family concerns, but rather narrowing the scope of his interests so as not to conflict with them.

Throughout the early fifties, Junior continued to come to the Office whenever he was in town and sit for long hours at the great Jacobean desk taking care of business he thought important and trying to get an idea of the affairs in which his sons were gradually involving themselves and the family. If nothing else, he still had had the power of the purse, controlling the almost $200 million of the great fortune not set aside in trust funds for his descendants. If his sons wanted ready money for one of their projects and did not want to invade the principal of their trusts, they still came to him. He was the one who paid the bills of the Office. He was still the patriarch, as he had in a way been since he was a young man, yet his powers were fading day by day.

For years he had shunned public recognition. But by the mid-1950s he capitulated to becoming a celebrity, acknowledging the fact that the apotheosis begun some forty years earlier by an obscure chain of events on the wind-swept plains of southern Colorado was now complete. His name was the best one an organization like the United Negro College Fund could have on its letterhead; his presence at a ceremonial occasion gave the event a moral authority nobody else could have provided. In 1956 his friend Henry Luce put him on the cover of *Time;* the feature story, entitled "The Good Man," noted that "it is because John D. Rockefeller Junior's is a life of constructive social giving that he ranks as an authentic American hero, just as certainly as any general who ever won a victory for an American army or any statesman who triumphed in behalf of U.S. diplomacy."

He had been devastated by Abby's death in 1948. Not long after the funeral, he had invited the entire staff of Room 5600 to Pocantico. With a black shawl on his shoulders he had shown them around the house and gardens, talking incessantly about his dead wife and telling them how much he had cared for her. He was terribly lonely, almost lost, without her, and his sons had breathed a sigh of relief when, in 1951, Junior married Martha Baird Allen, 56-year-old widow of Arthur Allen, an old college friend from Brown. All the Brothers liked "Aunt Martha," although later, as their father got weaker, relations became strained when they felt she monopolized Junior and made it difficult for them to see him. They knew the remarriage was no slight to their mother's memory. It provided Junior with companionship, as well as a way of arranging his residual estate for tax purposes. (Experts in the Office had arrived at a means of avoiding any estate tax at all, by stipulating that half would go to his wife and half to the tax-exempt Rockefeller Brothers Fund—a device that became known in the accounting trade as a "Rockefeller will.")

Yet as he grew older Junior had not completely embraced that autumnal period of reconciliation said to come with old age, at least not as far as his errant son, Winthrop, was concerned. Winthrop's early failures, his playboy antics, and his climactic fall into disgrace with his marriage and divorce might be forgiven but would never be forgotten.

There was no open break between them; in fact, relations were cordial during Winthrop's frequent visits to New York. Yet Junior never went to Arkansas to see Winrock Farm, or to appreciate his son's other achievements in his new home. It was clear to everyone that Winthrop needed his father's benediction to help resolve the guilt that still lingered from his past; but Junior always declined his invitations, saying that it was far too demanding a trip, even though he and Martha traveled to Arizona each winter. One observer close to the family later said, "Mr. Rockefeller would go to the ends of the earth for the 'well-being of mankind,' as everybody knew, but he wouldn't go three hundred miles out of his way for the well-being of his son."

The patriarchy Junior still exercised at Pocantico revolved around Sunday dinners, which were held in the Big House, with each of his son's families alternating in attendance. When he gave his grandchildren money for their birthdays, the check was usually accompanied by some bit of homiletic advice through which he attempted to transmit the ideals of the family mission to the new generation. The young people meant a great deal to him. Once his friend Fosdick found him unusually happy and asked why. Junior replied that he had just gone out to buy twenty-two Bibles, one for each of the grandchildren. When he agreed to allow his biography to be written, he stipulated that it was only so that his children could "know the sort of man I tried to be."

His last years were given over to thoughts about the family name now that he had finished his own mission. Although to the public he was the anonymous Rockefeller, little more than a bridge between a notorious father and famous sons, he had done his part. He had protected and replenished his inheritance, but also used it so that future generations would inherit an awesome name. It might not have occurred to him to use the word "dynasty." Yet there was something—a moral and social ambience—stemming from his own efforts to distinguish his family from other families of great wealth who might have bequeathed large gifts to society but had never dedicated themselves to the merger of national and personal ambition in quite the way he had.

In 1959 he had a prostate operation. By early 1960, he was eighty-six and increasingly feeble, the bones sticking out prominently from his face, and his knobby fingers shaking so badly from palsy that he could hardly write. He often sat by the window, a blanket tucked around his knees, the spring sun streaming in to warm him as he received old friends for what they both knew were last visits. His work done through his sons, he suddenly seemed to have little use for them and bewildered them by his desire to be alone. On May 11, 1960, Mr. Junior died, having paid so long and so well for his father's transgressions that the entire world was now in his debt.

He was the archetypal Rockefeller, and his passing came at a time when his greatest creation, the family itself, was at its high point. Yet it was possible for some to see that his death left the family poorer than it had been, and weakened it against the future. His grandson, John D. Rockefeller IV, who flew home from studies in Japan to attend the memorial service, recalled later: "It was quite powerful, the whole experience of grandfather's death. I remember feeling strongly the idea that more than my grandfather had died. It was the end of an era. It was history itself passing on."

Junior's passing, however, did not affect his sons the way their mother's had. The bargain between the old man and his boys had hinged on achievement, not affection, a contract involving the fulfillment of his family design. He had been a sponsor and a Pygmalion; in return, they had taken on the responsibilities he had accumulated. They mourned discreetly, yet far from being overcome with grief, the third Rockefeller generation seemed to heave an unconscious sigh of relief with the passing of the man who had been father, taskmaster, and symbol.

CHAPTER 17

Nelson had hardly achieved his first electoral triumph, than he was running for office again. In his inaugural address as governor, he had urged New Yorkers to show the way to a better world, as though they were but the advance guard in his larger constituency. Barely two months after spending his first full day as governor arranging his favorite Picassos and Légers on the walls of the Executive Mansion, he had converted a pair of town houses he owned on 55th Street into a New York political office. There he installed a large staff with the go-ahead to pursue discreetly the 1960 Republican presidential nomination. The operation was soon in high gear and running so well that, as T. H. White later remarked, John F. Kennedy's own efforts that same spring were "by comparison a Montana roadshow."

Nelson knew he had ignited the fancy of citizen Republicans all over the country in his 1958 campaign; and he knew, too, that a poll commissioned by Nixon's own people showed him leading the Vice-President 40 percent to 38 percent among rank-and-file voters. The question was how the party bosses would regard him and his upstart challenge. Beginning in May, he embarked on a highly publicized national speaking tour that also offered occasions to duck into smoke-filled rooms and receive his answer.

Nelson's eye had been on the White House at least since leaving the Eisenhower administration. The thought of the alternative, Richard Nixon, had only strengthened his resolve. Nelson had not been reluctant to make his low opinion of the Vice-President well-known. Nixon had the wrong ideas, the wrong friends, the wrong reasons for seeking power. He had no vision of the Republican party, let alone the presidency. In challenging the iron law of politics that said Nixon was heir apparent to the nomination, Nelson felt he was justified because, as T. H. White later wrote, the party was "almost a dependency of the Rockefeller family, like the Rockefeller Foundation or Rockefeller University." Nelson was not above taking the skeptical aside, pulling a neatly folded piece of paper with a dollar figure on it out of his breast pocket, and telling them that the astoundingly high sum they saw written on it in blue ink was the Rockefellers' bounty to Republicans over the years.

The people who came to see Nelson on his tour liked his enthusiasm and the populist twang in his voice. Yet the county chairmen and other party caciques were less enthusiastic. Nixon had sedulously worked the vineyards of state and local campaigns during the previous six years as a stand-in for a President who was not, in their oblique phrase, "politically conditioned." They owed him, and payment of their debt was the oil that made party machinery work. Yet they might have been persuaded to forget this if they had not had doubts about Rockefeller's version of Republicanism, which seemed so far from the cautiousness of the midwestern heartland that Ike had tapped for eight good years.

For the first time in his political career, Nelson began to feel the latent strength of that wing of the party for which Robert Taft had long been spokesman—oriented to the middle of the country; suspicious of internationalism, Wall Street, and the East; not comfortable with big ideas and big budgets. Even Wall Street, his own natural constituency, was not willing to gamble on him. One of Nelson's first probing acts had been to get his brother David and J. R. Dilworth of the Family Office to canvass the financial community. They found big business Republicans solidly behind Nixon. It was not because they especially liked him (they knew, in fact, that there was little ideological space between the two men and that Nixon, of all the Eisenhower administration, had been most receptive to Nelson's hard-line ideas); it was rather that they saw the Vice-President as a political *tabula rasa* on which they could write their own interests. A Rockefeller, on the other hand, immune from controls imposed by begging for contributions, might be destructively headstrong.

The route was still open for Nelson to enter the primaries and prove what he had been saying all along to party professionals—that Nixon couldn't win with the voters. Yet this would have involved running head-on against Eisenhower himself. As much as he felt that the administration had been an indecisive and incompetent interlude between the New Deal and the future, Nelson didn't need convincing that it would be political suicide for him to repudiate publicly the past eight years.

The campaign committee he had assembled continued to work for some kind of leverage. Emmet Hughes, a prominent journalist and former Eisenhower speech writer, joined Henry Kissinger as Nelson's chief ideologue and worked to establish positions that would put Nixon on the defensive. Yet toward the end of 1959, after six discouraging months of "taking soundings," Nelson realized he was in a no-win position. The day after Christmas he read a statement prepared by Hughes announcing his withdrawal from a contest he had never formally entered.

Yet he still hoped. When the Summit meeting of heads of state collapsed on May 17, 1960, following the downing of a U-2 spy plane over Russia and Eisenhower's refusal to apologize for the incident, Nelson saw the chance he had been waiting for. He had his friend and adviser Oren Root study the possibilities of organizing a draft movement like the one Root had as a young man put together for Wendell Willkie; and he allowed his operative L. Judson Morhouse to spread the word he was available, and that he had decided to attend the convention after all. On Memorial Day, only seven weeks before the delegates were scheduled to meet in Chicago, Nelson closeted himself with Hughes for a long brainstorming session. He emerged to launch a *Blitzkrieg* against the Republican party and Nixon. "I am deeply concerned," Rockefeller told the press in his opening barrage on June 8, "that those now assuming control of the Republican Party have failed to make clear where this party is heading and where it proposes to lead the nation." Referring to a "dangerous missile gap" between the United States and the Soviet Union, he called for a $5 billion increase in defense spending, a $500 million increase in civil defense, and a stepping up of the national growth rate by 50 percent.

Rockefeller's decisive assault on the Republican party and its heir apparent continued right up to the convention. Nixon, who had justified his nomination by a series of victories in the primaries, viewed the governor's attacks with mounting apprehension. Then, only a few days before the convention opening, Rockefeller announced that the party platform—a document which in normal circumstances would get little public attention—was unsatisfactory and indicated that there would be a floor fight to change it. Desperate to avoid any disunity, Nixon instructed former Attorney General Herbert Brownell to call the governor's aides and request a meeting to talk things over. Rockefeller then laid down the conditions that would continue to rankle his rival in years to come, as their political paths and personalities became more deeply entangled than either of them imagined possible: the Vice-President would have to call Nelson personally to request the meeting; it would have to take place at a location of Nelson's choosing; and Rockefeller would control the press release announcing the outcome.

On July 23, two days before the Republican convention was scheduled to open, Nixon made the humiliating journey to New York. Starting with dinner at Nelson's 32-room *pied-à-terre* apartment with Nelson flatly refusing to consider taking the vice-presidential nomination, the two men worked until three A.M. rewriting the platform to include fourteen of Nelson's points—among them his tougher defense position and more liberal posturing on civil rights. When they were finished, they relayed the decision over a special telephone trunk line Nelson had had installed for the occasion to the astonished platform committee, which had already wrapped up its work after deliberating for weeks in Chicago.

The Compact of Fifth Avenue, as it was called, angered Eisenhower because it seemed like a repudiation of his eight years in office, and seemed especially harshly critical of his handling of foreign and military affairs. From the conservative camp, Senator Barry Goldwater called it "the Munich of the Republican Party." To Nelson such charges only confirmed the fact he had won. Waving the agreement in front of newsmen when he arrived at the convention in Chicago, he said, "If you don't think this represents my views, you're crazy." Not bothering to calculate the number or the bitterness of the enemies he was making, Nelson climaxed a virtuoso performance when he agreed to appear before the convention on the final night (he had refused to nominate Nixon) to introduce the candidate. With the audience gasping in surprise, he capped the usual litany of hortatory clauses by saying, ". . . and the man who will succeed Dwight D. Eisenhower next January—Richard E. Nixon!"

Yet despite the gaffe (which he would arrange to have corrected in the official transcript of the speech), Nelson returned to New York jubilant. If Nixon was elected in November, he could take credit for having steered the party in the right direction; if Nixon lost, he could say that it was because he had not leaned far enough in his direction. Either way he would stand in a commanding position the next time Republicans selected a presidential nominee. Nor was Nelson's prestige hurt when John F. Kennedy told confidants after his election that if Rockefeller had been his opponent the Republicans probably would have won.

It was a heady time for Nelson. His popularity was still high in New York, despite a tax increase, and his administration was embarking on a program of public construction that would change the state's physical appearance almost as drastically as its finances. Some of the commitments he undertook in his first term as governor seemed calculated as demonstration projects for the rest of the nation. He moved to make New York the capital of the nation's nuclear industry by creating the State Atomic Research and Development Authority. He also prepared for the possibility of less peaceful uses of atomic energy by proposing a $100 million bomb-shelter program. The New Frontier could not help being interested in what he was doing. After all, many of its characteristic innovations were based on programs and ideas Nelson had done much to pioneer. In fact, the Kennedy administration's main effort—a dramatic escalation in the country's military posture including a multibillion-dollar annual increase in defense spending, emergency step-up in ICBMs, and the development of a counterinsurgency capability that would shortly be tested in Vietnam—was almost a point-by-point implementation of the recommendations of the Rockefeller Brothers Panel Studies.

Nelson was flattered by the President's evident regard. But he was also more obsessed than ever with the dream of someday having his own inaugural parade down Pennsylvania Avenue, especially since Nixon's loss had left the party leadership open. A week after Kennedy's election, Nelson sat down at Pocantico with Emmet Hughes, Harrison and other trusted aides to begin long-range planning for 1964. The group became a sort of shadow Cabinet; its regular meetings were based on the assumption that Nelson's only problem would be overcoming the Kennedy charisma in the general election. Yet Nelson had earned himself a reputation as a renegade and had made a lot of enemies among party regulars and conservatives in Chicago. Bridges had to be repaired, and Nelson set out on the campaign trail once again, this time to woo the Republican right.

His series of carefully calculated moves began with Barry Goldwater, who was then the leader of the conservative wing of the party. Nelson invited the Arizona senator to intimate lunches at his Foxhall Road mansion in Washington to explain his political philosophy and views. By the beginning of 1962 (according to Washington reporter Robert Evans) Goldwater was telling his conservative friends, "Rocky's really not such a bad fellow. He's more conservative than you would imagine. You ought to talk to him someday." A year later he was ready to fade out of the presidential picture because of his newfound faith in the New York governor.

Nelson's ambitions were coming to fruition with a speed that satisfied even him. Yet those who were close to him knew there was a time bomb in his personal life that might well go off at any moment. It was his marriage to Tod, which had been on the rocks for some time. Over the years, she had withdrawn more and more into the role of Calpurnia, the features of her long face congealing into a stoical mask as rumors of her husband's persistent infidelities circulated just within range of her hearing. She had grown accustomed to walking into suddenly hushed conversations about her husband—who he was with now, how he had sent so-and-so on some elaborate fact-finding junket to foreign countries so that he could enjoy the man's wife during his absence.

It could be accepted as part of the seemingly inevitable pornography of political life, although it made the role of Caesar's wife even more unbearable for her than it in any case would have been. Everything in her upbringing recoiled at the vulgarities of the political arena, the meaningless pleasantries of the reception line and of official dinners and entertainments. She was not, in campaign language, "a political asset." Moreover, she could not accept what family friend George Gilder describes as the Great Man Complex: "Tod was smart—smarter and wittier than Nelson, in fact. As he became absorbed in his political career and started believing his campaign literature, it was increasingly difficult for him to come home every night to an amused skeptic, who knew him as he used to be, before he was 'great.'"

Nelson himself had long since realized that the marriage was not working and had settled instead for an arrangement in which appearances would be observed: publicly he would play the role of husband and father; in return Tod would cause no scenes. Privately they would each go their way. But shortly before his first campaign for governor, the rules under which they had managed to live for years ceased to apply when Nelson fell seriously in love and decided that he had to have a divorce. But, in the course of a long meandering automobile ride, he allowed himself to be convinced by his friend Frank Jamieson that it would be political suicide. Nelson's children were grown, and even though he had vast resources for carrying on his current affair, including a "hideaway" on the Pocantico estate, the whole thing had become clumsy. As his emotional and political waves crested together, he felt that it was time to clear the decks.

The first public sign of his troubled marital life came on March 3, 1961, when the Executive Mansion caught fire late one night, and observers noted that firemen escorted Tod to safety from a wing opposite the one where her husband slept. After that, she never returned to Albany, although the separation was not announced. It went unnoticed that Nelson was living alone and shunning social occasions because attention was focused on his entrance into New York City politics, where he hoped to elect Attorney General Louis Lefkowitz mayor and thus not only improve his own chances of carrying the city when he ran for reelection but also show that he was the one Republican capable of dueling JFK for the urban centers in 1964.

On Saturday, November 18, 1961, after this adventure in king making had been beaten back by Mayor Robert Wagner, Nelson officially announced the separation from Tod. He knew there would be repercussions. It was one thing for someone like his brother Winthrop to marry and divorce a lower-class fortune hunter. It was something else entirely for the governor of New York to leave a wife of more than thirty years and the mother of his five children.

Yet the next day something more dramatic forced the separation out of the headlines. Nelson was lunching with his brother David, discussing the impact the news would have on his political future, when the telephone rang. There was a scrambled, terrifying conversation with Dutch officials in New Guinea. It was about Nelson's son Michael, who, with Dutch anthropologist Rene Wassing, had been on a field trip into the Asmat, a remote jungle area rarely visited by white men. The two had rigged a catamaran and begun sailing down the coast of the Arafura Sea, when their craft had been blown off course and out into the open sea. Voices on the other end of the echoing telephone connection said that three days ago Michael had strapped two empty gasoline cans to his back for flotation, left his partner clinging to the wreckage of the boat, and plunged into the shark-infested waters, beginning the eleven-mile swim to shore. Although Wassing had been rescued, nothing had been seen or heard of Michael since.

With this news flaying him as if in retribution for the previous day's announcement about the breakup of his marriage, Nelson chartered a plane and hurriedly left for New Guinea with Michael's twin sister, Mary. For a week they combed the area, coordinating with Dutch search parties as they hedgehopped in light planes over the impenetrable jungle, hoping for some sign that the 23-year-old youth was alive. On November 26 they gave up and began the long return home. At Idlewild Nelson was met by family, state officials, and some two hundred journalists. Afterward he went to his estranged wife's apartment to meet with her and his children. "You had a hard trip, Nels," she greeted him.

"Yes, I'm sorry to bring home such bad news, Tod," he replied.

The broken family was momentarily knit together again by the tragedy as Nelson spread a map of New Guinea on the floor in front of the fireplace and told of the search. After it was over, he got up looking gray and worn, kissed Tod on the cheek, and went home alone.

Michael's death placed an unspoken moratorium on discussions of Nelson's marital situation. In February 1962, Tod went to Reno to file for divorce on grounds of mental cruelty. Nelson brushed off rumors that he was romantically involved with someone else and set out to win reelection, hoping for such a large plurality over his little-known Democratic opponent, Robert Morgenthau, that it would prove conclusively his appeal had not been lessened by the divorce.

Although failing to achieve the million-vote margin he had expected, or even to equal the margin by which he had won in 1958, Nelson was reelected by more than 500,000 votes. Coupled with Nixon's loss in California's gubernatorial race and his vituperative withdrawal from politics, Nelson's triumph in the midst of personal problems that might have sunk another politician gave him an aura of invincibility. Walter Lippmann looked ahead to 1964 and wrote that he was "in the position of a man so certain to be nominated that he could not prevent it if he wanted to." Yet even before the assassination of Kennedy altered America's political course forever, Nelson made what hindsight would prove to be the most disastrous decision in his life: to marry the woman he had loved secretly for more than five years. The last step on the path that began with his separation from Tod, this decision might have had the portentous quality of a trope from classical tragedy if Nelson had possessed the self-recognition necessary for heroic stature. Even though he didn't, the act would come in time to seem as though it contained an element of fate.

The family took the news as a severe blow. Winthrop flew up from Arkansas to argue against it. David was devastated. His daughter Abby recalls: "The remarriage was the most distressing thing to him that ever happened in the world. Nelson was supposed to be the pivot around which the family would build its identity. That was why they all saw it as such a disaster." Neither Winthrop, nor David, nor John attended the wedding, nor did Nelson's four surviving children.

It took place at high noon on May 4, 1963, in the living room of Laurance's home at Pocantico. Nelson seemed younger than his fifty-four years as he stood in front of the minister from the family church at Pocantico Hills exchanging vows with Margaretta ("Happy") Murphy, a pretty 36-year-old society matron with honey-brown hair and a fresh-scrubbed, almost virginal look set off by a blue silk afternoon dress with a demure bow at the neck.

She and the husband she had divorced a month earlier were no strangers to the Rockefeller family. Dr. James ("Robin") Murphy was the son of an old friend of Junior's, and when he had married Happy in 1948, the couple had journeyed to see the Rockefeller patriarch at the Eyrie in Maine. Junior had been much taken with the attractive young couple and took them under his wing, arranging to have the ambitious Robin appointed to a research project of the Rockefeller Medical Institute in San Francisco. The following year Robin wanted to move to New York, and David, who was now the head of the Rockefeller Medical Institute, got him a permanent position at the Institute headquarters. In time, David arranged an unprecedented privilege for the young couple: Happy and Robin would be invited to build a home within the Pocantico Estate. As the family's architect in residence, Nelson naturally conferred with the Murphys at length about the sort of home they planned to build.

Outwardly Happy and Robin were the perfect couple, their relationship seemingly cemented over the years by four children. They were among the few outsiders allowed within the Rockefellers' charmed circle. Yet the taste of intimacy only created an appetite for more. Ironically, it was Robin Murphy who took the lead. As a close Rockefeller friend recalls: "Robin was the chief force in courting Nelson. He truckled to him, laughed too hard at his jokes, praised his art collection too unctuously. He was obvious. Usually the Rockefellers saw through such fawning."

One of the reasons Nelson bore it was the liaison with Happy, begun in the mid-1950s and intensifying after she went to work as a volunteer in his gubernatorial campaign and stayed on as a paid member of his staff. To facilitate the arrangement, Nelson appointed Robin—who privately raged

John D. Rockefeller, Sr., and Laura Spelman ("Cettie") Rockefeller founded the dynasty that became institutionalized in the next generation—represented by John D., Jr., posing below with his family at Seal Harbor, Maine, in 1920. From left: Laurance, Babs, JDR3, Abby with David, Winthrop, Junior, and Nelson.

At far left, Senior and Junior share a purposeful stroll in New York City; below, left, the five Brothers in November 1967, one of their last public appearances together; from left: David, Nelson, Winthrop, Laurance, and JDR3. In his last years Winthrop cultivated a flowing gray beard; at left, as he looked in 1972 shortly before his death. Below, Nelson appears with his bride Happy in May 1963.

The David Rockefellers' children, and two in-laws, from the family's 1973 Christmas card; below, left, Nelson and daughter Mary return from their fruitless search for Michael in 1961; below, right, Jay campaigning in West Virginia.

at Happy, but attempted to maintain outward appearances—to a position in the state health office in Albany. "I'm not sure I really deserve it," he confided pathetically to a family intimate. "I don't know how I'm qualified for it. I guess I must really have impressed Nelson with my work at the Rockefeller Institute or something."

Happy was different from the other women with whom he'd been involved. "Nelson was really deeply in love, and would get terribly romantic, almost sentimental, in talking about Happy during those years he thought he couldn't have her," recalls Frank Jamieson's widow. Happy had youth, beauty, and the rare ability to embody the unattainable.

"She was just dazzling in those days," George Gilder remembers. "She had a way of glowing at you, and her glow made you feel you were the most brilliant man in the world." She took on an almost symbolic quality in Nelson's life. Even as the couple jetted off for a seventeen-day honeymoon at Nelson's 18,000-acre Monte Sacro estate in the Venezuela mountains, Rockefeller's conservative opponents in the GOP—never fully convinced by his attempts after 1960 to mend fences with them—began to see that they might bring him down from his high perch in the party's future by pinning a morals charge on him. Divorce was one thing; remarriage was something else again, especially when the bride had to give up custody of four small children in her hasty trip to the altar. A Gallup Poll taken three weeks afterward confirmed that it had indeed done significant damage to Nelson's political hopes. The 43 to 26 percent lead he had enjoyed over Barry Goldwater before the wedding announcement had now vanished, and he trailed the Arizona senator 35 to 30 percent.

The new situation would have demanded a new strategy. He could not promote party unity as he would have if he had been the favorite; only a bloodletting could win him the prize. He would now declare war in the name of liberal values on the right wing he had covertly courted for the past two years. On July 14, 1963, he unveiled his new position with a bombshell declaration against Goldwater (whom he did not yet name) and the "well-drilled extremists" whom he had suddenly discovered "boring from within the party."

By September 15 a Gallup Poll showed that Goldwater was leading Rockefeller by a 59 to 41 percent margin among Republican voters. Yet the Rockefeller camp, fueled by its leader's inexhaustible determination and resources, was emphatically optimistic. "There is nothing wrong with Rockefeller," declared Charles F. Moore, who had left a spectacular career at Ford to manage Rockefeller's public relations in the primaries, "that can't be cured by a win in New Hampshire."

By early 1964, as the primaries were about to begin, Rockefeller had assembled the most elaborate political apparatus ever seen for a primary struggle in the history of American presidential elections. Before it was over, his official campaign would spend $8 million, the bulk of it from his own and his family's funds. He would get Laurance and the crestfallen David to make generous contributions, and he would receive others from Junior's widow, Martha Baird. Once he officially announced his candidacy, his paid campaign staff was increased from seventy to three hundred, and it was operating out of Rockefeller Center, the West 55th Street brownstones, an entire floor of an office building at 521 Fifth Avenue, and a suite of rooms in the United Rubber Building on West 49th Street.

New Hampshire was supposed to be a political weather vane, showing how public opinion would sort out Nelson's remarriage and his attacks on Goldwater's ideology. Rockfeller spent weeks slogging through the snows of the state with the pregnant Happy beside him. It was a bone-wearying effort that wound up inconclusively. Rockefeller forces spent hundreds of thousands of dollars, but when the votes were in, Henry Cabot Lodge, a write-in candidate, had scored 35 percent of the vote, Goldwater 23 percent, and Nelson 20 percent.

Yet he was undaunted. Setting out for Oregon like a driven man, he waged an exhausting campaign that left him gray and drawn, but rewarded him with a bracing primary victory over Lodge. The stage was set for the climactic battle in California.

Nearly half of the $3 million Nelson had budgeted for the primaries was spent in California, publicizing select Goldwaterisms about the bomb, Social Security, Medicare, and civil rights. One of these, a pamphlet titled *Whom Do You Want in the Room with the H-Bomb Button?*, was distributed to two million California voters.

It was a cruel campaign for Rockefeller, who had to run through the heartland of the John Birch Society and the radical right in Orange County. There were bomb threats; a tea party attended by Nelson and Happy was crashed by thugs; and there were endless organized calls to radio talk shows complaining about the remarriage and describing the liberal Republican candidate as morally unfit for the presidency. But for a while it looked as though Nelson might pull off his miracle. The Friday before the primary, the prestigious Field Poll showed Rockefeller leading Goldwater 49 percent to 40 percent. But then came the final ironic twist in the crooked path leading from the decision to divorce Tod. On Saturday night, three days before the primary, Happy Rockefeller entered a

New York hospital to give birth to a son—Nelson, Jr. The following day, a new Field Poll showed Rockefeller and Goldwater even. And when the voters went to the polls on Tuesday, the momentum caused by this reminder of Nelson's marital escapades gave his opponent a narrow victory and the 1964 presidential nomination.

Thrust into the unaccustomed role of loser, Rockefeller returned to San Francisco a month later as titular head of the anti-Goldwater forces at the convention. When he stood defiantly before the convention whose candidate he had denigrated and whose philosophy he had mocked, he was even more the enemy than Democratic candidate Lyndon Johnson. It was as if Nelson had decided that if he couldn't have their affection, he would at least have their hatred, and he baited them into howling at him and interrupting his speech ("This is still a democracy, ladies and gentlemen," he lectured them) as if to prove on national television that they were the wrathful, intolerant zealots he had all along claimed them to be.

If 1964 was a time when he won a large following among those who interpreted his confrontation with Goldwater as a courageous moral stand, it also seemed to be the end of whatever realistic hopes Nelson may have had of being nominated by his party for the presidency. He would never be able to give up his quest, but he could no longer believe as he had that it would naturally come to him. After the November Democratic landslide, old comrades like Senator Jacob Javits urged Nelson to remove himself from future presidential contention. They didn't want a repeat of 1964. And they told him so.

Politics, which had always been enjoyable for him, a true recreation, now came to seem a harsh exercise in survival. At the 1965 Governors' Conference, he announced his withdrawal from national politics to help unify the party. But this gesture got him little thanks from those whom he had used so cavalierly for his own ends. When, that same year, he gave John Lindsay half a million in loans, which Lindsay had demanded to run as Nelson's hand-picked candidate in the New York mayoralty race, it was because he knew that the glow had worn off his own administration, especially with the upstate conservatives irritated at the massive debt with which he was saddling the state. He would have to count on heavy support from the city in his next campaign.

When he himself entered the 1966 gubernatorial contest, it was against a Democratic candidate who was far ahead in the polls. It was not that Frank O'Connor was popular, but that Nelson's appeal had slipped to the point where early polls had shown him getting only 25 percent of the vote against *any* candidate.

Realizing that he was in the fight of his political life, Nelson spent an incredible $5.2 million on the gubernatorial race, almost ten times as much as O'Connor. The focus of Nelson's campaign was a devastating two-stage media attack. In its first weeks, when he was 26 percentage points behind O'Connor in the polls, Rockefeller advertisements stressed the achievements of his two terms: overhauling and dramatic expansion of the state university system, building tens of thousands of miles of new highways, and the like. Then, in the last weeks of the campaign, as he began to pull even, he turned to attacks on his opponent, who had failed to adopt his "tough" attitude on urban crime. During the final days of the campaign, television viewers were blitzed with commercials showing a syringe entering the main line, or hoodlums walking menacingly on dark, rain-slicked streets. The voice-over was that of Nelson, and it rasped: "Want to keep the crime rate high? Vote for O'Connor."

Nelson's media blitz would later be studied as a textbook example of the way an unprincipled use of television could affect the outcome of a campaign. Yet the campaign itself, regarded as one of the most ruthless in recent New York history, was successful. The usually infallible New York *Daily News* straw poll picked O'Connor, but Nelson's narrow victory proved it wrong for the first time in thirty years.

In postelection statements, Nelson again disclaimed any intention to run for the presidency in 1968. Bill Moyers was correct in his assessment of these weary disavowals of ambition: "I believe Rocky when he says he's lost his ambition. I also believe he remembers where he put it."

A week after his defeat of O'Connor, in fact, Nelson was running again. Of the new generation of Republican moderates clamoring for a chance at the nomination of 1968, Governor George Romney, who had won resounding victories in Michigan in three successive elections, was the leader. And it was Romney that Rockefeller invited to join him at his brother Laurance's Dorado Beach Hotel in December for conversations about the party's future.

Romney was far and away the leader in the polls. It was true that he had a reputation for making confusing statements and lacked a clear perspective of foreign affairs, but since he was the front-runner, and the last thing Nelson could afford was to create a schism within the moderate wing of the party, he urged him to get his candidacy going early. During the days they talked in the Puerto Rico sun, Nelson promised Romney the backing of the Republican governors (whose titular head he was) as well as money, workers, and the wide range of other resources that went into a typical Rockefeller campaign.

One Republican leader later said that the Michigan governor's campaign for the presidency had been like "watching a duck try to make love to a football." His most inept maneuver (although events would ultimately vindicate him in an odd way) had been his offhand statement in August 1967 that he had been "brainwashed" by U.S. generals while touring Vietnam. By the end of 1967, his credibility had sunk so low and he was lagging so far behind Nixon in the polls that he came to Nelson and asked to be relieved of his commitment to run. But Rockefeller, fearing that a premature Romney withdrawal could result in the moderates' anointing someone like Charles Percy, held him to his word and urged him to hold on through the New Hampshire primary. Only after he was humiliated there did Nelson release him from his obligation.

Yet Rockefeller, still gun-shy from 1964 and aware that he could not risk a primary loss to Nixon, hesitated about his own candidacy in what would strike some of those close to him as an odd and disturbing indecision. In March he formally took himself out of the contest. In April 1968, after LBJ's withdrawal, he announced with equal suddenness that he was a candidate and tried quickly to reassemble his dismantled campaign team, once again conscripting Emmet Hughes and Kissinger.

Hughes made a top-secret trip to California to meet with Ronald Reagan and form the strategy of cooperating to try to squeeze Nixon out of a first-ballot victory. Meanwhile Kissinger attempted to create a Vietnam position for Rockefeller that at least seemed different from the Johnson administration's policies, and prepared a highly confidential "Black Book on Nixon" as a casebook for Nelson to use in attacks on his old rival in the months between April and the convention. (This document, with provocative chapter headings like "The Tricky Dick Syndrome" and "The Loser Image," would remain locked in a closet in Room 5600 long after Kissinger had become the brightest luminary of the Nixon administration and Nelson one of the President's staunchest supporters.)

Yet until June 5, the Rockefeller campaign suffered from an indecisiveness that had uncharacteristically overtaken the candidate. It was as if his political personality, so sharply defined by events four years earlier was now out of focus. He searched for a foothold in space that other politicians occupied more dramatically. It was only when news of Bobby Kennedy's death flashed through New York that Nelson saw an opening in the role of charismatic maverick bucking the establishment and quickly decided to fill it.

Within forty-eight hours of the assassination Nelson had prepared a speech to be followed by a series of newspaper ads saying that he alone now offered a choice between "a new leadership and old politics," and he began a whirlwind tour that took him into cities all over the country, where he would plunge recklessly into crowds, allow young people to rip off his cuff links, and try to build pressure on delegates from below.

By the time he got to Miami, Nelson's attempt to ride past the party bosses on the shoulders of the people had clearly failed. He had spent $8 million in an effort to wrest the nomination away from Richard Nixon, but all he had really done was to help dramatize a convention whose conclusions had been foregone for months, since those crucial moments earlier in the spring when he had equivocated and lost the support of figures like Spiro Agnew who might have helped put him over despite the united opposition of the party regulars who remembered 1964.

Nelson had come a long distance from that time eight years earlier when he had been able to rewrite the Republican party's platform to suit his pleasure. But most of the way had been downhill. As Nixon was nominated on the first ballot, the prize Nelson had been striving after for more than a decade seemed finally out of his reach. If Nixon defeated Humphrey, as seemed likely, there would doubtless be a clamor among party regulars for four more years in 1972. By 1976, Nelson would be sixty-seven years old—young for a Rockefeller, perhaps, but old for a presidential hopeful. It seemed that he, like Tantalus, would have to learn to live with a raging thirst even while standing waist-deep in the lake.

CHAPTER 18

Nixon's inauguration coincided with a moment when the Rockefellers passed over an epic cusp into an age with new laws of motion slowing the movement that had elevated the family with such velocity during the previous half-century. As if overnight, they began to realize that something had gone out of their world; the pinnacle they had strained so hard to attain was suddenly now behind them, and in the future their children would handle the name and its responsibilities far differently from the way they had. They still had the power they had been born to, but in exercising it they were filled with a foreboding that affected them all in a deep and personal way.

If they did not confront the crisis directly, it was not because they were strangers to crisis. The family had faced and overcome awesome dilemmas in the past. But this was no crisis that they could stage-manage in such a way as to turn guilt into redemption. In fact, there was no single event they could focus on and hold responsible for the malaise that now took hold of them. It was something that was happening to them, not *because* of them.

One of its manifestations was the resurgence of an anti-Rockefeller zeal that had not been seen since World War I. The revival was due partly to Nelson's political campaigns, his readiness to use the immense resources at his command to achieve ends that were obviously connected to his own ambitions and desires. In his reckless flaunting of self, as in his opting for a political career in the first place, he had violated his father's lessons in pragmatic morality. Only if the Rockefellers stayed in the background and strenuously drained personality from their acts could the hatred of the Rockefeller wealth be kept dormant. Nelson had stirred up sleeping dragons.

The conservative Republican heartlands, which periodically had seen their presidential favorites blocked by the powerful caucus of eastern finance, had come to see that power personified in Rockefeller and the Rockefeller institutions. A pamphlet that served as the call to arms of the Goldwater campaign described how "the secret New York kingmakers" had controlled every Republican nominee since 1936, "to insure control of the largest cash market in the world: the Executive Branch of the United States Government." and how Nixon's 1960 "surrender in Manhattan" to Nelson was but the latest phase of their long, undemocratic *coup*.

Nelson was the immediate target, but in the long run such arguments were aimed at the name itself as the symbolic expression of forces drastically affecting American life. Whether the discussion was about big government or big business, the Rockefellers were potent representatives of both. Even the bizarre linking of the Rockefellers with the Communist conspiracy in right-wing demonologies seemed to make sense when it was coupled with the view that Socialism was not a share-the-wealth program but a method to consolidate and control economic life.

Underlying this unease was a sense that things were increasingly out of control, that "insiders" manipulated the government through interlocking directorates and elite organizations, like the Council on Foreign Relations, which dominated policy while operating outside the democratic process. "They" controlled things but were not accountable. And among those who conspired to run the world from behind the scenes, the secretive Rockefellers ranked at the very top.

Nor was the right wing alone in seeing the family as a symbol of unchecked plutocratic power and conspiratorial control. The left also revived the anti-Rockefeller tradition going back to the muckrakers, as the cold war consensus that had dominated the thought of the preceding decade foundered on the shoals of Vietnam, and readmitted critiques of wealth, power, and corporate predation into the cultural mainstream.

Consequently, although they were doing nothing different from what they had done for decades, the Rockefeller Brothers suddenly found themselves demonstrated against and denounced, the subject of "underground" exposés and ingenious diagrams which showed the interests and institutions interlocking them with apartheid in South Africa, militarism in Latin America, war in Indochina.

The family's secrecy and its global involvements could plausibly suggest a Byzantine network of control, feeding the right's fear of conspiracy on the one hand and left-wing paranoia about the Rockefellers on the other. When economist Victor Perlo claimed that the family directly controlled financial and industrial corporations worth more than $60 billion, this improbable figure was quickly accepted as an article of faith.

If they had not been so conditioned to accept the mythology that enveloped their lives and careers, the Brothers might have realized that a critical juncture had been passed in the dynasty they now controlled. They might have convened a summit meeting at the Playhouse (as they often did to discuss personal matters), away from the employees who stood guard over the Rockefeller myths like harem eunuchs, and tried to unravel the process that was cutting a jagged swath through American history and dragging them behind it. They would have had to step out of the ceremonial roles they had learned to play, and look at themselves objectively—as they might at the priceless artifacts they collected. They would have had to discard the books written by authors they had paid or sanctioned, and try to strip the presumption of manifest destiny from their history and come to grips with the peculiar series of events that had produced their unique family.

It would have been like reconstructing a true version of the family dialectic. It would have to begin with the grandfather—not the venerable old eccentric they had known as boys or the moral paragon their father had spoken of reverently, but the flinty industrialist who had terrorized his competitors and bent the country's economic system to his iron will, even at the cost of becoming a national outcast, as hated as he was feared. Next had come their father, the prim little man who had dedicated his life and the tainted fortune he inherited to changing the adverse view of the family created by the excesses of the Standard trust. He found that he could best ensure against the future hatred of the Rockefeller name by welding the family's destiny to the new political and economic order pro-pelling the nation to a position of global leadership and empire. As he did so, something seemed to lock, and a myth of epic proportions began to take shape.

Far from questioning the symbiosis between their family's destiny and the country's, the Brothers had devoted their careers to forging even stronger links that allowed them power of a kind their grandfather never could have hoped for, and also a kind of invulnerability, as the family's identification with America became so strong that it almost seemed trea-sonable to attack them. The fifties had been *their* era—the time when they came of age and first began to know the impact they might have on the world—and the sixties had begun even more auspiciously. Kennedy was President, but the Brothers had spent years building outposts in that area he now proclaimed a New Frontier. They were representative men of an aristocracy of wealth and power that would influence his adminis-tration, and the others to follow.

They were still regarded as a valuable national resource by the people who counted. Their access to the important nodes of social and econom-ic power was undiminished. Yet there had been a fundamental change in the way the world perceived them. No longer were they knights *sans peur et sans reproche,* as they had been when they were young men making their debuts. Now they were simply men of power, and they found it in-creasingly difficult to use the myth their father had created to avoid being called to account for its exercise.

Not only were they suddenly questioned about things for which they were in some sense responsible—the policies of Standard Oil, the Chase Bank, the Rockefeller Foundation, and other institutions they were in-volved in—but they were also attacked for the sins of the system itself. They had become the most visible embodiments of that sinister power implicit in the "establishment," "power structure," "ruling class," and the host of other terms used to describe the continuum of economic interest and ideological commitment people could not see but felt was responsible for the social and moral chaos of the times. The Rockefellers were influ-ence, money, control, policy. They were power.

It was early in 1973 that the Rockefeller Brothers agreed to grant CBS permission to film a documentary about their lives. They had always re-jected such proposals in the past; but now, with the Watergate crisis and the disarray of the Republican party sharpening Nelson's presidential am-bitions once again and with news of Winthrop's terminal illness reminding them of their mortality, they decided that the time had come for a summary of their joint and individual accomplishments.

Once the decision was made, the filming itself became just another item on calendars already tightly scheduled far into the future. Over a period of several weeks, the Brothers allowed network crews to trail them through their crowded lives. They knew how to put themselves in the hands of experts when their purposes so required. They sat docilely where they were told, posed for background footage when asked, and answered Walter Cronkite's questions on cue. All but Laurance. He wanted to stage his own scenes, setting up his entrances and exits and suggesting that his career might be summarized by vignettes showing him emerging from a swim near his Virgin Islands resort, talking over problems with administrators at the Sloan-Kettering Memorial Cancer clinic, or in some other moment of crucial self-dramatization.

The role of director suited him. He liked orchestrating things and appearances, and a hint of theatricality had always been submerged just below the calm surface of his personality. Each of the Brothers had arrived at his own way of coping with his special vulnerability as a Rockefeller. Laurance's solution had been to create a mask through which he could look out at the world but not really be seen. The idea was to seem more formidable and mysterious than he was, and he had worked as a young man to fashion the poker player's eyes, the mouth turned up at the corners in an enigmatic smile, and the unruffled look of someone more interested in the mechanics of a problem than the morality. It was a face that had served him perfectly in the years when he was just back from the Navy and making his mark as an entrepreneur in the interstices of the military-industrial complex. He had assumed automatically that it would work just as well when he decided to go public as a conservationist. It was a rare miscalculation.

Laurance was quick to recognize that the Outdoor Recreation Resources and Review Commission, to which President Eisenhower appointed him in 1958, would be the bridge leading him from his entrepreneurial past to his conservationist future, and poured more of himself into it than he had previously into any other activity. He spent time in Washington getting to know the congressional leaders and private conservationists serving with him on the commission, the Interior Department sachems, and key businessmen. He smoothed the interfacing between the commission's work and his own private efforts, augmenting the commission staff with aides from his two conservation organizations, Jackson Hole Preserve, Inc., and the American Conservation Association. In

1962, after three years of hard work, he delivered a thick report and twenty-nine supplementary studies to President Kennedy.

Cursed by an ungraceful acronym (ORRRC) and working from a relatively narrow mandate—to inventory the nation's recreation needs and potential to the year 2,000—the commission was not one whose work captured the public imagination, particularly amid the dozens of more glamorous activities and programs of the New Frontier. Yet the conservation establishment around Washington, recognizing it had been several decades since so thorough an evaluation of the nation's Great Outdoors had been made, knew that ORRRC's findings would have resonance in the years to come—especially its recommendations to emphasize the urban centers instead of the western states in future spending for parks and recreation; to adopt a policy of "multiple use" encouraging mining, lumbering, grazing, and other industrial activities on recreation lands; and to create a Bureau of Outdoor Recreation within the Department of Interior to handle work formerly spread among twenty federal agencies.

Laurance moved quickly to capitalize on ORRRC's impact. Even as the report was being delivered to the President, his own American Conservation Association (which would spend nearly $800,000 between 1962 and 1964 promoting the commission's report) gathered over 150 leaders from business, labor, and public affairs into the Citizens' Committee for the ORRRC Report; its aim was to make sure the recommendations got the widest possible circulation and acceptance. If it kept the commission's work in public view, this sort of publicity also kept Laurance's name in front of those who mattered, and when President Kennedy announced a Cabinet-level Advisory Council on Recreation, he appointed Laurance to be its head.

The Outdoor Recreation Resources and Review Commission was the vehicle by which Laurance transformed himself from a gentleman conservationist into a statesman in the emerging environmental movement. By the time ORRRC made its recommendations, in fact, the conservation movement was already developing. When it had first attracted Laurance's serious attention in the mid-1950s, it had been an adventitious outgrowth of the cold war and America's concern about strategic materials. But in the years since the Materials Policy Commission first raised the specter of a resources famine, the emphasis had shifted. The crisis of the next decade would not be based on strategic foreign materials like tin and tungsten, but on the basic resources of air, water, and land, which were increasingly threatened by pollution. The crisis was summarized in the phrase "quality of life," which John Kenneth Galbraith, among others, saw as threatened by a business economy that created artificial consumer wants and failed to calculate the social costs of its production.

Laurance accepted without reservation the idea that growth and conservation could be familiar bedfellows. And, as one straddling the fence between business and environment, he knew he could be an effective salesman of the concept of conservationist concern, allaying the fears of industrial leaders that the push for protection masked an antibusiness attitude. In a 1963 address to the seventieth annual meeting of the Congress of American Industry in New York, he tried to assure businessmen that nothing in the new concern for pure water and air threatened them. "Business can take this development in stride," he counseled, "in the same way it has, over the years, taken in its stride other steps which seemed like broad social rather than economic obligations. Like so many of the others it will turn out in the end to be just plain good business."

While this task force was meeting, Lady Bird Johnson became interested in beautification and indicated it would be her own special area of concern as First Lady. She sought out Laurance's advice. He enthusiastically supported Mrs. Johnson's ideas and helped launch the campaign, traveling with her in her "beautification bus" and later inviting her to become a trustee of Jackson Hole Preserve, Inc.

Lady Bird became one of Laurance's greatest boosters, speaking glowingly of his contributions to beautification and calling him "that number-one conservationist" and "America's leading citizen-conservationist." Early in 1965 LBJ sent Congress a strong message making it clear that conservation would have a high priority in his administration and announcing a White House Conference on Natural Beauty, to be headed by Laurance. One of the conference's results was the creation of a Citizens' Advisory Committee on Recreation and Natural Beauty, with Laurance serving as chairman and charged with advising the White House on environmental matters.

His ascent into the upper reaches of public policy as the President's privy counselor on the environment was remarkably rapid, even for a Rockefeller. He had penetrated officialdom deeply enough to be mentioned as a possible future Secretary of the Interior. But even as he was reaching this pinnacle, his name had ceased to inspire confidence among rank-and-file conservationists, who had turned out to be far more stubborn and independent than was ever contemplated. The grass-roots movement that emerged during the social turmoil of the sixties had a systemic view of the crisis (and a new concept—"ecology"—to describe it), which was not quite what Laurance, "Fair" Osborn, and the others had in mind when they helped christen and launch the bandwagon for environmental quality. Yet when they realized that the movement that had once been made up of weekend hikers and bird watchers was out of control, it was too late to do anything about it. The genie was out of the bottle.

Most of the great conservation battles of the mid-1960s would involve Laurance in some way or another. A harbinger had come in the controversy over Storm King, the massive granite bluff looming up dramatically at the gateway to the Hudson River Highlands. Local residents admired the mountain's weather-beaten face and were unaware that Consolidated Edison had drafted plans to drill into Storm King and hollow it out for a huge hydroelectric pumping station whose reservoir and generators would stand in reserve in case of emergency power needs in Manhattan.

By mid-1962, when the plan was finally made public, Nelson enthusiastically backed it, having been recruited to the project by Building and Trades Union boss Peter Brennan and others whom he had come to depend on as his political base inside organized labor. Nelson praised the plan as "an imaginative, long-term solution for the energy problem"; Laurance followed suit. After meeting with Con Ed executives to make sure that they did not intend to intrude upon the lands of the nearby Palisades Park and to convince them to change plans that had originally called for stringing unsightly transmission lines across Storm King gorge, he announced that he felt the utility's project could actually be "an exercise in democratic planning." Laurance brought his growing national reputation and his prestige as a Palisades Park commissioner and as head of the State Council on Parks (a post to which Nelson had appointed him in 1963 after forcing the aging Robert Moses out of the job) to the decision to back Con Ed. Moreover, as a trustee of the respected Hudson River Conservation Society, a patrician organization that had stood guard over the river since the early 1900s, Laurance was able to persuade its president, William Osborn, to endorse the plan.

Support for Storm King by the state's leading conservationist and the region's leading conservation organization seemed to give the project an indisputable seal of approval. But there were some residents—the sort of people who could generally be counted on as conservative and Republican on most issues—who had doubts. Tentatively at first, and then with growing certainty, they began speaking out against the project, forming an organization they called the Scenic Hudson Preservation Conference. Later they would develop impressive data showing how the pumping station would destroy the Hudson's marine environment, but they began with the same opposition to the disfigurement of the area that had led a wealthy man like John D. Rockefeller, Jr., to begin buying up the Palisades decades earlier to save them from the quarryman's dynamite.

The controversy simmered for a year and then erupted into a *cause célèbre*. As the public became aware of its fight, Scenic Hudson was joined by celebrities like James Cagney, Pete Seeger, and Nelson's son Steven; it hired attorneys to take the matter into court. Meanwhile, its publicists made much of such ironies as the fact that it would take one and a half times as much energy to pump water up to the storage reservoir as would be generated when the water was released. In March 1965, however, the Federal Power Commission ruled against Scenic Hudson, granting Con Ed permission to proceed with construction; one factor that weighed heavily in their decision was the backing Laurance had given it.

In explaining how the man who had been called the country's leading conservationist could be in the opposition camp, Scenic Hudson researchers raised the question of conflict of interest. "Governor Rockefeller and his brother Laurance agreed to that plant through private negotiations with the company," charged one of the organization's founders in the *Cornwall Local*. The purpose of the secrecy, he implied, was to conceal the connection between the agreement and a substantial stock interest in the utility company. Nelson and Laurance's Great-Uncle William Rockefeller had been, in fact, one of the original owners of Con Ed, and based on figures Junior had given investigators in 1937, the family's current holdings would amount to better than $10 million. Yet financial advantage—which in any case would have meant only a fractional increase in the Rockefeller fortune—was not the source of their support for Con Ed. A more plausible reason was later offered to author Robert Boyle by a prominent New York Republican: "The people who own Con Ed are his [Laurance's] people. They're in the same club." It was a philosophical kinship with the project, a belief in the "efficient use" of natural resources and the importance of industrial growth, that committed Nelson and Laurance to their course.

The Storm King battle would rage on in the appeals courts for the next decade. By early 1965, however, the issues it had already raised led an ambitious young Westchester congressman named Richard Ottinger to demand that the Interior Department make the Hudson River Valley a federal preserve, implying it was not safe in its present hands. Later in the year he introduced a bill to make the Hudson and a one-mile strip on either side a national scenic riverway under the jurisdiction of the Interior Department.

The Rockefellers responded quickly to what they regarded as a challenge to their proprietary authority. It was, after all, an area where their father had invested millions in projects like the Palisades Interstate Park and the Sleepy Hollow Restorations (which included the purchase for public use of the famous Philipsburg and Van Cortlandt manors, and Sunnyside, Washington Irving's home) and where he had helped build their family demesne. With $25,000 from his executive chamber budget, and a matching grant from Laurance's American Conservation Association, Nelson created a state watchdog agency called the Hudson River Valley Commission "to protect the river and its surrounding area." Made up of leading citizens like Averell Harriman, IBM's Thomas Watson, and Ford Foundation head Henry Heald, the commission was an attempt to head off federal intervention. Laurance, whom Nelson had named chairman of the new agency, said, "It's a matter of who can best save the Hudson. The Federal government acts in default of state responsibility. The burden should not be shifted to it as long as the State demonstrates the capacity to do the job."

The struggle for authority over the region came to a head in 1965 when the state of New York announced that north-south traffic between the Hudson Valley and Manhattan was becoming a problem and, since Route 9A could not handle it, a superhighway connecting New York City to Croton-on-Hudson must be constructed along the bank of the river. With this, the Rockefeller family's past and present conservation philanthropies—which had made conservationists reluctant to suspect their motives at the onset of the Storm King struggle—ceased to shield them from attack.

Conservationists opposing the damage the highway would do to the Hudson were quick to point out that the planned road had apparently been drawn with the family's Pocantico estate in mind. Indeed, in 1957, when Interstate 87 (as the road was known) first entered the state Department of Transportation's long-term planning, the idea that it might be built along the Hudson, involving an expensive dredge-and-fill operation, was not even seriously considered. At that time, it had been thought that the most economical and logical route would be up through the Pocantico Hills area. The version of I-87 planned during the Harriman administration would have bisected the Rockefeller estate so neatly that Nelson's house would have been on one side of the road and Laurance's on the other. Immediately after Nelson's election, needless to say, these plans were scrapped and the redrawn proposal for I-87 (now called "the Hudson Expressway") moved it five miles west of Pocantico, which placed it parallel to the east bank of the river.

A confidential Interior Department memorandum done at the height of the highway controversy and entitled "Benefits to the Rockefellers from the Expressway" said: "Probably the greatest financial benefit to the Rockefeller family would accrue from the fact that the Expressway, together with the extension of Route 117 from the Expressway to U.S. Highway 9, will open up the Rockefeller holdings to people as far away as New York City." Their father had been interested only in keeping people *away* from Pocantico. Yet Nelson and Laurance were looking ahead to a time when taxes and upkeep would make the family's 3,600-acres a financial burden. Land for residential development in the area was selling for as much as $100,000 an acre, and the two brothers were intrigued with the idea of Pocantico's potential for tasteful condominium and single-family dwellings. The proposed expressway would make the area more available to Manhattan executives.

But the expressway was another of those projects Nelson and Laurance would have supported even if personal considerations had not been in the background. In their view, it was a case where growth was not only desirable but inevitable, and could best be handled by careful planning. "Compatible development" was the term Laurance used to defend it, arguing that the Hudson River area would certainly develop, if not under the state's master plan, then in a spontaneous sprawl. In its 1966 report, the state's Hudson River Valley Commission, as was to be expected, backed the project, claiming that it would "not constitute a significant impairment of the natural resources of the river," but would in fact increase and improve the public's access to the Hudson.

The Rockefellers were oblivious to opposition. New York State Assemblyman Laurance Cabot later told of one occasion when he personally brought a load of anti-expressway mail from his constituents to Nelson's office. Rockefeller glanced perfunctorily at the huge mound of letters, listened to Cabot's speech, and then shrugged. "That's odd," he said, "I haven't heard a single objection to the expressway."

Because of the Hudson River Compact (Ottinger's bill had passed into law in 1966), the Interior Department had to approve the project and grant the U.S. Army Corps of Engineers permission to issue a permit for the construction. Conservationists had assembled a compelling case suggesting that while people would no doubt use the expressway once it was built, there was not enough real demand to justify its construction. They had also commissioned studies from fisheries experts showing how silt deposits from the dredge-and-fill operations would devastate the spawning runs of the shad, striped bass, sturgeon, and other game fish of the area, while also wiping out the propagation beds of native shell-fish. Interior Secretary Stewart Udall seemed persuaded; he was already on record as opposing the road and had written: "Such an expressway in the highly scenic and significantly historic corridor along the Hudson River would seriously impair the values we are all trying to preserve." But as the infighting intensified, the Rockefellers exerted leverage on Udall. It would have taken a stronger man to withstand their pressure.

Udall had already begun to waver on January 25, 1968, when he was summoned to New York for a meeting at Nelson's apartment with the Rockefellers and their aides. Even if he had been willing to buck the governor, it would have been hard to deny a man like Laurance, who was known to have the President's ear on conservation matters. As Udall now says, "It seemed to me that Laurance and the governor were wrong. I didn't really like the highway. But at that meeting they came in with all kinds of charts and reports. It was the *complete* presentation. During the meeting and after, Laurance leaned on me very hard not to interrupt the plans he and Nelson had for the Hudson. He picked up all the outstanding due bills on this one." It was not long after the meeting that Udall told Ed Crafts, director of the Bureau of Outdoor Recreation and a long-time friend of Laurance, that he had now changed his opinion and would no longer oppose the expressway.

When Udall publicly announced his decision to allow the Corps of Engineers to grant a dredge-and-fill permit, the Sierra Club and Citizens Committee for the Hudson Valley (an *ad hoc* group formed in 1965 in Ottinger's district to fight the road) moved into federal district court and were granted an injunction prohibiting construction. The complex legal battle that followed finally ended two years later in 1970 when the U.S. Supreme Court declined to hear New York's appeal on the matter, thus driving a final nail through the heart of the Rockefellers' highway plan.

Laurence's role in these struggles over the Hudson had been hard to pinpoint. His influence was felt, yet he was very much a background figure in a group photograph. Compared to the other starkly defined people, he seemed slightly out of focus, his motion not quite frozen by the camera's shutter. When he was captured, it was not looking ahead full face, but glancing over his brother's shoulder at someone else in the group, the habitual look of detached amusement on his face.

In the summer of 1968, when Senators Henry Jackson, Edmund Muskie, and other conservation leaders in Congress joined in a special meeting to discuss formulating a national policy on the environment, they invited

Laurance to be the opening speaker. In his remarks he suggested that the President should appoint a special Commission on Environmental Organization. His listeners assumed that Laurance would be the ideal man to head such a commission. It would have been a final feather in his cap, and a way of recovering the prestige lost in the conservation infighting of the past few years. But the President was deeply mired in his own difficulties over Vietnam and never got around to setting up the commission.

Laurance would continue to be an important figure in Washington's environmental establishment. He was a large contributor to Nixon's 1968 campaign, and after the new administration took office, he remained head of the Citizens' Advisory Committee on Environment Quality (as the new President had renamed Johnson's Committee on Recreation and Natural Beauty). He continued to have a formidable reputation in government circles. In the early 1970s a discreetly unsigned memorandum circulated through the upper reaches of the Interior Department regarding Laurance's influence; as author Allan Talbot observed, it sounded like an FBI dossier on some Mafia don. The memorandum noted that he "controlled" two conservation organizations and had "infiltrated" eleven more, while eight others were "suspect." He had the same sort of proprietary relationship with the increasingly important Bureau of Outdoor Recreation that his father had had with the National Park Service.

Yet, the memo was already behind the times. Though it might be difficult to see with the naked eye, Laurance's stock as a conservationist, which had risen precipitously in the go-go years of the Johnson administration, had begun a slow decline. After Earth Day 1970 brought ecology to the foreground of the public conscience and stimulated the growth of environmental action groups all across the country, Laurance's dilemma became clear. He may have privately abhorred the oil spills that blackened the beaches of Santa Barbara and San Francisco, but he could not publicly align himself with people picketing the oil companies and making antibusiness statements. He found himself involved in negotiations for a Golden Gateway National Recreation Area to preserve San Francisco Bay at the same time that his brother David was involved in Westbay Associates, a joint venture with Lazard Freres and the Crocker Land Company that proposed to fill in 4,800 acres of the bay to provide a foundation for a $3 billion real estate project. While environmental organizations like Friends of the Earth (which he purported to admire) were fighting to make the public aware of the potential disasters inherent in the plans for the commercial use of nuclear power, Laurance continued to put venture capital into nuclear technology, and, along with Nelson and

David, fully backed the efforts of Con Ed and other utility companies in their deployment of nuclear reactors.

It had always been Laurance's special pride both to be in the avant-garde of whatever movement he happened to be involved in and to feel that he had mastered the contradictions in his life by a sheer act of will. Yet now, at least in the conservation movement, his ideas and style of operation were passé. And as for the contradictions, they seemed to have slipped out of control.

His life had taken on a strangely circular quality. He had begun his career without any particular commitment, made a serious bid for fame and influence, and, when this entailed more controversy than he had anticipated, retracted back into the "creative dilettantism" of his younger days. He continued to be active in environmental affairs, but it was primarily as an emeritus removed from the everyday struggles.

Outwardly he was much the same as he had always been. His features had been sharpened by the onset of old age, and the side of one cheek was occasionally blotched below his ear from a skin cancer Sloan-Kettering doctors assured him was under control. He was pipe-smoking and philosophical, always ready with a graceful quip and anxious to keep up with the trendy epiphenomena of pop culture. Yet inwardly he had changed. From his youth he had been the Brother with the best chance to step outside the viscous mystique with which Junior had surrounded the Rockefeller family. This latency, the sense that he could be different if he *wanted* to, had always marked Laurance off from the other Brothers who accepted the Rockefellers' manifest destiny and its implications for their personal lives as an item of faith. Yet, as this latency remained bottled up in Laurance, it fermented into a cynicism. Beneath the debonair manner was a nihilism none of the other Brothers was capable of, perhaps because none of them was as aware as Laurance of the awesome price he had paid to be a Rockefeller.

Laurance's life continued to be encased by the insulation common to all men of affairs: endless conferences, board meetings, and briefings. But all his activity rotated around a core of emptiness. Off the record, some of his aides admitted as much, although to say so publicly was impermissible. His children were under no such constraints. His daughter Laura says regretfully, "I feel sad for him in a way. He missed the boat. Daddy could have been creative."

Laurance was aware of the fact that his life lacked a center of balance. He referred to it obliquely in comments which had once seemed nicely ironic, but as he grew older acquired a tone of desperate flippancy, as in the reply he gave when an interviewer noted that his career seemed to lack a plan: "Yes, my life has been almost Zen-like, finding without seeking." Since his undergraduate days at Princeton, Laurance had always professed to believe that a man was the sum of his contradictions, yet in himself it was increasingly difficult to tell what exactly it all added up to.

CHAPTER 19

It was early February 1974, and David Rockefeller was off on another of his globe-trotting journeys. Midway through his visit, David got a telephone call from the White House chief of staff, General Alexander Haig. The President had just received the resignation of Treasury Secretary George Shultz, effective as soon as a replacement could be found. Haig's voice quavered over the connection; could David fly back immediately to talk about taking the job? Speaking in the precise manner that made his ordinary conversation sound as if he were dictating a business letter, David replied that he would come to Washington as soon as he could.

While David was flattered by Haig's offer, it was no novelty for him to be called for this job. He had been sounded out for the Treasury post by Kennedy and offered it outright by Lyndon Johnson. He had accepted neither, however, because at the time he didn't want to interrupt his rise to the top at the Chase with a term of government service and also because his wife, Peggy, was adamantly opposed to living in Washington.

With the economy badly shaken by the oil crisis and inflation, and with the Watergate scandal poisoning the atmosphere in Washington, the post was in many ways less attractive than it had been. It was no secret, moreover, that President Nixon did not like Rockefellers.

Still, as he flew back to the United States in his private jet, David found himself seriously considering the offer. He arrived home in New York at eleven P.M. on a Wednesday night. By nine-fifteen the next morning he was in Haig's office in Washington talking about the authority he would insist on having and demanding assurance that he would be allowed to make economic policy free from interference by tactical considerations stemming from the Watergate affair. That night, leaning toward accepting the job, he went to a state dinner on the Middle East attended by Secretary of State Kissinger and the President. The President greeted him and shook hands cordially, but there was no mention of the new post, nor were there the expected words of encouragement urging David to come aboard. Things did not seem right. Within the next few days, the two men had occasion to meet again, and the President again failed to mention the post. David went back to his advisers to reappraise the situation. Perhaps it was just a mental lapse by Nixon, a result of the stress that had been so visible on the drawn grayness of his face; yet without the President's firm encouragement, the offer seemed too dangerous, given the risks.

The next day David called Haig from New York and told him that he would have to decline the offer. When the chief of staff pressed for his reason, Rockefeller paused for a moment, then with his usual diplomatic tact said that his decision was based on his fears that too many people secretly blamed his family for the energy crisis for him to be able to do an effective job at that point in time.

Others might have swallowed their doubts and taken the job on faith, but David didn't operate that way. In the nearly two decades he had worked in the Chase, he had long since come to occupy—in the words of *Finance* magazine—"the equivalent of cabinet rank in the society of his peers." This was a status that didn't change when a new administration moved into Washington or the nation's economy tumbled into chaos. It reflected a basic reality of the systems of power guiding the nation, and his own place in that arrangement.

In David's world, institutions occupied a primary place; and after the family, the Chase was the institution that mattered most of all. David realized that while he had been making his way up the executive ladder of the Chase, a crucial drama was taking place in the postwar American economy. It was the growing dominance of financial over industrial institutions, and of large institutional investors over shareholding individuals as the legal owners of the country's leading corporations. These trends intersected in the emergence of banks as the epicenter of the economy. Controlling huge trusts and even larger pension funds, they had become the great powers of the economic order. Among the powerful, the Chase Manhattan ranked very near the top. At the time David was deciding to turn down Nixon's offer of the Treasury post, he chaired a board of directors interlocked with the boards of dozens of other corporate giants. The Chase was a leading stockholder in CBS, Jersey Standard, Atlantic Richfield, United Airlines, and a galaxy of other corporations. The power this stockholding position conferred was immense.

The fruits of this brave new world of banking were still before him in 1960, when at the age of forty-five David Rockefeller had been appointed president of the Chase and given a one-half share of the chief executive officer's job. The other half went to the man who had succeeded John J.

McCloy as chairman of the board, George Champion. Tall, graying, distinguished, Champion had gained a solid reputation over the years as a commercial banker. He was more than ten years Rockefeller's senior, and in many ways his intellectual opposite. Yet the two men agreed on the basic issues confronting the bank. Their amiable relationship was based on the understanding that there were things about which they must simply agree to disagree, notably Champion's religious fundamentalism and David's penchant for modern art. When Billy Graham came to New York, David's contribution to his campaign was generous enough not to seem perfunctory; when Rockefeller began filling the bank with abstract expressionism, the traditional-minded Champion insisted only that the avant-garde sculpture constructed of auto fenders and other materials he considered unseemly be kept out of view of his office.

The relationship between the two men was smoothed by the fact that they knew their joint tenancy would be over in seven years when the 58-year-old Champion reached the mandatory retirement age and David assumed the full control of the bank he had been destined for from the moment his Uncle Winthrop had hired him. The Chase's new headquarters at 1 Chase Manhattan Plaza, in fact, seemed an aluminum and glass monument manifesting his destiny. Sixty stories high, David's $150 million slab jutting up above its neighbors was the first skyscraper completed in David's planned renovation of lower Manhattan. It was the biggest bank building in the world, with the biggest battery of computers and the biggest vault—a superbly equipped machine able to handle any sum of money or power.

On the 17th floor, guards moved inconspicuously up and down the corridors while executives sat in the barber shop getting their weekly trim or waited for the express elevator to whisk them to the aerie high above, where they lunched in executive dining rooms. Here David might be glimpsed darting out of his own private elevator—he moved with surprising quickness for a big man—and disappearing through the push-button, sliding glass doors into his private office, an opulent mélange of Cézannes, Wyeths, Rothkos, Etruscan pottery, and African sculpture. He was probably oblivious to the fact that the three hundred vice-presidents working under him regard this as the *sanctum sanctorum*, a spot not approached without a properly humbled heart.

He was the most peculiar of the Brothers, strangely vacuous for an important man, and definitely a throwback to his father's Victorian *beau ideal* in which emotion is always submerged beneath the agreeably formal façade of the rational man. He seemed almost characterless, someone whose views were bounded by what men of his station were supposed to say and whose acts were dictated by his sense of what it was appropriate to do. But if this made him frustrating for family and close friends, it also made him the perfect man to head one of the most powerful financial institutions in the world. The predictable, carefully measured quality that made him privately appear to be manipulated by some hidden ventriloquist also made him the consummate public spokesman for the community of which the Chase was a part. He knew the language and forms of the communication required of him and could articulate the point of view with perfect impersonality. He had learned well how to envelop himself in the double majesty coming from being a Rockefeller *and* head of the Chase, and how to use this institutional, semisymbolic power his own personality alone might not have won him.

David was like his brothers in that he had been prepared by his unique upbringing for every kind of adversity in life except failure. As he drew close to his sixtieth year, however, this possibility had begun to penetrate his unflappable exterior. It was nothing to put a finger on, but there were signs that things weren't quite turning out the way they should according to the unfinished idyll his father had scripted for the family. The virulence of the attacks on the Rockefeller name upset him and the irreverent attitude of his children, which he took to be a repudiation of his values and family traditions, wounded him deeply. "I think I have as interesting and exciting a job as anyone could have," he said plaintively to an interviewer, "but I don't think I have really convinced my children of the fact, at least not to the point where they're anxious to go into business." Yet these factors could be accounted to irrationality—the common reaction to public figures and parents.

The bank was finally the high ground where he chose to make his stand. His character was submerged in its conservatism, and he took a special pride in the fact that (as he put it to an interviewer) he was "the first member of the family since Grandfather who has had a regular job in a company and has devoted a major part of his time to being in business." Yet failure was in the air at three-thirty P.M. on the miserably chilly and rainy day of October 12, 1972, when David strode into the Chase boardroom, the muscles in his cheek twitching from the clench of his jaws. He glanced at the flock of reporters who had been summoned only three hours earlier by the public relations staff for what was billed as a major announcement. They had quickly noted that David was not accompanied by the bank's president, Herbert Patterson, appointed with great fanfare only three years earlier when George Champion had retired and David had made his final move to the top as chairman of the board and chief executive officer.

Those assembled knew that the Chase had not been doing well lately. In the first six months of 1972, its earnings had increased only 1 percent as compared to 16 percent for its great rival, the First National City, now incorporated as the Citibank. This was just part of a larger trend. Among the articles appearing recently in the pages of the financial press about the bank's difficulties, the most widely discussed had been a feature in *The New York Times* financial section, which had run underneath the foreboding headline, "The Chase at Ebb Tide."

It took David only a moment to drop the expected bombshell. In view of the slipping competitive position of the Chase, its executive committee had decided that Patterson should be replaced as president by Vice-Chairman Willard Butcher. "It was a stunning move by Rockefeller," commented *Business Week*, "—indeed a brutal one by the standards of big business and big banks, where discarded top managers are allowed to gently fade away." Wall Streeters were critical of the way the matter was handled, especially given the fact that Patterson, a Chase officer for twenty years, so clearly appeared to be a scapegoat for ills that proceeded from sources higher up. "Somebody had to take the rap," a dealer in bank stocks observed, "and it wasn't going to be the guy who owns the bank."

David's fellow bankers were not so circumspect in assigning responsibility for the Chase's problems. John R. Bunting, chief executive officer for the First Pennsylvania Bank, one of the largest financial institutions in the country, says of David: "He's got the best name in the world, the absolute best name in the world, or at least the best name in this country. Rockefeller. . . . He's got the bank with the—I would say—most prestige in the country going for him. And he's running a third-rate bank. Walter Wriston in First National City is beating the hell out of him."

At the end of 1968, just before David took over as chairman, the Chase's assets were $19 billion. It was slightly less than Citibank's $19.6 billion, but the Chase was slightly ahead in total deposits. Yet, a year after Patterson's replacement, Wriston's Citibank had built an enormous lead in assets ($41 billion to $27 billion), in deposits ($32 billion to $26 billion), and in profits, which, at $250 million, were 50 percent more than those of the Chase.

It was already several years since the Chase had lost its position as New York's largest bank to First National City because of the latter's commanding position in overseas areas. As an added humiliation, it had also lost the lead in domestic banking that it had always enjoyed among the giants of New York's money market. More recently, it had fallen behind in correspondent banking (banking for other banks, an area it had long regarded as one of its greatest strengths) to Manufacturers Hanover Trust, an institution with only half the overall volume of the Chase. At the same time, a number of key senior Chase executives had left the bank for other jobs. As one of them told the *Times*: "These offers come in all the time; you don't listen to them when you're happy."

The very fact that the Chase's difficulties extended across such a wide range of activities indicated the basic nature of the problem: for many years the bank had simply been outmanaged, outclassed, and outdone as a profit-making institution by its rivals in the commercial banking field. "The Chase of late, has come to resemble a lumbering giant—huge but neither quick nor shrewd," commented *Business Week*. "It has lost its verve, its momentum, its fine competitive edge." The Citibank had beaten the Chase into the bank holding-company field and its diversification moves had set the pattern that other banks were copying. It was ahead in fields of mortgage banking and management consulting, and its lucrative traveler's check operation had no equivalent at the Chase.

It was ironic, however, that it was in David's specialty—international banking—that the Chase should be most significantly outdistanced. While David was visiting heads of state of various countries in meetings where the advantage to the Chase was often in intangible good will, Walter Wriston was moving ahead without fanfare all over the world. In an area where bank profits were growing twice as fast as at home, the Citicorp had three foreign offices for every one belonging to the Chase. The Chase had attempted to cut the effects of Citibank's lead in foreign branches by making investments in 17 subsidiary banks with operations in 74 countries, but the strategy had not paid off. It was hard for the Chase to control banks in which it had less than a majority interest, and in some cases where there were both subsidiary banks and Chase foreign branches in the same area, Chase executives found themselves in the odd position of competing against themselves.

Inevitably David's extrabanking activities came in for some sharp criticism as a source of the Chase's difficulties. "Rockefeller is viewed by the investment community as a great world figure, a friend of kings and presidents," *Business Week* summed up, "but not as a skilled commercial banker." A harsher judgment was made by *Fortune* senior editor Sanford Rose: "David Rockefeller knows the banking business and the monetary system of this country very well. The central problem is that he doesn't pay attention to the Chase Manhattan. He is best described as a man who goes from global concern to global concern in an air-conditioned limousine, and occasionally in the midst of these global considerations, pauses to make a decision about the bank, and goofs. You can't spend all that time being an important international figure and still run a bank like the Chase. Rockefeller has permitted a situation to develop at the Chase that has led to widespread demoralization."

David faced the storm with the same placid exterior that he brought to every other potentially trying situation. Three months before firing Patterson, he had told the *Times*: "At no time in the twenty-six years I've been with the bank have I felt more optimistic about its future than I do at this moment." Sanford Rose responds: "He's totally unflappable. You could come up to him and say, 'Listen, I just heard that your wife is sleeping with Walter Wriston,' and he'd look back at you and say, 'Well, I'm sure there are rumors to that effect.'"

By the 1970s, David had become an almost allegorical figure: Chairman of the Board of the Establishment; Midas at the top of the power structure; a pudgy Cardinal Richelieu in a three-piece suit implicated in events as diverse as the Sharpeville Massacre in South Africa and the overthrow of Chile's Salvador Allende. He was the long historical shadow of his grandsire, and as events inexorably dragged the Rockefellers back toward the controversy with which they had started, David's name was used to conjure up the specter of irresponsible power for the Age of Aquarius in the way that the first John D.'s had been for the Gilded Age.

His power—less as a man, perhaps, than as an idea—was such that he had become the archetypal Rockefeller. His brother Nelson was still the dominant figure inside the family and always would be. Yet in his public life Nelson had spent himself too prodigally over the years. The lines and wrinkles on his face mapped all the frantic campaigns for the presidency and indicated a sharp yearning that lacked fulfillment, even after his selection in 1974 as Vice-President. Nelson's strength was in the sheer animal force with which he assaulted his environment; David's in the more passive way he had allowed himself to be the lightning rod discharging the static energy hanging in an immense cloud above the Rockefellers' family, financial, and policy-making institutions. The power he wielded cost him far less than that which Nelson had sought. And while his older brother was soaring like Icarus across the fiery horizon of American politics during the sixties—peaking, stalling, and then gliding downward and only partially recovering—David was always moving methodically up, usually in the shadows, always building a solid foothold before taking the next step, and never allowing his task to get out of hand.

Nelson reveled in the image, yet for David the open aspiration of power was unseemly and vulgar. The lesson David learned from his brother was the obvious truth about power and money: they stained anyone grasping them too avidly. Yet like money, power had its perverse fascination. An enterprising publisher had managed to promote a book about David onto the best-seller lists by quoting its line that "for David Rockefeller, the presidency of the United States would be a demotion." Despite the book's inaccuracies and distortions—it was a diatribe done from newspaper clips—David still seemed to take a secret pleasure in the *fact* of the book. When his son Richard asked how he stayed calm in the face of such abuse, David told him the family had long since learned it was best not to dignify such attacks with a response. "People will believe what they will believe, and if people believe I'm powerful, that's useful too."

CHAPTER 20

On January 12, 1971, the governor of Arkansas stood before the state legislature to deliver his farewell address. Gripping the podium with whitened knuckles and speaking in halting sentences, Winthrop Rockefeller was much changed from the man who had taken the oath of office four years earlier. Confidently youthful in that brief moment of triumph and vindication, he had since put on pounds and lost hair; tiny networks of ruptured capillaries reddened his puffy face; his jaundiced eyes seemed covered with a thin film, giving him the look of one who was getting more information than he could process. The optimism of the first inaugural was gone too, having been scaled down by what for any other man would have been called sobering experiences. This farewell speech had a plaintive quality. "When the history of the last few years is written," went the phrase that particularly stuck in listeners' minds, "I hope the historian will think of me as more than a political phenomenon."

It was more than the usual political valedictory. Those who had followed Winthrop's career and knew his background realized it was a deeper appeal—not merely for applause, but for understanding and even forgiveness. It was clear to everyone that the brief rebirth he had enjoyed in Arkansas was over now; much had happened in his seventeen years in the state, yet it all seemed a fairy tale. That tale had ended, leaving him in the condition in which he had arrived in Arkansas: defeated, divorced, revealed as an alcoholic, and hoping that those who judged him (surrogates of the father who withheld approval on into eternity) would weigh his human qualities in the balance and not be too severe.

In the beginning, his naturally genial nature had bloomed in the red dirt of Arkansas. It was far from the family and the standards he had never quite managed to live up to. He was no longer the least successful of a remarkable group of Brothers. He was *the* Rockefeller and he could make his own way at his own speed. And for the backward state of Arkansas, the mark he had made was very broad indeed. It was as if some giant had come to live there; Arkansas had watched in awe as he sliced off the top of Petit Jean Mountain to build his immense home of stone and glass, raised barns, outbuildings, a huge auditorium where he kept his collection of antique cars, built homes for his chief assistants and apartments for the other help—all of it equal to a good-sized Arkansas town. Winrock Farm had its own airfield, fire department, and shortwave radio; it flew its own flag. The flamboyant initials WR were branded onto objects all over the 900-acre estate—from the coasters on which the perspiring martinis appeared early every afternoon, to the shining rumps of the prize-winning Santa Gertrudis cattle, which breeders from all over the world came to bid on at auction time.

It began as an exile from failure but developed into a time of reorientation and success. Winthrop's personal life seemed to straighten out. In 1956 he had flown to Idaho to marry 37-year-old Jeannette Edris, who brought a ready-made family of two children by a prior marriage back to Winrock with her. Winthrop adopted them as his own. The photographs taken at the time show him standing beside the swimming pool with his new family, looking prouder and more confident than ever before.

Inside the Rockefeller family, Winthrop's primary virtues—simplicity and a capacity for spontaneous warmth—had always been seen as a weakness, and he had grown embarrassed by these feelings, hiding them as if they were overlarge hands or some other clumsy defect. But in Arkansas he found a kind of space he hadn't had before, and was no longer forced into the role of Mr. Junior's ungainly, wastrel son. His natural warmth reappeared. And from the moment he arrived in the state, Winthrop had begun looking around for a way of achieving what he had not been able to back in New York.

It was clear to everyone in Arkansas that he represented a political potential. In 1955, Governor Orval Faubus tried to capitalize on it for his administration by making Winthrop chairman of the Arkansas Industrial Development Commission (AIDC). This gave him a chance to do something about joblessness, the most urgent of the state's many problems. Mechanization of the cotton farms had thrown large numbers of people out of work. What industries there were—lumber, clothing, and furniture manufacture—were so underdeveloped, depressed, and low paying they couldn't attract skilled workers. College graduates routinely went to other states to find work fitting their education. With little industrial growth, Arkansas was steadily losing population and, next to Mississippi, had the lowest per capita income in the nation.

Winthrop threw himself into the task with a gusto he had not been able to summon for any of the responsibilities his father had thrust on him. It was *his* job to succeed or fail at, and there was no abstract standard by which his performance would be measured. While working to compile an impressive record during the commission's first year—73 new plants located in the state, creating 7,236 new jobs—Winthrop formed Winrock Enterprises, a multimillion-dollar venture capital company involved in agriculture, the manufacture of plastic pipe, and housing developments. Its demonstration projects were intended to show interested corporations that Arkansas's attractive tax laws could support industrial innovation.

It was also in 1956 that he began his Rockwin Fund to handle his philanthropy. Arkansas was unlike New York in that even relatively small sums could have a large impact. A $1.5 million grant built and equipped a model school in Morrilton, a small town near Winrock; it soon became a sort of educational laboratory for the state. Winthrop also equipped and supported a Perry County medical clinic, gave a series of college fellowships, and raised $1 million to help build the Arkansas Art Center while also buying an Artmobile to carry culture to the hills and hollows of the Ozarks. His arrival in Arkansas seemed a godsend. It was as Orval Faubus had said at a conference of southern governors when one of them asked how a person might go about getting a Rockefeller for his state. "I don't know," the Arkansas governor replied, "but you keep your cotton-pickin' fingers off mine."

Winthrop reveled in the acclaim his efforts brought him. It was a far cry from the humiliation of his past, and he gave his move to Arkansas a finality by transferring all his personal papers there and taking his investments and trust funds out of the management of Room 5600, putting them into the hands of the team of personal advisers he assembled in Little Rock. Yet his move out of New York was never quite complete. His work in Arkansas was in some sense a mime performed for the approval of a faraway group, which would ultimately have to sanction his new identity. However much he liked to travel through his adopted state in a stetson and hand-tooled cowboy boots, Winthrop would always be involved in what his advisers called the "pin-striped suit syndrome." Several times each year he got into the Falcon jet and flew east for family reunions, meetings of the Rockefeller Brothers Fund, and other family affairs where he found, if not respect, at least a surprised relief on the part of the family.

He had been seen as a potential candidate for governor since settling in Arkansas, and as the impact of his AIDC work and his Rockwin Fund philanthropies reverberated through the state, it became merely a question of when he would make his bid. Arkansas recognized what an anomaly he was: a Republican among Democrats, a liberal among conservatives, a rich man from the big city among rural populists, an impulsive and self-indulgent man among people whose circumstances had made them taciturn and self-denying. Unaware of the specifics of the family conflict that had bankrupted his life in New York and sent him fleeing to their state to lick his emotional wounds, Arkansans wondered why anyone should leave such a world of boardrooms, yachts, and nightlife to build a rambling aerie on top of a desolate mountain and spend his money and energies on their impoverished state. What was it he *wanted*?

Yet if they were suspicious of him, as of other "carpetbaggers," they knew not to look a gift horse in the mouth—even if he was a thoroughbred who had been a trustee of the Urban League and had publicly criticized Governor Faubus in 1957 for using National Guardsmen to prevent the integration of Little Rock's Central High. A certain pride went hand in hand with the suspiciousness. What other Arkansan could be seen on the front pages of newspapers across the country riding in a carriage with Queen Elizabeth and Prince Philip during their 1957 royal visit, or would be visited by Edward R. Murrow's "Person to Person"?

Despite his resources (and it would later be estimated that he had poured more than $10 million into his political career during the 1960s), Winthrop faced a formidable task. Changing over to the Democratic party would have been a greater break with family tradition than leaving New York and Room 5600, and was additionally impossible because of the adverse effect it would have had on Nelson's political career. So Winthrop undertook the rebuilding of the state Republican party, the tiny vestige of Reconstruction now shrunk to the point where it was little more than a tattered umbrella under which a few individuals collected every four years to receive patronage from the national party apparatus, although they rarely managed even to field a complete slate of candidates for state offices.

Shedding 35 pounds to reach a trim 207, Rockefeller began a tradition he would follow three times in the future when, in 1964, he journeyed to the small Arkansas hamlet of Winthrop in Little River County to announce that he would run for governor. He had proved his loyalty. It was through his efforts that the AIDC had brought 600 new businesses into the state, providing 90,000 new jobs and $270 million in payrolls and being largely responsible for the fact that the per capita income had risen 50 percent in Arkansas in the previous eight years. But while he could hardly call Winthrop a carpetbagger, Faubus could exploit his great riches and the civil rights issue. Although Winthrop told voters that he, like Barry Goldwater (whom he endorsed in San Francisco after vainly trying to steer the immovable Arkansas delegation to his brother Nelson), would have voted against the Civil Rights Act of 1964, Faubus made much of the fact that Rockefeller had once addressed a national convention of the NAACP and was known to have Negro friends.

Winthrop lost to Faubus, but he got 43 percent of the vote, a respectable enough showing for him to assure supporters, even while conceding defeat, that he was ready to begin the next campaign immediately. And for the next two years he continued to travel through the state, the closest thing to a celebrity Arkansas had. By 1966 the civil rights issue had been cooled somewhat by the humiliating national publicity the South had received. There was a widespread feeling that Arkansas must cultivate a more moderate image. Faubus was retiring after six terms, but old-guard Democrats managed to nominate an even more rabid segregationist in his place, James D. ("Justice Jim") Johnson, former state supreme court judge, founder of the White Citizen's Council, and ardent backer of Alabama Governor George Wallace. If Johnson, who opened and closed campaign rallies with rebel yells and taunted Rockefeller as a "liberal lush" and a "prissy sissy," came to personify the strong gravity of history attempting to pull the state back into the heyday of Jim Crow, Winthrop willingly adopted the role of Arkansas's usher into the twentieth century. Traveling through the state in a bus that was modest on the outside, but fitted with elaborate sleeping quarters, bar, and kitchen inside, he put together a fragile coalition of blacks, liberals, moderate Democrats, urban dwellers, and mountain Republicans. He beat Johnson with 57 percent of the vote to become the first Republican governor of Arkansas since Reconstruction.

On January 1, 1967, he took office in a jubilant mood of vindication—it seemed more a personal than a political triumph to him—taking his oath of office with his hand resting on his mother's Bible. It was as if he had at last joined the Rockefeller family, although his close friends would soon be looking back on the ceremony and saying that it was probably the high point of Winthrop's life.

Given that only 3 of the state's 135 legislators were Republicans, it was clear from the outset that Winthrop's legislative plan—a country-cousin version of Nelson's program in New York—would have troubles. Arkansas was too impoverished for such high-rise dreams, and the legislators were unwilling to raise taxes to make them a reality. At the very beginning of his governorship, therefore, Winthrop saw it would be necessary to substitute a symbolic program of crusades for a real legislative effort.

The first such crusade was the Arkansas penal system, renowned as the most barbaric in the nation. News of the atrocities in the dark recesses of Arkansas prisons had begun to leak out toward the end of Faubus's last term in office, and though only a few details were known, it was enough to suggest an American Devil's Island had grown up in the heart of the state. The work gangs labored under heartless conditions; torture was an everyday occurrence; a vicious and corrupt trusty system was the means of maintaining internal order. Winthrop had said bluntly, "Our prisons stink," and he hired Thomas Murton, a young criminologist from Illinois, to supervise reforms.

Meanwhile, the governor's office had also declared war on gambling operations. Winthrop put a former FBI man named Lynn Davis in charge of the state troopers and sent him on an assault against illicit gambling throughout the state. For weeks, Arkansas newspapers were filled with pictures of the flamboyant Davis in full dress uniform raiding gambling establishments in Warm Springs and elsewhere, dismantling slot machines with sledgehammers, and feeding them to raging bonfires.

The conditions he exposed shocked Arkansans, and they gave Winthrop their support on penal reform and gambling. On the question of civil rights, however, they did not. Nonetheless, although he eventually recanted his probussing stand and minimized the degree to which he had been involved in organizations like the Urban League, Winthrop did begin his administration by forcing state agencies to hire blacks in professional and supervisory jobs, and for the first time the state civil service in his administration had a sprinkling of black faces. When the legislature refused to give Winthrop the civil rights commission he had requested, he created one by executive order and gave it space in his own office. After Martin Luther King's murder, he went to the steps of the state capitol building and joined hands with black leaders in mourning there.

Winthrop was reelected in 1968, but by a narrowed majority and without appreciably increasing Republicans' strength in the legislature, as he had hoped to. Aides began to get the impression that he had wanted to be *elected* governor more than actually to *be* governor. Reports of his immoderate drinking filtered into the public press. In reporting on Winthrop's appearance before the state legislature on behalf of a mixed-drink bill, the *Pine Bluff Commercial* of June 2, 1968, noted that "the legislators were paying little attention to his message. They were snickering over what they assumed to be the governor's inebriation."

In addition to drinking, Winthrop rarely came to the governor's offices on the second floor of the capitol building, preferring to stay at Winrock, rising late in the morning and working late into the night in his office there or climbing aboard his Falcon jet for the five-minute ride into Little Rock, where he was chauffeured by his bodyguard in a maroon Lincoln limousine to the suite of offices he maintained in the Tower Building (the city's first skyscraper, which he had built).

It was as if dark forces beyond his knowledge, much less control, were pulling him back into that vortex of failure which had dizzied him most of his life. He almost seemed to expect to fail. When his bills were rejected by the legislature and he ran into problems that couldn't be solved with a flourish, it started a disenchantment that finally avalanched into a despair smothering all aspects of his life.

After the 1968 reelection, it was clear to close observers that his marriage was feeling the strain. For Jeannette Edris Rockefeller, politics had been an enemy, stirring up forces in her husband she thought were buried for good and destroying the life they had enjoyed in their first years at Winrock. As the moodiness, drinking bouts, and fits of bitterness increased, the mutual friends she and Winthrop had made began drifting away. She tried to accompany him on his political tours in and out of the state, but the large retinue traveling with them had proved too unwieldy and the pleasures of the rubber chicken circuit too sparse. Soon she began staying home. By 1969 she and Winthrop were living apart and had agreed on a divorce.

As Winthrop and his wife eyed each other coldly from opposite wings of the house, Winrock became less a home than a tourist attraction and convention center. There were banquet-sized dinners two or three times a week, and continual meetings, not only of political organizations, but of groups in which Winthrop was interested personally or which he thought might benefit the state. The climactic event of the year was the weekend of the annual cattle sale, when Winthrop flew in hundreds of VIPs in his private jet, housed them at Winrock, and fed and entertained them at opulent buffets in the huge circus tents set up in the "backyard." One part business and one part bacchanal, these weekends were renowned throughout the Southwest and attracted an exotic mix of celebrities, business people, and the social set.

Defying all political auguries as well as the increasing chaos of his private life, Winthrop decided to run for a third team in 1970. If nothing else, his presence in the state had forced the Democratic party to streamline its image and structure, and purge the old guard from its leadership. This time they put up no Jim Crow reactionary, but a young moderate named Dale Bumpers.

Bumpers clearly outcampaigned Winthrop. Previous opponents had called attention to his notorious drinking problem, but Bumpers didn't have to; audiences saw ample evidence of it for themselves in Winthrop's personal appearances and on television. At best he had been an undistinguished speaker, so halting and tongue-tied that reporters—most of them friendly because he was both amiable and available—often left his press conferences in bewilderment, wondering how to reconstruct what he had just said. But in 1970 it was not just sentences left dangling perilously in the air or metaphors twisted into exotic shapes; now it was the serious incoherence of a man who was often not sure what he was saying.

Winthrop, beaten badly by Bumpers, made his farewell to the legislature and withdrew to Winrock. If he had little hope of the eventual comeback that eases most defeated politicians' reentry into private life, he did have a complex empire of investments and interests in the state that could occupy him. Winrock Farms—which had purchased nearly 50,000 additional acres of grazing land in Texas and Oklahoma—was now producing revenues of $20 million a year. Winrock Enterprises had grown from a demonstration project into a large, diversified corporation building shopping centers in Albuquerque and elsewhere in the Southwest, producing trailer homes and plastic pipe, and leading Arkansas in the construction of single-family dwellings.

By 1972 he was sixty years old, although with his teeth mottled brown from years of smoking unfiltered Picayune cigarettes and a tic making his head bob and weave as he began sentences, he looked older. Falling into the role of the old man on the top of his mountain, he cultivated a flowing gray beard peppered with black that set off the sad and pensive eyes women had once found so attractive. He told aides that he felt he was on the threshold of the most creative period of his life. Yet a kind of resignation and randomness had crept into his days. In between drinking sprees he walked around the farm by himself, occasionally standing at the long flagstone walk with biblical quotations set in stone or walking over the grounds strewn with statues that had once belonged to his mother, carrying pruning shears to sculpture the trees and improve the view of the Arkansas River snaking through the valley below Petit Jean Mountain.

His 24-year-old son, Winthrop Paul, the relative stranger who was the first descendent of Mr. Junior to grow up outside the Rockefeller ethos, had come to Winrock to work his way into his father's affairs. Winthrop spent time trying to get to know the boy and find ways of integrating him into his own large activities and into the Rockefeller family as well.

In the summer of 1972, the former governor went to Miami as a delegate to the Republican convention. A few weeks later, after returning to Arkansas to help set up the campaign that would allow Richard Nixon to become the first Republican since U.S. Grant to carry the state in a presidential election, his private physician discovered a cyst under his arm and removed it. After a biopsy showed it to be malignant, Winthrop flew to Sloan-Kettering for extensive surgery and a course of chemotherapy. He returned to Arkansas late in October looking thin and shaky, although he buoyantly told reporters who met his plane the doctors had probably stopped the cancer.

Privately he knew that they had not, and that his time was short. By New Year's he had grown weak. His housekeeper Margaret Black remembers him spending much of that cold month staring bleakly out at the snow and dragging himself through the many rooms of the huge house to sort out clothes and personal belongings and tell her who they should go to in the ritual lottery he knew always followed death in the Rockefeller family. The chemicals pumped into him at Sloan-Kettering to fight the spread of the cancer made him feel constantly chilled, and in mid-February he flew to his home in Palm Springs to warm himself in the desert sun. While there he lapsed into a coma, and on February 22, 1973, the Rockefeller brother who had been last all his life was the first to die.

The funeral was a state occasion, taking place on top of Winthrop's mountain in the huge hall housing his collection of antique cars. The governors of Arkansas, Virginia, and West Virginia were there, along with Vice-President Spiro Agnew and his squad of Secret Service men, and various state dignitaries. Winthrop had scripted much of the funeral service before his death—one last attempt to control his image—and it was primarily a family drama. Rockefellers came from all over the country—Charleston and Cambridge, Palo Alto and Pocantico—setting down in a drizzling rain on the slick runway of the Petit Jean airport in commercial planes and private jets. The Brothers and their wives were ushered to the front row. Behind them were the larger group of fourth-generation Rockefellers known as the Cousins. Sitting behind them, in their accustomed role of buffer between the family and the rest of the world, were key members of the staff who had been flown down for the occasion from New York. The pathos of the situation was clear to Laurance's daughter Marion: "He was always issuing these general invitations—'y'all come down.' He was terribly lonely. Yet the only time the family showed up was for his funeral."

When Nelson rose to give the main eulogy, his remarks struck listeners as almost too smooth and polished, lacking any felt sense of loss. What few people in the room knew was that the words he read had been written a few days before the funeral by one of his speech writers, who had been instructed to call the Rockefeller Family Office to get the pertinent facts about Winthrop's life. Nelson had not seen the speech until midway in flight between Albany and Winrock.

Yet it hardly mattered. Winthrop was gone—in death as in life a sacrificial offering confirming the unity of the rest of his brothers. It was with a realism absent from the funeral oratory that Margaret Black later pointed out the only truth to be learned from his passing. "That poor, poor man," she said with an edge of bitterness in her voice, "he was just fair game for everybody—for strangers and family too."

CHAPTER 21

To the Rockefellers, Arkansas was *terra incognita,* a haven for exiles who could not function in the world of affairs. Winrock Farm had the eerie feeling of a place built by someone who seemed to have a detailed knowledge of what it was to be a Rockefeller but had not quite been able to attain their exquisite taste and sophistication. With its biblical quotations set in stone, its sculptured trees and other arabesques, Winrock seemed less a successful imitation of Pocantico than a parody of it, slightly embarrassing in the way Winthrop himself had been.

The Rockefellers felt the pathos and waste of their dead brother's life, yet they had grown so accustomed to regarding themselves as the type and him as the variant that it was hard not to share the attitude lying just below the patina of polished impersonality in Nelson's eulogy. As a direct descendant of the first John D., Winthrop had to have a state funeral; but whatever the words said over him, the family knew that the terminal disease had not been cancer at all, but weakness. In death, as in life, he had broken ranks and compromised them all.

Soon after returning to New York, JDR3 began tidying up his affairs and readying his collection of more than three hundred pieces of Oriental art for donation to the Asia Society. Laurance startled his children at a family gathering celebrating his fortieth wedding anniversary by telling them what each one's share of his estate would be. Not soon after, David began to do the same in individual conferences with his children.

Nelson could not help making some of these deferential gestures toward mortality. He seemed already to have lived two lives, one that ended in the late fifties after he left the Eisenhower administration, and the other that began when he became governor. He had watched the associates and friends of the earlier era die or wear out. The children of Nelson's first marriage had grown up, married, and had children of their own and, led by Rodman were themselves poised on the edge of middle age.

Nelson was no longer the handsome, blue-eyed, irrepressible young man who had popped like a champagne cork into public life thirty-five years earlier. Liver-spotted and wrinkled despite being hovered over by personal physicians, he now looked his sixty-six years. His features had settled into the square mass that recalled his father in old age, and with his heavy black-rimmed glasses and his gravelly voice, he looked and sounded like a WASP George Burns.

Yet at a profound level of his character, he could not accept growing old. As the elaborate machinery sustaining his public and private life wore down, he replaced it, finding younger people to serve as prosthetic extensions of himself. He had gotten a new set of young aides. He had a young wife and two young sons (Nelson, Jr., ten, and Mark, eight) on whom he lavished rides in the family helicopter, moments alone with him in his office sharing Oreo cookies, and other evidences of an almost grandfatherly affection. He was fond of saying to those who asked him about his age, "My grandfather lived to be ninety-seven and my father to be eighty-six. I plan to make it to a hundred." As friends watched the husky figure walking with Happy and the children along the beach at Seal Harbor, the rolling flat-footed gait reminded them of an old boxer who knows only one way to move—forward. His friend Jacob Javits had once said: "Nothing stands in Rockefeller's way. Nothing. He always gets what he wants."

When Nelson was asked if he felt this was true, he responded with a parable. "I remember bidding at an auction on a Modigliani once and losing to the Museum of Modern Art, of which I was then president. And years later another one came on the market and I was fortunate enough to get it. So it shows if you've got patience and persistence, even though you're thwarted at one point, you can [get what you want]."

Yet patience and persistence, he had to believe after 1968, would not get him the prize he had sought throughout his political career. For one of the rare times in his life he was in a position of having no alternatives. He could not let go of the ambition that had driven him through public life, but its fulfillment now clearly depended on some miracle that he was unable, as had always been his custom, to *make* happen. He could only wait for some divine intervention and prepare to take advantage of it—should it occur—by supporting and even toadying to Richard Nixon, a man he not only loathed but also felt was mentally unstable. And as the presidency receded from his grasp, a new element of bitterness entered his character. It was as if the world had undergone an elementary mitosis, splitting into the two opposing camps of friends and enemies.

He had the wealth to buy loyalty and the breeding to buy it in such a way that neither party in the transaction had to admit a deal had taken place. Rockefeller loyalists could count on jobs not only in the state government but also in the larger world of private patronage that Nelson controlled. If he had always known how to reward his friends, after 1968 he took a new kind of pleasure in finding ways to punish his enemies.

The celebrated feud with John Lindsay was a case in point. At the core of the conflict was a question of loyalty—personal and political—regarding how much exactly the mayor owed Nelson. The beginning of their struggle went back to 1965, when Rockefeller had helped convince Lindsay to abandon his congressional seat and enter the mayoralty race. In agreeing, Lindsay stipulated that he had to be assured of a campaign war chest of $1 million.

In giving the $450,000 he raised from his family, and in the other help he gave to make Lindsay's victory possible, Nelson naturally assumed he had gotten something he had been hoping for since first becoming governor: a Republican mayor of New York through whom he could control the city *in absentia*. Yet Lindsay soon began to go his own way, with youthful vitality, charisma, and an apparently bright future—exactly those things Nelson's own life now lacked.

The flash point came in 1968, when Rockefeller not only ignored Lindsay's request to call out the National Guard to pick up the mountains of garbage left by striking city sanitation workers, but settled the strike over the mayor's head. In return, Lindsay denounced Rockefeller for "cowardice" and "capitulation to blackmail." Nelson chose to believe that

Lindsay's outburst had been calculated to embarrass him and that it had actually been a critical factor in his loss of the presidential nomination to Nixon at Miami Beach. The following year he refused to endorse Lindsay in his reelection campaign, and the mayor reciprocated by endorsing Democrat Arthur Goldberg for governor in 1970. From then on it was open warfare, with Nelson using the full reach of his official and private leverage in the struggle that ended with Lindsay leaving the Republican party and, ultimately, public office.

It was not unique that Nelson should be involved in a struggle for power, but the amount of personal venom this particular conflict brought out in him did surprise those who had watched him over the years. He not only wanted to defeat Lindsay, he wanted to crush him as well.

People who had been in politics with him for twenty years began to see a new side of Nelson that was far different from the young man whose sins had once seemed to spring only from an excess of enthusiasm. He had grown irritable and wintry, and a calculating vindictiveness joined thwarted ambition as his prime traits. He ruled New York like a modern pharaoh, cajoling, wheedling, threatening, and intimidating legislators into supporting his programs and doing whatever was necessary to gain his ends.

He had grown increasingly cavalier and arrogant. His first move against Robert Moses—for decades regarded as the most powerful man in the state—was not begun for any reason of policy, or even of personality. Nelson simply wanted the chairmanship of the State Parks Commission for his brother Laurance. Nelson got the resignation from Moses, but it would be several years before the struggle between the two came to a head. When, in the late sixties, Nelson decided to centralize a state transportation empire under his aide William J. Ronan, Moses's last and seemingly most impregnable fortress—the Triborough Bridge Authority—stood in the way. The wall around this fortress consisted of the bondholders' covenants, which secured Moses's position and which not even a governor backed by the legislature could break—except that in this case the bondholders' trustee was the Chase Manhattan Bank. When the time came to merge the Triborough Bridge Authority into Nelson's superagency, he sat down with David in his 55th Street town house and within an hour concluded the arrangement.

There was nothing new in this mutuality. Nelson had always been ready to help David while advancing his own best interests. From the outset of his first administration, he had pushed for a liberalization of the laws on bank mergers and branch banking, and for the creation of bank holding companies, which would allow the banks to expand into other forms of business. Nelson also stepped in when the World Trade Center seemed about to become a costly white elephant. Though the Port Authority had floated $850 million in bonds to build it, and David and the Downtown Association had pressured the city into taking some major planning decisions to make it possible, as it neared completion it was finding it difficult to attract tenants. Nelson helped out by moving more than two dozen state offices into the Center buildings, taking out a 40-year state lease on 60 full floors of one of its 110-story twin towers. By 1974 the state was paying $18.3 million a year in rent to the Port Authority, and investigation by the Comptroller's Office was already under way to look into why the state was paying $4 million more annually on its rented space than private tenants were paying for comparable footage.

All of this was done with a brazen indifference for the consequences and regardless of whether the victims were powerful, like Moses, or impotent, like the vast unfathoming public who paid the bills. It was as William Farrell, former *New York Times* Albany bureau chief, said: "Nelson is a true democrat. He has contempt for *everyone* regardless of race, color, creed, religion or anything else." Aides who felt the sting of his increasingly foul moods called him "Fang" behind his back. Political opponents, T. H. White remarked, "called him the most ruthless man in politics."

Rockefeller still mixed with the people every four years, presenting his stage version of a plebeian style and filling up on ethnic foods; yet he realized as well as the voters that the persona of "Rocky" had become something like a joke whose punch line was too well known. He was almost as tired of running for office as New Yorkers were of having him run, and his campaigns came more and more to rely on massive infusions of money and lavish use of the media. Once gala affairs, they had become as predictable as a tank corps offensive rolling inexorably across the desert.

A more imaginative opponent might have taken advantage of New Yorkers' readiness to be convinced that Rockefeller was not an inevitability. Yet Arthur Goldberg's starchy pompousness only made Nelson seem more colorful than he was. The inability to take advantage of Rockefeller's weaknesses on issues went deeper than the yawning gap in resources between the two campaigns, although this was a large factor in Goldberg's defeat. The former Supreme Court Justice's ineptitude seemed to spring from a more profound source. Long after the campaign was over, aides were still speculating about it. One of them, speech writer Paul Weissman, feels that a vision of the family's awesome power had given

Rockefeller a kind of political voodoo over Goldberg: "I frankly think the campaign was over when Arthur was invited up to Pocantico late in the primary. The note came after it was pretty clear that he was going to be the Democratic nominee. It was cordial and handwritten, and Arthur accepted. He came back from the meeting terribly shaken. It was not, as some of us assumed at first, because of threats or anything like that, but just because for the first time in his political life he had seen what *real* power was, what it could buy, how it lived. Really, I don't think he was ever the same afterwards."

By early fall of 1970 Rockefeller had pulled even with Goldberg in the polls and in November he easily won an unprecedented fourth term. As always, victory was sweet, yet it was not like old times. People voted for him, he understood, but they didn't particularly like him. His status as the golden boy of American politics had long since slipped. As late as the 1968 presidential campaign, this diminished appeal had enough vestigial strength to inspire talk in political circles about how the country *needed* Nelson. His appalling record on civil liberties in New York was minimized, and his hard-line views on Vietnam were discounted the minute he began to make his ambiguous overtures to the antiwar sentiment that had crystallized around the candidacy of Robert Kennedy. People had willingly suspended their disbelief and made the sort of allowances for him they would not have made for any other politician in America. Underneath the pragmatism necessary to his profession, they said, was a man of basic humanity and liberal instinct, who just might be able to pull the nation out of its self-lacerating trauma and bind up its wounds.

As the seventies began, the myth of Nelson's liberalism could no longer be sustained. During the campaign against Goldberg, Nelson had emphasized his support of Nixon's Vietnamization plan, and when Senator Charles Goodell (whom he had appointed to Bobby Kennedy's seat in 1968) introduced his troop withdrawal plan, Nelson opposed it, saying, "It can only undermine the effectiveness of the President's bargaining position in negotiations with the North Vietnamese." In domestic affairs, he had inveighed against "welfare cheats," ordering audits of the relief rolls. He had announced cuts in Medicaid. Appealing to the silent majority in New York, he would remind audiences on the hustings that he had been "Spiro Agnew's first choice for President." Political observers interpreted these moves as a calculated "turn rightward," an attempt to make peace with the conservative wing of the Republican party and to accommodate the new interest in "law and order."

Nelson was in Washington, D.C., on September 9, 1971, attending a meeting of the Foreign Advisory Committee on International Intelligence, when he first got word from Commissioner of Corrections Russell Oswald that a rebellion had occurred at the state prison at Attica, and that 1,300 prisoners were holding 38 officials and guards in D Yard. Assuring Oswald that he had faith in his ability to handle the situation but cautioning him to avoid the appearance of "vacillation and indecision" in negotiations with inmates, Rockefeller told him that he would return to Pocantico the next day and assign his chief counsel "Bobby" Douglass to stay in contact with the situation. But when Oswald was unable to make headway in the discussion of inmate grievances, negotiations were taken over by an informal team of observers that included Congressman Herman Badillo, *New York Times* editor Tom Wicker, black State Assemblyman Arthur Eve, attorney William Kunstler, and others.

Discussions broke down on the issue of amnesty, which became especially crucial to inmates after a prison guard died of injuries suffered in the takeover. Equally crucial was whether Nelson would come to the scene of the crisis. On Sunday, four days after the rebellion first erupted, it appeared that troopers would be ordered to storm the prison. The observers broadcast a message over New York radio begging Rockefeller to intervene: "The committee of observers in Attica Prison is now convinced a massacre of prisoners and guards may take place in this institution. For the sake of our common humanity we call on everyone who hears these words to implore the Governor to come to Attica."

That afternoon, Wicker, Badillo, and State Senator John Dunne (who had Nelson's private phone number at Pocantico) talked with Rockefeller by phone for two hours, stressing that they wanted him on the scene at Attica. The conversation became a mini-campaign speech, as Tom Wicker later recalled in his book *A Time to Die.*

"'Governor,' said Wicker, 'I'm up here at Attica.'

"'I know you are,' Rockefeller broke in, 'and I just want you to know how grateful I am and how much I really admire what you and the others are doing up there. I know you've all worked hard and I appreciate it. I really do. It's just great. Just great.'"

But the bottom line was that he wasn't coming.

That evening Oswald too called the governor to ask him to come to the prison. Rockefeller replied that he had been in touch with Bobby Douglass and they had decided that he didn't have the constitutional authority to grant amnesty to the prisoners, so that a visit would be pointless. "In life," he told his commissioner of corrections, "it's not easy to face a hard decision, particularly when human lives are involved. . . . But I think that we have to look at these things not only in terms of the immediate but in terms of the large implication of what we are doing in our society."

The next morning Oswald called Nelson once more to ask if his mind was still made up. When Nelson said it was, orders went out to begin the offensive against the inmates assembled in D Yard. Without warning, a helicopter swooped down over the yard dropping a thick cloud of pepper gas. At this signal, snipers atop the prison battlegrounds let loose a hail of fire against the prisoners trapped in the yard, and an army of hundreds of state troopers and correction officers armed with shotguns and high-powered rifles began a volley of concentrated gunfire that lasted six minutes. When it was over, and the cease-fire order given, ten of the hostages and twenty-nine inmates lay dead or dying in the yard. (In all, forty-three would die at Attica at the hands of the assault squads and eighty would suffer gunshot wounds.) As the McKay Commission, which investigated the events afterward, commented, it was "with the exception of Indian massacres in the late 19th century . . . the bloodiest one-day encounter between Americans since the Civil War."

From the governor's office, a press release was issued following the attack; even those who had been sympathetic to Rockefeller's dilemma found it chilling: "Our hearts go out to the families of the hostages who died at Attica. The tragedy was brought on by the highly organized, revolutionary tactics of militants who rejected all efforts at a peaceful settlement, forced a confrontation and carried out cold-blooded killings they had threatened from the outset." When Rockefeller met the press two days later, however, autopsies had revealed that hostages did not die from having their throats slashed by their captors, as had first been suggested by prison officials, but from the troopers' deadly fire. Yet Nelson was not going to relinquish an inch of the ground he had staked out. He noted that when he was telephoned with the news that the remaining hostages had been brought out alive, he was "absolutely overwhelmed" with joy.

A reporter interjected, "What does this tell you about the prisoners, the fact that so many men [hostages] emerged unharmed?"

Rockefeller snapped back, "What it tells me is the use of this gas is a fantastic instrument in a situation of this kind."

Nelson's actions had a political reference that was wider than Attica, and which he never lost sight of. Shortly after the uprising was quelled, Nixon sent Rockefeller a telegram praising his "courage." William Safire, then still a Nixon aide, told political writer Richard Reeves: "The assault on Attica was a moral disgrace, but politically he did what our people wanted."

Attica was an ultimate indication of the extent to which Rockefeller had made his peace with the Republican party's mainstream. He could even veto antibussing and antiabortion measures passed by the New York legislature without being accused of backsliding, so firm was his conversion. On the larger issues—war and peace, crime and punishment—he was, in a favorite phrase of the Nixon administration, "on board."

Trying to assess the impact of the Rockefeller years in New York was like trying to analyze the aftereffects of a tornado. On coming to the governorship, Nelson had quickly grasped that there were two kinds of money available from the taxpayers: money for social services and money for construction. It was the second type that interested him. Like his father, he was intrigued by the sight of buildings going up, especially buildings that bore his stamp. And he realized that this kind of money had greater velocity and passed through more hands than social service money, reaching more of the people likely to help him in organizing a power base in the state. Construction money, as one person noted, could act "like a shot of cortisone on New York's metabolism." Never mind that too much cortisone might weaken New York's defenses of the body politic, as it could the human body. On becoming governor Nelson had assumed he wouldn't be in Albany long enough to face the consequences.

During nearly four terms in Albany, Rockefeller had repeatedly defended his increase of state expenditures as an effort to enhance what he called New York's "proud progressive tradition of services to our people." Yet the bulk of the monies he had spent had gone into monuments that had little relation to the pressing needs of New York's population—most notably the $1.2 billion Albany Mall. This sum was eerily close to the total benefaction of Senior and Junior combined, given over the course of nearly one hundred years—now taken back in one daring raid by the leader of the third Rockefeller generation.

In the field of narcotics, Nelson's failure was perhaps even more vivid than in the construction debacle at Albany. The 1966 civil commitment law was a shambles; the Narcotic Addiction Control Commission was itself a travesty of its original intentions. By 1972, almost three-quarters of the $224 million it had spent had gone into the construction of residential facilities. Some of them never opened; those that did spent $30 million a year on payroll and had more employees than addicts, although only a tiny fraction of the employees were physicians and psychiatrists. Of 5,172 individuals treated and released under the NACC's compulsory treatment program, only 141 were drug-free at the end of a year and a half, which meant each cure had cost New Yorkers about $1.6 million.

In his 1973 state of the state message to the legislature, Rockefeller acknowledged that the program had been a failure, that despite the nearly $500 million spent on drug control during his years in office, heroin-related deaths had risen by 32 percent and drug use had reached "epidemic proportions." Yet if the compulsory commitment program of 1966 had struck many New Yorkers as an extremist measure, he now proposed to replace it with one that was if anything even more severe. Almost in the same breath as admitting the failure of the 1966 law, Nelson announced a new program based on giving mandatory life sentences for persons convicted of possessing or selling drugs, with "bounties" paid to informants whose tips led to drug convictions.

As Nelson left office, draconian drug laws and other stiff rhetoric could hardly divert attention from the fact that the state was in moral and fiscal chaos; its political functions had atrophied and its future was weighed down under the burden of financial obligations that would tie its legislators' hands indefinitely. New Yorkers were already paying dearly for his public and private works—those they had approved at the ballot box and those on which they never had a chance to vote. Taxes of one kind or another had gone up in 8 of his 15 years in office, although his earliest and firmest pledge to New York voters had been that there would be no increases. Taxes amounted to $94 per person when he came to power, $460 per person when he left. When he came to Albany, there was no state sales tax; now there was one of 4 percent; the 3-cent cigarette tax had jumped to 15 cents a pack; the state gasoline tax had doubled.

The state budget had increased by 300 percent, but the state debt had increased by 400 percent. The semipublic authorities Nelson had brought into wide use now operated, according to State Comptroller Arthur Levitt, "on a scale so massive that, in some instances, they overshadow the fiscal operations of the state itelf." By the time Nelson left office, these authorities had an outstanding debt of $10 billion, with $50 million a year required merely to pay the interest. It was as if Nelson had taken a huge mortgage on New York's future to finance the expensive therapy required by what was now widely recognized as his "edifice complex."

Nelson blamed the federal government for the state's fiscal chaos. Noting that New Yorkers got only fourteen cents returned from their federal tax dollar in services, he went to Washington and became a persistent witness at congressional hearings into revenue sharing. Yet even here he was trapped in his own history, which prohibited him from seeking a real solution, for while he favored transferring services provided by the federal government to the state, he opposed any cuts in the defense budget—which accounted for most of the tax dollar and which he, as much as any living American, had helped elevate to its outrageous levels.

Yet it was not just radicals, Gay Libbers, and Right-to-Lifers who were disenchanted with Nelson. When they had a chance, the mass of New Yorkers were increasingly voting no on Rockefeller. Two transportation bond issues he had deemed especially vital—one for $2.5 billion in 1971 and one for $3.5 billion two years later—were roundly rejected by the electorate. The machinery seemed to be slipping out of his control. Even institutions like the Museum of Modern Art that had always been under his family's and his own control began to get obstreperous. At a 1971 exhibit of kinetic sculpture, one of the pieces was a whimsical voting machine designed by sculptor Hans Haake: people passing it could pause, look, and then cast a vote *against* Nelson Rockefeller.

In December 1973, Nelson announced that he was resigning from the governorship before the expiration of his term. By resigning when he did, Nelson accomplished several things at once. He spared himself from having to run for reelection in 1974 and defend his record in New York, although his control over New York politics was by now so complete that he probably didn't have to worry. To Lieutenant Governor Malcolm Wilson—descibed by Albany Mayor Erastus Corning as a man who had spent fifteen years "playing second fiddle in a one man band"—he gave the chance to run as an incumbent. He nonetheless still maintained control over the Republican state organization and delegation for the 1976 convention. Finally, he freed himself to spend the next three years gaining national visibility and meeting potential delegates across the country as chairman of two important federal commissions.

One was the National Commission on Water Quality. Established in 1972 with a budget of $2.5 million, it had a mandate to investigate the implementation of water pollution control standards and to report in two years. The other and more important was the Commission on Critical Choices for Americans. It had begun as a state commission studying New York's planning for the future, but as the convulsions within the Republican party gave Nelson new hope for 1976, he persuaded President Nixon to give it federal standing and a new mandate to report on the nation's prospects as it entered its third century.

The idea was that, as Nelson was now free of Albany, he could crisscross the country in his capacity as commission chairman, holding public hearings and allowing potential convention delegates to catch a glimpse of his new conservative ideas and image. And by July 4, 1976, when the nation was celebrating its two-hundredth anniversary and Republicans were getting ready to meet to select their standard-bearer, Rockefeller's commission would deliver the first part of its report prescribing a "way out" of what Americans had grown used to as their perennially changing and deepening national crisis.

The scenario might have been scripted in Hollywood. There was no margin for error; everything depended on Nixon's success in stonewalling through the Watergate investigations and surviving to the end or almost the end of his second term so that Gerald Ford could not establish himself as a legitimate national figure. (As late as February 11, 1974, Nelson was still defending this position, telling journalists that those who would "harass and drive a President out of office by resignation would not only circumvent but abrogate the Constitution of the United States.") He had been identified as a wrecker so long that he could no longer take his chances in mounting an insurgent campaign for the nomination at some future time. For Ronald Reagan, perhaps, such a campaign could be interpreted as an exercise in conviction; in Rockefeller it would only rattle old skeletons in his political closet. As it became clear that Nixon's days were numbered, Nelson decided to seize the main chance and began lobbying vigorously to fill the soon-to-be-vacant number-two position. After Nixon resigned, the newly inaugurated Gerald Ford held a *pro forma* consultation with party leaders and surprised nobody by announcing that Nelson Rockefeller was his choice as Vice-President.

Nelson's acceptance of the vice-presidential nomination was oddly anticlimactic. How many times had he claimed that he was "not cut out to be Number Two"? How often had he scoffed at the idea that he, a Rockefeller, should become "standby equipment"? Yet his moment of truth had come: he knew this was his last, best shot at the prize he otherwise had little chance of winning. This way he would at least have a seat at the table where the high-stakes game was going on and be in a position to take advantage of the country's volatile politics.

As so often in the past, however, Nelson's euphoria about his political career was not shared by family members. Laurance, as always, was an exception, and David was able to accept it reluctantly as part of the necessary burden of his family's stewardly responsibility. But the rest of the Rockefellers were not very pleased; many were not even particularly proud. For the Cousins—most of whom were actively opposed to Nelson and his politics—the nomination meant only an annoying alteration in their life-style. The must now become conscious of security (the Secret Service had soon contacted them all) in a way that further emphasized the vast distance between them and others, a distance they had spent much of their lives trying to narrow. It had been one thing for Nelson to be elected to office; it was quite another to accept an appointment that meant submitting to a a nationally televised grilling which would inevitably involve the rest of them, their careers and riches. As one aide in Room 5600 put it, "There is a strong feeling among the Rockefeller family that they want their privacy. And they would rather that Nelson was not Vice-President if the central trusts were exposed."

Yet it was with relish for exactly these details that the capital waited impatiently for hearings to begin. Nelson was not just another rich man like John Kennedy—he was part of a vast agglomeration of wealth and influence. As *New York Times* Washington correspondent William Shannon wrote, "Not since Lady Godiva rode naked through the streets of Coventry have the inhabitants of any town itched to see something usually hidden as people here now desire to see the extent of the Rockefeller fortune." But those who hoped the hearing would become a significant inquiry into the way the premier family in America used its immense wealth and power to influence national policy soon found that Nelson's strategy was to give the senators just enough hint of his family's fortune to awe them into submission.

Dressed in one of his inconspicuously elegant dark blue pin-striped suits, he sauntered into the Senate caucus room on the morning of August 23, occasionally breaking out of the flying wedge of aides to grab at some legislator or friend with the two-handed handshake he uses when he wants to emphasize the warmth of his feelings. Sitting in the same red leather chair where witnesses little more than a year earlier had begun the long death of the Nixon presidency, he spread a jumble of scrawled notes to himself on the green table, checked with aides as to what files they carried, and smiled at a phrase in Senator Jacob Javits' introduction: "If you gave a civil service examination for President, at the head of the class would be Nelson Rockefeller." The only sign of nervousness was the speed with which he attacked the carafe of water in front of him, emptying it in the first two hours of his testimony; yet there was no hesitancy in the 72-page history of the Rockefeller family that stood as his opening statement.

It was the Rockefellers' money that people were primarily interested in. The figures had always been held on to as tightly as classified government secrets. How much exactly had Senior left Junior? What had he done with it? How much did the Brothers have? What had they done with it? How much of the American economy did they now control with their purse strings?

The family had always avoided rendering an accounting not only because to do so would be to violate the most guarded principles of individual privacy, but primarily because it would involve giving up some intangible yet essential part of their power, draining a crucial element of mystery from it and robbing the myth of part of its animating spirit. Yet this secrecy now stood as an obstacle in Nelson's way, and he did not hesitate to sacrifice it. As he told the senators, "This myth about the power which my family exercises needs to be brought out into the light. . . . It just does not exist. I have to tell you I do not wield economic power."

All during the week before he began his testimony, Rockefeller had been chuckling to reporters who asked him about his personal fortune, hinting that they should be prepared to be disappointed in their extravagant expectations. One unconvincingly low figure of $22 million had been leaked. Now it was time for the truth. After finishing his historical sketch, Nelson turned to the financial data. Junior had gotten $465 million from Senior. Of this he had put $240 million into the Chase in trusts for his sons and grandchildren. Nelson's own share of these trusts, which had grown huge over the years, was $116 million in a depressed market. (The '34 Trust had, in fact, dropped $20 million in two months.) In addition, he itemized $62 million in personal assets, which was in the main made up of his huge art collection ($33 million), real estate ($11 million), and securities ($12 million); added to the trusts, this made a total of almost $179 million. Later, an IRS audit would raise the value of his real estate, and his total fortune would then stand at $218 million.

It was a phenomenal sum by most standards. Yet it was dwarfed by the billion-dollar personal fortunes of a J. Paul Getty, Howard Hughes, or H. Ross Perot. The Rockefellers had a lot of money, but it certainly wasn't equal to the reputation of riches it carried; nor was it enough to control the economy in a way it was alleged that they did. This became even more evident (and the revelation even more disappointing) as Nelson went on to describe the current holdings in Standard Oil.

Nelson's disclosures exploded the myth of the family's mega-wealth and its vast portfolio power. Yet the point was not, as he implied, that they lacked the power attributed to them, but that this power lay elsewhere. Its nature was far more potent and complex than indicated by net worth. In a striking consensus of views, Wall Streeters interviewed by *The New York Times* in the wake of Nelson's statement agreed that the Rockefeller portfolio was only the merest tip of the ïceberg. "If you go just on his holdings of stock," commented one investment banker talking about the family influence, "it's piddling. But let's face it, the Rockefellers are the Rockefellers." Another financier observed, "In family power in the United States, there is nothing that even faintly resembles the Rockefellers. They have tremendous power."

The nature of the power showed how successful Junior had been in his attempt to consolidate the dynasty. It did not spring from money, but from the unique network of Rockefeller institutions and associations, beginning in the economy but now stretching across all the political, cultural, and intellectual boundaries of the national enterprise. As a result of Junior's colossal investment in diverse fields and institutions and the Brothers' lifetime of activities in an even more kaleidoscopic range of endeavors, there was hardly a significant arena of decision making in which their employees, protégés, or institutions did not exert a major influence. Even the Rockefeller Foundation, in which they were no longer paramount, was run by men they had had a hand in appointing and who had experienced a profound sense of obligation to the family for its largesse. If the underlying trend of power in the nation was from individuals to institutions, the dynasty Junior had created was enmeshed in the syndication of such networks and gave the Brothers an unrivaled influence in national affairs. The Mellons and a few other American families may have been richer, but among the power elite whose rule stretched from Wall Street to Washington the Rockefellers were without peer.

Yet no one on the Senate Rules Committee could (or would) pierce the veil. West Virginia Senator Robert Byrd, alone in appearing not totally awed by Nelson, attempted to get the witness to be more candid about his family's power, but the line of questioning was spiked by Senate Minority Leader Hugh Scott, who acted almost as Rockefeller's attorney on the committee. His support made Nelson even bolder in his evasions of the issues at hand. When pressed by Senator Byrd about potential conflicts of interest should he be confirmed, he began by denying the existence of a "Rockefeller empire" and proceeded to confuse the issue with a lecture on the American system itself. The free enterprise system had made America "the greatest nation in the world," he said. "This system is not an empire. It is a democracy."

This was the characteristic way Nelson dealt with the conflict-of-interest question when it reappeared throughout the hearings. He would simply assert that he loved his country, or that he would take an oath of office and this in itself would dispose of the issue. Did the senators mean to be so discourteous as to imply that he who had dedicated his life to public service could intend anything venal or self-interested in fulfilling his duties? Rockefeller's assumption of a posture of almost divine rectitude and innocence made the questions about power appear increasingly defensive and apologetic.

After several frustrating attempts to establish that the accession to the vice-presidency must result in a vast concentration of Rockefeller power, Senator Byrd finally reduced his interrogation to a modest effort to pry from Nelson the admission that the combining of his great economic wealth and the great political power of the office would mean "a far greater power" for him than "for the average occupant whose financial means is much less than yours." Yet Nelson's reaction was so obtuse that he answered even this in the negative. From that point it would have been embarrassing to proceed, and no one was willing to cause embarrassment to the meticulously courteous figure before them. The issue of power and its potential for conflicts was left behind, everyone realizing that the Rockefellers' conflicts of interest were so pervasive and in a sense unintentional that they exemplified the conflicts inherent in the system itself.

At the end of the first day of testimony, Nelson gathered up his papers, put his silver pen in his pocket, and told reporters, "I thought it was great," as the television klieg lights went off and he pushed his way out of the room. The next two days went equally well. He presented his family as people so deeply involved in their individual pursuits that they had no time to come together for the sort of planning for control that only the paranoid could assume they did. In addition to their relatively "small" holdings in the Chase Bank, the Standard companies, and some other industries, and except for some of Laurance's venture capital companies, there was no enterprise in which they held more than 2 percent. With Republican Senators Scott and Marlow Cook running interference, Nelson was not only able to fend off questions concerning individual and family conflicts of interest, but also such suggestions of failure as the handling of Attica, the virtual bankruptcy of the state of New York, and other matters involving his record. Questioning on his commitments in foreign affairs, the most crucial part of his political personality, was almost nil.

By September 15 the senators had finished. Immediately after Ford had nominated him, White House and congressional mail had been overwhelmingly opposed to the choice, but the only noteworthy opposition during the hearing came from Angela Davis, the Liberty Lobby (which remained convinced that the Rockefellers had bankrolled the international Communist conspiracy), and Right-to-Life groups still seething over his veto of the repeal of New York's liberalized abortion law. This strange mélange seemed only to underline his inevitability.

Feeling he was as good as confirmed, Nelson took a quick vacation following the Senate hearings. It was while Nelson was on the West Coast that disquieting leaks began to appear. New material had turned up in investigations by Congress, the IRS, and the FBI (which would ultimately have 300 agents on the Rockefeller case). In quick order it was revealed that audits showed he owed nearly $1 million in back taxes; that in 1970 he had gotten his brother Laurance to put $60,000 into a dummy corporation to finance a derogatory biography of gubernatorial opponent Arthur Goldberg by right-wing columnist Victor Lasky; that he and his family had spent some $20 million on his political career alone, not to mention contributions to other candidates; and most damning of all, that he had made loans or gifts (or some combination of the two) to public officials totaling several millions including $50,000 to Henry Kissinger, $250,000 to New York Urban Development Corporation head Ed Logue, and $625,000 to MTA chief William Ronan.

On October 20 Nelson's staff released a list of his philanthropies over the preceding seventeen years. It was a use of the philanthropic gesture which his grandfather would have approved, yet the total of $24.7 million illustrated how diminished charitable activity had become in the family over the years. The list itself hardly showed a broad-gauged interest in the well-being of mankind. About 70 percent of Nelson's giving involved what were basically gifts to himself, his family, and their institutional extensions, Jackson Hole Preserve, Inc., the Rockefeller Brothers Fund, the Museum of Primitive Art, the Museum of Modern Art, the state of New York (to landscape the grounds of the Executive Mansion and furnish the governor's quarters in the style to which he was accustomed).

The publication of the list and the illness of Happy served to dampen some of the mounting criticism against him, but he was worried. The news leaks breaking all around him had managed to levitate the unexorcised ghost of Watergate, and Nelson now found his nomination in trouble. Appealing personally to Committee Chairman Howard Cannon, he tried to get the hearings rolling again. He publicly demanded that the Senate Rules Committee reconvene to allow him a chance to answer charges against him. But he had to wait for the completion of the elections, and for a month he was like a beached whale. All he could do was wage a war of press releases, finally using even the news of Happy's operation to board the brief wave of sympathy Betty Ford's mastectomy had won the administration.

It was not until November 13, after the Republican debacle that had swallowed up his friend Malcolm Wilson and many others, that Nelson was back on the stand. Unruffled, his opening statement was to remind people that he was no Nixon operating in the back alleys of the system, but a member of the mainstream. "It is the unbought voice of the American people that here ultimately determines everything," he lectured.

Yet in the material that had emerged, the public got its first chance to see the approximate features of the real Rockefeller. The face was far different from that of the sophisticated charmer of the first round of hearings. The issues had been placed into a new framework. Nelson was no longer "clean as a hound's tooth," in the phrase so frequently used in the days following his selection by Gerald Ford. Nor could he continue to press the implication that the great advantage he offered over other politicians was that he was too rich to be bought. What had been shown was something more sinister (yet ironically less blameworthy, according to current political standards) than being bought; being rich enough to do the buying. The information that had surfaced between the first and second rounds of hearings showed him to be as much a ruthless operator in politics as his grandfather had been in oil.

Of the charges that had been made against him, taxes were the easiest to field. In the past 10 years, he had paid more than $11 million. The additional $1 million the IRS now wanted came from exaggerated deductions of office expenses and for costs claimed for the management of his investments. In some sense it was palliated by Nixon's recent tax innovations. As *The New York Times* wrote: "In dollar terms, Mr. Nixon's big tax reducing devices were the illegal ones. It appears that the amounts Mr. Rockefeller saved in taxes by pushing right to the outer limits of the law—and possibly past them—were small compared with those he saved simply by using the special privileges that were available to him within the law." His financial statement indicated that he received about $1 million a year in interest on tax-exempt municipal bonds, some of them from the very authorities by which he had built his expensive public works monuments while governor. (His trust, held by the Chase, included 3,254,000 shares of New York State Housing Authority bonds; 3.2 million shares of New York State Power Authority bonds; and 1 million shares of Port of New York Authority construction bonds.) Other rich men's deductions Nelson was able to use included his art and his Standard Oil stock. When he gave a painting to a museum (even though he usually stipulated it would remain in his possession for the rest of his life), he deducted the market value instead of the purchase price. Overall, *The New York Times* estimated

427

that the true cost of his $24 million in charitable donations from 1957 to 1974 was closer to $8 million, since if he had not made them, in his tax bracket he would have paid $16 million more in federal taxes.

The Lasky book may have been poorly researched and shoddily written, as Nelson claimed, yet it smacked of one of Donald Segretti's dirty tricks. Moreover, Nelson's denial of knowledge of the book was as much an issue as his commissioning of it. When first asked about it under oath by the FBI, he had denied any knowledge of or involvement with the biography. On October 10, after information leaked to the effect that he had indeed been involved, he issued a statement to the press again denying responsibility, this time blaming Laurance for backing the project in an excess of brotherly loyalty: "Evidently what happened was that my brother had agreed to participate as an investor in underwriting a book that was expected to sell well. . . . Had he only told me about it at the time, I would have been totally opposed to it and would have strongly advised against his participation in any form." In the same press release Laurance validated this statement to cover for his brother, although privately he had been upset by the attempt to make him a fall guy. He visited his daughter Lucy in Washington shortly after the announcement and (in her words) "appeared extremly downcast." He told her that he had not masterminded the Lasky book and promised that the blame would soon be taken from his shoulders. When he reappeared before the committee, Nelson issued a "clarifying" statement completely changing his position and admitting that it was actually he who had recommended Laurance make the investment in the book.

If it had been another man, the perjury and the lies might have been taken seriously. But when Nelson took the stand, he described the bewildering maze that had led to the "unfortunate" decision: how Jack Wells (Lasky's attorney and an old political operative of Nelson's) came to him with the proposal, was sent to family attorney Donal O'Brien, who got Laurance involved and then got J. R. Dilworth to set up the investment through a dummy corporation in Philadelphia. The message seemed to be that this was the way decisions got made in the rarefied atmosphere of Room 5600, where another man's perjury was a Rockefeller's bureaucratic snafu. After being led through that bureaucracy, the senators tired of the matter and gave up. When Arthur Goldberg appeared at the hearings to testify, Nelson rushed up to shake his hand and said, "Thanks for coming." It was as if his former opponent had come to a Rockefeller testimonial dinner.

It was the question of political contributions that tended to contradict most dramatically Nelson's previous testimony that the economic power of his family was a myth. By his own figures, Nelson had contributed some $3,265,373 in his years in politics, much of it to himself. Yet Nelson's own giving was just the beginning. Other family members had chipped in every four years (or every two when he was running for President) as if by prescribed tithe and regularly enough to refute Nelson's previous testimony that the family rarely acted in concert. In all, they had contributed something over $20 million, with JRD3 giving the least and Laurance the most, and with nearly $11 million coming from the Martha Baird Rockefeller trusts, which had been established under the Brothers' control to handle their stepmother's residual estate.

Yet it was the series of gifts and loans that most showed the Rockefeller style. When news of the several millions given to aides and operatives first broke, it conjured up visions of a Renaissance prince throwing bags of gold to his retainers and awarding small kingdoms to his liege lords. "Rockefeller benefactions to federal officials," editorialized The New York Times, ". . . are aspects of private government more appropriate to Florence in the days of Lorenzo the Magnificent than to democratic America." Although subjected to stiff questioning, however, Nelson insisted these were the result rather of simple human decency stemming from the family's philanthropic ethic and the "American tradition" of sharing. He had been taught, he testified, that when he had a basket of apples and others did not, he ought to share his apples with them.

From what he said, it might have seemed that the men he had gathered around him had been victims of contagion or disaster. Yet on the whole, they were not poor men. William Ronan, for instance, was making over $100,000 a year while getting the last of his hardship loans from Nelson. It was the case of L. Judson Morhouse, however, that was most indicative of the puzzling and disquieting nature of Nelson's largesse.

The relationship went far back—to 1958, when Morhouse, as chairman of the State Republican Committee, played a key role in getting Nelson the gubernatorial nomination. After he was elected, Nelson lent Morhouse $100,000 for a business investment and persuaded Laurance to lend him $49,000 to buy some stock in a gas transmission company whose shares would soon yield a $100,000 windfall profit when put on the open market. Before the committee, the reason given for this charity was that Morhouse was unable to make ends meet; yet, between 1959 and 1963, he had made $231,000 as a lobbyist in Albany.

In 1966 Morhouse was convicted of taking a bribe in a scandal surrounding the State Liquor Authority. In 1970, after appeals were exhausted and he was about to start serving a term in prison, Nelson pardoned him because he had terminal cancer; at the time of the hearings, nearly five years later, Morhouse was still alive. In 1973, Nelson forgave him the $100,000 he had lent him. This caused some to wonder what it was Morhouse had done to deserve this loyalty and whether the gift had played any role as hush money in the Liquor Authority case. In any event, Morhouse managed to get from Rockefeller what the Watergate burglars were never quite able to extract from Nixon: a full pardon and a cash payoff.

The discussion in the hearings revolved around the question of what exactly Nelson had gotten from Morhouse and the others to whom he had made immense loans and gifts, and whether this largesse put them on call should he ask for favors afterward. Yet the hearings never really penetrated to the deeper commitment, for these monies represented far more than a simple cash transaction. Nelson did not make the deals in order to buy Kissinger, Ronan, Logue, and the others: in a large sense he already owned them as the patron of their rise to the heights they now enjoyed. The cash was more a reminder of who was lord and who the vassal.

By the end of the Senate hearings, Nelson had managed to dissipate a good deal of the myth his father had devoted a life to building. It was not the sense of the family's power that had been destroyed; if anything the mystique had been augmented by the spectacle of U.S. senators paying such deference to it. It was the philanthropic core of the myth that suffered by Nelson's exposure. His father had labored a lifetime to prove that Rockefeller gifts were something more than bribery; in a few memorable moments of the hearings, by presenting what certainly appeared to be political payoffs as pure-minded philanthropy, Nelson undid the effort.

In part because of this, in part because of the ill will stirred up by the disclosures, the rest of the Rockefellers had become increasingly agitated as the hearings progressed; their anxiety increased as it began to seem possible that one or more of them in addition to Laurance (who had appeared with his usual obtuse urbanity before the Senate Rules Committee) might be called to testify.

Nelson himself didn't seem much to care. There was a certain relish evident in his manner during his second appearance before the Senate Rules Committee. His answers to the questions flung at him did not remove the shadow of doubt that now covered his career and personality. Far from it, the image remaining after the hearings were over was that of a ruthless man of power possessed by an almost obsessive ambition. But it was not that of a corruptionist. Moreover, if great wealth in itself was not a disqualification for the office (as all the senators agreed), then there was finally little to be said. For everything Nelson had been and done had resulted from the immensity of his resources and his resolution to use them in a maximum way.

By the time the hearings passed on to the House on November 21, all doubts about confirmation had disappeared. It was nearly two months since the original revelations—if they could be called that—had placed his career in a moral penumbra. Rather than beginning an avalanche of damning corroboration, the original news leaks had summarized what was to come. Nothing further had been revealed. There was a growing mood to speed things up and get Nelson into the vacancy, especially as Gerald Ford floundered in his first months in office. Whatever his personal defects, so went the one myth left standing, Nelson had access to the "best people" in the country. Perhaps he, with his immense resources, could shore things up at the White House.

Nelson was to get his stiffest questioning in the House hearings, where he was handled with less deference than in the Senate. Yet with the doubts about confirmation all but gone, he gave back as good as he got, as he sat joking and sipping at a glass filled with Gatorade.

Casual observers couldn't have known it, but the climax of the hearing came midway through the House inquiry. Two University of California professors, Charles Schwartz and William Domhoff, had sent each congressman a paper entitled "Probing the Rockefeller Fortune." The paper laid out the thesis that the Rockefeller fortune, though vested in individual members of the family, was actually centrally coordinated by Room 5600 and represented a vast concentration of economic power. They had determined that 15 family employees working out of Room 5600 sat on the boards of some 100 corporations with combined assets of $70 *billion*.

The rebuttal witness was the silver-haired head of the family office J. Richardson Dilworth. In the Senate hearings, he had appeared as one peripherally involved in the corporate subterfuge surrounding the Goldberg book. Here he was appearing as the head of Room 5600, and the material he presented was a sop thrown to those who might otherwise have clamored for an appearance by David to testify about the uses of his power at the Chase, and respond to persistent rumors that Rockefeller political allies and friends had been given preferential treatment by the bank in a wide variety of services.

For three days beforehand, Dilworth had been on the phone with his clients, the Brothers and the Cousins. He had called to inform each of them that he would be a witness and that circumstances now compelled him to do something he had hoped would not be necessary, in fact something that went profoundly against his grain—list all the family's property and holdings as a way of laying to rest the questions that had arisen as a result of rumors and the Schwartz-Domhoff testimony concerning the family's economic power.

It was Tuesday morning, November 26, when Dilworth came before the House Rules Committee armed with five charts showing the way Room 5600 managed the $244 million in charities under its control and how it manipulated the family securities. The assets of the 84 family members calculated from Dilworth's figures and from previously provided information came to nearly $1.3 billion. The list of securities that Dilworth presented was an unprecedented accounting. Never before in the history of America's great fortunes had any of the proprietors disclosed the true extent of their ownings and wealth. "It may be of interest to this committee," Dilworth observed, underlining the obvious, "that this is the first time that any attempt has been made to aggregate the financial holdings of this family in this or any other manner." Dilworth's testimony left many questions unanswered, but it did show what basically had happened to the fortune that had once been America's greatest.

Although the $1.3 billion it came to was less than a quarter of the sum that had generally been projected, it was hardly a case of "shirtsleeves to shirtsleeves in three generations" as Junior had once worried might be the case. He and his father had given more than $1 billion to the great corporate philanthropies which had brought unparalleled acclaim to the family name. He and his sons had probably spent an equal sum supporting themselves in a style of regal splendor and in maintaining the dynastic retinue that operated out of Rockefeller Center and extended their reach into the vast complex of establishment institutions and associations that constituted a private caucus on the nation's destiny and progress. And yet, as a result of the surplus the fortune continued to generate, its total was slightly more than it had been at its highest point sixty-five years earlier. It was having your cake and eating it too on an epic scale.

Although many of Dilworth's answers were evasive in a manner not unnatural for a man whose responsibility was managing a great accumulation of wealth, his data were such as to confirm the impression previously conveyed by Nelson that the Rockefeller family holdings were diffuse and did not represent the vast concentration of ownership control in major American corporations that Rockefeller critics had talked about for years. Among the Rockefeller holdings in corporations with over $300 million in sales, only three amounted to more than 2 percent of the stock. As Dilworth himself noted, this contrasted with other great families who were known to hold controlling shares of 10 to 20 percent in four or five corporations more than twice the size of these. Excluding their holdings in IBEC, the Standard Oil companies, the Chase, and Rockefeller Center, the Rockefellers' largest cash investment was the more than 300,000 shares they held in IBM. This stock was worth more than $70 million; yet this was only one-quarter of 1 percent of outstanding IBM shares.

In his testimony, Dilworth also sought to pare down the number of interlocking directorates generated by the economic power of the family. He picked Nelson's aide George Hinman as an illustrative case, since Hinman's directorship of IBM accounted for several billion of the $70 billion aggregate of corporations listed by Domhoff and Schwartz. It was true that Hinman had worked for Nelson for years and was still a consultant to the Office and even designated to inform the Office of the situation of the company. Yet, as Dilworth explained, Hinman was a director of IBM not because of his Rockefeller relationship, but because his father-in-law was Thomas Watson, the founder of IBM.

Dilworth's observations were meant to lay to rest the ghost of the Rockefellers' "empire." In a sense they did, yet they also raised the specter of a much more imposing network of interlocking relationships than was intimated by shareholdings in the Rockefeller portfolio. If the son-in-law of the founder of IBM and one of its biggest stockholders considered working as a Rockefeller aide a worthy career, what did that suggest about the reach of Rockefeller power? This power was certainly based on the primary place the family had long occupied in international banking and oil. But clearly it did not end there.

In one sense the powers of the Rockefellers were the generic powers of the rich: possession of the means by which individuals rose, institutions developed, and elites prospered. But there was another dimension of their power, one that made them different from even the wealthiest of their peers. If it had a corporate identity, it was the billion-dollar investment that Junior and Senior had made in the superstructures of the social order. Directorships in one or a hundred business corporations had little to do with the ability of the Rockefellers to lift an academic like Henry Kissinger or Dean Rusk into the stratospheres of national power and policy, or to put together a prestigious body like the Rockefeller panels and establish the framework of national defense strategies over a decade.

If there were interlocking relationships that reflected their influence, they were the interlocks with government and philanthropy, with the scientific and cultural establishments, with top leadership in business and politics, which made the descendants of John D. Rockefeller more potent as a family than the richer Du Ponts and Mellons. In the end it was the dynastic ambition, the lifetime spent in "public service," and the active assumption of leadership roles that tied these threads of influence together and knit them into a formidable social force. It was the network of interconnections *across* the realms of business, culture, and politics—all of it institutionalized in Room 5600—that gave them what one Wall Streeter described to *The New York Times* as "a position in the sun." This position was beyond the will or ability of the Congress to probe.

The House hearings finally dragged to a conclusion. Shortly afterward, Nelson was confirmed. The doubts remained, but there was nothing that could be done about them. On December 10, with his young sons Nelson, Jr. and Mark squirming alongside Happy in the gallery, Nelson placed his hand on his grandmother Cettie Rockefeller's Bible—the one he had used four times previously in Albany—and took the oath of office. Reporters present claimed that they saw him lift his glasses and wipe a tear away before he began his speech accepting the great responsibility now officially thrust upon him.

Nelson had reached a vantage point he badly wanted, however ambiguous his triumph would become over the next few months. To get to the vice-presidency, he had looted the family mythology, trading the awe and mystery of the Rockefeller name for the satisfaction of this last ambition. He had picked up the last remaining IOU, scraped up the last of the goodwill his father had stored up for the family. His ambition and the question of the Rockefeller's future had been fatefully entwined since he was a young man musing on the coincidence that he had been born on the same day as his famous grandfather. Now he had dealt the tradition that flowed from the first John D. a mortal blow even as he was fulfilling its dictates. He was, in a sense, the last Rockefeller. As he was making his way toward the summit one last time, a new Rockefeller generation was watching from below with something like revulsion for the spectacle he had made of them all.

THE COUSINS

CHAPTER 22

Looking as though it had somehow run off the tracks of Western Pacific's Feather River line and tumbled to a stop in the freshly mown field, red caboose number 694 stands rusty and flaking in the moist warmth of the northern California summer. Smoke curls out of a stovepipe poking up from its roof. The only sounds are the busy noise of bees from a nearby hive, the territorial screech of red-winged blackbirds, and the muted bump of a car driving up a nearby dirt road.

A blond woman emerges from the back of the caboose where she has just finished cooking over a wood-burning stove. Her hair is gathered off her pretty sun-freckled face into an old green cloth serving as a bandanna; a thin coating of dust clings to her handmade ankle-length skirt. Trailed by a barefooted four-year-old with light hair and faded blue eyes that resemble her own, she spreads some dinner scraps on a compost pile and then walks over to shade herself for a moment in a stand of locust trees. Sweating slightly and looking out over the mesa rising above the California coastline, she resembles a character from *The Emigrants*, as content in respite as in labor.

Someone who knew her might easily shatter the illusion by asking what the great-granddaughter of John D. Rockefeller and potentially one of the richest and most powerful women in the country is doing in a place like this. But for Marion, second daughter of Laurance, the answer comes easily and without affectation. "It feels good here," she says in her soft, serious way. "Very good. The work, everything. Things seem to be coming out all right. More and more I feel that I control my life, that it's *my* life and not in hock to the family."

Marion lives here in the caboose only on weekends and in the summer. The rest of the time is spent in Berkeley, where her husband, Warren, is finishing a Ph.D. thesis in English at the university. The plan is to move here permanently when he finishes, and complete the organic farm foreshadowed in the two acres of pumpkins and cherry tomatoes whose fruits are sold in the fall at a roadside stand. In the meantime, they work hard to be self-sufficient and to keep a tight budget. So far they manage on $700 a month for a family of four, the first Rockefellers in more than a hundred years to live below the national average. The next goal, when they move to the farm, will be $300, bartering their produce with neighboring farmers for eggs and meat, and then as close to absolute self-sufficiency as possible. It is close to the spirit of the first John D.'s Ledger A, except that Marion, unlike previous Rockefellers, is trying to be free of the money, not worthy of it. A convert to Thoreau's idea that one is rich in proportion to the number of things he can do without, she supplements Warren's income as a teaching assistant by babysitting and weaving, and by growing comfrey in the backyard of the Berkeley house and selling it to local health food stores who have no idea that they are paying 50 cents a plant to a Rockefeller with a $10 million trust fund and the promise of many times that to come.

Although she is perhaps stronger in her determination to establish her own relationship to the world, she is like her other cousins in her attitude toward money: the wrestling is symbolic of an effort to gain control over the terms of her life; its aim, as she puts it, is "to get off the breast." Most of the fourth Rockefeller generation have spent long years with psychiatrists in their efforts to grapple with the money and the family, the taint and the promise. Marion explores inner space in her own way—among other things by attending to the promptings of an uncreated consciousness that finds expression in her dreams. Many of them are explicitly about her family, and almost literary in their attempt to fix the dilemma.

"Our family was all together," she recounts one of them. "We were dressed in flowing and very expensive clothes, with golden thread and thick, rich fabric. We are all walking down this road; it is beautiful, smooth, and very pleasant, and we're gliding over it. But suddenly I see out of the corner of my eye that there are people in the pastures on both sides of us, people we never knew were there, just regular people looking at us with envy and curiosity. I feel embarrassed and want to tell them something. Somehow I manage to get away from my family. Then, the next thing I know, I'm in the field with the regular people, watching the Rockefellers on parade. I feel glad that I'm not one of *them*."

But the biggest dream of all takes place in her waking hours. It is to have the Rockefeller identity totally behind her. "The fortune should be made extinct," she says passionately. "I was with my father in Woodstock recently, and he was talking about making up his will. I don't want his money passed on to me. I don't want it passed on to my children. I don't want them to have to deal with what I've had to deal with. I hope the social revolution will come soon and take away from us the necessity of having to deal with it."

The extremism of the formulation might bother some of her cousins, but she is far from alone in her desire to experience the Horatio Alger myth in reverse. To some degree they are all princes and princesses yearning to be paupers.

Speaking of the contemporary Vanderbilts, Cleveland Amory once said that it was "impossible to tell them from anybody else." When the Cousins (as the fourth generation is known) gather at Pocantico every June and December for their semiannual meetings, there is no doubt they are

Rockefellers. Running like leitmotifs through their faces are the telltale square jaw of John D. Rockefeller, Jr., and his wife Abby's generous mouth. Features from the Brothers' generation are also present in new combinations: the pointed nose and high cheekbones of the David family; the greyhound leanness and regal bearing of JDR3 and Blanchette; Nelson's solid body and Mary Clark's long face and jutting chin; Laurance's steady eye and rising forehead.

Yet this group of Rockefellers is separated from the past by facts that have played a large role in their unusual development. There are twenty-one Cousins, as dramatic an increase over the previous generation as one of the population charts from JDR3's desk. Only one-third of the Cousins are male, in a family that has always been patriarchal. Only four of them live in New York City. And finally, there are substantial differences in age and outlook that not only divide them into two groups on opposite sides of the generation gap (the oldest Cousin, Babs's daughter Mitzi, 46, could be the mother of David's youngest, the 22-year-old Eileen) but also preclude the unified view of things that led their fathers into public life.

Rodman, 42, Nelson's son and the oldest male, is the president of IBEC, a dedicated businessman, and the only member of his generation living off his salary. The 37-year-old John D. Rockefeller IV (Jay) is the Cousin's most famous member because of his career in West Virginia politics. Marion's sister Lucy, a Washington, D.C., psychiatrist, is interested in the La Leche League and other organizations having to do with parenthood. David's daughter Peggy, 27, has been involved in Cambridge's radical circles since the early days of SDS.

Political opinions range from the conservative Republicanism of Winthrop's son, Win Paul, to the Marxism of David's daughter Abby; lifestyles, from Marion's part-time existence in caboose number 694 to the Oyster Bay opulence of Mitzi, or the upper east side chic of Nelson's daughter Mary. Yet they are united by something thicker than blood itself: a searching look, an unremitting seriousness, a wariness so habitual and ingrained that it cannot be relaxed even in each other's presence. They have the look of people who have grown up with a burden they still aren't sure how to handle even though most are well on their way through adulthood. Whether to pick it up and heft it gingerly, or to decide in advance that it is too heavy and stand back from it: this is their choice.

Except for a few, like Marion, who have chosen the path of most resistance. Not only has she walked away from the family responsibility she was supposed to accept as a sacred trust, but she has come to see the mission itself as corrupt and destructive, and has spent much of her life scouring the missionary impulse and imperative out of her temperament. The path to the caboose standing in solitude in the shadow of the California mesa was a tortuous one. It led from the Brearley School for Girls to debutante balls, through periods of dark self-questioning and a strange kind of penance as a volunteer worker in madhouses and hospitals. "You grow up feeling that you can't ever make up for all the guilt and all the evil, and that you just have to be saintly," Marion says. "So you martyr yourself. That's how I entered the adult world. I wanted to be near people who were suffering, and to help them in some way. I worked as an art therapist in a home for retarded adults. Then I did the same thing in a terminal cancer ward, and then I worked in a sort of ghetto situation. The scarier the better. It was the only way I could feel better about things.

"The whole name problem is so strange. To be truthful, it was a great relief for me when I got married and didn't have to carry it around anymore. Now it's not the first thing that hits somebody when you first meet them. It's great to be free of that. I make my friends and later on my background seeps out and it's okay because we've had time to get to know each other on a different level. But it has been terribly hard to get to this point. And then with ourselves, we don't even get that far. Within the family, one hardly ever talks directly about who we are without our Rockefeller identity, our social identity, very little about love or hate or anger, without all these other damned attachments. It's really tragic. I think that's one of the sadder things about our family."

For each of the Cousins, being a Rockefeller has seemed like an Oriental puzzle of shadow and act, of opposites flowing into and out of each other. It is a blessing, bestowing more wealth and power on one at birth than most others accumulate in a lifetime; it is a curse, for the riches can be possessed only at an awesome spiritual cost. All of the Cousins have been tantalized by the Rockefeller identity, yet all have thought at one time or another that to be born into this dynasty was like having an exotic and utterly incurable hereditary disease.

"It's a preposterous name," says David's oldest daughter, Abby. "I remember as a child having it whispered that we were rich," she recalls. "I have vague memories of my classmates talking and then all of a sudden, the name Rockefeller looming as something beyond. Very quickly I came to feel that it wasn't my name. I never felt integrated with it, never felt connected to it. I always said it as if everyone would know it wasn't my name, and eventually I came to dread saying it, because of the fear of being seen as some other *thing*."

The Cousins are not a rebellious generation, and yet in their paralysis and painful attempts to locate themselves in the middle of the drama that has been unfolding over the last hundred years, they have surprisingly brought its plot to a sudden end. It is a peculiar finish for the morality play which had the first John D. representing Worldly Riches, redeemed by Junior's Good Works, with the Brothers stepping forth as gilt-edged Everymen. One thing the Cousins could be said to agree on is that to be an Everyman is finally to be a kind of no man, and that to put on the Rockefeller role is ultimately to drain oneself of humanity, concreteness, and connection. If they are part of the drama, it is only as a kind of Gothic epilogue, played out in cabooses settled down into western soil and other exotic settings. The action of this part of the plot is summarized by Abby: "The problem of disentangling oneself from a tradition and creating a new sense of self is unbelievably difficult and confusing. If you're a Rockefeller it is doubly so. You need an exorcism."

Marion's dream world, abounding in family images, often settles on Pocantico. "I was a stranger in some foreign land. I was the only blond— everyone else had black hair—and I was definitely a stranger. I sat at a table with those cold black-haired people I didn't know. At one point the women among them were picking up bouquets and throwing them in a heap, as if at a funeral. They asked me about myself, and I told them the truth. I also told them what my feelings were now. They asked, 'And who owns the estate now? Do the Cousins own the estate?' And I said, 'No, no, the uncles own the estate, and it's going to be sold.' As I said this I was flooded with a bittersweet feeling. I was glad that we were getting rid of it, but nostalgic because I remembered my childhood there."

The Cousins grew up as their fathers had: weekdays were spent in New York City, yet every weekend, vacation, and summer was spent at the estate. It was where the free time, the time that mattered, was spent. Though they would later reevaluate their growing up, there would always be good memories.

Mitzi, Rodman, and a couple of the other older ones have vague recollections of great-grandfather—the thinly delicate parchment-skinned founder of Standard Oil. Yet for most, he was only an image in the old Pathé newsreels the Family Office had spliced together in a kind of elaborate home movie to show at Christmas parties—an oddly Chaplinesque figure doffing his hat and dropping dimes into the outstretched hands of children. For most of the Cousins, the earliest memories were of the period just after the first John D.'s death, the war years when their own fathers (with the exception of Nelson) were gone for long periods, suddenly reappearing in striking dress uniforms, their arms filled with presents. Only their Uncle Winthrop had any war stories. The Cousins who were old enough to remember recall the excitement caused by news that he had been wounded in the battle for Okinawa.

Pocantico felt the pinch of the war only slightly. The Rockefellers had no stamp books and carried no grease to the butcher. It literally took the family three days to open all their Christmas presents. Yet fear of rationing did midwife the rebirth of farming at Pocantico, which had declined since the days when Senior had insisted on having produce from the estate shipped to him whenever he was at his three other homes. An immense vegetable patch was planted—the Rockefeller variant of the victory garden. Junior bought ninety head of beef and sundry other livestock, which were housed in the rambling structure known as the "farm barns." The Cousins often went after milking time to get the still-warm milk or newly churned butter. Sometimes they stayed to watch in fascinated horror as a steer was slaughtered, dressed out, and then smoked or placed in the estate's large freezers to be apportioned among the families or shipped by railway express to the city or to the vacation retreat at Seal Harbor.

During the war and for some time after, Pocantico was a society of women, children, and servants. The Cousins went with head groundsman Tom Pyle each spring to dig out fox dens and see the newborn kits. They were taught to ride by the Prussian riding master Joe Plick, who kept their grandfather's stables and named the newborn colts Roddy, Mitzi, and other Cousins' names. Bouncing up and down in English saddles behind him on the elaborate network of bridlepaths, they learned the rules for riding, which were broken the moment they were on their own. There was jumping and steeplechase competitions organized by their grandmother and by Aunt Blanchette and in these there were always the same number of ribbons as entrants in each category.

There were certain things that didn't make sense, such as the time Nelson's son Michael was attacked by one of the savage guard dogs patrolling the periphery of the estate and suffered a badly mauled arm. This and other similar incidents would cause them to look back later and wonder (in the words of one Cousin) if Pocantico had been a paradise or a prison. Yet when they were young, there was no doubt. It was Eden, and they were innocent. Marion remembers: "It was carpeted in green and very beautiful. I had my cousins for my friends, and the beauty of the place was wonderful. There were deer, raccoons, foxes, other animals living in our woods. We were almost like Indians. We roamed and roamed at will on our horses. Mine was named Queenie, a raggedy palomino I got when I was ten. When I got Queenie I'd take off by myself without saddle or bridle. Just take off. Somewhere I'd meet my cousins and we'd just go all day. We took off most of our clothes and rode half-naked. We covered all the trails. Sometimes we rode on Great-Grandfather's golf course. Once our horses' hooves gouged chunks of sod out of his putting greens."

Their Grandmother Abby Aldrich had died too soon for most of the Cousins to have any more than a slender memory of a handsome woman smelling of lilac and wearing extravagant hats, who became thick at the ankles and frequently ill in her last years. But memories of their grandfather—Mr. Junior—were firm. Even when well into his eighties, he controlled Pocantico with an iron hand, acting as "the Laird of Kikjuit" in a way his own father had not. He was generous with the cornucopia of good things at the estate, but left no doubt that they were his to give or withhold. The shiny, perfectly combed and cared-for horses Joe Plick kept in the central stable were taken out only by Grandfather's permission. The armada of electric cars sailing soundlessly over the estate were his to command. The bounty of food every family received from the farm barns and vegetable garden came from him. He alone controlled the allegiance of the small army of workers tending the estate.

The Cousins noted that this arrangement did not satisfy their fathers, and that they chafed under Junior's rule. Yet they themselves rarely experienced their grandfather as a disciplinarian. To them, he was a shy and increasingly fragile man whose uniform of dark suit and tie and starched white shirt was unvarying whether he was meeting with associates from New York City, or going for a Sunday afternoon drive with Martha Baird, the old family friend he had married after Abby's death.

He was the center of the world of Pocantico. Either in the massive stone house or driving around the estate in a horse and buggy or a limousine with a blanket over his lap (often stopping and walking with Martha into the fiery autumn woods with the uniformed chauffeur waiting a discreet distance away beside the idling car), he was the patriarch.

The massive fortune he had inherited intact from his father had been distributed. Much had gone into the corporate philanthropies and institutions that had been his lifework. It had bought important future assets like Rockefeller Center, and created the huge trusts for his sons in 1934. Yet he realized that being a Rockefeller involved having a piece of Standard Oil. In 1952 he took 120,000 of his remaining shares of Standard of New Jersey stock and set up trust funds for each of his grandchildren. This amounted to 20,000 shares for each family, split evenly between the children in it. In David's family of six children, for instance, each one got proportionately less than in JDR3's family of four or Babs's of two. But in any case all would have a comfortable sum of $5 million to $9 million each on attaining their majority. When they reached their twenty-first year, they learned about the trusts, as part of their "financial rights."

None of them ever really got to know this prim little man very well. Yet if not in his life, then in his death they grasped his meaning. After he was gone, the central stables, garden, and livestock operation of Pocantico were all shut down. Each individual family retreated a little farther into itself. It was as if the force holding them all together had gone out of the estate—and the world.

Winthrop's son, Win Paul, grew up in his mother's custody and away from the other Cousins. Babs's daughters, Mitzi and Marilyn, had grown up as Miltons, not Rockefellers, and were more like visitors at Pocantico than residents. Of the four Brothers whose families lived there, JDR3's was farthest from the others, both in terms of space and emotion. The children who grew up at Fieldwood Farm were more a self-contained unit than the others. The firstborn was Sandra, who as a child seemed wispy, easily frightened, almost neurasthenic. Next came a boy, Jay, only half a namesake because his father (in a covert act of rebellion against the responsibility he had borne so faithfully and at such a cost) named him simply John Rockefeller and said he could have the option of adopting the dynastic designation carried by the middle name Davison and number IV when he came of age. Hope grew into a tall, statuesque blond. Alida, born eleven years later in 1949 when her father was nearing middle age, had the same aristocratic good looks. All of the children had a regal quality; it was instilled by Blanchette, who seemed to hope to recapture in their generation the rule of primogeniture she felt Nelson had stolen from her husband.

JDR3 was away during much of their youth. "He traveled at least three months a year while I was growing up," Alida says. "Every winter he and mother went to Asia for a couple of months and I stayed with a nurse." Yet the psychic distance was always greater than the actual miles. Hope recalls him as always being in between appointments or projects. "One of the things I remember best about my father was the careful measuring of time. There was a certain time set aside for exercise, a certain time for receiving guests, and so on. If someone stayed too long, for instance, I noticed that my mother got extremely nervous."

When he was with them, he resembled his own father in that the role that was most comfortable for him was that of instructor. Hope recalls him setting out to teach her to drive in an old Jeep and retaining his serene patience as the vehicle gnashed gears and bucked like a Brahma bull over the dirt roads behind Fieldwood Farm.

Like his brothers, JDR3 felt that there were certain stones in the family past better left unturned. His daughter Alida remembers being twelve and pulling into a Mobil station for gas with a carload of her friends; when they started making the inevitable jokes about how she wouldn't have to pay, she couldn't understand and had trouble convincing them that she really didn't know that the family fortune was connected with this company. Yet her father was the one Rockefeller Brother sincerely interested in passing on the tradition of philanthropy to his children, even if only as an exercise in *noblesse oblige*. "Ever since I was very young," Alida says, "I remember Father talking to me about responsibility. I was made to think I was special from the beginning, that I had a special duty. From the time I was five years old I got an allowance that gradually increased from fifteen cents to five dollars a week. There were three little jewelry boxes. I got fifteen cents to spend, fifteen cents to save, and fifteen cents to give away. Every Christmas season, my father would sit down with me and we'd decide who I'd give the money in the third box to. Usually some went to Riverside Church, and always to one of the one hundred neediest cases in *The New York Times*. We read the cases together and decided which to give to. It was a real ritual, one of the times we were closest."

Laurance's children were more tentative than JDR3's. To the degree that their father did not know himself, he cut the ground from under them; it was as if they were confused by his ironies and kaleidoscope of moods. Laura, the oldest, dealt with Laurance by trying to master his casuistry; she debated him constantly. Marion was as withdrawn and mystical as her mother. Lucy showed some of the independence of her namesake, the half-deaf and aged Great-Aunt Lucy Aldrich. She defied her father, who thought that everything she wanted (her own pets, her own friends, and her freedom from family rituals) came too soon. The boy, Larry, grew up extremely cautious watching his mercurial father occupying all the spaces where he tried to expand.

Like JDR3, Laurance was absent during much of their growing up. Yet he was a power to be reckoned with even when gone, protean in the psychological shapes he could assume, hard to pin down, able to cut down a child's adventuresome inquiry with one quick stroke. He was the dominant fact in their lives, yet the tone of the family came from the mother. Mary French Rockefeller, in odd complement to her agnostic and very secular husband, spent much time reading the Bible and meditating by herself. If Laurance defused emotion through irony, she suppressed it through silence. "She never raised her voice when we were young," her daughter Marion recalls. "She never said much at all, the idea being that if you were in communication with God, you didn't *need* to communicate. During the arguments she never spoke. We practically used to hurl things at her—words and objects—and she'd just take it stoically."

The children of the Laurance household would look back in a kind of anger at their growing up. Lucy now lives in a stylish Chevy Chase house whose front yard is littered with children's toys. Along with her involvement in the La Leche League (which seeks to promote the breast feeding of infants) and in organizations emphasizing parental responsibility, this hints at the fact that she is still sorting out the past. "We were not so much isolated as children as we were encased in a vacuum," she said. "Nobody wanted to communicate. Nobody bothered to orient us to the world. Nothing was really talked about at home. They operated on the theory that you don't talk about important things to your animals, or servants, and you don't tell them to your children."

In each of the households, servants and nurses provided the close contact, while the mothers orchestrated and the fathers came and went. This too had an impact: "My struggle is for recognition," says Laura. "I was never recognized for myself by my parents. The servants gave us individual presents. Our parents gave us tons of presents, but never any that were for *me*. I became fond of the maids and the servants, and then when I heard my parents talk to them as though they were nonpeople, I vowed I would never treat anyone like that."

Laurance's children were inevitably drawn to Nelson's house. It was warmer and more open than their own, yet hardly informal by any standards other than those their grandfather had established as the norm of Pocantico. As Steven recalls, "Our lives were actually highly regulated. If you didn't show up in time for a meal, you didn't get it. Bells were rung and then you had five minutes to show up. If you didn't make it, you didn't get fed."

Rodman was somewhat detached from his brothers and sisters and also the other Cousins, made haughty (they felt) by his status as first male of their generation. Ann was the quietest of Nelson's children; Steven, a natural leader in a way Roddy was not. Everyone was especially fond of the twins, Mary and Michael, whose high spirits and constant exuberance reminded relatives of Nelson when he was young.

Nelson dominated his family, much as he dominated everything else, with his steamroller enthusiasms. (Not without a faint irony his sons called him "Chief.") His brothers John and Laurance let the forms of their own growing up slide in their children's youth, but Nelson did not. He made his children sit still for the Sunday devotions and Bible readings he himself had so chafed at under Junior's regime. Although they took lunches and dinners with their nurses, he made a point of being present—as Junior had—at breakfast. He explained about Great-Grandfather's Ledger A and made them keep accounts of their own. ("He was not overly strict," his son Steven recalls, "but he definitely implanted the idea in us that accounts were very important. The threat was mainly that if they didn't balance, we wouldn't get our allowance.") He was nonchalant about material things, and his children could lose a tennis racket and expect that another one would replace it. This contrasted with their mother's attitude, which was that they should not be spoiled just because they were Rockefellers.

Nelson was insistent about what he regarded as moral questions, and his displeasure was withering. His daughter Mary recalls: "I've never heard Father raise his voice to any one of us. When he got angry he'd just turn to stone. He would go cold and this stone quality would just enter his voice and manner. It was terrifying."

All the Cousins (but especially Laurance's children) were fond of Tod. Aunt Mary (as they called her) had an athletic grace and whimsical good humor the world at large didn't often see. Marion remembers seeking her out time after time, while she knelt at work in her gardens, to ask her questions and wait for the amusing replies to float up like bubbles from under the voluminous sunbonnet. A good part of what the Nelson children were to become stemmed from their mother's quiet, intelligent strength, which was unique in the increasingly diverse society of Pocantico. The qualities that made Tod fail as Nelson's wife helped her succeed with the children.

But it was "the Davids" who were generally reckoned by family observers to be the most interesting group at Pocantico. David took fatherhood seriously in a way that JDR3, Laurance, and Nelson did not, perhaps because he was the only Brother to accept uncritically the Rockefeller myth and to assume the necessity for instructing the young to shoulder its burdens. Yet he was absent from his children's growing up even more than his brothers were—especially during their childhood, when he was traveling in the foreign department of the Chase. With characteristic obtuseness, he emphasized these absences by bringing home toys he had obtained in the countries he visited.

It was, however, the mother who had the greatest impact on the children. Peggy McGrath Rockefeller was perhaps not as intellectual as Tod or as sophisticated as Blanchette, but she was by far the most independent and spirited woman to marry into the Rockefeller family. Blessed with resilient good looks, she came into the family an intuitive rebel with an often violent temper, an unadmitted hunger for independence, and a secret skepticism regarding much of the Rockefeller pomp. The other Brothers' wives were from pedigreed familes; Peggy McGrath's was well-off, but several rungs down the social ladder. To her, marriage to a Rockefeller had been a dramatic step up, and though she understood that it had involved something of a Faustian compact in regard to her private life, she never seemed to make her accommodation complete. In some sense she remained ambivalent, fearful that she might become a concubine to the famous name, poised for flight from its complexity to something simpler. While her husband was on one of his globe-circling tours, she would often be on Buckle Island, a small seven-acre island a half-day's sail from Seal Harbor. She had bought it with her own money; the only structure was a small prefab house she had built, where she stayed alone, away from the retinue of servants, gardening in solitude.

She was capable of breaking through the *noblesse oblige* that hung over the family like a fog with one swift gesture. It was in contrast to her husband's remote and condescending good manners, a veneer of humility whose solicitousness toward lesser beings seemed actually calculated to prove the reverse—how much better he was and how deserving of the privilege he enjoyed. Peggy treated the servants with a hauteur that earned her their hatred. She assigned her children to weed pulling and other tasks, as if unconsciously trying to sweat the Rockefeller pretension out of them.

"When we were young," says Abby of her mother, "she was the center of everyone's interest and of our frantic desire to win approval." But the attitude toward the father was more complex, especially since his mood of equanimity was taken as the family norm mother and children were guilty of violating. The children coveted his attention when he was available. Every Friday afternoon, when the family tumbled out of the Manhattan town house and piled into the large limousine with nurses and pets to begin the trip to Pocantico, there was a struggle among them for the privilege of sitting next to him in the front seat. Yet they had what approached disdain for him as well. He was good on beetle-collecting trips, where the information he dispensed was crisp and specific and gained him their complete respect. But otherwise he seemed to convey attitudes rather than data, speaking in the code of platitudinous gentility that was totally different from Peggy's continual attempts to define and discriminate. He seemed predictable, superficial, obtuse, his religious observances and ideas on the sanctity of the family almost comical. More than any of the other Cousins, David's children had the impulse to probe and understand; yet when they managed to penetrate their father's placid reserve, they found only give. There was one uniform mood, one tone of voice that carefully skirted conflict. "To our loss," said his son Richard, "*emotional* was seen as the antithesis of reasonable, which made it bad. Repress emotion. Control yourselves. These were the lessons we learned."

David commanded them to go to church even though his wife's absence—she was an atheist—silently condemned it as hypocrisy. As in other matters, however, they tried to serve mother and father at once. They dutifully squirmed through the sermons at the Pocantico Hills church, watching rainbows of sunlight stream through the stained glass windows Henri Matisse had done as a memorial for their grandmother; then after the service was over they chivied the Reverend Hansen with youthful Humean skepticism about the existence of God.

If the religion that had been such a great factor in the Rockefeller saga was breaking down, the great fortune was not. It represented an even more fundamental puritanism. They learned early that it was a threat to those who dared approach it too directly. "I remember when my brother David had just learned that our father was a millionaire," Abby recalls. "He was ten or eleven. He took a vulgar enthusiasm in telling the rest of us about it. We listened with as perverse and lustful an interest as we did when we heard for the first time about sex in the Playhouse alcove. It was wildly illegitimate and pleasurable." When David, Jr., later asked his father how much money he had, the response was cold and angry. Abby says, "My father said that such talk was *not nice.* The way he said these words made me glad I had not been the one to ask the question. Early on I picked up the signals that I shouldn't be proud of the money. Should I be grateful? No, that was wrong, too. So was pride, and contentment. There was no attitude in our childhood that we were allowed to have with respect to that money that was appropriate. We weren't allowed to discuss it; we weren't allowed to gloat; we couldn't do anything. And so it was like a festering sore. Like a thing that was going to pop later on."

The David family was marked by insight and intelligence. Yet its unique atmosphere created hungers that it could not satisfy. As Peggy recalls of her growing up, "We ate shepherd's pie with our nurses in the kitchen while our parents ate steak in the dining room. When we went in to say good night, we would hang on them, begging for food off their plates. Strangely enough, we had a sense of there not being enough to go around—not enough food, not enough love."

The Cousins' growing up had been in many ways idyllic. Yet there were elements of uncertainty from the beginning, questions that began increasingly to demand answers as they grew older. Why should relatives be their only friends? Why did they play behind patrolled gates? Why was family history a tabooed subject? (As Lucy later said, "It was considered indelicate to ask about our past. It was like sex, a forbidden topic. And like sex, we found out about it piecemeal from other sources.")

Nelson's oldest children, Rodman and Ann, followed in their father's footsteps to Lincoln School for a few years. But Lincoln School, which had been so important a part of the Brothers' youth, finally closed down in 1948. Even if it hadn't, the other Cousins probably still would have gone to schools more befitting their class. For the boys it was grade school in institutions like Buckley, then on to Exeter, Choate, or Deerfield. For the girls, it was fashionable schools like Brearley or Miss Chapin's School for Girls, then on to a prep school like Milton or Farmington Academy. Their parents thought they might be sheltered by such schools, but being there only added to the cognitive dissonance of their youth. It had been emphasized that they were normal children, no better than anyone else except perhaps in the extent of their obligations to benefit their fellow man. Yet now they found themselves in institutions that were training them to rule.

Even among the children of Du Ponts and Fords, the Rockefellers bore a special name. It was like being a crown prince or princess, but their parents had not prepared them for the notoriety they encountered. JDR3's daughter Alida recalls: "When I was about eleven and at a summer camp in Maine, people found out who I was. One came up and asked if I lit my cigars with million-dollar bills. Another came up and asked for my autograph. I gave it to her."

Whatever their school, the problem was the same. They were curiosities. They had the sense that they were constantly on stage, that other people were watching them and evaluating their actions for signs of selfishness or pride, on the one hand, or artificality on the other. Everyone they met seemed to know more about them and their family than they themselves did. Upon being introduced, they became accustomed to the name producing a flicker in the eye of the beholder. It froze them and instantly set them apart. From the time they entered grade school, they were the focus of hostility, obsequiousness, and ironies that were felt but often not understood. The extent to which they were different was something communicated silently, almost subliminally, by teachers and schoolmates. As Lucy later said, "It seemed as though my friends were always apologizing because their china wasn't as fine as ours." It was a situation calculated to drain their attempts to create distinct personalities and to set up walls between them and others. As Abby says, "Being a Rockefeller was an enormous, pervasive, and central issue for me. From the second grade onwards, it had me worrying all the time. My whole being was organized to try to repulse situations created by it."

School was an ordeal. "When I heard the family name mentioned," says Lucy, "I used to just blank out. I didn't take American history for that reason: I didn't want to hear about the Rockefellers." Her sister Marion's recollection of driving to Brearley in a chauffeured Cadillac is far different from the carefree days when her father and uncles had skipped or rollerskated up Fifth Avenue until they were tired and then climbed into the limousine Junior had ordered to crawl along beside them. "The closer we got to school," Laurance's daughter remembers, "the lower we sank into the back seat of the car. By the time we were almost there, we were begging the chauffeur to please drive a few blocks further and then let us out so we could arrive at school on foot, anonymously."

It was all the worse because it could not be discussed. The Brothers continued to promote the idea that being a Rockefeller was actually no different from being a Smith or a Jones, except that you were to be more responsible, and—it was never spoken, but always understood—better. Yet their children couldn't buy either the expectations or the illusion that they were the same as any other teenagers. On the contrary, for no reason they could quite pinpoint they began to feel ashamed of their name and connections. They were attracted to the privilege and the power, but ashamed of succumbing to such a base emotion. "The problem," recalls Abby, "was trying to figure out where the balance lay between the perverse pleasure of the magic in it, and the pain of alienation from it. I never got anything but a shameful pleasure from my name. I never got a clean sense of pride. To the extent that I ever felt privileged, I felt guilty and ashamed and embarrassed for the privilege."

It was an odd predicament. They had private planes, yachts, constant travel abroad, servants, vacation homes from the tip of the Caribbean to the Maine woods, from Venezuela to Wyoming, dinner conversation with princes, prime ministers, and some of the most celebrated commoners in the world; they had more than any other group of young people in

America. Laura, an attractive 38-year-old woman with three children, who is finishing a Ph.D. and writing a brief history of the Rockefellers, summarizes the problem: "How in the world do you ask for sympathy when you've got all the things that are *supposed* to make you happy?" They were conscious of falling into the stereotype of the poor little rich boy or girl and felt that they could not talk about their troubles.

As this confusion surrounded them, it naturally altered their view of their heritage. Laura was popular enough to be elected president of her class in high school, yet during those years and the college years that followed, she was almost afraid to bring people home with her. "You had the awful feeling that when you invited friends home and took them through the gates at Pocantico, they wouldn't love you anymore. Those goddamned gates! The messages they conveyed about the world. The world must be a pretty scary place if it is necessary to have police dogs and armed guards prowling around behind closed gates!"

It was possible to rebel against aspects of their growing up. As in the David family, they could flaunt the tradition exemplified in the account books, the church-going, and even ridicule some of the more fatuous aspects of their father's behavior and beliefs. Yet questioning the accumulated weight of the name they had been born with made about as much sense as questioning their height or facial structure. The Cousins' anxiety, therefore, was not in rejecting the family and its role and privilege but in safely finding a way to accept it. The Rockefeller image might be swollen as from elephantiasis, making living up to it impossible, but in the unrelenting system of moral accounting perfected by their grandfather, this debt was owed.

The Cousins couldn't behave as if their name were Smith and quickly finish college so they could get jobs and begin making money. They had to have plans worthy of them. There were pressures—especially on the males—to take posts of responsibility in the family empire, to flow smoothly into the dynasty and do their part to enlarge its influence. Some of the older ones tried to live up to the challenge; but most of them perfected strategies for stalling, creating alternatives, gaining time to organize their lives and prepare for the big decision ahead.

When Nelson's daughter Mary was in her first year at Vassar, she discussed her depression and unhappiness with her twin brother, Michael. After they had talked for hours about the wall that existed between them and others, Michael suggested that she get away for a time, go someplace where nobody knew who she was. (Her sister, Ann, had already spent time doing social work in London's East End.) In the turmoil of her freshman year, her uncertainty had so disoriented her and sapped her vitality that she had been put on probation. She agreed that she needed a change of scene. She didn't actually have to look for something to do; as soon as the word went out that there was a Rockefeller looking for a summer's obscurity, she had alternatives to choose from. She decided to join a team of Cornell researchers setting up a public health project on a Navajo reservation. Even now, after fifteen years, Mary becomes animated when discussing the experience. "We lived in a trailer and ate out of cans and lived among people who had never heard of a Rockefeller." She calls it, without qualification, "the turning point of my life."

Peggy went to Brazil, a country that knew of Rockefellers through Nelson's IBEC and David's travels for the Chase. For three summers while she was an undergraduate at Radcliffe, she did social work there. In the third summer she moved from the mansion where she'd lived with friends of her father to a *favella*, existing amid grinding poverty. When the local press found out about her and arrived at the shack of the poor family with whom she lived, she and a friend escaped through the back door to avoid being interviewed, taking a 1,200-mile bus trip through the Brazilian countryside to preserve her incognita.

Jay Rockefeller spent three years in Japan, mastering the language and culture in anonymity while living with a family in Tokyo. Marion went to territory as distant when she spent months working in hospitals for the retarded and terminally ill. After graduating from Harvard, her brother, Larry, lived in an East Harlem tenement for three years while working as a VISTA volunteer.

These odysseys were not purely escapism. They were also calisthenics for the future, part of a search for the "real" self the Cousins felt must exist beneath the artifice of their Rockefeller-ness. It was in this context that Michael decided to get away from his family.

He was accounted one of the "best adjusted" of the Cousins, a favorite of everyone in the family. With sandy hair, thick glasses, and an unaffected warmth, he was an athletic youth (he had lettered in lacrosse and was an excellent swimmer) who reminded family friends of the young Nelson. Although his temperament lacked his father's sharp edges, he seemed to have Nelson's ability to project himself past the obstacle of the name. "When you first enter a group," he once said, "people are curious; but when they find out you're human, it's okay again."

Michael, the most purely aesthetic member of the family, according to his sister Ann, had hoped to study architecture, but had been forced to yield to parental pressure and take up economics. He was just finishing his senior thesis at Harvard on his Great-Grandfather Nelson Aldrich and banking reform when a roommate told him about an expedition planned by the Film Study Center at Harvard's Peabody Museum. A small group of anthropologists and a film crew were going to the Baliem Valley in Dutch New Guinea to make a record of tribes whose primitive agricultural society was as yet untouched by Western culture. It was a rare opportunity to set foot in a place where few whites had ever gone, to step back into the Stone Age.

Michael had worked for IBEC in Puerto Rico and served as a ranch hand at his father's Venezuelan estate during summer vacations. He had once told his parents, "I want to do something romantic and adventuresome now while there are still faraway frontiers to explore." This seemed exactly the opportunity he had been waiting for. He was an accomplished photographer, and this competence (along with the influence trickling down from his Uncle David's status as an overseer at Harvard) helped him finesse his way aboard the expedition.

For different reasons, his older brothers, Rodman and Steven, had not worked out as heirs to Laurance's role as the Rockefeller who kept an eye on the family business. Michael knew that he had now become the male Cousin the Brothers agreed was best suited for leadership of the family in the coming generation. To his father and uncles, he explained the trip as a valuable experience for the future, as well as a chance to obtain artifacts for the Museum of Primitive Art, of which he was already a board member. His brother Steven later said, "The trip was acceptable to the Brothers because they were made to feel that it might be a prelude to a career in international business. Actually to Michael it was a way of buying time."

From the moment the expedition took off, Michael was galvanized by the prospects ahead. He carried out his job of photographer with zeal and also took on the job of sound man. He impressed his colleagues with his appetite for work and his lack of pretense. As one of them later said, "He suffered from the family complex of feeling that he had to work even harder than the rest to prove himself." If they noted any flaw at all in his character, it was a failure to calculate consequence, a kind of recklessness.

He managed to pack a lot of observation of life and death into his few weeks among the Kurelu tribesmen, photographing babies being born, warfare with other tribes, the death of wounded warriors, and the ceremony preparatory to the cremation that sent the dead to oblivion. He enjoyed observing and trying to understand the human cement that joined tribesmen to others. "Michael really found himself over there," one friend in the expedition later told a reporter. He grew a soft, dun-colored beard and decided that when he returned home he would enroll as a graduate student in anthropology.

Having heard of the Papaguan tribes in the coastal Asmat, he went there on a side trip in mid-August and became "wildly excited" by the artifacts he saw. The Peabody expedition had officially concluded, but Michael decided to put off his return to America. He was making preparations for a second, longer trip into the coastal area when he received a cable warning that his parents had decided to make public their intention to seek a divorce.

Michael immediately returned home. It took him only a week in New York to recognize that there was nothing he could do for them. He told them about his decision to become an anthropologist and then hopped aboard a plane and flew to Hollandia (now Djajapura). There he met with Dutch anthropologist Rene Wassing, and together they went on to New Guinea to begin two months of field work.

Moving in and out of the rivers of the Asmat in a catamaran powered by two 18 horsepower motors and able to carry a large load of trade goods, he and Wassing covered a lot of territory. The artifacts they collected— exquisitely carved shields and canoe figureheads, along with a good selection of shrunken heads—made Michael dream of returning home in triumph with the most complete record of primitive life ever assembled.

On November 18, after several weeks in the field, Michael and Wassing decided to travel to a large village on the other side of the South Eilander River. Instead of going by way of the complex system of inland waterways, they thought to save time by venturing out into the coastal waters and then going up the South Eilander. In the middle of this passage, which local traders had warned them was a dangerous one in the best of circumstances, a large wave swamped the catamaran, drowning the engine and sweeping most of Michael's field notes overboard. The two men clung to the foundering craft overnight, slowly being carried out to the open sea by the tide. The next morning Michael decided to try to make the eleven-mile swim to shore. Wassing pleaded with him not to, pointing out that the crococile- and shark-infested waters would make it an almost impossible task to reach the shore. But as the middle-aged Dutch anthropologist later said, "He listened to me, but I knew in advance that he would go ahead. It was very difficult to make him change his mind." Stripping to his undershorts, tying his glasses around his neck, and strapping old fuel cans over his shoulders for flotation, Michael looked at

Wassing one last time, said, "I think I can make it," and then plunged into the sea. He was never seen again.

Nelson and Michael's twin sister, Mary, flew to the area and participated in several exhausting days of searching along with elements of the Royal Dutch Air Force. There was no sign of him. Finally they returned home having accepted the verdict of authorities in the area. The official view was that Michael had almost certainly drowned in the treacherous tides; yet almost immediately rumors began filtering out of the wild, impenetrable jungle and were carried to civilization by Dutch missionaries in the area. One that gained some acceptance was that Michael did indeed make it to shore and, as he emerged from the exhausting swim, stumbled onto a party of warriors from the village of Otsjanep. He assumed that they would be friendly to a white man and hailed them, not knowing that Dutch soldiers had earlier killed several members of their tribe in a pacification campaign. According to this version, he was killed on sight and later eaten. For years travelers returning from the Asmat brought back lurid stories of having seen natives wearing Michael Rockefeller's broken glasses around their neck and of having been shown what was purported to be his shrunken skull.

To the world at large, Michael's disappearance was a compelling interlude in the drama of Nelson Rockefeller's divorce and remarriage. It was the story of a romantic, daring young man who had lost his life in pursuit of adventure. Only the Rockefeller Cousins could appreciate the true nature of his quest. They decided to pay tribute to his memory by endowing the Michael Rockefeller Fellowship at Harvard. It was the first institution they had formed and funded by themselves. (They did not ask the Brothers to contribute to it until it had been going for several years.) The language in the statement of intent (written by Steven) had a special meaning to them: "The primary purpose of the Fellowship is the development of an individual's understanding of himself and his world through involvement with people of a culture not his own."

Michael would always be the special Cousin, loved and admired by the others for daring to journey to the heart of darkness in pursuit of selfhood. (And perhaps he was secretly envied by the other Cousins because his early death came at a time when he was not yet compromised by the decisions they would all soon have to make.) His death highlighted the necessity of reaching some sort of accommodation with their dilemma. "Every one of us has thought at one time or another of getting away from the name, the whole thing," Hope says, "yet we all know deep down that there's no escape."

CHAPTER 23

In midsummer 1970, Room 5600 arranged to have a number of questions regarding the Rockefellers inserted into the regular Gallup Poll.
From the responses, they extrapolated what they called "The Public Attitudes Toward the Rockefellers." Bound, stamped "confidential," and
handed out to the family members, its findings showed that although Nelson was the only Rockefeller with whom the public was very familiar (re-
spondents had difficulty distinguishing the other Brothers from each other and from their father), the public image of the family, because of the
philanthropies with which it was associated, was generally good. The report concluded with an exhortation aimed indirectly at the Cousins:

> Here is a family whose vast wealth might be expected to generate envy, jealousy,
> and hatred; but instead it is seen predominantly by now as one dedicated to public
> and humanitarian service for the good of mankind. . . . The current generation
> of the family and their advisors have done their job, have made their impact; they
> have scaled about as far up their heights of esteem as it is humanly possible for the
> Rockefellers to attain. What is most needed now is that the younger generation
> proceed to carry on, with devotion, the good works of their forbears.

This was an exact summary of their dilemma. The good works expected
of them could take place only within the context of institutions pioneered
by their grandfather and perfected by their fathers. Even if the Cousins
hadn't had doubts about the enterprise, they would have felt that the
heights had been scaled and the possibilities for self-discovery exhausted.
Much of their reluctance about the tradition into which they had been
born centered exactly on the fact that its epic bulk smothered their individual attempts to locate themselves within it. Yet, whatever doubts
they had about being Rockefellers, they did want to *do* something with
their lives. To accept the scenario implicit in the survey's conclusions,
however, would be to become little more than curators in the museum of
past Rockefeller accomplishments. It was not enough.

Even had the Cousins been able to formulate this sense of dread, the
Brothers would have had trouble understanding, let alone accepting it.
They found it hard to accept the fact that the Cousins had been scarred
by growing up Rockefellers; it was as if to do so would somehow equivocate their own lives and accomplishments and call for a reevaluation of
the tradition and responsibility they had accepted. *We were up to it, why
aren't you?* This was the attitude the Cousins—particularly the male
Cousins—sensed in their fathers and uncles.

As one after another of his and the other Brothers' children went into therapy, Laurance (who had refined his own tenuousness into a life-style) sneered that they were "copping out." In few areas was the generation gap felt more acutely than in the question of seeking psychiatric help. David's younger son, Richard, smiles bitterly: "My father doesn't understand what a hang-up is. He and his brothers feel that if you're down, you should go and clean up your room and then you'll feel better."

If the Brothers didn't understand how their children felt oppressed by the Rockefeller identity and all it portended, they also failed to calculate the extent to which the Cousins were children of their own time, an era of protest over imperial war, racial inequality, and social injustice. The generation they identified with was challenging exactly those powers and assumptions on which the family tradition was based. The Brothers' insistence that the Cousins should be Rockefellers in the same sense they had been, showed how isolated the third generation had become.

It seemed natural that the female Cousins should take the lead, running interference for their more cautious and in some ways more burdened brothers. One Harvard SDS friend recalls how David's daughter Peggy, an early supporter of the Cambridge antiwar movement, came to his room, tears streaming down her face. It was 1966, at the time of the Vietnam teach-ins. He asked her what was wrong. "My father just asked me to go abroad with him to attend an opening of a branch of the bank," she replied.

"What's so bad about that? You've done it before," he comforted her.

Peggy answered, "The branch is in Saigon."

Peggy's older sister Abby was the only Cousin whose life would ultimately be profoundly changed through her involvement in the new politics. For many of the others, however, such involvement would be an important step in their struggle to locate themselves in the context of the family and to win freedom from its oppressive expectations. Like Peggy and Abby, Laura became an early sponsor of SDS during its participatory democracy stages (and remains a funder of the Cambridge Institute, which specializes in designing decentralized alternatives to capitalist forms of business and social organization); nearly a decade later, Alida, one of the last of the fourth generation to reach college age, stood sympathetically on the periphery of the Third World movement that swept over the Stanford campus. In between, Rockefeller women poured hundreds of thousands of dollars into movement causes ranging from *Ramparts* magazine and the film *Milhouse* to the *Venceremos* Brigade and Vietnam Veterans Against the War.

In some of this there was an element of "radical chic." Yet for this family above all others, politics is a metaphor for identity; it summarizes in solemn mummery the differences in sensibility and world view between the generations. The dialogue was particularly lively in the David family. He was not only the Brother most completely identified with the "system," but also the one who most felt that it (and by implication himself) must be defended against the onslaught of the younger generation. Peggy remembers heated discussions about the Chase Bank's involvement in South Africa and David's defense of reactionary regimes in Brazil and elsewhere around the world. "He always tried to justify support for dictatorships via the notion that the economic growth which stability brought to these countries made the average person there better off," she says, with a smile that betrays her embarrassment at the naïveté of it, and a certain shame at the complicity it defends.

As the war in Vietnam escalated, there were ever more violent discussions about it. They usually ended with Peggy shouting or bursting helplessly into tears while her father continued to defend some particularly indefensible aspect of official policy, like the domino theory, by claiming that he got his information from privileged communications with Bob McNamara or someone else who represented what he called the "horse's mouth." Peggy says, "He always insists that he gets his facts from some high-up source. This was true about Vietnam and later about Watergate. He claimed that McGovern had inflated the break-in out of all proportion and that people around the President had personally assured him that Nixon knew nothing about any part of it."

It was in part her activities around Cambridge radical circles that led Peggy to drop her last name. "My brother Dickie was always getting in political hassles because of the name," she said. "It got in the way of the things I was trying to do. In this country, Kennedy is the only other name I associate with such hassles: money, power, politics, philanthropy, buildings. The name got in the way of the things I was trying to do."

Always, whatever was involved, it came back to the name. Sandra, JDR3's oldest child, had been the first to jettison it, becoming plain Sandra Ferry in 1959. It was an attempt to solve the dilemma in one swift move; at the same time she dropped her last name, Sandra also tried to give away her money. Yet the trust fund was more firmly affixed to her than the name. She became the eccentric among the Cousins, the one whose name always brought a raised eyebrow or a shrug of incomprehension. By the early sixties she had moved to Cambridge and become a recluse and valetudinarian, still avoiding the family and the name, although now accepting the money. She lived behind multiple locks like a woman twice her age, being visited regularly by a psychiatrist and a music therapist. According to family lore, she once spent five years recovering from a broken toe.

Most of the female Cousins took a less direct route of changing their name: they married. Throughout the early sixties, formal weddings were becoming frequent affairs at the small Pocantico Hills church, brides being given away by their celebrated fathers to a series of commoners. Soon there were announcements heralding the arrival of the fifth generation of Rockefellers, bearing last names like Case, Hamlin, Kaiser, Strawbridge and Spencer. Yet time would show that more had been involved than young love. Since divorced and remarried, Laura now says, "I got married when I was nineteen because it was a way to lose the name."

Marriage got rid of the name, but at awesome emotional costs. By the mid-1960s, the handsome young couples who had said their vows a few years earlier were breaking up. Of seven such marriages launched in this period, five resulted in divorce. The process became not a solution but another step in the search.

The male Cousins have been aided by their sisters' rebelliousness (politically and personally), which provided a kind of protective coloration for their more moderate efforts to find a spot for themselves outside the family. The sons had also discovered that the Brothers themselves had unwittingly expanded the area in which a Rockefeller could maneuver without being guilty of an outright break. It had not been intentional, but occurred as a by-product of *their* accommodation to the name and the role as younger men. By subordinating everything else to his own career, Nelson had created a precedent for the Cousins' struggle to pursue individual goals. Most of all, there had been Winthrop. As Steven says, "Win paid a great price for it, but he rebelled rather forcefully and went his own way. Without breaking completely, he attempted to start a whole new life for himself. In a certain way, he was a model for us all. This is especially true of someone like Jay, of course."

The smoothly handsome 37-year-old Jay would agree that he is the most direct beneficiary of Winthrop's small rebellion. He recalls spending long nights with his lonely uncle at Winrock, watching him drink Scotch from water tumblers, listening to his rambling stories, and feeling his pathos. A towering six foot six, Jay is so thin that West Virginians call him "the beanpole politician." Yet he moves with a kind of grace befitting one who played basketball at Exeter and then on Harvard's freshman team.

In his third undistinguished year at college, as he began to feel that he was falling into the narrow part of the funnel and would soon find himself out of school and working in the Office if something weren't done, things came to a head. Feeling miserable about what he calls "the general sludge of Harvard," he went to see Professor Edwin O. Reischauer, former ambassador to Japan and a friend to JDR3. "I told him I really wasn't happy with my life and didn't feel I was doing the right thing with it. I told him I wished I could get off the track I was on, and do something different, something that was not just pushing blindly ahead." It was natural that their conversation should get around to the Orient. Jay had gone there with his father on one of JDR3's annual tours, and mentioned that he had most enjoyed Japan. Reischauer suggested that he consider taking a year off to go there and study. It was the perfect solution: it had the feel of conforming to family tradition, yet he would be going there not as a symbolic figure interpreting America to the Japanese, as his father had, but as an anonymous American student.

He left in 1958 and moved in with a middle-class family in Tokyo. He would come out of hiding and use the Rockefeller identification to his advantage when he wanted to attend diplomatic functions or needed respite from anonymity. Otherwise he was like anyone else. "When I got there," he says, glancing involuntarily at the large hand-painted Japanese screen on the wall of his office, "I worked hard. I threw myself into it totally. I was like a monk. Every morning I was up by five-thirty sitting crosslegged on a bamboo mat in my room, surrounded by books. I took courses, talked to students, read constantly. After a while, things began to change for me. I began to feel better about things."

The three years he spent in Japan were a respite during which he prepared himself for the ordeal ahead, the lifetime of being a Rockefeller. Yet it was also a time when he began to understand that if he could claim some territory that was uniquely his, the name might be as much a help as a hindrance. He says, "It wasn't on the surface of my mind, but I suppose I was resolving whatever doubts I had about being a Rockefeller. All the problems I'd had before seemed to get taken care of, although I don't recall really *doing* it myself." At about the same time that his sister Sandra was trying to renounce her name and heritage, Jay embraced his. John Rockefeller became John D. Rockefeller IV.

The first of two trips he made back to the United States during his stay in Japan came when his father wrote asking him to visit his namesake, who was critically ill. The second trip came when he was cabled of Junior's death. He got on a plane for New York, attended the memorial services for Junior, and hardly pausing for breath, flew back to Japan. The sleeplessness helped give the whole experience a kind of hallucinatory quality, convincing Jay that he had done the right thing in deciding not to swim against the current of the tradition that bore him along. "I remembered writing Grandfather when I was twenty-one, asking him for formal permission to use the whole name. He'd written back a very strong letter, proud of my request. It was very powerful, the whole experience of his death. It was more than a man passing on; it was history itself."

Part of the history that passed on, as it worked out, was that which in his father's generation had entailed a special obligation on the man bearing the dynastic name. Jay might now feel positively about being the fourth John D. Rockefeller, but this didn't change the independent course he had set himself. Though he knew that the Brothers felt he was an ideal candidate to go to work in Room 5600, when he returned from Tokyo it was not to New York but to Cambridge. Reentering Harvard in 1961 as a serious student, he quickly went through all the Japanese language, literature, and history classes the college offered, while also beginning to study Chinese. He was in such a big hurry that he went down to enroll in Yale (where he had been admitted as a graduate student in Oriental Studies) even before Harvard's commencement ceremonies.

He had originally planned to finish his Ph.D. in four years, but after the first year he lost the enthusiasm as suddenly as he had gotten it. It was as if the obsession with things Oriental had fulfilled its task, burning out his uncertainty about being a Rockefeller male, and could now be discarded. As Jay says, "It was like the fever had passed and I didn't need that kind of intense involvement anymore." Understanding intuitively that he had passed the stage where his only two choices were the equally impossible ones of turning his back on his family or being used by it, he cast about for ways in which his status as a Rockefeller might satisfy his inborn need, as he puts it, "to do something worthwhile," if not for all humanity—in traditional Rockefeller fashion—at least for himself.

The New Frontier was a logical beginning for someone with Jay's ambition and connections. ("Out of deference to my Uncle Nelson, I had first registered as a Republican—any news to the contrary would have embarrassed him politically—but I'd voted for Kennedy and considered myself part of the new things happening around the Democratic party.") In 1962, leaving graduate school, he took a job as Sargent Shriver's special assistant. One of his tasks was interviewing people for Peace Corps staff positions overseas. He recalls one occasion when he got a phone call from Attorney General Robert Kennedy, who said he was sending over a good candidate for a choice Peace Corps positon. Jay interviewed him, but wrote him off. "About ten days later, I got another call. The Attorney General said, 'Look, I feel pretty strongly about this.' I told him I felt pretty strongly too. We agreed to a standoff. It was the beginning of a pretty good relationship with Bobby."

For a young professional, as Jay had by that time begun to regard himself, the Peace Corps was perfect. "Papers moved fast, so did promotions and careers. Since going to Japan, I had fantasized constantly about being the first U.S. ambassador to the People's Republic—fantasized so much that I actually believed it would happen. I left the Peace Corps for the State Department to get some 'real' experience in foreign affairs." This was in 1963. For the next few months he worked as special assistant to Roger Hilsman and third man on the Indonesia desk.

When Hilsman was fired by Lyndon Johnson for not exhibiting sufficient enthusiasm about Vietnam, Jay was faced with a decision. He could have had a career in foreign affairs; his father's connections in the State Department guaranteed that. Yet it would begin at a lower level than he was interested in, and it would not give him the sense he was his own man. He was attracted to the world of politics, and he convinced himself that it was not the same world inhabited by his Uncle Nelson, but the newer politics of the Kennedys, which had transformed Washington society and given an existential touch to the wheeling and dealing and frantic mobilization of personal power that went on there. Jay decided he'd like to return to Washington someday—by election.

The question was where he should begin. He realized that it had to be removed from the New York-Washington axis—removed spatially and intellectually—if he were to keep from constantly tripping over his family. While he was pondering this, an old friend from the Peace Corps suggested West Virginia, whose Appalachia had become a symbolic area.

Getting to West Virginia in some legitimate capacity that did not have the word "carpetbagger" written in golden letters all over it was a problem. But as his goals became clearer, any reluctance he might have had to pull Rockefeller strings to get what he wanted was disappearing. He called Bobby Kennedy, who arranged to have him appointed to the Presidential Commission on Juvenile Delinquency, which had an agency (Action for Appalachian Youth) in West Virginia.

He arrived in Charleston in 1964 to find a desk job waiting for him in the state office building. Yet the kind of future he envisioned depended on being about among the people. He picked an area fifty miles away from the state capital. It was Emmons County, where (he says) "only thirteen of the two hundred fifty-six families weren't either ex-employed or working in some nonunion doghole." He bought and parked a small house trailer there so he could stay longer hours and work to overcome the suspicion these mountain people usually reserved for Republican organizers and revenue agents. His time there stretched into two years. He says, "Not necessarily because of me, the community began to get together. Once we found out that a nearby town had condemned an elementary school and was going to tear it down. We bought it for seventy-five dollars and reassembled it in Emmons as a community center."

His work among the poor in Emmons County was the initiation providing Jay with the credentials and the excuse—clearly, there were systemic problems community organization could not change—to do what had been in the back of his mind since he first came there: run for elective office. Early in 1966 he had changed his registration to Democratic; in November he was elected to the state's House of Delegates by a large margin—the first step on the road to the governorship he won in 1976.

He was a West Virginian in the way his Uncle Winthrop was an Arkansan: admired as a celebrity; coveted as a resource; tolerated as an outsider. If he didn't control enough of the great family fortune to focus it on the state's problems as Winthrop had in pumping some $35 million into his adopted home, it was widely *assumed* that he could, and that the magic of the Rockefeller name would attract a cornucopia of investment capital and government grants. Jay also performed a similar symbolic function to Winthrop's in indicating that the twentieth century had finally come to West Virginia and in bringing glamour to the state.

It came in 1967 when he married Sharon Percy, the honey-blond daughter of the Illinois Senator whom Jay had met when she was working in the office of then-Congressman John Lindsay. The wedding showed that Jay had not completely forsaken his family identity for the hills and hollows of Appalachia. Although he gallantly insisted that it was a "Percy affair," its ritual was distinctly Rockefeller. It was performed in the Rockefeller Chapel of the University of Chicago, named after his great-grandfather. The wedding march was played on the huge carrillon donated by Junior.

Jay did not follow his Uncle Winthrop's example and build himself a Jayrock. Even if he had had the money, which he didn't, this was not the style of his generation: none of the Cousins had the need to re-create Pocantico. Instead he and his bride moved into a relatively modest—for a Rockefeller—rambling country home on Barberry Lane in Charleston (the lotus fragility of the Oriental art he had collected in Japan was mixed with Early American antiques by a New York decorator to create what

Sharon Percy Rockefeller called "a young house"), and he bought a thousand acres in Pocahontas County where he would eventualy build a country home. In 1969 Sharon had their first child. He was named John (to be called "Jamie") and would also have the option of including "Davison" and "V" when turning twenty-one.

CHAPTER 24

The Family Office had changed greatly from what it had been when the Brothers returned from the war. Then it had still been a relic of Junior's years of achievement, an extended personal staff designed to serve him and achieve the ends to which he had devoted his life. The Brothers had remodeled it, making it a better receptacle for the increased wealth and influence their careers were designed to accumulate. When they finished, it was as if its Victorian structure had been streamlined by the Bauhaus technicians of whom Nelson was so fond: the Office had become a thoroughly efficient instrument suited to modern occasions. By the time the Cousins came of age, its structure was less that of a group of personal Associates than of a corporation operating by flow chart and the committee system, holding significant power and conscious of its own bureaucratic ends.

To the world at large, even the skeptical world of Wall Street, the combination of secrecy and mystique attached to its operations imparted an air of Byzantine intrigue: the *mysterium tremendum* of the Rockefeller Dynasty. Room 5600 was the place where the Brothers gathered with their illuminati of friends and advisers to make the decisions that would shake the world; it was Merlin's cave, where proposals for new ventures were carefully screened and the decision made to apply the alchemy the Name possessed above all others in the country and thereby turn the lucky few to gold. The mystique was enhanced by the fact that few had ever passed behind the glass doors of Room 5600, walked down the long halls lined with art works, and sat in the boardrooms where decisions were made regarding its unique product—the Rockefeller family.

The nerve center of the power radiating through the corridors of Room 5600 is the private office of J. Richardson Dilworth. After being lured away from Kuhn, Loeb in 1958 by David and Laurance, Dilworth became part of the troika running Room 5600 that included John Lockwood and Frank Jamieson (and, for a time after Jamieson's death, Emmet Hughes).

By the early sixties, as the Office took on more and more of a corporate character, Dilworth emerged as its "chief operating officer" responsible to a board of managers, which included the five Brothers and a few Cousins, and involved working closely with Laurance. Dilworth is in charge of the total daily operation of the Office, although his specialty is the heavy financial matters the Brothers have gotten into over the years.

As the Brothers' chief aide and heir to the role of confidant and privy councilor played by the Reverend Frederick T. Gates and attorney Thomas Debevoise in the previous two generations, Dilworth affects a bemused distance from the Cousins' difficulties. ("In a sense at least," he says in the genteel, highly qualified language used by all family aides, "the pressure they feel is a figment of their imagination; actually their parents are enormously supportive of their children's difficulties.") Yet clearly the fourth generation has been foremost among the "human problems" the chief operating officer has faced.

Not without an eye toward its own survival, the Office has attempted to make itself amenable to the Cousins. Realizing their skittishness and anxiety about being swallowed up in its machinery, it has tried to accommodate to them, making itself into a place they can "plug into" if or when they want, yet not coercing them into involvement. The Brothers and their advisers recognized that whether or not individual Cousins stepped forward to take over in the Office, the Chase, Rockefeller Center, and othe institutions, it was still necessary to link the members of the generation to each other and to the family. The best way to do this was to give them their own institution, following the precedent of the Brothers Fund. In 1968, with grants from three of the Brothers totaling more than $300,000, the Family Fund was begun. It started on a very modest basis; yet, as in everything else, it was recognized that there was more to come.

If the meager sum with which the Fund was endowed expressed the fathers' caution in making even this gesture to their reluctant children, the fact that David, Sr., was its first president and that Laurance also sat on the finance committee made its purpose clear. Alida calls it "a training institution to show us how it's done." It was a clever stroke. The Family Fund did indeed give the Cousins a financial stream where they could get their feet wet, and it soon became a neutral ground which some of them occupied when returning to the family fold after years of radical activity and criticism. The Family Fund developed five areas of emphasis (education, institutional awareness, women, conservation, and the arts) so that it would not overlap with the Brothers Fund and so that each Cousin could find something he or she could become enthusiastic about.

Yet the problem of Room 5600 remained. The Cousins had managed to extricate themselves from their families and begun to pursue individual lives and careers, but the Office continued to function *in loco parentis,* a bureaucratic guardian of elaborately complex proportions handling everything legal and financial for its wards, from doling out their income to preparing their tax returns, and even to relatively simple tasks like the purchase of automobiles and house insurance. (Except for spending-money, they hardly had to touch their fortunes.) By insulating the Cousins from the facts and process of their wealth, it made them dependent to an extraordinary degree, adding a sense of helplessness to the sense of guilt they already felt as recipients of the awesome legacy.

When solicited for a gift, a Cousin needed only to phone the appropriate person in the Office to decide the form in which the gift would be made, whether and how tax advantages would be derived, and the details of its transference. Or if the individual did not want to be bothered with such decisions in the first place, the Office offered the services of its philanthropic staff to suggest areas and projects in which the tax-deductible portion of one's income might be invested.

The operation of the Office had a dual effect. On the surface it made the Cousins' relationship to their wealth appear casual and it encouraged them in the comforting illusion that money really mattered less to them than to their fathers, who were preoccupied with its getting and spending. Yet in the end, they could not suppress the realization that their ignorance did not make the money insignificant, and that they were as dependent on it for survival as they were on the Office for making it work.

The very manner in which they received their income symbolized the predicament. The Brothers had given each of their children a sizable sum on their coming of age, but the bulk of their income came from the "Fidelity Trust" (so called because it was held in New Jersey's Fidelity Union Trust Company), which Junior had set up in 1952 with 120,000 shares of Jersey Standard stock.

The terms of the trust vary among each of the Brothers' families. The income is graded, almost as if to assure a slow maturing of the recipient's sense of responsibility. In Laurance's family, for instance, the Cousins receive $5,000 a year income from the trust on turning 21; by the age of 24 it has risen to $10,000, increasing at the rate of $5,000 a year until age 30, when it jumps to $65,000. After that, or upon marriage, the heir can get all the income from the trust, ranging from $200,000 to $300,000. In David's family, by contrast, a a stipulation limits the amount of income receivable, and the trustees are mandated to reinvest a portion of it. It is

David's way of inculcating the puritan ethic, and although he did not follow it in practice, Laurance approves. When some of David's children pressed for a greater share of income from their trusts, Laurance supported his brother's refusal. Noting that for years he had to pick up crumbs from his father's table, he asked, "What's all this talk of wanting it now?"

Anyone over thirty can invade the principal of the trust, but only for approved purposes and only after solemn application to the trustees, headed by Amyas Ames, the president of Lincoln Center, and including such notables as William McChesney Martin, former head of the Federal Reserve; Albert L. Nickerson, former president of Socony Mobil; and Nathan Pusey, former president of Harvard. The idea behind all the majestic legal machinery is that that part of the great fortune which was bestowed on each of the Cousins was not really *theirs*, but only held by them in trust for their children—whether or not they had or intended to have them. It was like a particularized expression of Junior's philanthropic idea that the great Standard Oil fortune was held by the Rockefellers in trust for the benefit of mankind. The Cousins were confronted by this limitation of their inheritance whenever they sought money in excess of the trust income (which, in the case of the David family, was quite modest, but in all cases hardly up to the Rockefeller standard set by their parents) for purposes not approved. "I was given a severe lecture by an accountant in the Office," recalls one of the Cousins about one such occasion, "for having spent what I had spent previously in the way that I had spent it. I was told explicitly that the money was not mine, that the trustees were responsible for what they did, and that if they approved something irresponsible they would be held accountable."

Just as the small army of accountants, analysts, and lawyers controlled the Cousins' trust, so a public relations department in Room 5600 controlled their official statements and vital statistics, and the archives controlled their history. Larry came into the archives one day to look through his file and was surprised to find a cache of letters he had written as a boy after Abby's death addressed "To Grandmother in Heaven." Along with other personal information and material, he had no recollection of writing them, much less any idea that they had been kept. Often the Cousins worried that the Office seemed to know more about them than they knew about themselves.

Yet for all their doubts, they found it hard to wean themselves from the benign management of Room 5600. They had grown up relying on Office staff to be the buffer between them and the world at large in ways they hadn't fully realized; they had allowed it to take care of the problems in their daily lives, and it had become an addiction. But if they were addicted to the Office, they resented it. They were ambivalent about Room 5600, and the Office (for it was almost impossible not to personify it) was equally so about them. It wanted them to be involved, yet it also wanted to keep them passively vibrating the strands of the web. Abby recalls an instance when she went to Room 5600 to find out exactly how much money she had, how it was invested, and how she went about getting control over it. "There was a surreal meeting with Don O'Brien, Dilworth, seven or eight assorted people from the Office, and an accountant named Joe Lee. They handed out a little red portfolio with all 'my' investments in it. Everything was so altogether done that I could hardly feel like a participant. Dilworth suggested to Lee that he run through my investments. He did, giving me a little synopsis of what each one was doing. He got to Exxon and said, 'Well, here's an old friend.' Then came Mobil, and he says, 'Now Mobil is a kind of little sister to Exxon.' That kind of stuff. Good-humored, but clearly meant to put distance between me and the money and to leave in question the degree to which it is *mine*. It worked. I felt like I had a mask over my face and was being laid out ready for an operation. Room 5600 is an institutional replica of my father's manner; it prevents one from asking questions that might explain its inner logic."

In Abby's opinion the Office is composed of two separate classes, which she calls *obsequiators* and *patronizers*. "The obsequiators are usually the junior members. They fawn over anyone whose name is, was, or even might be Rockefeller. They do it, but feel demeaned by it. They try to do the Cousins' will and the Brothers' at once, not admitting the conflicts that exist between them. The Brothers pay the bills and are in charge now, but on the off chance that we might take over someday, the obsequiators have to hedge their bets. The patronizers are those like Dilworth for whom the Office *is* the Brothers—they are men without qualms about power. To them, the Cousins are just aging wards incapable of making a serious bid for power, and are to be treated as such."

Other Cousins are similarly wary about Room 5600. When Marion asked Dilworth why she got such a small percentage of her trust at a time when she wanted income to further a land reform project she was interested in, she got a phone call from Dilworth. "He started talking and I said, 'Excuse me, I'm going to get Warren,' because I really couldn't believe what he was saying. He was the epitome of indirectness, the epitome of a language that I hardly even understand."

As much as anything else, it has been the shared problem of the Office that welded the Cousins together into a group: the desire to face Dilworth and the others with a united front that would keep them from being over-powered as in their one-to-one dealings. It was a desire that dominated the mood, if not the actual discussions, of the annual meetings they came to hold at Pocantico.

These Cousins' meetings had begun as informal get-togethers, presided over by Mitzi and Rodman as the elders of the generation and originally intended as initiation ceremonies meant primarily to induct Cousins who had reached their majority into the mysteries of their "financial rights." As time passed and more Cousins turned twenty-one, the meetings took on a social quality, and an attempt was made to forget the past few years of individual anguish and recapture some of the closeness of their youth. By the late sixties, however, as almost all of the Cousins began attending the meetings and the external pressures on them became severe, they began to discuss issues.

Some were internal matters, like the Brothers' plan for Pocantico. Although no Cousin except Rodman was interested in maintaining a home there in the style of the Brothers, some of the Cousins indicated they would like to have home sites, especially if the isolation of their youth was replaced with a more open situation. (One suggestion was to allow small communities of a few hundred people each to locate throughout the 3,600 acres.) Since this expression of interest came at a time when Laurance and Nelson were interested in developing parts of the estate, the Brothers agreed to commission a study of the possibilities. The Rouse Plan, as it was called, proposed that some "Cousins' Sites" of 20 acres each be developed around the "park" area, and that some 650 acres in the northern part of Pocantico be developed into two good-sized towns with 7,500 people, schools, recreational areas, and other support facilities.

Even for Laurance and Nelson the question was not so much making money from Pocantico as properly disposing of it after their generation was gone. After the Rouse Plan (whose attempt to accommodate both Cousins and Brothers had pleased neither group), Nelson Aldrich, the Brothers' cousin and David's architect-in-residence, was called upon to propose a comprehensive scheme that was to eliminate the idea of having planned communities in the estate. Yet a third plan was broached in 1968; this one was not architectural but financial. It called on stockholders of the Hill Realty Company (namely the Brothers), which owned Pocantico, to sell their stock to the '34 Trusts; the trusts, in turn, would hold it until they were dissolved in the fifth generation.

It was at this point that Steven and, to a lesser extent, Larry began arguing against the Brothers' plans. "In order to inherit Pocantico," Steven recalls, "the Cousins would have had to pay such heavy taxes that it wouldn't really be worth it. The question was whether to sell it and make as much money as possible, or to just agree that this extremely beautiful piece of land should be preserved for everyone to enjoy. I argued that the family didn't need the money. For us to divide Pocantico and sell it would be as great a crime as breaking up a work of art and burning it for the heat it would give during one evening."

The Cousins agreed. So did JDR3, who had always been against the kind of development Laurance and Nelson (with David's acquiscence) had been considering for Pocantico. The issue became symbolic of the differences in philosophy between the generations. Finally, architect Harmon Goldstone (who had worked with the family in other matters over the years) was brought in as a mediator to conceive a plan acceptable to all. The idea of ultimately giving Pocantico to the state for public use— announced in 1970 by Nelson in his role as family spokesman—was the resulting compromise beteen the Cousins and Brothers.

The estate, however, was a unique issue. When Steven and other Cousins tried to mobilize the fourth generation for a public stand against the war in Vietnam, they got nowhere. As a group they were fearful of doing something that would be interpreted as a repudiation of their fathers, all of whom supported the war. Yet the problem remained: in the criticism of the family that cropped up with increasing frequency in the late sixties, the Cousins were implicated as Rockefellers along with their elders; and unlike their fathers, they were not intellectually sealed off from the effects of this criticism, nor content to bifurcate reality so that wielding power was separate from doing good.

The issues were very much on Steven's mind and also Marion's. She and her husband had already informed the Internal Revenue Service of their intention to stop paying that proportion of their taxes that went to what they called, in their letter, "this government's murderous violence in Vietnam and other parts of Indochina." Telling the IRS it would have to get its taxes without their cooperation, they sent the money instead to antiwar groups. In 1971 Marion wrote a letter to Dana Creel, head of the Office's philanthropic division, in which she raised the issues of the lack of coherence in family policy:

Dear Mr. Creel,
 My sister Laura just sent me a copy of her letter to you and I want to say that what she had indicated about the necessity of inter-relationship between the phi-

lanthropist and the investor parts of us is, I believe, extremely important. I join her in feeling that we must take a hard look at our investment policy. . . . For example, I am very anxious to see this war end and the amount of money presently spent on defense decrease. I have given part of my income toward the work of various peace groups. But part of my income comes from dividends from investments in industries such as Westinghouse, Dupont, General Electric and Dow—companies who help make this war possible and hold substantial defense contracts. Likewise I am concerned about pollution and I support with part of my income various ecological groups and yet such a large part of this income results from investments in Standard Oil of New Jersey. I think as a family we could put pressure on Standard Oil to mend its ways . . . . I think our consciousness as a family will slowly grow as to the necessary relationship between our responsibilities as investors and philanthropists. It should become increasingly evident that it is nonsense to create with one hand and destroy with the other. I would appreciate your thoughts on all this.

The answer was not forthcoming, and other Cousins fretted about the same issues. If taking political stands as a group was out, they nonetheless felt that they had to at least try to seize the initiative over their money from Room 5600 and make sure it was not invested in corporations profiting from the war, supporting the South African economy, or exploiting the environment.

It was in their Cousins' meeting of June 1972 that these issues interacted with the personal anguish they had hacked their way through as individuals. Arriving from all over the country with their families, the Cousins' invasion made the estate look as though it had been rented to a summit meeting of McGovern staff workers. Some of them wore faded denims and long hair and had scruffily dressed children in tow. Most had, in fact, contributed generously to the campaign of the Democratic candidate, but this weekend they were worried only about family politics. It was on their minds from the moment that Sharon Percy Rockefeller, their elected president, stood up in the Playhouse Junior had built for their fathers half a century earlier, to call the meeting to order.

It was as if the doggedness with which they had borne their dissatisfaction for so many years suddenly collapsed, allowing the unhappiness to escape. There was resentment over the way the Office was organized to keep them infantilized. As the employees from Room 5600 appeared at the estate to make their yearly presentations, they were surprised to find themselves grilled with unusual force. The Cousins requested that Dilworth prepare a family directory completely blue-printing the workings of the Office. They talked about their individual frustrations in trying to manage their own money. The discussion snowballed until they found themselves appointing an Investment Committee of four Cousins instructed to work with Room 5600 in figuring out ways to bring their portfolio into line with their social values. The committee was headed by Jay, who had good reason for concern: he was in the middle of a race for the West Virginia governorship on a platform of independence from the mining interests that controlled the state, and had already faced a crisis when critics pointed out that the Rockefeller Foundation, of which he was a trustee, was a large shareholder in the Consolidation Coal Company, one of the biggest of the coal operators and a company that had been charged with lax safety regulations in respect to the prevalence of black lung disease among the miners.

Once the genie was out, it seemed impossible to entice it back into the bottle. After discussing investments, the Cousins broke up into men's and women's groups. In the men's groups, the "in-laws" spoke up about the problem of having the money and power reside with the women (even those husbands who had been divorced from Rockefeller women had gotten "alimony" in the form of property settlements), while the male Cousins compared notes on how they had avoided involvement in Room 5600.

But it was the women's group that provided the real drama. The women discussed their broken marriages and the question of women's liberation. One of Laurance's daughters said that their troubles sprang from a confusion that was learned in the family—or, at least, that the female role learned in her family was quite simple: "Daddy likes his women quiet and religious."

Laura, who was gathering data on the early childhoods of the older generation and therefore knew with what reverence the Brothers regarded their mother, observed that Abby Aldrich had been a wonderful person, who seemed to handle the role well.

She was immediately challenged by Babs's daughter Mitzi, who stood under the portrait of her mother and said with an ominous tone in her voice: "You don't know what grandmother was like." And then, with tears in her eyes, she talked about how her mother's life was "ruined" by Abby because, from the time she was a little girl, she was put off in a corner; it was only her sons that Abby cared for. As a result, her mother had no avenue of self-fulfillment or self-esteem; she had become reclusive and ineffective, as one of the other Cousins later observed, "an addendum to the Brothers' generation."

As the meeting concluded, the Cousins were left in a state of surprise over what had happened. At first there was euphoria. Hope said soon after, "There's an impulse not to take orders anymore or to agree automatically that this is a good firm and that a good investment, just because Room 5600 says so. This was the first time we flexed our own muscles."

Her brother, Jay, agreed: "As the Cousins come to see each other with mature curiosity and affection, we are better able to handle our relationship to the Office. It used to be that the Cousins would always be calling up Room 5600 and saying, 'I've lost my dog, what shall I do?' or 'I need a new refrigerator, how do I go about getting one?' No more of that."

At the time it occurred, the 1972 meeting was seen as a breakthrough by the Cousins, both in terms of the level of personal revelation—a mode not easy for any Rockefeller—and in terms of the challenge to the Office. Yet there was an uneasiness as well, a feeling that they had overreached, a sense that this meeting had really been delayed reaction to the ferment of the late sixties and that they had spontaneously taken a more extreme position than they really meant to follow through.

Those who misinterpreted the signs and thought that their generation was ready to issue a serious challenge to the Brothers soon found that the last thing the majority of the Cousins wanted was for their meetings to become a Jacobin Society. Marion and her husband, who arranged to show a Quaker-supported research group's slide presentation of the effects of the air war on Vietnam, were not encouraged in their efforts to follow it up. They found themselves continually frustrated when it came to any action, however modest, the Cousins might take as a group. When Alida, the youngest Cousin present, saw the film *State of Siege*, she became upset because Rockefeller was the only U.S. name introduced in the panorama of brutality and repression. "I wrote a letter telling the Cousins that everyone should see it before we have our next meeting, just because I think it's really a super eye-opener about the family and the possibility of how our money might be influencing things in ways we're not even aware of. It was like an accusation of murder." Yet when Alida attempted to get a discussion of the movie put on the agenda at the next Cousins meeting, she was told that it was not the place for "personal hobby-horses," and that she should talk to the Cousins individually.

Even the Investment Committee's visit to Dilworth resulted in little or no tangible result. There was no change in the management of the portfolio, but a woman, Catherine Tracy, was hired to work in Room 5600, gathering information about developments in the field of corporate responsibility. She was to keep abreast of all the stockholder resolutions proposed by church and consumer groups in their efforts to change or modify corporate policies. Several times a year she sent summaries of these struggles to the Cousins so they could act if they wished.

Far from advancing the Cousins' cause, her presence seemed meant only to disarm their concern. As an employee of the Brothers responsible to Dilworth, she had certainly not been hired to encourage the Cousins to assert themselves on behalf of greater conscience in the management of family finances. Her officially formulated memos, summarizing in neutral tones the views of the corporate rebels, both complicated the issues and removed from the Cousins any sense of moral crisis they might have had. After passing over her desk, the burning social issues of the time came to seem like complex problems of social management in which there were no simple rights or wrongs. At the same time, by making contacts herself with the young activists in church and consumer groups, Catherine Tracy insulated the Cousins from having to experience the urgent concern of their peers and prevented them from having to confront the issues directly.

When a few of them decided to act in spite of this they found their freedom to do so severely limited. Thus when Marion, in the spring of 1974, requested that the shares in one of her smaller trusts at the Chase Manhattan Bank be voted on behalf of several stockholder resolutions, including one inspired by the Watergate revelations then reaching their denouement, she received the following communication from Catherine Tracy: "Chase Manhattan Bank—Mr. Daniel Dorney—advises me that they voted for proposals 2 and 3 [as per Marion's request] on the IBM proxy. However, they would not take our suggestion that they vote in favor of the Project on Corporate Responsibility's resolution prohibiting corporate campaign contributions on the ITT proxy. Sorry!"

Though the Cousins were forced to backtrack, the reverberations from the June 1972 meeting continued to spread long after it was over. By the fall, the Cousins received one of the items they had requested from Room 5600. It was a detailed thirty-page family directory, which showed the form and function of Room 5600. It was accompanied by the caveat, "As you might suspect, the confidential nature of the work performed by the Office presents problems in delineating each job." Yet even the part of the leviathan it showed was impressive. There were more than 200 employees. The exact figure of the budget was not given (one of Laurance's aides, Peter Crips, noted that "it is confidential in nature") but was an estimated $6 million a year. The charts illustrating lines of authority showed how completely the Office personality had come to be dominated by investments. The Brothers Fund and Family Fund were not independent, as was implied, but subordinate to Dilworth. The division of the budget dollar (the percentages were given even though the total expenditures were not) also reflected the proportionate importance of philanthropy in Room 5600: investment accounted for 30 percent of the budget; accounting and taxes for 20 percent; the Legal Department for 18 percent; management and public relations for 8.6 percent; rent and telephone for the Brothers' offices, 5.8 percent; miscellaneous, 9.2 percent. This left a little over 8 percent of the total expenses of Room 5600 devoted to the philanthropic unit.

These facts were sobering for the Cousins. They showed how vast and complex was the operation which they presumed to alter to conform to their sensitivities and tastes. The Cousins realized that the Office was too formidable an enterprise and too strongly headed in the direction their fathers had sent it to be purified in the manner they wanted. The issues they had raised in their 1972 meeting would now be disposed of once and for all, ironically enough, in the one institution in the Office the Cousins theoretically controlled.

In the years since the Family Fund had begun operation in 1969, it had grown into a fairly large foundation, the result of a bequest of $10 million in Martha Baird's will. (When she died in 1970, Junior's widow left all of the $72 million he had willed her to various family philanthropies.) From the beginning, some of the Cousins feared the Fund would become just another Rockefeller institution. Marion and her husband wrote the other Cousins when its five areas of emphasis were being decided upon: "We are quite excited about the possibilities of the Family Fund. We hope very much that it will serve as an alternative to the usual channels and mode of giving. Focusing on environmental ecology, for example, is in our opinion a marvelous idea, but only if this (or any other cause the Fund supports) is not treated as though it were an area of concern like education, the arts, health and so on. In our view, to adopt such an attitude, which we sense in the communications we have had about the Fund so far, is merely to play the old role of philanthropist with a somewhat new twist. The times demand something more than one more tax deductible foundation. The task as we see it is often to attack the very political and economic forces which perpetuate the deductible contribution. . . . We think the Fund has an obligation to seek out organizations like American Friends Service Committee, Friends of the Earth, Pacifica stations, American Documentary Films et al. and support them regardless of their tax status."

Yet most of the Cousins were not ready to insist that these principles be adhered to, especially if it meant once again troubling the smooth waters they had so recently passed into. They accommodated themselves to what they felt were the realities of the situation. One of these realities was the presence of David, Sr., and Laurance on the board of trustees and investment committee of the Fund.

By spring of 1974, Catherine Tracy had sifted through the proposals of various insurgent stockholder groups and presented the Cousins with some they could act on with respect to the Fund's portfolio. The three issues addressed by the stockholders' resolutions were strip mining in the Rocky Mountain area by Exxon; insufficient minority hiring by General Electric and Caterpillar Tractors; and the South African policies of IBM. The Family Fund's investment committee dealt with these questions in executive session. There was unanimous agreement that Exxon's explanation of its strip-mining policies and its promise to reseed the gouged-out areas were adequate. On the question of minority hiring, the committee accepted David, Sr.'s suggestion that instead of giving proxies to the church groups challenging GE and Caterpillar, they should vote with the management, while also writing a letter for the record emphasizing the Rockefeller family's commitment to equal opportunities. When it was suggested by one of the Cousins that the letter also be used to request that the companies put the results of minority hiring programs in future annual reports, David objected, saying that he thought this was really "asking too much." Jay agreed, seconding his motion not to make this request part of the letter, which then passed unanimously.

At issue in the IBM stockholders' resolution was whether or not there should be complete disclosure of information on the company's activities in South Africa. David brought up a *Fortune* article stating that IBM was one of the more progressive firms in South Africa. The members of the Family Fund Investment Committee agreed with him when he then stated that if they were to vote with the dissident stockholders in favor of compelling disclosure, they would appear not to support IBM's progressive stance on some of South Africa's internal matters. The Fund voted only to write a mild letter outlining their views.

In addition to setting the tone for the Family Fund's responses to these specific stockholders issues, David also settled the general problem of the Fund's investment policy. The Cousins had assumed that the organization's investment would be consistent with its philanthropic policy, and had moved to instruct the company managing the Family Fund's portfolio to do so in a way that would reflect their generation's commitment to "corporate responsibility." However, "Uncle David" again interposed a strong opinion: if they didn't give the investment company a free rein to

475

make as much money as it could they wouldn't get anything out of it at all and the Fund's endowment might diminish. Unless they were willing to contest the assumptions behind this statement, which they weren't, they couldn't argue against its logic. They deferred on this question too.

The Brothers had resigned themselves to the fact that the Cousins' group identity would be in philanthropy and that if they were to extend the family's influence, it would be in that way. To a certain extent the Cousins were like Junior. In the strange dialectic expressed in the alternating generations of the family, their role was to atone for the sins of their fathers. Yet unlike Junior, their giving was not part of anything more than personal redemption. They had no dynastic objectives. Their philanthropy was actually only an aspect of a continuum of behavior in which they sought "liberation." One of them might occasionally make a gesture of bravado about philanthropy, as in the case of Laura's statement: "It's very hard to get rid of the money in a way that does more good than harm. One of the ways is to subsidize people who are trying to change the system and get rid of people like us." Yet in the last analysis giving occupied only a small part of the Cousins' energy.

At the 1974 Cousins' meeting Steven raised the question of whether the family beyond his generation wanted to continue to function as an institution. The issue had gradually shifted in the years of their growing up from whether and how they would participate in the Rockefeller dynasty, to whether or not the dynasty itself had a future. The Office, which had always been the engine powering the dynasty, was itself faced with this problem. Winthrop's death had shocked everyone concerned into the realization that Room 5600 was every bit as mortal as the Brothers themselves. It was expensive to operate. The Cousins weren't aggressively generating the income that would justify an effort to keep it going. Increasingly there was talk about the Office's being dissolved or radically modified after the next Brother died.

J. R. Dilworth attempts to discount the talk. "There's really no accurate way to predict what will become of the Office. It depends on the future. Even if the Cousins decided to go off on their own entirely, they'd have to come back at least once a year—at tax time. We've got services here for the next generation that they couldn't normally find, services they couldn't get by going off to any ordinary banker or lawyer. It's all here in the Office. We seem to have the best way of handling the complex business situation they're involved in—investment of their funds and, from a separate pocket, giving away a certain amount of their money. If by some catastrophe, all the remaining Brothers died today, moreover, it would take seven or eight years just to disband the present operation and unravel things satisfactorily."

Yet despite this, there was a feeling of waiting for the second shoe to fall. After the funeral at Winrock, the long corridors of Room 5600 were filled with speculation. Would the investments be curtailed and the Office consolidated into a philanthropic and accounting operation, the minimum functions necessary to handle taxes? Would the present scope of operations be maintained in skeletal form? There was a kind of *fin de siècle* mood that was heightened by Nelson's unraveling the family secrets before the Congress in a last desperate attempt to gain national office, and by the pain his confirmation hearings caused them all. Whatever the Cousins did or didn't do with the Office, its days seemed clearly numbered.

This might have caused pangs of nostalgia among others, but not among the Cousins. Even if they were not prepared to stand up against the family juggernaut, they were more than willing to be the passive beneficiaries of history. They thought what prior Rockefeller generations would have regarded as unthinkable. Steven says, "Someday somebody is going to have to go down there and figure out what to do with the Office. That's the main reason our periodic Cousins meetings are important. We're learning to work together, to make decisions, so that we'll be ready when the time comes. The question ultimately will be whether or not the family will be preserved as an institution in the form of Room 5600."

As he talks, the words begin to sound like a benediction. "The family institutions—first the Foundation and now increasingly the Brothers Fund, which the new laws say must put outsiders on the board—are getting out of the family's control. As with these institutional children so with the real children. They're getting out on their own now, away from the family; and once they're out, I don't see any way to get them back."

EPILOGUE

At least since William Avery's brushes with the law in the wilds of up-state New York, the fate of the Rockefellers has been synthesized out of the unpredictable chemistry of parents and children. Even more than their predecessors, however, the Cousins have grown up in an oedipal brier patch. For them the simplest acts have been fraught with heavy significance; the paths to maturity have been strewn with the emotional detritus of past struggles between fathers and sons. Repossession of self is not only a rebellion against the parents; it is magnified into a killing blow against the family, its rules and traditions. In their world of shadow and act, where each gesture is inflated out of all human proportion, the symbolic parricide becomes an act of murder against history itself.

Living in a family of immense silences where there are abundances of everything except feeling, the Cousins have tried to make as few decisions as possible. But even their modest desire to be individuals first and Rockefellers second has been interpreted as a mortal affront to the dynasty their grandfather consolidated. With an unintended acuity, this desire has cut through the religious awe surrounding the family and its special mission. In standing back from the responsibility of the role and the obligations of the power, the Cousins—without meaning something so portentous—have pierced the dynastic illusion. As if by some monstrous Freudian slip, the intention to say that the only thing they want is to be themselves has come out sounding like the last thing they want to be is Rockefellers. Apart from the human aspects of the dilemma, the Cousins have become a living fossil preserving the skeleton of a unique history.

At the core of Mr. Junior's dynastic project was a shrewd piece of moral calculation. Through his philanthropic efforts, the taint in the family fortune would be expunged, the blot on the name scoured away. Beginning with an obsessive need to believe his father pure, Junior's life gradually developed into a prolonged exercise in self-justification. The family became the vehicle of his quest to prove that the money, of which he was now the custodian, was not only fairly gotten, but well-deserved. Junior's idea was that future Rockefellers would earn their inheritance by assuming responsibility for what the Reverend Gates had called "the well-being of mankind." Instead of wealth coming, however obliquely, as a reward for individual effort, the individual would pay a life-term debt of service to the wealth itself and thus earn it after the fact. The concept of stewardship implied in Senior's claim that God had given him his money was refined by Junior into a comprehensive morality whose terms his heirs would come to understand quite well: power, like money, was an obligation; like money, it was a necessary part of the legacy.

Junior was a classicist, shaping nature to his requirements. Construction was always his favorite outlet: the materials were inert and tractable, willing co-conspirators in the process of creation. He did well also in those vast fields of endeavor his Associates discovered for him; these too could be shaped by careful infusions of capital and the gardener's clinical

478

detachment. But while he might order and even alter the nature of things, he could not control human nature. *That* would be the only volatile element in the Rockefeller enterprise.

JDR3's foundering in the role of heir apparent would become obvious when he tried to grow beyond it, beyond the task of being his father's representative. The meaning of Laurance's inability to step decisively from the background and of Winthrop's self-destructiveness would become clear toward the end of their lives. The message of David's stately rise at the Chase was that finally Junior's institutions supplied the energy for the Rockefeller aura, not the other way around. And Nelson's ambition, like some devouring metabolic disorder, finally turned upon the traditions at the very marrow of the family's morality, consuming them indiscriminately along with everything else.

Part of the Brothers' failing was their unblinking acceptance of the sense of manifest destiny with which their father had imbued the family. They believed in it completely, not only for themselves, but for their children as well. The ignored the impact of the social upheavals of the sixties on the Cousins, assuming that their alienation from the family myths was a temporary phase in their development, a sort of stage fright comparable to their own youthful hesitation to step into the giant future that had awaited them. They failed to see that, without really willing it, their children had been severed by events from the sense of family mission which, in the harsh light of Vietnam and then Watergate, would itself come to seem not only exaggerated and archaic, but culpable, even tainted. The peculiar burden of the fourth generation would be to look with a kind of nostalgia at past Rockefeller power and grandeur and yet realize that it was not for them. They would be forced to see the family and its myths with the eyes of outsiders and thus to realize that the family's place in the sun was an achievement of power, not of desert. And this perception was the single ragged thread that unraveled the whole fabric of Mr. Junior's elaborate moral tapestry.

The Rockefeller Foundation is the paradigm for the fate of the institutions designed to buttress Junior's dynasty into eternity. Though no longer within the closed circle of the family proper, it continues to stand at the epicenter of American wealth and power, its trustees drawn from among Rockefeller friends and institutional kin. It is *by* the family, but no longer *of* it, a formula that applies even more strongly to those companies led by Standard of New Jersey, now, more than a generation after the last Rockefeller has left it, once again the biggest corporation in the world. The dynasty is mortal; the institutions have a life of their own.

The process that began when the commission merchant firm of Clark & Rockefeller made its first venture into oil is far from over, yet the shape it will ultimately take is foreshadowed in the attitudes of the present generation. Perhaps some of the Cousins' children will retrace their Uncle Jay's course and harness the considerable energy lingering in the money, name and connections to achieve positions of personal power. Others will be content to enjoy the wealth, at least to the degree that such enjoyment is possible for a Rockefeller heir. A few will persist in the eccentricity of rebellion. Meanwhile, the critical mass will move toward a merger with the nation's general aristocracy of wealth, and the benign drift away from dynastic imperatives will continue year by year.

Instead of *the* family, there will be five families—those of each of the male heirs of the Brothers. Long after the Brothers have died, their grandchildren—the fifth generation—will finally inherit the vestige of Senior's fortune, the '34 Trusts, which terminate by law when they reach maturity. The aging Cousins will no doubt worry over the impact this sudden wealth will have on their children and what it will portend for the Rockefellers and their concept of service. But by that time the sense in which this has been the most royal of America's families will have passed, and the question will be largely academic.

There is thus a strange circularity to the Rockefeller saga. It is as if the entire effort since the founding of Standard Oil were an extravagant mummery on the theme of the vanity of human wishes. Junior set out to prove to the world that the wealth he inherited was morally just; in the end his efforts failed even to convince his grandchildren. He built a dynastic identity meant to close the distance between the Rockefellers and the rest of mankind; in the end his efforts only magnified the space separating the Rockefellers from everyone else and, in a final irony, divided the family even from itself.

The Cousins' attempt to recapture a personal identity from the family is too tentative and stumbling, and finally too mundane, to be seen as a heroic enterprise. Yet the end of this dynasty does have an epic quality, even if it is as symbol rather than event. For more than a hundred years, the Rockefellers have molded their ambition to the imperial course of the nation itself. Now their decline comes into view at the time that the American Century too is ending, over fifty years before its term. Far from what Junior envisioned, in neither fact is there much cause for regret.